on overdue items.

Bilingual Dictionary

English-Ukrainian
Ukrainian-English
Dictionary

Compiled by
Katerina Volobuyeva

STAR Foreign Language BOOKS
55, Warren Street, LONDON W1T 5NW (UK)

© Publishers

ISBN : 978 1 908357 18 2

First Edition: 2012

Published by
STAR Foreign Language BOOKS
a unit of ibs BOOKS (UK)
55, Warren Street, LONDON W1T 5NW (UK)
E-mail : starbooksuk@aol.com
www.foreignlanguagebooks.co.uk

Printed in India at
Star Print-O-Bind, New Delhi-110020

About this Dictionary

Developments in science and technology today have narrowed down distances between countries, and have made the world a small place. A person living thousands of miles away can learn and understand the culture and lifestyle of another country with ease and without travelling to that country. Languages play an important role as facilitators of communocation in this respect.

To promote such an understanding, **STAR Foreign Language BOOKS** has planned to bring out a series of bilingual dictionaries in which important English words have been translated into other languages, with Roman transliteration in case of languages that have different scripts. This is a humble attempt to bring people of the word closer through the medium of language, thus making communication easy and convenient.

Under this series of *one-to-one dictionaries*, we have published over 35 languages, the list of which has been given in the opening pages. These have all been compiled and edited by teachers and scholars of the relative languages.

Publishers.

Bilingual Dictionaries in this Series

English-Afrikaans / Afrikaans-English	Abraham Venter
English-Amharic / Amharic-English	Girun Asanke
English-Arabic / Arabic-English	Rania-al-Qass
English-Bengali / Bengali-English	Amit Majumdar
English-Bosnian / Bosnian-English	Boris Kazanegra
English-Bulgarian / Bulgarian-English	Vladka Kocheshkova
English-Cantonese / Cantonese-English	Nisa Yang
English-Chinese (Mandarin) / Chinese (Mandarin)-Eng	Y. Shang & R. Yao
English-Croatian / Croatin-English	Vesna Kazanegra
English-Czech / Czech-English	Jindriska Poulova
English-Dari / Dari-English	Amir Khan
English-Estonian / Estonian-English	Lana Haleta
English-Farsi / Farsi-English	Maryam Zaman Khani
English-Greek / Greek-English	Lina Stergiou
English-Gujarati / Gujarati-English	Sujata Basaria
English-Hindi / Hindi-English	Sudhakar Chaturvedi
English-Hungarian / Hungarian-English	Lucy Mallows
English-Latvian / Latvian-English	Julija Baranovska
English-Lithuanian / Lithuanian-English	Regina Kazakeviciute
English-Marathi / Marathi-English	Sahard Thackerey
English-Nepali / Nepali-English	Anil Mandal
English-Pashto / Pashto-English	Amir Khan
English-Polish / Polish-English	Magdalena Herok
English-Punjabi / Punjabi-English	Teja Singh Chatwal
English-Romanian / Romanian-English	Georgeta Laura Dutulescu
English-Russian / Russian-English	Katerina Volobuyeva
English-Serbian / Serbian-English	Vesna Kazanegra
English-Slovak / Slovak-English	Zozana Horvathova
English-Somali / Somali-English	Ali Mohamud Omer
English-Tagalog / Tagalog-English	Jefferson Bantayan
English-Tamil / Tamil-English	Sandhya Mahadevan
English-Thai / Thai-English	Suwan Kaewkongpan
English-Turkish / Turkish-English	Nagme Yazgin
English-Ukrainian / Ukrainian-English	Katerina Volobuyeva
English-Urdu / Urdu-English	S. A. Rahman
English-Vietnamese / Vietnamese-English	Hoa Hoang

More languages in print

STAR Foreign Language BOOKS

55, Warren Street, LONDON W1T 5NW (UK)

ENGLISH-UKRAINIAN

A

abolish *v.t* покласти кінець
poklasty kinets
abominable *a* жахливий
zhakhlyvyi
abound *v.i.* бути у великій
кількості buty u velykii kilkosti
about *adv* кругом kruhom
about *prep* про pro
above *adv* нагорі nahori
above *prep.* над nad
abreast *adv* в ряд v riad
abridge *v.t* скорочувати
skorochuvaty
abridgement *n* скорочення
skorochennia
abroad *adv* за кордоном za
kordonom
abscond *v.i* уникати unykaty
absence *n* відсутність vidsutnist
absent *a* відсутній vidsutnii
absent *v.t* не бути ne buty
absolute *a* абсолютний
absoliutnyi
absolutely *adv* абсолютно
absoliutno
absorb *v.t* поглинати pohlynaty
abstract *v.t* абстрагувати
abstrahuvaty
abstract *a* абстрактний
abstraktnyi
abstract *n* абстракція abstraktsiia
abstraction *n.* узагальнення
uzahalnennia
absurd *a* абсурдний absurdnyi
absurdity *n* безглуздість
bezhluzdist
abundance *n* надлишок
nadlyshok
abundant *a* більш ніж достатній
bilsh nizh dostatnii

abuse *n* зловживання
zlovzhyvannia
abuse *v.t.* ображати obrazhaty
abusive *a* жорстокий zhorstokyi
academic *a* науковий naukovyi
academy *n* академія akademiia
accede *v.t.* приєднуватися
pryiednuvatysia
accelerate *v.t* прискорювати
pryskoriuvaty
acceleration *n* прискорення
pryskorennia
abaction *n* скотокрадство
skotokradstvo
abactor *n* скотокрад skotokrad
abandon *v.t.* покидати pokydaty
abase *v.t.* понижувати
ponyzhuvaty
abasement *n* приниження
prynyzhennia
abash *v.t.* соромити soromyty
abate *v.t.* ослабляти oslabliaty
abatement *n.* послаблення
poslablennia
abbey *n.* абатство abatstvo
abbreviate *v.t.* скорочувати
skorochuvaty
abbreviation *n* абревіатура
abreviatura
abdicate *v.t,* відрікатися
vidrikatysia
abdication *n* зречення
zrechennia
abdomen *n* черево cherevo
abdominal *a.* черевний cherevnyi
abduct *v.t.* викрадати vykradaty
abduction *n* викрадення
vykradennia
abed *adv.* у ліжку u lizhku
aberrance *n.* відхилення
vidkhylennia
abet *v.t.* підбурювати pidburiuvaty
abetment *n.* сприяння spryiannia

abeyance *n.* стан непевності stan nepevnosti
abhor *v.t.* ненавидіти nenavydity
abhorrence *n.* відраза vidraza
abide *v.i* очікувати ochikuvaty
abiding *a* постійний postiinyi
ability *n* здатність zdatnist
abject *a.* підлий pidlyi
ablactate *v. t* віднімати від грудей vidnimaty vid hrudei
ablactation *n* відібрання дитини від грудей vidibrannia dytyny vid hrudei
ablaze *adv.* палаючий palaiuchyi
able *a* спроможній spromozhnii
ablepsy *n* сліпота slipota
ablush *adv* збентежений zbentezhenyi
ablution *n* обмивання obmyvannia
abnegate *v. t* відмовляти собі в чому-небудь vidmovliaty sobi v chomu-nebud
abnegation *n* відмова vidmova
abnormal *a* ненормальний nenormalnyi
aboard *adv* на борту na bortu
abode *n* житло zhytlo
abolition *n.* анулювання anuliuvannia
aboriginal *a* аборигенний aboryhennyi
aborigines *n. pl* аборигени aboryheny
abort *v.i* перервати perervaty
abortion *n* аборт abort
abortive *adv* викидень vykyden
abrogate *v. t.* анулювати anuliuvaty
abrupt *a* раптовий raptovyi
abruption *n* розрив rozryv
abscess *n* абсцес abstses
absolve *v.t* звільняти zvilniaty

absonant *adj* різкий rizkyi
abstain *v.i.* утримуватися utrymuvatysia
abutted *v* прилягати pryliahaty
abyss *n* безодня bezodnia
acarpous *adj.* що не має плодів shcho ne maie plodiv
accent *n* акцент aktsent
accent *v.t* виділяти vydiliaty
accept *&* приймати pryimaty
acceptable *a* прийнятний pryiniatnyi
acceptance *n* прийняття pryiniattia
access *n* доступ dostup
accession *n* вступ vstup
accessory *n* співучасник spivuchasnyk
accident *n* випадок vypadok
accidental *a* випадковий vypadkovyi
accipitral *adj* хижий khyzhyi
acclaim *v.t* бурхливо аплодувати burkhlyvo aploduvaty
acclaim *n* гучне вітання huchne vitannia
acclamation *n* вітальні вигуки vitalni vyhuky
acclimatise *v.t* акліматизуватися aklimatyzuvatysia
accommodate *v.t* пристосовувати prystosovuvaty
accommodation *n.* приміщення prymishchennia
accompaniment *n* супровід suprovid
accompany *v.t.* супроводжувати suprovodzhuvaty
accomplice *n* спільник spilnyk
accomplish *v.t.* здійснювати zdiisniuvaty
accomplished *a* доповнений dopovnenyi

accomplishment *n.* освіченість osvichenist

accord *n.* згода zhoda

accord *v.t.* узгоджувати uzhodzhuvaty

accordingly *adv.* відповідно vidpovidno

account *v.t.* вважати за vvazhaty za

account *n.* рахунок rakhunok

accountable *a* відповідальний vidpovidalnyi

accountancy *n.* бухгалтерська справа bukhhalterska sprava

accountant *n.* відповідач vidpovidach

accredit *v.t.* уповноважувати upovnovazhuvaty

accrementition *n* розростання тканини rozrostannia tkanyny

accrete *v.t.* зростатися zrostatysia

accrue *v.i.* збільшуватися zbilshuvatysia

accumulate *v.t.* акумулювати akumuliuvaty

accumulation *n* акумуляція akumuliatsiia

accuracy *n.* точність tochnist

accurate *a.* точний tochnyi

accursed *a.* проклятий prokliatyi

accusation *n* звинувачення zvynuvachennia

accuse *v.t.* обвинувачити obvynuvachyty

accused *n.* обвинувачений obvynuvachenyi

accustom *v.t.* привчати pryvchaty

accustomed *a.* звиклий zvyklyi

ace *n* туз tuz

acentric *adj* той, що не має центру toi, shcho ne maie tsentru

acephalous *adj.* позбавлений голови pozbavlenyi holovy

acephalus *n.* безголовий bezholovyi

acetify *v.* перетворюватися на оцет peretvoriuvatysia na otset

ache *n.* біль bil

ache *v.i.* хворіти khvority

achieve *v.t.* досягати dosiahaty

achievement *n.* виконання vykonannia

achromatic *adj* ахроматичний akhromatychnyi

acid *a* кислий kyslyi

acid *n* кислота kyslota

acidity *n.* кислотність kyslotnist

acknowledge *v.* усвідомлювати usvidomliuvaty

acknowledgement *n.* визнання vyznannia

acne *n* прищ pryshch

acorn *n.* жолудь zholud

acoustic *a* акустичний akustychnyi

acoustics *n.* акустика akustyka

acquaint *v.t.* познайомити poznaiomyty

acquaintance *n.* знайомство znaiomstvo

acquest *n* набуття чинності nabuttia chynnosti

acquiesce *v.i.* неохоче згоджуватися neokhoche zhodzhuvatysia

acquiescence *n.* покірність pokirnist

acquire *v.t.* набувати nabuvaty

acquirement *n.* придбання prydbannia

acquisition *n.* привласнення pryvlasnennia

acquit *v.t.* виносити виправдальний вирок vynosyty vypravdalnyi vyrok

acquittal *n.* виправдання vypravdannia

acre *n.* акр akr

acreage *n.* площа землі в акрах ploshcha zemli v akrakh

acrimony *n* жовчність zhovchnist

acrobat *n.* акробат akrobat

across *adv.* впоперек vpoperek

across *prep.* через cherez

act *n.* акт akt

act *v.i.* діяти diiaty

acting *n.* виконання vykonannia

action *n.* вчинок vchynok

activate *v.t.* активувати aktyvuvaty

active *a.* активний aktyvnyi

activity *n.* діяльність diialnist

actor *n.* актор aktor

actress *n.* актриса aktrysa

actual *a.* фактичний faktychnyi

actually *adv.* фактично faktychno

acumen *n.* кмітливість kmitlyvist

acute *a.* різкий rizkyi

adage *n.* прислів'я pryslivia

adamant *n.* адамант adamant

adamant *a.* непохитний nepokhytnyi

adapt *v.t.* адаптуватися adaptuvatysia

adaptation *n.* адаптація adaptatsiia

adays *adv* щоденно shchodenno

add *v.t.* додати dodaty

addict *v.t.* залежати zalezhaty

addict *n.* наркоман narkoman

addiction *n.* залежність zalezhnist

addition *n.* додаток dodatok

additional *a.* додатковий dodatkovyi

addle *adj* зіпсований zipsovanyi

address *n.* адреса adresa

address *v.t.* звернутися zvernutysia

addressee *n.* адресат adresat

adduce *v.t.* наводити докази navodyty dokazy

adept *n.* знавець znavets

adept *a.* обізнаний obiznanyi

adequacy *n.* адекватність adekvatnist

adequate *a.* адекватний adekvatnyi

adhere *v.i.* дотримуватися dotrymuvatysia

adherence *n.* дотримання dotrymannia

adhesion *n.* прилипання prylypannia

adhesive *n.* клей klei

adhesive *a.* клейкий kleikyi

adhibit *v.t.* прикладати prykladaty

adieu *interj.* прощавай(те)! proshchavai(te)!

adieu *n.* прощання proshchannia

adiure *v.t.* благати blahaty

adjacent *a.* прилеглий prylehlyi

adjective *n.* прикметник prykmetnyk

adjoin *v.t.* примикати prymykaty

adjourn *v.t.* відкладати vidkladaty

adjournment *n.* відкладення vidkladennia

adjudge *v.t.* виносити вирок vynosyty vyrok

adjunct *n.* доповнення dopovnennia

adjuration *n* благання blahannia

adjust *v.t.* упорядковувати uporiadkovuvaty

adjustment *n.* врегулювання vrehuliuvannia

administer *v.t.* управляти upravliaty

administration *n.* управління upravlinnia

administrative *a.* адміністративний administratyvnyi

administrator *n.* адміністратор administrator

admirable *a.* прекрасний prekrasnyi

admiral *n.* адмірал admiral

admiration *n.* предмет захоплення predmet zakhoplennia

admire *v.t.* захоплюватися zakhopliuvatysia

admissible *a.* допустимий dopustymyi

admission *n.* допущення dopushchennia

admit *v.t.* допускати dopuskaty

admittance *n.* доступ dostup

admonish *v.t.* застерігати zasterihaty

admonition *n.* застереження zasterezhennia

adnascent *adj.* той, що зростає toi, shcho zrostaie

ado *n.* шум shum

adobe *n.* цегла повітряного сушіння tsehla povitrianoho sushinnia

adolescence *n.* молодість molodist

adolescent *a.* юний yunyi

adopt *v.t.* переймати pereimaty

adoption *n* добір dobir

adorable *a.* обожнюваний obozhniuvanyi

adoration *n.* обожнювання obozhniuvannia

adore *v.t.* обожнювати obozhniuvaty

adorn *v.t.* прикрашати prykrashaty

adscititious *adj* привнесений pryvnesenyi

adscript *adj.* приписаний prypysanyi

adulation *n* лестощі lestoshchi

adult *n.* доросла людина dorosla liudyna

adult *a* дорослий doroslyi

adulterate *v.t.* перелюбствувати pereliubstvuvaty

adulteration *n.* перелюб pereliub

adultery *n.* адюльтер adiulter

advance *n.* аванс avans

advance *v.t.* крокувати krokuvaty

advancement *n.* прогрес prohres

advantage *v.t.* давати перевагу davaty perevahu

advantage *n.* перевага perevaha

advantageous *a.* виграшний vyhrashnyi

advent *n.* прихід prykhid

adventure *n* авантюра avantiura

adventurous *a.* авантюрний avantiurnyi

adverb *n.* прислівник pryslivnyk

adverbial *a.* прислівниковий pryslivnykovyi

adversary *n.* противник protyvnyk

adverse *a* несприятливий nespryiatlyvyi

adversity *n.* негаразди neharazdy

advert *v.* звертатися zvertatysia

advertise *v.t.* рекламувати reklamuvaty

advertisement *n* реклама reklama

advice *n* порада porada

advisability *n* доцільність dotsilnist

advisable *a.* доцільний dotsilnyi
advise *v.t.* консультувати konsultuvaty
advocacy *n.* адвокатура advokatura
advocate *n* адвокат advokat
advocate *v.t.* захищати zakhyshchaty
aerial *n.* антена antena
aerial *a.* повітряний povitrianyi
aeriform *adj.* газоподібний hazopodibnyi
aerify *v.t.* аерувати aeruvaty
aerodrome *n* аеродром aerodrom
aeronautics *n.pl.* аеронавтика aeronavtyka
aeroplane *n.* аероплан aeroplan
aesthetic *a.* естетичний estetychnyi
aesthetics *n.pl.* естетика estetyka
aestival *adj* річний richnyi
afar *adv.* удалині udalyni
affable *a.* привітний pryvitnyi
affair *n.* справа sprava
affect *v.t.* впливати vplyvaty
affectation *n* афектація afektatsiia
affection *n.* поразка porazka
affectionate *a.* люблячий liubliachyi
affidavit *n* письмове свідчення pysmove svidchennia
affiliation *n.* приєднання pryiednannia
affinity *n* спорідненість sporidnenist
affirm *v.t.* стверджувати stverdzhuvaty
affirmation *n* затвердження zatverdzhennia
affirmative *a* ствердний stverdnyi
affix *v.t.* наклеювати nakleiuvaty

afflict *v.t.* засмучувати zasmuchuvaty
affliction *n.* гіркота hirkota
affluence *n.* достаток dostatok
affluent *a.* який вільно тече yakyi vilno teche
afford *v.t.* давати davaty
afforest *v.t.* засадити лісом zasadyty lisom
affray *n* бешкет beshket
affront *n* ганьба hanba
affront *v.t.* образити obrazyty
afield *adv.* у полі u poli
aflame *adv.* у вогні u vohni
afloat *adv.* на воді na vodi
afoot *adv.* в русі v rusi
afore *prep.* вище vyshche
afraid *a.* переляканий pereliakanyi
afresh *adv.* знову znovu
after *prep.* за za
after *conj.* згідно з zhidno z
after *a* майбутній maibutnii
after *adv* позаду pozadu
afterwards *adv.* згодом zhodom
again *adv.* з другого боку z druhoho boku
against *prep.* проти proty
agamist *n* переконаний холостяк perekonanyi kholostiak
agape *adv.*, роззявивши рот rozziavyvshy rot
agaze *adv* у подиві u podyvi
age *n.* вік vik
aged *a.* літній litnii
agency *n.* агентство ahentstvo
agenda *n.* повістка povistka
agent *n* агент ahent
aggravate *v.t.* ускладнювати uskladniuvaty
aggravation *n.* загострення zahostrennia
aggregate *v.t.* збирати zbyraty

aggression *n* агресія ahresiia
aggressive *a.* агресивний ahresyvnyi
aggressor *n.* агресор ahresor
aggrieve *v.t.* кривдити kryvdyty
aghast *a.* вражений жахом vrazhenyi zhakhom
agile *a.* рухливий rukhlyvyi
agility *n.* спритність sprytnist
agist *v.t.* брати на відгодівлю braty na vidhodivliu
agitate *v.t.* агітувати ahituvaty
agitation *n* агітація ahitatsiia
aglow *adv.* палаючий palaiuchyi
agnus *n* Агні Ahni
ago *adv.* тому tomu
agog *adj.* збуджений zbudzhenyi
agonist *n* суперник supernyk
agonize *v.t.* мучитися muchytysia
agony *n.* агонія ahoniia
agoraphobia *n.* агорафобія ahorafobiia
agrarian *a.* аграрний ahrarnyi
agree *v.i.* погоджуватися pohodzhuvatysia
agreeable *a.* згодний zhodnyi
agreement *n.* угода uhoda
agricultural *a* сільськогосподарський silskohospodarskyi
agriculture *n* сільське господарство silske hospodarstvo
agriculturist *n.* агроном ahronom
agronomy *n.* агрономія ahronomiia
ague *n* гарячковий озноб hariachkovyi oznob
ahead *adv.* попереду poperedu
aheap *adv* в купі v kupi
aid *n* допомога dopomoha
aid *v.t* допомогти dopomohty
aigrette *n* плюмаж pliumazh

ail *v.t.* турбувати turbuvaty
ailment *n.* хвороба khvoroba
aim *n.* мета meta
aim *v.i.* цілити tsilyty
air *n* повітря povitria
aircraft *n.* літальний апарат litalnyi aparat
airy *a.* повітряний povitrianyi
ajar *adv.* відкритий vidkrytyi
akin *a.* споріднений sporidnenyi
alacrious *adj* запопадливий zapopadlyvyi
alacrity *n.* жвавість zhvavist
alamort *adj.* при смерті pry smerti
alarm *v.t* сигнальний syhnalnyi
alarm *n* тривога tryvoha
alas *interj.* на жаль na zhal
albeit *conj.* хоча khocha
albion *n* Альбіон Albion
album *n.* альбом albom
albumen *n* яєчний білок yaiechnyi bilok
alchemy *n.* алхімія alkhimiia
alcohol *n* алкоголь alkohol
ale *n* ель el
alegar *n* солодовий оцет solodovyi otset
alert *a.* насторожений nastorozhenyi
alertness *n.* настороженість nastorozhenist
algebra *n.* алгебра alhebra
alias *adv.* інакше inakshe
alias *n.* прізвисько prizvysko
alibi *n.* алібі alibi
alien *a.* прибулець prybulets
alienate *v.t.* відчужувати vidchuzhuvaty
aliferous *adj.* крилатий krylatyi
alight *v.i.* злізти zlizty
align *v.t.* вибудовувати в лінію vybudovuvaty v liniiu

alignment *n.* регулювання rehuliuvannia
alike *adv* подібно podibno
alike *a.* схожий skhozhyi
aliment *n.* зміст zmist
alimony *n.* аліменти alimenty
alin *adj* благородний blahorodnyi
aliquot *n.* певна кількість pevna kilkist
alive *a* живий zhyvyi
alkali *n* луг luh
all *a.* весь ves
all *pron* все vse
all *n* всі vsi
all *adv* цілком tsilkom
allay *v.t.* вгамовувати vhamovuvaty
allegation *n.* твердження tverdzhennia
allege *v.t.* посилатися на posylatysia na
allegiance *n.* вірність virnist
allegorical *a.* алегоричний alehorychnyi
allegory *n.* алегорія alehoriia
allergy *n.* алергія alerhiia
alleviate *v.t.* пом'якшувати pomiakshuvaty
alleviation *n.* полегшення polehshennia
alley *n.* алея aleia
alliance *n.* альянс alians
alligator *n* алігатор alihator
alliterate *v.* алітерувати aliteruvaty
alliteration *n.* алітерація aliteratsiia
allocate *v.t.* призначати pryznachaty
allocation *n.* асигнування asyhnuvannia
allot *v.t.* наділяти nadiliaty
allotment *n.* наділ nadil

allow *v.t.* дозволяти dozvoliaty
allowance *n.* порція portsiia
alloy *n.* сплавляти splavliaty
allude *v.i.* зposилатися zposylatysia
alluminate *v.t.* висвітлювати vysvitliuvaty
allure *v.t.* заманювати zamaniuvaty
allurement *n* спокуса spokusa
allusion *n* натяк natiak
allusive *a.* алегоричний alehorychnyi
ally *v.t.* вступати у союз vstupaty u soiuz
ally *n.* союзник soiuznyk
almanac *n.* альманах almanakh
almighty *a.* всемогутній vsemohutnii
almond *n.* мигдаль myhdal
almost *adv.* майже maizhe
alms *n.* милостиня mylostynia
aloft *adv.* в горі v hori
alone *a.* самотній samotnii
along *adv.* уздовж uzdovzh
along *prep.* через cherez
aloof *adv.* осторонь ostoron
aloud *adv.* вголос vholos
alp *n.* гірська вершина hirska vershyna
alpha *n* альфа alfa
alphabet *n.* алфавіт alfavit
alphabetical *a.* алфавітний alfavitnyi
alphonsion *n.* берікс beriks
alpinist *n* альпініст alpinist
already *adv.* вже vzhe
also *adv.* також takozh
altar *n.* вівтар vivtar
alter *v.t.* переробляти pererobliaty
alteration *n* зміна zmina
altercation *n.* сперечання sperechannia

alternate *a.* переміжний peremizhnyi

alternate *v.t.* чергувати cherhuvaty

alternative *n.* альтернатива alternatyva

alternative *a.* змінний zminnyi

although *conj.* хоча khocha

altimeter *n* альтиметр altymetr

altitude *n.* висота vysota

altivalent *adj* той, що високо літає toi, shcho vysoko lытaie

alto *n* альт alt

altogether *adv.* всі разом vsi razom

aluminium *n.* алюміній aliuminii

alumna *n* колишня вихованка kolyshnia vykhovanka

alveary *n* зовнішній слуховий прохід zovnishnii slukhovyi prokhid

alvine *adj.* кишковий kyshkovyi

always *adv* завжди zavzhdy

am *adv* актор-аматор aktor-amator

amalgam *n* амальгама amalhama

amalgamate *v.t.* зливатися zlyvatysia

amalgamation *n* злиття zlyttia

amass *v.t.* скупчувати skupchuvaty

amateur *n.* любитель liubytel

amatory *adj* аматорський amatorskyi

amauriosis *n* сліпота slipota

amaze *v.t.* дивувати dyvuvaty

amazement *n.* дивування dyvuvannia

ambassador *n.* посол posol

amberite *n.* амберіт amberit

ambient *adj.* навколо navkolo

ambiguity *n.* двозначність dvoznachnist

ambiguous *a.* двозначний dvoznachnyi

ambition *n.* честолюбство chestoliubstvo

ambitious *a.* честолюбний chestoliubnyi

ambry *n.* комора komora

ambulance *n.* машина швидкої допомоги mashyna shvydkoi dopomohy

ambulant *adj* що переходить з одного місця на інше shcho perekhodyt z odnoho mistsia na inshe

ambulate *v.t* пересуватися peresuvatysia

ambush *n.* засідка zasidka

ameliorate *v.t.* поліпшуватися polipshuvatysia

amelioration *n.* амеліорація amelioratsiia

amen *interj.* амінь! amin!

amenable *a* зговірливий zhovirlyvyi

amend *v.t.* змінити zminyty

amendment *n.* зміна zmina

amends *n.pl.* поправки popravky

amenorrhoea *n* аменорея amenoreia

amiability *n.* люб'язність liubiaznist

amiable *a.* люб'язний liubiaznyi

amicable *adj.* доброзичливий dobrozychlyvyi

amid *prep.* в середені v seredeni

amiss *adv.* невірно nevirno

amity *n.* дружні стосунки druzhni stosunky

ammunition *n.* боєприпаси boieprypasy

amnesia *n* амнезія amneziia

amnesty *n.* амністія amnistiia

among *prep.* серед sered

amongst *prep.* між mizh
amoral *a.* аморальний amoralnyi
amorous *a.* влюбливий vliublyvyi
amount *v.* зводитися zvodytysia
amount *v.i* становити stanovyty
amount *n* сума suma
amour *n* любовний зв'язок liubovnyi zviazok
ampere *n* Ампер Amper
amphibious *adj* десантний desantnyi
amphitheatre *n* амфітеатр amfiteatr
ample *a.* місткий mistkyi
amplification *n* зусилля zusyllia
amplifier *n* підсилювач pidsyliuvach
amplify *v.t.* перебільшувати perebilshuvaty
amuck *adv.* шалений shalenyi
amulet *n.* амулет amulet
amuse *v.t.* забавляти zabavliaty
amusement *n* звеселяння zveseliannia
an *art* невизначений артикль nevyznachenyi artykl
anabaptism *n* анабаптизм anabaptyzm
anachronism *n* анахронізм anakhronizm
anaclisis *n* анаклаза anaklaza
anadem *n* гірлянда hirlianda
anaemia *n* анемія anemiia
anaesthesia *n* анестезія anesteziia
anaesthetic *n.* анестетик anestetyk
anal *adj.* анальний analnyi
analogous *a.* подібний podibnyi
analogy *n.* аналогія analohiia
analyse *v.t.* аналізувати analizuvaty
analysis *n.* аналіз analiz

analyst *n* аналітик analityk
analytical *a* аналітичний analitychnyi
anamnesis *n* пригадування pryhaduvannia
anamorphous *adj* анаморфний anamorfnyi
anarchism *n.* анархізм anarkhizm
anarchist *n* анархіст anarkhist
anarchy *n* анархія anarkhiia
anatomy *n.* анатомія anatomiia
ancestor *n.* предок predok
ancestral *a.* спадковий spadkovyi
ancestry *n.* походження pokhodzhennia
anchor *n.* якір yakir
anchorage *n* якірна стоянка yakirna stoianka
ancient *a.* стародавній starodavnii
ancon *n* лікоть likot
and *conj.* і i
androphagi *n.* андрофаг androfah
anecdote *n.* анекдот anekdot
anemometer *n* анемометр anemometr
anew *adv.* по-новому po-novomu
anfractuous *adj* кривий kryvyi
angel *n* янгол yanhol
anger *n.* гнів hniv
angina *n* ангіна anhina
angle *n.* кут kut
angle *n* точка зору tochka zoru
angry *a.* злий zlyi
anguish *n.* страждання strazhdannia
angular *a.* кутовий kutovyi
anigh *adv.* близько blyzko
animal *n.* тварина tvaryna
animate *a.* натхненний natkhnennyi
animate *v.t.* оживити ozhyvyty

animation *n* пожвавлення pozhvavlennia
animosity *n* ворожість vorozhist
animus *n* намір namir
aniseed *n* аніс anis
ankle *n.* гомілка homilka
anklet *n* ножний браслет nozhnyi braslet
annalist *n.* літописець litopysets
annals *n.pl.* літописі litopysi
annectant *adj.* проміжний promizhnyi
annex *v.t.* крило krylo
annexation *n* анексія aneksiia
annihilate *v.t.* знищувати znyshchuvaty
annihilation *n* знищення znyshchennia
anniversary *n.* річниця richnytsia
announce *v.t.* оголошувати oholoshuvaty
announcement *n.* оголошення oholoshennia
annoy *v.t.* досаждати dosazhdaty
annoyance *n.* досада dosada
annual *a.* щорічний shchorichnyi
annuitant *n* аннуітент annuitent
annuity *n.* щорічна рента shchorichna renta
annul *v.t.* анулювати anuliuvaty
annulet *n* поясок колони poiasok kolony
anoint *v.t.* мазати mazaty
anomalous *a* неправильний nepravylnyi
anomaly *n* аномалія anomaliia
anon *adv.* скоро skoro
anonymity *n.* анонімність anonimnist
anonymity *n.* безликість bezlykist
anonymous *a.* анонімний anonimnyi
another *a* інший inshyi

answer *n* вирішення vyrishennia
answer *v.t* відповісти vidpovisty
answerable *a.* який несе відповідальність yakyi nese vidpovidalnist
ant *n* мураха murakha
antacid *adj.* антацидний antatsydnyi
antagonism *n* антагонізм antahonizm
antagonist *n.* антагоніст antahonist
antagonize *v.t.* ворогувати vorohuvaty
antarctic *a.* антарктичний antarktychnyi
antecede *v.t.* передувати pereduvaty
antecedent *n.* минуле mynule
antecedent *a.* апріорний apriornyi
antedate *n* датувати більш раннім числом datuvaty bilsh rannim chyslom
antelope *n.* антилопа antylopa
antenatal *adj.* який відбувся до народження yakyi vidbuvsia do narodzhennia
antennae *n.* чуття chuttia
antenuptial *adj.* дошлюбний doshliubnyi
anthem *n* гімн himn
anthology *n.* антологія antolohiia
anthropoid *adj.* людиноподібний liudynopodibnyi
anti *pref.* анти anty
anti-aircraft *a.* зенітний zenitnyi
antic *n* гримаси hrymasy
anticardium *n* ямка під грудьми yamka pid hrudmy
anticipate *v.t.* передбачити peredbachyty
anticipation *n.* побоювання poboiuvannia

antidote *n.* антидот antydot
antinomy *n.* протиріччя в законі
protyrichchia v zakoni
antipathy *n.* антипатія antypatiia
antiphony *n.* антифон antyfon
antipodes *n.* антиподи antypody
antiquarian *n* антиквар antykvar
antiquarian *a.* антикварний
antykvarnyi
antiquary *n.* збирач старовинних
речей zbyrach starovynnykh
rechei
antiquated *a.* старезний stareznyi
antique *a.* давній davnii
antiquity *n.* старовина starovyna
antiseptic *n.* антисептик
antyseptyk
antiseptic *a.* антисептичний
antyseptychnyi
antitheist *n* атеїст ateist
antithesis *n.* антитеза antyteza
antler *n.* оленячий ріг oleniachyi
rih
antonym *n.* антонім antonim
anus *n.* задній прохід zadnii
prokhid
anvil *n.* ковадло kovadlo
anxiety *n* тривога tryvoha
anxious *a.* заклопотаний
zaklopotanyi
any *adv.* взагалі vzahali
any *a.* який-небудь yakyi-nebud
anyhow *adv.* так чи інакше tak
chy inakshe
apace *adv.* швидко shvydko
apart *adv.* на віддалі na viddali
apartment *n.* квартира kvartyra
apathy *n.* апатія apatiia
ape *n* мавпа mavpa
ape *v.t.* мавпувати mavpuvaty
aperture *n.* отвір otvir
apex *n.* верхівка verkhivka
aphorism *n* афоризм aforyzm

apiary *n.* пасіка pasika
apiculture *n.* бджільництво
bdzhilnytstvo
apish *a.* мавпячий mavpiachyi
apnoea *n* задуха zadukha
apologize *v.i.* вибачатися
vybachatysia
apologue *n* повчальна база
povchalna baza
apology *n.* вибачення
vybachennia
apostle *n.* апостол apostol
apostrophe *n.* апостроф apostrof
apotheosis *n.* прославляння
proslavliannia
apparatus *n.* апарат aparat
apparel *n.* предмети одягу
predmety odiahu
apparel *v.t.* споряджати
sporiadzhaty
apparent *a.* видимий vydymyi
appeal *v.t.* апеляція apeliatsiia
appeal *n.* заклик zaklyk
appear *v.i.* показуватися
pokazuvatysia
appearance *n* поява poiava
appease *v.t.* полегшувати
polehshuvaty
appellant *n.* аппелянт appeliant
append *v.t.* приєднувати
pryiednuvaty
appendage *n.* придаток prydatok
appendicitis *n.* апендицит
apendytsyt
appendix *n.* апендикс apendyks
appendix *n.* додаток dodatok
appetence *n.* потяг potiah
appetent *adj.* спраглий sprahlyi
appetite *n.* апетит apetyt
appetite *n.* пристрасть prystrast
appetizer *n* аперитив aperytyv
applaud *v.t.* аплодувати
aploduvaty

applause *n.* оплески oplesky
apple *n.* яблуко yabluko
appliance *n.* прилад prylad
applicable *a.* застосовний zastosovnyi
applicant *n.* заявник zaiavnyk
application *n.* застосовність zastosovnist
apply *v.t.* застосовувати zastosovuvaty
appoint *v.t.* затверджувати zatverdzhuvaty
appointment *n.* побачення pobachennia
apportion *v.t.* розподіляти rozpodiliaty
apposite *a.* відповідний vidpovidnyi
apposite *adj* доречно dorechno
appositely *adv* до речі do rechi
appraise *v.t.* розцінювати roztsiniuvaty
appreciable *a.* помітний pomitnyi
appreciate *v.t.* усвідомлювати usvidomliuvaty
appreciation *n.* оцінка otsinka
apprehend *v.t.* передчувати peredchuvaty
apprehension *n.* розуміння rozuminnia
apprehensive *a.* кмітливий kmitlyvyi
apprentice *n.* підмайстер pidmaister
apprise *v.t.* сповіщати spovishchaty
approach *n.* підхід pidkhid
approach *v.t.* підходити pidkhodyty
approbate *v.t* санкціонувати sanktsionuvaty
approbation *n.* схвалення skhvalennia

appropriate *a.* доречний dorechnyi
appropriate *v.t.* привласнювати pryvlasniuvaty
appropriation *n.* асигнування asyhnuvannia
approval *n.* розгляд rozhliad
approve *v.t.* затверджувати zatverdzhuvaty
approximate *a.* приблизно pryblyzno
appurtenance *n* приналежність prynalezhnist
apricot *n.* абрикос abrykos
apron *n.* фартух fartukh
apt *a.* здібний zdibnyi
aptitude *n.* придатність prydatnist
aquarium *n.* акваріум akvarium
aquarius *n.* Водолій Vodolii
aqueduct *n* аведук akveduk
arable *adj* орний ornyi
arbiter *n.* арбітр arbitr
arbitrary *a.* довільний dovilnyi
arbitrate *v.t.* виносити третейське рішення vynosyty treteiske rishennia
arbitration *n.* третейський суд treteiskyi sud
arbitrator *n.* третейський суддя treteiskyi suddia
arc *n.* арка arka
arcade *n* аркада arkada
arch *n.* звід zvid
arch *v.t.* згинати zhynaty
arch *a* опуклий opuklyi
archaic *a.* архаїчний arkhaichnyi
archangel *n* архангел arkhanhel
archbishop *n.* архієпископ arkhiiepyskop
archer *n* лучник luchnyk
architect *n.* архітектор arkhitektor
architecture *n.* архітектура arkhitektura

archives *n.pl.* архіви arkhivy
Arctic *n* Арктика Arktyka
ardent *a.* палкий palkyi
ardour *n.* запал zapal
arduous *a.* важкий vazhkyi
area *n* площа ploshcha
areca *n* арека areka
arefaction *n* осушення osushennia
arena *n* місце подій mistse podii
argil *n* глина hlyna
argue *v.t.* сперечатися sperechatysia
argument *n.* довід dovid
argute *adj* гострий hostryi
arid *adj.* сухий sukhyi
aries *n* Овен Oven
aright *adv.* вірно virno
aright *adv* правильно pravylno
arise *v.i.* виникати vynykaty
aristocracy *n.* аристократія arystokratiia
aristocrat *n.* аристократ arystokrat
aristophanic *adj* той, що відноситься до Аристофана toi, shcho vidnosytsia do Arystofana
arithmetic *n.* арифметика aryfmetyka
arithmetical *a.* числовий chyslovyi
ark *n* ящик yashchyk
arm *v.t.* озброювати ozbroiuvaty
arm *n.* рука ruka
armada *n.* армада armada
armament *n.* озброєння ozbroiennia
armature *n.* арматура armatura
armistice *n.* припинення військових дій prypynennia viiskovykh dii
armlet *a* нарукавник narukavnyk

armour *n.* броня bronia
armoury *n.* склад зброї sklad zbroi
army *n.* армія armiia
around *adv* крізь kriz
around *prep.* по ро
arouse *v.t.* будити budyty
arraign *v.* притягати до суду prytiahaty do sudu
arrange *v.t.* влаштовувати vlashtovuvaty
arrangement *n.* впорядкування vporiadkuvannia
arrant *n.* запеклий zapeklyi
array *n.* бойовий порядок boiovyi poriadok
array *v.t.* вишиковувати в бойовий порядок vyshykovuvaty v boiovyi poriadok
arrears *n.pl.* борги borhy
arrest *n.* арешт aresht
arrest *v.t.* заарештовувати zaareshtovuvaty
arrival *n.* прибуття prybuttia
arrive *v.i.* прибути prybuty
arrogance *n.* гордовитість hordovytist
arrogant *a.* зарозумілий zarozumilyi
arrow *n* стріла strila
arrowroot *n.* арроурут arrourut
arsenal *n.* арсенал arsenal
arsenic *n* арсен arsen
arson *n* підпал pidpal
art *n.* мистецтво mystetstvo
artery *n.* магістраль mahistral
artful *a.* вправний vpravnyi
arthritis *n* артрит artryt
artichoke *n.* артишок artyshok
article *n* стаття stattia
articulate *a.* артикулювати artykuliuvaty

artifice *n.* винахід vynakhid
artificial *a.* штучний shtuchnyi
artillery *n.* артилерія artyleriia
artisan *n.* ремісник remisnyk
artist *n.* художник khudozhnyk
artistic *a.* художній khudozhnii
artless *a.* простий prostyi
as *conj.* так як tak yak
as *adv.* як yak
as *pron.* який yakyi
asafoetida *n.* асафетида
  asafetyda
asbestos *n.* азбест azbest
ascend *v.t.* сходити skhodyty
ascent *n.* сходження
  skhodzhennia
ascertain *v.t.* з'ясовувати
  ziasovuvaty
ascetic *n.* аскет asket
ascetic *a.* аскетичний asketychnyi
ascribe *v.t.* приписувати
  prypysuvaty
ash *n.* попіл popil
ashamed *a.* совісно sovisno
ashore *adv.* до берега do bereha
aside *n.* зауваження, зроблене
  «про себе» zauvazhennia,
  zroblene «pro sebe»
aside *adv.* окремо okremo
asinine *adj.* ослячий osliachyi
ask *v.t.* просити prosyty
asleep *adv.* сплячий spliachyi
aspect *n.* аспект aspekt
asperse *v.* ганьбити hanbyty
aspirant *n.* честолюбець
  chestoliubets
aspiration *n.* прагнення
  prahnennia
aspire *v.t.* прагнути prahnuty
ass *n.* дупа dupa
assail *v.* штурмувати shturmuvaty
assassin *n.* вбивця vbyvtsia
assassinate *v.t.* вбити vbyty

assassination *n* вбивство
  vbyvstvo
assault *v.t.* атакувати atakuvaty
assault *n.* напад napad
assemble *v.t.* збиратися
  zbyratysia
assembly *n.* асамблея asambleia
assent *n.* дозвіл dozvil
assent *v.i.* згоджуватися
  zhodzhuvatysia
assert *v.t.* відстоювати
  vidstoiuvaty
assess *v.t.* визначати vyznachaty
assessment *n.* обкладання
  obkladannia
asset *n.* актив aktyv
assibilate *v.* вимовляти з
  шипінням vymovliaty z
  shypinniam
assign *v.t.* уповноважувати
  upovnovazhuvaty
assignee *n.* уповноважений
  upovnovazhenyi
assimilate *v.* засвоювати
  zasvoiuvaty
assimilation *n* засвоєння
  zasvoiennia
assist *v.t.* допомагати
  dopomahaty
assistance *n.* сприяння
  spryiannia
assistant *n.* асистент asystent
associate *a.* асоціативний
  asotsiatyvnyi
associate *v.t.* асоціювати
  asotsiiuvaty
associate *n.* спільник spilnyk
association *n.* асоціація
  asotsiatsiia
assoil *v.t.* виправдовувати по
  суду vypravdovuvaty po sudu
assort *v.t.* сортувати sortuvaty

assuage *v.t.* заспокоїти zaspokoity

assume *v.t.* удавати udavaty

assumption *n.* самовпевненість samovpevnenist

assurance *n.* страхування strakhuvannia

assure *v.t.* завіряти zaviriaty

astatic *adj.* нестабільний nestabilnyi

asterisk *n.* зірочка zirochka

asterism *n.* астеризм asteryzm

asteroid *adj.* зіркоподібний zirkopodibnyi

asthma *n.* астма astma

astir *adv.* що перебуває в русі shcho perebuvaie v rusi

astonish *v.t.* вражати vrazhaty

astonishment *n.* здивування zdyvuvannia

astound *v.i.* дивуватися dyvuvatysia

astray *adv.,* той, що заблукав toi, shcho zablukav

astrologer *n.* астролог astroloh

astrology *n.* астрологія astrolohiia

astronaut *n.* астронавт astronavt

astronomer *n.* астроном astronom

astronomy *n.* астрономія astronomiia

asunder *adv.* нарізно narizno

asylum *n* психіатрична лікарня psykhiatrychna likarnia

at *prep.* при pry

atheism *n* атеїзм ateizm

atheist *n* безбожник bezbozhnyk

athirst *adj.* прагнучий prahnuchyi

athlete *n.* атлет atlet

athletic *a.* атлетичний atletychnyi

athletics *n.* атлетика atletyka

athwart *prep.* наперерік napererik

atlas *n.* атлас atlas

atmosphere *n.* атмосфера atmosfera

atoll *n.* атол atol

atom *n.* атом atom

atomic *a.* атомний atomnyi

atone *v.i.* спокутувати spokutuvaty

atonement *n.* спокута spokuta

atrocious *a.* звірячий zviriachyi

atrocity *n* звірство zvirstvo

attach *v.t.* вкладати vkladaty

attache *n.* аташе atashe

attachment *n.* вкладення vkladennia

attack *v.t.* нападати napadaty

attack *n.* наступ nastup

attain *v.t.* домагатися domahatysia

attainment *n.* досягнення dosiahnennia

attaint *v.t.* оголошувати поза законом oholoshuvaty poza zakonom

attempt *v.t.* намагатися namahatysia

attempt *n.* спроба sproba

attend *v.t.* відвідувати vidviduvaty

attendance *n.* відвідуваність vidviduvanist

attendant *n.* відвідувач vidviduvach

attention *n.* увага uvaha

attentive *a.* уважний uvazhnyi

attest *v.t.* свідчити svyidchyty

attire *n.* наряд nariad

attire *v.t.* наряджати nariadzhaty

attitude *n.* ставлення stavlennia

attorney *n.* прокурор prokuror

attract *v.t.* залучати zaluchaty

attraction *n.* принада prynada

attractive *a.* привабливий pryvablyvyi

attribute *n.* визначення vyznachennia

attribute *v.t.* приписувати prypysuvaty

auction *v.t.* продавати з аукціону prodavaty z auktsionu

auction *n* торг torh

audible *a* чутний chutnyi

audience *n.* публіка publika

audit *n.* аналіз analiz

audit *v.t.* перевіряти звітність pereviriaty zvitnist

auditive *adj.* слуховий slukhovyi

auditor *n.* аудитор audytor

auditorium *n.* зал для глядачів zal dlia hliadachiv

auger *n.* шнек shnek

aught *n.* щось shchos

augment *v.t.* збільшувати zbilshuvaty

augmentation *n.* збільшення zbilshennia

august *a.* величний velychnyi

August *n.* серпень serpen

aunt *n.* тітка titka

auriform *adj.* що має форму вуха shcho maie formu vukha

aurilave *n.* апарат для промивання вуха aparat dlia promyvannia vukha

aurora *n* ранкова зоря rankova zoria

auspicate *v.t.* починати pochynaty

auspice *n.* заступництво zastupnytstvo

auspicious *a.* сприятливий spryiatlyvyi

austere *a.* суворий suvoryi

authentic *a.* достовірний dostovirnyi

author *n.* автор avtor

authoritative *a.* авторитетний avtorytetnyi

authority *n.* влада vlada

authorize *v.t.* уповноважувати upovnovazhuvaty

autobiography *n.* автобіографія avtobiohrafiia

autocracy *n* самодержавство samoderzhavstvo

autocrat *n* самодержець samoderzhets

autocratic *a* самодержавний samoderzhavnyi

autograph *n.* автограф avtohraf

automatic *a.* несвідомий nesvidomyi

automobile *n.* автомобіль avtomobil

autonomous *a* автономний avtonomnyi

autumn *n.* осінь osin

auxiliary *a.* допоміжний dopomizhnyi

auxiliary *n.* допоміжний механізм dopomizhnyi mekhanizm

avail *v.t.* бути корисним buty korysnym

available *a* наявний naiavnyi

avale *v.t.* опускати opuskaty

avarice *n.* скупість skupist

avenge *v.t.* мстити mstyty

avenue *n.* проспект prospekt

average *a.* звичайний zvychainyi

average *n.* середня величина serednia velychyna

average *v.t.* усереднювати useredniuvaty

averse *a.* неприхильний neprykhylnyi

aversion *n.* відраза vidraza

avert *v.t.* відвести vidvesty

aviary *n.* пташник ptashnyk

aviation *n.* авіація aviatsiia

aviator *n.* пілот pilot

avid *adj.* жадібний zhadibnyi

avidity *n.* пожадливість pozhadlyvist
avidly *adv* жадібно zhadibno
avoid *v.t.* уникати unykaty
avoidance *n.* уникнути unyknuty
avow *v.t.* визнавати vyznavaty
avulsion *n.* відрив vidryv
await *v.t.* чекати chekaty
awake *a* бадьорий badoryi
awake *v.t.* пробуджуватися probudzhuvatysia
award *n.* нагорода nahoroda
award *v.t.* нагороджувати nahorodzhuvaty
aware *a.* свідомий svidomyi
away *adv.* геть het
awe *n.* благоговіння blahohovinnia
awful *a.* що викликає страх shcho vyklykaie strakh
awhile *adv.* ненадовго nenadovho
awkward *a.* незграбний nezhrabnyi
axe *n.* сокира sokyra
axis *n.* вісь vis
axle *n.* вісь vis

babble *n.* лепет lepet
babble *v.i.* лепетати lepetaty
babe *n.* маля malia
babel *n* галас halas
baboon *n.* бабуїн babuin
baby *n.* дитина dytyna
bachelor *n.* холостяк kholostiak
back *adv.* назад nazad
back *n.* спина spyna
backbite *v.t.* обмовляти obmovliaty
backbone *n.* хребет khrebet
background *n.* фон fon

backhand *n.* тильна сторона руки tylna storona ruky
backslide *v.i.* відмовлятися від переконань vidmovliatysia vid perekonan
backward *adv.* на гірше na hirshe
backward *a.* темний temnyi
bacon *n.* сало salo
bacteria *n.* бактерія bakteriia
bad *a.* зіпсований zipsovanyi
badge *n.* значок znachok
badger *n.* борсук borsuk
badly *adv.* погано pohano
badminton *n.* бадмінтон badminton
baffle *v. t.* спантеличувати spantelychuvaty
bag *n.* сумка sumka
bag *v. i.* класти у мішок klasty u mishok
baggage *n.* майно maino
bagpipe *n.* волинка volynka
bail *v. t.* брати на поруки braty na poruky
bail *n.* застава zastava
bailable *a.* який має право на звільнення з ув'язнення під заставу yakyi maie pravo na zvilnennia z uviaznennia pid zastavu
bailiff *n.* судовий пристав sudovyi prystav
bait *n* наживка nazhyvka
bait *v.t.* перепочинок perepochynok
bake *v.t.* пекти pekty
baker *n.* пекар pekar
bakery *n* пекарня pekarnia
balance *n.* баланс balans
balance *v.t.* балансувати balansuvaty
balcony *n.* балкон balkon
bald *a.* лисий lysyi

bale *v.t.* в'язати у вузли viazaty u vuzly
bale *n.* зв'язка zviazka
baleen *n.* китовий вус kytovyi vus
baleful *a.* ліховісний likhovisnyi
ball *n.* м'яч miach
ballad *n.* балада balada
ballet *sn.* балет balet
balloon *n.* повітряна куля povitriana kulia
ballot *n* бюлетень biuleten
ballot *v.i.* голосувати holosuvaty
balm *n.* бальзам balzam
balsam *n.* розрада rozrada
bam *n.* розіграш rozihrash
bamboo *n.* бамбук bambuk
ban *n* анафема anafema
ban *n.* заборона zaborona
banal *a.* банальний banalnyi
banana *n.* банан banan
band *n.* стрічка strichka
bandage *~n.* бинт bynt
bandage *v.t* бинтувати byntuvaty
bandit *n.* розбійник rozbiinyk
bang *v.t.* стукнути stuknuty
bang *n.* удар udar
bangle *n.* браслет braslet
banish *v.t.* виганяти vyhaniaty
banishment *n.* висилка vysylka
banjo *n.* банджо bandzho
bank *n.* банк bank
bank *v.t.* згрібати в купу zhribaty v kupu
banker *n.* банкір bankir
bankrupt *n.* банкрут bankrut
bankruptcy *n.* неспроможність nespromozhnist
banner *n.* прапор prapor
banquet *n.* банкет banket
banquet *v.t.* бенкетувати benketuvaty
bantam *n.* забіяка-коротун zabiiaka-korotun

banter *v.t.* добродушно жартувати dobrodushno zhartuvaty
banter *n.* жартівлива бесіда zhartivlyva besida
bantling *n.* кодло kodlo
banyan *n.* баніан banian
baptism *n.* хрещення khreshchennia
baptize *+v.t.* хрестити khrestyty
bar *n.* бочка bochka
bar *v.t* виключати, не рахуючи vykliuchaty, ne rakhuiuchy
barb *n.* колючка koliuchka
barbarian *n.* варвар varvar
barbarian *a.* варварський varvarskyi
barbarism *n.* варварство varvarstvo
barbarity *n* нелюдяність neliudianist
barbarous *a.* дикий dykyi
barbed *a.* колючий koliuchyi
barber *n.* перукар perukar
bard *n.* бард bard
bare *a.* голий holyi
bare *v.t.* оголювати oholiuvaty
barely *adv.* ледь led
bargain *n.* угода uhoda
bargain *v.t.* укладати угоду ukladaty uhodu
barge *n.* баржа barzha
bark *n.* кора kora
bark *v.t.* нарощувати кору naroshchuvaty koru
barley *n.* ячмінь yachmin
barn *n.* сарай sarai
barnacles *n* докучлива людина dokuchlyva liudyna
barometer *n* барометр barometr
barouche *n.* ландо lando
barrack *n.* барак barak
barrage *n.* гребля hreblia

barrator *ns.* хабарник khabarnyk
barrel *n.* бочка bochka
barren *n* пустир pustyr
barricade *n.* барикада barykada
barrier *n.* бар'єр barier
barrister *n.* адвокат найвищого рангу advokat naivyshchoho ranhu
barter1 *v.t.* міняти miniaty
barter2 *n.* товарообмін tovaroobmin
barton *n.* садиба sadyba
basal *adj.* що лежить в основі shcho lezhyt v osnovi
base *a.* базовий bazovyi
base *v.t.* заснувати zasnuvaty
base *n.* основа osnova
baseless *a.* безпідставний bezpidstavnyi
basement *n.* підстава pidstava
bashful *a.* сором'язливий soromiazlyvyi
basial *adv.* базіоальвеолярний bazioalveoliarnyi
basic *a.* головний holovnyi
basil *n.* базилік bazylik
basin *n.* резервуар rezervuar
basis *n.* базис bazys
bask *v.i.* грітися hritysia
basket *n.* кошик koshyk
baslard *n.* кинджал kyndzhal
bass *n.* бас bas
bastard *n.* ублюдок ubliudok
bastard *a* позашлюбний pozashliubnyi
bat *v. i* бити палицею byty palytseiu
bat *n* дубина dubyna
bat *n* кажан kazhan
batch *n* пачка pachka
bath *n* ванна vanna
bathe *v. t* купати kupaty
baton *n* жезл zhezl

batsman *n.* гравець биткою hravets bytkoiu
battalion *n* дивізіон dyvizion
battery *n* батарея batareia
battle *n* бій bii
battle *v. i.* боротися borotysia
bawd *n.* звідник zvidnyk
bawl *n.* крик kryk
bawn *n.* загін для худоби zahin dlia khudoby
bay *n* бухта bukhta
bayard *n.* відчайдушна голова vidchaidushna holova
bayonet *n* багнет bahnet
be *pref.* обез- obez-
be *v.t.* бути buty
beach *n* пляж pliazh
beacon *n* маяк maiak
bead *n* бусинка busynka
beadle *n.* церковний сторож tserkovnyi storozh
beak *n* дзьоб dzob
beaker *n* кубок kubok
beam *n* промінь promin
beam *v. i* сяяти siaiaty
bean *n.* квасоля kvasolia
bear *n* ведмідь vedmid
bear *v.t* переносити perenosyty
beard *n* борода boroda
bearing *n* народження narodzhennia
beast *n* чудовисько chudovysko
beastly *a* тваринний tvarynnyi
beat *v. t.* бити byty
beat *n* удар udar
beautiful *a* красивий krasyvyi
beautify *v. t* прикрашати prykrashaty
beauty *n* краса krasa
beaver *n* бобер bober
because *conj.* тому що tomu shcho
beck *n.* кивок kyvok

beckon *v.t.* вабити vabyty
beckon *v. t* зробити знак zrobyty
znak
become *v. i* ставати stavaty
becoming *a* який пасує yakyi
pasuie
bed *n* ліжко lizhko
bedding *n.* постільні
приналежності postilni
prynalezhnosti
bedevil *v. t* мучити muchyty
bedight *v.t.* одягати odiahaty
bed-time *n.* час лягати спати
chas liahaty spaty
bee *n.* бджола bdzhola
beech *n.* бук buk
beef *n* яловичина yalovychyna
beehive *n.* вулик vulyk
beer *n* пиво pyvo
beet *n* буряк buriak
beetle *n* жук zhuk
befall *v. t* траплятися trapliatysia
before *prep* до do
before *adv.* перш persh
before *conj* швидше, ніж
shvydshe, nizh
beforehand *adv.* завчасно
zavchasno
befriend *v. t.* ставитися дружньо
stavytysia druzhno
beg *v. t.* благати blahaty
beget *v. t* народжувати
narodzhuvaty
beggar *n* жебрак zhebrak
begin *v.t.* розпочинати
rozpochynaty
beginning *n.* початок pochatok
begird *v.t.* оперізувати
operizuvaty
beguile *v. t* сорочити sorochyty
behalf *n* підтримка pidtrymka
behave *v. i.* надходити
nadkhodyty

behaviour *n* поведінка povedinka
behead *v. t.* обезголовити
obezholovyty
behind *prep* позаду pozadu
behind *adv* ззаду zzadu
behold *v. t* бачити bachyty
being *n* буття buttia
belabour *v. t* лупцювати
luptsiuvaty
belated *adj.* запізнілий zapiznilyi
belch *v. t* вивергати vyverhaty
belch *n* відрижка vidryzhka
belief *n* віра vira
believe *v. t* вірити viryty
bell *n* дзвін dzvin
belle *n* красуня krasunia
bellicose *a* войовничий
voiovnychyi
belligerency *n* стан війни stan
viiny
belligerent *a* той, що
знаходиться в стані війни toi,
shcho znakhodytsia v stani viiny
belligerent *n* учасник бійки
uchasnyk biiky
bellow *v. i* ревіти revity
bellows *n.* міхи mikhy
belly *n* живіт zhyvit
belong *v. i* належати nalezhaty
belongings *n.* деталі detali
beloved *n* коханий kokhanyi
beloved *a* улюблений uliublenyi
below *adv* нижче nyzhche
below *prep* нижче nyzhche
belt *n* ремінь remin
belvedere *n* альтанка altanka
bemask *v. t* замовчувати
zamovchuvaty
bemire *v. t* забризкувати брудом
zabryzkuvaty brudom
bemuse *v. t* приголомшити
pryholomshyty
bench *n* лава lava

bend *n* згин zhyn
bend *v. t* напружувати
napruzhuvaty
beneath *adv* внизу vnyzu
beneath *prep* під pid
benefaction *n.* благодіяння
blahodiiannia
benefice *n* бенефіцій benefitsii
beneficial *a* благотворний
blahotvornyi
benefit *n* привілей pryvilei
benefit *v. t.* мати користь maty
koryst
benevolence *n* доброзичливість
dobrozychlyvist
benevolent *a* доброзичливий
dobrozychlyvyi
benight *v. t* ввергати у морок
vverhaty u morok
benign *adj* милостивий
mylostyvyi
benignly *adv* милостиво
mylostyvo
benison *n* благословення
blahoslovennia
bent *n* схильність skhylnist
bequeath *v. t.* заповідати
zapovidaty
bereave *v. t.* віднімати vidnimaty
bereavement *n* втрата vtrata
berth *n* койка koika
beside *prep.* поруч з poruch z
besides *prep* крім krim
besides *adv* крім того krim toho
besiege *v. t* облягати obliahaty
beslaver *v. t* слинити slynyty
bestow *v. t* дарувати daruvaty
bestrew *v. t* всипати vsypaty
bet *v.i* сперечатися sperechatysia
bet *n* ставка stavka
betel *n* бетель betel
betray *v.t.* зраджувати
zradzhuvaty

betrayal *n* зрада zrada
betroth *v. t* обручити obruchyty
betrothal *n.* заручини zaruchyny
better *a* кращий krashchyi
better *adv.* набагато nabahato
better *v. t* поліпшувати
polipshuvaty
betterment *n* видатки на
збільшення вартості власності
vydatky na zbilshennia vartosti
vlasnosti
between *prep* між mizh
beverage *n* напій napii
bewail *v. t* оплакувати oplakuvaty
beware *v.i.* берегтися berehtysia
bewilder *v. t* заплутувати
zaplutuvaty
bewitch *v.t* зачарувати
zacharuvaty
beyond *prep.* за za
beyond *adv.* понад ponad
bi *pref* бі bi
biangular *adj.* двуугольний
dvuuholnyi
bias *v. t* настроювати nastroiuvaty
bias *n* нахил nakhyl
biaxial *adj* двохосьовий
dvokhosovyi
bibber *n* п'яниця pianytsia
bible *n* біблія bibliia
bibliographer *n* бібліограф
bibliohraf
bibliography *+n* бібліографія
bibliohrafiia
bicentenary *adj* двохсотріччя
dvokhsotrichchia
biceps *n* біцепс bitseps
bicker *v. t* сперечатися
sperechatysia
bicycle *n.* велосипед velosyped
bid *v.t* пропонувати ціну
proponuvaty tsinu

bid *n* конкурсна пропозиція konkursna propozytsiia
bidder *n* учасник торгів uchasnyk torhiv
bide *v. t* проживати prozhyvaty
biennial *adj* дворічний dvorichnyi
bier *n* одр odr
big *a* великий velykyi
bigamy *n* двоєженство dvoiezhenstvo
bight *n* закрут zakrut
bigot *n* фанатик fanatyk
bigotry *n* фанатизм fanatyzm
bile *n* жовч zhovch
bilingual *a* двомовний dvomovnyi
biliteral *adj* двобуквений dvobukvenyi
bilk *v. t.* вислизати vyslyzaty
bill *n* список spysok
billion *n* мільярд miliard
billow *v.i* здійматися zdiimatysia
billow *n* лавина lavyna
bimenasl *adj* оманливий omanlyvyi
bimonthly *adj.* двічі на місяць dvichi na misiats
binary *adj* двійковий dviikovyi
bind *v.t* пов'язувати poviazuvaty
binding *a* сполучний spoluchnyi
binocular *n.* бінокулярний binokuliarnyi
biographer *n* біограф biohraf
biography *n* біографія biohrafiia
biologist *n* біолог bioloh
biology *n* біологія biolohiia
bioscope *n* біоскоп bioskop
biped *n* двоноге dvonohe
birch *n.* береза bereza
bird *n* птах ptakh
birdlime *n* пташиний клей ptashynyi klei
birth *n.* зародження zarodzhennia
biscuit *n* печиво pechyvo

bisect *v. t* ділити навпіл dilyty navpil
bisexual *adj.* двостатевий dvostatevyi
bishop *n* єпископ yepyskop
bison *n* бізон bizon
bisque *n* фора в тенісі fora v tenisi
bit *n* шматок shmatok
bitch *n* самка samka
bite *v. t.* жалити zhalyty
bite *n* укус ukus
bitter *a* гіркий hirkyi
bi-weekly *adj* раз на два тижні raz na dva tyzhni
bizarre *adj* химерний khymernyi
blab *v. t. & i* базікати bazikaty
black *a* чорний chornyi
blacken *v. t.* чорнити chornyty
blackmail *n* шантаж shantazh
blackmail *v.t* шантажувати shantazhuvaty
blacksmith *n* коваль koval
bladder *n* сечовий міхур sechovyi mikhur
blade *n.* лезо lezo
blain *n* нарив naryv
blame *v. t* вважати винним vvazhaty vynnym
blame *n* осуд osud
blanch *v. t. & i* відбілювати vidbiliuvaty
bland *adj.* ввічливий vvichlyvyi
blank *a* порожній porozhnii
blank *n* пробіл probil
blanket *n* ковдра kovdra
blare *v. t* сурмити surmyty
blast *n* вибух vybukh
blast *v.i* шкодити shkodyty
blaze *n* полум'я polumia
blaze *v.i* палати palaty
bleach *v. t* відбілювати vidbiliuvaty

blear *v. t* затуманювати zatumaniuvaty
bleat *n* бекання bekannia
bleat *v. i* бекати bekaty
bleb *n* пухир pukhyr
bleed *v. i* кровоточити krovotochyty
blemish *n* недолік nedolik
blend *v. t* змішувати zmishuvaty
blend *n* суміш sumish
bless *v. t* благословляти blahoslovliaty
blether *v. i* тріщати trishchaty
blight *n* занепад zanepad
blind *a* сліпий slipyi
blindage *n* бліндаж blindazh
blindfold *v. t* зав'язувати очі zaviazuvaty ochi
blindness *n* сліпота slipota
blink *v. t. & i* блимати blymaty
bliss *n* блаженство blazhenstvo
blister *n* пузир puzyr
blizzard *n* заметіль zametil
bloc *n* блок blok
block *n* колода koloda
block *v.t* примусити prymusyty
blockade *n* затор zator
blockhead *n* дурень duren
blood *n* кров krov
bloodshed *n* кровопролиття krovoprolyttia
bloody *a* кривавий kryvavyi
bloom *n* розквіт rozkvit
bloom *v.i.* розквітати rozkvitaty
blossom *v.i* цвісти tsvisty
blossom *n* цвітіння tsvitinnia
blot *v. t* бруднити brudnyty
blot *n.* ляпка liapka
blouse *n* блуза bluza
blow *v.i.* надути naduty
blow *n* удар udar
blue *a* блакитний blakytnyi
blue *n* синій колір synii kolir

bluff *n* блеф blef
bluff *v. t* блефувати blefuvaty
blunder *n* промах promakh
blunder *v.i* промахуватися promakhuvatysia
blunt *a* тупий tupyi
blur *n* неразні обриси nerazni obrysy
blurt *v. t* бовкнути bovknuty
blush *n* рум'янець rumianets
blush *v.i* червоніти chervonity
boar *n* кабан kaban
board *v. t.* сісти на корабель sisty na korabel
board *n* управління upravlinnia
boast *v.i* хвастати khvastaty
boast *n* хвастощі khvastoshchi
boat *v.i* кататися на човні katatysia na chovni
boat *n* човен choven
bodice *n* корсаж korsazh
bodily *adv.* особисто osobysto
bodily *a* цілком tsilkom
body *n* тіло tilo
bodyguard *n.* охоронець okhoronets
bog *n* трясовина triasovyna
bog *v.i* вигинати спину vyhynaty spynu
bogle *n* страховище strakhovyshche
bogus *a* підроблений pidroblenyi
boil *n* кипіння kypinnia
boil *v.i.* кипіти kypity
boiler *n* бак bak
bold *a.* зухвалий zukhvalyi
boldness *n* сміливість smilyvist
bolt *v. t* замикати на засув zamykaty na zasuv
bolt *n* засув zasuv
bomb *n* бомба bomba
bomb *v. t* бомбити bombyty

bombard *v. t* бомбардувати bombarduvaty
bombardment *n* бомбардування bombarduvannia
bomber *n* бомбардувальник bombarduvalnyk
bonafide *a* сумлінний sumlinnyi
bonafide *adv* сумлінно sumlinno
bond *n* кайдани kaidany
bondage *n* кабала kabala
bone *n.* кістка kistka
bonfire *n* багаття bahattia
bonnet *n* капот kapot
bonten *n* хутро khutro
bonus *n* премія premiia
book *v. t.* записуватися zapysuvatysia
book *n* книга knyha
bookish *n.* книжковий knyzhkovyi
book-keeper *n* бухгалтер bukhhalter
booklet *n* буклет buklet
book-mark *n.* закладка zakladka
book-seller *n* книгопродавець knyhoprodavets
book-worm *n* книжковий хробак knyzhkovyi khrobak
boon *n* добродіяння dobrodiiannia
boor *n* мужик muzhyk
boost *v. t* прискорювати pryskoriuvaty
boost *n* рекламування reklamuvannia
boot *n* чобіт chobit
booth *n* палатка palatka
booty *n* видобуток vydobutok
booze *v. i* випивка vypyvka
border *n* кордон kordon
border *v.t* межувати mezhuvaty
bore *n* калібр kalibr
bore *v. t* набридати nabrydaty
born *v.* перенести perenesty

born rich *adj.* багатий за народженням bahatyi za narodzhenniam
borne *adj.* обмежений obmezhenyi
borrow *v. t* запозичувати zapozychuvaty
bosom *n* груди hrudy
boss *n* бос bos
botany *n* ботаніка botanika
botch *v. t* робити недбало robyty nedbalo
both *pron* і один і другий i odyn i druhyi
both *adj.* обидва obydva
both *conj* так само, як tak samo, yak
bother *v. t* набридати nabrydaty
botheration *n* неспокій nespokii
bottle *n* пляшка pliashka
bottler *n* розливочна машина rozlyvochna mashyna
bottom *n* дно dno
bough *n* сук suk
boulder *n* валун valun
bouncer *n* хвалько khvalko
bound *n.* кидок kydok
boundary *n* межа mezha
bountiful *a* щедрий shchedryi
bounty *n* щедрість shchedrist
bouquet *n* букет buket
bout *n* мах makh
bow *v. t* гнутися hnutysia
bow *n* лук для стрільби luk dlia strilby
bow *n* уклін uklin
bowel *n.* кишечник kyshechnyk
bower *n* дача dacha
bowl *v.i* подавати м'яч podavaty miach
bowl *n* чаша chasha
box *n* коробка korobka
boxing *n* бокс boks

boy *n* хлопчик khlopchyk
boycott *n* бойкот boikot
boycott *v. t.* бойкотувати boikotuvaty
boyhood *n* отроцтво otrotstvo
brace *n* скоба skoba
bracelet *n* браслет braslet
brag *n* хвалько khvalko
brag *v. i* хвастати khvastaty
braille *n* шрифт Брайля shryft Brailia
brain *n* мозок mozok
brake *n* гальмо halmo
brake *v. t* гальмувати halmuvaty
branch *n* філія filiia
brand *n* головешка holoveshka
brandy *n* бренді brendi
brangle *v. t* шумно сваритися shumno svarytysia
brass *n.* латунь latun
brave *a* хоробрий khorobryi
bravery *n* хоробрість khorobrist
brawl *v. i. & n* сваритися svarytysia
bray *n* ревіння revinnia
bray *v. i* пронизливо кричати pronyzlyvo krychaty
breach *n* порушення porushennia
bread *n* хліб khlib
breaden *v. t. & i* панірувати paniruvaty
breadth *n* ширина shyryna
break *v. t* ламати lamaty
break *n* прорив proryv
breakage *n* поломка polomka
breakdown *n* аварія avariia
breakfast *n* сніданок snidanok
breakneck *n* запаморочлива швидкість zapamorochlyva shvydkist
breast *n* джерело харчування dzherelo kharchuvannia
breath *n* дихання dykhannia

breathe *v. i.* дихати dykhaty
breeches *n.* бриджі brydzhi
breed *n* порода poroda
breed *v.t* розводити rozvodyty
breeze *n* бриз bryz
breviary *n.* скорочення skorochennia
brevity *n* стислість styslist
brew *v. t.* варити пиво varyty pyvo
brewery *n* пивоварня pyvovarnia
bribe *v. t.* давати хабар davaty khabar
bribe *n* хабар khabar
brick *n* цегла tsehla
bride *n* наречена narechena
bridegroom *n.* жених zhenykh
bridge *n* міст mist
bridle *n* узда uzda
brief *a.* короткий korotkyi
brigade *n.* бригада bryhada
brigadier *n* бригадир bryhadyr
bright *a* яскравий yaskravyi
brighten *v. t* кращати krashchaty
brilliance *n* яскравість yaskravist
brilliant *a* блискучий blyskuchyi
brim *n* край krai
brine *n* розсіл rozsil
bring *v. t* нести nesty
brinjal *n* баклажан baklazhan
brink *n.* берег bereh
brisk *adj* жвавий zhvavyi
bristle *n* щетина shchetyna
british *adj* британський brytanskyi
brittle *a.* тендітний tenditnyi
broad *a* широкий shyrokyi
broadcast *n* радіопередача radioperedacha
broadcast *v. t* транслювати transliuvaty
brocade *n* парча parcha
broccoli *n.* броколі brokkoli
brochure *n* брошура broshura

brochure *n* брошура broshura
broker *n* брокер broker
bronze *n. & adj* бронза bronza
brood *n* виводок vyvodok
brook *n.* струмок strumok
broom *n* мітла mitla
broth *n* юшка yushka
brothel *n* бордель bordel
brother *n* брат brat
brotherhood *n* братство bratstvo
brow *n* брова brova
brown *a* коричневий korychnevyi
brown *n* коричневий колір
korychnevyi kolir
browse *n* огляд ohliad
bruise *n* синяк syniak
bruit *n* чутки chutky
brush *n* пензлик penzlyk
brustle *v. i* тріщати trishchaty
brutal *a* брутальний brutalnyi
brute *n* тварина tvaryna
bubble *n* міхур mikhur
bucket *n* відро vidro
buckle *n* пряжка priazhka
bud *n* брунька brunka
budge *v. i. & n* ворушитися
vorushytysia
budget *n* бюджет biudzhet
buff *n* буйволяча шкіра
buivoliacha shkira
buffalo *n.* буйвол buivol
buffoon *n* блазень blazen
bug *n.* блошиця bloshytsia
bugle *n* ріжок rizhok
build *n* будова тіла budova tila
build *v. t* будувати buduvaty
building *n* будівництво
budivnytstvo
bulb *n.* лампа lampa
bulk *n* обсяг obsiah
bulky *a* громіздкий hromizdkyi
bull *n* бик byk

bull's eye *n* точний постріл
tochnyi postril
bulldog *n* бульдог buldoh
bullet *n* куля kulia
bulletin *n* зведення zvedennia
bullock *n* віл vil
bully *v. t.* задирати zadyraty
bully *n* хуліган khulihan
bulwark *n* бастіон bastion
bumper *n.* бампер bamper
bumpy *adj* вибоїстий vyboistyi
bunch *n* компанія kompaniia
bundle *n* вузол vuzol
bungalow *n* бунгало bunhalo
bungle *v. t* невміло працювати
nevmilo pratsiuvaty
bungle *n* погана робота pohana
robota
bunk *n* спальне місце spalne
mistse
bunker *n* ямка yamka
buoy *n* буй bui
buoyancy *n* плавучість plavuchist
burden *n* ноша nosha
burden *v. t* обтяжувати
obtiazhuvaty
burdensome *a* обтяжливий
obtiazhlyvyi
Bureacracy *n.* бюрократія
biurokratiia
bureau *n.* бюро biuro
bureaucrat *n* бюрократ biurokrat
burglar *n* зломщик zlomshchyk
burglary *n* крадіжка зі зломом
kradizhka zi zlomom
burial *n* захоронення
zakhoronennia
burk *v. t* дуже тверда брила
duzhe tverda bryla
burn *v. t* горіти hority
burn *n* опік opik
burrow *n* нора nora
burst *v. i.* зламувати zlamuvaty

burst *n* спалах spalakh
bury *v. t.* ховати khovaty
bus *n* автобус avtobus
bush *n* кущ kushch
business *n* бізнес biznes
businessman *n* бізнесмен biznesmen
bustle *v. t* підганяти pidhaniaty
busy *a* зайнятий zainiatyi
but *prep* але ale
but *conj.* але ale
butcher *v. t* забивати zabyvaty
butcher *n* м'ясник miasnyk
butter *v. t* мазати mazaty
butter *n* масло maslo
butterfly *n* метелик metelyk
buttermilk *n* пахта pakhta
buttock *n* зад zad
button *n* ґудзик gudzyk
button *v. t.* застібати zastibaty
buy *v. t.* купувати kupuvaty
buyer *n.* покупець pokupets
buzz *v. i* дзижчати dzyzhchaty
buzz *n.* дзижчання dzyzhchannia
by *prep* біля bilia
by *adv* біля bilia
bye-bye *interj.* бувай buvai
by-election *n* додаткові вибори dodatkovi vybory
bylaw, bye-law *n* постанова postanova
bypass *n* обхід obkhid
by-product *n* субпродукти subprodukty
byre *n* корівник korivnyk
byword *n* приказка prykazka

cab *n.* таксі taksi
cabaret *n.* кабаре kabare
cabbage *n.* капуста kapusta
cabin *n.* хатина khatyna

cabinet *n.* група міністрів hrupa ministriv
cable *v. t.* закріплювати канатом zakripliuvaty kanatom
cable *n.* кабель kabel
cache *n* тайник tainyk
cachet *n* відбиток vidbytok
cackle *v. i* кудкудакати kudkudakaty
cactus *n.* кактус kaktus
cad *n* хам kham
cadet *n.* курсант kursant
cadge *v. i* жебракувати zhebrakuvaty
cadmium *n* кадмій kadmii
cafe *n.* кафе kafe
cage *n.* клітина klityna
cain *n* братовбивця bratovbyvtsia
cake *n.* пиріг pyrih
calamity *n.* біда bida
calcium *n* кальцій kaltsii
calculate *v. t.* розраховувати rozrakhovuvaty
calculation *n.* обчислення obchyslennia
calculator *n* калькулятор kalkuliator
calendar *n.* календар kalendar
calf *n.* теля telia
call *v. t.* кликати klykaty
call *n.* дзвінок dzvinok
caller *n* візитер vizyter
calligraphy *n* каліграфія kalihrafiia
calling *n.* покликання poklykannia
callous *a.* черствий cherstvyi
callow *adj* незрілий nezrilyi
calm *v. t.* заспокоювати zaspokoiuvaty
calm *n.* спокій spokii
calm *n.* заспокоєння zaspokoiennia

calmative *adj* заспокійливий zaspokiilyvyi
calorie *n.* калорія kaloriia
calumniate *v. t.* обумовлювати obumovliuvaty
camel *n.* верблюд verbliud
camera *n.* камера kamera
camlet *n* камлот kamlot
camp *v. i.* розбивати табір rozbyvaty tabir
camp *n.* табір tabir
campaign *n.* кампанія kampaniia
camphor *n.* камфора kamfora
can *v.* бути в змозі buty v zmozi
can *v. t.* могти mohty
can *n.* бідон bidon
canal *n.* канал kanal
canard *n* качка kachka
cancel *v. t.* закреслювання zakresliuvannia
cancellation *n* скасування skasuvannia
cancer *n.* рак rak
candid *a.* щирий shchyryi
candidate *n.* кандидат kandydat
candle *n.* свічка svichka
candour *n.* відвертість vidvertist
candy *v. t.* зацукровувати zatsukrovuvaty
candy *n.* цукерка tsukerka
cane *v. t.* плести з очерету plesty z ocheretu
cane *n.* ціпок tsipok
canister *n.* каністра kanistra
cannon *n.* гармата harmata
cannonade *v. t.* обстрілювати артилерійським вогнем obstriliuvaty artyleriiskym vohnem
canon *n* критерій kryterii
canopy *n.* полог poloh
canteen *n.* їдальня yidalnia
canter *n* ханжа khanzha

canton *n* кантон kanton
cantonment *n.* розквартирування rozkvartyruvannia
canvas *n.* парусина parusyna
canvass *v. t.* агітувати ahituvaty
cap *v. t.* закривати кришкою zakryvaty kryshkoiu
cap *n.* кепка kepka
capability *n.* здібність zdibnist
capable *a.* здатний zdatnyi
capacious *a.* ємний yemnyi
capacity *n.* місткість mistkist
cape *n.* накидка nakydka
capital *n.* столиця stolytsia
capital *a.* столичний stolychnyi
capitalist *n.* капіталіст kapitalist
capitulate *v. t* капітулювати kapituliuvaty
caprice *n.* каприз kapryz
capricious *a.* вередливий veredlyvyi
Capricorn *n* Козеріг Kozerih
capsicum *n* перець червоний perets chervonyi
capsize *v. i.* перекидатися perekydatysia
capsular *adj* капсульний kapsulnyi
captain *n.* капітан kapitan
captaincy *n.* звання капітана zvannia kapitana
caption *n.* титр tytr
captivate *v. t.* полонити polonyty
captive *a.* полонений polonenyi
captive *n.* бранець branets
captivity *n.* полонення polonennia
capture *n.* здобич zdobych
capture *v. t.* захоплювати силою zakhopliuvaty syloiu
car *n.* вагон трамвая vahon tramvaia
carat *n.* карат karat

caravan *n.* караван karavan

carbide *n.* карбід karbid

carbon *n.* вуглець vuhlets

card *n.* гральна карта hralna karta

cardamom *n.* кардамон kardamon

cardboard *n.* картон karton

cardiacal *adjs* серцевий sertsevyi

cardinal *n.* кардинал kardynal

cardinal *a.* головний holovnyi

care *v. i.* піклуватися pikluvatysia

care *n.* догляд dohliad

career *n.* кар'єра kariera

careful *a* ретельний retelnyi

careless *a.* недбалий nedbalyi

caress *v. t.* пестити pestyty

cargo *n.* вантаж vantazh

caricature *n.* карикатура karykatura

carious *adj* каріозний karioznyi

carl *n* селюк seliuk

carnage *n* кривава бійня kryvava biinia

carnival *n* карнавал karnaval

carol *n* весела пісня vesela pisnia

carpal *adj* кистьовий kystovyi

carpenter *n.* тесляр tesliar

carpentry *n.* теслярські роботи tesliarski roboty

carpet *n.* килим kylym

carriage *n.* коляска koliaska

carrier *n.* носильник nosylnyk

carrot *n.* морква morkva

carry *v. t.* триматися trymatysia

cart *n.* візок vizok

cartage *n.* перевезення perevezennia

carton *n* картонка kartonka

cartoon *n.* мультфільм multfilm

cartridge *n.* патрон patron

carve *v. t.* вирізати vyrizaty

cascade *n.* водоспад vodospad

case *n.* положення polozhennia

cash *v. t.* перетворювати в готівку peretvoriuvaty v hotivku

cash *n.* готівка hotivka

cashier *n.* касир kasyr

casing *n.* кожух kozhukh

cask *n* барило barylo

casket *n* шкатулка shkatulka

cassette *n.* касета kaseta

cast *v. t.* метати metaty

cast *n.* тип typ

caste *n* каста kasta

castigate *v. t.* карати karaty

casting *n* кидання kydannia

cast-iron *n* чавун chavun

castle *n.* замок zamok

castor oil *n.* касторове масло kastorove maslo

castral *adj* табірний tabirnyi

casual *a.* тимчасовий tymchasovyi

casualty *n.* втрати vtraty

cat *n.* кішка kishka

catalogue *n.* каталог kataloh

cataract *n.* каскад kaskad

catch *n.* піймання piimannia

catch *v. t.* ловити lovyty

categorical *a.* категорічний katehorichnyi

category *n.* категорія katehoriia

cater *v. i* поставляти провізію postavliaty proviziiu

caterpillar *n* гусениця husenytsia

cathedral *n.* собор sobor

catholic *a.* католицький katolytskyi

cattle *n.* худоба khudoba

cauliflower *n.* кольорова капуста kolorova kapusta

causal *adj.* причинний prychynnyi

causality *n* причинність prychynnist

cause *v.t* заподіювати zapodiiuvaty

cause *n.* підстава pidstava

causeway *n* бруківка brukivka

caustic *a.* уїдливий uidlyvyi

caution *v. t.* робити попередження robyty poperedzhennia

caution *n.* застереження zasterezhennia

cautious *a.* передбачливий peredbachlyvyi

cavalry *n.* кавалерія kavaleriia

cave *n.* печера pechera

cavern *n.* дупло duplo

cavil *v. t* чіплятися chipliatysia

cavity *n.* порожнина porozhnyna

caw *v. i.* каркати karkaty

caw *n.* каркання karkannia

cease *v. i.* переставати perestavaty

ceaseless ~*a.* невпинний nevpynnyi

cedar *n.* кедр kedr

ceiling *n.* стеля stelia

celebrate *v. t. & i.* святкувати sviatkuvaty

celebration *n.* святкування sviatkuvannia

celebrity *n* славетна людина slavetna liudyna

celestial *adj* небесний nebesnyi

celibacy *n.* безшлюбність bezshliubnist

celibacy *n.* целібат tselibat

cell *n.* осередок oseredok

cellar *n* погріб pohrib

cellular *adj* клітинний klitynnyi

cement *v. t.* цементувати tsementuvaty

cement *n.* цемент tsement

cemetery *n.* цвинтар tsvyntar

cense *v. t* кадити kadyty

censer *n* кадило kadylo

censor *v. t.* цензурувати tsenzuruvaty

censor *n.* цензор tsenzor

censorious *adj* прискіпливий pryskiplyvyi

censorship *n.* цензура tsenzura

censure *n.* цензура tsenzura

censure *v. t.* осуджувати osudzhuvaty

census *n.* перепис perepys

cent *n* цент tsent

centenarian *n* довгожитель dovhozhytel

centenary *n.* сторіччя storichchia

centennial *adj.* столітній stolitnii

center *n* центр tsentr

centigrade *a.* стоградусний stohradusnyi

centipede *n.* сороконіжка sorokonizhka

central *a.* центральний tsentralnyi

centre *n* центр tsentr

centrifugal *adj.* відцентровий vidtsentrovyi

centuple *n. & adj* стократний stokratnyi

century *n.* століття stolittia

ceramics *n* кераміка keramika

cerated *adj.* воскований voskovanyi

cereal *a* злаковий zlakovyi

cereal *n.* каша kasha

cerebral *adj* церебральний tserebralnyi

ceremonial *a.* церемоніальний tseremonialnyi

ceremonious *a.* церемонний tseremonnyi

ceremony *n.* церемонія tseremoniia

certain *a* якийсь yakyis

certainly *adv.* звичайно zvychaino

certainty *n.* безсумнівний факт
bezsumnivnyi fakt
certificate *n.* сертифікат sertyfikat
certify *v. t.* засвідчувати
zasvidchuvaty
cerumen *n* вушна сірка vushna
sirka
cesspool *n.* вигрібна яма
vyhribna yama
chaice *n* чаша chasha
chain *n* ланцюг lantsiuh
chair *n.* стілець stilets
chairman *n* головуючий
holovuiuchyi
chaise *n* фаетон faeton
challenge *v. t.* викликати
vyklykaty
challenge *n.* виклик vyklyk
chamber *n.* кімната kimnata
chamberlain *n* камергер
kamerher
champion *v. t.* захищати
zakhyshchaty
champion *n.* чемпіон chempion
chance *n.* шанс shans
chancellor *n.* канцлер kantsler
chancery *n* канцелярія
kantseliariia
change *n.* заміна zamina
change *v. t.* переробляти
pererobliaty
channel *n* річище richyshche
chant *n* хорал khoral
chaos *n.* хаос khaos
chaotic *adv.* хаотичний
khaotychnyi
chapel *n.* каплиця kaplytsia
chapter *n.* глава hlava
character *n.* характер kharakter
charge *n.* заряд zariad
charge *v. t.* заряджати
zariadzhaty

chariot *n* легка коляска lehka
koliaska
charitable *a.* благодійний
blahodiinyi
charity *n.* милосердя myloserdia
charm1 *n.* чарівність charivnist
charm2 *v. t.* заклинати zaklynaty
chart *n.* графік hrafik
charter *n* грамота hramota
chase1 *v. t.* погоня pohonia
chase2 *n.* полювання poliuvannia
chaste *a.* цнотливий tsnotlyvyi
chastity *n.* цнотливість tsnotlyvist
chat1 *n.* бесіда besida
chat2 *v. i.* розмовляти rozmovliaty
chatter *v. t.* цокотіти tsokotity
chauffeur *n.* шофер shofer
cheap *a* дешевий deshevyi
cheapen *v. t.* дешевшати
deshevshaty
cheat *n.* шахрайство shakhraistvo
cheat *v. t.* шахраювати
shakhraiuvaty
check *n* відмітка vidmitka
check *v. t.* зазначити zaznachyty
checkmate *n* шах і мат shakh i
mat
cheek *n* щока shchoka
cheep *v. i* пропищати
propyshchaty
cheer *v. t.* вітати vitaty
cheer *n.* схвальний вигук
skhvalnyi vyhuk
cheerful *a.* безжурний bezzhurnyi
cheerless *a* сумовитий sumovytyi
cheese *n.* сир syr
chemical *n.* хімікат khimikat
chemical *a.* хімічний khimichnyi
chemise *n* жіноча сорочка
zhinocha sorochka
chemist *n.* хімік khimik
chemistry *n.* хімія khimiia
cheque *n.* чек chek

cherish v. t. плекати plekaty
cheroot n сигара syhara
chess n. віконна рама vikonna rama
chest n ящик yashchyk
chestnut n. каштан kashtan
chevalier n кавалер kavaler
chew v. t жувати zhuvaty
chicken n. курча kurcha
chide v. t. сварити svaryty
chief a. головний holovnyi
chieftain n. вождь vozhd
child n маля malia
childhood n. дитинство dytynstvo
childish a. дитячий dytiachyi
chiliad n. тисяча tysiacha
chill n. холод kholod
chilli n. перець гострий perets hostryi
chilly a мерзлякуватий merzliakuvatyi
chimney n. труба truba
chimpanzee n. шимпанзе shympanze
chin n. підборіддя pidboriddia
china n. фарфор farfor
chirp n цвірінькання tsvirinkannia
chirp v.i. цвірінькати tsvirinkaty
chisel v. t. працювати стамескою pratsiuvaty stameskoiu
chisel n стамеска stameska
chit n. крихта krykhta
chivalrous a. лицарський lytsarskyi
chivalry n. лицарство lytsarstvo
chlorine n хлор khlor
chloroform n хлороформ khloroform
chocolate n шоколад shokolad
choice n. асортимент asortyment
choir n хор khor
choke v. t. душитися dushytysia
cholera n. холера kholera

choose v. t. вибирати vybyraty
chop v. t кришити kryshyty
chord n. струна struna
choroid n судинна оболонка sudynna obolonka
chorus n. хор khor
Christ n. Христос Khrystos
Christendom n. християнський світ khrystyianskyi svit
Christian n християнин khrystyianyn
Christian a. християнський khrystyianskyi
Christianity n. християнство khrystyianstvo
Christmas n Різдво Rizdvo
chrome n жовта фарба zhovta farba
chronic a. хронічний khronichnyi
chronicle n. хроніка khronika
chronograph n хронограф khronohraf
chronology n. хронологія khronolohiia
chuckle v. i посміюватися posmiiuvatysia
chum n приятель pryiatel
church n. церква tserkva
churchyard n. кладовище kladovyshche
churl n селюк seliuk
churn n. олійниця oliinytsia
churn v. t. & i. збивати zbyvaty
cigar n. сигара syhara
cigarette n. сигарета syhareta
cinema n. кінотеатр kinoteatr
cinnabar n кіновар kinovar
cinnamon n кориця korytsia
cipher, cipher n. шифр shyfr
circle n. коло kolo
circuit n. кругообіг kruhoobih
circular a круговой kruhovoi
circular n. циркуляр tsyrkuliar

circulate *v. i.* циркулювати tsyrkuliuvaty
circulation *n* круговорот kruhovorot
circumference *n.* коло kolo
circumfluence *n.* обтікання obtikannia
circumspect *adj.* обережний oberezhnyi
circumstance *n* обставина obstavyna
circus *n.* цирк tsyrk
cist *n* гробниця hrobnytsia
citadel *n.* цитадель tsytadel
cite *v. t* згадувати zhaduvaty
citizen *n* громадянин hromadianyn
citizenship *n* громадянство hromadianstvo
citric *adj.* лимонний lymonnyi
city *n* місто misto
civic *a* цивільний tsyvilnyi
civics *n* основи громадянськості osnovy hromadianskosti
civil *a* цивільний tsyvilnyi
civilian *n* цивільна особа tsyvilna osoba
civilization *n.* цивілізація tsyvilizatsiia
civilize *v. t* цивілізувати tsyvilizuvaty
clack *n. & v. i* тріщати trishchaty
claim *v. t* вимагати vymahaty
claim *n* позов pozov
claimant *n* позивач pozyvach
clamber *v. i* дертися dertysia
clamour *v. i.* бурхливо виражати протест burkhlyvo vyrazhaty protest
clamour *n* шум shum
clamp *n* хомут khomut
clandestine *adj.* таємний taiemnyi

clap *n* бавовна bavovna
clap *v. i.* ляпати liapaty
clarification *n* прояснення proiasnennia
clarify *v. t* прояснити proiasnyty
clarion *n.* звук ріжка zvuk rizhka
clarity *n* чистота chystota
clash *v. t.* зіштовхуватися zishtovkhuvatysia
clash *n.* зіткнення zitknennia
clasp *n* застібка zastibka
class *n* клас klas
classic *n* класик klasyk
classic *a* класичний klasychnyi
classical *a* гуманітарний humanitarnyi
classification *n* класифікація klasyfikatsiia
classify *v. t* класифікувати klasyfikuvaty
clause *n* стаття stattia
claw *n* пазур pazur
clay *n* глинозем hlynozem
clean *v. t* чистити chystyty
clean чистий chystyi
cleanliness *n* чистота chystota
cleanse *v. t* чистити chystyty
clear *a* чистий chystyi
clear *v. t* очищати ochyshchaty
clearance *n* очищення ochyshchennia
clearly *adv* ясно yasno
cleft *n* тріщина trishchyna
clergy *n* духовенство dukhovenstvo
clerical *a* клерикальний klerykalnyi
clerk *n* клерк klerk
clever *a.* розумний rozumnyi
clew *n.* клубок klubok
click *n.* клацання klatsannia
client *n..* клієнт kliient
cliff *n.* стрімчак strimchak

climate *n.* клімат klimat
climax *n.* клімакс klimaks
climb *v.i* видиратися vydyratysia
climb1 *n.* підйом pidiom
cling *v. i.* прилипати prylypaty
clinic *n.* клініка klinika
clink *n.* віршик virshyk
cloak *n.* плащ plashch
clock *n.* годинник hodynnyk
clod *n.* ком kom
cloister *n.* монастир monastyr
close *v. t* закрити zakryty
close *a.* закритий zakrytyi
close *n.* завершення
zavershennia
closet *n.* кабінет kabinet
closure *n.* закриття zakryttia
clot *n.* грудка hrudka
clot *v. t* запікатися zapikatysia
cloth *n* тканина tkanyna
clothe *v. t* вкривати vkryvaty
clothes *n.* убрання ubrannia
clothing *n* обмундирування
obmundyruvannia
cloud *n.* хмара khmara
cloudy *a* хмарний khmarnyi
clove *n* гвоздика hvozdyka
clown *n* клоун kloun
club *n* клуб klub
clue *n* ключ kliuch
clumsy *a* нетактовний
netaktovnyi
cluster *v. i.* зростати гронами
zrostaty hronamy
cluster *n* китиця kytytsia
clutch *n* зчеплення zcheplennia
clutter *v. t* спричиняти безлад
sprychyniaty bezlad
coach *n* тренер trener
coachman *n* кучер kucher
coal *n* вугілля vuhillia
coalition *n* коаліція koalitsiia
coarse *a* грубий hrubyi

coast *n* узбережжя uzberezhzhia
coat *n* пальто palto
coating *n* шар shar
coax *v. t* умовляти umovliaty
cobalt *n* кобальт kobalt
cobbler *n* швець shvets
cobra *n* кобра kobra
cobweb *n* павутина pavutyna
cocaine *n* кокаїн kokain
cock *n* півень piven
cocker *v. t* балувати baluvaty
cockle *v. i* морщитися
morshchytysia
cock-pit *n.* кокпіт kokpit
cockroach *n* тарган tarhan
coconut *n* кокос kokos
code *n* код kod
co-education *n.* спільне
навчання spilne navchannia
coefficient *n.* коефіцієнт
koefitsiient
co-exist *v. i* співіснувати
spivisnuvaty
co-existence *n* співіснування
spivisnuvannia
coffee *n* кава kava
coffin *n* труна truna
cog *n* зубець zubets
cogent *adj.* переконливий
perekonlyvyi
cognate *adj* споріднений
sporidnenyi
cognizance *n* знання znannia
cohabit *v. t* співмешкати
spivmeshkaty
coherent *a* зчеплений zcheplenyi
cohesive *adj* здатний до
зчеплення zdatnyi do
zcheplennia
coif *n* стрижка stryzhka
coin *n* монета moneta
coinage *n* карбування монети
karbuvannia monety

coincide v. i збігатися zbihatysia
coir n кокосові волокна kokosovi volokna
coke v. t кокс koks
cold n холод kholod
cold a холодний kholodnyi
collaborate v. i співпрацювати spivpratsiuvaty
collaboration n співробітництво spivrobitnytstvo
collapse v. i обвал obval
collar n комір komir
colleague n колега koleha
collect v. t колекціонувати kolektsionuvaty
collection n колекція kolektsiia
collective a колективний kolektyvnyi
collector n складальник skladalnyk
college n коледж koledzh
collide v. i. зіштовхувати zishtovkhuvaty
collision n сутичка sutychka
collusion n таємна угода taiemna uhoda
colon n двокрапка dvokrapka
colon n Колон Kolon
colonel n. полковник polkovnyk
colonial a колоніальний kolonialnyi
colony n колонія koloniia
colour v. t розфарбовувати rozfarbovuvaty
colour n колір kolir
colter n різак rizak
column n колона kolona
coma n. голова комети holova komety
comb n гребінь hrebin
combat v. t. боротися borotysia
combat1 n сутичка sutychka
combatant a. стройовий stroiovyi

combatant1 n той, хто бореться toi, khto boretsia
combination n комбінація kombinatsiia
combine v. t комбінувати kombinuvaty
come v. i. приходити prykhodyty
comedian n. комедіант komediant
comedy n. комедія komediia
comet n комета kometa
comfit n. драже drazhe
comfort v. t втішати vtishaty
comfort1 n. комфорт komfort
comfortable a зручний zruchnyi
comic n комік komik
comic a комічний komichnyi
comical a смішний smishnyi
comma n кома koma
command n команда komanda
command v. t командувати komanduvaty
commandant n комендант komendant
commander n командир komandyr
commemorate v. t. відзначати vidznachaty
commemoration n. святкування sviatkuvannia
commence v. t починатися pochynatysia
commencement n набуття nabuttia
commend v. t рекомендувати rekomenduvaty
commendable a. похвальний pokhvalnyi
commendation n похвала pokhvala
comment n коментар komentar
comment v. i коментувати komentuvaty

commentary *n* коментар komentar

commentator *n* коментатор komentator

commerce *n* торгівля torhivlia

commercial *a* торговий torhovyi

commiserate *v. t* співчувати spivchuvaty

commission *n.* доручення doruchennia

commissioner *n.* уповноважений upovnovazhenyi

commissure *n.* спайка spaika

commit *v. t.* доручати doruchaty

committee *n* комітет komitet

commodity *n.* товар tovar

common *a.* загальний zahalnyi

commoner *n.* людина незнатного походження liudyna neznatnoho pokhodzhennia

commonplace *a.* загальне місце zahalne mistse

commonwealth *n.* держава derzhava

commotion *n* хвилювання khvyliuvannia

commove *v. t* турбувати turbuvaty

communal *a* комунальний komunalnyi

commune *v. t* спілкуватися spilkuvatysia

communicate *v. t* спілкуватися spilkuvatysia

communication *n.* комунікація komunikatsiia

communiqué *n.* комюніке komiunike

communism *n* комунізм komunizm

community *n.* суспільство suspilstvo

commute *v. t* перемикати peremykaty

compact *n.* договір dohovir

compact *a.* щільний shchilnyi

companion *n.* супутник suputnyk

company *n.* компанія kompaniia

comparative *a* порівняльний porivnialnyi

compare *v. t* порівнювати porivniuvaty

comparison *n* порівняння porivniannia

compartment *n.* купе kupe

compass *n* компас kompas

compassion *n* співчуття spivchuttia

compel *v. t* змушувати zmushuvaty

compensate *v.t* компенсувати kompensuvaty

compensation *n* компенсація kompensatsiia

compete *v. i* конкурувати konkuruvaty

competence *n* компетентність kompetentnist

competent *a.* компетентний kompetentnyi

competition *n.* змагання zmahannia

competitive *a* конкурентоспроможний konkurentospromozhnyi

compile *v. t* компілювати kompiliuvaty

complacent *adj.* послужливий posluzhlyvyi

complain *v. i* скаржитися skarzhytysia

complaint *n* скарга skarha

complaisance *n.* ввічливість vvichlyvist

complaisant *adj.* послужливий posluzhlyvyi

complement *n* повний комплект
povnyi komplekt
complementary *a* неконкуруючий
nekonkuruiuchyi
complete *v. t* завершувати
zavershuvaty
complete *a* повний povnyi
completion *n.* вивершення
vyvershennia
complex *n* комплекс kompleks
complex *a* комплексний
kompleksnyi
complexion *n* колір обличчя kolir
oblychchia
compliance *n.* щзгода shchzhoda
compliant *adj.* сумісний sumisnyi
complicate *v. t* ускладнювати
uskladniuvaty
complication *n.* складність
skladnist
compliment *n.* комплімент
kompliment
compliment *v. t* хвалити khvalyty
comply *v. i* підкорятися
pidkoriatysia
component *adj.* складовий
skladovyi
compose *v. t* складати skladaty
composition *n* складання
skladannia
compositor композитор
kompozytor
compost *n* удобрювати
компостом udobriuvaty
kompostom
composure *n.* холоднокровність
kholodnokrovnist
compound *a* складений
skladenyi
compound *n* сполука spoluka
compound *v. i* з'єднувати
ziednuvaty

compound *n* сполучення
spoluchennia
compounder *n.* мировий
посередник myrovyi
poserednyk
comprehend *v. t* включати
vkliuchaty
comprehension *n* розуміння
rozuminnia
comprehensive *a* всебічний
vsebichnyi
compress *v. t.* стискати styskaty
compromise *v. t* компрометувати
komprometuvaty
compromise *n* компроміс
kompromis
compulsion *n* примус prymus
compulsory *a* обов'язковий
oboviazkovyi
compunction *n.* каяття kaiattia
computation *n.* розрахунок
rozrakhunok
compute *v.t.* рахувати rakhuvaty
comrade *n.* товариш tovarysh
conation *n.* здатність до
вольового руху zdatnist do
volovoho rukhu
concave *adj.* увігнутий uvihnutyi
conceal *v. t.* ховати khovaty
concede *v.t.* погоджуватися
pohodzhuvatysia
conceit *n* марнославство
marnoslavstvo
conceive *v. t* задумувати
zadumuvaty
concentrate *v. t* концентруватися
kontsentruvatysia
concentration *n.* концентрація
kontsentratsiia
concept *n* концепція kontseptsiia
conception *n* задум zadum
concern *n* справа sprava

concern *v. t* стосуватися stosuvatysia
concert *n.* концерт kontsert
concert2 *v. t* змовлятися zmovliatysia
concession *n* поступка postupka
conch *n.* абсида absyda
conciliate *v.t.* примиряти prymyriaty
concise *a* стислий styslyi
conclude *v. t* укладати ukladaty
conclusion *n.* висновок vysnovok
conclusive *a* заключний zakliuchnyi
concoct *v. t* куховарити kukhovaryty
concoction *n.* куховарство kukhovarstvo
concord *n.* узгодження uzhodzhennia
concrescence *n.* зрощення zroshchennia
concrete *n* бетон beton
concrete *a* бетонний betonnyi
concrete *v. t* твердіти tverdity
concubinage *n.* позашлюбне співжиття pozashliubne spivzhyttia
concubine *n* співмешанка spivmeshanka
conculcate *v.t.* топати topaty
condemn *v. t.* засудити zasudyty
condemnation *n* вирок vyrok
condense *v. t* згущувати zhushchuvaty
condite *v.t.* солити solyty
condition *n* умова umova
conditional *a* обумовлений obumovlenyi
condole *v. i.* співчувати spivchuvaty
condolence *n* співчуття spivchuttia

condonation *n.* потурання poturannia
conduct *v. t* вести vesty
conduct *n* керувати keruvaty
conductor *n* кондуктор konduktor
cone *n.* шишка shyshka
confectioner *n* кондитер kondyter
confectionery *n* кондитерські вироби kondyterski vyroby
confer *v. i* радитися radytysia
conference *n* конференція konferentsiia
confess *v. t.* сповідувати spoviduvaty
confession *n* сповідь spovid
confidant *n* довірена особа dovirena osoba
confide *v. i* довіряти doviriaty
confidence *n* довіра dovira
confident *a.* впевнений vpevnenyi
confidential *a.* конфіденційний konfidentsiinyi
confine *v. t* обмежувати obmezhuvaty
confinement *n.* позбавлення волі pozbavlennia voli
confirm *v. t* санкціонувати sanktsionuvaty
confirmation *n* підтвердження pidtverdzhennia
confiscate *v. t* конфіскувати konfiskuvaty
confiscation *n* конфіскація konfiskatsiia
conflict *v. i* бути в конфлікті buty v konflikti
conflict *n.* конфлікт konflikt
confluence *n* скупчення народу skupchennia narodu
confluent *adj.* який зливається yakyi zlyvaietsia

conformity *n.* погодженість
pohodzhenist

conformity *n.* підпорядкування
pidporiadkuvannia

confraternity *n.* товариство
tovarystvo

confrontation *n.* конфронтація
konfrontatsiia

confuse *v. t* змішувати
zmishuvaty

confusion *n* замішування
zamishuvannia

confute *v.t.* спростовувати
sprostovuvaty

conge *n.* наказ nakaz

congenial *a* сприятливий
spryiatlyvyi

conglutinat *v.t.* склеювати
skleiuvaty

congratulate *v. t* поздоровляти
pozdorovliaty

congratulation *n* поздоровлення
pozdorovlennia

congress *n* конгрес konhres

conjecture *n* здогад zdohad

conjecture *v. t* гадати hadaty

conjugal *a* шлюбний shliubnyi

conjugate *v.t. & i.* відмінюватися
vidminiuvatysia

conjunct *adj.* з'єднаний ziednanyi

conjunctiva *n.* кон'юнктива
koniunktyva

conjuncture *n.* кон'юктура
koniuktura

conjure *v.i.* заклинати zaklynaty

conjure *v.t.* чаклувати chakluvaty

connect *v. t.* з'єднуватися
ziednuvatysia

connection *n* зв`язок zv`iazok

connivance *n.* попуск popusk

conquer *v. t* завойовувати
zavoiovuvaty

conquest *n* завоювання
zavoiuvannia

conscience *n* совість sovist

conscious *a* який усвідомлює
yakyi usvidomliuie

consecrate *v.t.* присвячувати
prysviachuvaty

consecutive *adj.* послідовний
poslidovnyi

consecutively *adv* послідовно
poslidovno

consensus *n.* згода zhoda

consent *v. i* дозволяти dozvoliaty

consent *n.* угода uhoda

consent3 *v.t.* бути задоволеним
buty zadovolenym

consequence *n* наслідок naslidok

consequent *a* логічний lohichnyi

conservative *n* консерватор
konservator

conservative *a* консервативний
konservatyvnyi

conserve *v. t* консервувати
konservuvaty

consider *v. t* обмірковувати
obmirkovuvaty

considerable *a* достатній
dostatnii

considerate *a.* уважний uvazhnyi

consideration *n* розгляд rozhliad

considering *prep.* враховуючи
vrakhovuiuchy

consign *v. t.* доручати doruchaty

consign *v.i.* ввіряти vviriaty

consignment *n.* партія partiia

consist *v. i* полягати poliahaty

consistence,-cy *n.* логічність
lohichnist

consistent *a* щільний shchilnyi

consolation *n* утіха utikha

console *v. t* заспокоювати
zaspokoiuvaty

consolidate v. t. консолідувати
konsoliduvaty
consolidation n консолідація
konsolidatsiia
consonance n. співзвуччя
spivzvuchchia
consonant n. приголосний
pryholosnyi
consort n. чоловік cholovik
conspectus n. конспект konspekt
conspicuous a. показний
pokaznyi
conspiracy n. змова zmova
conspirator n. змовник zmovnyk
conspire v. i. вчиняти змову
vchyniaty zmovu
constable n констебль konstebl
constant a сталий stalyi
constellation n. сукупність
sukupnist
constipation n. закреп zakrep
constituency n електорат
elektorat
constituent n. виборець vyborets
constituent adj. який обирає
yakyi obyraie
constitute v. t складати skladaty
constitution n конституція
konstytutsiia
constrict v.t. стискати styskaty
construct v. t. конструювати
konstruiuvaty
construction n спорудження
sporudzhennia
consult v. t довідуватися
doviduvatysia
consultation n консультація
konsultatsiia
consume v. t споживати
spozhyvaty
consumption n витрата vytrata
consumption n споживання
spozhyvannia

contact n. контакт kontakt
contact v. t контактувати
kontaktuvaty
contagious a заразливий
zarazlyvyi
contain v.t. містити mistyty
contaminate v.t. забруднювати
zabrudniuvaty
contemplate v. t споглядати
spohliadaty
contemplation n споглядання
spohliadannia
contemporary a сучасний
suchasnyi
contempt n презирство
prezyrstvo
contemptuous a презирливий
prezyrlyvyi
contend v. i твердити tverdyty
content a. який голосує «за»
yakyi holosuie «za»
content n. задоволення
zadovolennia
content v. t задовольняти
zadovolniaty
content n суть sut
contention n твердження
tverdzhennia
contentment n задоволеність
zadovolenist
contest v. t оскаржувати
oskarzhuvaty
contest n. суперечка superechka
context n контекст kontekst
continent n континент kontynent
continental a континентальний
kontynentalnyi
contingency n. випадковість
vypadkovist
continual adj. безперервний
bezperervnyi
continuation n. продовження
prodovzhennia

continue v. i. продовжувати
prodovzhuvaty
continuity n безперервність
bezperervnist
continuous a безперервний
bezperervnyi
contour n контур kontur
contra pref. проти- proty-
contraception n. контрацепція
kontratseptsiia
contract n контракт kontrakt
contract v. t скорочувати
skorochuvaty
contractor n підрядник pidriadnyk
contradict v. t суперечити
superechyty
contradiction n протиріччя
protyrichchia
contrapose v.t. протиставляти
protystavliaty
contrary a супротивний
suprotyvnyi
contrast n контраст kontrast
contrast v. t суперечити
superechyty
contribute v. t сприяти spryiaty
contribution n внесок vnesok
control n контроль kontrol
control v. t контролювати
kontroliuvaty
controller n. контролер kontroler
controversy n спір spir
contuse v.t. контузія kontuziia
conundrum n. загадка zahadka
convene v. t скликати sklykaty
convener n керівник конференції
kerivnyk konferentsii
convenience n. зручність
zruchnist
convenient a придатний
prydatnyi

convent n католіцька жіноча
школа katolitska zhinocha
shkola
convention n. угода uhoda
conversant adj. добре знайомий
dobre znaiomyi
conversant a досвічений
dosvichenyi
conversation n бесіда besida
converse v.t. спілкуватися
spilkuvatysia
conversion n зміна zmina
convert v. t перетворювати
peretvoriuvaty
convert n новонавернений
novonavernenyi
convey v. t. переправляти
perepravliaty
conveyance n перевізни засоби
perevizny zasoby
convict n арештант areshtant
convict v. t. визнанти винним
vyznanty vynnym
conviction n переконаність
perekonanist
convince v. t переконати
perekonaty
convivial adj. бенкетний
benketnyi
convocation n. скликання
sklykannia
convoke v.t. скликати sklykaty
convolve v.t. згортати zhortaty
coo n воркування vorkuvannia
coo v. i ніжно воркувати nizhno
vorkuvaty
cook v. t готувати hotuvaty
cook n кухар kukhar
cooker n кухонна плита
kukhonna plyta
cool v. i. охолоджувати
okholodzhuvaty
cool a прохолодний prokholodnyi

cooler n холодильник kholodylnyk
coolie n чорнороб chornorob
co-operate v. i співпрацювати spivpratsiuvaty
co-operation n співробітництво spivrobitnytstvo
co-operative a кооперативний kooperatyvnyi
co-ordinate v.t координувати koordynuvaty
co-ordinate a координований koordynovanyi
co-ordination n координація koordynatsiia
coot n. лисуха lysukha
co-partner n член товариства chlen tovarystva
cope v. i справитися spravytysia
coper n. баришник baryshnyk
copper n мідь mid
coppice n. підлісок pidlisok
coprology n. копрологія koprolohiia
copulate v.i. спаровуватися sparovuvatysia
copy n копія kopiia
copy v. t копіювати kopiiuvaty
coral n корал koral
corbel n. кронштейн kronshtein
cord n шнур shnur
cordate adj. серцеподібний sertsepodibnyi
cordial a серцевий sertsevyi
core n. ядро yadro
coriander n. коріандр koriandr
Corinth n. Коринф Korynf
cork n. затикати zatykaty
cormorant n. ненажера nenazhera
corn n зерно zerno
cornea n рогівка rohivka
corner n район raion

cornet n. корнет kornet
cornicle n. вусик vusyk
coronation n коронація koronatsiia
coronet n. віночок vinochok
corporal a тілесний tilesnyi
corporate adj. корпоративний korporatyvnyi
corporation n корпорація korporatsiia
corps n корпус korpus
corpse n труп trup
correct v. t виправляти vypravliaty
correct a правильний pravylnyi
correction n виправлення vypravlennia
correlate v.t. зіставляти zistavliaty
correlation n. взаємозв'язок vzaiemozviazok
correspond v. i відповідати vidpovidaty
correspondence n. відповідність vidpovidnist
correspondent n. кореспондент korespondent
corridor n. коридор korydor
corroborate v.t. підтверджувати pidtverdzhuvaty
corrosive adj. корозійний koroziinyi
corrupt v. t. спотворювати spotvoriuvaty
corrupt a. зіпсований zipsovanyi
corruption n. псування psuvannia
cosier n. затишне місце zatyshne mistse
cosmetic n. косметика kosmetyka
cosmetic a. косметичний kosmetychnyi
cosmic adj. космічний kosmichnyi
cost n. вартість vartist
cost v.t. коштувати koshtuvaty

costal *adj.* реберний rebernyi
costly *a.* дорогий dorohyi
costume *n.* одяг odiah
cosy *a.* приємний pryiemnyi
cot *n.* дитяче ліжко dytiache lizhko
cote *n.* хлів khliv
cottage *n* котедж kotedzh
cotton *n.* бавовна bavovna
couch *n.* диван dyvan
cough *n.* кашель kashel
cough *v. i.* кашляти kashliaty
council *n.* рада rada
councillor *n.* радник radnyk
counsel *v. t.* дати пораду daty poradu
counsel *n.* обговорення obhovorennia
counsellor *n.* радник radnyk
count *n.* позовна pozovna
count *v. t.* підраховувати pidrakhovuvaty
countenance *n.* обличчя oblychchia
counter *n.* прилавок prylavok
counter *v. t* протистояти protystoiaty
counteract *v.t.* протидіяти protydiiaty
countercharge *n.* зустрічне звинувачення zustrichne zvynuvachennia
counterfeit *a.* підробляти pidrobliaty
counterfeiter *n.* підроблювач pidrobliuvach
countermand *v.t.* відкликати vidklykaty
counterpart *n.* двійник dviinyk
countersign *v. t.* скріплювати підписом skripliuvaty pidpysom
countess *n.* графиня hrafynia

countless *a.* незчисленний nezchyslennyi
country *n.* країна kraina
county *n.* жителі графства zhyteli hrafstva
coup *n.* подвиг podvyh
couple *n* пара para
couple *v. t* спаруватися spariuvatysia
couplet *n.* куплет kuplet
coupon *n.* відривний талон vidryvnyi talon
courage *n.* хоробрість khorobrist
courageous *a.* сміливий smilyvyi
courier *n.* кур'єр kurier
course *n.* курс kurs
court *v. t.* спокушати spokushaty
court *n.* суд sud
courteous *a.* чемний chemnyi
courtesan *n.* куртизанка kurtyzanka
courtesy *n.* чемність chemnist
courtier *n.* придворний prydvornyi
courtship *n.* залицяння zalytsiannia
courtyard *n.* двір dvir
cousin *n.* двоюрідний брат dvoiuridnyi brat
covenant *n.* домовленість domovlenist
cover *v. t.* закривати zakryvaty
cover *n.* покришка pokryshka
coverlet *n.* покривало pokryvalo
covet *v.t.* жадати zhadaty
cow *v. t.* залякувати zaliakuvaty
cow *n.* корова korova
coward *n.* боягуз boiahuz
cowardice *n.* боягузтво boiahuztvo
cower *v.i.* зіщулюватися zishchuliuvatysia
cozy *adj.* затишний zatyshnyi

crab *n* краб krab
crack *v. i* розтріскування roztriskuvannia
crack *n* тріск trisk
cracker *n* сухар sukhar
crackle *v.t.* потріскувати potriskuvaty
cradle *n* колиска kolyska
craft *n* ремесло remeslo
craftsman *n* вправний майстер vpravnyi maister
crafty *a* хитрий khytryi
cram *v. t* втискувати vtyskuvaty
crambo *n*. ріфмоплетство rifmopletstvo
crane *n* підйомний кран pidiomnyi kran
crankle *v.t.* звиватися zvyvatysia
crash *v. i* розбити з грюкотом rozbyty z hriukotom
crash *n* тріск trыsk
crass *adj.* повний povnyi
crate *n.* кліть klit
crave *v.t.* палко бажати palko bazhaty
craw *n.* зоб zob
crawl *n* повзання povzannia
crawl *v. t* плентатися plentatysia
craze *n* манія maniia
crazy *a* божевільний bozhevilnyi
creak *v. i* скрипіти skrypity
creak *n* скрип skryp
cream *n* вершки vershky
crease *n* складка skladka
create *v. t* створювати stvoriuvaty
creation *n* створення stvorennia
creative *adj.* творчий tvorchyi
creator *n* творець tvorets
creature *n* створіння stvorinnia
credible *a* ймовірний ymovirnyi
credit *n* кредит kredyt
creditable *a* похвальний pokhvalnyi

creditor *n* кредитор kredytor
credulity *adj.* довірливість dovirlyvist
creed *n*. кредо kredo
creed *n* віросповідання virospovidannia
creek *n*. струмок strumok
creep *v. i* плазувати plazuvaty
creeper *n* повзуча рослина povzucha roslyna
cremate *v. t* кремувати kremuvaty
cremation *n* кремація krematsiia
crest *n* гребінець hrebinets
crevet *n*. плавильна чаша plavylna chasha
crew *n*. екіпаж ekipazh
crib *n*. ясла yasla
cricket *n* цвіркун tsvirkun
crime *n* злочин zlochyn
criminal *n* злочинець zlochynets
criminal *a* кримінальний kryminalnyi
crimp *n* агент, що вербує на військову службу обманом ahent, shcho verbuie na vыiskovu sluzhbu obmanom
crimple *v.t.* робити складки robyty skladky
crimson *n* малиновий колір malynovyi kolir
cringe *v. i.* раболіпствувати rabolipstvuvaty
cripple *n* каліка kalika
crisis *n* криза kryza
crisp *a* розсипчастий rozsypchastyi
criterion *n* мірило mirylo
critic *n* критик krytyk
critical *a* критичний krytychnyi
criticism *n* критика krytyka
criticize *v. t* критикувати krytykuvaty
croak *n*. кумкання kumkannia

crockery *n.* посуд posud
crocodile *n* крокодил krokodyl
croesus *n.* Крез Krez
crook *a* несправедливий nespravedlyvyi
crop *n* урожай urozhai
cross *v. t* перетинати peretynaty
cross *a* поперечний poperechnyi
cross *n* хрест khrest
crossing *n.* перетин peretyn
crotchet *n.* гачок hachok
crouch *v. i.* раболіпствувати rabolipstvuvaty
crow *n* ворона vorona
crow *v. i* кукурікати kukurikaty
crowd *n* натовп natovp
crown *v. t* вінчати vinchaty
crown *n* корона korona
crucial *adj.* вирішальний vyrishalnyi
crude *a* необроблений neobroblenyi
cruel *a* жорстокий zhorstokyi
cruelty *n* жорстокість zhorstokist
cruise *v.i.* круїз kruiz
cruiser *n* крейсер kreiser
crumb *n* крихітка krykhitka
crumble *v. t* кришити kryshyty
crump *adj.* зхрусткий zkhrustkyi
crusade *n* похід pokhid
crush *v. t* роздавити rozdavyty
crust *n.* скоринка skorynka
crutch *n* опора opora
cry *n* благання blahannia
cry *v. i* кричати krychaty
cryptography *n.* криптографія kryptohrafiia
crystal *n* кришталь kryshtal
cub *n* дитинча dytyncha
cube *n* куб kub
cubical *a* кубічний kubichnyi
cubiform *adj.* кубовидний kubovydnyi

cuckold *n.* рогоносець rohonosets
cuckoo *n* зозуля zozulia
cucumber *n* огірок ohirok
cudgel *n* дрючок driuchok
cue *n* репліка replika
cuff *v. t* бити рукою byty rukoiu
cuff *n* манжета manzheta
cuisine *n.* кулінарне мистецтво kulinarne mystetstvo
cullet *n.* склобій sklobii
culminate *v.i.* досягати найвищої точки dosiahaty naivyshchoi tochky
culpable *a* винний vynnyi
culprit *n* винуватець vynuvatets
cult *n* культ kult
cultivate *v. t* обробляти obrobliaty
cultrate *adj.* загострений zahostrenyi
cultural *a* культурний kulturnyi
culture *n* культура kultura
culvert *n.* дренажна труба drenazhna truba
cunning *a* хитрий khytryi
cunning *n* хитрість khytrist
cup *n.* чашка chashka
cupboard *n* буфет bufet
Cupid *n* Купідон Kupidon
cupidity *n* скнарість sknarist
curable *a* виліковний vylikovnyi
curative *a* цілющий tsiliushchyi
curb *v. t* приборкувати pryborkuvaty
curb *n* узбіччя uzbichchia
curcuma *n.* куркума kurkuma
curd *n* сир syr
cure *v. t.* виліковувати vylikovuvaty
cure *n* ліки liky
curfew *n* комендантська година komendantska hodyna
curiosity *n* цікавість tsikavist

curious *a* цікавий tsikavyi
curl *n.* локон lokon
currant *n.* смородина smorodyna
currency *n* валюта valiuta
current *n* електричний струм elektrychnyi strum
current *a* поточний potochnyi
curriculum *n* навчальний план navchalnyi plan
curse *v. t* проклинати proklynaty
curse *n* прокляття prokliattia
cursory *a* поверховий poverkhovyi
curt *a* уривчастий uryvchastyi
curtail *v. t* скорочувати skorochuvaty
curtain *n* заслона zaslona
curve *v. t* вигинати vyhynaty
curve *n* дуга duha
cushion *n* диванна подушка dyvanna podushka
cushion *v. t* підкладати подушку pidkladaty podushku
custard *n* заварний крем zavarnyi krem
custodian *n* зберігач zberihach
custody *v* опіка opika
custom *n.* звичай zvychai
customary *a* звичайний zvychainyi
customer *n* замовник zamovnyk
cut *n* поріз poriz
cut *v. t* різати rizaty
cutis *n.* шкіра shkira
cuvette *n.* кювета kiuveta
cycle *n* цикл tsykl
cyclic *a* циклічний tsyklichnyi
cyclist *n* велосипедист velosypedyst
cyclone *n.* циклон tsyklon
cyclostyle *n* розмножувальний апарат rozmnozhuvalnyi aparat

cyclostyle *v. t* розмножувати rozmnozhuvaty
cylinder *n* циліндр tsylindr
cynic *n* цинік tsynik
cypher cypress *n* кипарис kyparys

dabble *v. i.* займатися чимсь поверхово zaimatysia chyms poverkhovo
dacoit *n.* бандит bandyt
dacoity *n.* розбій rozbii
dad, daddy *n* тато, татусь tato, tatus
daffodil *n.* нарцис жовтий nartsys zhovtyi
daft *adj.* божевільний bozhevilnyi
dagger *n.* кинджал kyndzhal
daily *n.* щоденна газета shchodenna hazeta
daily *a* щоденний shchodennyi
daily *adv.* щоденно shchodenno
dainty *a.* витончений vytonchenyi
dainty *n.* ласощі lasoshchi
dairy *n* маслоробня maslorobnia
dais *n.* поміст pomist
daisy *n* маргаритка marharytka
dale *n* ділянка землі dilianka zemli
dam *n* дамба damba
damage *v. t.* пошкоджувати poshkodzhuvaty
damage *n.* пошкодження poshkodzhennia
dame *n.* дама dama
damn *v. t.* лаятися laiatysia
damnation *n.* проклін proklin
damp *a* вологий volohyi
damp *v. t.* сиріти syrity
damp *n* вогкість vohkist
damsel *n.* грілка hrilka

dance *n* танець tanets
dance *v. t.* танцювати tantsiuvaty
dandelion *n.* кульбаба kulbaba
dandle *v.t.* гойдати hoidaty
dandruff *n* лупа lupa
dandy *n* денді dendi
danger *n.* небезпека nebezpeka
dangerous *a* небезпечний nebezpechnyi
dangle *v. t* гойдатися hoidatysia
dank *adj.* неприємно вологий nepryiemno volohyi
dap *v.i.* ударяти про землю udariaty pro zemliu
dare *v. i.* сміти smity
daring *n.* сміливість smilyvist
daring *a* хоробрий khorobryi
dark *n* таємниця taiemnytsia
dark *a* темний temnyi
darkle *v.i.* темніти temnity
darling *n* улюбленець uliublenets
darling *a* улюблений uliublenyi
dart *n.* стріла strila
dash *v. i.* жбурнути zhburnuty
dash *n* рішучість rishuchist
date *n* дата data
date *v. t* ставити число stavyty chyslo
daub *n.* мазок mazok
daub *v. t.* обмазувати obmazuvaty
daughter *n* дочка dochka
daunt *v. t* приборкати pryborkaty
dauntless *a* безстрашний bezstrashnyi
dawdle *v.i.* байдикувати baidykuvaty
dawn *n* світанок svitanok
dawn *v. i.* світати svitaty
day *n* день den
daze *v. t* здивувати zdyvuvaty
daze *n* подив podyv
dazzle *v. t.* засліплювати блиском zaslipliuvaty blyskom

dazzle *n* сліпучий блиск slipuchyi blysk
deacon *n.* диякон dyiakon
dead *a* мертвий mertvyi
deadlock *n* тупик tupyk
deadly *a* смертельний smertelnyi
deaf *a* глухий hlukhyi
deal *n* справа sprava
deal *v. i* роздати rozdaty
dealer *n* дилер dyler
dealing *n.* роздача rozdacha
dean *n.* декан dekan
dear *a* милий mylyi
dearth *n* голод holod
death *n* смерть smert
debar *v. t.* не дозволяти ne dozvoliaty
debase *v. t.* знижувати якість znyzhuvaty yakist
debate *v. t.* дебатувати debatuvaty
debate *n.* дебати debaty
debauch *n* дебош debosh
debauch *v. t.* спокушати spokushaty
debauchee *n* розпусник rozpusnyk
debauchery *n* оргія orhiia
debility *n* слабкість slabkist
debit *n* дебет debet
debit *v. t* дебетувати debetuvaty
debris *n* уламки ulamky
debt *n* борг borh
debtor *n* боржник borzhnyk
decade *n* група з десяти hrupa z desiaty
decadent *a* занепадницький zanepadnytskyi
decamp *v. i* тікати tikaty
decay *v. i* руйнуватися ruinuvatysia
decay *n* розпад rozpad
decease *v. i* померти pomerty

decease *n* смерть smert
deceit *n* хитрість khytrist
deceive *v. t* навмисно вводити
в оману navmysno vvodyty v
omanu
december *n* грудень hruden
decency *n* пристойність
prystoinist
decennary *n*. десятиліття
desiatylittia
decent *a* славний slavnyi
deception *n* облуда obluda
decide *v. t* вирішувати vyrishuvaty
decillion *n*. деціліон detsillion
decimal *a* десятковий desiatkovyi
decimate *v.t.* стратити stratyty
decision *n* рішення rishennia
decisive *a* певний pevnyi
deck *n* палуба paluba
deck *v. t* настилати палубу
nastylaty palubu
declaration *n* заява zaiava
declare *v. t.* визнавати vyznavaty
decline *n* занепад zanepad
decline *n* захід zakhid
decline *v. t.* відхиляти vidkhyliaty
declivous *adj.* похилий pokhylyi
decompose *v. t.* розкладати
rozkladaty
decomposition *n*. розкладання
rozkladannia
decontrol *v.t.* зняти контроль
zniaty kontrol
decorate *v. t* нагороджувати
орденами nahorodzhuvaty
ordenamy
decoration *n* декорація
dekoratsiia
decorum *n* благопристойність
blahoprystoinist
decrease *n* зниження znyzhennia
decrease *v. t* знижувати
znyzhuvaty

decree *n* рішення rishennia
decree *v. i* видавати декрет
vydavaty dekret
decrement *n*. зменшення
zmenshennia
dedicate *v. t.* відкривати
vidkryvaty
dedication *n* відданість viddanist
deduct *v.t.* утримувати
utrymuvaty
deed *n* документ про передачу
права власності dokument pro
peredachu prava vlasnosti
deem *v.i.* вважати vvazhaty
deep *a.* глибокий hlybokyi
deer *n* олень olen
defamation *n* наклеп naklep
defame *v. t.* брехати brekhaty
default *n*. замовчування
zamovchuvannia
defeat *n* припинення prypynennia
defeat *v. t.* перемогти peremohty
defect *n* дефект defekt
defence *n* аргументація захисту
arhumentatsiia zakhystu
defend *v. t* обороняти oboroniaty
defendant *n* підсудний pidsudnyi
defensive *adv.* оборона oborona
deference *n* повага povaha
defiance *n* зухвала поведінка
zukhvala povedinka
deficient *adj.* недостатній
nedostatnii
deficit *n* дефіцит defitsyt
defile *n.* дефіле defile
define *v. t* характеризувати
kharakteryzuvaty
definite *a* певний pevnyi
definition *n* дефініція definitsiia
deflation *n.* дефляція defliatsiia
deflect *v.t. & i.* заломлювати
zalomliuvaty
deft *adj.* моторний motornyi

degrade v. t деградувати dehraduvaty

degree n ступінь stupin

dehort v.i. переконувати perekonuvaty

deist n. деїст deist

deity n. божество bozhestvo

deject v. t пригнічувати pryhnichuvaty

dejection n зневіра znevira

delay v.t. & i. затримувати zatrymuvaty

delegate v. t делегувати delehuvaty

delegation n делегація delehatsiia

delete v. t видалити vydalyty

delibate v.t. зменшувати zmenshuvaty

deliberate a обдуманий obdumanyi

deliberate v. i обговорювати obhovoriuvaty

deliberation n нарада narada

delicate a слабкий slabkyi

delicious a дуже смачний duzhe smachnyi

deligate1 n пов'язка poviazka

delight n захват zakhvat

delight v. t. захоплювати zakhopliuvaty

deliver v. t доставляти dostavliaty

delivery n доставка dostavka

delta n дельта delta

delude n.t. зваблювати zvabliuvaty

delusion n. зваба zvaba

demand n вимога vymoha

demand v. t висувати вимогу vysuvaty vymohu

demarcation n. демаркація demarkatsiia

dement v.t зводити з розуму zvodyty z rozumu

demerit n вада vada

democracy n демократія demokratiia

democratic a демократичний demokratychnyi

demolish v. t. зносити znosyty

demon n. демон demon

demonetize v.t. вилучати з обігу vyluchaty z obihu

demonstrate v. t демонструвати demonstruvaty

demonstration n. демонстрація demonstratsiia

demoralize v. t. деморалізувати demoralizuvaty

demur n вагання vahannia

demur v. t вагатися vahatysia

demurrage n. плата за простій plata za prostii

den n притон pryton

dengue n. тропічна лихоманка tropichna lykhomanka

denial n заперечення zaperechennia

denote v. i позначати poznachaty

denounce v. t доносити donosyty

dense a густий hustyi

density n щільність shchilnist

dentist n дантист dantyst

denude v.t. позбавляти pozbavliaty

denunciation n. донос donos

deny v. t. заперечувати zaperechuvaty

depart v. i. відбувати vidbuvaty

department n відділення viddilennia

departure n виліт vylit

depauperate v.t. виснажувати vysnazhuvaty

depend v. i. залежати zalezhaty

dependant *n* нахлібник nakhlibnyk
dependence *n* підпорядкованість pidporiadkovanist
dependent *a* залежний zalezhnyi
depict *v. t.* зображати zobrazhaty
deplorable *a* прикрий prykryi
deploy *v.t.* розгортати rozhortaty
deponent *n.* свідок, який дає показання під присягою svidok, yakyi daie pokazannia pid prysiahoiu
deport *v.t.* депортувати deportuvaty
depose *v. t* позбавити влади pozbavyty vlady
deposit *n.* депозит depozyt
deposit *v. t* класти в банк klasty v bank
depot *n* депо depo
depreciate *v.t.i.* знецінювати znetsiniuvaty
depredate *v.t.* спустошувати spustoshuvaty
depress *v. t* пригноблювати pryhnobliuvaty
depression *n* депресія depresiia
deprive *v. t* позбавити pozbavyty
depth *n* глибина hlybyna
deputation *n* депутація deputatsiia
depute *v. t* доручати doruchaty
deputy *n* депутат deputat
derail *v. t.* пускати під укіс puskaty pid ukis
derive *v. t.* виводити vyvodyty
descend *v. i.* зійти ziity
descendant *n* нащадок nashchadok
descent *n.* спуск spusk
describe *v. t* описувати opysuvaty
description *n* опис opys
descriptive *a* описовий opysovyi

desert *v. t.* залишати zalyshaty
desert *n* пустеля pustelia
deserve *v. t.* бути гідним buty hidnym
design *n.* намір namir
design *v. t.* проектувати proektuvaty
desirable *a* бажаний bazhanyi
desire *v.t* бажати bazhaty
desire *n* предмет бажання predmet bazhannia
desirous *a* бажаючий bazhaiuchyi
desk *n* парта parta
despair *n* відчай vidchai
despair *v. i* зневірятися zneviriatysia
desperate *a* відчайдушний vidchaidushnyi
despicable *a* мерзенний merzennyi
despise *v. t* зневажати znevazhaty
despot *n* деспот despot
destination *n* призначення pryznachennia
destiny *n* доля dolia
destroy *v. t* знищити znyshchyty
destruction *n* руйнування ruinuvannia
detach *v. t* відряджати vidriadzhaty
detachment *n* відряджання vidriadzhannia
detail *n* деталь detal
detail *v. t* деталізувати detalizuvaty
detain *v. t* тримати під вартою trymaty pid vartoiu
detect *v. t* виявляти vyiavliaty
detective *a* детектив detektyv
detective *n.* детективний detektyvnyi

determination *n.* рішимість
rishymist
determine *v. t* вимірювати
vymiriuvaty
dethrone *v. t* скидати з трону
skydaty z tronu
develop *v. t.* розвивати rozvyvaty
development *n.* розвиток
rozvytok
deviate *v. i* відхилятися
vidkhyliatysia
deviation *n* девіація deviatsiia
device *n* метод metod
devil *n* диявол dyiavol
devise *v. t* вигадати vyhadaty
devoid *a* позбавлений
pozbavlenyi
devote *v. t* віддаватися
viddavatysia
devotee *n* прихильник prykhylnyk
devotion *n* відданість viddanist
devour *v. t* знищувати
znyshchuvaty
dew *n.* роса rosa
diabetes *n* цукровий діабет
tsukrovyi diabet
diagnose *v. t* діагностувати
diahnostuvaty
diagnosis *n* діагноз diahnoz
diagram *n* графік hrafik
dial *n.* циферблат tsyferblat
dialect *n* діалект dialekt
dialogue *n* діалог dialoh
diameter *n* диметр dymetr
diamond *n* діамант diamant
diarrhoea *n* пронос pronos
diary *n* щоденник shchodennyk
dice *n.* гральні кості hralni kosti
dice *v. i.* грати в кості hraty v kosti
dictate *v. t* диктувати dyktuvaty
dictation *n* диктування
dyktuvannia
dictator *n* диктатор dyktator

diction *n* дикція dyktsiia
dictionary *n* словник slovnyk
dictum *n* вислів vysliv
didactic *a* дидактичний
dydaktychnyi
die *n* гральна кість hralna kist
die *v. i* померти pomerty
diet *n* дієта diieta
differ *v. i* відрізнятися
vidrizniatysia
difference *n* різниця riznytsia
different *a* відмінний vidminnyi
difficult *a* складний skladnyi
difficulty *n* труднощі trudnoshchi
dig *v.t.* копати kopaty
dig *n* тичок tychok
digest *v. t.* переварювати
perevariuvaty
digest *n.* збірник zbirnyk
digestion *n* травлення travlennia
digit *n* цифра tsyfra
dignify *v.t* облагороджувати
oblahorodzhuvaty
dignity *n* гідність hidnist
dilemma *n* дилема dylema
diligence *n* старанність starannist
diligent *a* старанний starannyi
dilute *a* розбавлений rozbavlenyi
dilute *v. t* розбавляти rozbavliaty
dim *a* матовий matovyi
dim *v. t* потьмяніти potmianity
dimension *n* вимір vymir
diminish *v. t* опадати opadaty
din *n* гомін homin
dine *v. t.* вечеряти vecheriaty
dinner *n* вечеря vecheria
dip *n.* занурення zanurennia
dip *v. t* занурюватися
zanuriuvatysia
diploma *n* диплом dyplom
diplomacy *n* дипломатія
dyplomatiia
diplomat *n* дипломат dyplomat

diplomatic *a* дипломатичний dyplomatychnyi
dire *a* жахливий zhakhlyvyi
direct *a* безпосередній bezposerednii
direct *v. t* направляти napravliaty
direction *n* напрям napriam
director *n.* директор dyrektor
directory *n* довідник dovidnyk
dirt *n* бруд brud
dirty *a* нечесний nechesnyi
disability *n* нездатність nezdatnist
disable *v. t* робити непридатним robyty neprydatnym
disabled *a* непрацездатний nepratsezdatnyi
disadvantage *n* збиток zbytok
disagree *v. i* не сходитися в поглядах ne skhodytysia v pohliadakh
disagreeable *a.* неприємний nepryiemnyi
disagreement *n.* розбіжність rozbizhnist
disappear *v. i* зникнути znyknuty
disappearance *n* зникнення znyknennia
disappoint *v. t.* розчаровувати rozcharovuvaty
disapproval *n* несхвалення neskhvalennia
disapprove *v. t* не схвалювати ne skhvaliuvaty
disarm *v. t* обеззброювати obezzbroiuvaty
disarmament *n.* роззброєння rozzbroiennia
disaster *n* катастрофа katastrofa
disastrous *a* катастрофічний katastrofichnyi
disc *n.* диск dysk
discard *v. t* звільняти zvilniaty

discharge *n.* розвантажування rozvantazhuvannia
discharge *v. t* розряджати rozriadzhaty
disciple *n* апостол apostol
discipline *n* дисципліна dystsyplina
disclose *v. t* розкрити rozkryty
discomfort *n* незручність nezruchnist
disconnect *v. t* роз'єднувати roziednuvaty
discontent *n* незадоволеність nezadovolenist
discontinue *v. t* припиняти prypyniaty
discord *n* розлад rozlad
discount *n* знижка znyzhka
discourage *v. t.* відраджувати vidradzhuvaty
discourse *n* мова mova
discourteous *a* непоштивий neposhtyvyi
discover *v. t* знаходити znakhodyty
discovery *n.* відкриття vidkryttia
discretion *n* розсуд rozsud
discriminate *v. t.* дискримінувати dyskryminuvaty
discrimination *n* дискримінація dyskryminatsiia
discuss *v. t.* обговорювати obhovoriuvaty
disdain *v. t.* нехтувати nekhtuvaty
disdain *n* зневажання znevazhannia
disease *n* захворювання zakhvoriuvannia
disguise *n* маскування maskuvannia
disguise *v. t* маскувати maskuvaty
dish *n* блюдо bliudo

dishearten v. t приводити у відчай pryvodyty u vidchai
dishonest a нечесний nechesnyi
dishonesty n. несумлінність nesumlinnist
dishonour v. t безчестити bezchestyty
dishonour n безчестя bezchestia
dislike v. t не любити ne liubyty
dislike n неприязнь nepryiazn
disloyal a нелояльний neloialnyi
dismiss v. t. відпускати vidpuskaty
dismissal n зняття zniattia
disobey v. t не підкорятися ne pidkoriatysia
disorder n безлад bezlad
disparity n нерівність nerivnist
dispensary n диспансер dyspanser
disperse v. t розбігатися rozbihatysia
displace v. t витісняти vytisniaty
display n прояв proiav
display v. t проявляти proiavliaty
displease v. t не подобатися ne podobatysia
displeasure n невдоволеність nevdovolenist
disposal n розпорядження rozporiadzhennia
dispose v. t розташовувати roztashovuvaty
disprove v. t спростовувати sprostovuvaty
dispute v. i сперечатися sperechatysia
dispute n спір spir
disqualification n дискваліфікація dyskvalifikatsiia
disqualify v. t. дискваліфікувати dyskvalifikuvaty

disquiet n хвилювання khvyliuvannia
disregard n зневага znevaha
disregard v. t знехтувати znekhtuvaty
disrepute n погана слава pohana slava
disrespect n неповага nepovaha
disrupt v. t зривати zryvaty
dissatisfaction n невдоволення nevdovolennia
dissatisfy v. t. викликати нэвдоволення vyklykaty nevdovolennia
dissect v. t розсікати rozsikaty
dissection n розсічення rozsichennia
dissimilar a несхожий neskhozhyi
dissolve v.t розчиняти rozchyniaty
dissuade v. t відмовляти vidmovliaty
distance n відстань vidstan
distant a далекий dalekyi
distil v. t гнати hnaty
distillery n спиртогорілчаний завод spyrtohorilchanyi zavod
distinct a чіткий chitkyi
distinction n відмінність vidminnist
distinguish v. i розрізняти rozrizniaty
distort v. t спотворювати spotvoriuvaty
distress n нужда nuzhda
distress v. t крушити krushyty
distribute v. t роздавати rozdavaty
distribution n розподіл rozpodil
district n округ okruh
distrust n сумнів sumniv
distrust v. t. сумніватися sumnivatysia

disturb v. t турбувати turbuvaty
ditch n канава kanava
ditto n. точна копія tochna kopiia
dive v. i пірнати pirnaty
dive n кубло kublo
diverse a різноманітний riznomanitnyi
divert v. t відволікати vidvolikaty
divide v. t розділяти rozdiliaty
divine a божествений bozhestvenyi
divinity n богослов'я bohoslovia
division n дівізія diviziia
divorce v. t розлучати rozluchaty
divorce n розлучення rozluchennia
divulge v. t оприлюднити opryliudnyty
do v. t робити robyty
docile a тямущий tiamushchyi
dock n. док dok
doctor n лікар likar
doctorate n докторська ступінь doktorska stupin
doctrine n доктрина doktryna
document n документ dokument
dodge n виверт vyvert
dodge v. t лукавити lukavyty
doe n лань lan
dog n собака sobaka
dog v. t цькувати собаками tskuvaty sobakamy
dogma n догма dohma
dogmatic a догматичний dohmatychnyi
doll n лялька lialka
dollar n долар dolar
domain n область oblast
dome n купол kupol
domestic a домашній domashnii
domestic n домашня робота domashnia robota

domicile n постійне місце проживання postiine mistse prozhyvannia
dominant a домінуючий dominuiuchyi
dominate v. t домінувати dominuvaty
domination n панування panuvannia
dominion n домініон dominion
donate v. t жертвувати zhertvuvaty
donation n. дар dar
donkey n осел osel
donor n донор donor
doom n загибель zahybel
doom v. t. прирікати pryrikaty
door n двері dveri
dose n доза doza
dot v. t ставити крапки над stavyty krapky nad
dot n точка tochka
double n двійник dviinyk
double a подвійний podviinyi
double v. t. роздвоюватися rozdvoiuvatysia
doubt n сумнів sumniv
doubt v. i сумніватися sumnivatysia
dough n тісто tisto
dove n голуб holub
down v. t збити zbyty
down adv вниз vnyz
down prep по ро
downfall n розвал rozval
downpour n злива zlyva
downright a повний povnyi
downright adv явно yavno
downward adv донизу donyzu
downward a який спускається yakyi spuskaietsia
downwards adv під уклон pid uklon

dowry *n* придане prydane
doze *v. i* дрімати drimaty
doze *n.* дрімота drimota
dozen *n* дюжина diuzhyna
draft *n* креслення kreslennia
draft *v. t* робити ескіз robyty eskiz
draftsman *n* укладач ukladach
drag *n* волочіння volochinnia
drag *v. t* тягти tiahty
dragon *n* дракон drakon
drain *n* відтік vidtik
drain *v. t* осушувати osushuvaty
drainage *n* дренаж drenazh
dram *n* драхма drakhma
drama *n* драма drama
dramatic *a* драматичний
  dramatychnyi
dramatist *n* драматург dramaturh
draper *n* драпірувальник
  drapiruvalnyk
drastic *a* сильнодійний
  sylnodiinyi
draught *n* складати
  законопроект skladaty
  zakonoproekt
draw *n* розіграш rozihrash
draw *v.t* малювати maliuvaty
drawback *n* перешкода
  pereshkoda
drawer *n* буфетник bufetnyk
drawing *n* креслення kreslennia
drawing-room *n* вітальня vitalnia
dread *n* жуть zhut
dread *v.t* боятися boiatysia
dread *a* страхатися strakhatysia
dream *v. i.* мріяти mriiaty
dream *n* сон son
drench *v. t* доза ліків doza likiv
dress *n* плаття plattia
dress *v. t* причісувати
  prychisuvaty
dressing *n* прикраса prykrasa
drill *v. t.* свердлити sverdlyty

drill *n* свердло sverdlo
drink *v. t* випивати vypyvaty
drink *n* питво pytvo
drip *n* капання kapannia
drip *v. i* капати kapaty
drive *n* виїзд vyizd
drive *v. t* водити автомобіль
  vodyty avtomobil
driver *n* водій vodii
drizzle *n* мжичка mzhychka
drizzle *v. i* мрячити mriachyty
drop *v. i* крапати krapaty
drop *n* крапля kraplia
drown *v.i* тонути tonuty
drug *n* медикамент medykament
druggist *n* фармацевт farmatsevt
drum *n* барабан baraban
drum *v.i.* бити в барабан byty v
  baraban
drunkard *n* алкоголік alkoholik
dry *n* посуха posukha
dry *v. i.* сохнути sokhnuty
dry *a* сухий sukhyi
dual *a* двоїстий dvoistyi
duck *n.* качка kachka
duck *v.i.* присідати prysidaty
due *n* належне nalezhne
due *adv* належний nalezhnyi
due *a* належний nalezhnyi
duel *n* дуель duel
duel *v. i* битися на дуелі bytysia
  na dueli
duke *n* герцог hertsoh
dull *a* тупий tupyi
dull *v. t.* притуплятися
  prytupliatysia
duly *adv* належним чином
  nalezhnym chynom
dumb *a* німий nimyi
dunce *n* йолоп yolop
dung *n* кал kal
duplicate *n* дублікат dublikat

duplicate *v. t* дублювати dubliuvaty
duplicate *a* запасний zapasnyi
duplicity *n* лукавість lukavist
durable *a* довговічний dovhovichnyi
duration *n* тривалість tryvalist
during *prep* під час pid chas
dusk *n* сутінковий sutinkovyi
dust *n* пил pyl
dust *v.t.* порошити poroshyty
duster *n* ганчірка hanchirka
dutiful *a* покірний pokirnyi
duty *n* податок podatok
dwarf *n* зупиняти розвиток zupyniaty rozvytok
dwell *v. i* мешкати meshkaty
dwelling *n* оселя oselia
dwindle *v. t* скорочуватися skorochuvatysia
dye *n* барвник barvnyk
dye *v. t* фарбувати farbuvaty
dynamic *a* динамічний dynamichnyi
dynamics *n.* динаміка dynamika
dynamite *n* динаміт dynamit
dynamo *n* генератор henerator
dynasty *n* династія dynastiia
dysentery *n* дизентерія dyzenteriia

E

each *pron.* один одного odyn odnoho
each *a* кожен kozhen
eager *a* старанний starannyi
eagle *n* орел orel
ear *n* вухо vukho
early *a* ранній rannii
early *adv* рано rano
earn *v. t* заробляти zarobliaty

earnest *a* переконаний perekonanyi
earth *n* земля zemlia
earthen *a* земний zemnyi
earthly *a* земляний zemlianyi
earthquake *n* землетрус zemletrus
ease *n* легкість lehkist
ease *v. t* полегшувати polehshuvaty
east *adv* на схід na skhid
east *n* схід skhid
east *a* східний skhidnyi
easter *n* великдень velykden
eastern *a* східний skhidnyi
easy *a* легкий lehkyi
eat *v. t* є ye
eatable *n.* їстівне yistivne
eatable *a* їстівний yistivnyi
ebb *n* відлив vidlyv
ebb *v. i* відлити vidlyty
ebony *n* чорне дерево chorne derevo
echo *n* луна luna
echo *v. t* лунати lunaty
eclipse *n* затемнення zatemnennia
economic *a* економічний ekonomichnyi
economical *a* ощадливий oshchadlyvyi
economics *n.* економіка ekonomika
economy *n* економія ekonomiia
edge *n* грань hran
edible *a* придатний для їжи prydatnyi dlia yizhy
edifice *n* будівля budivlia
edit *v. t* редагувати redahuvaty
edition *n* видання vydannia
editor *n* видавець vydavets
editorial *a* редакторскій redaktorckii

editorial *n* передовиця peredovytsia

educate *v. t* давати освіту davaty osvitu

education *n* освіта osvita

efface *v. t* стерти sterty

effect *v. t* впливати vplyvaty

effect *n* ефект efekt

effective *a* ефективний efektyvnyi

effeminate *a* подібний до жінки podibnyi do zhinky

efficacy *n* дієвість diievist

efficiency *n* ефективність efektyvnist

efficient *a* ефективний efektyvnyi

effigy *n* зображення zobrazhennia

effort *n* спроба sproba

egg *n* яйце yaitse

ego *n* егоїзм ehoizm

egotism *n* зарозумілість zarozumilist

eight *n* вісім visim

eighteen *n* вісімнадцять visimnadtsiat

eighty *n* вісімдесят visimdesiat

either *a.*, або ... або abo ... abo

either *adv.* будь-який bud-iakyi

eject *v. t.* вигнати vyhnaty

elaborate *a* вдосконалений vdoskonalenyi

elaborate *v. t* детально розробляти detalno rozrobliaty

elapse *v. t* проходити prokhodyty

elastic *a* еластичний elastychnyi

elbow *n* підлокітник pidlokitnyk

elder *n* староста starosta

elder *a* старший starshyi

elderly *a* похилого віку pokhyloho viku

elect *v. t* обрати obraty

election *n* вибори vybory

electorate *n* контингент виборців kontynhent vybortsiv

electric *a* електричний elektrychnyi

electricity *n* електрика elektryka

electrify *v. t* електрифікувати elektryfikuvaty

elegance *n* елегантність elehantnist

elegant *adj* елегантний elehantnyi

elegy *n* елегія elehiia

element *n* елемент element

elementary *a* елементарний elementarnyi

elephant *n* слон slon

elevate *v. t* підвищувати по службі pidvyshchuvaty po sluzhbi

elevation *n* піднесення pidnesennia

eleven *n* одинадцять odynadtsiat

elf *n* ельф elf

eligible *a* підхожий pidkhozhyi

eliminate *v. t* усувати usuvaty

elimination *n* усунення usunennia

elope *v. i* втекти vtekty

eloquence *n* красномовство krasnomovstvo

eloquent *a* красномовний krasnomovnyi

else *adv* а то a to

else *a* інший inshyi

elucidate *v. t* з'ясувати ziasuvaty

elude *v. t* уникати unykaty

elusion *n* викрут vykrut

elusive *a* невловимий nevlovymyi

emancipation *n.* емансипація emansypatsiia

embalm *v. t* забальзамувати zabalzamuvaty

embankment *n* насип nasyp

embark *v. t* вантажити на корабель vantazhyty na korabel

embarrass *v. t* ускладнювати
uskladniuvaty
embassy *n* посольство posolstvo
embitter *v. t* озлобляти ozlobliaty
emblem *n* емблема emblema
embodiment *n* втілення vtilennia
embody *v. t.* втілювати vtiliuvaty
embolden *v. t.* заохочувати
zaokhochuvaty
embrace *n* обійми obiimy
embrace *v. t.* обійняти obiiniaty
embroidery *n* вишивання
vyshyvannia
embryo *n* ембріон embrion
emerald *n* смарагд smarahd
emerge *v. i* з'явитися ziavytysia
emergency *n* крайність krainist
eminance *n* високе положення
vysoke polozhennia
eminent *a* іменитий imenytyi
emissary *n* шпигун shpyhun
emit *v. t* видавати vydavaty
emolument *n* заработок
zarobotok
emotion *n* емоція emotsiia
emotional *a* емоційний emotsiinyi
emperor *n* імператор imperator
emphasis *n* акцентування
aktsentuvannia
emphasize *v. t* акцентувати
aktsentuvaty
emphatic *a* виразний vyraznyi
empire *n* імперія imperiia
employ *v. t* наймати naimaty
employee *n* працівник pratsivnyk
employer *n* роботодавець
robotodavets
employment *n* зайнятість
zainiatist
empower *v. t* уповноважити
upovnovazhyty
empress *n* імператриця
imperatrytsia

empty *v* спорожнити sporozhnyty
empty *a* марний marnyi
emulate *v. t* змагатися
zmahatysia
enable *v. t* давати можливість
davaty mozhlyvist
enact *v. t* пропонувати
proponuvaty
enamel *n* емаль emal
enamour *v. t* закохувати
zakokhuvaty
encase *v. t* укладати ukladaty
enchant *v. t* чарувати charuvaty
encircle *v. t.* обводити obvodyty
enclose *v. t* оточувати otochuvaty
enclosure *n.* огорожа ohorozha
encompass *v. t* стосуватися
stosuvatysia
encounter *v. t* зустріти zustrity
encounter *n.* сутичка sutychka
encourage *v. t* підбадьорювати
pidbadoriuvaty
encroach *v. i* зазіхати zazikhaty
encumber *v. t.* забудовувати
zabudovuvaty
encyclopaedia *n.* енциклопедія
entsyklopediia
end *v. t* кінчатися kinchatysia
end *n.* смерть smert
endanger *v. t.* піддавати
небезпеці piddavaty nebezpetsi
endear *v.t* пеститися pestytysia
endearment *n.* ласка laska
endeavour *v.i* спроба sproba
endeavour *n* старання starannia
endorse *v. t.* надписувати
nadpysuvaty
endow *v. t* забезпечувати
постійним доходом
zabezpechuvaty postiinym
dokhodom
endurable *a* стерпний sterpnyi

endurance *n.* терплячість terpliachist
endure *v.t.* витерпіти vyterpity
enemy *n* ворог voroh
energetic *a* енергійний enerhiinyi
energy *n.* енергія enerhiia
enfeeble *v. t.* послаблювати poslabliuvaty
enforce *v. t.* нав'язувати naviazuvaty
enfranchise *v.t.* відпускати на волю vidpuskaty na voliu
engage *v. t* привертати pryvertaty
engagement *n.* зобов'язання zoboviazannia
engine *n* двигун dvyhun
engineer *n* інженер inzhener
English *n* англійська мова anhliiska mova
engrave *v. t* гравірувати hraviruvaty
engross *v.t* скупити skupyty
engulf *v.t* засмоктувати zasmoktuvaty
enigma *n* таємниця taiemnytsia
enjoy *v. t* отримувати задоволення otrymuvaty zadovolennia
enjoyment *n* задоволення zadovolennia
enlarge *v. t* розширювати rozshyriuvaty
enlighten *v. t.* просвіщати prosvishchaty
enlist *v. t* завербуватися zaverbuvatysia
enliven *v. t.* оживляти ozhyvliaty
enmity *n* ворожнеча vorozhnecha
ennoble *v. t.* надавати дворянський титул nadavaty dvorianskyi tytul
enormous *a* величезний velycheznyi

enough *adv.* досить dosyt
enough *adv* достатньо dostatno
enrage *v. t* бісити bisyty
enrapture *v. t* викликати захоплення vyklykaty zakhoplennia
enrich *v. t* збагачувати zbahachuvaty
enrol *v. t* вносити до списку vnosyty do spysku
enshrine *v. t* зберігати zberihaty
enslave *v.t.* поневолювати ponevoliuvaty
ensue *v.i* слідувати sliduvaty
ensure *v. t* гарантувати harantuvaty
entangle *v. t* замішувати zamishuvaty
enter *v. t* входити vkhodyty
enterprise *n* ініціативність initsiatyvnist
entertain *v. t* розважати rozvazhaty
entertainment *n.* видовище vydovyshche
enthrone *v. t* зводити на престол zvodyty na prestol
enthusiasm *n* ентузіазм entuziazm
enthusiastic *a* захоплений zakhoplenyi
entice *v. t.* спокушати spokushaty
entire *a* цілий tsilyi
entirely *adv* повністю povnistiu
entitle *v. t.* надавати право nadavaty pravo
entity *n* суб'єкт sub'iekt
entomology *n.* ентомологія entomolohiia
entrails *n.* нутрощі nutroshchi
entrance *n* вхід vkhid
entrap *v. t.* заманити zamanyty
entreat *v. t.* молити molyty

entreaty *n.* прохання prokhannia
entrust *v. t* надавати nadavaty
entry *n* вступ vstup
enumerate *v. t.* переписувати
perepysuvaty
envelop *v. t* огортати ohortaty
envelope *n* конверт konvert
enviable *a* завидний zavydnyi
envious *a* заздрісний zazdrisnyi
environment *n.* навколишнє
середовище navkolyshnie
seredovyshche
envy *v. t* заздрити zazdryty
envy *n* об`єкт заздрощів ob`iekt
zazdroshchiv
epic *n* епічна поема epichna
poema
epidemic *n* епідемія epidemiia
epigram *n* епіграма epihrama
epilepsy *n* епілепсія epilepsiia
epilogue *n* епілог epiloh
episode *n* епізод epizod
epitaph *n* епітафія epitafiia
epoch *n* доба doba
equal *n* рівня rivnia
equal *v. t* дорівнювати
dorivniuvaty
equal *a* однаковий odnakovyi
equality *n* рівність rivnist
equalize *v. t.* зрівнювати
zrivniuvaty
equate *v. t* зрівнювати zrivniuvaty
equation *n* рівняння rivniannia
equator *n* екватор ekvator
equilateral *a* рівносторонній
rivnostoronnii
equip *v. t* екіпірувати ekipiruvaty
equipment *n* обладнання
obladnannia
equitable *a* справедливий
spravedlyvyi
equivalent *a* еквівалентний
ekvivalentnyi

equivocal *a* неясний neiasnyi
era *n* епоха epokha
eradicate *v. t* викорінювати
vykoriniuvaty
erase *v. t* прати praty
erect *a* піднятий pidniatyi
erect *v. t* спорудити sporudyty
erection *n* спорудження
sporudzhennia
erode *v. t* знецінюватися
znetsiniuvatysia
erosion *n* ерозія eroziia
erotic *a* еротичний erotychnyi
err *v. i* помилятися pomyliatysia
errand *n* завдання zavdannia
erroneous *a* неправильний
nepravylnyi
error *n* помилка pomylka
erupt *v. i* вивергатися
vyverhatysia
eruption *n* виверження
vyverzhennia
escape *n* минути mynuty
escape *v.i* тікати tikaty
escort *n* конвой konvoi
escort *v. t* супроводжувати
suprovodzhuvaty
especial *a* особливий osoblyvyi
essay *v. t.* випробовувати
vyprobovuvaty
essay *n.* есе ese
essayist *n* есеїст eseist
essence *n* есенція esentsiia
essential *a* істотний istotnyi
establish *v. t.* закладати
zakladaty
establishment *n* пристрій prystrii
estate *n* майно maino
esteem *n* шана shana
esteem *v. t* поважати povazhaty
estimate *n.* кошторис koshtorys
estimate *v. t* складати кошторис
skladaty koshtorys

estimation *n* розрахунок
rozrakhunok
etcetera *a* і так далі i tak dali
eternal *a* вічний vichnyi
eternity *n* вічність vichnist
ether *n* ефір efir
ethical *a* етичний etychnyi
ethics *n.* етика etyka
etiquette *n* етикет etyket
etymology *n.* етимологія
etymolohiia
eunuch *n* євнух yevnukh
evacuate *v. t* евакуювати
evakuiuvaty
evacuation *n* евакуація
evakuatsiia
evade *v. t* уникати unykaty
evaluate *v. t* атестувати
atestuvaty
evaporate *v. i* випаровувати
vyparovuvaty
evasion *n* ухиляння ukhyliannia
even *v. t* вирівнювати vyrivniuvaty
even *a* рівномірний rivnomirnyi
even *adv* хоча khocha
evening *n* вечір vechir
event *n* випадок vypadok
eventually *adv.* врешті-решт
vreshti-resht
ever *adv* коли-небудь koly-nebud
evergreen *n* вічнозелена
рослина vichnozelena roslyna
evergreen *a* вічнозелений
vichnozelenyi
everlasting *a.* безсмертний
bezsmertnyi
every *a* будь-який bud-iakyi
evict *v. t* виселяти vyseliaty
eviction *n* виселення vyselennia
evidence *n* доказ dokaz
evident *a.* очевидний ochevydnyi
evil *a* лихий lykhyi
evil *n* лихо lykho

evoke *v. t* витребувати справу
з нижчого суду до вищого
vytrebuvaty spravu z nyzhchoho
sudu do vyshchoho
evolution *n* розвиток rozvytok
evolve *v.t* виділяти vydiliaty
ewe *n* вівця vivtsia
exact *a* точний tochnyi
exaggerate *v. t.* перебільшувати
perebilshuvaty
exaggeration *n.* перебільшення
perebilshennia
exalt *v. t* звеличувати
zvelychuvaty
examination *n.* дослідження
doslidzhennia
examine *v. t* розглядати
rozhliadaty
examinee *n* екзаменований
ekzamenovanyi
examiner *n* екзаменатор
ekzamenator
example *n* приклад pryklad
excavate *v. t.* рити ryty
excavation *n.* розкопка rozkopka
exceed *v.t* перевищувати
perevyshchuvaty
excel *v.i* перевищувати
perevyshchuvaty
excellence *n.* висока якість
vysoka yakist
excellency *n* ясновельможність
yasnovelmozhnist
excellent *a.* відмінний vidminnyi
except *v. t* виключати vykliuchaty
except *prep* за винятком za
vyniatkom
exception *n* виняток vyniatok
excess *a* зайвий zaivyi
excess *n* надлишок nadlyshok
exchange *n* обмін obmin
exchange *v. t* обмінювати
obminiuvaty

excise *n* акциз aktsyz
excite *v. t* хвилювати khvyliuvaty
exclaim *v.i* вигукувати vyhukuvaty
exclamation *n* вигук vyhuk
exclude *v. t* вимикати vymykaty
exclusive *a* винятковий vyniatkovyi
excommunicate *v. t*. відлучити від церкви vidluchyty vid tserkvy
excursion *n.* екскурсія ekskursiia
excuse *n* звільнення від обов'язку zvilnennia vid oboviazku
excuse *v.t* прощати proshchaty
execute *v. t* стратити stratyty
execution *n* страта strata
executioner *n.* кат kat
exempt *v. t*. вилучати vyluchaty
exempt *a* звільнений від zvilnenyi vid
exercise *n.* вправа vprava
exercise *v. t* виправляти vypravliaty
exhaust *v. t*. вичерпувати vycherpuvaty
exhibit *n.* експонат eksponat
exhibit *v. t* виявляти vyiavliaty
exhibition *n.* виставка vystavka
exile *n.* засланець zaslanets
exile *v. t* заслати zaslaty
exist *v.i* бути buty
existence *n* існування isnuvannia
exit *n.* смерть smert
expand *v.t.* розвивати rozvyvaty
expansion *n.* експансія ekspansiia
ex-parte *a* односторонній odnostoronnii
ex-parte *a* який йде лише від однієї сторони yakyi yde lyshe vid odniiei storony
expect *v. t* чекати chekaty

expectation *n.* очікування ochikuvannia
expedient *a* раціональний ratsionalnyi
expedite *v. t*. швидко виконувати shvydko vykonuvaty
expedition *n* експедиція ekspedytsiia
expel *v. t*. виштовхувати vyshtovkhuvaty
expend *v. t* витрачати vytrachaty
expenditure *n* споживання spozhyvannia
expense *n.* ціна tsina
expensive *a* який дорого коштує yakyi doroho koshtuie
experience *v. t*. довідатися з досвіду dovidatysia z dosvidu
experience *n* досвід dosvid
experiment *n* експеримент eksperiment
expert *a* знаючий znaiuchyi
expert *n* експерт ekspert
expire *v.i.* кінчатися kinchatysia
expiry *n* витікання vytikannia
explain *v. t.* пояснювати poiasniuvaty
explanation *n* пояснення poiasnennia
explicit *a.* явний yavnyi
explode *v. t.* вибухнути vybukhnuty
exploit *v. t* експлуатувати ekspluatuvaty
exploit *n* подвиг podvyh
exploration *n* розвідка rozivdka
explore *v.t* досліджувати doslidzhuvaty
explosion *n.* вибух vybukh
explosive *n.* вибухова речовина vybukhova rechovyna
explosive *a* вибуховий vybukhovyi

exponent *n* інтерпретатор interpretator

export *n* вивезення vyvezennia

export *v. t.* вивозити vyvozyty

expose *v. t* викладати vykladaty

express *v. t.* висловлювати vyslovliuvaty

express *a* кур'єрський kurierskyi

express *n* нарочний narochnyi

expression *n.* вираз vyraz

expressive *a.* який служить до вираження yakyi sluzhyt do vyrazhennia

expulsion *n.* вигнання vyhnannia

extend *v. t* спростягати sprostiahaty

extent *n.* ступінь stupin

external *a* зовнішній zovnishnii

extinct *a* згаслий zhaslyi

extinguish *v.t* гасити hasyty

extol *v. t.* розхвалювати rozkhvaliuvaty

extra *adv* додатково dodatkovo

extra *a* спеціальний spetsialnyi

extract *v. t* витягати vytiahaty

extract *n* настій nastii

extraordinary *a.* екстраординарний ekstraordynarnyi

extravagance *n* марнотратність marnotratnist

extravagant *a* марнотратний marnotratnyi

extreme *a* екстремальний ekstremalnyi

extreme *n* надмірність nadmirnist

extremist *n* екстреміст ekstremist

exult *v. i* тріумфувати triumfuvaty

eye *n* око oko

eyeball *n* очне яблуко ochne yabluko

eyelash *n* вія viia

eyelet *n* петелька petelka

eyewash *n* окозамилювання okozamyliuvannia

fable *n.* байка baika

fabric *n* матерія materiia

fabricate *v.t* вигадувати vyhaduvaty

fabrication *n* виготовлення vyhotovlennia

fabulous *a* нечуваний nechuvanyi

facade *n* фасад fasad

face *n* лице lytse

face *v.t* стояти обличчям до stoiaty oblychchiam do

facet *n* аспект aspekt

facial *a* лицьовий lytsovyi

facile *a* гнучкий hnuchkyi

facilitate *v.t* полегшувати polehshuvaty

facility *n* нескладність neskladnist

facsimile *n* факсиміле faksymile

fact *n* факт fakt

faction *n* фракція fraktsiia

factious *a* фракційний fraktsiinyi

factor *n* фактор faktor

factory *n* фабрика fabryka

faculty *n* факультет fakultet

fad *n* коник konyk

fade *v.i* в'янути vianuty

faggot *n* в'язанка viazanka

fail *v.i* зазнавати невдачі zaznavaty nevdachi

failure *n* неуспіх neuspikh

faint *a* слабкий slabkyi

faint *v.i* слабнути slabnuty

fair *a* справедливий spravedlyvyi

fair *n.* ярмарок yarmarok

fairly *adv.* чесно chesno

fairy *n* фея feia

faith *n* довіра dovira

faithful *a* вірний virnyi
falcon *n* сокіл sokil
fall *v.i.* падати padaty
fall *n* падіння padinnia
fallacy *n* омана omana
fallow *n* земля під паром zemlia
　pid parom
false *a* штучний shtuchnyi
falter *v.i* зам'яти zamiaty
fame *n* слава slava
familiar *a* знайомий znaiomyi
family *n* сім'я simia
famine *n* голодовка holodovka
famous *a* славетний slavetnyi
fan *n* віяло viialo
fanatic *n* фанатик fanatyk
fanatic *a* фанатичний fanatychnyi
fancy *n* уява uiava
fancy *v.t* фантазійний fantaziinyi
fantastic *a* фантастичний
　fantastychnyi
far *n* далека відстань daleka
　vidstan
far *adv.* далеко daleko
far *a* дальній dalnii
farce *n* фарс fars
fare *n* вартість проїзду vartist
　proizdu
farewell *interj.* прощавай!
　proshchavai!
farewell *n* прощальний прийом
　гостей proshchalnyi pryiom
　hostei
farm *n* ферма ferma
farmer *n* фермер fermer
fascinate *v.t* зачаровувати
　поглядом zacharovuvaty
　pohliadom
fascination *n.* чарівність
　charivnist
fashion *n* мода moda
fashionable *a* модний modnyi
fast *n* голодування holoduvannia

fast *v.i* голодувати holoduvaty
fast *a* пісний pisnyi
fast *a* швидкий shvydkyi
fasten *v.t* зав'язувати zaviazuvaty
fat *n* жир zhyr
fat *a* масний masnyi
fatal *a* фатальний fatalnyi
fate *n* фатум fatum
father *n* батько batko
fathom *n* морська сажень morska
　sazhen
fathom *v.t* вимірювати глибину
　vymiriuvaty hlybynu
fatigue *n* втома vtoma
fatigue *v.t* стомлювати
　stomliuvaty
fault *n* хиба khyba
faulty *a* недосконалий
　nedoskonalyi
fauna *n* фауна fauna
favour *v.t* сприяти spryiaty
favour1 *n* прихильність
　prykhylnist
favourable *a* сприятливий
　spryiatlyvyi
favourite *a* улюблений uliublenyi
favourite *n* фаворит favoryt
fear *v.i* побоюватися
　poboiuvatysia
fear *n* страх strakh
fearful *a.* страшний strashnyi
feasible *a* здійсненний
　zdiisnennyi
feast *n* бенкет benket
feast *v.i* вшановувати
　vshanovuvaty
feat *n* фах fakh
feather *n* перо pero
feature *n* ознака oznaka
February *n* лютий liutyi
federal *a* федеральний federalnyi
federation *n* федерація
　federatsiia

fee *n* гонорар honorar
feeble *a* слабкий slabkyi
feed *n* годування hoduvannia
feed *v.t* годувати hoduvaty
feel *v.t* відчувати vidchuvaty
feeling *n* почуття pochuttia
feign *v.t* прикидатися
  prykydatysia
felicitate *v.t* бажати щастя
  bazhaty shchastia
felicity *n* вдалість vdalist
fell *v.t* валити valyty
fellow *n* хлопець khlopets
female *a* жіночий zhinochyi
female *n* самиця samytsia
feminine *a* властивий жінкам
  vlastyvyi zhinkam
fence *v.t* огороджувати
  ohorodzhuvaty
fence *n* паркан parkan
fend *v.t* відображати vidobrazhaty
ferment *v.t* бродити brodyty
ferment *n* фермент ferment
fermentation *n* бродіння
  brodinnia
ferocious *a* лютий liutyi
ferry *v.t* переганяти літаки
  perehaniaty litaky
ferry *n* переправа pereprava
fertile *a* рясний riasnyi
fertility *n* родючість rodiuchist
fertilize *v.t* удобрювати
  udobriuvaty
fertilizer *n* добриво dobryvo
fervent *a* гарячий hariachyi
fervour *n* палкість palkist
festival *n* свято sviato
festive *a* святковий sviatkovyi
festivity *n* веселість veselist
festoon *n* фестон feston
fetch *v.t* принести prynesty
fetter *n* кайдани kaidany
fetter *v.t* сковувати skovuvaty

feud *n.* тривала ворожнеча
  tryvala vorozhnecha
feudal *a* феодальний feodalnyi
fever *n* лихоманка lykhomanka
few *a* нечисленний nechyslennyi
fiasco *n* фіаско fiasko
fibre *n* волокно volokno
fickle *a* мінливий minlyvyi
fiction *n* вигадка vyhadka
fictitious *a* вигаданий vyhadanyi
fiddle *v.i* хімічити khimichyty
fiddle *n* скрипка skrypka
fidelity *n* лояльність loialnist
fie *interj* фу fu
field *n* поле pole
fiend *n* лиходій lykhodii
fierce *a* шалений shalenyi
fiery *a* вогненний vohnennyi
fifteen *n* п'ятнадцять piatnadtsiat
fifty *n.* п'ятьдесят piatdesiat
fig *n* інжир inzhyr
fight *v.t* битися bytysia
fight *n* боротьба borotba
figment *n* фікція fiktsiia
figurative *a* фігуральний
  fihuralnyi
figure *v.t* зобразити zobrazyty
figure *n* фігура fihura
file *v.i.* пересуватися колоною
  peresuvatysia kolonoiu
file *n* досьє dosie
file *v.t* підшити pidshyty
file *v.t* пиляти pyliaty
file *n* справа sprava
file *n* файл fail
fill *v.t* заповнювати zapovniuvaty
film *n* плівка plivka
film *v.t* покривати тонкою
  плівкою pokryvaty tonkoiu
  plivkoiu
filter *n* фільтр filtr
filter *v.t* фільтрувати filtruvaty
filth *n* мерзота merzota

filthy *a* мерзотний merzotnyi
fin *n* плавник plavnyk
final *a* остаточний ostatochnyi
finance *n* фінансова справа finansova sprava
finance *v.t* фінансувати finansuvaty
financial *a* фінансовий finansovyi
financier *n* фінансист finansyst
find *v.t* знаходити znakhodyty
fine *a* тонкий tonkyi
fine *n* штраф shtraf
fine *v.t* штрафувати shtrafuvaty
finger *v.t* встановити vstanovyty
finger *n* палець palets
finish *n* закінчення zakinchennia
finish *v.t* закінчувати zakinchuvaty
finite *a* особовий osobovyi
fir *n* ялина yalyna
fire *n* вогонь vohon
fire *v.t* запалювати zapaliuvaty
firm *a* міцний mitsnyi
firm *n.* фірма firma
first *a* перший pershyi
first *n* перший примірник pershyi prymirnyk
first *adv* по-перше po-pershe
fiscal *a* фіскальний fiskalnyi
fish *v.i* вудити vudyty
fish *n* риба ryba
fisherman *n* рибалка rybalka
fissure *n* тріщина trishchyna
fist *n* кулак kulak
fistula *n* фістула fistula
fit *v.t* годитися hodytysia
fit *n* підгонка pidhonka
fit *n* припадок prypadok
fitful *a* переривчастий pereryvchastyi
fitter *n* придатний prydatnyi
five *n* п'ять piat
fix *n* угода uhoda

fix *v.t* фіксувати fiksuvaty
flabby *a* відвислий vidvyslyi
flag *n* стяг stiah
flagrant *a* жахливий zhakhlyvyi
flame *n* полум'я polumia
flame *v.i* полум'яніти polumianity
flannel *n* фланель flanel
flare *n* блискотіння blyskotinnia
flare *v.i* яскраво спалахнути yaskravo spalakhnuty
flash *v.t* виблискувати vyblyskuvaty
flash *n* спалах spalakh
flask *n* фляга fliaha
flat *a* млявий mliavyi
flat *n* площина ploshchyna
flatter *v.t* лестити lestyty
flattery *n* самообман samoobman
flavour *n* смак smak
flaw *n* тріщина trishchyna
flea *n.* блоха blokha
flee *v.i* бігти bihty
fleece *n* руно runo
fleece *v.t* стригти овець stryhty ovets
fleet *n* флот flot
flesh *n* плоть plot
flexible *a* гнучкий hnuchkyi
flicker *n* мерехтіння merekhtinnia
flicker *v.t* мерехтіти merekhtity
flight *n* переліт perelit
flimsy *a* неміцний nemitsnyi
fling *v.t* рішуче братися rishuche bratysia
flippancy *n* легковажність lehkovazhnist
flirt *n* флірт flirt
flirt *v.i* фліртувати flirtuvaty
float *v.i* плавати plavaty
flock *n* пушинка pushynka
flock *v.i* скупчуватися skupchuvatysia
flog *v.t* стьобати stobaty

flood *v.t* затопляти zatopliaty
flood *n* повінь povin
floor *v.t* настилати підлогу
nastylaty pidlohu
floor *n* підлога pidloha
flora *n* флора flora
florist *n* квітникар kvitnykar
flour *n* борошно boroshno
flourish *v.i* розростатися
rozrostatysia
flow *n* потік potik
flow *v.i* текти tekty
flower *n* квітка kvitka
flowery *a* барвистий barvystyi
fluent *a* вільний vilnyi
fluid *n* флюїд fliuid
fluid *a* текучий tekuchyi
flush *v.i* бити струминою byty
strumynoiu
flush *n* приступ prystup
flute *v.i* грати на флейті hraty na
fleiti
flute *n* флейта fleita
flutter *n* пурхання purkhannia
flutter *v.t* махати крилами
makhaty krylamy
fly *v.i* летіти letity
fly *n* муха mukha
foam *n* піна pina
foam *v.t* вспінювати vspiniuvaty
focal *a* фокальний fokalnyi
focus *n* фокус fokus
focus *v.t* фокусуватися
fokusuvatysia
fodder *n* фураж furazh
foe *n* недруг nedruh
fog *n* туман tuman
foil *v.t* фольга folha
fold *n* складка skladka
fold *v.t* схрещувати
skhreshchuvaty
foliage *n* листя lystia
follow *v.t* послідувати posliduvaty

follower *n* послідовник
poslidovnyk
folly *n* дурість durist
foment *v.t* підбурювати
pidburiuvaty
fond *a* марний marnyi
fondle *v.t* голубити holubyty
food *n* їжа yizha
fool *n* блазень blazen
foolish *a* нерозсудливий
nerozsudlyvyi
foolscap *n* блазенський ковпак
blazenskyi kovpak
foot *n* нога noha
for *prep* для dlia
for *conj.* протягом protiahom
forbid *v.t* не дозволяти ne
dozvoliaty
force *v.t* примушувати
prymushuvaty
force *n* сила syla
forceful *a* дієвий diievyi
forcible *a* насильницький
nasylnytskyi
forearm *v.t* заздалегідь
озброюватися zazdalehid
ozbroiuvatysia
forearm *n* передпліччя
peredplichchia
forecast *v.t* завбачення
zavbachennia
forecast *n* прогноз prohnoz
forefather *n* прабатько prabatko
forefinger *n* вказівний палець
vkazivnyi palets
forehead *n* лоб lob
foreign *a* іноземний inozemnyi
foreigner *n* іноземець inozemets
foreknowledge *n.* передбачення
peredbachenrіa
foreleg *n* передня лапа perednia
lapa
forelock *n* чуб chub

foreman *n* майстер maister
foremost *a* передовий peredovyi
forenoon *n* час до полудня chas do poludnia
forerunner *n* попередник poperednyk
foresee *v.t* передбачити peredbachyty
foresight *n* мушка mushka
forest *n* ліс lis
forestall *v.t* передбачати peredbachaty
forester *n* лісник lisnyk
forestry *n* лісництво lisnytstvo
foretell *v.t* завбачати zavbachaty
forethought *n* передбачливість peredbachlyvist
forever *adv* назавжди nazavzhdy
forewarn *v.t* попереджати заздалегідь poperedzhaty zazdalehid
foreword *n* передмова peredmova
forfeit *v.t* позбутися pozbutysia
forfeit *n* штраф shtraf
forfeiture *n* позбавлення pozbavlennia
forge *v.t* кувати kuvaty
forge *n* кузня kuznia
forgery *n* фальсифікація falsyfikatsiia
forget *v.t* забувати zabuvaty
forgetful *a* забудькуватий zabudkuvatyi
forgive *v.t* вибачати vybachaty
forgo *v.t* утримуватися від utrymuvatysia vid
forlorn *a* нещасний neshchasnyi
form *v.t.* утворювати utvoriuvaty
form *n* форма forma
formal *a* формальний formalnyi
format *n* формат format

formation *n* формування formuvannia
former *a* колишній kolyshnii
former *n.* укладач ukladach
formerly *adv* раніше ranishe
formidable *a* грізний hriznyi
formula *n* формула formula
formulate *v.t* формулювати formuliuvaty
forsake *v.t.* відмовлятися vidmovliatysia
forswear *v.t.* зарікатися zarikatysia
fort *n.* піднесеність pidnesenist
forte *n.* сильна сторона sylna storona
forth *adv.* вперед vpered
forthcoming *a.* наступний nastupnyi
forthwith *adv.* зараз zaraz
fortify *v.t.* зводити укріплення zvodyty ukriplennia
fortitude *n.* сила духу syla dukhu
fort-night *n.* два тижні dva tyzhni
fortress *n.* фортеця fortetsia
fortunate *a.* щасливий shchaslyvyi
fortune *n.* стан stan
forty *n.* сорок sorok
forum *n.* збори zbory
forward *v.t* передавати peredavaty
forward *a.* передовий peredovyi
forward *adv* уперед upered
fossil *n.* скам'яніліст skamianilist
foster *v.t.* виховувати vykhovuvaty
foul *a.* брудний brudnyi
found *v.t.* засновувати zasnovuvaty
foundation *n.* установа ustanova
founder *n.* засновник zasnovnyk
foundry *n.* плавильня plavylnia

fountain *n.* фонтан fontan

four *n.* чотири chotyry

fourteen *n.* чотирнадцять chotyrnadtsiat

fowl *n.* птиця ptytsia

fowler *n.* птахолов ptakholov

fox *n.* лисиця lysytsia

fraction *n.* частка chastka

fracture *v.t* розколюватися rozkoliuvatysia

fracture *n.* пролом prolom

fragile *a.* тендітний tenditnyi

fragment *n.* фрагмент frahment

fragrance *n.* аромат aromat

fragrant *a.* ароматний aromatnyi

frail *a.* крихкий krykhkyi

frame *v.t.* обрамовувати obramovuvaty

frame *n* рама rama

franchise *n.* привілей pryvilei

frank *a.* щирий shchyryi

frantic *a.* шалений shalenyi

fraternal *a.* братерський braterskyi

fraternity *n.* громада hromada

fratricide *n.* братовбивство bratovbyvstvo

fraud *n.* шахрайство shakhraistvo

fraudulent *a.* шахрайський shakhraiskyi

fraught *a.* обтяжений obtiazhenyi

fray *n* сварка svarka

free *a.* відкритий vidkrytyi

free *v.t* визволяти vypzvoliaty

freedom *n.* свобода svoboda

freeze *v.i.* заморожувати zamorozhuvaty

freight *n.* фрахт frakht

French *a.* французький frantsuzkyi

French *n* французька мова frantsuzka mova

frenzy *n.* божевілля bozhevillia

frequency *n.* частота chastota

frequent *a.* частий chastyi

fresh *a.* свіжий svizhyi

fret *v.t.* підточувати pidtochuvaty

fret *n.* хвилювання khvyliuvannia

friction *n.* тертя tertia

Friday *n.* п'ятниця piatnytsia

fridge *n.* холодильник kholodylnyk

friend *n.* приятель pryiatel

fright *n.* жах zhakh

frighten *v.t.* налякати naliakaty

frigid *a.* холодний kholodnyi

frill *n.* оборка oborka

fringe *n.* бахрома bakhroma

fringe *v.t* облямовувати obliamovuvaty

frivolous *a.* легковажний lehkovazhnyi

frock *n.* плаття plattia

frog *n.* жаба zhaba

frolic *n.* пустощі pustoshchi

frolic *v.i.* пустувати pustuvaty

from *prep.* від vid

front *a* передній perednii

front *v.t* виходити на vykhodyty na

front *n.* чоло cholo

frontier *n.* рубіж rubizh

frost *n.* мороз moroz

frown *n.* похмурий погляд pokhmuryi pohliad

frown *v.i* хмуритися khmurytysia

frugal *a.* скромний skromnyi

fruit *n.* фрукт frukt

fruitful *a.* плідний plidnyi

frustrate *v.t.* розладнувати rozladnuvaty

frustration *n.* розлад rozlad

fry *n* смажене smazhene

fry *v.t.* смажити smazhyty

fuel *n.* паливо palyvo

fugitive *a.* побіжний pobizhnyi

fugitive *n.* утікач utikach
fulfill *v.t.* виконувати vykonuvaty
fulfilment *n.* здійснення
  zdiisnennia
full *a.* нескорочений
  neskorochenyi
full *adv.* пухкий pukhkyi
fullness *n.* повнота povnota
fully *adv.* цілком tsilkom
fumble *v.i.* нишпорити nyshporyty
fun *n.* розвага rozvaha
function *v.i* функціонувати
  funktsionuvaty
function *n.* функція funktsiia
functionary *n.* функціонер
  funktsioner
fund *n.* фонд fond
fundamental *a.*
  фундаментальний
  fundamentalnyi
funeral *n.* похорон pokhoron
fungus *n.* грибок hrybok
funny *n.* забавний zabavnyi
fur *n.* хутро khutro
furious *a.* скажений skazhenyi
furl *v.t.* кріпити kripyty
furlong *n.* восьма частина милі
  vosma chastyna myli
furnace *n.* горн horn
furnish *v.t.* обставляти obstavliaty
furniture *n.* обстановка
  obstanovka
furrow *n.* борозна borozna
further *adv.* подалі podali
further *a* подальший podalshyi
further *v.t* сприяти spryiaty
fury *n.* лють liut
fuse *v.t.* плавити plavyty
fuse *n* плавка plavka
fusion *n.* плавлення plavlennia
fuss *v.i* метушитися metushytysia
fuss *n.* метушня metushnia
futile *a.* марний marnyi

futility *n.* марність marnist
future *a.* майбутній maibutnii
future *n* майбутнє maibutnie

gabble *v.i.* бурмотати burmotaty
gadfly *n.* сліпень slipen
gag *v.t.* затикати рот zatykaty rot
gag *n.* кляп kliap
gaiety *n.* нарядність nariadnist
gain *n* виграш vyhrash
gain *v.t.* здобувати zdobuvaty
gainsay *v.t.* суперечити
  superechyty
gait *n.* хода khoda
galaxy *n.* галактика halaktyka
gale *n.* шторм shtorm
gallant *a.* галантний halantnyi
gallant *n* кавалер kavaler
gallantry *n.* галантність halantnist
gallery *n.* галерея halereia
gallon *n.* галон halon
gallop *n.* галоп halop
gallop *v.t.* скакати skakaty
gallows *n.* . шибениця
  shybenytsia
galore *adv.* удосталь udostal
galvanize *v.t.* гальванізувати
  halvanizuvaty
gamble *n* азартна гра azartna hra
gamble *v.i.* грати в азартні ігри
  hraty v azartni ihry
gambler *n.* гравець hravets
game *n.* гра hra
game *v.i* грати hraty
gander *n.* йолоп yolop
gang *n.* банда banda
gangster *n.* гангстер hanhster
gap *n* пролом prolom
gape *v.i.* позіхати pozikhaty
garage *n.* гараж harazh
garb *n.* одіяння odiiannia

garb *v.t* одягатися odiahatysia
garbage *n.* сміття smittia
garden *n.* сад sad
gardener *n.* садівник sadivnyk
gargle *v.i.* полоскати poloskaty
garland *n.* вінок vinok
garland *v.t.* прикрашати гірляндою prykrashaty hirliandoiu
garlic *n.* часник chasnyk
garment *n.* предмет одягу predmet odiahu
garter *n.* підв'язка pidviazka
gas *n.* газ haz
gasket *n.* набивка nabyvka
gasp *v.i* важко дихати vazhko dykhaty
gasp *n.* утруднене дихання utrudnene dykhannia
gassy *a.* балакучий balakuchyi
gastric *a.* шлунковий shlunkovyi
gate *n.* ворота vorota
gather *v.t.* рвати rvaty
gaudy *a.* яскравий yaskravyi
gauge *n.* розмір rozmir
gauntlet *n.* рукавиця rukavytsia
gay *a.* безтурботний bezturbotnyi
gaze *v.t.* дивитися dyvytysia
gaze *n* погляд pohliad
gazette *n.* газета hazeta
gear *n.* швидкість shvydkist
geld *v.t.* обкладати податком obkladaty podatkom
gem *n* коштовність koshtovnist
gender *n.* рід rid
general *a.* широкий shyrokyi
generally *adv.* як правило yak pravylo
generate *v.t.* породжувати porodzhuvaty
generation *n.* покоління pokolinnia

generator *n.* джерело енергії dzherelo enerhii
generosity *n.* щедрість shchedrist
generous *a.* щедрий shchedryi
genius *n.* геній henii
gentle *a.* м'який miakyi
gentleman *n.* джентльмен dzhentlmen
gentry *n.* дрібнопомісне дворянство dribnopomisne dvorianstvo
genuine *a.* справжній spravzhnii
geographer *n.* географ heohraf
geographical *a.* географічний heohrafichnyi
geography *n.* географія heohrafiia
geological *a.* геологічний heolohichnyi
geologist *n.* геолог heoloh
geology *n.* геологія heolohiia
geometrical *a.* геометричний heometrychnyi
geometry *n.* геометрія heometriia
germ *n.* мікроб mikrob
germicide *n.* бактерицид bakterytsyd
germinate *v.i.* прорости prorosty
germination *n.* пророщування proroshchuvannia
gerund *n.* герундій herundii
gesture *n.* жест zhest
get *v.t.* приносити prynosyty
ghastly *a.* мертво-блідий mertvo-blidyi
ghost *n.* тінь tin
giant *n.* гігант hihant
gibbon *n.* гібон hibon
gibe *n* колючість koliuchist
gibe *v.i.* насміхатися nasmikhatysia
giddy *a.* запаморочливий zapamorochlyvyi

gift *n.* дар dar
gifted *a.* обдарований obdarovanyi
gigantic *a.* гігантський hihantskyi
giggle *v.i.* хихикати khykhykaty
gild *v.t.* прикрашати prykrashaty
gilt *a.* позолота pozolota
ginger *n.* імбир imbyr
giraffe *n.* жираф zhyraf
gird *v.t.* підперізувати pidperizuvaty
girder *n.* перекладина perekladyna
girdle *v.t* кільцювати kiltsiuvaty
girdle *n.* кушак kushak
girl *n.* дівчина divchyna
girlish *a.* дівочий divochyi
gist *n.* суть sut
give *v.t.* піддатливість piddatlyvist
glacier *n.* льодовик lodovyk
glad *a.* приємний pryiemnyi
gladden *v.t.* радувати raduvaty
glamour *n.* чарівність charivnist
glance *v.i.* окинути поглядом okynuty pohliadom
glance *n.* швидкий погляд shvydkyi pohliad
gland *n.* залоза zaloza
glare *n.* блискуча мішура blyskucha mishura
glare *v.i* пильно дивитися pylno dyvytysia
glass *n.* скло sklo
glaucoma *n.* глаукома hlaukoma
glaze *n* глазур hlazur
glaze *v.t.* склити sklyty
glazier *n.* скляр skliar
glee *n.* радість radist
glide *v.t.* плавно рухатися plavno rukhatysia
glider *n.* глісер hliser
glimpse *n.* просвіт prosvit
glitter *n* блиск blysk

glitter *v.i.* виблискувати vyblyskuvaty
global *a.* глобальний hlobalnyi
globe *n.* глобус hlobus
gloom *n.* заволікатися zavolikatysia
gloomy *a.* темний temnyi
glorification *n.* вихваляння vykhvaliannia
glorify *v.t.* славити slavyty
glorious *a.* славний slavnyi
glory *n.* слава slava
gloss *n.* лиск lysk
glossary *n.* глосарій hlosarii
glossy *a.* лискучий lyskuchyi
glove *n.* рукавичка rukavychka
glow *v.i.* розжарюватися rozzhariuvatysia
glow *n* спека speka
glucose *n.* глюкоза hliukoza
glue *n.* клей klei
glut *v.t.* завалювати товарами zavaliuvaty tovaramy
glut *n* затоварення zatovarennia
glutton *n.* росомаха rosomakha
gluttony *n.* обжерливість obzherlyvyst
glycerine *n.* гліцерин hlitseryn
go *v.i.* йти yty
goad *v.t* спонукати sponukaty
goad *n.* стимул stymul
goal *n.* завдання zavdannia
goat *n.* коза koza
gobble *n.* жерти zherty
goblet *n.* келих kelykh
god *n.* бог boh
goddess *n.* богиня bohynia
godhead *n.* божественність bozhestvennist
godly *a.* праведний pravednyi
godown *n.* склад товарів sklad tovariv
godsend *n.* удача udacha

goggles *n.* здивований погляд zdyvovanyi pohliad
gold *n.* золото zoloto
golden *a.* золотий zolotyi
goldsmith *n.* ювелір yuvelir
golf *n.* гольф holf
gong *n.* гонг honh
good *a.* добрий dobryi
good *n.* товар tovar
good-bye *interj.* до побачення do pobachennia
goodness *n.* доброта dobrota
goodwill *n.* благовоління blahovolinnia
goose *n.* гусак husak
gooseberry *n.* аґрус agrus
gorgeous *a.* яскравий yaskravyi
gorilla *n.* горила horyla
gospel *n.* проповідь propovid
gospel *n.* Євангеліє Yevanheliie
gossip *n.* плітка plitka
gourd *n.* горлянка horlianka
gout *n.* подагра podahra
govern *v.t.* управляти upravliaty
governance *n.* керівництво kerivnytstvo
governess *n.* гувернантка huvernantka
government *n.* управління upravlinnia
governor *n.* губернатор hubernator
gown *n.* сукня suknia
grab *v.t.* хапати khapaty
grace *n.* грація hratsiia
grace *v.t.* удостоювати udostoiuvaty
gracious *a.* милостивий mylostyvyi
gradation *n.* градація hradatsiia
grade *v.t* сортувати sortuvaty
grade *n.* ступінь stupin
gradual *a.* поступовий postupovyi

graduate *v.i.* випускати vypuskaty
graduate *n* випускний vypusknyi
graft *v.t* пересаджувати peresadzhuvaty
graft *n.* щеплення shcheplennia
grain *n.* крупи krupy
grammar *n.* граматика hramatyka
grammarian *n.* граматисти hramatysty
gramme *n.* грам hram
gramophone *n.* грамофон hramofon
granary *n.* житниця zhytnytsia
grand *a.* грандіозний hrandioznyi
grandeur *n.* велич velych
grant *n* видача vydacha
grant *v.t.* надавати nadavaty
grape *n.* виноград vynohrad
graph *n.* крива kryva
graphic *a.* графічний hrafichnyi
grapple *n.* сутичка sutychka
grapple *v.i.* чепляти chepliaty
grasp *v.t.* розібратися rozibratysia
grasp *n* стискання styskannia
grass *n* трава trava
grate *n.* ґрати graty
grate *v.t* терти terty
grateful *a.* благодатний blahodatnyi
gratification *n.* винагорода vynahoroda
gratis *adv.* безкоштовний bezkoshtovnyi
gratitude *n.* подяка podiaka
gratuity *n.* грошовий подарунок hroshovyi podarunok
grave *a.* вагомий vahomyi
grave *n.* могила mohyla
gravitate *v.i.* тяжіти tiazhyty
gravitation *n.* гравітація hravitatsiia
gravity *n.* серйозність sierioznist
graze *v.i.* пасти pasty

graze *n* садно sadno
grease *n* мастило mastylo
grease *v.t* змастити zmastyty
greasy *a.* жирний zhyrnyi
great *a* значний znachnyi
greed *n.* жадібність zhadibnist
greedy *a.* пожадливий pozhadlyvyi
Greek *n.* грецька мова hretska mova
Greek *a* грецький hretskyi
green *a.* зелений zelenyi
green *n* зелений колір zelenyi kolir
greenery *n.* оранжерея oranzhereia
greet *v.t.* вітатися vitatysia
grenade *n.* граната hranata
grey *a.* сірий siryi
greyhound *n.* хортиця khortytsia
grief *n.* горе hore
grievance *n.* скарга skarha
grieve *v.t.* горювати horiuvaty
grievous *a.* сумний sumnyi
grind *v.i.* размелювати razmeliuvaty
grinder *n.* шліфувальник shlifuvalnyk
grip *n* затиснення zatysnennia
grip *v.t.* схоплювати skhopliuvaty
groan *n* стогін stohin
groan *v.i.* стогнати stohnaty
grocer *n.* бакалійник bakaliinyk
grocery *n.* бакалійна лавка bakaliina lavka
groom *n.* грум hrum
groom *v.t* чистити коня chystyty konia
groove *n.* вибоїна vyboina
groove *v.t* жалоби zhaloby
grope *v.t.* намацувати namatsuvaty
gross *n.* брутто brutto

gross *a* огрядний ohriadnyi
grotesque *a.* гротеск hrotesk
ground *n.* майданчик maidanchyk
group *n.* група hrupa
group *v.t.* групувати hrupuvaty
grow *v.t.* робитися robytysia
grower *n.* садівник sadivnyk
growl *n* бурчання burchannia
growl *v.i.* бурчати burchaty
growth *n.* зростання zrostannia
grudge *n* заздрість zazdrist
grudge *v.t.* шкодувати shkoduvaty
grumble *v.i.* гуркотіти hurkotity
grunt *n.* рохкання rokhkannia
grunt *v.i.* рохкати rokhkaty
guarantee *n.* поручитель poruchytel
guarantee *v.t* ручатися ruchatysia
guard *n.* охорона okhorona
guard *v.i.* охороняти okhoroniaty
guardian *n.* страж strazh
guava *n.* гуава huava
guerilla *n.* партизан partyzan
guess *n.* здогадка zdohadka
guess *v.i* здогадуватися zdohaduvatysia
guest *n.* гість hist
guidance *n.* керівництво kerivnytstvo
guide *v.t.* провести provesty
guide *n.* розвідник rozvidnyk
guild *n.* гільдія hildiia
guile *n.* підступність pidstupnist
guilt *n.* провина provyna
guilty *a.* винуватий vynuvatyi
guise *n.* личина lychyna
guitar *n.* гітара hitara
gulf *n.* затока zatoka
gull *v.t* дурити duryty
gull *n* чайка chaika
gull *n.* чайка chaika
gulp *n.* ковток kovtok
gum *n.* десна desna

gun *n.* зброя zbroia
gust *n.* шквал shkval
gutter *n.* жолоб zholob
guttural *a.* горловий horlovyi
gymnasium *n.* гімнастичний зал himnastychnyi zal
gymnast *n.* гімнаст himnast
gymnastic *a.* гімнастичний himnastychnyi
gymnastics *n.* гімнастика himnastyka

habeas corpus *n.* судовий наказ про передачу арештованого до суду для належного судового розгляду sudovyi nakaz pro peredachu areshtovanoho do sudu dlia nalezhnoho sudovoho rozhliadu
habit *n.* будова тіла budova tila
habitable *a.* придатний для житла prydatnyi dlia zhytla
habitat *n.* батьківщина batkivshchyna
habitation *n.* проживання prozhyvannia
habituate *v. t.* привчати pryvchaty
hack *v.t.* мотика motyka
hag *n.* чаклунка chaklunka
haggard *a.* виснажений vysnazhenyi
haggle *v.i.* торгуватися torhuvatysia
hail *v.t* поздоровляти pozdorovliaty
hail *v.i* сипатися sypatysia
hail *n.* слава slava
hair *n* волосся volossia
hale *a.* здоровий zdorovyi
half *n.* половина polovyna
half *a* половинний polovynnyi

hall *n.* зал zal
hallmark *n.* проба proba
hallow *v.t.* шанувати shanuvaty
halt *v. t.* зробити привал zrobyty pryval
halt *n* привал pryval
halve *v.t.* поділити навпіл podilyty navpil
hamlet *n.* селище selyshche
hammer *n.* молоток molotok
hammer *v.t* прибивати prybyvaty
hand *v.t* передати peredaty
hand *n* рука ruka
handbill *n.* рекламний листок reklamnyi lystok
handbook *n.* довідник туриста dovidnyk turysta
handcuff *v.t* надіти наручники nadity naruchnyky
handcuff *n.* наручник naruchnyk
handful *n.* жменя zhmenia
handicap *n* фізична вада fizychna vada
handicap *v.t.* ускладнювати uskladniuvaty
handicraft *n.* ручна робота ruchna robota
handiwork *n.* ручна робота ruchna robota
handkerchief *n.* носовичок nosovychok
handle *v.t* поратися poratysia
handle *n.* рукоятка rukoiatka
handsome *a.* гарний harnyi
handy *a.* портативний portatyvnyi
hang *v.t.* вішати vishaty
hanker *v.i.* прагнути prahnuty
haphazard *a.* необдуманий neobdumanyi
happen *v.t.* статися statysia
happening *n.* подія podiia
happiness *n.* щастя shchastia
happy *a.* щасливий shchaslyvyi

harass *v.t.* турбувати turbuvaty
harassment *n.* залякування zaliakuvannia
harbour *n.* гавань havan
harbour *v.t* стати на якір staty na yakir
hard *a.* жорсткий zhorstkyi
harden *v.t.* робити твердим robyty tverdym
hardihood *n.* зухвальство zukhvalstvo
hardly *adv.* насилу nasylu
hardship *n.* нестатки nestatky
hardy *adj.* відважний vidvazhnyi
hare *n.* заєць zaiets
harm *n.* шкода shkoda
harm *v.t* шкодити shkodyty
harmonious *a.* гармонійний harmoniinyi
harmonium *n.* фісгармонія fisharmoniia
harmony *n.* гармонія harmoniia
harness *v.t* запрягати zapriahaty
harness *n.* упряж upriazh
harp *n.* арфа arfa
harsh *a.* твердий tverdyi
harverster *n.* збирач врожаю zbyrach vrozhaiu
harvest *n.* урожай urozhai
haste *n.* поспіх pospikh
hasten *v.i.* поспішати pospishaty
hasty *a.* запальний zapalnyi
hat *n.* капелюх kapeliukh
hatchet *n.* сокирка sokyrka
hate *v.t.* ненавидіти nenavydity
hate *n.* ненависть nenavyst
haughty *a.* гордовитий hordovytyi
haunt *n* улюблене місце uliublene mistse
haunt *v.t.* часто бувати chasto buvaty
have *v.t.* мати maty
haven *n.* притулок prytulok

havoc *n.* спустошення spustoshennia
hawk *n* яструб yastrub
hawker *n* сокільник sokilnyk
hawthorn *n.* глід hlid
hay *n.* сіно sino
hazard *n.* загроза zahroza
hazard *v.t* ставити на карту stavyty na kartu
haze *n.* легкий туман lehkyi tuman
hazy *a.* туманний tumannyi
he *pron.* він vin
head *n.* голова holova
head *v.t* вести vesty
headache *n.* головний біль holovnyi bil
heading *n.* заголовок zaholovok
headlong *adv.* невтримний nevtrymnyi
headstrong *a.* свавільний svavilnyi
heal *v.i.* сприяти заєнню spryiaty zaienniu
health *n.* здоров'я zdorovia
healthy *a.* корисний korysnyi
heap *n.* купа kupa
heap *v.t* нагромаджувати nahromadzhuvaty
hear *v.t.* чути chuty
hearsay *n.* слух slukh
heart *n.* серце sertse
hearth *n.* вогнище vohnyshche
heartily *adv.* серцево sertsevo
heat *v.t* зігрівати zihrivaty
heat *n.* спека speka
heave *v.i.* піднімати pidnimaty
heaven *n.* небеса nebesa
heavenly *a.* священний sviashchennyi
hedge *n.* дивопліт dyvoplit
hedge *v.t* підрізати живопліт podrizaty zhyvoplit

heed *v.t.* звернути увагу zvernuty uvahu
heed *n* увага uvaha
heel *n.* п'ята piata
hefty *a.* неабиякий neabyiakyi
height *n.* зріст zrist
heighten *v.t.* підвищувати pidvyshchuvaty
heinous *a.* огидний ohydnyi
heir *n.* спадкоємець spadkoiemets
hell *a.* пекло peklo
helm *n.* кермо kermo
helmet *n.* шолом sholom
help *v.t.* допомагати dopomahaty
help *n* помічник pomichnyk
helpful *a.* корисний korysnyi
helpless *a.* безпомічний bezpomichnyi
helpmate *n.* товариш tovarysh
hemisphere *n.* півкуля pivkulia
hemp *n.* пенька penka
hen *n.* курка kurka
hence *adv.* звідси zvidsy
henceforth *adv.* з цього часу z tsoho chasu
henceforward *adv.* відтепер vidteper
henchman *n.* зброєносець zbroienosets
henpecked *n.* підкаблучник pidkabluchnyk
her *a* її yii
her *pron.* їй yii
herald *n.* вісник visnyk
herald *v.t* сповіщати spovishchaty
herb *n.* трава trava
herculean *a.* дуже сильний duzhe sylnyi
herd *n.* стадо stado
herdsman *n.* пастух pastukh
here *adv.* тут tut

hereabouts *adv.* десь поруч des poruch
hereafter *adv.* тут і далі tut i dali
hereditary *a.* спадковий spadkovyi
heredity *n.* спадковість spadkovist
heritable *a.* наслідуваний nasliduvanyi
heritage *n.* спадщина spadshchyna
hermit *n.* самітник samitnyk
hermitage *n.* пустинь pustyn
hernia *n.* грижа hryzha
hero *n.* герой heroi
heroic *a.* героїчний heroichnyi
heroine *n.* героїня heroinia
heroism *n.* героїзм heroizm
herring *n.* оселедець oseledets
hesitant *a.* коливний kolyvnyi
hesitate *v.i.* коливатися kolyvatysia
hesitation *n.* коливання kolyvannia
hew *v.t.* прорубувати prorubuvaty
heyday *n.* розквіт rozkvit
hibernation *n.* зимівля zymivlia
hiccup *n.* гикавка hykavka
hide *n.* укриття ukryttia
hide *v.t* ховати khovaty
hideous *a.* потворний potvornyi
hierarchy *n.* ієрархія iierarkhiia
high *a.* високий vysokyi
highly *adv.* дуже duzhe
Highness *n.* височість vysokist
highway *n.* шосе shose
hilarious *a.* галасливий halaslyvyi
hilarity *n.* гучні веселощі huchni veseloshchi
hill *n.* пагорб pahorb
hillock *n.* горбок horbok
him *pron.* йому yomu
hinder *v.t.* заважати zavazhaty

hindrance *n.* завада zavada
hint *v.i* натякати natiakaty
hint *n.* натяк natiak
hip *n* стегно stehno
hire *v.t* знімати znimaty
hire *n.* наймання naimannia
hireling *n.* найманець naimanets
his *pron.* його yoho
hiss *n* шипіння shypinnia
hiss *v.i* шипіти shypity
historian *n.* історик istoryk
historic *a* . історичний istorychnyi
historical *a.* пов'язаний з
    історією poviazanyi z ictoriieiu
history *n.* історія istoriia
hit *n* удар udar
hit *v.t.* ударяти udariaty
hitch *n.* ривок ryvok
hither *adv.* сюди siudy
hitherto *adv.* досі dosi
hive *n.* саджати у вулик sadzhaty
    u vulyk
hoarse *a.* хрипкий khrypkyi
hoax *v.t* дурити duryty
hoax *n.* містифікація mistyfikatsiia
hobby *n.* хобі khobi
hobby-horse *n.* коник konyk
hockey *n.* хокей khokei
hoist *v.t.* підняти pidniaty
hold *n.* володіння volodinnia
hold *v.t* тримати trymaty
hole *n* діра dira
hole *v.t* дірявити diriavyty
holiday *n.* день відпочинку den
    vidpochynku
hollow *v.t* видовбувати
    vydovbuvaty
hollow *a.* глухий hlukhyi
hollow *n.* пустота pustota
holocaust *n.* масове винищення
    masove vynyshchennia
holy *a.* святий sviatyi

homage *n.* шанування
    shanuvannia
home *n.* будинок budynok
homeopathy *n.* гомеопатія
    homeopatiia
homicide *n.* позбавлення життя
    pozbavlennia zhyttia
homoeopath *n.* гомеопат
    homeopat
homogeneous *a.* однорідний
    odnoridnyi
honest *a.* чесний chesnyi
honesty *n.* чесність chesnist
honey *n.* мед med
honeycomb *n.* медові соти
    medovi soty
honeymoon *n.* медовий місяць
    medovyi misiats
honorarium *n.* винагорода
    vynahoroda
honorary *a.* почесний pochesnyi
honour *n.* честь chest
honour *v. t* поважати povazhaty
honourable *a.* шановний
    shanovnyi
hood *n.* капюшон kapiushon
hoodwink *v.t.* ввести в оману
    vvesty v omanu
hoof *n.* бити копитом byty
    kopytom
hook *n.* гак hak
hooligan *n.* хуліган khulihan
hoot *n.* гикання hykannia
hoot *v.i* улюлюкати uliuliukaty
hop *v. i* стрибати strybaty
hop *n* стрибок strybok
hope *n* надія nadiia
hope *v.t.* сподіватися spodivatysia
hopeful *a.* який сподівається
    yakyi spodivaietsia
hopeless *a.* безнадійний
    beznadiinyi
horde *n.* орда orda

horizon *n.* горизонт horyzont
horn *n.* ріг rih
hornet *n.* шершень shershen
horrible *a.* бридкий brydkyi
horrify *v.t.* шокувати shokuvaty
horror *n.* огида ohyda
horse *n.* коняка koniaka
horticulture *n.* садівництво sadivnytstvo
hose *n.* шланг shlanh
hosiery *n.* панчішні вироби panchishni vyroby
hospitable *a.* гостинний hostynnyi
hospital *n.* лікарня likarnia
hospitality *n.* гостинність hostynnist
host *n.* господар hospodar
hostage *n.* заручник zaruchnyk
hostel *n.* гуртожиток hurtozhytok
hostile *a.* ворожий vorozhyi
hostility *n.* вороже ставлення vorozhe stavlennia
hot *a.* пекучий pekuchyi
hotchpotch *n.* рагу з м'яса з овочами rahu z miasa z ovochamy
hotel *n.* готель hotel
hound *n.* мисливський собака myslyvskyi sobaka
hour *n.* година hodyna
house *v.t* надавати житло nadavaty zhytlo
house *n* хата khata
how *adv.* як yak
however *adv.* тим не менш tym ne mensh
however *conj* при цьому pry tsomu
howl *v.t.* вити vyty
howl *n* завивання zavyvannia
hub *n.* втулка vtulka
hubbub *n.* шум shum

huge *a.* величезний velycheznyi
hum *n* гудіння hudinnia
hum *v.* і гудіти hudity
human *a.* людський liudskyi
humane *a.* гуманний humannyi
humanitarian *a* гуманітарій humanitarii
humanity *n.* людство liudstvo
humanize *v.t.* олюднювати oliudniuvaty
humble *a.* скромний skromnyi
humdrum *a.* загальне місце zahalne mistse
humid *a.* сирий syryi
humidity *n.* вологість volohist
humiliate *v.t.* принижувати prynyzhuvaty
humiliation *n.* приниженість prynyzhenist
humility *n.* покірність pokirnist
humorist *n.* гуморист humoryst
humorous *a.* гумористичний humorystychnyi
humour *n.* гумор humor
hunch *n.* горб horb
hundred *n.* сотня sotnia
hunger *n* тривале недоїдання tryvale nedoidannia
hungry *a.* голодний holodnyi
hunt *n* полювання poliuvannia
hunt *v.t.* полювати poliuvaty
hunter *n.* мисливець myslyvets
huntsman *n.* єгер yeher
hurdle1 *n.* ратка hatka
hurdle2 *v.t* обгороджувати тином obhorodzhuvaty tynom
hurl *v.t.* жбурляти zhburliaty
hurrah *interj.* ура ura
hurricane *n.* ураган urahan
hurry *n* квапливість kvaplyvist
hurry *v.t.* квапити kvapyty
hurt *v.t.* заподіювати біль zapodiiuvaty bil

hurt *n* образа obraza
husband *n* чоловік cholovik
husbandry *n.* землеробство
  zemlerobstvo
hush *v.i* змушувати замовчати
  zmushuvaty zamovchaty
hush *n* тиша tysha
husk *n.* лушпайка lushpaika
husky *a.* сухий sukhyi
hut *n.* хатина khatyna
hyaena, hyena *n.* гієна hiiena
hybrid *n* гібрид hibryd
hybrid *a.* гібридний hibrydnyi
hydrogen *n.* водень voden
hygiene *n.* гігієна hihiiena
hygienic *a.* гігієнічний
  hihiienichnyi
hymn *n.* церковний гімн
  tserkovnyi himn
hyperbole *n.* гіпербола hiperbola
hypnotism *n.* гіпнотизм
  hipnotyzm
hypnotize *v.t.* гіпнотизувати
  hipnotyzuvaty
hypocrisy *n.* лицемірство
  lytsemirstvo
hypocrite *n.* лицемір lytsemir
hypocritical *a.* лицемірний
  lytsemirnyi
hypothesis *n.* гіпотеза hipoteza
hypothetical *a.* можливий
  mozhlyvyi
hysteria *n.* істерія isteriia
hysterical *a.* істеричний
  isterychnyi

I *pron.* я ya
ice *n.* лід lid
iceberg *n.* айсберг aisberh
icicle *n.* бурулька burulka
icy *a.* крижаний kryzhanyi

idea *n.* ідея ideia
ideal *n* ідеал ideal
ideal *a.* ідеальний idealnyi
idealism *n.* ідеалізм idealizm
idealist *n.* ідеаліст idealist
idealistic *a.* ідеалістичний
  idealistychnyi
idealize *v.t.* ідеалізувати
  idealizuvaty
identical *a.* ідентичний
  identychnyi
identify *v.t.* ідентифікувати
  identyfikuvaty
identity *n.* ідентичність
  identychnist
ideocy *n.* ідіотизм idiotyzm
idiom *n.* ідіома idioma
idiomatic *a.* ідіоматичний
  idiomatychnyi
idiot *n.* ідіот idiot
idiotic *a.* ідіотський idiotskyi
idle *a.* незайнятий nezainiatyi
idleness *n.* ледарство ledarstvo
idler *n.* нероба neroba
idol *n.* ідол idol
idolater *n.* ідолопоклонник
  idolopoklonnyk
if *conj.* якщо yakshcho
ignoble *a.* низький nyzkyi
ignorance *n.* неуцтво neutstvo
ignorant *a.* неосвічений
  neosvichenyi
ignore *v.t.* ігнорувати ihnoruvaty
ill *a.* хворий khvoryi
ill *adv.* навряд чи navriad chy
ill *n* шкода shkoda
illegal *a.* незаконний nezakonnyi
illegibility *n.* неможливість
  прочитати nemozhlyvist
  prochytaty
illegible *a.* який важко читається
  yakyi vazhko chytaietsia

illegitimate *a.* неправильний nepravylnyi
illicit *a.* недозволений nedozvolenyi
illiteracy *n.* неграмотність nehramotnist
illiterate *a.* неписьменний nepysmennyi
illness *n.* хвороба khvoroba
illogical *a.* нелогічний nelohichnyi
illuminate *v.t.* опромінювати oprominiuvaty
illumination *n.* ілюмінація iliuminatsiia
illusion *n.* ілюзія iliuziia
illustrate *v.t.* ілюструвати iliustruvaty
illustration *n.* ілюстрація iliustratsiia
image *n.* образ obraz
imagery *n.* різьба rizba
imaginary *a.* уявний uiavnyi
imagination *n.* уява uiava
imaginative *a.* творчий tvorchyi
imagine *v.t.* уявляти uiavliaty
imitate *v.t.* копіювати kopiiuvaty
imitation *n.* наслідування nasliduvannia
imitator *n.* наслідувач nasliduvach
immaterial *a.* нематеріальний nematerialnyi
immature *a.* нестиглий nestyhlyi
immaturity *n.* незрілість nezrilist
immeasurable *a.* незмірний nezmirnyi
immediate *a* спішний spishnyi
immemorial *a.* древній drevnii
immense *a.* неосяжний neosiazhnyi
immensity *n.* безмір bezmir
immerse *v.t.* занурювати zanuriuvaty

immersion *n.* занурення zanurennia
immigrant *n.* іммігрант immihrant
immigrate *v.i.* іммігрувати immihruvaty
immigration *n.* імміграція immihratsiia
imminent *a.* насувається nasuvaietsia
immodest *a.* нескромне neskromne
immodesty *n.* нескромність neskromnist
immoral *a.* розпутний rozputnyi
immorality *n.* аморальність amoralnist
immortal *a.* безсмертний bezsmertnyi
immortality *n.* безсмертя bezsmertia
immortalize *v.t.* увічнити uvichnyty
immovable *a.* байдужий baiduzhyi
immune *a.* імунний imunnyi
immunity *n.* несприйнятливість nespryiniatlyvist
immunize *v.t.* імунізувати imunizuvaty
impact *n.* імпульс impuls
impart *v.t.* давати davaty
impartial *a.* неупереджений neuperedzhenyi
impartiality *n.* неупередженість neuperedzhenist
impassable *a.* непрохідний neprokhidnyi
impasse *n.* безвихідне становище bezvykhidne stanovyshche
impatience *n.* нетерпимість neterpymist

impatient *a.* дратівливий
drativlyvyi
impeach *v.t.* брати під сумнів
braty pid sumniv
impeachment *n.* вияв сумніву
vyiav sumnivu
impede *v.t.* затримувати
zatrymuvaty
impediment *n.* ускладнення
uskladnennia
impenetrable *a.* недоступний
nedostupnyi
imperative *a.* наказовий
nakazovyi
imperfect *a.* незавершений
nezavershenyi
imperfection *n.* недосконалість
nedoskonalist
imperial *a.* імперський imperskyi
imperialism *n.* імперіалізм
imperializm
imperil *v.t.* наражати на
небезпеку narazhaty na
nebezpeku
imperishable *a.* нерушимий
nerushymyi
impersonal *a.* безособовий
bezosobovyi
impersonate *v.t.* уособлювати
uosobliuvaty
impersonation *n.* уособлення
uosoblennia
impertinence *n.* зухвалість
zukhvalist
impertinent *a.* нахабний
nakhabnyi
impetuosity *n.* імпульсивність
impulsyvnist
impetuous *a.* стрімкий strimkyi
implement *n.* знаряддя
znariaddia

implement *v.t.* щзабезпечувати
інструментами
shchzabezpechuvaty
instrumentamy
implicate *v.t.* вплутувати
vplutuvaty
implication *n.* залучення
zaluchennia
implicit *a.* котрого kotroho
implore *v.t.* просити prosyty
imply *v.t.* містити в собі mistyty
v sobi
impolite *a.* неввічливий
nevvichlyvyi
import *n.* імпорт import
import *v.t.* імпортувати
importuvaty
importance *n.* важливість
vazhlyvist
important *a.* важливий vazhlyvyi
impose *v.t.* накласти naklasty
imposing *a.* імпозантний
impozantnyi
imposition *n.* накладення
nakladennia
impossibility *n.* неможливість
nemozhlyvist
impossible *a.* неможливий
nemozhlyvyi
impostor *n.* обманщик
obmanshchyk
imposture *n.* обман obman
impotence *n.* безсилля bezsyllia
impotent *a.* слабкий slabkyi
impoverish *v.t.* довести до
бідності dovesty do bidnosti
impracticability *n.*
нездійсненність nezdiisnennist
impracticable *a.* нездійсненний
nezdiisnennyi
impress *v.t.* віддруковувати
viddrukovuvaty

impression *n.* враження
vrazhennia
impressive *a.* вражаючий
vrazhaiuchyi
imprint *v.t.* удруковане
udrukovane
imprint *n.* штамп shtamp
imprison *v.t.* ув'язнювати
uviazniuvaty
improper *a.* невідповідний
nevidpovidnyi
impropriety *n.* недоречність
nedorechnist
improve *v.t.* вдосконалювати
vdoskonaliuvaty
improvement *n.* поліпшення
polipshennia
imprudence *n.* нерозсудливість
nerozsudlyvist
imprudent *a.* необережний
neoberezhnyi
impulse *n.* збудження
zbudzhennia
impulsive *a.* імпульсивний
impulsyvnyi
impunity *n.* безкарність
bezkarnist
impure *a.* нечистий nechystyi
impurity *n.* нечистота nechystota
impute *v.t.* ставити stavyty
in *prep.* у u
inability *n.* нездібність nezdibnist
inaccurate *a.* помилковий
pomylkovyi
inaction *n.* бездіяльність
bezdiialnist
inactive *a.* бездіяльний
bezdiialnyi
inadmissible *a.* неприпустимий
neprypustymyi
inanimate *a.* неживий nezhyvyi
inapplicable *a.* непридатний
neprydatnyi

inattentive *a.* неуважний
neuvazhnyi
inaudible *a.* нечутний nechutnyi
inaugural *a.* урочиста промова
urochysta promova
inauguration *n.* урочисте
відкриття urochyste vidkryttia
inauspicious *a.* зловісний
zlovisnyi
inborn *a.* уроджений urodzhenyi
incalculable *a.* незліченні
nezlichenni
incapable *a.* невмілий nevmilyi
incapacity *n.* нездатність
nezdatnist
incarnate *a.* втілений vtilenyi
incarnate *v.t.* втілювати vtiliuvaty
incarnation *n.* уособлення
uosoblennia
incense *v.t.* дратувати dratuvaty
incense *n.* ладан ladan
incentive *n.* спонукання
sponukannia
inception *n.* народження
narodzhennia
inch *n.* дюйм diuim
incident *n.* інцидент intsydent
incidental *a.* побічний pobichnyi
incite *v.t.* порушувати
porushuvaty
inclination *n.* нахилення
nakhylennia
incline *v.i.* схиляти skhyliaty
include *v.t.* включати vkliuchaty
inclusion *n.* включення
vkliuchennia
inclusive *a.* містить mistyt
incoherent *a.* незв'язних
nezviaznykh
income *n.* дохід dokhid
incomparable *a.* непорівнянний
neporivniannyi

incompetent *a.* некомпетентний nekompetentnyi
incomplete *a.* неповний nepovnyi
inconsiderate *a.* необдуманий neobdumanyi
inconvenient *a.* незручний nezruchnyi
incorporate *a.* об'єднаний obiednanyi
incorporate *v.t.* реєструвати reiestruvaty
incorporation *n.* корпорація korporatsiia
incorrect *a.* невірний nevirnyi
incorrigible *a.* невиправний nevypravnyi
incorruptible *a.* псується psuietsia
increase *n* збільшуватися zbilshuvatysia
increase *v.t.* зростати zrostaty
incredible *a.* неймовірний neimovirnyi
increment *n.* приріст pryrist
incriminate *v.t.* інкримінувати inkryminuvaty
incubate *v.i.* висиджувати vysydzhuvaty
inculcate *v.t.* впроваджувати vprovadzhuvaty
incumbent *n.* особа, що займає посаду osoba, shcho zaimaie posadu
incumbent *a* покладений pokladenyi
incur *v.t.* брати на себе braty na sebe
incurable *a.* невиліковний nevylikovnyi
indebted *a.* знаходиться в боргу znakhodytsia v borhu

indecency *n.* безсоромна дія bezsoromna diia
indecent *a.* непорядний neporiadnyi
indecision *n.* нерішучість nerishuchist
indeed *adv.* невже nevzhe
indefensible *a.* незахищений nezakhyshchenyi
indefinite *a.* невизначений nevyznachenyi
indemnity *n.* гарантія від збитків harantiia vid zbytkiv
indentification *n.* ідентифікація identyfikatsiia
independence *n.* незалежність nezalezhnist
independent *a.* самостійний samostiinyi
indescribable *a.* неясний neiasnyi
index *n.* покажчик pokazhchyk
Indian *a.* індійський indiiskyi
indicate *v.t.* вказувати vkazuvaty
indication *n.* вказівка vkazivka
indicative *a.* який вказує yakyi vkazuie
indicator *n.* індикатор indykator
indict *v.t.* висувати обвинувачення vysuvaty obvynuvachennia
indictment *n.* обвинувальний акт obvynuvalnyi akt
indifference *n.* байдужість baiduzhist
indifferent *a.* байдужий baiduzhyi
indigenous *a.* місцевий mistsevyi
indigestible *a.* нестравний nestravnyi
indigestion *n.* порушення травлення porushennia travlennia
indignant *a.* обурений oburenyi

indignation *n.* обурення oburennia

indigo *n.* індиго indyho

indirect *a.* непрямий nepriamyi

indiscipline *n.* недисциплінованість nedystsyplinovanist

indiscreet *a.* нескромний neskromnyi

indiscretion *n.* нечемність nechemnist

indiscriminate *a.* нерозбірливий nerozbirlyvyi

indispensable *a.* необхідний neobkhidnyi

indisposed *a.* неприхильність neprykhylnist

indisputable *a.* безперечний bezperechnyi

indistinct *a.* неясний neiasnyi

individual *a.* особистий osobystyi

individualism *n.* індивідуалізм indyvidualizm

individuality *n.* індивідуальність indyvidualnist

indivisible *a.* неподільний nepodilnyi

indolent *a.* пустопорожнє pustoporozhnie

indomitable *a.* неприборканий nepryborkanyi

indoor *a.* внутрішній vnutrishnii

indoors *adv.* всередині vseredyni

induce *v.t.* спонукати sponukaty

inducement *n.* спонукання sponukannia

induct *v.t.* вводити в посаду vvodyty v posadu

induction *n.* офіційно вводити на посаду ofitsiino vvodyty na posadu

indulge *v.t.* давати собі волю davaty sobi voliu

indulgence *n.* поблажливість poblazhlyvist

indulgent *a.* поблажливий poblazhlyvyi

industrial *a.* виробничий vyrobnychyi

industrious *a.* працьовитий pratsovytyi

industry *n.* виробництво vyrobnytstvo

ineffective *a.* безрезультатний bezrezultatnyi

inert *a.* інертний inertnyi

inertia *n.* сила інерції syla inertsii

inevitable *a.* неминучий nemynuchyi

inexact *a.* неточний netochnyi

inexorable *a.* невблаганний nevblahannyi

inexpensive *a.* недорогий nedorohyi

inexperience *n.* недосвідченість nedosvidchenist

inexplicable *a.* незрозумілий nezrozumilyi

infallible *a.* безпомилковий bezpomylkovyi

infamous *a.* має погану репутацію maie pohanu reputatsiiu

infamy *n.* ганьба hanba

infancy *n.* раннє дитинство rannie dytynstvo

infant *n.* немовля nemovlia

infanticide *n.* дітовбивство ditovbyvstvo

infantile *a.* інфантільний infantilnyi

infantry *n.* піхота pikhota

infatuate *v.t.* закрутити голову zakrutyty holovu

infatuation *n.* сліпе захоплення slipe zakhoplennia

infect *v.t.* заражати zarazhaty
infection *n.* зараження zarazhennia
infectious *a.* інфекційний infektsiinyi
infer *v.t.* укладати ukladaty
inference *n.* виведення vyvedennia
inferior *a.* підлеглий pidlehlyi
inferiority *n.* неповноцінність nepovnotsinnist
infernal *a.* пекельний pekelnyi
infinite *a.* безмежний bezmezhnyi
infinity *n.* нескінченність neskinchennist
infirm *a.* немічний nemichnyi
infirmity *n.* неміч nemich
inflame *v.i.* запалюватися zapaliuvatysia
inflammable *a.* горюча речовина horiucha rechovyna
inflammation *n.* займання zaimannia
inflammatory *a.* збудливий zbudlyvyi
inflation *n.* надування naduvannia
inflexible *a.* негнучкий nehnuchkyi
inflict *v.t.* наносити nanosyty
influence *n.* вплив vplyv
influence *v.t.* впливова особа vplyvova osoba
influential *a.* впливовий vplyvovyi
influenza *n.* грип hryp
influx *n.* приплив pryplyv
inform *v.t.* повідомляти povidomliaty
informal *a.* неофіційний neofitsiinyi
information *n.* інформація informatsiia

informative *a.* інформаційний informatsiinyi
informer *n.* інформатор informator
infringe *v.t.* посягати posiahaty
infringement *n.* обмеження obmezhennia
infuriate *v.t.* приводити в лють pryvodyty v liut
infuse *v.t.* вливати vlyvaty
infusion *n.* вливання vlyvannia
ingrained *a.* проникаючий pronykaiuchyi
ingratitude *n.* невдячність nevdiachnist
ingredient *n.* інгредієнт inhrediient
inhabit *v.t.* населяти naseliaty
inhabitable *a.* жилий zhylyi
inhabitant *n.* житель zhytel
inhale *v.i.* вдихати vdykhaty
inherent *a.* властивий vlastyvyi
inherit *v.t.* успадковувати uspadkovuvaty
inheritance *n.* успадкування uspadkuvannia
inhibit *v.t.* забороняти zaboroniaty
inhibition *n.* стримування strymuvannia
inhospitable *a.* негостинний nehostynnyi
inhuman *a.* нелюдський neliudskyi
inimical *a.* неприязний nepryiaznyi
inimitable *a.* неповторний nepovtornyi
initial *n.* ініціал initsial
initial *a.* початковий pochatkovyi
initial *v.t* ставити ініціали stavyty initsialy

initiate *v.t.* ознайомити oznaiomyty

initiative *n.* ініціатива initsiatyva

inject *v.t.* вводити vvodyty

injection *n.* упорскування uporskuvannia

injudicious *a.* несвоєчасний nesvoiechasnyi

injunction *n.* припис prypys

injure *v.t.* забити zabyty

injurious *a.* шкідливий shkidlyvyi

injury *n.* рана rana

injustice *n.* неправосуддя nepravosuddia

ink *n.* чорнило chornylo

inkling *n.* слабка підозра slabka pidozra

inland *adv.* углиб країни uhlyb krainy

inland *a.* розташований усередені країни roztashovanyi useredeni krainy

in-laws *n.* свояки svoiaky

inmate *n.* мешканець meshkanets

inmost *a.* лежить глибоко усередині lezhyt hlyboko useredyni

inn *n.* трактир traktyr

innate *a.* вроджений vrodzhenyi

inner *a.* інтелектуальний intelektualnyi

innermost *a.* найглибший naihlybshyi

innings *n.* подача podacha

innocence *n.* невинність nevynnist

innocent *a.* безвинний bezvynnyi

innovate *v.t.* запроваджувати нововведення zaprovadzhuvaty novovvedennia

innovation *n.* нововведення novovvedennia

innovator *n.* новатор novator

innumerable *a.* незлічний nezlichnyi

inoculate *v.t.* робити щеплення robyty shcheplennia

inoculation *n.* щеплення shcheplennia

inoperative *a.* недіючий nediiuchyi

inopportune *a.* недоречний nedorechnyi

input *n.* введення vvedennia

inquest *n.* слідство slidstvo

inquire *v.t.* розпитувати rozpytuvaty

inquiry *n.* запит zapyt

inquisition *n.* вивчення vyvchennia

inquisitive *a.* допитливий dopytlyvyi

insane *a.* душевнохворий dushevnokhvoryi

insanity *n.* божевілля bozhevillia

insatiable *a.* ненаситно nenasytno

inscribe *v.t.* вписувати vpysuvaty

inscription *n.* напис napys

insect *n.* комаха komakha

insecticide *n.* інсектицид insektytsyd

insecure *a.* небезпечний nebezpechnyi

insecurity *n.* небезпечність nebezpechnist

insensibility *n.* нечутливість nechutlyvist

insensible *a.* нечутливий nechutlyvyi

inseparable *a.* нероздільний nerozdilnyi

insert *v.t.* вставляти vstavliaty

insertion *n.* вкладання
vkladannia
inside *a* прихований prykhovanyi
inside *adv.* у середині u seredyni
inside *prep.* усередині useredyni
inside *n.* внутрішня сторона
vnutrishnia storona
insight *n.* інтуїція intuitsiia
insignificance *n.* незначність
neznachnist
insignificant *a.* дрібний dribnyi
insincere *a.* нещирий neshchyryi
insincerity *n.* нещирість
neshchyrist
insinuate *v.t.* непомітно вселяти
nepomitno vseliaty
insinuation *n.* інсинуація
insynuatsiia
insipid *a.* несмачний nesmachnyi
insipidity *n.* відсутність смаку
vidsutnist smaku
insist *v.t.* наполягати napoliahaty
insistence *n.* нестійкість nestiikist
insistent *a.* наполегливий
napolehlyvyi
insolence *n.* нахабство
nakhabstvo
insolent *a.* пихатий pykhatyi
insoluble *n.* нерозчинний
nerozchynnyi
insolvency *n.* банкрутство
bankrutstvo
insolvent *a.* неплатоспроможний
neplatospromozhnyi
inspect *v.t.* уважно оглядати
uvazhno ohliadaty
inspection *n.* інспекція inspektsiia
inspector *n.* інспектор inspektor
inspiration *n.* натхнення
natkhnennia
inspire *v.t.* навіювати naviiuvaty
instability *n.* несталість nestalist

install *v.t.* офіційно празначувати
на посаду ofitsiino
praznachuvaty na posadu
installation *n.* інтсоляція
intsoliatsiia
instalment *n.* випуск vypusk
instance *n.* інстанція instantsiia
instant *a.* миттєвий myttievyi
instant *n.* мить myt
instantaneous *a.* негайний
nehainyi
instantly *adv.* відразу vidrazu
instigate *v.t.* спонукати sponukaty
instigation *n.* підбурювання
pidburiuvannia
instil *v.t.* вливати по краплині
vlyvaty po kraplyni
instinct *n.* інстинкт instynkt
instinctive *a.* інстинктивний
instynktyvnyi
institute *n.* інститут instytut
institution *n.* установа ustanova
instruct *v.t.* вчити vchyty
instruction *n.* інструктаж
instruktazh
instructor *n.* інструктор instruktor
instrument *n.* інструмент
instrument
instrumental *a.*
інструментальний
instrumentalnyi
instrumentalist *n.*
інструменталіст instrumentalist
insubordinate *a.* непокірливий
nepokirlyvyi
insubordination *n.* непокора
nepokora
insufficient *a.* незадовільний
nezadovilnyi
insular *a.* острівний ostrivnyi
insularity *n.* відособленість
vidosoblenist
insulate *v.t.* роз'єднати roziednaty

insulation *n.* відокремлення vidokremlennia
insulator *n.* ізолятор izoliator
insult *v.t.* завдавати образи zavdavaty obrazy
insult *n.* знущання znushchannia
insupportable *a.* нестерпний nesterpnyi
insurance *n.* страховка strakhovka
insure *v.t.* страхувати strakhuvaty
insurgent *n.* повстанець povstanets
insurgent *a.* повсталий povstalyi
insurmountable *a.* непереборний neperebornyi
insurrection *n.* заколот zakolot
intact *a.* незайманий nezaimanyi
intangible *a.* невідчутний nevidchutnyi
integral *a.* всеосяжний vseosiazhnyi
integrity *n.* прямота priamota
intellect *n.* інтелект intelekt
intellectual *a.* розумовий rozumovyi
intellectual *n.* інтелігент intelihent
intelligence *n.* розвідка rozvidka
intelligent *a.* кмітливий kmitlyvyi
intelligentsia *n.* інтелігенція intelihentsiia
intelligible *a.* зрозумілий zrozumilyi
intend *v.t.* мати намір maty namir
intense *a.* вразливий vrazlyvyi
intensify *v.t.* посилюватися posyliuvatysia
intensity *n.* інтенсивність intensyvnist
intensive *a.* інтенсивний intensyvnyi
intent *n.* призначення pryznachennia

intent *a.* схильний skhylnyi
intention *n.* прагнення prahnennia
intentional *a.* навмисний navmysnyi
intercept *v.t.* перехопити perekhopyty
interception *n.* перехоплювання perekhopliuvannia
interchange *v.* обмінюватися obminiuvatysia
interchange *n.* операції operatsii
intercourse *n.* спілкування spilkuvannia
interdependence *n.* взаємозалежність vzaiemozalezhnist
interdependent *a.* взаємозалежний vzaiemozalezhnyi
interest *n.* інтерес interes
interested *a.* упереджений uperedzhenyi
interesting *a.* цікавий tsikavyi
interfere *v.i.* перешкоджати pereshkodzhaty
interference *n.* втручання vtruchannia
interim *n.* інтервал interval
interior *a.* віддалений від моря viddalenyi vid moria
interior *n.* внутрішність vnutrishnist
interjection *n.* втручання vtruchannia
interlock *v.t.* блокування blokuvannia
interlude *n.* антракт antrakt
intermediary *n.* посередник poserednyk
intermediate *a.* проміжний promizhnyi

interminable *a.* нескінченний neskinchennyi

intermingle *v.t.* спілкуватися spilkuvatysia

intern *v.t.* стажист stazhyst

internal *a.* національний natsionalnyi

international *a.* міжнародний mizhnarodnyi

interplay *n.* взаємодія vzaiemodiia

interpret *v.t.* тлумачити tlumachyty

interpreter *n.* перекладач perekladach

interrogate *v.t.* допитувати dopytuvaty

interrogation *n.* питання pytannia

interrogative *n* дізнання diznannia

interrogative *a.* питальний pytalnyi

interrupt *v.t.* переривати pereryvaty

interruption *n.* перерва pererva

intersect *v.t.* перетинатися peretynatysia

intersection *n.* перехрестя perekhrestia

interval *n.* проміжок promizhok

intervene *v.i.* втручатися vtruchatysia

intervention *n.* інтервенція interventsiia

interview *v.t.* проводити співбесіду provodyty spivbesidu

interview *n.* співбесіда spivbesida

intestinal *a.* кишковий kyshkovyi

intestine *n.* кишка kyshka

intimacy *n.* тісний зв'язок tisnyi zviazok

intimate *v.t.* говорити натяками hovoryty natiakamy

intimate *a.* інтимний intymnyi

intimation *n.* повідомлення povidomlennia

intimidate *v.t.* лякати liakaty

intimidation *n.* залякування zaliakuvannia

into *prep.* у u

intolerable *a.* непереносний neperenosnyi

intolerance *n.* нетолерантність netolerantnist

intolerant *a.* нетерпимий neterpymyi

intoxicant *n.* токсична речовина toksychna rechovyna

intoxicate *v.t.* одурманювати odurmaniuvaty

intoxication *n.* сп'яніння spianinnia

intransitive *a. (verb)* непехідний neperekhidnyi

intrepid *a.* відважний vidvazhnyi

intrepidity *n.* сміливість smilyvist

intricate *a.* заплутаний zaplutanyi

intrigue *n* інтрига intryha

intrigue *v.t.* інтригувати intryhuvaty

intrinsic *a.* інстінктивний instinktyvnyi

introduce *v.t.* знайомити znaiomyty

introduction *n.* знайомство znaiomstvo

introductory *a.* вступний vstupnyi

introspect *v.i.* дивитися всередину dyvytysia vseredynu

introspection *n.* інтроспекція introspektsiia

intrude *v.t.* вторгатися vtorhatysia

intrusion *n.* вторгнення vtorhnennia

intuition *n.* інтуїція intuitsiia

intuitive *a.* інтуїтивний intuityvnyi

invade *v.t.* вражати vrazhaty
invalid *a.* необґрунтований neobhruntovanyi
invalid *n* інвалід invalid
invalid *a.* недійсний nediisnyi
invalidate *v.t.* позбавляти законної сили pozbavliaty zakonnoi syly
invaluable *a.* неоціненний neotsinennyi
invasion *n.* навала navala
invective *n.* лайка laika
invent *v.t.* винаходити vynakhodyty
invention *n.* створення stvorennia
inventive *a.* винахідливий vynakhidlyvyi
inventor *n.* винахідник vynakhidnyk
invert *v.t.* перевертати perevertaty
invest *v.t.* інвестувати investuvaty
investigate *v.t.* розслідувати rozsliduvaty
investigation *n.* розслідування rozsliduvannia
investment *n.* інвестиції investytsii
invigilate *v.t.* наглядати nahliadaty
invigilation *n.* спостереження за тими, хто проходить іспит sposterezhennia za tymy, khto prokhodyt ispyt
invigilator *n.* той, кто слідкує за тим, щоб студенти не списували під час іспитів toi, kto slidkuie za tym, shchob studenty ne spysuvaly pid chas ispytiv
invincible *a.* непереможний neperemozhnyi

inviolable *a.* який користується недоторнканістю yakyi korystuietsia nedotornkanistiu
invisible *a.* невидимий nevydymyi
invitation *n.* запрошення zaproshennia
invite *v.t.* запрошувати zaproshuvaty
invocation *n.* заклинання zaklynannia
invoice *n.* рахунок-фактура rakhunok-faktura
invoke *v.t.* закликати zaklykaty
involve *v.t.* ускладнювати uskladniuvaty
inward *a.* внутрішній vnutrishnii
inwards *adv.* усередину useredynu
irate *a.* гнівний hnivnyi
ire *n.* роздратування rozdratuvannia
Irish *n.* ірландська мова irlandska mova
Irish *a.* ірландський irlandskyi
irksome *a.* дратівний drativnyi
iron *v.t.* залізний zaliznyi
iron *n.* праска praska
ironical *a.* іронічний ironichnyi
irony *n.* іронія ironiia
irradiate *v.i.* роз'яснити roziasnyty
irrational *a.* нераціональний neratsionalnyi
irreconcilable *a.* непримиренний neprymyrennyi
irrecoverable *a.* непоправний nepopravnyi
irrefutable *a.* незаперечний nezaperechnyi
irregular *a.* нерегулярний nerehuliarnyi
irregularity *n.* неправильність nepravylnist

irrelevant *a.* недоречний
nedorechnyi
irrespective *a.* незалежний
nezalezhnyi
irresponsible *a.*
невідповідальний
nevidpovidalnyi
irrigate *v.t.* зрошувати zroshuvaty
irrigation *n.* зрошення zroshennia
irritable *a.* дратівливий drativlyvyi
irritant *a.* касувальний kasuvalnyi
irritant *n.* подразник podraznyk
irritate *v.t.* дратувати dratuvaty
irritation *n.* роздратування
rozdratuvannia
irruption *n.* набіг nabih
island *n.* острів ostriv
isle *n.* острівець ostrivets
isobar *n.* изобар yzobar
isolate *v.t.* ізолювати izoliuvaty
isolation *n.* ізоляція izoliatsiia
issue *n.* виходити vykhodyty
issue *v.i.* закінчуватися
zakinchuvatysia
it *pron.* воно vono
Italian *a.* італійський italiiskyi
Italian *n.* італійська мову italiiska
movu
italic *a.* курсивний kursyvnyi
italics *n.* курсив kursyv
itch *n.* свербіж sverbizh
itch *v.i.* свербіти sverbity
item *n.* параграф parahraf
ivory *n.* бивень byven
ivy *n* плющ pliushch

jab *v.t.* пхати pkhaty
jabber *v.t.* плескати язиком
pleskaty yazykom
jack *v.t.* залишити zalyshyty
jack *n.* простолюдин prostoliudyn

jackal *n.* шакал shakal
jacket *n.* куртка kurtka
jade *n.* шкапа shkapa
jail *n.* в'язниця viaznytsia
jailer *n.* тюремник tiuremnyk
jam *n.* джем dzhem
jam *v.t.* затискати zatyskaty
jar *n.* неприємний звук
nepryiemnyi zvuk
jargon *n.* жаргон zharhon
jasmine, jessamine *n.* жасмин
zhasmyn
jaundice *v.t.* викликати ревнощі
vyklykaty revnoshchi
jaundice *n.* жовтяниця
zhovtianytsia
javelin *n.* метальний спис
metalnyi spys
jaw *n.* щелепа shchelepa
jay *n.* базіка bazika
jealous *a.* ревнивий revnyvyi
jealousy *n.* ревнощі revnoshchi
jean *n.* джинсова тканина
dzhynsova tkanyna
jeer *v.i.* глумитися hlumytysia
jelly *n.* желе zhele
jeopardize *v.t.* ризикувати
ryzykuvaty
jeopardy *n.* небезпека nebezpeka
jerk *n.* різкий рух rizkyi rukh
jerkin *n.* жакет zhaket
jerky *a.* труський truskyi
jersey *n.* фуфайка fufaika
jest *n.* дотеп dotep
jest *v.i.* кепкувати kepkuvaty
jet *n.* реактивний двигун
reaktyvnyi dvyhun
Jew *n.* єврей yevrei
jewel *v.t.* вставляти камені
vstavliaty kameni
jewel *n.* дорогоцінний камінь
dorohotsinnyi kamin
jeweller *n.* ювелір yuvelir

jewellery *n.* коштовності koshtovnosti
jingle *v.i.* дзвеніти dzvenity
jingle *n.* передзвін peredzvin
job *n.* робота robota
jobber *n.* маклер makler
jobbery *n.* спекуляція spekuliatsiia
jocular *a.* жартівливий zhartivlyvyi
jog *v.t.* штовхати shtovkhaty
join *v.t.* приєднуватися pryiednuvatysia
joiner *n.* столяр stoliar
joint *n.* шов shov
jointly *adv.* спільно spilno
joke *n.* жарт zhart
joke *v.i.* жартувати zhartuvaty
joker *n.* насмішник nasmishnyk
jollity *n.* гулянка hulianka
jolly *a.* жвавий zhvavyi
jolt *n.* трясіння triasinnia
jolt *v.t.* трясти triasty
jostle *n.* давка davka
jostle *v.t.* натрапити natrapyty
jot *n.* йота yota
jot *v.t.* стисло записати styslo zapysaty
journal *n.* журнал zhurnal
journalism *n.* журналістика zhurnalistyka
journalist *n.* журналіст zhurnalist
journey *v.i.* подорожувати podorozhuvaty
journey *n.* поїздка poizdka
jovial *a.* товариський tovaryskyi
joviality *n.* товариськість tovaryskist
joy *n.* успіх uspikh
joyful, joyous *a.* щасливий shchaslyvyi
jubilant *a.* задоволений zadovolenyi

jubilation *n.* торжество torzhestvo
jubilee *n.* свято sviato
judge *n.* суддя suddia
judge *v.i.* судити sudyty
judgement *n.* розум rozum
judicature *n.* судочинство sudochynstvo
judicial *a.* судовий sudovyi
judiciary *n.* судоустрій sudoustrii
judicious *a.* розсудливий rozsudlyvyi
jug *n.* глечик hlechyk
juggle *v.t.* обманювати obmaniuvaty
juggler *n.* фокусник fokusnyk
juice *n* сік sik
juicy *a.* соковитий sokovytyi
jumble *n.* тряска triaska
jumble *v.t.* трястися triastysia
jump *v.i* стрибати strybaty
jump *n.* стрибок strybok
junction *n.* злиття zlyttia
juncture *n.* стан справ stan sprav
jungle *n.* джунглі dzhunhli
junior *a.* молодий molodyi
junior *n.* молодший за званням molodshyi za zvanniam
junk *n.* утиль utyl
jupiter *n.* Юпітер Yupiter
jurisdiction *n.* юрисдикція yurysdyktsiia
jurisprudence *n.* юриспруденція yurysprudentsiia
jurist *n.* юрист yuryst
juror *n.* член журі chlen zhuri
jury *n.* журі zhuri
juryman *n.* присяжний prysiazhnyi
just *a.* справедливий spravedlyvyi
just *adv.* тільки tilky
justice *n.* справедливість spravedlyvist

justifiable *a.* законний zakonnyi
justification *n.* обставини, що виправдовують obstavyny, shcho vypravdovuiut
justify *v.t.* виправдовувати vypravdovuvaty
justly *adv.* недарма nedarma
jute *n.* джут dzhut
juvenile *a.* юнацький yunatskyi

K

keen *a.* тонко сприймаючий tonko spryimaiuchyi
keenness *n.* гострота hostrota
keep *v.t.* тримати trymaty
keeper *n.* сторож storozh
keepsake *n.* подарунок на пам'ять podarunok na pamiat
kennel *n.* будка budka
kerchief *n.* хустка khustka
kernel *n.* зернятко zerniatko
kerosene *n.* гас has
ketchup *n.* кетчуп ketchup
kettle *n.* чайник chainyk
key *v.t* замикати zamykaty
key *n.* ключ kliuch
kick *v.t.* вдарити ногою vdaryty nohoiu
kick *n.* удар ногою udar nohoiu
kid *n.* дитя dytia
kidnap *v.t.* викрасти vykrasty
kidney *n.* характер kharakter
kill *v.t.* вбивати vbyvaty
kill *n.* здобич zdobych
kiln *n.* промислова піч для сушіння promyslova pich dlia sushinnia
kin *n.* рідня ridnia
kind *n.* різновид riznovyd
kind *a* сорт sort
kindergarten ; *n.* дитячий сад dytiachyi sad

kindle *v.t.* загорітися zahoritysia
kindly *adv.* доброзичливо dobrozychlyvo
king *n.* король korol
kingdom *n.* королівство korolivstvo
kinship *n.* спорідненість sporidnenist
kiss *n.* поцілунок potsilunok
kiss *v.t.* цілувати tsiluvaty
kit *n.* екіпірування ekipiruvannia
kitchen *n.* кухня kukhnia
kite *n.* паперовий змій paperovyi zmii
kith *n.* друзі druzi
kitten *n.* кошеня koshenia
knave *n.* шахрай shakhrai
knavery *n.* шахрайство shakhraistvo
knee *n.* коліно kolino
kneel *v.i.* стояти на колінах stoiaty na kolinakh
knife *n.* ніж nizh
knight *n.* лицар lytsar
knight *v.t.* посвячувати в лицарі posviachuvaty v lytsari
knit *v.t.* в'язати viazaty
knock *v.t.* стукати stukaty
knot *n.* бант bant
knot *v.t.* зав'язати вузлом zaviazaty vuzlom
know *v.t.* знати znaty
knowledge *n.* пізнання piznannia

label *v.t.* позначати poznachaty
label *n.* ярлик yarlyk
labial *a.* губний hubnyi
laboratory *n.* лабораторія laboratoriia
laborious *a.* стомлюючий stomliuiuchyi

labour *v.i.* працювати pratsiuvaty
labour *n.* праця pratsia
laboured *a.* вимучений vymuchenyi
labourer *n.* чорнороб chornorob
labyrinth *n.* лабіринт labirynt
lac, lakh *n* сто тисяч sto tysiach
lace *v.t.* шнурувати shnuruvaty
lace *n.* мереживо merezhyvo
lacerate *v.t.* рвати rvaty
lachrymose *a.* плаксивий plaksyvyi
lack *v.t.* відчувати брак vidchuvaty brak
lack *n.* нестача nestacha
lackey *n.* лакей lakei
lacklustre *a.* тьмяний tmianyi
laconic *a.* лаконічний lakonichnyi
lactate *v.i.* виділяти молоко vydiliaty moloko
lactometer *n.* лактометр laktometr
lactose *n.* лактоза laktoza
lacuna *n.* прогалина prohalyna
lacy *a.* мереживний merezhyvnyi
lad *n.* хлопець khlopets
ladder *n.* сходи skhody
lade *v.t.* вантажити vantazhyty
ladle *n.* ківш kivsh
ladle *v.t.* черпати cherpaty
lady *n.* леді ledi
lag *v.i.* запізнюватися zapizniuvatysia
laggard *n.* телепень telepen
lagoon *n.* лагуна lahuna
lair *n.* барліг barlih
lake *n.* озеро ozero
lama *n.* лама lama
lamb *n.* ягня yahnia
lambaste *v.t.* шмагати shmahaty
lambkin *n.* ягнятко yahniatko
lame *v.t.* калічити kalichyty
lame *a.* кульгавий kulhavyi

lament *n* скарги skarhy
lament *v.i.* стогнати stohnaty
lamentable *a.* сумний sumnyi
lamentation *n.* нарікання narikannia
laminate *v.t.* розщеплювати на тонкі шари rozshchepliuvaty na tonki shary
lamp *n.* світило svytylo
lampoon *n.* зла сатира zla satyra
lampoon *v.t.* писати памфлети pysaty pamflety
lance *v.t.* пронизувати списом pronyzuvaty spysom
lance *n.* спис spys
lancer *n.* улан ulan
lancet *a.* ланцет lantset
land *v.i.* висаджувати vysadzhuvaty
land *n.* суша susha
landing *n.* висадка vysadka
landscape *n.* ландшафт landshaft
lane *n.* стежка stezhka
language *n.* стиль styl
languish *v.i.* слабшати slabshaty
lank *a.* худий khudyi
lantern *n.* ліхтар likhtar
lap *n.* пола pola
lapse *v.i.* впадати vpadaty
lapse *n* плин plyn
lard *n.* свиняче сало svyniache salo
large *a.* крупний krupnyi
largesse *n.* щедрий дар shchedryi dar
lark *n.* проказа prokaza
lascivious *a.* хтивий khtyvyi
lash *n* канчук kanchuk
lash *v.t.* хльостати khlostaty
lass *n.* дівчинка divchynka
last *adv.* після всіх pislia vsikh
last *n* кінець kinets

last *v.i.* продовжуватися prodovzhuvatysia
last1 *a.* крайній krainii
lasting *a.* тривалість tryvalist
lastly *adv.* на закінчення na zakinchennia
latch *n.* клямка kliamka
late *a.* пізній piznii
late *adv.* пізно pizno
lately *adv.* останнім часом ostannim chasom
latent *a.* латентний latentnyi
lath *n.* рейка reika
lathe *n.* верстат verstat
lathe *n.* токарний верстат tokarnyi verstat
lather *n.* мильна піна mylna pina
latitude *n.* широта shyrota
latrine *n.* відхоже місце vidkhozhe mistse
latter *a.* недавній nedavnii
lattice *n.* решітка reshitka
laud *v.t.* прославляти proslavliaty
laud *n* хвала khvala
laudable *a.* доброякісний dobroiakisnyi
laugh *n.* сміх smikh
laugh *v.i* сміятися smiiatysia
laughable *a.* смішний smishnyi
laughter *n.* регіт rehit
launch *n.* спуск spusk
launch *v.t.* спускати spuskaty
launder *v.t.* прати і прасувати praty i prasuvaty
laundress *n.* прачка prachka
laundry *n.* пральня pralnia
laureate *a.* видатний vydatnyi
laureate *n* лауреат laureat
laurel *n.* лавр lavr
lava *n.* лава lava
lavatory *n.* туалет tualet
lavender *n.* лаванда lavanda
lavish *a.* щедрий shchedryi

lavish *v.t.* щедро раздавати shchedro razdavaty
law *n.* закон zakon
lawful *a.* законний zakonnyi
lawless *a.* беззаконний bezzakonnyi
lawn *n.* галявина haliavyna
lawyer *n.* юрист yuryst
lax *a.* слабкий slabkyi
laxative *n.* проносний засіб pronosnyi zasib
laxative *a* проносний pronosnyi
laxity *n.* слабкість slabkist
lay *n* коротенька пісенька korotenka pisenka
lay *v.t.* класти klasty
lay *a.* непрофесійний neprofesiinyi
layer *n.* шар shar
layman *n.* мирянин myrianyn
laze *v.i.* ледарювати ledariuvaty
laziness *n.* лінь lin
lazy *n.* лінивий linyvyi
lea *n.* пасовищі pasovyshchi
leach *v.t.* ропа ropa
lead *n.* грузило hruzylo
lead *n.* провідна позиція providna pozytsiia
lead *v.t.* управляти upravliaty
leaden *a.* свинцевий svyntsevyi
leader *n.* керівник kerivnyk
leadership *n.* керівна посада kerivna posada
leaf *n.* листок lystok
leaflet *n.* листочок lystochok
leafy *a.* покритий листям pokrytyi lystiam
league *n.* ліга liha
leak *n.* витік vytik
leak *v.i.* текти tekty
leakage *n.* просочування prosochuvannia
lean *v.i.* притуляти prytuliaty

lean *n.* худий khudyi
leap *v.i.* стрибати strybaty
leap *n* стрибок strybok
learn *v.i.* вчитися vchytysia
learned *a.* вчений vchenyi
learner *n.* учень uchen
learning *n.* навчання navchannia
lease *v.t.* здавати в оренду zdavaty v orendu
lease *n.* оренда orenda
least *a.* малий malyi
least *adv.* менш за все mensh za vse
leather *n.* шкіра shkira
leave *n.* дозвіл dozvil
leave *v.t.* припиняти prypyniaty
lecture *n.* лекція lektsiia
lecture *v* читати лекцію chytaty lektsiiu
lecturer *n.* лектор lektor
ledger *n.* надгробна плита nadhrobna plyta
lee *n.* укриття ukryttia
leech *n.* п'явка piavka
leek *n.* цибуля-порей tsybulia-porei
left *a.* лівий livyi
left *adv.* ліво livo
leftist *n* лівак livak
leg *n.* нога noha
legacy *n.* спадщина spadshchyna
legal *a.* дозволений dozvolenyi
legality *n.* легальність lehalnist
legalize *v.t.* узаконити uzakonyty
legend *n.* легенда lehenda
legendary *a.* легендарний lehendarnyi
leghorn *n.* італійська соломка italiiska solomka
legible *a.* розбірливий rozbirlyvyi
legibly *adv.* розбірливо rozbirlyvo
legion *n.* легіон lehion
legionary *n.* легіонер lehioner

legislate *v.i.* видавати закони vydavaty zakony
legislation *n.* законодавство zakonodavstvo
legislative *a.* законодавчий zakonodavchyi
legislator *n.* законодавець zakonodavets
legislature *n.* законодавча влада zakonodavcha vlada
legitimacy *n.* законність zakonnist
legitimate *a.* закононароджений zakononarodzhenyi
leisure *n.* вільний час vilnyi chas
leisure *n.* дозвілля dozvillia
leisurely *a.* неквапливий nekvaplyvyi
leisurely *adv.* неквапливо nekvaplyvo
lemon *n.* лимон lymon
lemonade *n.* лимонад lymonad
lend *v.t.* позичати pozychaty
length *n.* довжина dovzhyna
lengthen *v.t.* подовжувати podovzhuvaty
lengthy *a.* тривалий tryvalyi
lenience, leniency *n.* м'якість miakist
lenient *a.* терпимий terpymyi
lens *n.* лінза linza
lentil *n.* сочевиця sochevytsia
Leo *n.* Лев Lev
leonine *a* левиний levynyi
leopard *n.* леопард leopard
leper *n.* парія pariia
leprosy *n.* проказа prokaza
leprous *a.* прокажений prokazhenyi
less *prep.* без bez
less *adv.* за вирахуванням za vyrakhuvanniam
less *a.* маленький malenkyi

less *adv.* менше menshe
lessee *n.* наймач naimach
lessen *v.t* зменшуватися
zmenshuvatysia
lesser *a.* менший menshyi
lesson *n.* урок urok
lest *conj.* щоб... не shchob... ne
let *v.t.* здавати внайм zdavaty
vnaim
lethal *a.* летальний letalnyi
lethargic *a.* летаргічний
letarhichnyi
lethargy *n.* млявість mliavist
letter *n* лист lyst
level *n.* рівень riven
level *a* плоский ploskyi
level *v.t.* робити рівним robyty
rivnym
lever *n.* важіль vazhil
lever *v.t.* піднімати за допомогою
важіля pidnimaty za
dopomohoiu vazhilia
leverage *n.* дія важеля diia
vazhelia
levity *n.* недоречна веселість
nedorechna veselist
levy *v.t.* обкладати obkladaty
levy *n.* збирання zbyrannia
lewd *a.* безсоромний
bezsoromnyi
lexicography *n.* лексикографія
leksykohrafiia
lexicon *n.* лексикон leksykon
liability *n.* відповідальність
vidpovidalnist
liable *a.* зобов'язаний
zoboviazanyi
liaison *n.* взаємодія vzaiemodiia
liar *n.* брехун brekhun
libel *n.* пасквіль paskvil
libel *v.t.* писати пасквілі pysaty
paskvili
liberal *a.* ліберальний liberalnyi

liberalism *n.* лібералізм
liberalizm
liberality *n.* щедрість shchedrist
liberate *v.t.* віизволяти viyzvoliaty
liberation *n.* визволення
vyzvolennia
liberator *n.* визволитель
vyzvolytel
libertine *n.* вільнодумець
vilnodumets
liberty *n.* свобода svoboda
librarian *n.* бібліотекар bibliotekar
library *n.* бібліотека biblioteka
licence *n.* ліцензія litsenziia
license *v.t.* ліцензувати
litsenzuvaty
licensee *n.* ліцензіат litsenziat
licentious *a.* розпущений
rozpushchenyi
lick *v.t.* лизати lyzaty
lick *n* облизування oblizuvannia
lid *n.* кришка kryshka
lie *n* брехня brekhnia
lie *v.i* брехати brekhaty
lie *v.i.* лежати lezhaty
lien *n.* заставне право zastavne
pravo
lieu *n.* місце mistse
lieutenant *n.* лейтенант leitenant
life *n* життя zhyttia
lifeless *a.* нудний nudnyi
lifelong *a.* довічний dovichnyi
lift *n.* ліфт lift
lift *v.t.* скасовувати skasovuvaty
light *v.t.* засвічувати zasvichuvaty
light *a* світлий svitlyi
light *n.* світло svitlo
lighten *v.i.* полегшувати
polehshuvaty
lightening *n.* освітлення
osvitlennia
lighter *n.* легше lehshe
lightly *adv.* злегка zlehka

lignite *n.* буре вугілля bure vuhillia
like *adv.* начебто nachebto
like *v.t.* любити liubyty
like *a.* схожий skhozhyi
like *n.* щось подібне shchos podibne
likelihood *n.* ймовірність ymovirnist
likely *a.* багатонадійний bahatonadiinyi
liken *v.t.* уподібнювати upodibniuvaty
likeness *n.* подібність podibnist
likewise *adv.* також takozh
liking *n.* смак smak
lilac *n.* бузок buzok
lily *n.* лілія liliia
limb *n.* кінцівка kintsivka
limber *v.t.* робити гнучким robyty hnuchkym
limber *n* сучкоруб suchkorub
lime *n.* лайм laim
lime *v.t* білити вапном bilyty vapnom
lime *n.* вапно vapno
limelight *n.* центр уваги tsentr uvahy
limit *v.t.* встановлювати межі vstanovliuvaty mezhi
limit *n.* границя hranytsia
limitation *n.* строк давності strok davnosti
limited *a.* з обмеженою відповідальністю z obmezhenoiu vidpovidalnistiu
limitless *a.* безмежний bezmezhnyi
line *v.t.* лініювати liniiuvaty
line *n.* лінія liniia
line *v.t.* проводити лінію provodyty liniiu
lineage *n.* родовід rodovid

linen *n.* полотно polotno
linger *v.i.* затримуватися zatrymuvatysia
lingo *n.* іноземна мова inozemna mova
lingua franca *n.* лінгва франка linhva franka
lingual *a.* мовний movnyi
linguist *n.* лінгвіст linhvist
linguistic *a.* лінгвістичний linhvistychnyi
linguistics *n.* мовознавство movoznavstvo
lining *n* підкладка pidkladka
link *n.* посилання posylannia
link *v.t* посилатися posylatysia
linseed *n.* лляне насіння lliane nasinnia
lintel *n.* перемички peremychky
lion *n* лев lev
lioness *n.* левиця levytsia
lip *n.* губа huba
liquefy *v.t.* перетворювати на рідину peretvoriuvaty na ridynu
liquid *n* рідка їжа ridka yizha
liquid *a.* рідкий ridkyi
liquidate *v.t.* ліквідувати likviduvaty
liquidation *n.* ліквідація likvidatsiia
liquor *n.* алкогольний напій alkoholnyi napii
lisp *v.t.* шепелявити shepeliavyty
lisp *n* шепелявість shepeliavist
list *v.t.* вносити до списку vnosyty do spysku
list *n.* список spysok
listen *v.i.* слухати slukhaty
listener *n.* слухач slukhach
listless *a.* апатичний apatychnyi
lists *n.* арена arena
literacy *n.* грамотність hramotnist
literal *a.* буквальний bukvalnyi

literary *a.* літературний literaturnyi
literate *a.* освічений osvichenyi
literature *n.* література literatura
litigant *n.* сторона у справі storona u spravi
litigate *v.t.* судитися sudytysia
litigation *n.* судовий процес sudovyi protses
litre *n.* літр litr
litter *v.t.* виносити на ношах vynosyty na noshakh
litter *n.* ноші noshi
litterateur *n.* літератор literator
little *n.* невелика кількість nevelyka kilkist
little *adv.* мало malo
little *a.* слабкий slabkyi
littoral *a.* прибережний pryberezhnyi
liturgical *a.* літургійний liturhiinyi
live *a.* діяльний diialnyi
live *v.i.* жити zhyty
livelihood *n.* зарплатня zarplatnia
lively *a.* швидкий shvydkyi
liver *n.* печінка pechinka
livery *n.* ліврея livreia
living *a.* невгаслий nevhaslyi
living *n* спосіб життя sposib zhyttia
lizard *n.* ящірка yashchirka
load *n.* навантаження navantazhennia
load *v.t.* навантажувати navantazhuvaty
loadstar *n.* Полярна зірка Poliarna zirka
loadstone *n.* магнетит mahnetyt
loaf *n.* буханець bukhanets
loaf *v.i.* ледарювати ledariuvaty
loafer *n.* ледар ledar
loan *v.t.* давати в борг davaty v borh

loan *n.* позика pozyka
loath *a.* неохочий neokhochyi
loathe *v.t.* ненавидіти nenavydity
loathsome *a.* що викликає відразу shcho vyklykaie vidrazu
lobby *n.* фойє foiie
lobe *n.* мочка вуха mochka vukha
lobster *n.* омар omar
local *a.* місцевий mistsevyi
locale *n.* місце дії mistse dii
locality *n.* місцевість mistsevist
localize *v.t.* локалізувати lokalizuvaty
locate *v.t.* розмістити rozmistyty
location *n.* місце розташування mistse roztashuvannia
lock *v.t* замикати на замок zamykaty na zamok
lock *n.* замок zamok
lock *n* засув zasuv
locker *n.* шафа shafa
locket *n.* медальйон medalion
locomotive *n.* локомотив lokomotyv
locus *n.* місцеположення mistsepolozhennia
locust *n.* сарана sarana
locution *n.* ідіома idioma
lodge *n.* будиночок budynochok
lodge *v.t.* тимчасово жити tymchasovo zhyty
lodging *n.* тимчасове житло tymchasove zhytlo
loft *n.* горище horyshche
lofty *a.* ставний stavnyi
log *n.* колода koloda
logarithim *n.* логарифм loharyfm
loggerhead *n.* болван bolvan
logic *n.* логіка lohika
logical *a.* логічний lohichnyi
logician *n.* логік lohik
loin *n.* поперек poperek

loiter *v.i.* тинятися без діла tyniatysia bez dila

loll *v.i.* ніжитися nizhytysia

lollipop *n.* льодяник на паличці lodianyk na palychtsi

lone *a.* відокремлений vidokremlenyi

loneliness *n.* самотність samotnist

lonely *a.* який навіває тугу yakyi navivaie tuhu

lonesome *a.* занедбаний zanedbanyi

long *adv* довго dovho

long *v.i* сумувати sumuvaty

long *a.* довгий dovhyi

longevity *n.* довговічність dovhovichnist

longing *n.* сильне бажання sylne bazhannia

longitude *n.* довгота dovhota

look *v.i* глянути hlianuty

look *n.* зовнішність zovnishnist

loom *v.i.* маячити maiachyty

loom *n* ткацький верстат tkatskyi verstat

loop *n.* петля petlia

loop-hole *n.* бійниця biinytsia

loose *a.* вільний vilnyi

loose *v.t.* розв'язувати rozviazuvaty

loosen *v.t.* розв'язувати rozv'iazuvaty

loot *v.i.* забирати нагробоване добро zabyraty nahrabovane dobro

loot *n.* трофей trofei

lop *v.t.* обкраяти obkraiaty

lop *n.* суки suky

lord *n.* пан pan

lordly *a.* панський panskyi

lordship *n.* світлість svitlist

lore *n.* практичні знання praktychni znannia

lorry *n.* вантажівка vantazhivka

lose *v.t.* втрачати vtrachaty

loss *n.* втрата vtrata

lot *n.* багато bahato

lot *n.* жереб zhereb

lotion *n.* лосьйон losion

lottery *n.* лотерея lotereia

lotus *n.* лотос lotos

loud *a.* гучний huchnyi

lounge *v.i.* розсістися rozsistysia

lounge *n.* хол khol

louse *n.* воша vosha

lovable *a.* привабливий pryvablyvyi

love *v.t.* любити liubyty

love *n* любов liubov

lovely *a.* прекрасний prekrasnyi

lover *n.* коханець kokhanets

loving *a.* люблячий liubliachyi

low *n.* низина nyzyna

low *v.i.* волати volaty

low *n.* мукання mukannia

low *a.* ниций nytsyi

lower *v.t.* нижче nyzhche

lowliness *n.* смиренність smyrennist

lowly *a.* невибагливий nevybahlyvyi

loyal *a.* лояльний loialnyi

loyalist *n.* вірнопідданий virnopiddanyi

loyalty *n.* лояльність loialnist

lubricant *n.* примиритель prymyrytel

lubricate *v.t.* мастити mastyty

lubrication *n.* змащування zmashchuvannia

lucent *a.* яскравий yaskravyi

lucerne *n.* люцерна liutserna

lucid *a.* ясний yasnyi

lucidity *n.* ясність yasnist

luck *n.* удача udacha
luckily *adv.* на щастя na shchastia
luckless *a.* невдачливий nevdachlyvyi
lucky *a.* щасливий shchaslyvyi
lucrative *a.* прибутковий prybutkovyi
lucre *n.* корисливість koryslyvist
luggage *n.* багаж bahazh
lukewarm *a.* теплий teplyi
lull *n.* затишшя zatyshshia
lull *v.t.* колихати kolykhaty
lullaby *n.* колискова kolyskova
luminary *n.* знаменитість znamenytist
luminous *a.* світиться svitytsia
lump *v.t.* важко ступати vazhko stupaty
lump *n.* шматок shmatok
lunacy *n.* сомнабулізм somnabulizm
lunar *a.* місячний misiachnyi
lunatic *n.* безумець bezumets
lunatic *a.* схиблений skhyblenyi
lunch *n.* обід obid
lunch *v.i.* обідати obidaty
lung *n* легке lehke
lunge *n.* випад vypad
lunge *v.i* робити випад robyty vypad
lurch *n.* крен kren
lurch *v.i.* кренитися krenytysia
lure *n.* приманка prymanka
lure *v.t.* приманювати prymaniuvaty
lurk *v.i.* таїтися taitysia
luscious *a.* солодкий solodkyi
lush *a.* соковитий sokovytyi
lust *n.* жага zhaha
lustful *a.* хтивий khtyvyi
lustre *n.* слава slava

lustrous *a.* глянсуватий hliansuvatyi
lusty *a.* здоровий zdorovyi
lute *n.* лютня liutnia
luxuriance *n.* буйний ріст buinyi rist
luxuriant *a.* пишний pyshnyi
luxurious *a.* який любит розкіш yakyi liubyt rozkish
luxury *n.* насолода nasoloda
lynch *v.t.* лінчувати linchuvaty
lyre *n.* ліра lira
lyric *n.* ліричний вірш lirychnyi virsh
lyric *a.* ліричний lirychnyi
lyrical *a.* захоплений zakhoplenyi
lyricist *n.* лірик liryk

maddle *v.i.* звихнутися zvykhnutysia
magical *a.* магічний mahichnyi
magician *n.* маг mah
magisterial *a.* суддівський suddivskyi
magistracy *n.* магістратура mahistratura
magistrate *n.* суддя suddia
magnanimity *n.* великодушність velykodushnist
magnanimous *a.* великодушний velykodushnyi
magnate *n.* магнат mahnat
magnet *n.* магніт mahnit
magnetic *a.* магнітний mahnitnyi
magnetism *n.* магнетизм mahnetyzm
magnificent *a.* пишний pyshnyi
magnify *v.t.* збільшувати zbilshuvaty
magnitude *n.* величина velychyna

magpie *n.* сорока soroka

mahogany *n.* червоне дерево chervone derevo

mahout *n.* погонич слонів pohonych sloniv

maid *n.* покоївка pokoivka

maiden *n.* діва diva

maiden *a* незаміжня nezamizhnia

mail *v.t.* відправляти поштою vidpravliaty poshtoiu

mail *n* кореспонденція korespondentsiia

mail *n.* пошта poshta

main *n* відкрите море vidkryte more

main *a* основний osnovnyi

mainly *adv.* головним чином holovnym chynom

mainstay *n.* головна підтримка holovna pidtrymka

maintain *v.t.* підтримувати pidtrymuvaty

maintenance *n.* технічне обслуговування tekhnichne obsluhovuvannia

maize *n.* кукурудза kukurudza

majestic *a.* величний velychnyi

majesty *n.* величність velychnist

major *n* майор maior

major *a.* повнолітній povnolitnii

majority *n.* повноліття povnolittia

make *n* модель model

make *v.t.* робити robyty

maker *n.* виробник vyrobnyk

maladjustment *n.* невідповідність nevidpovidnist

maladministration *n.* неправильні адміністративні дії nepravylni administratyvni dii

maladroit *a.* невдалий nevdalyi

malady *n.* хвороба khvoroba

malafide *a.* несумлінний nesumlinnyi

malafide *adv* нечесно nechesno

malaise *n.* нездужання nezduzhannia

malaria *n.* малярія maliariia

malcontent *a.* незадоволений nezadovolenyi

malcontent *n* опозиціонер opozytsioner

male *n* чоловік cholovik

male *a.* чоловічий cholovichyi

malediction *n.* лайка laika

malefactor *n.* зловмисник zlovmysnyk

maleficent *a.* згубний zhubnyi

malice *n.* злий умисел zlyi umysel

malicious *a.* зловмисний zlovmysnyi

malign *v.t.* злословити zloslovyty

malign *a* злоякісний zloiakisnyi

malignancy *n.* злоякісність zloiakisnist

malignant *a.* злісний zlisnyi

malleable *a.* ковкий kovkyi

malmsey *n.* мальвазія malvaziia

malnutrition *n.* недоїдання nedoidannia

malpractice *n.* зловживання довірою zlovzhyvannia doviroiu

malt *n.* солод solod

mal-treatment *n.* ппогане поводження ppohane povodzhennia

mamma *n.* грудна залоза hrudna zaloza

mammal *n.* ссавець ssavets

mammary *a.* грудний hrudnyi

mammon *n.* багатство bahatstvo

mammoth *n.* мамонт mamont

mammoth *a* схожий на мамонта skhozhyi na mamonta

man *v.t.* ставити людей (до гармати) stavyty liudei (do harmaty)

man *n.* людина liudyna
manage *v.t.* управляти upravliaty
manageable *a.* керований kerovanyi
management *n.* управління upravlinnia
manager *n.* менеджер menedzher
managerial *a.* управлінський upravlinskyi
mandate *n.* мандат mandat
mandatory *a.* примусовий prymusovyi
mane *n.* грива hryva
manes *n.* патли patly
manful *a.* рішучий rishuchyi
manganese *n.* марганець marhanets
manger *n.* ясла yasla
mangle *v.t.* шматувати shmatuvaty
mango *n* манго manho
manhandle *v.t.* тягти tiahty
manhole *n.* люк liuk
manhood *n.* змужнілість zmuzhnilist
mania *n* маніакальний синдром maniakalnyi syndrom
maniac *n.* маніяк maniiak
manicure *n.* манікюр manikiur
manifest *v.t.* робити очевидним robyty ochevydnym
manifest *a.* явний yavnyi
manifestation *n.* виявлення vyiavlennia
manifesto *n.* маніфест manifest
manifold *a.* колектор kolektor
manipulate *v.t.* маніпулювати manipuliuvaty
manipulation *n.* маніпуляція manipuliatsiia
mankind *n.* людський рід liudskyi rid

manlike *a.* чоловічий cholovichyi
manliness *n* мужність muzhnist
manly *a.* мужній muzhnii
manna *n.* манна manna
mannequin *n.* манекен maneken
manner *n.* манера manera
mannerism *n.* манірність manirnist
mannerly *a.* з гарними манерами z harnymy maneramy
manoeuvre *n.* маневр manevr
manoeuvre *v.i.* маневрувати manevruvaty
manor *n.* маєток maietok
manorial *a.* маноріальний manorialnyi
mansion *n.* особняк osobniak
mantel *n.* камінна дошка kaminna doshka
mantle *n* мантія mantiia
mantle *v.t* огорнути ohornuty
manual *n* посібник posibnyk
manual *a.* ручний ruchnyi
manufacture *n* обробка obrobka
manufacture *v.t.* штампувати shtampuvaty
manufacturer *n* виробник vyrobnyk
manumission *n.* відпускна грамота vidpuskna hramota
manumit *v.t.* звільняти zvilniaty
manure *n.* органічне добриво orhanichne dobryvo
manure *v.t.* удобрювати udobriuvaty
manuscript *n.* рукопис rukopys
many *a.* багато хто bahato khto
map *v.t.* наносити на карту nanosyty na kartu
map *n* карта karta
mar *v.t.* спотворювати spotvoriuvaty
marathon *n.* марафон marafon

maraud *v.i.* мародерствувати maroderstvuvaty
marauder *n.* мародер maroder
marble *n.* мармур marmur
march *n.* березень berezen
march *n* марш marsh
march *v.i* марширувати marshyruvaty
mare *n.* кобила kobyla
margarine *n.* маргарин marharyn
margin *n.* маржа marzha
marginal *a.* граничний hranychnyi
marigold *n.* чорнобривці chornobryvtsi
marine *a.* морський morskyi
mariner *n.* моряк moriak
marionette *n.* маріонетка marionetka
marital *a.* сімейний simeinyi
maritime *a.* приморський prymorskyi
mark *v.t* позначати poznachaty
mark *n.* позначка poznachka
marker *n.* маркер marker
market *n* ринок rynok
market *v.t* ринок rynok
marketable *a.* товарний tovarnyi
marksman *n.* вправний стрілець vpravnyi strilets
marl *n.* мергель merhel
marmalade *n.* мармелад marmelad
maroon *v.t* залишатися в безвихідному становищі zalyshatysia v bezvykhidnomu stanovyshchi
maroon *a* темно-бордовий temno-bordovyi
maroon *n.* темно-бордовий колір temno-bordovyi kolir
marriage *n.* шлюб shliub
marriageable *a.* шлюбний shliubnyi

marry *v.t.* одружуватися odruzhuvatysia
Mars *n* Марс Mars
marsh *n.* болото boloto
marshal *n* маршал marshal
marshal *v.t* вибудовувати vybudovuvaty
marshy *a.* болотистий bolotystyi
marsupial *n.* сумчастий sumchastyi
mart *n.* аукціонний зал auktsionnyi zal
marten *n.* куниця kunytsia
martial *a.* військовий viiskovyi
martinet *n.* прихильник суворої дисципліни prykhylnyk suvoroi dystsypliny
martyr *n.* мученик muchenyk
martyrdom *n.* мучеництво muchenytstvo
marvel *v.i* дивуватися dyvuvatysia
marvel *n.* чудо chudo
marvellous *a.* незбагнений nezbahnenyi
mascot *n.* талісман talisman
masculine *a.* чоловічий cholovichyi
mash *v.t* роздавлювати rozdavliuvaty
mash *n.* пюре piure
mask *n.* маска maska
mask *v.t.* маскувати maskuvaty
mason *n.* муляр muliar
masonry *n.* кам'яна укладка kamiana ukladka
masquerade *n.* маскарад maskarad
mass *v.i* збиратися натовпом zbyratysia natovpom
mass *n.* маса masa
massacre *n.* масове вбивство masove vbyvstvo

massacre v.t. влаштувати
різанину vlashtuvaty rizanynu
massage n. масаж masazh
massage v.t. масажувати
masazhuvaty
masseur n. масажист masazhyst
massive a. масивний masyvnyi
massy a. солідний solidnyi
mast n. щогла shchohla
master v.t. володіти volodity
master n. хазяїн khaziain
masterly a. віртуозний virtuoznyi
masterpiece n. шедевр shedevr
mastery n. майстерність
maisternist
masticate v.t. пережовувати
perezhovuvaty
masturbate v.i. мастурбувати
masturbuvaty
mat n. циновка tsynovka
matador n. матадор matador
match n підбір pidbir
match v.i. співпадати spivpadaty
match n. матч match
matchless a. неоднаковий
neodnakovyi
mate v.t. зробити мат zrobyty mat
mate n мат mat
mate n. напарник naparnyk
mate v.t. поєднувати poiednuvaty
material n матеріал material
material a. речовий rechovyi
materialism n. матеріалізм
materializm
materialize v.t. матеріалізувати
materializuvaty
maternal a. властивий матері
vlastyvyi materi
maternity n. материнство
materynstvo
mathematical a. математичний
matematychnyi

mathematician n. математик
matematyk
mathematics n математика
matematyka
matinee n. денний спектакль
dennyi spektakl
matriarch n. матриарх matryarkh
matricidal a. матеревбивчий
materevbyvchyi
matricide n. матеревбивство
materevbyvstvo
matriculate v.t. зарахувати до
вищого навчального закладу
zarakhuvaty do vyshchoho
navchalnoho zakladu
matriculation n. атестат зрілості
atestat zrilosti
matrimonial a. матрімоніальний
matrimonialnyi
matrimony n. подружжя
podruzhzhia
matrix n матриця matrytsia
matron n. заміжня жінка
zamizhnia zhinka
matter v.i. означати oznachaty
matter n. предмет predmet
mattock n. киркомотика
kyrkomotyka
mattress n. матрац matrats
mature a. зрілий zrilyi
mature v.i зріти zrity
maturity n. зрілість zrilist
maudlin a сентиментальнй
sentymentalni
maul n. кувалда kuvalda
maul v.t терзати terzaty
maulstick n. муштабель
mushtabel
maunder v.t. незв'язно говорити
nezviazno hovoryty
mausoleum n. мавзолей
mavzolei
mawkish a. нудотний nudotnyi

maxilla *n.* верхня щелепа
verkhnia shchelepa
maxim *n.* сентенція sententsiia
maximize *v.t.* максимізувати
maksymizuvaty
maximum *n* максимум
maksymum
maximum *a.* максимальний
maksymalnyi
may *v* мати можливість maty
mozhlyvist
May *n.* травень traven
mayor *n.* мер mer
maze *n.* плутанина plutanyna
me *pron.* мені meni
mead *n.* луг luh
meadow *n.* лучка luchka
meagre *a.* убогий ubohyi
meal *n.* прийняття їжи pryiniattia
yizhy
mealy *a.* борошнистий
boroshnystyi
mean *n.* засіб zasib
mean *v.t* мати на увазі maty na
uvazi
mean *v.t.* призначатися
pryznachatysia
mean *a.* скупий skupyi
meander *v.i.* блукати навмання
blukaty navmannia
meaning *n.* сенс sens
meaningful *a.* багатозначний
bahatoznachnyi
meaningless *a.* безглуздий
bezhluzdyi
meanness *n.* підлість pidlist
means *n* кошти koshty
meanwhile *adv.* тим часом tym
chasom
measles *n* кір kir
measurable *a.* вимірний vymirnyi
measure *v.t* вимірювати
vymiriuvaty

measure *n.* міра mira
measureless *a.* безмірний
bezmirnyi
measurement *n.* нормування
normuvannia
meat *n.* м'ясо miaso
mechanic *a* автоматичний
avtomatychnyi
mechanic *n.* механік mekhanik
mechanical *a.* механічний
mekhanichnyi
mechanics *n.* механіка
mekhanika
mechanism *n.* механізм
mekhanizm
medal *n.* медаль medal
medallist *n.* медаліст medalist
median *a.* медіана mediana
mediate *v.i.* бути посередником
buty poserednykom
mediation *n.* посередництво
poserednytstvo
mediation *n.* посередництво
poserednytstvo
mediator *n.* посередник
poserednyk
medical *a.* медичний medychnyi
medicament *n.* ліки liky
medicinal *a.* лікарський likarskyi
medicine *n.* медицина medytsyna
medico *n.* доктор doktor
medieval *a.* середньовічний
serednovichnyi
medieval *a.* середньовічний
serednovichnyi
mediocre *a.* середній serednii
mediocrity *n.* посередність
poserednist
meditate *v.t.* міркувати mirkuvaty
meditative *a.* медитативний
medytatyvnyi
medium *n* шлях shliakh
medium *a* помірний pomirnyi

meek *a.* лагідний lahidnyi
meet *n.* збір zbir
meet *v.t.* зустрічатися zustrichatysia
meeting *n.* дуель duel
megalith *n.* мегаліт mehalit
megalithic *a.* мегалітичний mehalitychnyi
megaphone *n.* мегафон mehafon
melancholia *n.* меланхолія melankholiia
melancholic *a.* меланхолійний melankholiinyi
melancholy *n.* зневіра znevira
melancholy *adj* тужливий tuzhlyvyi
melee *n.* рукопашна rukopashna
meliorate *v.t.* меліорували melioruvaly
mellow *a.* спілий spilyi
melodious *a.* мелодійний melodiinyi
melodrama *n.* мелодрама melodrama
melodramatic *a.* мелодраматичний melodramatychnyi
melody *n.* мелодія melodiia
melon *n.* диня dynia
melt *v.i.* танути tanuty
member *n.* член chlen
membership *n.* членство chlenstvo
membrane *n.* мембрана membrana
memento *n.* сувенір suvenir
memoir *n.* мемуари memuary
memorable *a.* пам'ятний pamiatnyi
memorandum *n* меморандум memorandum
memorial *n.* меморіал memorial

memorial *a* меморіальний memorialnyi
memory *n.* пам'ять pamiat
menace *v.t* загрожувати zahrozhuvaty
menace *n* небезпека nebezpeka
mend *v.t.* лагодити lahodyty
mendacious *a.* брехливий brekhlyvyi
menial *a.* лакейський lakeiskyi
menial *n* слуга sluha
meningitis *n.* менінгіт meninhit
menopause *n.* менопауза menopauza
menses *n.* менструації menstruatsii
menstrual *a.* менструальний menstrualnyi
menstruation *n.* менструація menstruatsiia
mental *a.* розумовий rozumovyi
mentality *n.* менталітет mentalitet
mention *n.* згадка zhadka
mention *v.t.* згадувати zhaduvaty
mentor *n.* наставник nastavnyk
menu *n.* меню meniu
mercantile *a.* меркантильний merkantylnyi
mercenary *a.* корисливий koryslyvyi
mercerise *v.t.* мерсиризувати mersyryzuvaty
merchandise *n.* товар tovar
merchant *n.* купець kupets
merciful *a.* милосердний myloserdnyi
merciless *adj.* немилосердний nemyloserdnyi
mercurial *a.* ртутний rtutnyi
mercury *n.* ртуть rtut
mercy *n.* милосердя myloserdia
mere *a.* цілковитий tsilkovytyi
merge *v.t.* зливатися zlyvatysia

merger *n.* поглинення pohlynennia

meridian *a.* меридіан merydian

merit *n.* заслуга zasluha

merit *v.t* заслуговувати zasluhovuvaty

meritorious *a.* виграшний vyhrashnyi

mermaid *n.* русалка rusalka

merman *n.* водяний vodianyi

merriment *n.* веселощі veseloshchi

merry *a* веселий veselyi

mesh *n.* сіті siti

mesh *v.t* піймати в сіті piimaty v siti

mesmerism *n.* гіпноз hipnoz

mesmerize *v.t.* гіпнотизувати hipnotyzuvaty

mess *n.* безладдя bezladdia

mess *v.i* зробити безлад zrobyty bezlad

message *n.* лист lyst

messenger *n.* посильний posylnyi

messiah *n.* месія mesiia

Messrs *n.* Господа Hospoda

metabolism *n.* обмін речовин obmin rechovyn

metal *n.* метал metal

metallic *a.* металевйй metalevyi

metallurgy *n.* металургія metalurhiia

metamorphosis *n.* метаморфоза metamorfoza

metaphor *n.* метафора metafora

metaphysical *a.* метафізичний metafizychnyi

metaphysics *n.* метафізика metafizyka

mete *v.t* відміряти vidmiriaty

meteor *n.* метеор meteor

meteoric *a.* метеорний meteornyi

meteorologist *n.* метеоролог meteoroloh

meteorology *n.* метеорологія meteorolohiia

meter *n.* метр metr

method *n.* метод metod

methodical *a.* методичний metodychnyi

metre *n.* метр metr

metric *a.* метричний metrychnyi

metrical *a.* вимірювальний vymiriuvalnyi

metropolis *n.* метрополія metropoliia

metropolitan *n.* митрополит mytropolyt

metropolitan *a.* столичний stolychnyi

mettle *n.* характер kharakter

mettlesome *a.* завзятий zavziatyi

mew *n.* нявкання niavkannia

mew *v.i.* нявкати niavkaty

mezzanine *n.* мезонін mezonin

mica *n.* слюда sliuda

microfilm *n.* мікрофільм mikrofilm

micrology *n.* мікроскопія mikroskopiia

micrometer *n.* мікрометр mikrometr

microphone *n.* мікрофон mikrofon

microscope *n.* мікроскоп mikroskop

microscopic *a.* мікроскопічний mikroskopichnyi

microwave *n.* мікрохвильова піч mikrokhvylova pich

mid *a.* середній serednii

midday *n.* полудень poluden

middle *n* гуща hushcha

middle *a.* середній serednii

middleman *n.* комісіонер komisioner

middling *a.* другосортний druhosortnyi
midget *n.* карлик karlyk
midland *n.* центральний tsentralnyi
midnight *n.* північ pivnoch
mid-off *n.* польовий гравець на лівій стороні від боулера в крикеті polovyi hravets na livii storoni vid boulera v kryketi
mid-on *n.* польовий гравець на правій стороні від боулера в крикеті polovyi hravets na pravii storoni vid boulera v kryketi
midriff *n.* діафрагма diafrahma
midst серед sered
midsummer *n.* середина літа seredyna lita
midwife *n.* акушерка akusherka
might *n.* могутність mohutnist
mighty *adj.* могутній mohutnii
migraine *n.* мігрень mihren
migrant *n.* мігрант mihrant
migrate *v.i.* мігрувати mihruvaty
migration *n.* міграція mihratsiia
milch *a.* молочний molochnyi
mild *a.* несуворий nesuvoryi
mildew *n.* цвіль tsvil
mile *n.* миля mylia
mileage *n.* пробіг probih
milestone *n.* віха vikha
milieu *n.* оточення otochennia
militant *n* боєць boiets
militant *a.* бойовий boiovyi
military *n* війська viiska
military *a.* призовний pryzovnyi
militate *v.i.* свідчити проти svidchyty proty
militia *n.* міліція militsiia
milk *v.t.* доїти doity
milk *n.* молоко moloko
milky *a.* молочний molochnyi
mill *v.t.* молоти moloty

mill *n.* млин mlyn
millennium *n.* тисячоліття tysiacholittia
miller *n.* мельник melnyk
millet *n.* просо proso
milliner *n.* капелюшник kapeliushnyk
milliner *n.* модистка modystka
millinery *n.* модні товари modni tovary
million *n.* мільйон milion
millionaire *n.* мільйонер milioner
millipede *n.* багатоніжка bahatonizhka
mime *n.* мім mim
mime *v.i* наслідувати nasliduvaty
mimesis *n.* мімікрія mimikriia
mimic *n* імітатор imitator
mimic *v.t* імітувати imituvaty
mimic *a.* мімічний mimichnyi
mimicry *n* міміка mimika
minaret *n.* мінарет minaret
mince *v.t.* рубати м'ясо rubaty miaso
mind *v.t.* пам'ятати pamiataty
mind *n.* розум rozum
mindful *a.* уважний uvazhnyi
mindless *a.* дурний durnyi
mine *pron.* мій mii
mine *n* шахта shakhta
miner *n.* шахтар shakhtar
mineral *a* мінеральний mineralnyi
mineral *n.* мінерал mineral
mineralogist *n.* мінералог mineraloh
mineralogy *n.* мінералогія mineralohiia
mingle *v.t.* змішуватися zmishuvatysia
miniature *a.* мініатюрний miniatiurnyi
miniature *n.* мініатюра miniatiura

minim *n.* дрібна частка dribna chastka

minimal *a.* мінімальний minimalnyi

minimize *v.t.* мінімізувати minimizuvaty

minimum *a* мінімальний minimalnyi

minimum *n.* мінімум minimum

minion *n.* фаворит favoryt

minister *v.i.* сприяти spryiaty

minister *n.* міністр ministr

ministrant *a.* священик sviashchenyk

ministry *n.* міністерство ministerstvo

mink *n.* норка norka

minor *n* неповнолітній підліток nepovnolitnii pidlitok

minor *a.* неповнолітній nepovnolitnii

minority *n.* меншість menshist

minster *n.* кафедральний собор kafedralnyi sobor

mint *v.t.* карбувати karbuvaty

mint *n.* м'ята miata

mint *n* м'ятний miatnyi

minus *n* мінус minus

minus *a* негативний nehatyvnyi

minus *prep.* за мінусом za minusom

minuscule *a.* мізерний mizernyi

minute *a.* дріб'язковий dribiazkovyi

minute *n.* хвилина khvylyna

minutely *adv.* докладно dokladno

minx *n.* кокетка koketka

miracle *n.* чудо chudo

miraculous *a.* чудотворний chudotvornyi

mirage *n.* міраж mirazh

mire *v.t.* зав'язнути в багнюці zaviaznuty v bahniutsi

mire *n.* грязь hriaz

mirror *v.t.* відображати vidobrazhaty

mirror *n* дзеркало dzerkalo

mirth *n.* веселість veselist

mirthful *a.* радісний radisnyi

misadventure *n.* нещасний випадок neshchasnyi vypadok

misalliance *n.* мезальянс mezalians

misanthrope *n.* мізантроп mizantrop

misapplication *n.* зловживання zlovzhyvannia

misapprehend *v.t.* зрозуміти неправильно zrozumity nepravylno

misapprehension *n* непорозуміння neporozuminnia

misappropriate *v.t.* незаконно привласнювати nezzakonno pryvlasniuvaty

misappropriation *n.* незаконне привласнення nezakonne pryvlasnennia

misbehave *v.i.* погано поводитися pohano povodytysia

misbehaviour *n.* неналежна поведінка nenalezhna povedinka

misbelief *n.* помилкова думка pomylkova dumka

miscalculate *v.t.* прорахуватися prorakhuvatysia

miscalculation *n.* прорахунок prorakhunok

miscall *v.t.* невірно називати nevirno nazyvaty

miscarriage *n.* помилка pomylka

miscarry *v.i.* викинути vykynuty

miscellaneous *a.* різноманітний riznomanitnyi

miscellany *n.* мішанина mishanyna

mischance *n.* невдача nevdacha

mischief *n* витівка vytivka

mischievous *a.* пустотливий pustotlyvyi

misconceive *v.t.* мати неправильне уявлення maty nepravylne uiavlennia

misconception *n.* неправильне уявлення nepravylne uiavlennia

misconduct *n.* проступок prostupok

misconstrue *v.t.* неправильно тлумачити nepravylno tlumachyty

miscreant *n.* єретик yeretyk

misdeed *n.* злочин zlochyn

misdemeanour *n.* судово караний проступок sudovo karanyi prostupok

misdirect *v.t.* неправильно адресувати nepravylno adresuvaty

misdirection *n.* неправильне nepravylne

miser *n.* скнара sknara

miserable *a.* бідолашний bidolashnyi

miserly *a.* скупий skupyi

misery *n.* убозтво uboztvo

misfire *v.i.* давати осічку davaty osichku

misfit *n.* той, хто не підходить toi, khto ne pidkhodyt

misfortune *n.* невдача nevdacha

misgive *v.t.* вселяти побоювання vseliaty poboiuvannia

misgiving *n.* побоювання poboiuvannia

misguide *v.t.* вводити в оману vvodyty v omanu

mishap *n.* нещасний випадок neshchasnyi vypadok

misjudge *v.t.* недооцінювати nedootsiniuvaty

mislead *v.t.* збивати з шляху zbyvaty z shliakhu

mismanagement *n.* неправильне керівництво nepravylne kerivnytstvo

mismatch *v.t.* не відповідати ne vidpovidaty

misnomer *n.* неправильна назва nepravylna nazva

misplace *v.t.* класти не на місце klasty ne na mistse

misprint *v.t.* зробити помилку zrobyty pomylku

misprint *n.* друкарська помилка drukarska pomylka

misrepresent *v.t.* спотворювати spotvoriuvaty

misrule *n.* погане управління pohane upravlinnia

miss *v.t.* не потрапити ne potrapyty

miss *n.* осічка osichka

missile *n.* ракета raketa

mission *n.* місія misiia

missionary *n.* місіонер misioner

missis, missus *n..* місіс misis

missive *n.* послання poslannia

mist *n.* туман tuman

mistake *v.t.* помилятися pomyliatysia

mistake *n.* непорозуміння neporozuminnia

mister *n.* містер mister

mistletoe *n.* омела omela

mistreat *d* брутально поводитися brutalno povodytysia

mistress *n.* пані pani

mistrust *v.t.* не довіряти ne doviriaty

mistrust *n.* недовіра nedovira
misty *a.* туманний tumannyi
misunderstand *v.t.* неправильно зрозуміти nepravylno zrozumity
misunderstanding *n.* непорозуміння neporozuminnia
misuse *v.t.* зловживати zlovzhyvaty
misuse *n.* погане ставлення pohane stavlennia
mite *n.* гріш hrish
mite *n* кліщ klishch
mithridate *n.* протиотрута protyotruta
mitigate *v.t.* послабляти poslabliaty
mitigation *n.* пом'якшення pomiakshennia
mitre *n.* митра mytra
mitten *n.* рукавиця rukavytsia
mix *v.i* вводитися vvodytysia
mixture *n.* суміш sumish
moan *n.* стогін stohin
moan *v.i.* стогнати stohnaty
moat *v.t.* обносити ровом obnosyty rovom
moat *n.* кріпосний рів kriposnyi riv
mob *v.t.* товпитися tovpytysia
mob *n.* юрба yurba
mobile *a.* мобільний mobilnyi
mobility *n.* мобільність mobilnist
mobilize *v.t.* мобілізувати mobilizuvaty
mock *v.i.* знущатися znushchatysia
mock *adj* удаваний udavanyi
mockery *n.* знущання znushchannia
modality *n.* модальність modalnist
mode *n.* режим rezhym
model *v.t.* ліпити lipyty
model *n.* макет maket

moderate *a.* помірний pomirnyi
moderate *v.t.* стримувати strymuvaty
moderation *n.* сповільнення spovilnennia
modern *a.* сучасний suchasnyi
modernity *n.* сучасність suchasnist
modernize *v.t.* модернізувати modernizuvaty
modest *a.* скромний skromnyi
modesty *n* скромність skromnist
modicum *n.* трішки trishky
modification *n.* модифікація modyfikatsiia
modify *v.t.* змінювати zminiuvaty
modulate *v.t.* модулювати moduliuvaty
moil *v.i.* важка робота vazhka robota
moist *a.* дощовий doshchovyi
moisten *v.t.* зволожувати zvolozhuvaty
moisture *n.* волога voloha
molar *a* молярний moliarnyi
molar *n.* корінний зуб korinnyi zub
molasses *n* патока patoka
mole *n.* моль mol
molecular *a.* молекулярний molekuliarnyi
molecule *n.* молекула molekula
molest *v.t.* приставати prystavaty
molestation *n.* настирливість nastyrlyvist
molten *a.* розплавлений rozplavlenyi
moment *n.* момент moment
momentary *a.* короткочасний korotkochasnyi
momentous *a.* найважливіший naivazhlyvishyi

momentum *n.* рушійна сила rushiina syla
monarch *n.* монарх monarkh
monarchy *n.* монархія monarkhiia
monastery *n.* монастир monastyr
monasticism *n* чернецтво chernetstvo
Monday *n.* понеділок ponedilok
monetary *a.* монетний monetnyi
money *n.* гроші hroshi
monger *n.* торговець torhovets
mongoose *n.* мангуста manhusta
mongrel *a* нечістокровний nechistokrovnyi
monitor *n.* староста starosta
monitory *a.* застережливий zasterezhlyvyi
monk *n.* чернець chernets
monkey *n.* кривляка kryvliaka
monochromatic *a.* монохроматичний monokhromatychnyi
monocle *n.* монокль monokl
monocular *a.* монокуляр monokuliar
monody *n.* похоронна пісня pokhoronna pisnia
monogamy *n.* моногамія monohamiia
monogram *n.* монограма monohrama
monograph *n.* монографія monohrafiia
monogynous *a.* моногінний monohinnyi
monolatry *n.* поклоніння одному Богу pokloninnia odnomu Bohu
monolith *n.* моноліт monolit
monologue *n.* монолог monoloh
monopolist *n.* монополіст monopolist
monopolize *v.t.* монополізувати monopolizuvaty

monopoly *n.* монополія monopoliia
monostrous *a.* жахливо монотонний zhakhlyvo monotonnyi
monosyllabic *a.* односкладовий odnoskladovyi
monosyllable *n.* односкладове слово odnoskladove slovo
monotheism *n.* монотеїзм monoteizm
monotheist *n.* монотеїст monoteist
monotonous *a.* одноманітний odnomanitnyi
monotony *n* монотонність monotonnist
monsoon *n.* мусон muson
monster *n.* монстр monstr
monstrous *a.* величезний velycheznyi
month *n.* місяць misiats
monthly *n* щомісячник shchomisiachnyk
monthly *adv* щомісячно shchomisiachno
monthly *a.* щомісячний shchomisiachnyi
monument *n.* пам'ятник pamiatnyk
monumental *a.* монументальний monumentalnyi
moo *v.i* мукати mukaty
mood *n.* настрій nastrii
moody *a.* похмурий pokhmuryi
moon *n.* місяць misiats
moor *n.* мохове болото mokhove boloto
moor *v.t* швартуватися shvartuvatysia
moorings *n.* причал prychal

moot *n.* навчальний судовий процес navchalnyi sudovyi protses

mop *v.t.* чистити шваброю chystyty shvabroiu

mop *n.* швабра shvabra

mope *v.i.* хандрити khandryty

moral *n.* мораль moral

moral *a.* моральний moralnyi

morale *n.* бойовий дух boiovyi dukh

moralist *n.* мораліст moralist

morality *n.* моральність moralnist

moralize *v.t.* моралізувати moralizuvaty

morbid *a.* хворобливий khvoroblyvyi

morbidity *n* захворюваність zakhvoriuvanist

more *adv* більше bilshe

more *a.* численніший chyslennishyi

moreover *adv.* більше того bilshe toho

morganatic *a.* морганатичний morhanatychnyi

morgue *n.* морг morh

moribund *a.* вмираючий vmyraiuchyi

morning *n.* ранок ranok

moron *n.* слабоумний slaboumnyi

morose *a.* понурий ponuryi

morphia *n.* морфій morfii

morrow *n.* наступний день nastupnyi den

morsel *n.* шматочок shmatochok

mortal *n* смертний smertnyi

mortal *a.* смертний smertnyi

mortality *n.* смертність smertnist

mortar *v.t.* товкти в ступі tovkty v stupi

mortgage *v.t.* заставляти zastavliaty

mortgage *n.* заставна zastavna

mortgagee *n.* кредитор по заставній kredytor po zastavnii

mortgagor *n.* боржник за заставною borzhnyk za zastavnoiu

mortify *v.t.* вгамовувати vhamovuvaty

mortuary *n.* могильник mohylnyk

mosaic *n.* мозаїка mozaika

mosque *n.* мечеть mechet

mosquito *n.* комар komar

moss *n.* мох mokh

most *n* більшість bilshist

most *adv.* найбільш naibilsh

most *a.* самий samyi

mote *n.* цяточка tsiatochka

motel *n.* мотель motel

moth *n.* нічний метелик nichnyi metelyk

mother *v.t.* плекати plekaty

mother *n* матінка matinka

motherhood *n.* материнство materynstvo

motherlike *adj.* як мати yak maty

motherly *a.* материнський materynskyi

motif *n.* мотив motyv

motion *v.i.* показувати жестом pokazuvaty zhestom

motion *n.* рух rukh

motionless *a.* нерухомий nerukhomyi

motivate *v* мотивувати motyvuvaty

motivation *n.* мотивація motyvatsiia

motive *n.* мотив motyv

motley *a.* строкатий strokatyi

motor *v.i.* везти на автомобілі vezty na avtomobili

motor *n.* електромотор elektromotor

motorist *n.* автомобіліст avtomobilist

mottle *n.* цятка tsiatka

motto *n.* девіз deviz

mould *n* виливок vylyvok

mould *v.t.* відливати у форму vidlyvaty u formu

mould *n* форма forma

mould *n.* зліпок zlipok

mouldy *a.* заплісні лий zaplisnilyi

moult *v.i.* линька lynka

mound *n.* курган kurhan

mount *v.t.* встановлювати vstanovliuvaty

mount *n* установка ustanovka

mount *n.* гора hora

mountain *n.* маса masa

mountaineer *n.* альпініст alpinist

mountainous *a.* гористий horystyi

mourn *v.i.* сумувати sumuvaty

mourner *n.* плакальники plakalnyky

mournful *n.* скорботний skorbotnyi

mourning *n.* траур traur

mouse *n.* миша mysha

moustache *n.* вус vus

mouth *v.t.* вирікати vyrikaty

mouth *n.* рот rot

mouthful *n.* шматок shmatok

movable *a.* рухомий rukhomyi

movables *n.* рухоме майно rukhome maino

move *n.* зміна положення zmina polozhennia

move *v.t.* рухатися rukhatysia

movement *n.* пересування peresuvannia

mover *n.* рушійна сила rushiina syla

movies *n.* кіно kino

mow *v.t.* скиртувати skyrtuvaty

much *adv* майже maizhe

much *adv.* багато bahato

mucilage *n.* рослинний слиз roslynnyi slyz

muck *n.* погань pohan

mucous *a.* слизовий slyzovyi

mucus *n.* слиз slyz

mud *n.* твань tvan

muddle *v.t.* плутати plutaty

muddle *n.* безладдя bezladdia

muffle *v.t.* глушити hlushyty

muffler *n.* кашне kashne

mug *n.* гуртка hurtka

muggy *a.* важкий vazhkyi

mulatto *n.* мулат mulat

mulberry *n.* шовковиця shovkovytsia

mule *n.* мул mul

mulish *a.* впертий vpertyi

mull *v.t.* переплутати pereplutaty

mull *n.* тонкий муслін tonkyi muslin

mullah *n.* мулла mulla

mullion *n.* середник serednyk

multifarious *a.* багатогранний bahatohrannyi

multiform *a.* різноманітний riznomanitnyi

multilateral *a.* багатосторонній bahatostoronnii

multiparous *a.* та, що народжувала ta, shcho narodzhuvala

multiped *n.* тварина, що має багато ніг tvaryna, shcho maie bahato nih

multiple *n* стисле число stysle chyslo

multiple *a.* множинний mnozhynnyi

multiplex *a.* складний skladnyi

multiplicand *n.* множене mnozhene

multiplication *n.* множення mnozhennia
multiplicity *n.* множинність mnozhynnist
multiply *v.t.* помножити pomnozhyty
multitude *n.* безліч bezlich
mum *n* мама mama
mum *a.* мовчазний movchaznyi
mumble *v.i.* шамкати shamkaty
mummer *n.* фігляр fihliar
mummy *n* мамаша mamasha
mummy *n.* мумія mumiia
mumps *n.* свинка svynka
munch *v.t.* плямкати pliamkaty
mundane *a.* мирський myrskyi
municipal *a.* муніципальний munitsypalnyi
municipality *n.* муніципалітет munitsypalitet
munificent *a.* надзвичайно щедрий nadzvychaino shchedryi
muniment *n.* документ про права dokument pro prava
munitions *n.* спорядження sporiadzhennia
mural *n.* фреска freska
mural *a.* стінний stinnyi
murder *n.* навмисне вбивство navmysne vbyvstvo
murder *v.t.* вбивати vbyvaty
murderer *n.* убивця ubyvtsia
murderous *a.* вбивчий vbyvchyi
murmur *v.t.* нарікати narikaty
murmur *n.* бурмотання burmotannia
muscle *n.* м'яз miaz
muscovite *n.* москвич moskvych
muscular *a.* м'язистий miazystyi
muse *n* муза muza
muse *v.i.* споглядати spohliadaty
museum *n.* музей muzei

mush *n.* м'якуш m'iakush
mushroom *n.* гриб hryb
music *n.* музика muzyka
musical *a.* музичний muzychnyi
musician *n.* музикант muzykant
musk *n.* мускус muskus
musket *n.* мушкет mushket
musketeer *n.* мушкетер mushketer
muslin *n.* муслін muslin
must *n* зобов'зання zobovzannia
must *n.* необхідність neobkhidnist
must *v.* повинен povynen
mustache *n.* вуса vusa
mustang *n.* мустанг mustanh
mustard *n.* гірчиця hirchytsia
muster *n* переклик pereklyk
muster *v.t.* робити переклик robyty pereklyk
musty *a.* затхлий zatkhlyi
mutation *n.* мутація mutatsiia
mutative *a.* мутаційний mutatsiinyi
mute *a.* мовчазний movchaznyi
mute *n.* статист statyst
mutilate *v.t.* нівечити nivechyty
mutilation *n.* каліцтво kalitstvo
mutinous *a.* заколотний zakolotnyi
mutiny *v. i* бунтувати buntuvaty
mutiny *n.* заколот zakolot
mutter *v.i.* мимрити mymryty
mutton *n.* баранина baranyna
mutual *a.* взаємний vzaiemnyi
muzzle *v.t* надягати намордник nadiahaty namordnyk
muzzle *n.* морда morda
my *a.* мій mii
myalgia *n.* біль у м'язах bil u miazakh
myopia *n.* короткозорість korotkozorist

myopic *a.* короткозорий korotkozoryi
myosis *n.* міозіс miozis
myriad *a* незліченний nezlichennyi
myriad *n.* міріади miriady
myrrh *n.* мирра myrra
myrtle *n.* мирт myrt
myself *pron.* сам sam
mysterious *a.* таємничий taiemnychyi
mystery *n.* таємниця taiemnytsia
mystic *n* містик mistyk
mystic *a.* містичний mistychnyi
mysticism *n.* містицизм mistytsyzm
mystify *v.t.* містифікувати mistyfikuvaty
myth *n.* міф mif
mythical *a.* міфічний mifichnyi
mythological *a.* міфологічний mifolohichnyi
mythology *n.* міфологія mifolohiia

N

nab *v.t.* заарештувати zaareshtuvaty
nabob *n.* набоб nabob
nadir *n.* найнижчий рівень nainyzhchyi riven
nag *v.t.* чіплятися chipliatysia
nag *n.* шкапа shkapa
nail *v.t.* придушувати prydushuvaty
nail *n.* ніготь nihot
naive *a.* наївний naivnyi
naivete *n.* наївність naivnist
naivety *n.* простацтво prostatstvo
naked *a.* оголений oholenyi
name *n.* ім'я imia
name *v.t.* назвати nazvaty
namely *adv.* а саме a same

namesake *n.* тезка tezka
nap *n.* легкий сон lehkyi son
nap *n* начіс nachis
nap *v.i.* подрімати podrimaty
nape *n.* потилиця potylytsia
napkin *n.* серветка servetka
narcissism *n.* самозакоханість samozakokhanist
narcissus *n* нарцис nartsys
narcosis *n.* наркоз narkoz
narcotic *n.* наркотичний narkotychnyi
narrate *v.t.* оповідати opovidaty
narration *n.* розповідь rozpovid
narrative *a.* розповідний rozpovidnyi
narrative *n.* оповідання opovidannia
narrator *n.* розповідач rozpovidach
narrow *v.t.* звужувати zvuzhuvaty
narrow *a.* вузький vuzkyi
nasal *n* носова кістка nosova kistka
nasal *a.* носовий nosovyi
nascent *a.* який народжується yakyi narodzhuietsia
nasty *a.* противний protyvnyi
natal *a.* натальний natalnyi
natant *a.* плавучий plavuchyi
nation *n.* нація natsiia
national *a.* національний natsionalnyi
nationalism *n.* націоналізм natsionalizm
nationalist *n.* націоналістичний natsionalistychnyi
nationality *n.* національність natsionalnist
nationalization *n.* націоналізація natsionalizatsiia
nationalize *v.t.* націоналізувати natsionalizuvaty

native *n* місцевий житель mistsevyi zhytel
native *a.* рідний ridnyi
nativity *n.* гороскоп horoskop
natural *a.* природний pryrodnyi
naturalist *n.* натураліст naturalist
naturalize *v.t.* натуралізувати naturalizuvaty
naturally *adv.* природно pryrodno
nature *n.* природа pryroda
naughty *a.* неслухняний neslukhnianyi
nausea *n.* нудота nudota
nautic(al) *a.* морехідний morekhidnyi
naval *a.* військово-морський viiskovo-morskyi
nave *n.* неф nef
navigable *a.* судноплавний sudnoplavnyi
navigate *v.i.* літати litaty
navigation *n.* навігація navihatsiia
navigator *n.* навігатор navihator
navy *n.* військово-морський флот viiskovo-morskyi flot
nay *adv.* мало того malo toho
neap *a.* дишло dyshlo
near *v.i.* наближатися nablyzhatysia
near *adv.* поблизу poblyzu
near *prep.* мало не malo ne
near *a.* ближній blyzhnii
nearly *adv.* ледве не ledve ne
neat *a.* акуратний akuratnyi
nebula *n.* туманність tumannist
necessary *a* потрібний potribnyi
necessary *n.* необхідно neobkhidno
necessitate *v.t.* робити необхідним robyty neobkhidnym
necessity *n.* бідність bidnist
neck *n.* шия shyia

necklace *n.* намисто namysto
necklet *n.* боа boa
necromancer *n.* некромант nekromant
necropolis *n.* некрополь nekropol
nectar *n.* нектар nektar
need *v.t.* потребувати potrebuvaty
need *n.* необхідність neobkhidnist
needful *a.* необхідне neobkhidne
needle *n.* голка holka
needless *a.* непотрібний nepotribnyi
needs *adv.* потреби potreby
needy *a.* скрутний skrutnyi
nefandous *a.* невимовний nevymovnyi
nefarious *a.* підлий pidlyi
negation *n.* заперечення zaperechennia
negative *v.t.* відкидати vidkydaty
negative *n.* негатив nehatyv
negative *a.* заперечний zaperechnyi
neglect *n* зневага znevaha
neglect *v.t.* зневажати znevazhaty
negligence *n.* халатність khalatnist
negligent *a.* халатний khalatnyi
negligible *a.* який не береться до уваги yakyi ne beretsia do uvahy
negotiable *a.* оборотний oborotnyi
negotiate *v.t.* вести переговори vesty perehovory
negotiation *n.* переговори perehovory
negotiator *n.* учасник переговорів uchasnyk perehovoriv
negress *n.* негритянка nehrytianka
negro *n.* негр nehr

neigh *n.* іржання irzhannia
neigh *v.i.* іржати irzhaty
neighbour *n.* сусід susid
neighbourhood *n.* сусідство susidstvo
neighbourly *a.* добросусідський dobrosusidskyi
neither *a.* жоден zhoden
nemesis *n.* відплата vidplata
neolithic *a.* неолітичний neolitychnyi
neon *n.* неоновий neonovyi
nephew *n.* племінник pleminnyk
nepotism *n.* кумівство kumivstvo
Neptune *n.* Нептун Neptun
Nerve *n.* Нерв Nerv
nerveless *a.* боягузливий boiahuzlyvyi
nervous *a.* нервовий nervovyi
nescience *n.* незнання neznannia
nest *v.t.* гніздитися hnizdytysia
nest *n.* гніздо hnizdo
nestle *v.i.* притиснутися prytysnutysia
nestling *n.* пташеня ptashenia
net *v.t.* ловити сіткою lovyty sitkoiu
net *v.t.* покривати мережею pokryvaty merezheiu
net *a* чистий chystyi
net *n.* сіть sit
nether *a.* нижній nyzhnii
nettle *n.* кропива kropyva
nettle *v.t.* ужалити кропивою uzhalyty kropyvoiu
network *n.* мережа merezha
neurologist *n.* невролог nevroloh
neurology *n.* неврологія nevrolohiia
neurosis *n.* невроз nevroz
neuter *a.* неперехідний neperekhidnyi
neuter *n* середній рід serednii rid

neutral *a.* нейтральний neitralnyi
neutralize *v.t.* нейтралізувати neitralizuvaty
neutron *n.* нейтрон neitron
never *adv.* ніколи nikoly
nevertheless *conj.* хоча khocha
new *a.* недавній nedavnii
news *n.* новини novyny
next *adv.* потім potim
next *a.* наступний nastupnyi
nib *n.* кінчик пера kinchyk pera
nibble *n* клювання kliuvannia
nibble *v.t.* гризти hryzty
nice *a.* витончений vytonchenyi
nicety *n.* пунктуальність punktualnist
niche *n.* ніша nisha
nick *n.* зарубка zarubka
nickel *n.* нікель nikel
nickname *v.t.* прозвати prozvaty
nickname *n.* зменшене ім`я zmenshene im`ia
nicotine *n.* нікотин nikotyn
niece *n.* племінниця pleminnytsia
niggard *n.* скнара sknara
niggardly *a.* скупий skupyi
nigger *n.* чорношкірий chornoshkiryi
nigh *adv.* поруч poruch
nigh *prep.* майже maizhe
night *n.* ніч nich
nightie *n.* ночнушка nochnushka
nightingale *n.* соловей solovei
nightly *adv.* вночі vnochi
nightmare *n.* кошмар koshmar
nihilism *n.* нігілізм nihilizm
nil *n.* нуль nul
nimble *a.* спритний sprytnyi
nimbus *n.* німб nimb
nine *n.* дев'ять deviat
nineteen *n.* дев'ятнадцять deviatnadtsiat

nineteenth *a.* дев'ятнадцятого deviatnadtsiatoho
ninetieth *a.* дев'яностий devianostyi
ninety *n.* дев'яносто devianosto
ninth *a.* дев'ятий deviatyi
nip *v.t* щипати shchypaty
nipple *n.* сосок sosok
nitrogen *n.* азот azot
no *n* відмова vidmova
no *a.* ні ni
no *adv.* ніякий niiakyi
nobility *n.* дворянство dvorianstvo
noble *n.* ханжа khanzha
noble *a.* шляхетний shliakhetnyi
nobleman *n.* дворянин dvorianyn
nobody *pron.* ніхто nikhto
nocturnal *a.* нічний nichnyi
nod *v.i.* кивати головою kyvaty holovoiu
node *n.* вузловий пункт vuzlovyi punkt
noise *n.* шум shum
noisy *a.* шумний shumnyi
nomad *n.* кочівник kochivnyk
nomadic *a.* кочовий kochovyi
nomenclature *n.* номенклатура nomenklatura
nominal *a.* номінальний nominalnyi
nominate *v.t.* іменувати imenuvaty
nomination *n.* висування vysuvannia
nominee *n* претендент pretendent
non-alignment *n.* нейтралізм neitralizm
nonchalance *n.* безтурботність bezturbotnist
nonchalant *a.* недбалий nedbalyi
none *adv.* ні один ni odyn

none *pron.* жоден zhoden
nonentity *n.* нікчема nikchema
nonetheless *adv.* проте prote
nonpareil *n.* ідеал ideal
nonpareil *a.* незрівнянний nezrivniannyi
nonplus *v.t.* приводити в замішання pryvodyty v zamishannia
nonsense *n.* нісенітниця nisenitnytsia
nonsensical *a.* нісенітний nisenitnyi
nook *n.* затишний куточок zatyshnyi kutochok
noon *n.* полудень poluden
noose *v.t.* заарканити zaarkanyty
noose *n.* зашморг zashmorh
nor *conj* не ne
norm *n.* норма norma
norm *n.* стандарт standart
normal *a.* нормальний normalnyi
normalcy *n.* нормальність normalnist
normalize *v.t.* нормалізувати normalizuvaty
north *adv.* на північ na pivnich
north *a* який виходить на північ yakyi vykhodyt na pivnich
north *n.* північ pivnich
northerly *adv.* на північ na pivnich
northerly *a.* північний pivnichnyi
northern *a.* який дме з півночі yakyi dme z pivnochi
nose *v.t* чуття chuttia
nose *n.* ніс nis
nosegay *n.* букетик квітів buketyk kvitiv
nosey *a.* цікавий tsikavyi
nostalgia *n.* ностальгія nostalhiia
nostril *n.* ніздря nizdria
nostrum *n.* патентований засоб patentovanyi zasob

nosy *a.* пронирливий pronyrlyvyi
not *adv.* не ne
notability *n.* відома людина vidoma liudyna
notable *a.* примітний prymitnyi
notary *n.* нотаріус notarius
notation *n.* позначення poznachennia
notch *n.* паз paz
note *v.t.* зауважити zauvazhyty
note *n.* примітка prymitka
noteworthy *a.* визначний vyznachnyi
nothing *adv.* нічого nichoho
nothing *n.* порожнє місце porozhnie mistse
notice *v.t.* звертати увагу zvertaty uvahu
notice *v.t.* посилати повідомлення posylaty povidomlennia
notification *n.* попередження poperedzhennia
notify *v.t.* давати відомості davaty vidomosti
notion *n.* поняття poniattia
notional *a.* смисловий smyslovyi
notoriety *n.* особа, яка зажила дурної слави osoba, yaka zazhyla durnoi slavy
notorious *a.* горезвісний horezvisnyi
notwithstanding *prep.* всупереч vsuperech
notwithstanding *conj.* незважаючи на nezvazhaiuchy na
notwithstanding *adv.* однак odnak
nought *n.* нікчема nikchema
noun *n.* іменник imennyk
nourish *v.t.* живити zhyvyty
nourishment *n.* харчування kharchuvannia
novel *a.* новий novyi
novel *n.* роман roman
novelette *n.* повість povist
novelist *n.* романіст romanist
novelty *n.* новинка novynka
november *n.* листопад lystopad
novice *n.* початківець pochatkivets
now *conj.* коли koly
now *adv.* зараз zaraz
nowhere *adv.* ніде nide
noxious *a.* шкідливий shkidlyvyi
nozzle *n.* сопло soplo
nuance *n.* нюанс niuans
nubile *a.* шлюбний shliubnyi
nuclear *a.* ядерний yadernyi
nucleus *n.* ядро yadro
nude *n.* оголене тіло oholene tilo
nude *a.* голий holyi
nudge *v.t.* підштовхнути pidshtovkhnuty
nudity *n.* нагота nahota
nugget *n.* самородок samorodok
nuisance *n.* неприємність nepryiemnist
null *a.* нульовий nulovyi
nullification *n.* анулювання anuliuvannia
nullify *v.t.* скасувати skasuvaty
numb *a.* онімілий onimilyi
number *v.t.* випуск vypusk
number *n.* номер nomer
numberless *a.* що не має номера shcho ne maie nomera
numeral *a.* цифра tsyfra
numerator *n.* чисельник chyselnyk
numerical *a.* чисельний chyselnyi
numerous *a.* численний chyslennyi
nun *n.* монахиня monakhynia

nunnery *n.* жіночий монастир zhinochyi monastyr
nuptial *a.* шлюбний shliubnyi
nuptials *n.* весілля vesillia
nurse *v.t* вигодовувати дитину vyhodovuvaty dytynu
nurse *n.* медсестра medsestra
nursery *n.* розплідник rozplidnyk
nurture *v.t.* вирощувати vyroshchuvaty
nurture *n.* виховання vykhovannia
nut *n* горіх horikh
nutrition *n.* харчування kharchuvannia
nutritious *a.* живильний zhyvylnyi
nutritive *a.* поживний pozhyvnyi
nuzzle *v.* притиснутися prytysnutysia
nylon *n.* нейлон neilon
nymph *n.* німфа nimfa

oak *n.* дуб dub
oar *n.* весляр vesliar
oarsman *n.* майстер веслування maister vesluvannia
oasis *n.* оазис oazys
oat *n.* овес oves
oath *n.* присяга prysiaha
obduracy *n.* черствість cherstvist
obdurate *a.* заскнілий zasknilyi
obedience *n.* слухняність slukhnianist
obedient *a.* слухняний slukhnianyi
obeisance *n.* реверанс reverans
obesity *n.* ожиріння ozhyrinnia
obey *v.t.* коритися korytysia
obituary *a.* некролог nekroloh
object *v.t.* заперечувати zaperechuvaty

object *n.* об`єкт ob`iekt
objection *n.* несхвалення neskhvalennia
objectionable *a.* спірний spirnyi
objective *a.* об'єктивний obiektyvnyi
objective *n.* ціль tsil
oblation *n.* жертвопринесення zhertvoprynesennia
obligation *n.* облігація oblihatsiia
obligatory *a.* борговий borhovyi
oblige *v.t.* зобов'язувати zoboviazuvaty
oblique *a.* косий kosyi
obliterate *v.t.* викреслювати vykresliuvaty
obliteration *n.* облітерація obliteratsiia
oblivion *n.* забуття zabuttia
oblivious *a.* який не пам'ятає yakyi ne pamiataie
oblong *a.* довгастий dovhastyi
oblong *n.* довгастий предмет dovhastyi predmet
obnoxious *a.* неприємний nepryiemnyi
obscene *a.* хуліганський khulihanskyi
obscenity *n.* лайка laika
obscure *v.t.* затемнювати zatemniuvaty
obscure *a.* непомітний nepomitnyi
obscurity *n.* невідомість nevidomist
observance *n.* дотримання dotrymannia
observant *a.* спостережливий sposterezhlyvyi
observation *n.* спостереження sposterezhennia
observatory *n.* обсерваторія observatoriia

observe *v.t.* спостерігати
sposterihaty
obsess *v.t.* гнітити hnityty
obsession *n.* нав'язлива ідея
naviazlyva ideia
obsolete *a.* атрофований
atrofovanyi
obstacle *n.* перепона perepona
obstinacy *n.* упертість upertist
obstinate *a.* впертий vpertyi
obstruct *v.t.* чинити обструкцію
chynyty obstruktsiiu
obstruction *n.* непрохідність
neprokhidnist
obstructive *a.* перешкоджаючий
pereshkodzhaiuchyi
obtain *v.t.* досягати dosiahaty
obtainable *a.* доступний
dostupnyi
obtuse *a.* тупий tupyi
obvious *a.* неприхований
neprykhovanyi
occasion *v.t* давати привід
davaty pryvid
occasion *n.* можливість
mozhlyvist
occasional *a.* нерегулярний
nerehuliarnyi
occasionally *adv.* час від часу
chas vid chasu
occident *n.* країни Заходу krainy
Zakhodu
occidental *a.* західний zakhidnyi
occult *a.* окультний okultnyi
occupancy *n.* заняття zaniattia
occupant *n.* пожилець pozhylets
occupation *n.* вид дияльності
vyd dyialnosti
occupier *n.* окупант okupant
occupy *v.t.* захоплювати
zakhopliuvaty
occur *v.i.* відбуватися
vidbuvatysia

occurrence *n.* пригода pryhoda
ocean *n.* океан okean
oceanic *a.* океанічний
okeanichnyi
octagon *n.* восьмикутник
vosmykutnyk
octangular *a.* восьмикутний
vosmykutnyi
octave *n.* октава oktava
October *n.* жовтень zhovten
octogenarian *n.*
вісімдесятирічний старий
visimdesiatyrichnyi staryi
octogenarian *a.*
вісімдесятирічний
visimdesiatyrichnyi
octroi *n.* міська митниця miska
mytnytsia
ocular *a.* очний ochnyi
oculist *n.* окуліст okulist
odd *a.* непарний neparnyi
oddity *n.* дивина dyvyna
odds *n.* шанси shansy
ode *n.* ода oda
odious *a.* одіозний odioznyi
odium *n.* ганьба hanba
odorous *a.* запашний zapashnyi
odour *n.* запах zapakh
offence *n.* кривда kryvda
offend *v.t.* ображати obrazhaty
offender *n.* кривдник kryvdnyk
offensive *n* наступ nastup
offensive *a.* агресивний
ahresyvnyi
offer *n* наведення navedennia
offer *v.t.* траплятися trapliatysia
offering *n.* підношення
pidnoshennia
office *n.* офіс ofis
officer *n.* офіцер ofitser
official *n* чиновник chynovnyk
official *a.* офіційний ofitsiinyi
officially *adv.* офіційно ofitsiino

officiate *v.i.* виконувати обов'язки vykonuvaty oboviazky

officious *a.* офіціозний ofitsioznyi

offing *n.* узмор'я uzmoria

offset *n* зміщення zmishchennia

offset *v.t.* зводити баланс zvodyty balans

offshoot *n.* відгалуження vidhaluzhennia

offspring *n.* потомство potomstvo

oft *adv.* часто chasto

often *adv.* найчастіше naichastishe

ogle *v.t.* дивитися закоханими очима dyvytysia zakokhanymy ochyma

ogle *n* око oko

oil *v.t* змащувати zmashchuvaty

oil *n.* олія oliia

oily *a.* маслянистий maslianystyi

ointment *n.* мазь maz

old *a.* старий staryi

oligarchy *n.* олігархія oliharkhiia

olive *n.* оливковий olyvkovyi

olympiad *n.* олімпіада olimpiada

omega *n.* омега omeha

omelette *n.* омлет omlet

omen *n.* ознака oznaka

ominous *a.* загрозливий zahrozlyvyi

omission *n.* недогляд nedohliad

omit *v.t.* опустити opustyty

omnipotence *n.* всемогутність vsemohutnist

omnipotent *a.* всесильний vsesylnyi

omnipresence *n.* всюдисущість vsiudysushchist

omnipresent *a.* всюдисущий vsiudysushchyi

omniscience *n.* всевідання vsevidannia

omniscient *a.* всезнаючий vseznaiuchyi

on *adv.* на na

on *prep.* на na

once *adv.* раз raz

one *pron.* один odyn

one *a.* єдиний yedynyi

oneness *n.* тотожність totozhnist

onerous *a.* скрутний skrutnyi

onion *n.* цибуля tsybulia

on-looker *n.* глядач hliadach

only *conj.* лише lyshe

only *adv.* тільки tilky

only *a.* єдиний yedynyi

onomatopoeia *n.* звуконаслідування zvukonasliduvannia

onrush *n.* натиск natysk

onset *n.* натиск natysk

onslaught *n.* стрімка атака strimka ataka

onus *n.* тягар tiahar

onward *a.* поступальний postupalnyi

onwards *adv.* далі dali

ooze *v.i.* виділятися vydiliatysia

ooze *n.* липка грязь lypka hriaz

opacity *n.* непрозорість neprozorist

opal *n.* опал opal

opaque *a.* непрозорий neprozoryi

open *v.t.* відкрити vidkryty

open *a.* розкритий rozkrytyi

opening *n.* щілина shchylyna

openly *adv.* відкрито vidkryto

opera *n.* опера opera

operate *v.t.* діяти diiaty

operation *n.* операція operatsiia

operative *a.* оперативний operatyvnyi

operator *n.* оператор operator

opine *v.t.* висловлювати думку vyslovliuvaty dumku

opinion *n.* думка dumka
opium *n.* опіум opium
opponent *n.* опонент oponent
opportune *a.* сприятливий
spryiatlyvyi
opportunism *n.* опортунізм
oportunizm
opportunity *n.* перспектива
perspektyva
oppose *v.t.* виступати проти
vystupaty proty
opposite *a.* протилежний
protylezhnyi
opposition *n.* опозиція opozytsiia
oppress *v.t.* гнітити hnityty
oppression *n.* пригнічення
pryhnichennia
oppressive *a.* гнітючий hnitiuchyi
oppressor *n.* гнобитель hnobytel
opt *v.i.* робити вибір robyty vybir
optic *a.* оптичний optychnyi
optician *n.* оптик optyk
optimism *n.* оптимізм optymizm
optimist *n.* оптиміст optymist
optimistic *a.* оптимістичний
optymistychnyi
optimum *a* оптимальний
optymalnyi
optimum *n.* оптимум optymum
option *n.* опція optsiia
optional *a.* необов'язковий
neoboviazkovyi
opulence *n.* достаток dostatok
opulent *a.* багатий bahatyi
oracle *n.* оракул orakul
oracular *a.* догматичний
dohmatychnyi
oral *a.* усний usnyi
orally *adv.* усно usno
orange *a* помаранчевий
pomaranchevyi
orange *n.* апельсин apelsyn
oration *n.* благання blahannia

orator *n.* оратор orator
oratorical *a.* ораторський
oratorskyi
oratory *n.* ораторське мистецтво
oratorske mystetstvo
orb *n.* шар shar
orbit *n.* орбіта orbita
orchard *n.* фруктовий сад
fruktovyi sad
orchestra *n.* оркестр orkestr
orchestral *a.* оркестровий
orkestrovyi
ordeal *n.* випробування
vyprobuvannia
order *v.t* наказувати nakazuvaty
order *n.* порядок poriadok
orderly *n.* прибиральник вулиць
prybyralnyk vulyts
orderly *a.* упорядкований
uporiadkovanyi
ordinance *n.* указ ukaz
ordinarily *adv.* зазвичай
zazvychai
ordinary *a.* посередній poserednii
ordnance *n.* артилерія artyleriia
ore *n.* руда ruda
organ *n.* орган orhan
organic *a.* органічний orhanichnyi
organism *n.* організм orhanizm
organization *n.* організація
orhanizatsiia
organize *v.t.* організувати
orhanizuvaty
orient *v.t.* орієнтувати oriientuvaty
orient *n.* схід skhid
oriental *n* житель Сходу zhytel
Skhodu
oriental *a.* східний skhidnyi
orientate *v.t.* орієнтуватися
oriientuvatysia
origin *n.* джерело dzherelo
original *n* оригінал oryhinal

original *a.* початковий pochatkovyi

originality *n.* оригінальність oryhinalnist

originate *v.t.* започатковувати zapochatkovuvaty

originator *n.* творець tvorets

ornament *n.* орнамент ornament

ornament *v.t.* оздоблювати ozdobliuvaty

ornamental *a.* декоративний dekoratyvnyi

ornamentation *n.* оздоблення ozdoblennia

orphan *v.t* робити сиротою robyty syrotoiu

orphan *n.* сирота syrota

orphanage *n.* дитячий будинок dytiachyi budynok

orthodox *a.* ортодоксальний ortodoksalnyi

orthodoxy *n.* ортодоксальність ortodoksalnist

oscillate *v.i.* гойдатися hoidatysia

oscillation *n.* вібрація vibratsiia

ossify *v.t.* костеніти kostenity

ostracize *v.t.* піддавати остракізму piddavaty ostrakizmu

ostrich *n.* страус straus

other *a.* додатковий dodatkovyi

other *pron.* інакший inakshyi

otherwise *conj.* або ж abo zh

otherwise *adv.* в іншому випадку v inshomu vypadku

otter *n.* видра vydra

ottoman *n.* тахта takhta

ounce *n.* унція untsiia

our *pron.* наш nash

oust *v.t.* скидати skydaty

out *adv.* зовні zovni

out-balance *v.t.* перевершувати perevershuvaty

outbid *v.t.* перебити ціну perebyty tsinu

outbreak *n.* спалах spalakh

outburst *n.* спалах spalakh

outcast *a* знедолений znedolenyi

outcast *n.* вигнанець vyhnanets

outcome *n.* наслідок naslidok

outcry *n.* вигук vyhuk

outdated *a.* застарілий zastarilyi

outdo *v.t.* перевершити perevershyty

outdoor *a.* поза межами poza mezhamy

outer *a.* зовнішній zovnishnii

outfit *n.* обмундирування obmundyruvannia

outfit *v.t* обмундирувати obmundyruvaty

outgrow *v.t.* виростати з vyrostaty z

outhouse *n.* флігель flihel

outing *n.* прогулянка за мужі міста prohulianka za muzhi mista

outlandish *a.* дивовижний dyvovyzhnyi

outlaw *v.t* оголошувати поза законом oholoshuvaty poza zakonom

outlaw *n.* ізгой izhoi

outline *v.t.* окреслити okreslyty

outline *n.* обрис obrys

outlive *v.t.* пережити perezhyty

outlook *n.* плани на майбутнє plany na maibutnie

outmoded *a.* старомодний staromodnyi

outnumber *v.t.* перевершувати чисельно perevershuvaty chyselno

outpatient *n.* амбулаторний хворий ambulatornyi khvoryi

outpost *n.* аванпост avanpost

output *n.* зникнення znyknennia
outrage *n.* наруга naruha
outrage *v.t.* порушувати закон porushuvaty zakon
outright *a* цілеспрямований tsilespriamovanyi
outright *adv.* наповал napoval
outrun *v.t.* випереджати vyperedzhaty
outset *n.* гирло шахти hyrlo shakhty
outshine *v.t.* затьмарювати zatmariuvaty
outside *adv* за межами za mezhamy
outside *n* лицьова сторона lytsova storona
outside *prep* назовні nazovni
outside *a.* крайній krainii
outsider *n.* стороння людина storonnia liudyna
outsize *a.* нестандартний nestandartnyi
outskirts *n.* околиця okolytsia
outspoken *a.* відвертий vidvertyi
outstanding *a.* знаменитий znamenytyi
outward *adv* назовні nazovni
outward *a.* поверхневий poverkhnevyi
outwardly *adv.* зовні zovni
outwards *adv* за межі za mezhi
outweigh *v.t.* переважувати perevazhuvaty
outwit *v.t.* перехитрити perekhytryty
oval *n* футбольний м'яч futbolnyi miach
oval *a.* овальний ovalnyi
ovary *n.* яєчник yaiechnyk
ovation *n.* овація ovatsiia
oven *n.* піч pich
over *n* пух pukh

over *adv* через cherez
over *prep.* через cherez
overact *v.t.* переігравати perehravaty
overall *a* граничний hranychnyi
overall *n.* спецодяг spetsodiah
overawe *v.t.* вселяти шанобливий страх vseliaty shanoblyvyi strakh
overboard *adv.* за борт za bort
overburden *v.t.* переобтяжувати pereobtiazhuvaty
overcast *a.* хмарність khmarnist
overcharge *n* перезаряд perezariad
overcharge *v.t.* перезаряджати perezariadzhaty
overcoat *n.* шинель shynel
overcome *v.t.* п. олати podolaty
overdo *v.t.* перестаратися perestaratysia
overdose *v.t.* прийняти дуже велику дозу pryiniaty duzhe velyku dozu
overdose *n.* передозування peredozuvannia
overdraft *n.* овердрафт overdraft
overdraw *v.t.* перевитрачати perevytrachaty
overdue *a.* прострочений prostrochenyi
overhaul *n.* капітальний ремонт kapitalnyi remont
overhaul *v.t.* ремонтувати remontuvaty
overhear *v.t.* підслуховувати pidslukhovuvaty
overjoyed *a* дуже задоволений duzhe zadovolenyi
overlap *n* перекриття perekryttia
overlap *v.t.* перекривати perekryvaty
overleaf *adv.* на звороті na zvoroti

overload *n* перевантаження perevantazhennia

overload *v.t.* перевантажувати perevantazhuvaty

overlook *v.t.* упускати з уваги upuskaty z uvahy

overnight *a* що триває всю ніч shcho tryvaie vsiu nich

overnight *adv.* всю ніч vsiu nich

overpower *v.t.* пересилювати peresyliuvaty

overrate *v.t.* переоцінювати pereotsiniuvaty

overrule *v.t.* пересилювати peresyliuvaty

overrun *v.t* переливатися через край perelyvatysia cherez krai

oversee *v.t.* здійснявати нагляд zdiisniavaty nahliad

overseer *n.* наглядач nahliadach

overshadow *v.t.* затінювати zatiniuvaty

oversight *n.* нагляд nahliad

overt *a.* явний yavnyi

overtake *v.t.* наздогнати nazdohnaty

overthrow *n* повалення povalennia

overthrow *v.t.* перекидати perekydaty

overtime *n* понаднормовий час ponadnormovyi chas

overtime *adv.* понаднормовий ponadnormovyi

overture *n.* увертюра uvertiura

overwhelm *v.t.* сповнювати spovniuvaty

overwork *n.* перевтома perevtoma

overwork *v.i.* перевтомлюватися perevtomliuvatysia

owe *v.t* заборгувати zaborhuvaty

owl *n.* сова sova

own *v.t.* допускати dopuskaty

own *a.* власний vlasnyi

owner *n.* власник vlasnyk

ownership *n.* власність vlasnist

ox *n.* бик byk

oxygen *n.* кисень kysen

oyster *n.* устриця ustrytsia

pace *v.i.* ходити khodyty

pace *n* темп temp

pacific *a.* миролюбний myroliubnyi

pacify *v.t.* умиротворяти umyrotvoriaty

pack *n.* стос stos

pack *v.t.* упаковувати upakovuvaty

package *n.* упакування upakuvannia

packet *n.* пакет paket

packing *n.* упаковка upakovka

pact *n.* пакт pakt

pad *v.t.* набивати nabyvaty

pad *n.* подушка podushka

padding *n.* оббивка obbyvka

paddle *n* весло veslo

paddle *v.i.* гребти веслом hrebty veslom

paddy *n.* муляр muliar

page *v.t.* нумерувати сторінки numeruvaty storinky

page *n.* сторінка storinka

pageant *n.* видовище vydovyshche

pageantry *n.* пишність pyshnist

pagoda *n.* пагода pahoda

pail *n.* цеберка tseberka

pain *v.t.* хворіти khvority

pain *n.* страждання strazhdannia

painful *a.* хворобливий khvoroblyvyi

painstaking *a.* кропіткий kropitkyi
paint *v.t.* фарбувати farbuvaty
paint *n.* фарба farba
painter *n.* художник khudozhnyk
painting *n.* живопис zhyvopys
pair *n.* пара para
pair *v.t.* розташовуватися roztashovuvatysia
pal *n.* приятель pryiatel
palace *n.* палац palats
palanquin *n.* паланкін palankin
palatable *a.* смачний smachnyi
palatal *a.* піднебінний pidnebinnyi
palate *n.* піднебіння pidnebinnia
palatial *a.* палацовий palatsovyi
pale *a* блідий blidyi
pale *v.i.* бліднути blidnuty
pale *n.* кіл kil
palette *n.* палітра palitra
palm *n.* долонь dolon
palm *n.* пальма palma
palm *v.t.* підкидати pidkydaty
palmist *n.* хіромант khiromant
palmistry *n.* хіромантія khiromantiia
palpable *a.* відчутний vidchutnyi
palpitate *v.i.* тріпотіти tripotity
palpitation *n.* серцебиття sertsebyttia
palsy *n.* стан повної безпорадності stan povnoi bezporadnosti
paltry *a.* жалюгідний zhaliuhidnyi
pamper *v.t.* балувати baluvaty
pamphlet *n.* памфлет pamflet
pamphleteer *n.* памфлетист pamfletyst
panacea *n.* панацея panatseia
pandemonium *n.* стовпотворіння stovpotvorinnia
pane *n.* віконне скло vikonne sklo
panegyric *n.* панегірик panehiryk

panel *v.t.* обшивати панелями obshyvaty paneliamy
panel *n.* панель panel
pang *n.* гострий біль hostryi bil
panic *n.* паніка panika
panorama *n.* панорама panorama
pant *n.* пихтіння pykhtinnia
pant *v.i.* тіпатися tipatysia
pantaloon *n.* рейтузи reituzy
pantheism *n.* пантеїзм panteizm
pantheist *n.* пантеїст panteist
panther *n.* пантера pantera
pantomime *n.* пантоміма pantomima
pantry *n.* буфетна bufetna
papacy *n.* папство papstvo
papal *a.* папський papskyi
paper *n.* папір papir
par *n.* номінал nominal
parable *n.* притча prytcha
parachute *n.* парашут parashut
parachutist *n.* парашутист parashutyst
parade *v.t.* хизуватися khyzuvatysia
parade *n.* парад parad
paradise *n.* рай rai
paradox *n.* парадокс paradoks
paradoxical *a.* парадоксальний paradoksalnyi
paraffin *n.* парафін parafin
paragon *n.* парагон parahon
paragraph *n.* пункт punkt
parallel *v.t.* порівнювати porivniuvaty
parallel *a.* паралельний paralelnyi
parallelism *n.* паралелізм paralelizm
parallelogram *n.* паралелограм paralelohram
paralyse *v.t.* паралізувати paralizuvaty

paralysis *n.* параліч paralich
paralytic *a.* паралітичний
paralitychnyi
paramount *n.* першорядний
pershoriadnyi
paramour *n.* коханка kokhanka
paraphernalia *n.* супровідне
майно suprovidne maino
paraphrase *v.t.* переказувати
perekazuvaty
paraphrase *n.* парафраз parafraz
parasite *n.* паразит parazyt
parcel *v.t.* загортати в пакет
zahortaty v paket
parcel *n.* посилка posylka
parch *v.t.* підсушувати
pidsushuvaty
pardon *n.* помилування
pomyluvannia
pardon *v.t.* помилувати
pomyluvaty
pardonable *a.* простимий
prostymyi
parent *n.* названий батько
nazvanyi batko
parentage *n.* батьківство
batkivstvo
parental *a.* батьківський
batkivskyi
parenthesis *n.* кругла дужка
kruhla duzhka
parish *n.* прихід prykhid
parity *n.* паритет parytet
park *n.* парк park
park *v.t.* паркувати parkuvaty
parlance *n.* манера говорити
manera hovoryty
parley *v.i* вести переговори vesty
perehovory
parley *n.* переговори perehovory
parliament *n.* парламент
parlament

parliamentarian *n.*
парламентарій parlamentarii
parliamentary *a.* парламентський
parlamentskyi
parlour *n.* кабінет kabinet
parody *v.t.* пародіювати
parodiiuvaty
parody *n.* пародія parodiia
parole *v.t.* умовне звільнення
ув'язненого з в'язниці umovne
zvilnennia uviaznenoho z
viaznytsi
parole *n.* слово честі slovo chesti
parricide *n.* батьковбивство
batkovbyvstvo
parrot *n.* папуга papuha
parry *n.* парирування
paryruvannia
parry *v.t.* парирувати paryruvaty
parson *n.* священик sviashchenyk
part *v.t.* відокремлювати
vidokremliuvaty
part *n.* частина chastyna
partake *v.i.* брати участь braty
uchast
partial *a.* частковий chastkovyi
partiality *n.* упередженість
uperedzhenist
participant *n.* учасник uchasnyk
participate *v.i.* розподіляти
rozpodiliaty
participation *n.* участь uchast
particle *a.* префікс prefiks
particular *n.* приватність
pryvatnist
particular *a.* винятковий
vyniatkovyi
partisan *a.* партизанів partyzaniv
partisan *n.* партизанський
partyzanskyi
partition *v.t.* розділяти rozdiliaty
partition *n.* частина chastyna
partner *n.* партнер partner

partnership *n.* партнерство partnerstvo

party *n.* прийом гостей pryiom hostei

pass *n* пропуск propusk

pass *v.i.* проходити prokhodyty

passage *n.* проходження prokhodzhennia

passenger *n.* пасажир pasazhyr

passion *n.* вибух почуттів vybukh pochuttiv

passionate *a.* пристрасний prystrasnyi

passive *a.* пасивний pasyvnyi

passport *n.* паспорт pasport

past *n.* життя людини zhyttia liudyny

past *prep.* повз povz

past *a.* минулий mynulyi

paste *v.t.* клеїти kleity

paste *n.* паста pasta

pastel *n.* пастельний pastelnyi

pastime *n.* приємне проведення часу pryiemne provedennia chasu

pastoral *a.* пасторальний pastoralnyi

pasture *v.t.* паша pasha

pasture *n.* пасовищі pasovyshchi

pat *n* поплескування popleskuvannia

pat *adv* своєчасно svoiechasno

pat *v.t.* шльопати shlopaty

patch *n* клапоть klapot

patch *v.t.* латати lataty

patent *n* патент patent

patent *v.t.* патентувати patentuvaty

patent *a.* патентований patentovanyi

paternal *a.* по батькові po batkovi

path *n.* шлях shliakh

pathetic *a.* патетичний patetychnyi

pathos *n.* пафос pafos

patience *n.* терпіння terpinnia

patient *n* пацієнт patsiient

patient *a.* терплячий terpliachyi

patricide *n.* вбивство батька vbyvstvo batka

patrimony *n.* спадкоємне майно spadkoiemne maino

patriot *n.* патріот patriot

patriotic *a.* патріотичний patriotychnyi

patriotism *n.* патріотизм patriotyzm

patrol *n* патруль patrul

patrol *v.i.* патрулювати patruliuvaty

patron *n.* покровитель pokrovytel

patronage *n.* патронаж patronazh

patronize *v.t.* протегувати protehuvaty

pattern *n.* шаблон shablon

paucity *n.* брак brak

pauper *n.* злидар zlydar

pause *v.i.* робити паузу robyty pauzu

pause *n.* пауза pauza

pave *v.t.* мостити mostyty

pavement *n.* тротуар trotuar

pavilion *n.* павільйон pavilion

paw *v.t.* торкати лапою torkaty lapoiu

paw *n.* лапа lapa

pay *n* оплата oplata

pay *v.t.* платити platyty

payable *a.* до сплати do splaty

payee *n.* одержувач платежу oderzhuvach platezhu

payment *n.* сплата splata

pea *n.* горох horokh

peace *n.* мир myr

peaceable *a.* спокійний spokiinyi

peaceful *a.* мирний myrnyi
peach *n.* персик persyk
peacock *n.* павич pavych
peahen *n.* пава pava
peak *n.* пік pik
pear *n.* груша hrusha
pearl *n.* перлина perlyna
peasant *n.* селянин selianyn
peasantry *n.* селянство selianstvo
pebble *n.* галька halka
peck *v.i.* клювати kliuvaty
peck *n.* клювок kliuvok
peculiar *a.* своєрідний svoieridnyi
peculiarity *n.* особливість osoblyvist
pecuniary *a.* грошовий hroshovyi
pedagogue *n.* педагог pedahoh
pedagogy *n.* педагогіка pedahohika
pedal *v.t.* натискати педаль natyskaty pedal
pedal *n.* педаль pedal
pedant *n.* педант pedant
pedantic *n.* педантичний pedantychnyi
pedantry *n.* педантичність pedantychnist
pedestal *n.* п'єдестал piedestal
pedestrian *n.* пішохід pishokhid
pedigree *n.* родовід rodovid
peel *n.* шкірка shkirka
peel *v.t.* обдирати obdyraty
peep *n* швидкий погляд shvydkyi pohliad
peep *v.i.* підглядати pidhliadaty
peer *n.* рівний rivnyi
peerless *a.* неперевершуваний neperevershuvanyi
peg *v.t.* прикріплювати кілочком prykripliuvaty kilochkom
peg *n.* кілочок kilochok
pelf *n.* гроші hroshi

pell-mell *adv.* упереміш uperemish
pen *v.t.* творити tvoryty
pen *n.* ручка ruchka
penal *a.* карний karnyi
penalize *v.t.* робити карним robyty karnym
penalty *n.* штраф shtraf
pencil *v.t.* малювати олівцем maliuvaty olivtsem
pencil *n.* олівець olivets
pending *prep.* до do
pending *a* який розглядається yakyi rozhliadaietsia
pendulum *n.* маятник maiatnyk
penetrate *v.t.* проникати pronykaty
penetration *n.* прорив proryv
penis *n.* статевий член statevyi chlen
penniless *a.* без гроша bez hrosha
penny *n.* пенні penni
pension *v.t.* призначати пенсію pryznachaty pensiiu
pension *n.* пенсія pensiia
pensioner *n.* пенсіонер pensioner
pensive *a.* замислений zamyslenyi
pentagon *n.* п'ятикутник piatykutnyk
peon *n.* піхотинець pikhotynets
people *v.t.* заселяти zaseliaty
people *n.* люди liudy
pepper *n.* перець perets
pepper *v.t.* перчити perchyty
per *prep.* згідно zhidno
per cent *adv.* на сотню na sotniu
perambulator *n.* дитяча коляска dytiacha koliaska
perceive *v.t.* сприймати spryimaty
percentage *n.* відсоток vidsotok
perceptible *adj* помітно pomitno

perception *n.* сприйняття spryiniattia

perceptive *a.* сприйнятливий spryiniatlyvyi

perch *v.i.* влаштуватися vlashtuvatysia

perch *n.* окунь okun

perennial *n.* багаторічна рослина bahatorichna roslyna

perennial *a.* нев'янучий nevianuchyi

perfect *a.* досконалий doskonalyi

perfect *v.t.* удосконалювати udoskonaliuvaty

perfection *n.* удосконалення udoskonalennia

perfidy *n.* віроломство virolomstvo

perforate *v.t.* перфорувати perforuvaty

perforce *adv.* волею-неволею voleiu-nevoleiu

perform *v.t.* виконувати vykonuvaty

performance *n.* продуктивність produktyvnist

performer *n.* виконавець vykonavets

perfume *n.* духи dukhy

perfume *v.t.* напахувати парфумами napakhuvaty parfumamy

perhaps *adv.* можливо mozhlyvo

peril *v.t.* піддавати небезпеці piddavaty nebezpetsi

peril *n.* ризик ryzyk

perilous *a.* згубний zhubnyi

period *n.* період period

periodical *a.* періодичний periodychnyi

periodical *n.* періодичне видання periodychne vydannia

periphery *n.* периферія peryferiia

perish *v.i.* гинути hynuty

perishable *a.* швидкопсувний shvydkopsuvnyi

perjure *v.i.* лжесвідчити lzhesvidchyty

perjury *n.* лжесвідчення lzhesvidchennia

permanence *n.* сталість stalist

permanent *a.* залишковий zalyshkovyi

permissible *a.* дозволений dozvolenyi

permission *n.* дозвіл dozvil

permit *v.t.* дозволити dozvolyty

permit *n.* перепустка perepustka

permutation *n.* переміщення peremishchennia

pernicious *a.* шкідливий shkidlyvyi

perpendicular *n.* перпендикуляр perpendykuliar

perpendicular *a.* перпендикулярний perpendykuliarnyi

perpetual *a.* нескінченний neskinchennyi

perpetuate *v.t.* увічнювати uvichniuvaty

perplex *v.t.* спантеличувати spantelychuvaty

perplexity *n.* ускладнення uskladnennia

persecute *v.t.* впіддавати гонінням vpiddavaty honinniam

persecution *n.* цькування tskuvannia

perseverance *n.* наполегливість napolehlyvist

persevere *v.i.* упиратися upyratysia

persist *v.i.* зберігатися zberihatysia

persistence *n.* завзятість
zavziatist
persistent *a.* стійкий stiikyi
person *n.* людина liudyna
personage *n.* персонаж
personazh
personal *a.* персональний
personalnyi
personality *n.* особистість
osobystist
personification *n.* персоніфікація
personifikatsiia
personify *v.t.* уособлювати
uosobliuvaty
personnel *n.* персонал personal
perspective *n.* вид vyd
perspiration *n.* піт pit
perspire *v.i.* потіти potity
persuade *v.t.* відмовити
vidmovyty
persuasion *n.* переконання
perekonannia
pertain *v.i.* ставитися stavytysia
pertinent *a.* доречний dorechnyi
perturb *v.t.* хвилювати khvyliuvaty
perusal *n.* прочитання
prochytannia
peruse *v.t.* переглянути
perehlianuty
pervade *v.t.* просочувати
prosochuvaty
perverse *a.* збочений zbochenyi
perversion *n.* збочення
zbochennia
perversity *n.* збоченість
zbochenist
pervert *v.t.* збоченець zbochenets
pessimism *n.* песимізм
pesymizm
pessimist *n.* песиміст pesymist
pessimistic *a.* песимістичний
pesymistychnyi
pest *n.* шкідник shkidnyk

pesticide *n.* пестицид pestytsyd
pestilence *n.* пошесть poshest
pet *v.t.* обійматися obiimatysia
pet *n.* домашня тварина
domashnia tvaryna
petal *n.* пелюстка peliustka
petition *v.t.* подавати прохання
podavaty prokhannia
petition *n.* клопотання
klopotannia
petitioner *n.* прохач prokhach
petrol *n.* бензин benzyn
petroleum *n.* нафта nafta
petticoat *n.* нижня спідниця
nyzhnia spidnytsia
petty *a.* дрібний dribnyi
petulance *n.* дратівливість
drativlyvist
petulant *a.* заухвалий zaukhvalyi
phantom *n.* фантом fantom
pharmacy *n.* аптека apteka
phase *n.* фаза faza
phenomenal *a.* феноменальний
fenomenalnyi
phenomenon *n.* явище
yavyshche
phial *n.* фіал fial
philanthropic *a.* філантропічний
filantropichnyi
philanthropist *n.* філантроп
filantrop
philanthropy *n.* благодійність
blahodiinist
philological *a.* філологічний
filolohichnyi
philologist *n.* філолог filoloh
philology *n.* філологія filolohiia
philosopher *n.* філософ filosof
philosophical *a.* філософський
filosofskyi
philosophy *n.* філософія filosofiia
phone *n.* телефон telefon

phonetic *a.* фонетичний fonetychnyi
phonetics *n.* фонетика fonetyka
phosphate *n.* фосфат fosfat
phosphorus *n.* фосфор fosfor
photo *n* фото foto
photograph *n* фотографія fotohrafiia
photograph *v.t.* фотографувати fotohrafuvaty
photographer *n.* фотограф fotohraf
photographic *a.* фотографічний fotohrafichnyi
photography *n.* фотографування fotohrafuvannia
phrase *v.t.* висловити vyslovyty
phrase *n.* фраза fraza
phraseology *n.* фразеологія frazeolohiia
physic *v.t.* дати ліки daty liky
physic *n.* лікування likuvannia
physical *a.* фізичний fizychnyi
physician *n.* терапевт terapevt
physicist *n.* фізик fizyk
physics *n.* фізика fizyka
physiognomy *n.* фізіономія fizionomiia
physique *n.* статура statura
pianist *n.* піаніст pianist
piano *n.* піаніно pianino
pick *n.* кирка kyrka
pick *v.t.* відбирати vidbyraty
picket *v.t.* пікетувати piketuvaty
picket *n.* пікет piket
pickle *v.t* маринувати marynuvaty
pickle *n.* соління solinnia
picnic *v.i.* брати участь у пікніку braty uchast u pikniku
picnic *n.* пікнік piknik
pictorical *a.* ілюстрований iliustrovanyi
picture *v.t.* малювати maliuvaty

picture *n.* картина kartyna
picturesque *a.* мальовничий malovnychyi
piece *v.t.* з'єднувати ziednuvaty
piece *n.* шматок shmatok
pierce *v.t.* проколювати prokoliuvaty
piety *n.* благочестя blahochestia
pig *n.* свиня svynia
pigeon *n.* голуб holub
pigmy *n.* пігмей pihmei
pile *v.t.* навалювати navaliuvaty
pile *n.* паля palia
piles *n.* геморой hemoroi
pilfer *v.t.* красти krasty
pilgrim *n.* паломник palomnyk
pilgrimage *n.* паломництво palomnytstvo
pill *n.* пілюля piliulia
pillar *n.* стовп stovp
pillow *v.t.* служити подушкою sluzhyty podushkoiu
pillow *n* підкладка pidkladka
pilot *v.t.* пілотувати pilotuvaty
pilot *n.* досвідчений поводир dosvidchenyi povodyr
pimple *n.* вугор vuhor
pin *v.t.* приколювати prykoliuvaty
pin *n.* шпилька shpylka
pinch *n.* щіпка shchipka
pinch *v.t.* щипати shchypaty
pine *v.i.* нудитися nudytysia
pine *n.* сосна sosna
pineapple *n.* ананас ananas
pink *a* рожевий rozhevyi
pink *n.* рожевий rozhevyi
pinkish *a.* блідо-рожевий blido-rozhevyi
pinnacle *n.* вершина vershyna
pioneer *v.t.* прокладати шлях prokladaty shliakh
pioneer *n.* піонер pioner

pious *a.* благочестивий blahochestyvyi

pipe *v.i* пищати pyshchaty

pipe *n.* труба truba

piquant *a.* пікантний pikantnyi

piracy *n.* піратство piratstvo

pirate *v.t* розбійничати rozbiinychaty

pirate *n.* пірат pirat

pistol *n.* пістолет pistolet

piston *n.* поршень porshen

pit *v.t.* складати в яму skladaty v yamu

pit *n.* яма yama

pitch *v.t.* качати kachaty

pitch *n.* крок krok

pitcher *n.* брущатка brushchatka

piteous *a.* жалібний zhalibnyi

pitfall *n.* вибоїна vyboina

pitiable *a.* жалюгідний zhaliuhidnyi

pitiful *a.* сумний sumnyi

pitiless *a.* безжалісний bezzhalisnyi

pitman *n.* шатун shatun

pittance *n.* жалюгідні гроші zhaliuhidni hroshi

pity *v.t.* жаліти zhality

pity *n.* жалість zhalist

pivot *v.t.* перетворюватися peretvoriuvatysia

pivot *n.* стрижень stryzhen

place *v.t.* поміщати pomishchaty

place *n.* місце mistse

placid *a.* спокійний spokiinyi

plague *v.t.* насилати нещастя nasylaty neshchastia

plague *n.* чума chuma

plain *a.* невигадливий nevyhadlyvyi

plain *n.* рівнина rivnyna

plaintiff *n.* позивач pozyvach

plan *v.t.* планувати planuvaty

plan *n.* план plan

plane *v.t.* планерувати planeruvaty

plane *a.* плоский ploskyi

plane *n* проекція proektsiia

plane *n.* літак litak

planet *n.* планета planeta

planetary *a.* планетарний planetarnyi

plank *v.t.* настилати дошки nastylaty doshky

plank *n.* дошка doshka

plant *n.* рослина roslyna

plant *v.t.* саджати sadzhaty

plantain *n.* подорожник podorozhnyk

plantation *n.* плантація plantatsiia

plaster *v.t.* штукатурити shtukaturyty

plaster *n.* штукатурка shtukaturka

plate *n.* плита plyta

plate *v.t.* покривати металом pokryvaty metalom

plateau *n.* плато plato

platform *n.* платформа platforma

platonic *a.* платонічний platonichnyi

platoon *n.* взвод vzvod

play *v.i.* бавитися bavytysia

play *n.* спектакль spektakl

play card *n.* гральна карта hralna karta

player *n.* учасник гри uchasnyk hry

plea *n.* благання blahannia

plead *v.i.* виступати в суді vystupaty v sudi

pleader *n.* захисник zakhysnyk

pleasant *a.* приємний pryiemnyi

pleasantry *n.* жартівливість zhartivlyvist

please *v.i.* подобатися podobatysia

pleasure *n.* задоволення zadovolennia
plebiscite *n.* плебісцит plebistsyt
pledge *v.t.* запевняти zapevniaty
pledge *n.* тост tost
plenty *n.* надмір nadmir
plight *n.* заручини zaruchyny
plod *v.i.* тягтися tiahtysia
plot *v.t.* плести інтриги plesty intryhy
plot *n.* ділянка dilianka
plough *v.t.* орати oraty
plough *n.* плуг pluh
ploughman *n.* орач orach
pluck *n* смикання smykannia
pluck *v.t.* скубти skubty
plug *v.t.* затикати zatykaty
plug *n.* заглушка zahlushka
plum *n.* слива slyva
plumber *n.* водопровідник vodoprovidnyk
plunder *n* грабіж hrabizh
plunder *v.t.* пограбувати pohrabuvaty
plunge *n* пірнання pirnannia
plunge *v.t.* поринати porynaty
plural *a.* строкатий strokatyi
plurality *n.* сумісництво sumisnytstvo
plus *n* плюс plius
plus *a.* позитивний pozytyvnyi
ply *n* шар shar
ply *v.t.* засипати zasypaty
pneumonia *n.* пневмонія pnevmoniia
pocket *v.t.* привласнити pryvlasnyty
pocket *n.* кишеня kyshenia
pod *n.* стручок struchok
poem *n.* вірш virsh
poesy *n.* поезія poeziia
poet *n.* поет poet
poetaster *n.* віршомаз virshomaz

poetess *n.* поетеса poetesa
poetic *a.* поетичний poetychnyi
poetics *n.* поетика poetyka
poetry *n.* поетичність poetychnist
poignancy *n.* пікантність pikantnist
poignant *a.* пікантний pikantnyi
point *v.t.* указувати ukazuvaty
point *n.* точка tochka
poise *n* врівноваженість vrivnovazhenist
poise *v.t.* врівноважувати vrivnovazhuvaty
poison *v.t.* отруїти otruity
poison *n.* отрута otruta
poisonous *a.* отруйний otruinyi
poke *n.* тичок tychok
poke *v.t.* штовхати shtovkhaty
polar *n.* полярний poliarnyi
pole *n.* полюс polius
police *n.* поліція politsiia
policeman *n.* поліцейський politseiskyi
policy *n.* політика polityka
polish *n* поліровка polirovka
polish *v.t.* полірувати poliruvaty
polite *a.* витончений vytonchenyi
politeness *n.* чемність chemnist
politic *a.* політичний politychnyi
political *a.* пов'язаний з політикою poviazanyi z politykoiu
politician *n.* політик polityk
politics *n.* політика polityka
polity *n.* державний устрій derzhavnyi ustrii
poll *v.t.* підраховувати голоси pidrakhovuvaty holosy
poll *n.* голосування holosuvannia
pollen *n.* пилок pylok
pollute *v.t.* поганити pohanyty
pollution *n.* забруднення zabrudnennia

polo *n.* поло polo
polygamous *a.* полігамний polihamnyi
polygamy *n.* полігамія polihamiia
polyglot1 *n.* поліглот polihlot
polyglot2 *a.* багатомовний bahatomovnyi
polytechnic *n.* політехнікум politekhnikum
polytechnic *a.* політехнічний politekhnichnyi
polytheism *n.* багатобожжя bahatobozhzhia
polytheist *n.* політеїст politeist
polytheistic *a.* політеїстичний politeistychnyi
pomp *n.* пишнота pyshnota
pomposity *n.* помпезність pompeznist
pompous *a.* помпезний pompeznyi
pond *n.* ставок stavok
ponder *v.t.* зважувати zvazhuvaty
pony *n.* поні poni
poor *a.* бідний bidnyi
pop *v.i.* плескати pleskaty
pop *n* популярний populiarnyi
pope *n.* ляскання liaskannia
poplar *n.* тополя topolia
poplin *n.* поплін poplin
populace *n.* простий народ prostyi narod
popular *a.* популярний populiarnyi
popularity *n.* популярність populiarnist
popularize *v.t.* популяризувати populiaryzuvaty
populate *v.t.* населяти naseliaty
population *n.* населення naselennia
populous *a.* густонаселений hustonaselenyi

porcelain *n.* фарфор farfor
porch *n.* ганок hanok
pore *n.* пори pory
pork *n.* свинина svynyna
porridge *n.* вівсянка vivsianka
port *n.* порт port
portable *a.* переносний perenosnyi
portage *n.* провезення provezennia
portal *n.* портал portal
portend *v.t.* передвіщати peredvishchaty
porter *n.* провідник providnyk
portfolio *n.* портфель portfel
portico *n.* портик portyk
portion *v.t.* ділити dilyty
portion *n* частина chastyna
portrait *n.* опис opys
portraiture *n.* портретний живопис portretnyi zhyvopys
portray *v.t.* малювати портрет maliuvaty portret
portrayal *n* портрет portret
pose *n.* поза poza
pose *v.i.* позувати pozuvaty
position *n.* позиція pozytsiia
position *v.t.* визначати місцезнаходження vyznachaty mistseznakhodzhennia
positive *a.* позитивний pozytyvnyi
possess *v.t.* оволодівати ovolodivaty
possession *n.* залежна теріторія zalezhna teritoriia
possibility *n.* перспективи perspektyvy
possible *a.* імовірний imovirnyi
post *v.t.* відправляти vidpravliaty
post *v.t.* розклеювати rozkleiuvaty
post *n.* пост post
post *n* стовп stovp
post *adj.* спішно spishno

postage *n.* поштові витрати poshtovi vytraty

postal *a.* поштовий poshtovyi

post-date *v.t.* датувати пізнішим числом datuvaty piznishym chyslom

poster *n.* плакат plakat

posterity *n.* нащадки nashchadky

posthumous *a.* народжений після смерті батька narodzhenyi pislia smerti batka

postman *n.* листоноша lystonosha

postmaster *n.* поштмейстер poshtmeister

post-mortem *n.* аналіз гри після її закінчення analiz hry pislia yii zakinchennia

post-mortem *a.* посмертний posmertnyi

post-office *n.* поштове відділення poshtove viddilennia

postpone *v.t.* відтерміновувати vidterminovuvaty

postponement *n.* відстрочка vidstrochka

postscript *n.* постскриптум postskryptum

posture *n.* постава postava

pot *n.* горщик horshchyk

pot *v.t.* заготовлювати про запас zahotovliuvaty pro zapas

potash *n.* поташ potash

potassium *n.* калій kalii

potato *n.* картопля kartoplia

potency *n.* потенція potentsiia

potent *a.* потужний potuzhnyi

potential *n.* потенціал potentsial

potential *a.* потенційний potentsiinyi

potentiality *n.* потенційність potentsiinist

potter *n.* гончар honchar

pottery *n.* гончарні вироби honcharni vyroby

pouch *n.* сумка sumka

poultry *n.* домашня птиця domashnia ptytsia

pounce *n* наскок naskok

pounce *v.i.* накидатися nakydatysia

pound *n.* фунт funt

pound *v.t.* подрібнювати podribniuvaty

pour *v.i.* лити lyty

poverty *n.* бідність bidnist

powder *v.t.* пудрити pudryty

powder *n.* порошок poroshok

power *n.* міць mits

powerful *a.* потужний potuzhnyi

practicability *n.* здійсненність zdiisnennist

practicable *a.* прохідний prokhidnyi

practical *a.* практичний praktychnyi

practice *n.* практика praktyka

practise *v.t.* вправлятися vpravliatysia

practitioner *n.* практикуючий лікар praktykuiuchyi likar

pragmatic *a.* прагматичний prahmatychnyi

pragmatism *n.* прагматизм prahmatyzm

praise *n.* хвала khvala

praise *v.t.* хвалити khvalyty

praiseworthy *a.* гідний похвали hidnyi pokhvaly

prank *n.* жарт zhart

prattle *n.* белькотання belkotannia

prattle *v.i.* белькотати belkotaty

pray *v.i.* молитися molytysia

prayer *n.* молитва molytva

preach *v.i.* проповідувати
propoviduvaty

preacher *n.* проповідник
propovidnyk

preamble *n.* преамбула
preambula

precaution *n.* заходи безпеки
zakhody bezpeky

precautionary *a.*
попереджувальний
poperedzhuvalnyi

precede *v.* біти попереду bity
poperedu

precedence *n.* пріоритет priorytet

precedent *n.* прецедент
pretsedent

precept *n.* заповідь zapovid

preceptor *n.* учитель uchytel

precious *a.* дорогоцінний
dorohotsinnyi

precis *n.* конспект konspekt

precise *a.* точний tochnyi

precision *n.* точність tochnist

precursor *n.* ровісник rovisnyk

predecessor *n.* попередник
poperednyk

predestination *n.* приречення
pryrechennia

predetermine *v.t.* зумовлювати
zumovliuvaty

predicament *n.* скрутне
становище skrutne
stanovyshche

predicate *n.* предикат predykat

predict *v.t.* прогнозувати
prohnozuvaty

prediction *n.* прогноз prohnoz

predominance *n.* переважання
perevazhannia

predominant *a.* що переважає
shcho perevazhaie

predominate *v.i.* переважати
perevazhaty

pre-eminence *n.* вищість
vyshchist

pre-eminent *a.* видатний vydatnyi

preface *n.* пролог proloh

preface *v.t.* робити вступ robyty
vstup

prefect *n.* префект prefekt

prefer *v.t.* віддавати перевагу
viddavaty perevahu

preference *n.* преференція
preferentsiia

preferential *a.* пільговий pilhovyi

prefix *n.* префікс prefiks

prefix *v.t.* приставляти спереду
prystavliaty speredu

pregnancy *n.* вагітність vahitnist

pregnant *a.* вагітна vahitna

prehistoric *a.* доісторичний
doistorychnyi

prejudice *n.* упередження
uperedzhennia

prelate *n.* прелат prelat

preliminary *n* підготовчий захід
pidhotovchyi zakhid

preliminary *a.* попередній
poperednii

prelude *n.* прелюдія preliudiia

prelude *v.t.* служити вступом
sluzhyty vstupom

premarital *a.* передшлюбний
peredshliubnyi

premature *a.* передчасний
peredchasnyi

premeditate *v.t.* обмірковувати
obmirkovuvaty

premeditation *n.* навмисність
navmysnist

premier *a.* перший pershyi

premier *n* прем'єр-міністр
premier-ministr

premiere *n.* прем'єра premiera

premium *n.* плата plata

premonition *n.* передчуття
peredchuttia
preoccupation *n.* заклопотаність
zaklopotanist
preoccupy *v.t.* привертати увагу
pryvertaty uvahu
preparation *n.* підготовка
pidhotovka
preparatory *a.* підготовчий
pidhotovchyi
prepare *v.t.* підготовляти
pidhotovliaty
preponderance *n.*
перевалювання
perevaliuvannia
preponderate *v.i.* перевалювати
perevaliuvaty
preposition *n.* привід pryvid
prerequisite *n* умова umova
prerequisite *a.* який вимагається
заздалегідь yakyi vymahaietsia
zazdalehid
prerogative *n.* прерогатива
prerohatyva
prescience *n.* передбачення
peredbachennia
prescribe *v.t.* наказувати
nakazuvaty
prescription *n.* лікарський
рецепт likarskyi retsept
presence *n.* наявність naiavnist
present *v.t.* підносити pidnosyty
present *n.* подарунок podarunok
present *a.* справжній spravzhnii
presentation *n.* презентація
prezentatsiia
presently *adv.* за хвилину za
khvylynu
preservation *n.* збереження
zberezhennia
preservative *a.* запобіжний
zapobizhnyi

preservative *n.* консервант
konservant
preserve *v.t.* берегти berehty
preserve *n.* консерви konservy
preside *v.i.* головувати holovuvaty
president *n.* президент prezydent
presidential *a.* президентський
prezydentskyi
press *v.t.* здавити zdavyty
press *n* преса presa
pressure *n.* тиск tysk
pressurize *v.t.* герметизувати
hermetyzuvaty
prestige *n.* престиж prestyzh
prestigious *a.* престижний
prestyzhnyi
presume *v.t.* гадати hadaty
presumption *n.* презумпція
prezumptsiia
presuppose *v.t.* містити в собі
mistyty v sobi
presupposition *n.* передумова
peredumova
pretence *n.* удавання udavannia
pretend *v.t.* вдавати vdavaty
pretension *n.* претензійність
pretenziinist
pretentious *a.* претензійний
pretenziinyi
pretext *n* відмовка vidmovka
prettiness *n.* миловидність
mylovydnist
pretty *a* гарненький harnenkyi
pretty *adv.* досить dosyt
prevail *v.i.* існувати isnuvaty
prevalence *n.* панування
panuvannia
prevalent *a.* поширений
poshyrenyi
prevent *v.t.* запобігати zapobihaty
prevention *n.* відвернення
vidvernennia

preventive *a.* превентивний preventyvnyi

previous *a.* передчасний peredchasnyi

prey *n.* награбоване nahrabovane

prey *v.i.* терзати terzaty

price *v.t.* оцінювати otsiniuvaty

price *n.* ціна tsina

prick *v.t.* наколоти nakoloty

prick *n.* колоти koloty

pride *n.* гордість hordist

pride *v.t.* пишатися pyshatysia

priest *n.* священик sviashchenyk

priestess *n.* жриця zhrytsia

priesthood *n.* священство sviashchenstvo

prima facie *adv.* на перший погляд na pershyi pohliad

primarily *adv.* в першу чергу v pershu cherhu

primary *a.* первинний pervynnyi

prime *a.* квітучий kvituchyi

prime *n.* початок pochatok

primer *n.* ґрунтовка hruntovka

primeval *a.* первісний pervisnyi

primitive *a.* примітивний prymityvnyi

prince *n.* принц prynts

princely *a.* князівський kniazivskyi

princess *n.* принцеса pryntsesa

principal *n.* директор dyrektor

principal *a* провідний providnyi

principle *n.* принцип pryntsyp

print *n* друк druk

print *v.t.* друкувати drukuvaty

printer *n.* принтер prynter

prior *n* настоятель nastoiatel

prior *a.* вагоміший vahomishyi

prioress *n.* настоятелька nastoiatelka

priority *n.* старшинство starshynstvo

prison *n.* тюрма tiurma

prisoner *n.* ув'язнений uviaznenyi

privacy *n.* усамітнення usamitnennia

private *a.* приватний pryvatnyi

privation *n.* відсутність vidsutnist

privilege *n.* привілей pryvilei

prize *v.t.* високо цінувати vysoko tsinuvaty

prize *n.* приз pryz

probability *n.* можливість mozhlyvist

probable *a.* правдоподібний pravdopodibnyi

probably *adv.* ймовірно ymovirno

probation *n.* випробний термін vyprobnyi termin

probationer *n.* стажист stazhyst

probe *n* зонд zond

probe *v.t.* прощупувати proshchupuvaty

problem *n.* задача zadacha

problematic *a.* проблематичний problematychnyi

procedure *n.* процедура protsedura

proceed *v.i.* продовжити prodovzhyty

proceeding *n.* судовчинство sudovchynstvo

proceeds *n.* виручка vyruchka

process *n.* процес protses

procession *n.* процесія protsesiia

proclaim *v.t.* проголошувати proholoshuvaty

proclamation *n.* проголошення proholoshennia

proclivity *n.* схильність skhylnist

procrastinate *v.i.* прострочувати prostrochuvaty

procrastination *n.* зволікання zvolikannia

proctor *n.* проктор proktor

procure *v.t.* роздобути rozdobuty
procurement *n.* постачання postachannia
prodigal *a.* надмірний nadmirnyi
prodigality *n.* велика кількість velyka kilkist
produce *v.t.* виробляти vyrobliaty
produce *n.* продукція produktsiia
product *n.* продукт produkt
production *n.* продукція produktsiia
productive *a.* продуктивний produktyvnyi
productivity *n.* продуктивність produktyvnist
profane *v.t.* оскверняти oskverniaty
profane *a.* світський svitskyi
profess *v.t.* сповідувати spoviduvaty
profession *n.* професія profesiia
professional *a.* професійний profesiinyi
professor *n.* професор profesor
proficiency *n.* уміння uminnia
proficient *a.* обізнаний obiznanyi
profile *v.t.* профанувати profanuvaty
profile *n.* профіль profil
profit *n.* вигода vyhoda
profit *v.t.* нажити nazhyty
profitable *a.* корисний korysnyi
profiteer *v.i.* спекулювати spekuliuvaty
profiteer *n.* спекулянт spekuliant
profligacy *n.* розпуста rozpusta
profligate *a.* розпусний rozpusnyi
profound *a.* море more
profundity *n.* безодня bezodnia
profuse *a.* рясний riasnyi
profusion *n.* велика кількість velyka kilkist
progeny *n.* наслідок naslidok

programme *v.t.* запрограмувати zaprohramuvaty
programme *n.* програма prohrama
progress *n.* прогрес prohres
progress *v.i.* прогресувати prohresuvaty
progressive *a.* прогресивний prohresyvnyi
prohibit *v.t.* заважати zavazhaty
prohibition *n.* заборона zaborona
prohibitive *a.* заборонний zaboronnyi
prohibitory *a.* забороняючий zaboroniaiuchyi
project *v.t.* програма prohrama
project *n.* проект proekt
projectile *a* метальний metalnyi
projectile *n.* снаряд snariad
projection *n.* проекція proektsiia
projector *n.* проектор proektor
proliferate *v.i.* швидко поширюватися shvydko poshyriuvatysia
proliferation *n.* швидке збільшення shvydke zbilshennia
prolific *a.* плідний plidnyi
prologue *n.* пролог proloh
prolong *v.t.* продовжити prodovzhyty
prolongation *n.* відстрочка vidstrochka
prominence *n.* опуклість opuklist
prominent *a.* видний vydnyi
promise *v.t* обіцяти obitsiaty
promise *n* обіцянка obitsianka
promising *a.* багатообіцяючий bahatoobitsiaiuchyi
promissory *a.* який містить зобов'язання yakyi mistyt zoboviazannia
promote *v.t.* сприяти spryiaty

promotion *n.* просування prosuvannia

prompt *v.t.* спонукати sponukaty

prompt *a.* швидкий shvydkyi

prompter *n.* суфлер sufler

prone *a.* схильний skhylnyi

pronoun *n.* займенник zaimennyk

pronounce *v.t.* вимовляти vymovliaty

pronunciation *n.* вимова vymova

proof *n.* доказ dokaz

proof *a* непроникний nepronyknyi

prop *n.* підпірка pidpirka

prop *v.t.* підпирати pidpyraty

propaganda *n.* пропаганда propahanda

propagandist *n.* пропагандист propahandyst

propagate *v.t.* плодити plodyty

propagation *n.* розведення rozvedennia

propel *v.t.* стимулювати stymuliuvaty

proper *a.* належний nalezhnyi

property *n.* майно maino

prophecy *n.* пророцтво prorotstvo

prophesy *v.t.* пророкувати prorokuvaty

prophet *n.* пророк prorok

prophetic *a.* пророчий prorochyi

proportion *v.t.* розміряти rozmiriaty

proportion *n.* пропорція proportsiia

proportional *a.* пропорційний proportsiinyi

proportionate *a.* співрозмірний spivrozmirnyi

proposal *n.* освідчення osvidchennia

propose *v.t.* висувати vysuvaty

proposition *n.* справа sprava

propound *v.t.* висувати vysuvaty

proprietary *a.* власницький vlasnytskyi

proprietor *n.* господар hospodar

propriety *n.* доречність dorechnist

prorogue *v.t.* відстрочувати vidstrochuvaty

prosaic *a.* прозаїчний prozaichnyi

prose *n.* проза proza

prosecute *v.t.* переслідувати в судовому порядку peresliduvaty v sudovomu poriadku

prosecution *n.* кримінальне переслідування kryminalne peresliduvannia

prosecutor *n.* обвинувач obvynuvach

prosody *n.* просодія prosodiia

prospect *n.* панорама panorama

prospective *a.* перспективний perspektyvnyi

prospectus *n.* публікація publikatsiia

prosper *v.i.* процвітати protsvitaty

prosperity *n.* процвітання protsvitannia

prosperous *a.* процвітаючий protsvitaiuchyi

prostitute *v.t.* займатися проституцією zaimatysia prostytutsiieiu

prostitute *n.* проститутка prostytutka

prostitution *n.* проституція prostytutsiia

prostrate *v.t.* падати ниць padaty nyts

prostrate *a.* розпростертий rozprostertyi

prostration *n.* прострація prostratsiia

protagonist *n.* поборник pobornyk

protect *v.t.* захищати zakhyshchaty

protection *n.* протегування protehuvannia

protective *a.* захисний zakhysnyi

protector *n.* захисник zakhysnyk

protein *n.* білок bilok

protest *n.* протест protest

protest *v.i.* протестувати protestuvaty

protestation *n.* опротестування oprotestuvannia

prototype *n.* прототип prototyp

proud *a.* гордий hordyi

prove *v.t.* доводити dovodyty

proverb *n.* прислів'я pryslivia

proverbial *a.* провербіальний proverbialnyi

provide *v.i.* подавати podavaty

providence *n.* провидіння provydinnia

provident *a.* завбачливий zavbachlyvyi

providential *a.* провіденціальне providentsialne

province *n.* провінція provintsiia

provincial *a.* провінційний provintsiinyi

provincialism *n.* провінціалізм provintsializm

provision *n.* надання nadannia

provisional *a.* тимчасовий tymchasovyi

proviso *n.* умова umova

provocation *n.* провокація provokatsiia

provocative *a.* провокаційний provokatsiinyi

provoke *v.t.* провокувати provokuvaty

prowess *n.* доблесть doblest

proximate *a.* найближчий naiblyzhchyi

proximity *n.* близькість blyzkist

proxy *n.* довіреність dovirenist

prude *n.* ханжа khanzha

prudence *n.* розсудливість rozsudlyvist

prudent *a.* ощадливий oshchadlyvyi

prudential *a.* розважливий rozvazhlyvyi

prune *v.t.* підрізати pidrizaty

pry *v.i.* зламувати zlamuvaty

psalm *n.* псалом psalom

pseudonym *n.* псевдонім psevdonim

psyche *n.* дух dukh

psychiatrist *n.* психіатр psykhiatr

psychiatry *n.* психіатрія psykhiatriia

psychic *a.* психічний psykhichnyi

psychological *a.* психологічний psykholohichnyi

psychologist *n.* психолог psykholoh

psychology *n.* психологія psykholohiia

psychopath *n.* психопат psykhopat

psychosis *n.* психоз psykhoz

psychotherapy *n.* психотерапія psykhoterapiia

puberty *n.* статева зрілість stateva zrilist

public *a.* громадський hromadskyi

public *n.* громадськість hromadskist

publication *n.* опублікування opublikuvannia

publicity *n.* гласність hlasnist

publicize *v.t.* оголошувати oholoshuvaty

publish *v.t.* публікувати
publikuvaty
publisher *n.* видавець vydavets
pudding *n.* пудинг pudynh
puddle *v.t.* каламутити
kalamutyty
puddle *n.* калюжа kaliuzha
puerile *a.* незрілий nezrilyi
puff *v.i.* вдувати vduvaty
puff *n.* слойка sloika
pull *v.t.* дути поривами duty
poryvamy
pull *n.* смикання smykannia
pulley *n.* шків shkiv
pullover *n.* пуловер pulover
pulp *n.* м'якоть плоду miakot
plodu
pulp *v.t.* перетворити на м'яку
масу peretvoryty na miaku
masu
pulpit *a.* кафедра kafedra
pulpy *a.* м'ясистий miasystyi
pulsate *v.i.* пульсувати pulsuvaty
pulsation *n.* пульсація pulsatsiia
pulse *n.* пульс puls
pulse *v.i.* битися bytysia
pump *n.* насос nasos
pump *v.t.* працювати насосом
pratsiuvaty nasosom
pumpkin *n.* гарбуз harbuz
pun *n.* каламбур kalambur
pun *v.i.* каламбурити kalamburyty
punch *v.t.* пробити probyty
punch *n.* пунш punsh
punctual *a.* пунктуальний
punktualnyi
punctuality *n.* точність tochnist
punctuate *v.t.* перемежовувати
peremezhovuvaty
punctuation *n.* пунктуація
punktuatsiia
puncture *n.* прокол prokol

puncture *v.t.* пробивати отвір
probyvaty otvir
pungency *n.* їдкість yidkist
pungent *a.* гострокінцевий
hostrokintsevyi
punish *v.t.* карати karaty
punishment *n.* покарання
pokarannia
punitive *a.* каральний karalnyi
puny *a.* незначний neznachnyi
pupil *n.* зіниця zinytsia
puppet *n.* лялька lialka
puppy *n.* цуценя tsutsenia
purblind *n.* підсліпуватий
pidslipuvatyi
purchase *v.t.* купівля kupivlia
purchase *n.* покупка pokupka
pure *a* чистий chystyi
purgation *n.* очищення
кишечника ochyshchennia
kyshechnyka
purgative *n.* проносне pronosne
purgative *a* очисний ochysnyi
purgatory *n.* чистилище
chystylyshche
purge *v.t.* прочищати
prochyshchaty
purification *n.* ректифікація
rektyfikatsiia
purify *v.t.* очищатися
ochyshchatysia
purist *n.* пурист puryst
puritan *n.* пуританин purytanyn
puritanical *a.* пуританський
purytanskyi
purity *n.* чистота chystota
purple *adj.* фіолетовий fioletovyi
purport *n.* сенс sens
purpose *v.t.* замишляти
zamyshliaty
purpose *n.* намір namir
purposely *adv.* навмисно
navmysno

purr *n.* муркотання murkotannia
purr *v.i.* муркотіти murkotity
purse *v.t.* піджати pidzhaty
purse *n.* ридикюль rydykiul
pursuance *n.* переслідування
  peresliduvannia
pursue *v.t.* проводити provodyty
pursuit *n.* гонитва honytva
purview *n.* компетенція
  kompetentsiia
pus *n.* гній hnii
push *n.* поштовх poshtovkh
push *v.t.* штовхати shtovkhaty
put *v.t.* покласти poklasty
puzzle *n.* головоломка
  holovolomka
puzzle *v.t.* приводити в складне
  становище pryvodyty v skladne
  stanovyshche
pygmy *n.* карликовий karlykovyi
pyorrhoea *n.* піорея pioreia
pyramid *n.* піраміда piramida
pyre *n.* похоронне багаття
  pokhoronne bahattia
python *n.* пітон piton

quack *n* шарлатан sharlatan
quack *v.i.* крякати kriakaty
quackery *n.* шарлатанство
  sharlatanstvo
quadrangle *n.* чотирикутник
  chotyrykutnyk
quadrangular *a.* чотирикутний
  chotyrykutnyi
quadrilateral *a.* чотирикутний
  chotyrykutnyi
quadruped *n.* чотиринога
  тварина chotyrynoha tvaryna
quadruple *v.t.* множити на
  чотири mnozhyty na chotyry

quadruple *a.* четверний
  chetvernyi
quail *n.* перепел perepel
quaint *a.* химерний khymernyi
quake *n* тремтіння tremtinnia
quake *v.i.* тремтіти tremtity
qualification *n.* кваліфікація
  kvalifikatsiia
qualify *v.i.* кваліфікувати
  kvalifikuvaty
qualitative *a.* якісний yakisnyi
quality *n.* якість yakist
quandary *n.* скрутне становище
  skrutne stanovyshche
quantitative *a.* кількісний kilkisnyi
quantity *n.* кількість kilkist
quantum *n.* квантовий kvantovyi
quarrel *v.i.* сваритися svarytysia
quarrel *n.* сварка svarka
quarrelsome *a.* нісенітний
  nisenitnyi
quarry *v.i.* розробляти кар'єр
  rozrobliaty karier
quarry *n.* кар'єр karier
quarter *v.t.* розділити на чотири
  rozdilyty na chotyry
quarter *n.* чверть chvert
quarterly *a.* щоквартальний
  shchokvartalnyi
queen *n.* королева koroleva
queer *a.* дивний dyvnyi
quell *v.t.* заспокоювати
  zaspokoiuvaty
quench *v.t.* гартувати hartuvaty
query *v.t* піддавати сумніву
  piddavaty sumnivu
query *n.* сумнів sumniv
quest *v.t* здійснювати пошук
  zdiisniuvaty poshuk
quest *n.* пошук poshuk
question *v.t.* питати pytaty
question *n.* питання pytannia

questionable *a.* сумнівний sumnivnyi
questionnaire *n.* анкета anketa
queue *n.* черга cherha
quibble *v.i.* викрутас vykrutas
quibble *n.* ігра слів ihra sliv
quick *n* жива огорожа zhyva ohorozha
quick *a.* швидкий shvydkyi
quicksand *n.* пливун plyvun
quicksilver *n.* ртуть rtut
quiet *n.* мовчання movchannia
quiet *v.t.* стихнути stykhnuty
quiet *a.* тихий tykhyi
quilt *n.* стьобана ковдра stobana kovdra
quinine *n.* хінін khinin
quintessence *n.* квінтесенція kvintesentsiia
quit *v.t.* звільняти zvilniaty
quite *adv.* цілком tsilkom
quiver *v.i.* тріпотіти tripotity
quiver *n.* трепет trepet
quixotic *a.* донкіхотський donkikhotskyi
quiz *v.t.* провести опитування provesty opytuvannia
quiz *n.* вікторина viktoryna
quorum *n.* кворум kvorum
quota *n.* квота kvota
quotation *n.* цитата tsytata
quote *v.t.* цитувати tsytuvaty
quotient *n.* показник pokaznyk

R

rabato *n.* великий відкладний комір velykyi vidkladnyi komir
rabbit *n.* кролик krolyk
rabies *n.* сказ skaz
race *v.i* брати участь у скачках braty uchast u skachkakh
race *n.* гонки honky

racial *a.* расовий rasovyi
racialism *n.* расизм rasyzm
rack *n.* стелаж stelazh
rack *v.t.* класти на полицю klasty na polytsiu
racket *n.* рекет reket
radiance *n.* сяйво siaivo
radiant *a.* променистий promenystyi
radiate *v.t.* випромінювати vyprominiuvaty
radiation *n.* радіація radiatsiia
radical *a.* радикальний radykalnyi
radio *v.t.* передавати по радіо peredavaty po radio
radio *n.* радіо radio
radish *n.* редис redys
radium *n.* радій radii
radius *n.* радіус radius
rag *v.t.* дражнити drazhnyty
rag *n.* клапоть klapot
rage *v.i.* бушувати bushuvaty
rage *n.* скаженість skazhenist
raid *v.t.* здійснювати набіг zdiisniuvaty nabih
raid *n.* рейд reid
rail *v.t.* їхати залізницею yikhaty zaliznytseiu
rail *n.* перила peryla
railing *n.* поруччя poruchchia
raillery *n.* жарти zharty
railway *n.* залізниця zaliznytsia
rain *n* дощ doshch
rain *v.i.* литися lytysia
rainy *a.* дощовий doshchovyi
raise *v.t.* підвищення pidvyshchennia
raisin *n.* ізюм izium
rally *n* обʼєднання obiiednannia
rally *v.t.* оволодіти собою ovolodity soboiu
ram *v.t.* таранити taranyty
ram *n.* баран baran

ramble *n.* прогулянка prohulianka
ramble *v.t.* блукати без мети blukaty bez mety
rampage *n.* шаленство shalenstvo
rampage *v.i.* шаленіти shalenity
rampant *a.* нестямний nestiamnyi
rampart *n.* вал val
rancour *n.* злопам'ятність zlopamiatnist
random *a.* безладний bezladnyi
range *n.* діапазон diapazon
range *v.t.* ставити по порядку stavyty po poriadku
ranger *n.* лісничий lisnychyi
rank *a.* родючий rodiuchyi
rank *v.t.* шикувати в шеренгу shykuvaty v sherenhu
rank *n.* ранг ranh
ransack *v.t.* розграбувати rozhrabuvaty
ransom *v.t.* викуповувати vykupovuvaty
ransom *n.* викуп vykup
rape *v.t.* гвалтувати hvaltuvaty
rape *n.* згвалтування zhvaltuvannia
rapid *a.* швидкий shvydkyi
rapidity *n.* швидкість shvydkist
rapier *n.* рапіра rapira
rapport *n.* взаєморозуміння vzaiemorozuminnia
rapt *a.* зосереджений zoseredzhenyi
rapture *n.* вияв захоплення vyiav zakhoplennia
rare *a.* рідкісний ridkisnyi
rascal *n.* шахрай shakhrai
rash *a.* необачний neobachnyi
rat *n.* щур shchur
rate *n.* ставка stavka
rate *v.t.* обчислювати obchysliuvaty

rather *adv.* швидше shvydshe
ratify *v.t.* ратифікувати ratyfikuvaty
ratio *n.* співвідношення spivvidnoshennia
ration *n.* раціон ratsion
rational *a.* розсудливий rozsudlyvyi
rationale *n.* логічне пояснення lohichne poiasnennia
rationality *n.* раціональність ratsionalnist
rationalize *v.t.* раціоналізувати ratsionalizuvaty
rattle *n* брязкальце briazkaltse
rattle *v.i.* тріщати trishchaty
ravage *v.t.* спустошувати spustoshuvaty
ravage *n.* спустошення spustoshennia
rave *v.i.* марити maryty
raven *n.* ворон voron
ravine *n.* ущелина ushchelyna
raw *a.* неварений nevarenyi
ray *n.* проблиск problysk
raze *v.t.* зрівняти із землею zrivniaty iz zemleiu
razor *n.* бритва brytva
reach *v.t.* надходити nadkhodyty
react *v.i.* реагувати reahuvaty
reaction *n.* реакція reaktsiia
reactionary *a.* реакційний reaktsiinyi
read *v.t.* читати chytaty
reader *n.* читач chytach
readily *adv.* з готовністю z hotovnistiu
readiness *n.* спритність sprytnist
ready *a.* готовий hotovyi
real *a.* реальний realnyi
realism *n.* реалізм realizm
realist *n.* реаліст realist

realistic *a.* реалістичний realistychnyi

reality *n.* реальність realnist

realization *n.* реалізація realizatsiia

realize *v.t.* здійснити zdiisnyty

really *adv.* насправді naspravdi

realm *n.* королівство korolivstvo

ream *n.* накип nakyp

reap *v.t.* пожинати pozhynaty

reaper *n.* жнець zhnets

rear *v.t.* споруджувати sporudzhuvaty

rear *n.* огузок ohuzok

reason *v.i.* мислити myslyty

reason *n.* причина prychyna

reasonable *a.* обґрунтований obgruntovanyi

reassure *v.t.* переконувати perekonuvaty

rebel *v.i.* піднімати заколот pidnimaty zakolot

rebel *n.* бунтівник buntivnyk

rebellion *n.* бунт bunt

rebellious *a.* востанський vostanskyi

rebirth *n.* метемпсихоз metempsykhoz

rebound *n.* відскок vidskok

rebound *v.i.* рікошетувати rikoshetuvaty

rebuff *v.t.* давати відсіч davaty vidsich

rebuff *n.* відсіч vidsich

rebuke *n.* догана dohana

rebuke *v.t.* дорікати dorikaty

recall *n.* відкликання vidklykannia

recall *v.t.* відкликати vidklykaty

recede *v.i.* відступати vidstupaty

receipt *n.* отримання otrymannia

receive *v.t.* отримувати otrymuvaty

receiver *n.* одержувач oderzhuvach

recent *a.* останній ostannii

recently *adv.* недавно nedavno

reception *n.* прийом pryiom

receptive *a.* сприйнятливий spryiniatlyvyi

recess *n.* відокремлене місце vidokremlene mistse

recession *n.* рецесія retsesiia

recipe *n.* рецепт retsept

recipient *n.* реципієнт retsypiient

reciprocal *a.* аналогічний analohichnyi

reciprocate *v.t.* відповідати взаємністю vidpovidaty vzaiemnistiu

recital *n.* сольний концерт solnyi kontsert

recitation *n.* декламація deklamatsiia

recite *v.t.* декламувати deklamuvaty

reckless *a.* безрозсудний bezrozsudnyi

reckon *v.t.* підраховувати pidrakhovuvaty

reclaim *v.t.* робити кращим robyty krashchym

reclamation *n* виправлення vypravlennia

recluse *n.* самітник samitnyk

recognition *n.* дізнавання diznavannia

recognize *v.t.* дізнаватися diznavatysia

recoil *n.* віддача viddacha

recoil *v.i.* відскочити vidskochyty

recollect *v.t.* знову зібрати znovu zibraty

recollection *n.* спогад spohad

recommend *v.t.* радити radyty

recommendation *n.*
рекомендація rekomendatsiia
recompense *n.* відшкодування
vidshkoduvannia
recompense *v.t.*
винагороджувати
vynahorodzhuvaty
reconcile *v.t.* примиряти
prymyriaty
reconciliation *n.* примирення
prymyrennia
record *n.* запис zapys
record *v.t.* записувати zapysuvaty
recorder *n.* реєстратор reiestrator
recount *v.t.* розповідати
rozpovidaty
recoup *v.t.* відшкодувати
vidshkoduvaty
recourse *n.* звернення
zvernennia
recover *v.t.* видужувати
vyduzhuvaty
recovery *n.* відшкодування
vidshkoduvannia
recreation *n.* відпочинок
vidpochynok
recruit *v.t.* вербувати verbuvaty
recruit *n.* призовник pryzovnyk
rectangle *n.* прямокутник
priamokutnyk
rectangular *a.* прямокутний
priamokutnyi
rectification *n.* випрямлення
vypriamlennia
rectify *v.i.* ректіфікувати
rektifikuvaty
rectum *n.* пряма кишка priama
kyshka
recur *v.i.* рецидивувати
retsydyvuvaty
recurrence *n.* рецидив retsydyv
recurrent *a.* повторюваний
povtoriuvanyi

red *n.* червоний колір chervonyi
kolir
red *a.* червоний chervonyi
redden *v.t.* червоніти chervonity
reddish *a.* червонуватий
chervonuvatyi
redeem *v.t.* виплачувати
vyplachuvaty
redemption *n.* погашення
pohashennia
redouble *v.t.* подвоїти podvoity
redress *n* відшкодування
vidshkoduvannia
redress *v.t.* відновлювати
vidnovliuvaty
reduce *v.t.* зменшити zmenshyty
reduction *n.* перетворення
peretvorennia
redundance *n.* надмірність
nadmirnist
redundant *a.* надлишковий
nadlyshkovyi
reel *v.i.* мотати motaty
reel *n.* котушка kotushka
refer *v.t.* послатися poslatysia
referee *n.* судовий розпорядник
sudovyi rozporiadnyk
reference *n.* довідка dovidka
referendum *n.* референдум
referendum
refine *v.t.* удосконалювати
udoskonaliuvaty
refinement *n.* вишуканість
vyshukanist
refinery *n.* очисний завод
ochysnyi zavod
reflect *v.t.* відображати
vidobrazhaty
reflection *n.* відображення
vidobrazhennia
reflective *a.* рефлективний
reflektyvnyi
reflector *n.* відбивач vidbyvach

reflex *a* рефлекторний
reflektornyi
reflex *n.* рефлекс refleks
reflexive *a* зворотний zvorotnyi
reform *n.* реформа reforma
reform *v.t.* реформувати
reformuvaty
reformation *n.* реформування
reformuvannia
reformatory *n.* виправний заклад
vypravnyi zaklad
reformatory *a* виправний
vypravnyi
reformer *n.* реформатор
reformator
refrain *n* приспів pryspiv
refrain *v.i.* утримуватися
utrymuvatysia
refresh *v.t.* оновити onovyty
refreshment *n.* закуски та напої
zakusky ta napoi
refrigerate *v.t.* охолодити
okholodyty
refrigeration *n.* охолодження
okholodzhennia
refrigerator *n.* холодильник
kholodylnyk
refuge *n.* сховище skhovyshche
refugee *n.* біженець bizhenets
refulgence *n.* сяйво siaivo
refulgent *a.* сяючий siaiuchyi
refund *v.t.* відшкодовувати
vidshkodovuvaty
refund *n.* повертати гроші
povertaty hroshi
refusal *n.* опціон optsion
refuse *v.t.* відмовляти vidmovliaty
refuse *n.* покидьки pokydky
refutation *n.* спростування
sprostuvannia
refute *v.t.* спростувати
sprostuvaty
regal *a.* королівський korolivskyi

regard *n.* увага uvaha
regard *v.t.* розцінювати
roztsiniuvaty
regenerate *v.t.* регенерувати
reheneruvaty
regeneration *n.* регенерація
reheneratsiia
regicide *n.* царевбивство
tsarevbyvstvo
regime *n.* державний стрій
derzhavnyi strii
regiment *n.* полк polk
regiment *v.t.* формувати полк
formuvaty polk
region *n.* регіон rehion
regional *a.* регіональний
rehionalnyi
register *n.* реєстр reiestr
register *v.t.* реєструвати
reiestruvaty
registrar *n.* утримувач реєстру
utrymuvach reiestru
registration *n.* реєстрація
reiestratsiia
registry *n.* реєстратура
reiestratura
regret *n* жаль zhal
regret *v.i.* жалкувати zhalkuvaty
regular *a.* регулярний rehuliarnyi
regularity *n.* регулярність
rehuliarnist
regulate *v.t.* урегульовувати
urehulovuvaty
regulation *n.* норма norma
regulator *n.* регулятор rehuliator
rehabilitate *v.t.* реабілітувати
reabilituvaty
rehabilitation *n.* реабілітація
reabilitatsiia
rehearsal *n.* репетиція repetytsiia
rehearse *v.t.* репетирувати
repetyruvaty
reign *n* князювання kniaziuvannia

reign *v.i.* царювати tsariuvaty
reimburse *v.t.* сплачувати splachuvaty
rein *v.t.* правити pravyty
rein *n.* поводи povody
reinforce *v.t.* посилювати posyliuvaty
reinforcement *n.* армування armuvannia
reinstate *v.t.* відновлювати vidnovliuvaty
reinstatement *n.* відновлення vidnovlennia
reiterate *v.t.* повторити povtoryty
reiteration *n.* повторення povtorennia
reject *v.t.* відкидати vidkydaty
rejection *n.* неприйняття nepryiniattia
rejoice *v.i.* радіти radity
rejoin *v.t.* приєднатися pryiednatysia
rejoinder *n.* відповідь vidpovid
rejuvenate *v.t.* омолоджуватися omolodzhuvatysia
rejuvenation *n.* омолодження omolodzhennia
relapse *n.* повторення povtorennia
relapse *v.i.* знову робити znovu robyty
relate *v.t.* ставитися stavytysia
relation *n.* родичка rodychka
relative *n.* родич rodych
relative *a.* відносний vidnosnyi
relax *v.t.* розслаблятися rozslabliatysia
relaxation *n.* релаксація relaksatsiia
relay *v.t.* зміняти zminiaty
relay *n.* реле rele
release *n* звільнення zvilnennia

release *v.t.* дозволяти демонстрування dozvoliaty demonstruvannia
relent *v.i.* пом'якшуватися pomiakshuvatysia
relentless *a.* невідступний nevidstupnyi
relevance *n.* релевантність relevantnist
relevant *a.* релевантний relevantnyi
reliable *a.* надійний nadiinyi
reliance *n.* надія nadiia
relic *n.* реліквія relikviia
relief *n.* полегшення polehshennia
relieve *v.t.* позбавляти pozbavliaty
religion *n.* релігія relihiia
religious *a.* релігійний relihiinyi
relinquish *v.t.* відмовлятися vidmovliatysia
relish *n* насолода nasoloda
relish *v.t.* насолоджуватися nasolodzhuvatysia
reluctance *n.* небажання nebazhannia
reluctant *a.* неприхильний neprykhylnyi
rely *v.i.* покладатися pokladatysia
remain *v.i.* залишатися zalyshatysia
remainder *n.* залишок zalyshok
remains *n.* залишки zalyshky
remand *n* відрахування vidrakhuvannia
remand *v.t.* відрахувати vidrakhuvaty
remark *v.t.* помічати pomichaty
remark *n.* зауваження zauvazhennia
remarkable *a.* чудовий chudovyi
remedial *a.* лікувальний likuvalnyi

remedy *n.* відшкодування vidshkoduvannia

remedy *v.t* усувати usuvaty

remember *v.t.* дарувати daruvaty

remembrance *n.* сувенір suvenir

remind *v.t.* нагадувати nahaduvaty

reminder *n.* нагадування nahaduvannia

reminiscence *n.* спогад spohad

reminiscent *a.* нагадуючий nahaduiuchyi

remission *n.* ремісія remisiia

remit *v.t.* пробачити probachyty

remittance *n.* грошовий переказ hroshovyi perekaz

remorse *n.* докори совісті dokory sovisti

remote *a.* віддалений viddalenyi

removable *a.* змінний zminnyi

removal *n.* видалення vydalennia

remove *v.t.* прибирати prybyraty

remunerate *v.t.* оплачувати oplachuvaty

remuneration *n.* оплата праці oplata pratsi

remunerative *a.* вигідний vyhidnyi

renaissance *n.* ренесанс renesans

render *v.t.* віддати viddaty

rendezvous *n.* рандеву randevu

renew *v.t.* відновити vidnovyty

renewal *n.* оновлення onovlennia

renounce *v.t.* зрікатися zrikatysia

renovate *v.t.* реставрувати restavruvaty

renovation *n.* ремонт remont

renown *n.* слава slava

renowned *a.* знаменитий znamenytyi

rent *v.t.* брати в оренду braty v orendu

rent *n.* просвіт prosvit

renunciation *n.* самозречення samozrechennia

repair *n.* загоєння zahoiennia

repair *v.t.* відправлятися vidpravliatysia

reparable *a.* виправити vypravyty

repartee *n.* дотепна відповідь dotepna vidpovid

repatriate *n* репатріант repatriant

repatriate *v.t.* репатріювати repatriiuvaty

repatriation *n.* репатріація repatriatsiia

repay *v.t.* платити вдруге platyty vdruhe

repayment *n.* сплата splata

repeal *n* скасування skasuvannia

repeal *v.t.* скасовувати skasovuvaty

repeat *v.t.* повторювати povtoriuvaty

repel *v.t.* відштовхувати vidshtovkhuvaty

repellent *n* репелент repelent

repellent *a.* який відштовхує yakyi vidshtovkhuie

repent *v.i.* розкаюватися rozkaiuvatysia

repentance *n.* покаяння pokaiannia

repentant *a.* каянник kaiannyk

repercussion *n.* наслідки naslidky

repetition *n.* копія kopiia

replace *v.t.* замінювати zaminiuvaty

replacement *n.* заміщення zamishchennia

replenish *v.t.* поповнювати popovniuvaty

replete *a.* переповнений perepovnenyi

replica *n.* репродукція reproduktsiia

reply *v.i.* вживати відповідних заходів vzhyvaty vidpovidnykh zakhodiv

reply *n.* відзив vidzyv

report *n.* звіт zvit

report *v.t.* описувати opysuvaty

reporter *n.* репортер reporter

repose *v.i.* давати відпочинок davaty vidpochynok

repose *n.* спокій spokii

repository *n.* сховище skhovyshche

represent *v.t.* зображати zobrazhaty

representation *n.* зображення zobrazhennia

representative *a.* представницький predstavnytskyi

representative *n.* представник predstavnyk

repress *v.t.* класти край klasty krai

repression *n.* репресія represiia

reprimand *v.t.* робити догану robyty dohanu

reprimand *n.* догана dohana

reprint *n.* перевидання perevydannia

reprint *v.t.* передруковувати peredrukovuvaty

reproach *n.* докір dokir

reproach *v.t.* докоряти dokoriaty

reproduce *v.t.* відтворювати vidtvoriuvaty

reproduction *n* відтворення vidtvorennia

reproductive *a.* відтворювальний vidtvoriuvalnyi

reproof *n.* докір dokir

reptile *n.* рептилія reptyliia

republic *n.* республіка respublika

republican *n* республіканець respublikanets

republican *a.* республіканський respublikanskyi

repudiate *v.t.* зрікатися zrikatysia

repudiation *n.* зречення zrechennia

repugnance *n.* антипатія antypatiia

repugnant *a.* нестерпний nesterpnyi

repulse *n.* відмова vidmova

repulse *v.t.* відбивати vidbyvaty

repulsion *n.* відштовхування vidshtovkhuvannia

repulsive *a.* відразливий vidrazlyvyi

reputation *n.* репутація reputatsiia

repute *n.* загальна думка zahalna dumka

repute *v.t.* гадати hadaty

request *n* попит popyt

request *v.t.* попросити poprosyty

requiem *n.* реквієм rekviiem

require *v.t.* наказувати nakazuvaty

requirement *n.* необхідна умова neobkhidna umova

requisite *a.* належний nalezhnyi

requisite *n* потрібне potribne

requisition *n.* офіційне розпорядження ofitsiine rozporiadzhennia

requisition *v.t.* реквізувати rekvizuvaty

requite *v.t.* відплачувати vidplachuvaty

rescue *n* порятунок poriatunok

rescue *v.t.* звільняти zvilniaty

research *v.i.* збирати матеріал zbyraty material

research *n* ретельні пошуки retelni poshuky

resemblance *n.* схожість skhozhist

resemble *v.t.* бути схожим buty skhozhym

resent *v.t.* обурюватися oburiuvatysia

resentment *n.* почуття образи pochuttia obrazy

reservation *n.* резервування rezervuvannia

reserve *v.t.* оберігати oberihaty

reservoir *n.* водойма vodoima

reside *v.i.* проживати prozhyvaty

residence *n.* місце проживання mistse prozhyvannia

resident *n* резидент rezydent

resident *a.* який постійно мешкає yakyi postiino meshkaie

residual *a.* залишковий zalyshkovyi

residue *n.* частина chastyna

resign *v.t.* йти у відставку yty u vidstavku

resignation *n.* відставка vidstavka

resist *v.t.* чинити опір chynyty opir

resistance *n.* опір opir

resistant *a.* стійкий stiikyi

resolute *a.* непохитний nepokhytnyi

resolution *n.* рішучість rishuchist

resolve *v.t.* рішати rishaty

resonance *n.* резонанс rezonans

resonant *a.* резонансний rezonansnyi

resort *v.i.* вдаватися vdavatysia

resort *n* курорт kurort

resound *v.i.* звучати zvuchaty

resource *n.* ресурс resurs

resourceful *a.* спритний sprytnyi

respect *n.* повага povaha

respect *v.t.* шанувати shanuvaty

respectful *a.* шанобливий shanoblyvyi

respective *a.* турботливий turbotlyvyi

respiration *n.* вдих vdykh

respire *v.i.* вдихати vdykhaty

resplendent *a.* сяючий siaiuchyi

respond *v.i.* робити що-небудь у відповідь robyty shcho-nebud u vidpovid

respondent *n.* відповідач vidpovidach

response *n.* реагування reahuvannia

responsibility *n.* підопічний pidopichnyi

responsible *a.* важливий vazhlyvyi

rest *v.i.* відпочивати vidpochyvaty

rest *n* сон son

restaurant *n.* ресторан restoran

restive *a.* норовливий norovlyvyi

restoration *n.* ресторація restoratsiia

restore *v.t.* повертати povertaty

restrain *v.t.* стримувати strymuvaty

restrict *v.t.* тримати в певних межах trymaty v pevnykh mezhakh

restriction *n.* обмеження obmezhennia

restrictive *a.* обмежувальний obmezhuvalnyi

result *v.i.* витікати vytikaty

result *n.* результат rezultat

resume *v.t.* брати назад braty nazad

resume *n.* резюме reziume

resumption *n.* поверенння poverennnia

resurgence *n.* відродження
vidrodzhennia
resurgent *a.* який відроджується
yakyi vidrodzhuietsia
retail *adv.* в роздріб v rozdrib
retail *v.t.* продавати в роздріб
prodavaty v rozdrib
retail *n.* роздрібна торгівля
rozdribna torhivlia
retail *a* роздрібний rozdribnyi
retailer *n.* роздрібний торговець
rozdribnyi torhovets
retain *v.t.* оберігати oberihaty
retaliate *v.i.* помститися
pomstytysia
retaliation *n.* відплата vidplata
retard *v.t.* сповільнювати
spovilniuvaty
retardation *n.* уповільнення
upovilnennia
retention *n.* утримання
utrymannia
retentive *a.* який зберігає yakyi
zberihaie
reticence *n.* скритність skrytnist
reticent *a.* стриманий strymanyi
retina *n.* сітківка sitkivka
retinue *n.* свита svyta
retire *v.i.* йти на пенсію yty na
pensiiu
retirement *n.* вихід на пенсію
vykhid na pensiiu
retort *n.* заперечення
zaperechennia
retort *v.t.* різко заперечувати
rizko zaperechuvaty
retouch *v.t.* ретушувати
retushuvaty
retrace *v.t.* відновлювати у
пам`яті vidnovliuvaty u pam`iati
retread *v.t.* відновити протектор
vidnovyty protektor

retread *n.* новий протектор novyi
protektor
retreat *v.i.* відійти vidiity
retrench *v.t.* урізувати urizuvaty
retrenchment *n.* скорочення
skorochennia
retrieve *v.t.* витягувати
vytiahuvaty
retrospect *n.* погляд назад
pohliad nazad
retrospection *n.* ретроспекція
retrospektsiia
retrospective *a.* ретроспективний
retrospektyvnyi
return *n.* повернення
povernennia
return *v.i.* повернути povernuty
revel *n.* гуляння huliannia
revel *v.i.* пиячити pyiachyty
revelation *n.* одкровення
odkrovennia
reveller *n.* гуляка huliaka
revelry *n.* пиятика pyiatyka
revenge *v.t.* жадоба помсти
zhadoba pomsty
revenge *n.* помста pomsta
revengeful *a.* мстивий mstyvyi
revenue *n.* доходи dokhody
revere *v.t.* почитати pochytaty
reverence *n.* шанування
shanuvannia
reverend *a.* преподобний
prepodobnyi
reverent *a.* благоговійний
blahohoviinyi
reverential *a.* шанобливий
shanoblyvyi
reverie *n.* мрійливість mriilyvist
reversal *n.* анулювання
anuliuvannia
reverse *a.* зворотний zvorotnyi
reverse *v.t.* обертати obertaty

reverse *n* оборотна сторона oborotna storona
reversible *a.* реверсивний reversyvnyi
revert *v.i.* повертатися povertatysia
review *n* розгляд rozhliad
review *v.t.* оглядати ohliadaty
revise *v.t.* переглядати perehliadaty
revision *n.* перегляд perehliad
revival *n.* повернення до життя povernennia do zhyttia
revive *v.i.* відроджувати vidrodzhuvaty
revocable *a.* який підлягає скасуванню yakyi pidliahaie skasuvanniu
revocation *n.* ревокація revokatsiia
revoke *v.t.* брати назад braty nazad
revolt *v.i.* повставати povstavaty
revolt *n.* опір opir
revolution *n.* революція revoliutsiia
revolutionary *a.* революційний revoliutsiinyi
revolutionary *n* революціонер revoliutsioner
revolve *v.i.* обертатися obertatysia
revolver *n.* револьвер revolver
reward *n.* винагорода vynahoroda
reward *v.t.* винагороджувати vynahorodzhuvaty
rhetoric *n.* риторика rytoryka
rhetorical *a.* риторичний rytorychnyi
rheumatic *a.* ревматичний revmatychnyi
rheumatism *n.* ревматизм revmatyzm

rhinoceros *n.* носоріг nosorih
rhyme *n.* рима ryma
rhyme *v.i.* римувати rymuvaty
rhymester *n.* віршомаз virshomaz
rhythm *b.* ритм rytm
rhythmic *a.* ритмічний rytmichnyi
rib *n.* ребро rebro
ribbon *n.* стрічка strichka
rice *n.* рис rys
rich *a.* родючий rodiuchyi
riches *n.* скарби skarby
richness *n.* поживність pozhyvnist
rick *n.* стіг stih
rickets *n.* рахіт rakhit
rickety *a.* хиткий khytkyi
rickshaw *n.* рикша ryksha
rid *v.t.* рятувати riatuvaty
riddle *v.i.* говорити загадками hovoryty zahadkamy
riddle *n.* решето resheto
ride *n* поїздка poizdka
ride *v.t.* їздити yizdyty
rider *n.* вершник vershnyk
ridge *n.* хребет khrebet
ridicule *n.* насмішка nasmishka
ridicule *v.t.* піднімати на сміх pidnimaty na smikh
ridiculous *a.* смішний smishnyi
rifle *n* гвинтівка hvyntivka
rifle *v.t.* стріляти з гвинтівки striliaty z hvyntivky
rift *n.* тріщина trishchyna
right *v.t.* випрямитися vypriamytysia
right *a.* правий pravyi
right *adv* належним чином nalezhnym chynom
right *n* право pravo
righteous *a.* справедливий spravedlyvyi
rigid *a.* жорсткий zhorstkyi
rigorous *a.* суворий suvoryi

rigour *n.* строгість strohist
rim *n.* обід obid
ring *n.* кільце kiltse
ring *v.t.* оточити кільцем otochyty kiltsem
ringlet *n.* колечко kolechko
ringworm *n.* стригучий лишай stryhuchyi lyshai
rinse *v.t.* прополоскати propoloskaty
riot *v.t.* бешкетувати beshketuvaty
riot *n.* бунт bunt
rip *v.t.* розрізати rozrizaty
ripe *a* стиглий styhlyi
ripen *v.i.* дозрівати dozrivaty
ripple *n.* брижі bryzhi
ripple *v.t.* покривати брижами pokryvaty bryzhamy
rise *v.* вставати vstavaty
rise *n.* підйом pidiom
risk *n.* ризик ryzyk
risk *v.t.* наважуватися navazhuvatysia
risky *a.* ризикований ryzykovanyi
rite *n.* обряд obriad
ritual *n.* ритуал rytual
ritual *a.* ритуальний rytualnyi
rival *n.* суперник supernyk
rival *v.t.* суперничати supernychaty
rivalry *n.* суперництво supernytstvo
river *n.* річка richka
rivet *n.* заклепка zaklepka
rivet *v.t.* клепати klepaty
rivulet *n.* річечка richechka
road *n.* дорога doroha
roam *v.i.* тинятися tyniatysia
roar *n.* рев rev
roar *v.i.* ричати rychaty
roast *n* печеня pechenia
roast *a* смажений smazhenyi
roast *v.t.* смажити smazhyty

rob *v.t.* грабувати hrabuvaty
robber *n.* грабіжник hrabizhnyk
robbery *n.* пограбування pohrabuvannia
robe *v.t.* облачати oblachaty
robe *n.* халат khalat
robot *n.* робот robot
robust *a.* здоровий zdorovyi
rock *v.t.* коливати kolyvaty
rock *n.* скеля skelia
rocket *n.* реактивний снаряд reaktyvnyi snariad
rod *n.* лоза loza
rodent *n.* гризун hryzun
roe *n.* косуля kosulia
rogue *n.* шельма shelma
roguery *n.* шахрайство shakhraistvo
roguish *a.* шахрайський shakhraiskyi
role *n.* роль rol
roll *v.i.* котити kotyty
roll *n.* рулон rulon
roll-call *n.* перекличка pereklychka
roller *n.* валик valyk
romance *n.* романтика romantyka
romantic *a.* романтичний romantychnyi
romp *v.i.* возитися vozytysia
romp *n.* шибеник shybenyk
rood *n.* розп'яття rozpiattia
roof *n.* дах dakh
roof *v.t.* крити kryty
rook *n.* грак hrak
rook *v.t.* обдирати obdyraty
room *n.* приміщення prymishchennia
roomy *a.* місткий mistkyi
roost *v.i.* всістися на сідало vsistysia na sidalo
roost *n.* сідало sidalo
root *n.* корінь korin

root *v.i.* пускати коріння puskaty korinnia
rope *v.t.* зв'язати мотузкою zviazaty motuzkoiu
rope *n.* мотузка motuzka
rosary *n.* розарій rozarii
rose *n.* троянда troianda
roseate *a.* надмірно оптимістичний nadmirno optymistychnyi
rostrum *n.* трибуна trybuna
rosy *a.* рум'яний rumianyi
rot *n.* гниль hnyl
rot *v.i.* гнити hnyty
rotary *a.* обертальний obertalnyi
rotate *v.i.* чергуватися cherhuvatysia
rotation *n.* обертання obertannia
rote *n.* зубріння zubrinnia
rouble *n.* рубль rubl
rough *a.* необроблений neobroblenyi
round *a.* круглий kruhlyi
round *adv.* навколо navkolo
round *v.t.* огинати ohynaty
round *n.* щабель shchabel
rouse *v.i.* сердити serdyty
rout *v.t.* розбити вщент rozbyty vshchent
rout *n* розгром rozhrom
route *n.* маршрут marshrut
routine *a* поточний potochnyi
routine *n.* рутина rutyna
rove *v.i.* блукати blukaty
rover *n.* мандрівник mandrivnyk
row *n* веслування vesluvannia
row *v.t.* гребти hrebty
row *n.* ряд riad
row *n.* провулок provulok
rowdy *a.* буйний buinyi
royal *a.* царський tsarskyi
royalist *n.* рояліст roialist
royalty *n.* роялті roialti

rub *n* розтирання roztyrannia
rub *v.t.* терти terty
rubber *n.* гума huma
rubbish *n.* сміття smittia
rubble *n.* кругляк kruhliak
ruby *n.* рубін rubin
rude *a.* брутальний brutalnyi
rudiment *n.* рудимент rudyment
rudimentary *a.* рудиментарний rudymentarnyi
rue *v.t.* рута ruta
rueful *a.* сумний sumnyi
ruffian *n.* хуліган khulihan
ruffle *v.t.* рябити riabyty
rug *n.* килимок kylymok
rugged *a.* шорсткуватий shorstkuvatyi
ruin *n.* розорення rozorennia
ruin *v.t.* загибель zahybel
rule *v.t.* панувати panuvaty
rule *n.* правило pravylo
ruler *n.* правитель pravytel
ruling *n.* правлячий pravliachyi
rum *n.* ром rom
rum *a* чудний chudnyi
rumble *v.i.* грюкати hriukaty
rumble *n.* гуркіт hurkit
ruminant *a.* жуйний zhuinyi
ruminant *n.* жуйну тварина zhuinu tvaryna
ruminate *v.i.* жувати жуйку zhuvaty zhuiku
rumination *n.* роздум rozdum
rummage *n* пошуки poshuky
rummage *v.i.* ритися rytysia
rummy *n.* алкоголік alkoholik
rumour *v.t.* поширювати чутки poshyriuvaty chutky
rumour *n.* слух slukh
run *v.i.* бігати bihaty
run *n.* втеча vtecha
rung *n.* перекладини perekladyny
runner *n.* бігун bihun

rupee *n.* рупія rupiia
rupture *v.t.* проривати proryvaty
rupture *n.* пробій probii
rural *a.* сільський silskyi
ruse *n.* хитрість khytrist
rush *v.t.* діяти занадто поспішно diiaty zanadto pospishno
rush *n.* очерет ocheret
rush *n* схвалення skhvalennia
rust *n.* іржа irzha
rust *v.i* іржавіти irzhavity
rustic *n* селянин selianyn
rustic *a.* сільський silskyi
rusticate *v.t.* жити в селі zhyty v seli
rustication *n.* оселення в селі oselennia v seli
rusticity *n.* простота prostota
rusty *a.* іржавий irzhavyi
rut *n.* колія koliia
ruthless *a.* нещадний neshchadnyi
rye *n.* жито zhyto

sabbath *n.* шабаш shabash
sabotage *n.* саботаж sabotazh
sabotage *v.t.* саботувати sabotuvaty
sabre *v.t.* рубати шаблею rubaty shableiu
sabre *n.* шабля shablia
saccharin *n.* сахарин sakharyn
saccharine *a.* сахаріновий sakharinovyi
sack *v.t.* знімати з посади znimaty z posady
sack *n.* мішок mishok
sacrament *n.* таїнство tainstvo
sacred *a.* священний sviashchennyi

sacrifice *n.* пожертвування pozhertvuvannia
sacrifice *v.t.* приносити в жертву prynosyty v zhertvu
sacrificial *a.* жертовний zhertovnyi
sacrilege *n.* святотатство sviatotatstvo
sacrilegious *a.* блюзнірський bliuznirskyi
sacrosanct *a.* недоторканний nedotorkannyi
sad *a.* сумний sumnyi
sadden *v.t.* сумовати sumovaty
saddle *v.t.* сідлати sidlaty
saddle *n.* сідло sidlo
sadism *n.* садизм sadyzm
sadist *n.* садист sadyst
safe *a.* безпечний bezpechnyi
safe *n.* сейф seif
safeguard *n.* обережність oberezhnist
safety *n.* безпека bezpeka
saffron *n.* шафран shafran
saffron *a* шафранний shafrannyi
sagacious *a.* прозорливий prozorlyvyi
sagacity *n.* проникливість pronyklyvist
sage *n.* мудрець mudrets
sage *a.* мудрий mudryi
sail *v.i.* йти під вітрилами yty pid vitrylamy
sail *n.* вітрило vitrylo
sailor *n.* матрос matros
saint *n.* святий sviatyi
saintly *a.* святий sviatyi
sake *n.* саке sake
salable *a.* ходовий khodovyi
salad *n.* салат salat
salary *n.* оклад oklad
sale *n.* продаж prodazh

salesman *n.* продавець prodavets

salient *a.* випуклий vypuklyi

saline *a.* сольовий solovyi

salinity *n.* солоність solonist

saliva *n.* слина slyna

sally *n.* вилазка vylazka

sally *v.i.* робити вилазку robyty vylazku

saloon *n.* шинок shynok

salt *n.* сіль sil

salt *v.t* солити solyty

salty *a.* солоний solonyi

salutary *a.* цілющий tsiliushchyi

salutation *n.* привітання pryvitannia

salute *v.t.* привітати pryvitaty

salute *n* салют saliut

salvage *n.* вторинна сировина vtorynna syrovyna

salvage *v.t.* рятувати судно riatuvaty sudno

salvation *n.* порятунок poriatunok

same *a.* однаковий odnakovyi

sample *n.* взірець vzirets

sample *v.t.* відбирати пробу vidbyraty probu

sanatorium *n.* санаторій sanatorii

sanctification *n.* освячення osviachennia

sanctify *v.t.* освячувати osviachuvaty

sanction *v.t.* санкціонувати sanktsionuvaty

sanction *n.* санкція sanktsiia

sanctity *n.* святість sviatist

sanctuary *n.* святилище sviatylyshche

sand *n.* пісок pisok

sandal *n.* сандал sandal

sandalwood *n.* сандалове дерево sandalove derevo

sandwich *n.* бутерброд buterbrod

sandwich *v.t.* поміщати посередині pomishchaty poseredyni

sandy *a.* піщаний pishchanyi

sane *a.* нормальний normalnyi

sanguine *a.* сангвінічний sanhvinichnyi

sanitary *a.* санітарний sanitarnyi

sanity *n.* осудність osudnist

sap *n.* живиця zhyvytsia

sap *v.t.* длубатися dlubatysia

sapling *n.* паросток parostok

sapphire *n.* сапфір sapfir

sarcasm *n.* сарказм sarkazm

sarcastic *a.* саркастичний sarkastychnyi

sardonic *a.* сардонічний sardonichnyi

satan *n.* сатана satana

satchel *n.* ранець ranets

satellite *n.* супутник suputnyk

satiable *a.* який задовольняється yakyi zadovolniaietsia

satiate *v.t.* насичувати nasychuvaty

satiety *n.* ситість sytist

satire *n.* сатира satyra

satirical *a.* сатиричний satyrychnyi

satirist *n.* сатирик satyryk

satirize *v.t.* висміювати vysmiiuvaty

satisfaction *n.* сплата боргу splata borhu

satisfactory *a.* задовільний zadovilnyi

satisfy *v.t.* погашати pohashaty

saturate *v.t.* пронизувати pronyzuvaty

saturation *n.* насичення nasychennia

Saturday *n.* субота subota

sauce *n.* соус sous

saucer *n.* блюдце bliudtse
saunter *v.t.* проходжуватися prokhodzhuvatysia
savage *a.* варварський varvarskyi
savage *n* дикун dykun
savagery *n.* дикість dykist
save *prep* за винятком za vyniatkom
save *v.t.* уберігати uberihaty
saviour *n.* рятівник riativnyk
savour *n.* смак smak
savour *v.t.* смакувати smakuvaty
saw *n.* вислів vysliv
saw *v.t.* пиляти pyliaty
say *v.t.* сказати skazaty
say *n.* слово slovo
scabbard *n.* піхви pikhvy
scabies *n.* короста korosta
scaffold *n.* будівельні ліси budivelni lisy
scale *v.t.* зважувати zvazhuvaty
scale *n.* масштаб masshtab
scalp *n* скальп skalp
scamper *v.i* носитися nosytysia
scamper *n* пробіжка probizhka
scan *v.t.* сканувати skanuvaty
scandal *n* скандал skandal
scandalize *v.t.* шокувати shokuvaty
scant *a.* убогий ubohyi
scanty *a.* худий khudyi
scapegoat *n.* козел відпущення kozel vidpushchennia
scar *v.t.* залишати шрам zalyshaty shram
scar *n* шрам shram
scarce *a.* дефіцитний defitsytnyi
scarcely *adv.* навряд чи navriad chy
scarcity *n.* брак brak
scare *v.t.* налякати naliakaty
scare *n.* страх strakh
scarf *n.* шарф sharf

scatter *v.t.* розкидати rozkydaty
scavenger *n.* сміттяр smittiar
scene *n.* сцена stsena
scenery *n.* декорації dekoratsii
scenic *a.* сценічний stsenichnyi
scent *n.* запах zapakh
scent *v.t.* учувати uchuvaty
sceptic *n.* скептик skeptyk
sceptical *a.* скептичний skeptychnyi
scepticism *n.* скептицизм skeptytsyzm
sceptre *n.* скіпетр skipetr
schedule *n.* каталог kataloh
schedule *v.t.* скласти розклад sklasty rozklad
scheme *v.i.* замислити zamyslyty
scheme *n.* схема skhema
schism *n.* секта sekta
scholar *n.* вчений vchenyi
scholarly *a.* властивий вченим vlastyvyi vchenym
scholarship *n.* вченість vchenist
scholastic *a.* схоластичний skholastychnyi
school *n.* школа shkola
science *n.* наука nauka
scientific *a.* технічний tekhnichnyi
scientist *n.* науковець naukovets
scintillate *v.i.* іскритися iskrytysia
scintillation *n.* сцинтилляция stsyntylliatsyia
scissors *n.* ножиці nozhytsi
scoff *v.i.* знущатися znushchatysia
scoff *n.* посміховисько posmikhovysko
scold *v.t.* лаяти laiaty
scooter *n.* скутер skuter
scope *n.* намір namir
scorch *v.t.* палити palyty
score *v.t.* одержувати oderzhuvaty

score *n.* борг borh
scorer *n.* лічильний очків lichylnyi ochkiv
scorn *v.t.* зневажати znevazhaty
scorn *n.* об`єкт зневаги ob`iekt znevahy
scorpion *n.* скорпіон skorpion
Scot *n.* шотландець shotlandets
scotch *n.* скотч skotch
scotch *a.* шотландський shotlandskyi
scot-free *a.* безкарний bezkarnyi
scoundrel *n.* падлюка padliuka
scourge *n.* бич bych
scourge *v.t.* бичувати bychuvaty
scout *v.i* провести розвідку provesty rozvidku
scout *n* розвідник rozvidnyk
scowl *n.* похмурий вигляд pokhmuryi vyhliad
scowl *v.i.* хмуритися khmurytysia
scramble *n* видирання vydyrannia
scramble *v.i.* підніматися pidnimatysia
scrap *n.* клаптик klaptyk
scratch *v.t.* подряпати podriapaty
scratch *n.* подряпина podriapyna
scrawl *n* каракулі karakuli
scrawl *v.t.* нерозбірливо писати nerozbirlyvo pysaty
scream *n* зойк zoik
scream *v.i.* волати volaty
screen *v.t.* прикрити prykryty
screen *n.* екран ekran
screw *v.t.* пригвинчувати pryhvynchuvaty
screw *n.* гвинт hvynt
scribble *n.* карлючки karliuchky
scribble *v.t.* неакуратно писати neakuratno pysaty
script *n.* сценарій stsenarii

scripture *n.* Священне писання Sviashchenne pysannia
scroll *n.* сувій suvii
scrutinize *v.t.* вивчати vyvchaty
scrutiny *n.* розгляд rozhliad
scuffle *v.i.* битися bytysia
scuffle *n.* бійка biika
sculptor *n.* скульптор skulptor
sculptural *a.* скульптурний skulpturnyi
sculpture *n.* скульптура skulptura
scythe *v.t.* косити kosyty
scythe *n.* коса kosa
sea *n.* море more
seal *v.t.* ставити печатку stavyty pechatku
seal *n.* тюлень tiulen
seal *n.* печатка pechatka
seam *v.t.* з'єднати швами ziednaty shvamy
seam *n.* шов shov
seamy *a.* покритий швами pokrytyi shvamy
search *v.t.* шукати shukaty
search *n.* розшук rozshuk
season *v.t.* загартовувати zahartovuvaty
season *n.* сезон sezon
seasonable *a.* своєчасний svoiechasnyi
seasonal *a.* сезонний sezonnyi
seat *v.t.* сидіти sydity
seat *n.* сидіння sydinnia
secede *v.i.* відокремлюватися vidokremliuvatysia
secession *n.* розкол rozkol
secessionist *n.* сепаратист separatyst
seclude *v.t.* усамітнюватися usamitniuvatysia
secluded *a.* ізолювати izoliuvaty
seclusion *n.* усамітнення usamitnennia

second *a.* другий druhyi
second *v.t.* підтримувати pidtrymuvaty
second *n* секунда sekunda
secondary *a.* вторинний vtorynnyi
seconder *n.* той, хто підтримує кандидатуру toi, khto pidtrymuie kandydaturu
secrecy *n.* секретність sekretnist
secret *n.* секрет sekret
secret *a.* секретний sekretnyi
secretariat (e) *n.* секретаріат sekretariat
secretary *n.* секретар sekretar
secrete *v.t.* ховати khovaty
secretion *n.* секреція sekretsiia
secretive *a.* потайний potainyi
sect *n.* секта sekta
sectarian *a.* сектантський sektantskyi
section *n.* розділ rozdil
sector *n.* сектор sektor
secure *v.t.* застрахувати zastrakhuvaty
secure *a.* спокійний spokiinyi
security *n.* безпечність bezpechnist
sedan *n.* носилки nosylky
sedate *v.t.* присипляти prysypliaty
sedate *a.* статечний statechnyi
sedative *n* заспокійливе zaspokiilyve
sedative *a.* болезаспокійливий bolezaspokiilyvyi
sedentary *a.* сидячий sydiachyi
sediment *n.* відстій vidstii
sedition *n.* підбурювання до заколоту pidburiuvannia do zakolotu
seditious *a.* підбурювальний pidburiuvalnyi
seduce *n.* спокушати spokushaty
seduction *n.* зваба zvaba

seductive *a* спокусливий spokuslyvyi
see *v.t.* знаходити znakhodyty
seed *n.* насіння nasinnia
seed *v.t.* сіяти siiaty
seek *v.t.* шукати shukaty
seem *v.i.* здаватися zdavatysia
seemly *a.* пристойний prystoinyi
seep *v.i.* просочуватися prosochuvatysia
seer *n.* провидець provydets
seethe *v.i.* вирувати vyruvaty
segment *v.t.* ділити на сегменти dilyty na sehmenty
segment *n.* сегмент sehment
segregate *v.t.* ізолюватися izoliuvatysia
segregation *n.* ізоляція izoliatsiia
seismic *a.* сейсмічний seismichnyi
seize *v.t.* заволодіти zavolodity
seizure *n.* захоплення zakhoplennia
seldom *adv.* рідко ridko
select *a* добірний dobirnyi
select *v.t.* проводити відбір provodyty vidbir
selection *n.* вибір vybir
selective *a.* селективний selektyvnyi
self *n.* самість samist
selfish *a.* егоїстичний ehoistychnyi
selfless *a.* самовідданий samoviddanyi
sell *v.t.* продавати prodavaty
seller *n.* торговець torhovets
semblance *n.* зовнішність zovnishnist
semen *n.* сперма sperma
semester *n.* семестр semestr
seminal *a.* насіннєвий nasinnievyi
seminar *n.* семінар seminar

senate *n.* сенат senat
senator *n.* сенатор senator
senatorial *a* який стосується виборів у сенат yakyi stosuietsia vyboriv u senat
senatorial *a.* сенаторський senatorskyi
send *v.t.* послати poslaty
senile *a.* старечий starechyi
senility *n.* старість starist
senior *n.* начальник nachalnyk
senior *a.* старший starshyi
seniority *n.* трудовий стаж trudovyi stazh
sensation *n.* відчуття vidchuttia
sensational *a.* сенсаційний sensatsiinyi
sense *v.t.* усвідомлювати usvidomliuvaty
sense *n.* сенс sens
senseless *a.* безглуздий bezhluzdyi
sensibility *n.* чутливість chutlyvist
sensible *a.* відчутний vidchutnyi
sensitive *a.* чутливий chutlyvyi
sensual *a.* чуттєвий chuttievyi
sensualist *n.* сластолюбець slastoliubets
sensuality *n.* чуттєвість chuttievist
sensuous *a.* плотський plotskyi
sentence *v.t.* засуджувати zasudzhuvaty
sentence *n.* вирок vyrok
sentience *n.* здатність відчувати zdatnist vidchuvaty
sentient *a.* який відчуває yakyi vidchuvaie
sentiment *n.* настрій nastrii
sentimental *a.* сентиментальний sentymentalnyi
sentinel *n.* часовий chasovyi
sentry *n.* караул karaul

separable *a.* віддільний viddilnyi
separate *v.t.* відокремлювати vidokremliuvaty
separate *a.* окремий okremyi
separation *n.* поділ podil
sepsis *n.* сепсис sepsys
September *n.* вересень veresen
septic *a.* септичний septychnyi
sepulchre *n.* склеп sklep
sepulture *n.* поховання pokhovannia
sequel *n.* наслідок naslidok
sequence *n.* послідовність poslidovnist
sequester *v.t.* накладати арешт nakladaty aresht
serene *a.* безтурботний bezturbotnyi
serenity *n.* спокій spokii
serf *n.* кріпак kripak
serge *n.* саржа sarzha
sergeant *n.* сержант serzhant
serial *n.* серіал serial
serial *a.* серійний seriinyi
series *n.* серія seriia
serious *a* серйозний serioznyi
sermonize *v.i.* повчати povchaty
serpent *n.* змія zmiia
serpentine *n.* змійовик zmiiovyk
servant *n.* слуга sluha
serve *n.* подача м`яча podacha m`iacha
serve *v.t.* служити sluzhyty
service *v.t* обслуговувати obsluhovuvaty
service *n.* обслуговування obsluhovuvannia
serviceable *a.* справний spravnyi
servile *a.* рабський rabskyi
servility *n.* піднесливість pidneslyvist
session *n.* сесія sesiia
set *a* встановлений vstanovlenyi

set *n* набір nabir
set *v.t* ставити stavyty
settle *v.i.* врегулювати
vrehuliuvaty
settlement *n.* колонізація
kolonizatsiia
settler *n.* поселенець poselenets
seven *a* семирічний semyrichnyi
seven *n.* сім sim
seventeen *n.* сімнадцять
simnadtsiat
seventeenth *a.* сімнадцятий
simnadtsiatyi
seventh *a.* сьомий somyi
seventieth *a.* сімдесятий
simdesiatyi
seventy *n., a* сімдесят simdesiat
sever *v.t.* розривати rozryvaty
several *a* кілька kilka
severance *n.* відділення
viddilennia
severe *a.* твердий tverdyi
severity *n.* строгість strohist
sew *v.t.* шити shyty
sewage *n.* стічні води stichni vody
sewer *n* швець shvets
sewerage *n.* каналізація
kanalizatsiia
sex *n.* стать stat
sexual *a.* сексуальний seksualnyi
sexuality *n.* сексуальність
seksualnist
sexy *a.* сексапільний seksapilnyi
shabby *a.* потертий potertyi
shackle *v.t.* скувати skuvaty
shackle *n.* пута puta
shade *v.t.* штрихувати
shtrykhuvaty
shade *n.* тінь tin
shadow *v.t* спостерігати
sposterihaty
shadow *n.* тінь tin
shadowy *a.* темний temnyi

shaft *n.* ратище ratyshche
shake *n* тремтіння tremtinnia
shake *v.i.* трясти triasty
shaky *a.* хиткий khytkyi
shallow *a.* мілкий milkyi
sham *n* удавання udavannia
sham *a* фіктивний fiktyvnyi
sham *v.i.* симулювати symuliuvaty
shame *v.t.* соромити soromyty
shame *n.* сором sorom
shameful *a.* ганебний hanebnyi
shameless *a.* безсоромний
bezsoromnyi
shampoo *v.t.* мити шампунем
myty shampunem
shampoo *n.* шампунь shampun
shanty *n.* халупка khalupka
shape *v.t* надати форму nadaty
formu
shape *n.* форма forma
shapely *a.* стрункий strunkyi
share *n* акція aktsiia
share *v.t.* ділитися dilytysia
share *n.* пай pai
shark *n.* акула akula
sharp *adv.* сильно sylno
sharp *a.* виразний vyraznyi
sharpen *v.t.* точити tochyty
sharpener *n.* стругачка
struhachka
sharper *n.* шахрай shakhrai
shatter *v.t.* розстроюватися
rozstroiuvatysia
shave *n* гоління holinnia
shave *v.t.* голитися holytysia
shawl *n.* шаль shal
she *pron.* вона vona
sheaf *n.* сніп snip
shear *v.t.* зрушення zrushennia
shears *n. pl.* ножиці nozhytsi
shed *n* навіс navis
shed *v.t.* поширювати
poshyriuvaty

sheep *n.* паства pastva
sheepish *a.* дурнуватий durnuvatyi
sheer *a.* чистий chystyi
sheet *v.t.* покрити pokryty
sheet *n.* чохол chokhol
shelf *n.* шельф shelf
shell *v.t.* очищати від шкарлупи ochyshchaty vid shkarlupy
shell *n.* оболонка obolonka
shelter *v.t.* дати притулок daty prytulok
shelter *n.* укриття ukryttia
shelve *v.t.* відкласти vidklasty
shepherd *n.* чабан chaban
shield *v.t.* затуляти zatuliaty
shield *n.* щит shchyt
shift *n* зміна zmina
shift *v.t.* переміщати peremishchaty
shifty *a.* вивертий vyvertkyi
shilling *n.* шилінг shylinh
shilly-shally *v.i.* бути нерішучим buty nerishuchym
shilly-shally *n.* нерішучий nerishuchyi
shin *n.* рулька rulka
shine *n* сяяня siaiania
shine *v.i.* блищати blyshchaty
shiny *a.* лискучий lyskuchyi
ship *v.t.* занурити zanuryty
ship *n.* судно sudno
shipment *n.* відвантаження vidvantazhennia
shire *n.* графство hrafstvo
shirk *v.t.* ухилятися ukhyliatysia
shirker *n.* прогульник prohulnyk
shirt *n.* сорочка sorochka
shiver *v.i.* тремтіти tremtity
shoal *v.t.* міліти mility
shoal *n.* зграя zhraia
shock *v.t.* шокувати shokuvaty
shock *n.* шок shok

shoe *v.t.* взувати vzuvaty
shoe *n.* туфля tuflia
shoot *n* стрілянина strilianyna
shoot *v.t.* стріляти striliaty
shop *v.i.* робити покупки robyty pokupky
shop *n.* магазин mahazyn
shore *n.* берег bereh
short *adv.* коротко korotko
short *a.* низький nyzkyi
shortage *n.* недостача nedostacha
shortcoming *n.* дефект defekt
shorten *v.t.* скорочувати skorochuvaty
shortly *adv.* незабаром nezabarom
shorts *n. pl.* шорти shorty
shot *n.* постріл postril
shoulder *v.t.* проштовхуватися proshtovkhuvatysia
shoulder *n.* плече pleche
shout *v.i.* голосно говорити holosno hovoryty
shout *n.* вигук vyhuk
shove *n.* штовхання shtovkhannia
shove *v.t.* шпурляти shpurliaty
shovel *v.t.* вигрібати vyhribaty
shovel *n.* лопата lopata
show *n.* шоу shou
show *v.t.* показувати pokazuvaty
shower *v.t.* литися зливою lytysia zlyvoiu
shower *n.* душ dush
shrew *n.* землерийка zemleryika
shrewd *a.* проникливий pronyklyvyi
shriek *v.i.* верещати vereshchaty
shriek *n.* вереск veresk
shrill *a.* пронизливий pronyzlyvyi
shrine *n.* усипальниця usypalnytsia

shrink *v.i* скорочуватися skorochuvatysia

shrinkage *n.* усадка usadka

shroud *v.t.* загорнути в саван zahornuty v savan

shroud *n.* саван savan

shrub *n.* чагарник chaharnyk

shrug *n* знизування znyzuvannia

shrug *v.t.* знизувати плечима znyzuvaty plechyma

shudder *n* тремтіння tremtinnia

shudder *v.i.* здригатися zdryhatysia

shuffle *n.* човгання chovhannia

shuffle *v.i.* човгати chovhaty

shun *v.t.* уникати unykaty

shunt *v.t.* пересувати peresuvaty

shut *a.* шунтувальний shuntuvalnyi

shutter *n.* затвор zatvor

shuttle *v.t.* рухатися назад і вперед rukhatysia nazad i vpered

shuttle *n.* човник chovnyk

shuttlecock *n.* волан volan

shy *v.i.* полохатися polokhatysia

shy *n.* різкий випад rizkyi vypad

sick *a.* хворий khvoryi

sickle *n.* серп serp

sickly *a.* хворобливий khvoroblyvyi

sickness *n.* хвороба khvoroba

side *v.i.* вставати на чиюсь сторону vstavaty na chyius storonu

side *n.* сторона storona

siege *n.* облога obloha

siesta *n.* сієста siiesta

sieve *v.t.* відсівати vidsivaty

sieve *n.* сито syto

sift *v.t.* просівати prosivaty

sigh *v.i.* зітхати zitkhaty

sigh *n.* зітхання zitkhannia

sight *v.t.* побачити pobachyty

sight *n.* зір zir

sightly *a.* видний vydnyi

sign *v.t.* підписати pidpysaty

sign *n.* знак znak

signal *v.t.* сигналізувати syhnalizuvaty

signal *a.* сигнальний syhnalnyi

signal *n.* сигнал syhnal

signatory *n.* сторона, яка підписалася storona, yaka pidpysalasia

signature *n.* підпис pidpys

significance *n.* значення znachennia

significant *a.* багатозначний bahatoznachnyi

signification *n.* показ pokaz

signify *v.t.* виявляти vyiavliaty

silence *v.t.* заглушити zahlushyty

silence *n.* тиша tysha

silencer *n.* глушник hlushnyk

silent *a.* неактивний neaktyvnyi

silhouette *n.* силует syluet

silk *n.* шовк shovk

silken *a.* шовковий shovkovyi

silky *a.* шовковистий shovkovystyi

silly *a.* недоумкуватий nedoumkuvatyi

silt *v.t.* замулюватися zamuliuvatysia

silt *n.* шлам shlam

silver *v.t.* сріблити sriblyty

silver *n.* срібло sriblo

silver *a* срібний sribnyi

similar *a.* схожий skhozhyi

similarity *n.* тотожність totozhnist

simile *n.* порівняння porivniannia

similitude *n.* схожість skhozhist

simmer *v.i.* кипіти на повільному вогні kypity na povilnomu vohni

simple *a.* елементарний elementarnyi
simpleton *n.* простак prostak
simplicity *n.* простодушність prostodushnist
simplification *n.* спрощення sproshchennia
simplify *v.t.* спростити sprostyty
simultaneous *a.* одночасний odnochasnyi
sin *v.i.* грішити hrishyty
sin *n.* гріх hrikh
since *conj.* з тих пір z tykh pir
since *adv.* тому tomu
since *prep.* після pislia
sincere *a.* щиросердний shchyroserdnyi
sincerity *n.* щирість shchyrist
sinful *a.* грішний hrishnyi
sing *v.i.* співати spivaty
singe *n* опік opik
singe *v.t.* обпалювати obpaliuvaty
singer *n.* співак spivak
single *v.t.* відібрати vidibraty
single *n.* холостяк kholostiak
single *a.* самотній samotnii
singular *a.* одиничний odynychnyi
singularity *n.* незвичайність nezvychainist
singularly *adv.* особливо osoblyvo
sinister *a.* поганий pohanyi
sink *n* раковина rakovyna
sink *v.i.* топити topyty
sinner *n.* грішник hrishnyk
sinuous *a.* звивистий zvyvystyi
sip *n.* маленький ковток malenkyi kovtok
sip *v.t.* куштувати kushtuvaty
sir *n.* сер ser
siren *n.* сирена syrena
sister *n.* сестра sestra

sisterhood *n.* сестринство sestrynstvo
sisterly *a.* сестринський sestrynskyi
sit *v.i.* сидіти sydity
site *n.* сайт sait
situation *n.* ситуація sytuatsiia
six *n., a* шість shist
sixteen *n., a.* шістнадцять shistnadtsiat
sixteenth *a.* шістнадцятий shistnadtsiatyi
sixth *a.* шостий shostyi
sixtieth *a.* шістдесятий shistdesiatyi
sixty *n., a.* шістьдесят shistdesiat
sizable *a.* значний znachnyi
size *n.* розмір rozmir
size *v.t.* розставляти за величиною rozstavliaty za velychynoiu
sizzle *n.* шипіння shypinnia
sizzle *v.i.* шипіти shypity
skate *v.t.* кататися на ковзанах katatysia na kovzanakh
skate *n.* санчата sanchata
skein *n.* моток пряжі motok priazhi
skeleton *n.* скелет skelet
sketch *v.t.* накидати nakydaty
sketch *n.* ескіз eskiz
sketchy *a.* уривчастий uryvchastyi
skid *n* занос zanos
skid *v.i.* буксувати buksuvaty
skilful *a.* майстерний maisternyi
skill *n.* навик navyk
skin *v.t* покривати шкірою pokryvaty shkiroiu
skin *n.* шкіра shkira
skip *n* стрибок strybok
skip *v.i.* пропускати propuskaty
skipper *n.* шкіпер shkiper

skirmish *v.t.* зав'язати перестрілку zaviazaty perestrilku

skirmish *n.* перестрілка perestrilka

skirt *v.t.* обходити obkhodyty

skirt *n.* спідниця spidnytsia

skit *n.* пародія parodiia

skull *n.* череп cherep

sky *v.t.* вішати під стелю vishaty pid steliu

sky *n.* небо nebo

slab *n.* шматок shmatok

slack *a.* слабкий slabkyi

slacken *v.t.* слабшати slabshaty

slacks *n.* слабина slabyna

slake *v.t.* втамувати vtamuvaty

slam *n* удар udar

slam *v.t.* кидати зі стуком kydaty zi stukom

slander *n.* лихослів'я lykhoslivia

slander *v.t.* паплюжити papliuzhyty

slanderous *a.* наклепницький naklepnytskyi

slang *n.* сленг slenh

slant *n* схил skhyl

slant *v.t.* нахиляти nakhyliaty

slap *v.t.* шльопати shlopaty

slap *n.* ляпас liapas

slash *n* вирубка vyrubka

slash *v.t.* рубати rubaty

slate *n.* шифер shyfer

slattern *n.* грязнуля hriaznulia

slatternly *a.* неохайний neokhainyi

slaughter *v.t.* зарізати zarizaty

slaughter *n.* різанина rizanyna

slave *v.i.* працювати, як раб pratsiuvaty, yak rab

slave *n.* раб rab

slavery *n.* рабовласництво rabovlasnytstvo

slavish *a.* рабський rabskyi

slay *v.t.* убити ubyty

sleek *a.* гладкий hladkyi

sleep *n.* сон son

sleep *v.i.* спати spaty

sleeper *n.* соня sonia

sleepy *a.* сонний sonnyi

sleeve *n* рукав rukav

sleight *n.* спритність sprytnist

slender *n.* стрункий strunkyi

slice *v.t.* нарізати скибками narizaty skybkamy

slice *n.* скибочка skybochka

slick *a* мспритний msprytnyi

slide *n* ковзати kovzaty

slide *v.i.* каток katok

slight *a.* крихкий krykhkyi

slight *v.t.* нехтувати nekhtuvaty

slight *a.* тендітний tenditnyi

slim *v.i.* худнути khudnuty

slim *a.* тонкий tonkyi

slime *n.* слиз slyz

slimy *a.* слизовий slyzovyi

sling *n.* строп strop

slip *n.* сковзнути skovznuty

slip *v.i.* ковзання kovzannia

slipper *n. pl* тапочки tapochky

slippery *a.* слизький slyzkyi

slipshod *a.* недбалий nedbalyi

slit *v.t.* нарізати у довжину narizaty u dovzhynu

slit *n.* щілина shchilyna

slogan *n.* гасло haslo

slope *v.i.* хилитися khylytysia

slope *n.* схил skhyl

sloth *n.* лінощі linoshchi

slothful *n.* недбайливий nedbailyvyi

slough *v.t.* скинути шкіру skynuty shkiru

slough *n.* багно bahno

slough *n.* ковбаня kovbania

slovenly *a.* неохайний neokhainyi

slow *v.i.* зволікати zvolikaty
slow *a* повільний povilnyi
slowly *adv.* повільно povilno
slowness *n.* повільність povilnist
sluggard *n.* ледар ledar
sluggish *a.* ледачий ledachyi
sluice *n.* шлюз shliuz
slum *n.* нетрі netri
slumber *n.* сон son
slumber *v.i.* не діяти ne diiaty
slump *v.i.* різко падати rizko padaty
slump *n.* спад spad
slur *n.* чорниш chornysh
slush *n.* сльота slota
slushy *a.* сльотавий slotavyi
slut *n.* шльондра shlondra
sly *a.* хитрий khytryi
smack *n.* дзвінкий поцілунок dzvinkyi potsilunok
smack *v.t.* мати присмак maty prysmak
smack *v.i.* пахнути pakhnuty
smack *n* чмоканье chmokane
smack *n.* присмак prysmak
small *n* мала величина mala velychyna
small *a.* невеликий nevelykyi
smallness *n.* малість malist
smallpox *n.* віспа vispa
smart *v.i* відчувати сильний біль vidchuvaty sylnyi bil
smart *n* пекучий біль pekuchyi bil
smart *a.* різкий rizkyi
smash *n* нищівний удар nyshchivnyi udar
smash *v.t.* громити hromyty
smear *n.* пляма pliama
smear *v.t.* натирати natyraty
smell *v.t.* нюхати niukhaty
smell *n.* нюх niukh
smelt *v.t.* виплавляти vyplavliaty

smile *v.i.* посміхатися posmikhatysia
smile *n.* усмішка usmishka
smith *n.* коваль koval
smock *n.* халат khalat
smog *n.* смог smoh
smoke *v.i.* диміти dymity
smoke *n.* дим dym
smoky *a.* димчастий dymchastyi
smooth *v.t.* пригладжувати pryhladzhuvaty
smooth *a.* плавний plavnyi
smother *v.t.* задихнутися zadykhnutysia
smoulder *v.i.* тліти tlity
smug *a.* самовдоволений samovdovolenyi
smuggle *v.t.* провозити контрабандою provozyty kontrabandoiu
smuggler *n.* контрабандист kontrabandyst
snack *n.* закуска zakuska
snag *n.* уламок зуба ulamok zuba
snail *n.* равлик ravlyk
snake *v.i.* повзти povzty
snake *n.* зрадник zradnyk
snap *n* засувка zasuvka
snap *a* поспішний pospishnyi
snap *v.t.* клацати klatsaty
snare *v.t.* піймати в пастку piimaty v pastku
snare *n.* пастка pastka
snarl *v.i.* гарчати harchaty
snarl *n.* гарчання harchannia
snatch *n.* злодійство zlodiistvo
snatch *v.t.* урвати urvaty
sneak *n* злодюжка zlodiuzhka
sneak *v.i.* крастися krastysia
sneer *n* презирлива усмішка prezyrlyva usmishka
sneer *v.i* глузливо посміхнутися hluzlyvo posmikhnutysia

sneeze *n* чхання chkhannia
sneeze *v.i.* чхати chkhaty
sniff *n* сопіння sopinnia
sniff *v.i.* сопіти sopity
snob *n.* сноб snob
snobbery *n.* снобізм snobizm
snobbish *v* снобістський snobistskyi
snore *n* хропіння khropinnia
snore *v.i.* хропіти khropity
snort *n.* пирхання pyrkhannia
snort *v.i.* фиркати fyrkaty
snout *n.* рило rylo
snow *v.i.* заносити снігом zanosyty snihom
snow *n.* сніг snih
snowy *a.* сніжний snizhnyi
snub *n.* образа obraza
snub *v.t.* принизити prynyzyty
snuff *n.* нагар на свічці nahar na svichtsi
snug *n.* затишне містечко zatyshne mistechko
so *adv.* так tak
so *conj.* таким чином takym chynom
soak *n.* замочування zamochuvannia
soak *v.t.* вбирати vbyraty
soap *v.t.* намилити namylyty
soap *n.* мило mylo
soapy *a.* мильний mylnyi
soar *v.i.* парити paryty
sob *n* ридання rydannia
sob *v.i.* ридати rydaty
sober *a.* тверезий tverezyi
sobriety *n.* тверезість tverezist
sociability *n.* товариськість tovaryskist
sociable *a.* товариський tovaryskyi
social *n.* соціальний sotsialnyi
socialism *n* соціалізм sotsializm

socialist *n,a* соціаліст, соціалістичний sotsialist, sotsialistychnyi
society *n.* суспільство suspilstvo
sociology *n.* соціологія sotsiolohiia
sock *n.* шкарпетка shkarpetka
socket *n.* розетка rozetka
sod *n.* дерен deren
sodomite *n.* педераст pederast
sodomy *n.* содомія sodomiia
sofa *n.* софа sofa
soft *n.* ніжний nizhnyi
soften *v.t.* ослабляти опір противника oslabliaty opir protyvnyka
soil *v.t.* бруднитися brudnytysia
soil *n.* грунт hrunt
sojourn *n* тимчасове перебування tymchasove perebuvannia
sojourn *v.i.* тимчасово проживати tymchasovo prozhyvaty
solace *n.* заспокоєння zaspokoiennia
solace *v.t.* утішати utishaty
solar *a.* сонячний soniachnyi
solder *v.t.* зварювання zvariuvannia
solder *n.* припій prypii
soldier *v.i.* солдат soldat
soldier *n.* споювати spoiuvaty
sole *a* винятковий vyniatkovyi
sole *v.t* ставити підметку stavyty pidmetku
sole *n.* підошва pidoshva
solemn *a.* урочистий urochystyi
solemnity *n.* урочистість urochystist
solemnize *v.t.* святкувати sviatkuvaty

solicit *v.t.* клопотатися klopotatysia
solicitation *n.* чіпляння chipliannia
solicitor *n.* повірений povirenyi
solicitous *a.* повний бажання povnyi bazhannia
solicitude *n.* дбайливість dbailyvist
solid *n* твердий tverdyi
solid *a.* згуртований zhurtovanyi
solidarity *n.* тіло tilo
soliloquy *n.* внутрішній монолог vnutrishnii monoloh
solitary *a.* занедбаний zanedbanyi
solitude *n.* самота samota
solo *adv.* незалежно nezalezhno
solo *a.* сольний solnyi
solo *n* соло solo
soloist *n.* соліст solist
solubility *n.* розчинність rozchynnist
soluble *a.* розчинний rozchynnyi
solution *n.* розчин rozchyn
solve *v.t.* вирішити vyrishyty
solvency *n.* платоспроможність platospromozhnist
solvent *n* розчинник rozchynnyk
solvent *a.* що розчиняє shcho rozchyniaie
sombre *a.* темний temnyi
some *pron.* дехто dekhto
some *a.* якийсь yakyis
somebody *n.* будь-хто bud-khto
somebody *pron.* хтось khtos
somehow *adv.* якось yakos
someone *pron.* хтось khtos
somersault *v.i.* стрибати перевертом strybaty perevertom
somersault *n.* перекидання perekydannia

something *adv.* дещо deshcho
something *pron.* щось shchos
sometime *adv.* колись kolys
sometimes *adv.* іноді inodi
somewhat *adv.* трохи trokhy
somewhere *adv.* десь des
somnambulism *n.* сомнамбулізм somnambulizm
somnambulist *n.* лунатик lunatyk
somnolence *n.* сонливість sonlyvist
somnolent *a.* сонливий sonlyvyi
son *n.* син syn
song *n.* пісня pisnia
songster *n.* співак spivak
sonic *a.* звуковий zvukovyi
sonnet *n.* сонет sonet
sonority *n.* звучність zvuchnist
soon *adv.* скоро skoro
soot *v.t.* покрити сажею pokryty sazheiu
soot *n.* сажа sazha
soothe *v.t.* втішати vtishaty
sophism *n.* софізм sofizm
sophist *n.* софіст sofist
sophisticate *v.t.* перекручувати perekruchuvaty
sophisticated *a.* позбавлений простоти pozbavlenyi prostoty
sophistication *n.* витонченість vytonchenist
sorcerer *n.* чаклун chaklun
sorcery *n.* чаклунство chaklunstvo
sordid *a.* злиденний zlydennyi
sore *n* болячка boliachka
sore *a.* запалений zapalenyi
sorrow *v.i.* засмучуватися zasmuchuvatysia
sorrow *n.* печаль pechal
sorry *a.* засмучений zasmuchenyi
sort *n.* сорт sort
sort *v.t* сортувати sortuvaty

soul *n.* душа dusha
sound *v.i.* вимірювати глибину vymiriuvaty hlybunu
sound *n.* звук zvuk
sound *a.* міцний mitsnyi
soup *n.* суп sup
sour *v.t.* прокисати prokysaty
sour *a.* прокислий prokyslyi
source *n.* джерело dzherelo
south *n.* країни Півдня krainy Pivdnia
south *a.* південний pivdennyi
south *n.* південь pivden
southerly *a.* з півдня z pivdnia
southern *a.* зюйдовий ziuidovyi
souvenir *n.* сувенір suvenir
sovereign *a* суверенний suverennyi
sovereign *n.* суверен suveren
sovereignty *n.* суверенітет suverenitet
sow *n.* свиня svynia
sow *v.t.* сіяти siiaty
space *v.t.* розставити з проміжками rozstavyty z promizhkamy
space *n.* простір prostir
spacious *a.* просторий prostoryi
spade *v.t.* копати лопатою kopaty lopatoiu
spade *n.* заступ zastup
span *v.t.* простягатися prostiahatysia
span *n.* амплітуда amplituda
Spaniard *n.* іспанець ispanets
spaniel *n.* спанієль spaniiel
Spanish *n.* іспанська мова ispanska mova
Spanish *a.* іспанський ispanskyi
spanner *n.* вилочний ключ vylochnyi kliuch
spare *n.* запасні частини zapasni chastyny

spare *a* убогий ubohyi
spare *v.t.* економити ekonomyty
spark *n.* іскра iskra
spark *v.i.* іскритися iskrytysia
spark *n.* іскра iskra
sparkle *n.* іскріння iskrinnia
sparkle *v.i.* іскритися iskrytysia
sparrow *n.* горобець horobets
sparse *a.* рідкісний ridkisnyi
spasm *n.* спазм spazm
spasmodic *a.* спазматичний spazmatychnyi
spate *n.* раптова злива raptova zlyva
spatial *a.* просторовий prostorovyi
spawn *v.i.* метати ікру metaty ikru
spawn *n.* виплодок vyplodok
speak *v.i.* висловлюватися vyslovliuvatysia
speaker *n.* спікер spiker
spear *v.t.* бити остенем byty ostenem
spear *n.* спис spys
spearhead *v.t.* очолювати ocholiuvaty
spearhead *n.* вістря vistria
special *a.* спеціальний spetsialnyi
specialist *n.* спеціаліст spetsialist
speciality *n.* спеціальність spetsialnist
specialization *n.* спеціалізація spetsializatsiia
specialize *v.i.* спеціалізуватися spetsializuvatysia
species *n.* вид vyd
specific *a.* конкретний konkretnyi
specification *n.* специфікація spetsyfikatsiia
specify *v.t.* встановлювати vstanovliuvaty
specimen *n.* зразок zrazok
speck *n.* плямочка pliamochka

spectacle *n.* сцена stsena
spectacular *a.* захоплюючий zakhopliuiuchyi
spectator *n.* очевидець ochevydets
spectre *n.* примара prymara
speculate *v.i.* спекулювати spekuliuvaty
speculation *n.* міркування mirkuvannia
speech *n.* промова promova
speed *v.i.* квапити kvapyty
speed *n.* швидкість shvydkist
speedily *adv.* швидко shvydko
speedy *a.* швидкий shvydkyi
spell *v.t.* зачаровувати zacharovuvaty
spell *n* шарм sharm
spell *n.* чари chary
spend *v.t.* розтрачувати roztrachuvaty
spendthrift *n.* мот mot
sperm *n.* кашалот kashalot
sphere *n.* сфера sfera
spherical *a.* сферичний sferychnyi
spice *v.t.* приправляти prypravliaty
spice *n.* спеції spetsii
spicy *a.* пряний prianyi
spider *n.* павук pavuk
spike *v.t.* перестромлювати perestromliuvaty
spike *n.* шпилька shpylka
spill *n* затичка zatychka
spill *v.i.* проливати prolyvaty
spin *n.* кружляння kruzhliannia
spin *v.i.* ловити на блешню lovyty na bleshniu
spinach *n.* шпинат shpynat
spinal *a.* спинний spynnyi
spindle *n.* шпиндель shpyndel
spine *n.* хребет khrebet

spinner *n.* пряха priakha
spinster *n.* стара діва stara diva
spiral *a.* спіральний spiralnyi
spiral *n.* спіраль spiral
spirit *n.* дух dukh
spirited *a.* сміливий smilyvyi
spiritual *a.* духовний dukhovnyi
spiritualism *n.* спіритизм spirytyzm
spiritualist *n.* спіритуаліст spirytualist
spirituality *n.* духовність dukhovnist
spit *n* слина slyna
spit *v.i.* плювати pliuvaty
spite *n.* злість zlist
spittle *n* плювок pliuvok
spittoon *n.* плювальниця pliuvalnytsia
splash *n* сплеск splesk
splash *v.i.* плескатися pleskatysia
spleen *n.* селезінка selezinka
splendid *a.* блискучий blyskuchyi
splendour *n.* шляхетність shliakhetnist
splinter *v.t.* розщеплювати rozshchepliuvaty
splinter *n.* осколок oskolok
split *n* розщеплювання rozshchepliuvannia
split *v.i.* розколювати rozkoliuvaty
spoil *n* порожня порода porozhnia poroda
spoil *v.t.* балувати baluvaty
spoke *n.* поперечина poperechyna
spokesman *n.* промовець promovets
sponge *v.t.* чистити губкою chystyty hubkoiu
sponge *n.* губка hubka
sponsor *v.t.* спонсорувати sponsoruvaty

sponsor *n.* спонсор sponsor
spontaneity *n.* спонтанність spontannist
spontaneous *a.* спонтанний spontannyi
spoon *n.* ложка lozhka
spoon *v.t.* черпати ложкою cherpaty lozhkoiu
spoonful *n.* повна ложка povna lozhka
sporadic *a.* спорадичний sporadychnyi
sport *v.i.* гратися hratysia
sport *n.* спорт sport
sportive *a.* спортивний sportyvnyi
sportsman *n.* спортсмен sportsmen
spot *v.t.* плямувати pliamuvaty
spot *n.* прищик pryshchyk
spotless *a.* незаплямований nezapliamovanyi
spousal *n.* подружній podruzhnii
spouse *n.* чоловік cholovik
spout *v.i.* бити струменем byty strumenem
spout *n.* носик nosyk
sprain *n.* розтягнення суглоба roztiahnennia suhloba
sprain *v.t.* розтягнути зв'язки roztiahnuty zviazky
spray *n* гілка hilka
spray *v.t.* розпорошувати rozporoshuvaty
spray *n.* струмінь strumin
spread *n.* поширення poshyrennia
spread *v.i.* поширюватися poshyriuvatysia
spree *n.* запій zapii
sprig *n.* гілочка hilochka
sprightly *a.* бадьорий badoryi
spring *n* весна vesna
spring *v.i.* скакати skakaty

sprinkle *v. t.* бризкати bryzkaty
sprint *n* спринт sprynt
sprint *v.i.* спрінтовать sprintovat
sprout *n* пагін pahin
sprout *v.i.* проростати prorostaty
spur *v.t.* пришпорити pryshporyty
spur *n.* шпора shpora
spurious *a.* паразитний parazytnyi
spurn *v.t.* штофхати shtofkhaty
spurt *n* ривок ryvok
spurt *v.t.* викидати vykydaty
sputnik *n.* супутник suputnyk
sputum *n.* мокрота mokrota
spy *v.i.* шпигувати shpyhuvaty
spy *n.* шпигун shpyhun
squad *n.* загін zahin
squadron *n.* ескадрон eskadron
squalid *a.* убогий ubohyi
squalor *n.* убозтво uboztvo
squander *v.t.* розбазарювати rozbazariuvaty
square *v.t.* надавати квадратну форму nadavaty kvadratnu formu
square *a* квадратний kvadratnyi
square *n.* консерватор konservator
squash *n* тиснява tysniava
squash *v.t.* роздавлювати rozdavliuvaty
squat *v.i.* сидіти навпочіпках sydity navpochipkakh
squeak *n* скрип skryp
squeak *v.i.* скрипіти skrypity
squeeze *v.t.* стиснути stysnuty
squint *n* косоокість kosookist
squint *v.i.* дивитися скоса dyvytysia skosa
squire *n.* зброєносець zbroienosets
squirrel *n.* білка bilka
stab *n.* удар udar

stab *v.t.* втикати vtykaty
stability *n.* стабільність stabilnist
stabilization *n.* стабілізація stabilizatsiia
stabilize *v.t.* стабілізуватися stabilizuvatysia
stable *v.t.* ставити в стайню stavyty v stainiu
stable *n* стайня stainia
stable *a.* стабільний stabilnyi
stadium *n.* стадіон stadion
staff *v.t.* укомплектувати штат ukomplektuvaty shtat
staff *n.* кий kyi
stag *n.* біржовий брокер birzhovyi broker
stage *v.t.* інсценувати instsenuvaty
stage *n.* етап etap
stagger *n.* похитування pokhytuvannia
stagger *v.i.* хитатися khytatysia
stagnant *a.* застійний zastiinyi
stagnate *v.i.* застоюватися zastoiuvatysia
stagnation *n.* застій zastii
staid *a.* статечний statechnyi
stain *v.t.* забруднити zabrudnyty
stain *n.* барвник barvnyk
stainless *a.* нержавіючий nerzhaviiuchyi
stair *n.* сходинка skhodynka
stake *v.t.* ставити stavyty
stake *n* частина chastyna
stale *v.t.* спростовувати sprostovuvaty
stale *a.* черствий cherstvyi
stalemate *n.* безвихідне положення bezvykhidne polozhennia
stalk *v.i.* потай просуватися potai prosuvatysia
stalk *n* черешок chereshok

stalk *n.* стебло steblo
stall *v.t.* займати стійло zaimaty stiilo
stall *n.* стійло stiilo
stallion *n.* жеребець zherebets
stalwart *a.* рослий roslyi
stalwart *n* стійкий прихильник stiikyi prykhylnyk
stamina *n.* витривалість vytryvalist
stammer *n* заїкання zaikannia
stammer *v.i.* заїкатися zaikatysia
stamp *v.i.* ставити печатку stavyty pechatku
stamp *n.* штамп shtamp
stampede *v.i* панічно тікати panichno tikaty
stampede *n.* панічна втеча panichna vtecha
stand *n.* стояк stoiak
stand *v.i.* стояти stoiaty
standard *a* стандартний standartnyi
standard *n.* стандарт standart
standardization *n.* стандартизація standartyzatsiia
standardize *v.t.* стандартизувати standartyzuvaty
standing *n.* стоячий stoiachyi
standpoint *n.* точка зору tochka zoru
standstill *n.* зупинка zupynka
stanza *n.* строфа strofa
staple *a* основний osnovnyi
staple *n.* скоба skoba
star *v.t.* нагородити орденом nahorodyty ordenom
star *n.* зірка zirka
starch *v.t.* крохмалити krokhmalyty
starch *n.* крохмаль krokhmal
stare *n.* пильний погляд pylnyi pohliad

stare *v.i.* витріщатися
vytrishchatysia
stark *adv.* цілком tsilkom
stark *n.* задубілий zadubilyi
starry *a.* зоряний zorianyi
start *n* перевага perevaha
start *v.t.* вирушати в дорогу
vyrushaty v dorohu
startle *v.t.* налякати naliakaty
starvation *n.* голодна смерть
holodna smert
starve *v.i.* зголодніти zholodnity
state *v.t* стверджувати
stverdzhuvaty
state *n.* стан stan
stateliness *n.* величавість
velychavist
stately *a.* сповнений гідності
spovnenyi hidnosti
statement *n.* констатація
konstatatsiia
statesman *n.* державний діяч
derzhavnyi diiach
static *n.* статичний statychnyi
statics *n.* статика statyka
station *v.t.* направляти на місце
роботи napravliaty na mistse
roboty
station *n.* станція stantsiia
stationary *a.* стаціонарний
statsionarnyi
stationer *n.* торговець
канцелярським приладдям
torhovets kantseliarskym
pryladdiam
stationery *n.* канцелярські
товари kantseliarski tovary
statistical *a.* статистичний
statystychnyi
statistician *n.* статистик statystyk
statistics *n.* статистика statystyka
statue *n.* статуя statuia
stature *n.* фігура fihura

status *n.* статус status
statute *n.* статут statut
statutory *a.* законний zakonnyi
staunch *a.* стійкий stiikyi
stay *n* перебування perebuvannia
stay *v.i.* стримувати strymuvaty
steadfast *a.* стійкий stiikyi
steadiness *n.* стійкість stiikist
steady *v.t.* укріплювати
ukripliuvaty
steady *a.* стійкий stiikyi
steal *v.i.* крадена річ kradena rich
stealthily *adv.* крадькома
kradkoma
steam *v.i.* випускати пар
vypuskaty par
steam *n* пар par
steamer *n.* пароплав paroplav
steed *n.* кінь kin
steel *n.* сталь stal
steep *v.t.* вимочувати
vymochuvaty
steep *a.* крутий krutyi
steeple *n.* шпиль shpyl
steer *v.t.* управляти upravliaty
stellar *a.* зоряний zorianyi
stem *v.i.* відбутися vidbutysia
stem *n.* стебло steblo
stench *n.* сморід smorid
stencil *v.i.* фарбувати за
трафаретом farbuvaty za
trafaretom
stencil *n.* трафарет trafaret
stenographer *n.* стенографістка
stenohrafistka
stenography *n.* стенографія
stenohrafiia
step *v.i.* ступнути stupnuty
step *n.* хода khoda
steppe *n.* степ step
stereotype *v.t.* робити побитим
robyty pobytym

stereotype *n.* стереотип stereotyp

stereotyped *a.* стереотипний stereotypnyi

sterile *a.* стерильний sterylnyi

sterility *n.* стерильність sterylnist

sterilization *n.* стерилізація sterylizatsiia

sterilize *v.t.* стерилізувати sterylizuvaty

sterling *n.* стерлінг sterlinh

sterling *a.* надійний nadiinyi

stern *n.* хвіст khvist

stern *a.* суворий suvoryi

stethoscope *n.* стетоскоп stetoskop

stew *v.t.* тушкувати tushkuvaty

stew *n.* тушковане м'ясо tushkovane miaso

steward *n.* стюард stiuard

stick *v.t.* наклеїти nakleity

stick *n.* палиця palytsia

sticker *n.* наклейка nakleika

stickler *n.* прихильник prykhylnyk

sticky *n.* липкий lypkyi

stiff *n.* негнучкий nehnuchkyi

stiffen *v.t.* надавати жорсткості nadavaty zhorstkosti

stifle *v.t.* душити dushyty

stigma *n.* стигмат styhmat

still *adv.* до цих пір do tsykh pir

still *v.t.* переганяти perehaniaty

still *n.* фотокадр fotokadr

still *a.* непорушний neporushnyi

stillness *n.* нерухомість nerukhomist

stilt *n.* паля palia

stimulant *n.* стимулятор stymuliator

stimulate *v.t.* стимулювати stymuliuvaty

stimulus *n.* стимул stymul

sting *n.* укус ukus

sting *v.t.* відчувати гострий біль vidchuvaty hostryi bil

stingy *a.* скупий skupyi

stink *n.* сморід smorid

stink *v.i.* смердіти smerdity

stipend *n.* стипендія stypendiia

stipulate *v.t.* ставити умовою stavyty umovoiu

stipulation *n.* умова umova

stir *v.i.* переполох perepolokh

stirrup *n.* стремено stremeno

stitch *v.t.* стьобати stobaty

stitch *n.* стібок stibok

stock *a.* біржовий birzhovyi

stock *v.t.* зберігати на складі zberihaty na skladi

stock *n.* акції aktsii

stocking *n.* рівень запасів riven zapasiv

stoic *n.* стоїчний stoichnyi

stoke *v.t.* підтримувати вогонь pidtrymuvaty vohon

stoker *n.* кочегар kochehar

stomach *v.t.* стерпіти sterpity

stomach *n.* шлунок shlunok

stone *v.t.* мостити каменем mostyty kamenem

stone *n.* камінь kamin

stony *a.* кам'янистий kamianystyi

stool *n.* стілець stilets

stoop *n* сутулість sutulist

stoop *v.i.* сутулитися sutulytysia

stop *n* стоп stop

stop *v.t.* зупинити zupynyty

stoppage *n* затримка zatrymka

storage *n.* склад sklad

store *v.t.* вміщувати vmishchuvaty

store *n.* резерв rezerv

storey *n.* поверх poverkh

stork *n.* лелека leleka

storm *v.i.* штурмувати shturmuvaty

storm *n.* гроза hroza

stormy *a.* грозовий hrozovyi
story *n.* оповідання opovidannia
stout *a.* товстий tovstyi
stove *n.* піч pich
stow *v.t.* укладати ukladaty
straggle *v.i.* відставати vidstavaty
straggler *n.* відсталий vidstalyi
straight *adv.* прямо priamo
straight *a.* невигнутий nevyhnutyi
straighten *v.t.* випрямляти vypriamliaty
straightforward *a.* простий prostyi
straightway *adv.* негайно nehaino
strain *n* напруга napruha
strain *v.t.* натягувати natiahuvaty
strait *n.* протока protoka
straiten *v.t.* обмежувати obmezhuvaty
strand *n* пасмо pasmo
strand *v.i.* сісти на мілину sisty na milynu
strange *a.* дивний dyvnyi
stranger *n.* незнайомець neznaiomets
strangle *v.t.* задушити zadushyty
strangulation *n.* удушення udushennia
strap *v.t.* стягнути ременем stiahnuty remenem
strap *n.* ремінець reminets
strategem *n.* хитрість khytrist
strategic *a.* стратегічний stratehichnyi
strategist *n.* стратег strateh
strategy *n.* стратегія stratehiia
stratum *n.* шар shar
straw *n.* солома soloma
strawberry *n.* полуниця polunytsia
stray *n* бездомна собака bezdomna sobaka
stray *a* заблудлий zabludlyi

stray *v.i.* блудити bludyty
stream *v.i.* текти tekty
stream *n.* валка valka
streamer *n.* вимпел vympel
streamlet *n.* струмочок strumochok
street *n.* вулиця vulytsia
strength *n.* міцність mitsnist
strengthen *v.t.* зміцнювати zmitsniuvaty
strenuous *a.* напружений napruzhenyi
stress *v.t* ставити наголос stavyty naholos
stress *n.* стрес stres
stretch *n* розтягування roztiahuvannia
stretch *v.t.* розтягувати roztiahuvaty
stretcher *n.* носилки nosylky
strew *v.t.* посипати posypaty
strict *a.* суворий suvoryi
stricture *n.* стриктура stryktura
stride *n* великий крок velykyi krok
stride *v.i.* бігти маховим кроком bihty makhovym krokom
strident *a.* скрипучий skrypuchyi
strife *n.* розбрат rozbrat
strike *n* страйк straik
strike *v.t.* страйкувати straikuvaty
striker *n.* страйкарі straikari
string *v.t.* мотузка motuzka
string *n.* тасьма tasma
stringency *n.* строгість strohist
stringent *a.* суворий suvoryi
strip *v.t.* здирати zdyraty
strip *n.* полоса polosa
stripe *v.t.* наносити смуги nanosyty smuhy
stripe *n.* шеврон shevron
strive *v.i.* докладати зусилля dokladaty zusyllia

stroke *v.t.* погладжувати pohladzhuvaty
stroke *n* хід khid
stroke *n.* замах zamakh
stroll *n* мандри mandry
stroll *v.i.* мандрувати mandruvaty
strong *a.* сильний sylnyi
stronghold *n.* фортеця fortetsia
structural *a.* структурний strukturnyi
structure *n.* структура struktura
struggle *n* зусилля zusyllia
struggle *v.i.* відбиватися vidbyvatysia
strumpet *n.* повія poviia
strut *n* стояк stoiak
strut *v.i.* закріплювати zakripliuvaty
stub *n.* недопалок nedopalok
stubble *n.* стерня sternia
stubborn *a.* упертий upertyi
stud *v.t.* оббити obbyty
stud *n.* шпилька shpylka
student *n.* студент student
studio *n.* студія studiia
studious *a.* старанний starannyi
study *n.* вивчення vyvchennia
study *v.i.* вивчати vyvchaty
stuff *2 v.t.* нафарширувати nafarshyruvaty
stuff *n.* речовина rechovyna
stuffy *a.* задушливий zadushlyvyi
stumble *n.* запинки zapynky
stumble *v.i.* спотикатися spotykatysia
stump *v.t* обрубувати obrubuvaty
stump *n.* обрубок obrubok
stun *v.t.* оглушати ohlushaty
stunt *n* зупинка зростання zupynka zrostannia
stunt *v.t.* демонструвати сміливість demonstruvaty smilyvist

stupefy *v.t.* приголомшувати pryholomshuvaty
stupendous *a.* колосальний kolosalnyi
stupid *a* дурний durnyi
stupidity *n.* безглуздість bezhluzdist
sturdy *a.* стійкий stiikyi
sty *n.* свинарник svynarnyk
stye *n.* ячмінь на оці yachmin na otsi
style *n.* стиль styl
subdue *v.t.* скоряти skoriaty
subject *a* залежний zalezhnyi
subject *v.t.* піддавати piddavaty
subject *n.* тема tema
subjection *n.* віддання viddannia
subjective *a.* суб'єктивний subiektyvnyi
subjudice *a.* який перебуває на розгляді yakyi perebuvaie na rozhliadi
subjugate *v.t.* колонізувати kolonizuvaty
subjugation *n.* підкорення pidkorennia
sublet *v.t.* передавати в суборенду peredavaty v suborendu
sublimate *v.t.* сублімувати sublimuvaty
sublime *n* найвища точка naivyshcha tochka
sublime *a.* піднесений pidnesenyi
sublimity *n.* піднесеність pidnesenist
submarine *a* підводний pidvodnyi
submarine *n.* підводний човен pidvodnyi choven
submerge *v.i.* затоплюватися zatopliuvatysia
submission *n.* покора pokora
submissive *a.* покірний pokirnyi

submit *v.t.* представляти predstavliaty
subordinate *n* підлеглий pidlehlyi
subordinate *a.* підрядний pidriadnyi
subordinate *v.t.* підпорядковувати pidporiadkovuvaty
subordination *n.* субординація subordynatsiia
subscribe *v.t.* підписуватися pidpysuvatysia
subscription *n.* підписка pidpyska
subsequent *a.* який випливає yakyi vyplyvaie
subservience *n.* раболіпство rabolipstvo
subservient *a.* раболіпний rabolipnyi
subside *v.i.* спадати spadaty
subsidiary *a.* дочірня компанія dochirnia kompaniia
subsidize *v.t.* субсидіювати subsydiiuvaty
subsidy *n.* субсидія subsydiia
subsist *v.i.* існувати isnuvaty
subsistence *n.* існування isnuvannia
substance *n.* субстанція substantsiia
substantial *a.* тривкий tryvkyi
substantially *adv.* в значній мірі v znachnii miri
substantiate *v.t.* обґрунтовувати obgruntovuvaty
substantiation *n.* аргумент arhument
substitute *v.t.* замінити zaminyty
substitute *n.* замінник zaminnyk
substitution *n.* заміна zamina
subterranean *a.* підземний pidzemnyi

subtle *a.* тонкий tonkyi
subtlety *n.* тонкість tonkist
subtract *v.t.* відняти vidniaty
subtraction *n.* віднімання vidnimannia
suburb *n.* передмістя peredmistia
suburban *a.* заміський zamiskyi
subversion *n.* підривна діяльність pidryvna diialnist
subversive *a.* підривний pidryvnyi
subvert *v.t.* перевертати perevertaty
succeed *v.i.* домагатися успіху domahatysia uspikhu
success *n.* успіх uspikh
successful *a* успішний uspishnyi
succession *n.* наступність nastupnist
successive *a.* наступний nastupnyi
successor *n.* наступник nastupnyk
succour *v.t.* приходити на допомогу prykhodyty na dopomohu
succour *n.* допомога dopomoha
succumb *v.i.* піддаватися piddavatysia
such *pron.* той toi
such *a.* такий takyi
suck *n.* всмоктування vsmoktuvannia
suck *v.t.* смоктати smoktaty
suckle *v.t.* годувати грудьми hoduvaty hrudmy
sudden *n.* несподіванка nespodivanka
suddenly *adv.* раптово raptovo
sue *v.t.* порушувати справу porushuvaty spravu
suffer *v.t.* страждати strazhdaty
suffice *v.i.* вистачити vystachyty

sufficiency *n.* достатність
dostatnist

sufficient *a.* належний nalezhnyi

suffix *v.t.* додавати dodavaty

suffix *n.* суфікс sufiks

suffocate *v.t* душити dushyty

suffocation *n.* удушення
udushennia

suffrage *n.* виборче право
vyborche pravo

sugar *v.t.* обцукровувати
obtsukrovuvaty

sugar *n.* цукор tsukor

suggest *v.t.* підказувати
pidkazuvaty

suggestion *n.* вказівка vkazivka

suggestive *a.* навідний navidnyi

suicidal *a.* самогубний
samohubnyi

suicide *n.* самогубство
samohubstvo

suit *v.t.* задовольняти вимогам
zadovolniaty vymoham

suit *n.* костюм kostium

suitability *n.* доцільність dotsilnist

suitable *a.* придатний prydatnyi

suite *n.* почет pochet

suitor *n.* шанувальник
shanuvalnyk

sullen *a.* неяскравий neiaskravyi

sulphur *n.* сірка sirka

sulphuric *a.* сірчаний sirchanyi

sultry *a.* спекотний spekotnyi

sum *v.t.* складати skladaty

sum *n.* сума suma

summarily *adv.* сумарно sumarno

summarize *v.t.* підсумовувати
pidsumovuvaty

summary *a* сумарний sumarnyi

summary *n.* конспект konspekt

summer *n.* літо lito

summit *n.* саміт samit

summon *v.t.* покликати poklykaty

summons *n.* судова повістка
sudova povistka

sumptuous *a.* розкішний
rozkishnyi

sun *v.t.* гріти на сонці hrity na
sontsi

sun *n.* сонце sontse

Sunday *n.* неділя nedilia

sunder *v.t.* розколювати
rozkoliuvaty

sundry *a.* різний riznyi

sunny *a.* сонячний soniachnyi

sup *v.i.* відсьорбувати
vidsorbuvaty

superabundance *n.* надмірна
кількість nadmirna kilkist

superabundant *a.* зайвий zaivyi

superb *a.* вищої якості vyshchoi
yakosti

superficial *a.* наносний nanosnyi

superficiality *n.* поверховість
poverkhovist

superfine *a.* найтонший
naitonshyi

superfluity *n.* розкіш rozkish

superfluous *a.* зайвий zaivyi

superhuman *a.* надлюдський
nadliudskyi

superintend *v.t.* управляти
upravliaty

superintendence *n.* завідування
zaviduvannia

superintendent *n.* керівник
kerivnyk

superior *a.* вищий vyshchyi

superiority *n.* старшинство
starshynstvo

superlative *n.* кульмінація
kulminatsiia

superlative *a.* найвищий
naivyshchyi

superman *n.* супермен supermen

supernatural *a.* надприродний nadpryrodnyi

supersede *v.t.* міняти miniaty

supersonic *a.* надзвуковий nadzvukovyi

superstition *n.* марновірство marnovirstvo

superstitious *a.* забобонний zabobonnyi

supertax *n.* податок на надприбуток podatok na nadprybutok

supervise *v.t.* контролювати kontroliuvaty

supervision *n.* переливання perelyvannia

supervisor *n.* контролер kontroler

supper *n.* причастя prychastia

supple *a.* піддатливий piddatlyvyi

supplement *v.t.* доповнювати dopovniuvaty

supplement *n.* допоміжний засоб dopomizhnyi zasob

supplementary *a.* який доповнює yakyi dopovniuie

supplier *n.* постачальник postachalnyk

supply *n* запас zapas

supply *v.t.* постачати postachaty

support *n.* оплот oplot

support *v.t.* допомагати dopomahaty

suppose *v.t.* мати певні обов`язки maty pevni obov`iazky

supposition *n.* припущення prypushchennia

suppress *v.t.* забороняти zaboroniaty

suppression *n.* придушення prydushennia

supremacy *n.* верховенство verkhovenstvo

supreme *a.* верховний verkhovnyi

surcharge *v.t.* штрафувати shtrafuvaty

surcharge *n.* доплата doplata

sure *a.* впевнений vpevnenyi

surely *adv.* твердо tverdo

surety *n.* поручительство poruchytelstvo

surf *n.* прибій prybii

surface *n.* поверхня poverkhnia

surface *v.i* приганяти pryhaniaty

surfeit *n.* непомірність nepomirnist

surge *v.i.* хлинути khlynuty

surge *n.* хвилі khvyli

surgeon *n.* хірург khirurh

surgery *n.* хірургія khirurhiia

surmise *v.t.* припускати prypuskaty

surmise *n.* підозра pidozra

surmount *v.t.* долати dolaty

surname *n.* прізвище prizvyshche

surpass *v.t.* випереджати vyperedzhaty

surplus *n.* перевищення perevyshchennia

surprise *v.t.* наскочити naskochyty

surprise *n.* сюрприз siurpryz

surrender *n* капітуляція kapituliatsiia

surrender *v.t.* поступатися postupatysia

surround *v.t.* обступати obstupaty

surroundings *n.* околиці okolytsi

surtax *n.* додатковий податок dodatkovyi podatok

surveillance *n.* спостереження sposterezhennia

survey *n.* інспектування inspektuvannia

survey *v.t.* обдивлятися obdyvliatysia

survival *n.* виживання vyzhyvannia

survive *v.i.* виживати vyzhyvaty

suspect *n* підозрюваний pidozriuvanyi

suspect *a.* підозрілий pidozrilyi

suspect *v.t.* підозрювати pidozriuvaty

suspend *v.t.* призупиняти pryzupyniaty

suspense *n.* занепокоєння zanepokoiennia

suspension *n.* призупинення pryzupynennia

suspicion *n.* підозра pidozra

suspicious *a.* який має підозру yakyi maie pidozru

sustain *v.t.* живити сили zhyvyty syly

sustenance *n.* засоби до існування zasoby do isnuvannia

swagger *n* розв'язність rozviaznist

swagger *v.i.* хвастати khvastaty

swallow *n.* ковток kovtok

swallow *n.* ластівка lastivka

swallow *v.t.* ковтати kovtaty

swamp *v.t.* затоплювати zatopliuvaty

swamp *n.* болото boloto

swan *n.* лебідь lebid

swarm *v.i.* роїтися roitysia

swarm *n.* зграя zhraia

swarthy *a.* смаглявий smahliavyi

sway *n* влада vlada

sway *v.i.* гойдати hoidaty

swear *v.t.* лаятися laiatysia

sweat *v.i.* потіти potity

sweat *n.* піт pit

sweater *n.* светр svetr

sweep *n.* підмітання pidmitannia

sweep *v.i.* підмітати pidmitaty

sweeper *n.* чистильник chystylnyk

sweet *n* цукерка tsukerka

sweet *a.* солодкий solodkyi

sweeten *v.t.* підсолоджувати pidsolodzhuvaty

sweetmeat *n.* цукати tsukaty

sweetness *n.* солодкість solodkist

swell *n* здуття zduttia

swell *v.i.* набухати nabukhaty

swift *a.* швидкий shvydkyi

swim *n* запаморочення zapamorochennia

swim *v.i.* плавати в чомусь plavaty v chomus

swimmer *n.* плавець plavets

swindle *n.* ошукування oshukuvannia

swindle *v.t.* ошукувати oshukuvaty

swindler *n.* ошуканець oshukanets

swine *n.* нахаба nakhaba

swing *n* гойдалки hoidalky

swing *v.i.* вішати vishaty

swiss *a* швейцарський shveitsarskyi

swiss *n.* швейцарець shveitsarets

switch *v.t.* бити лозиною byty lozynoiu

switch *n.* перемикач peremykach

swoon *v.i* непритомніти neprytomnity

swoon *n.* непритомність neprytomnist

swoop *n* пікірування pikiruvannia

swoop *v.i.* спрямуватися вниз spriamuvatysia vnyz

sword *n.* меч mech

sycamore *n.* платан platan

sycophancy *n.* низькопоклонство nyzkopoklonstvo

sycophant *n.* підлабузник pidlabuznyk
syllabic *a.* складовий skladovyi
syllable *n.* склад sklad
syllabus *n.* конспект konspekt
sylph *n.* сильф sylf
sylvan *a.* лісовий lisovyi
symbol *n.* символ symvol
symbolic *a.* символічний symvolichnyi
symbolism *n.* символізм symvolizm
symbolize *v.t.* символізувати symvolizuvaty
symmetrical *a.* симетричний symetrychnyi
symmetry *n.* симетрія symetriia
sympathetic *a.* симпатичний sympatychnyi
sympathize *v.i.* співчувати spivchuvaty
sympathy *n.* співчуття spivchuttia
symphony *n.* симфонія symfoniia
symposium *n.* симпозіум sympozium
symptom *n.* симптом symptom
symptomatic *a.* симптоматичний symptomatychnyi
synonym *n.* синонім synonim
synonymous *a.* синонімічний synonimichnyi
synopsis *n.* синопсис synopsys
syntax *n.* синтаксис syntaksys
synthesis *n.* синтез syntez
synthetic *n* синтетичний продукт syntetychnyi produkt
synthetic *a.* синтетичний syntetychnyi
syringe *v.t.* спринцювати spryntsiuvaty
syringe *n.* шприц shpryts
syrup *n.* сироп syrop
system *n.* система systema

systematic *a.* систематичний systematychnyi
systematize *v.t.* систематизувати systematyzuvaty

table *v.t.* класти на стіл klasty na stil
table *n.* стіл stil
tablet *n.* таблетка tabletka
taboo *a* заборонений zaboronenyi
taboo *v.t.* забороняти zaboroniaty
taboo *n.* табу tabu
tabular *a.* табличний tablychnyi
tabulate *v.t.* зводити в таблицю zvodyty v tablytsiu
tabulation *n.* складання таблиць skladannia tablyts
tabulator *n.* табулятор tabuliator
tacit *a.* який мається на увазі yakyi maietsia na uvazi
taciturn *a.* неговіркий nehovirkyi
tackle *v.t.* закріпити снастями zakripyty snastiamy
tackle *n.* снасті snasti
tact *n.* тактовність taktovnist
tactful *a.* тактовний taktovnyi
tactician *n.* тактик taktyk
tactics *n.* тактика taktyka
tactile *a.* дотиковий dotykovyi
tag *v.t.* скріпити skripyty
tag *n.* ярлик yarlyk
tail *n.* хвіст khvist
tailor *v.t.* шити shyty
tailor *n.* кравець kravets
taint *v.t.* заразити zarazyty
taint *n.* зараза zaraza
take *v.t* брати braty
tale *n.* історія istoriia
talent *n.* талант talant
talisman *n.* талісман talisman

talk *n* розмова rozmova
talk *v.i.* говорити hovoryty
talkative *a.* говіркий hovirkyi
tall *a.* хвалькуватий khvalkuvatyi
tallow *n.* сало salo
tally *v.t.* підрахувати pidrakhuvaty
tally *n.* етикетка etyketka
tamarind *n.* тамаринд tamarynd
tame *v.t.* приручати pryruchaty
tame *a.* ручний ruchnyi
tamper *v.i.* вступати в таємні відносини vstupaty v taiemni vidnosyny
tan *n., a.* загар zahar
tan *v.i.* загоряти zahoriaty
tangent *n.* дотична dotychna
tangible *a.* осяжний osiazhnyi
tangle *v.t.* заплутувати zaplutuvaty
tangle *n.* конфлікт konflikt
tank *n.* цистерна tsysterna
tanker *n.* танкер tanker
tanner *n.* дубильник dubylnyk
tannery *n.* шкіряний завод shkirianyi zavod
tantalize *v.t.* віддавати на муки viddavaty na muky
tantamount *a.* рівносильний rivnosylnyi
tap *n.* кран kran
tap *v.t.* ставити кран stavyty kran
tape *v.t* зв'язати шнуром zviazaty shnurom
tape *n.* стрічка strichka
taper *n* конус konus
taper *v.i.* звужуватися до кінця zvuzhuvatysia do kintsia
tapestry *n.* гобелен hobelen
tar *v.t.* мазати дьогтем mazaty dohtem
tar *n.* дьоготь dohot
target *n.* об'єкт obiekt
tariff *n.* тариф taryf

tarnish *v.t.* тьмяність tmianist
task *v.t.* задати роботу zadaty robotu
task *n.* завдання zavdannia
taste *v.t.* випробувати vyprobuvaty
taste *n.* смак smak
tasteful *a.* зі смаком zi smakom
tasty *a.* смачний smachnyi
tatter *v.t* рвати на шматки rvaty na shmatky
tatter *n.* лахмітник lakhmitnyk
tattoo *v.i.* татуювати tatuiuvaty
tattoo *n.* татуювання tatuiuvannia
taunt *n* образливе глузування obrazlyve hluzuvannia
taunt *v.t.* дражнити drazhnyty
tavern *n.* таверна taverna
tax *v.t.* надмірно напружувати nadmirno napruzhuvaty
tax *n.* тягар tiahar
taxable *a.* оподатковуваний opodatkovuvanyi
taxation *n.* оподаткування opodatkuvannia
taxi *v.i.* їздити на таксі yizdyty na taksi
taxi *n.* таксі taksi
tea *n* чай chai
teach *v.t.* навчати navchaty
teacher *n.* вчитель vchytel
teak *n.* тик tyk
team *n.* бригада bryhada
tear *n.* сльоза sloza
tear *v.t.* роздирати rozdyraty
tear *n.* сльоза sloza
tearful *a.* плачущий plachushchyi
tease *v.t.* ворсувати vorsuvaty
teat *n.* сосок sosok
technical *n.* технічний tekhnichnyi
technicality *n.* формальність formalnist
technician *n.* технік tekhnik

technique *n.* техніка tekhnika
technological *a.* технологічний tekhnolohichnyi
technologist *n.* технолог tekhnoloh
technology *n.* технологія tekhnolohiia
tedious *a.* виснажливий vysnazhlyvyi
tedium *n.* нудьга nudha
teem *v.i.* рясніти riasnity
teenager *n.* підліток pidlitok
teens *n.* підлітковий вік pidlitkovyi vik
teethe *v.i.* намічатися namichatysia
teetotal *a.* непитущий nepytushchyi
teetotaller *n.* непитуща людина nepytushcha liudyna
telecast *v.t.* передавати по телебаченню peredavaty po telebachenniu
telecast *n.* телепередача teleperedacha
telecommunications *n.* далекий зв'язок dalekyi zviazok
telegram *n.* телеграма telehrama
telegraph *v.t.* телеграфувати telehrafuvaty
telegraph *n.* телеграфний telehrafnyi
telegraphic *a.* телеграфний telehrafnyi
telegraphist *n.* телеграфіст telehrafist
telegraphy *n.* телеграфія telehrafiia
telepathic *a.* телепатичний telepatychnyi
telepathist *n.* телепат telepat
telepathy *n.* телепатія telepatiia
telephone *v.t.* дзвонити dzvonyty

telephone *n.* телефон telefon
telescope *n.* телескоп teleskop
telescopic *a.* телескопічний teleskopichnyi
televise *v.t.* повідомляти по телебаченню povidomliaty po telebachenniu
television *n.* телебачення telebachennia
tell *v.t.* розказати rozkazaty
teller *n.* оповідач opovidach
temper *v.t.* регулювати rehuliuvaty
temper *n.* вдача vdacha
temperament *n.* темперамент temperament
temperamental *a.* темпераментний temperamentnyi
temperance *n.* помірність pomirnist
temperate *a.* стриманий strymanyi
temperature *n.* температура temperatura
tempest *n.* буря buria
tempestuous *a.* бурхливий burkhlyvyi
temple *n* скроня skronia
temple *n.* храм khram
temporal *a.* швидкоплинний shvydkoplynnyi
temporary *a.* тимчасовий tymchasovyi
tempt *v.t.* спокушати spokushaty
temptation *n.* спокуса spokusa
tempter *n.* спокусник spokusnyk
ten *n.* десять desiat
tenable *a.* обороноздатний oboronozdatnyi
tenacious *a.* чіпкий chipkyi
tenacity *n.* чіпкість chipkist

tenancy *n.* термін оренди termin orendy

tenant *n.* орендар orendar

tend *v.i.* мати схильність maty skhylnist

tendency *n.* тенденція tendentsiia

tender *a* ніжний nizhnyi

tender *v.t.* пропонувати виконання угоди proponuvaty vykonannia uhody

tender *n* тендер tender

tender *n* пропозиція propozytsiia

tenet *n.* принцип pryntsyp

tennis *n.* теніс tenis

tense *a.* збуджений zbudzhenyi

tense *n.* збудження zbudzhennia

tension *n.* напруженість napruzhenist

tent *n.* намет namet

tentative *a.* орієнтовний oriientovnyi

tenure *n.* володіння volodinnia

term *v.t.* виражати vyrazhaty

term *n.* термін termin

terminable *a.* строковий strokovyi

terminal *n* термінал terminal

terminal *a.* семестровий semestrovyi

terminate *v.t.* припиняти prypyniaty

termination *n.* припинення prypynennia

terminological *a.* термінологічний terminolohichnyi

terminology *n.* термінологія terminolohiia

terminus *n.* вокзал vokzal

terrace *n.* тераса terasa

terrible *a.* страшенний strashennyi

terrier *n.* тер'єр terier

terrific *a.* приголомшливий pryholomshlyvyi

terrify *v.t.* жахати zhakhaty

territorial *a.* територіальний terytorialnyi

territory *n.* територія terytoriia

terror *n.* терор teror

terrorism *n.* тероризм teroryzm

terrorist *n.* терорист teroryst

terrorize *v.t.* тероризувати teroryzuvaty

terse *a.* небагатослівний nebahatoslivnyi

test *n* тест test

test *v.t.* тестувати testuvaty

testament *n.* заповіт zapovit

testicle *n.* яєчко yaiechko

testify *v.i.* давати показання davaty pokazannia

testimonial *n.* свідоцтво svidotstvo

testimony *n.* показання pokazannia

tete-a-tete *n.* віч-на-віч vich-na-vich

tether *v.t.* прив'язати pryviazaty

tether *n.* прив'язь pryviaz

text *n.* текст tekst

textile *n* тканина tkanyna

textile *a.* текстильний tekstylnyi

textual *n.* текстовий tekstovyi

texture *n.* текстура tekstura

thank *v.t.* подякувати podiakuvaty

thankful *a.* вдячний vdiachnyi

thankless *a.* невдячний nevdiachnyi

thanks *n.* подяка podiaka

that *dem. pron.* ті, хто ti, khto

that *rel. pron.* той toi

that *conj.* що shcho

that *adv.* щоб shchob

that *a.* який yakyi

thatch *v.t.* крити соломою kryty
solomoiu
thatch *n.* солома soloma
thaw *n* відлига vidlyha
thaw *v.i* танути tanuty
theatre *n.* театр teatr
theatrical *a.* театральний
teatralnyi
theft *n.* крадіжка kradizhka
their *a.* їх yikh
theirs *pron.* їхній yikhnii
theism *n.* теїзм teizm
theist *n.* теїст teist
them *pron.* їм yim
thematic *a.* тематичний
tematychnyi
theme *n.* тема tema
then *a* тодішній todishnii
then *adv.* тоді todi
thence *adv.* звідти zvidty
theocracy *n.* теократія teokratiia
theologian *n.* богослов bohoslov
theological *a.* богословський
bohoslovskyi
theology *n.* богослов'я
bohoslovia
theorem *n.* теорема teorema
theoretical *a.* теоретичний
teoretychnyi
theorist *n.* теоретик teoretyk
theorize *v.i.* теоретизувати
teoretyzuvaty
theory *n.* теорія teoriia
therapy *n.* терапія terapiia
there *adv.* там tam
thereabouts *adv.* неподалік
nepodalik
thereafter *adv.* відтоді vidtodi
thereby *adv.* тим самим tym
samym
therefore *adv.* тому tomu
thermal *a.* тепловий teplovyi

thermometer *n.* термометр
termometr
thermos (flask) *n.* термос (колба)
termos (kolba)
thesis *n.* дисертація dysertatsiia
thick *adv.* густо husto
thick *a.* товстий tovstyi
thick *n.* центр tsentr
thicken *v.i.* згустити zhustyty
thicket *n.* гущавина hushchavyna
thief *n.* злодій zlodii
thigh *n.* стегно stehno
thimble *n.* наперсток naperstok
thin *v.t.* робити тонким robyty
tonkym
thin *a.* тонкий tonkyi
thing *n.* річ rich
think *v.t.* думати dumaty
thinker *n.* мислитель myslytel
third *n.* третина tretyna
third *a.* третій tretii
thirdly *adv.* по-третє po-tretie
thirst *v.i.* хотіти пити khotity pyty
thirst *n.* спрага spraha
thirsty *a.* спраглий sprahlyi
thirteen *n.* тринадцять trynadtsiat
thirteen *n.* число тринадцять
chyslo trynadtsiat
thirteenth *a.* тринадцятий
trynadtsiatyi
thirtieth *n* тринадцята частина
trynadtsiata chastyna
thirtieth *a.* тридцятий trydtsiatyi
thirty *n.* число тридцять chyslo
trydtsiat
thirty *n.* тридцять trydtsiat
thistle *n.* чортополох
chortopolokh
thither *adv.* туди tudy
thorn *n.* шип shyp
thorny *a.* тернистий ternystyi
thorough *a* ретельний retelnyi
thoroughfare *n.* проїзд proizd

though *adv.* втім vtim
though *conj.* хоча khocha
thought *n* мислення myslennia
thoughtful *a.* вдумливий vdumlyvyi
thousand *a* тисячний tysiachnyi
thousand *n.* тисяча tysiacha
thrall *n.* раб чогось rab chohos
thralldom *n.* рабство rabstvo
thrash *v.t.* молотити molotyty
thread *v.t* нанизувати nanyzuvaty
thread *n.* нитка nytka
threadbare *a.* пошарпаний posharpanyi
threat *n.* загроза zahroza
threaten *v.t.* погрожувати pohrozhuvaty
three *a* третій tretii
three *n.* три try
thresh *v.t.* стібати stibaty
thresher *n.* молотарка molotarka
threshold *n.* поріг porih
thrice *adv.* тричі trychi
thrift *n.* ощадливість oshchadlyvist
thrifty *a.* економний ekonomnyi
thrill *v.t.* тріпотіти tripotity
thrill *n.* трепет trepet
thrive *v.i.* цвісти tsvisty
throat *n.* горло horlo
throaty *a.* гортанний hortannyi
throb *n.* биття byttia
throb *v.i.* тріпотіти tripotity
throe *n.* нестерпний біль nesterpnyi bil
throne *v.t.* займати високе становище zaimaty vysoke stanovyshche
throne *n.* трон tron
throng *n.* товкотнеча tovkotnecha
throng *v.t.* товпитися tovpytysia
throttle *v.t.* стискати styskaty
throttle *n.* стопор stopor

through *adv.* зовсім zovsim
through *a* прямий priamyi
through *prep.* через cherez
throughout *prep.* усюди usiudy
throughout *adv.* по всьому ро vsomu
throw *n.* шарф sharf
throw *v.t.* кидати kydaty
thrust *n* удар udar
thrust *v.t.* тикати tykaty
thud *v.i.* ударятися із глухим стуком udariatysia iz hlukhym stukom
thud *n.* глухий стук hlukhyi stuk
thug *n.* головоріз holovoriz
thumb *v.t.* захватати zakhvataty
thumb *n.* великий палець velykyi palets
thump *v.t.* стукати stukaty
thump *n.* важкий удар vazhkyi udar
thunder *v.i.* гриміти hrymity
thunder *n.* грім hrim
thunderous *a.* громовий hromovyi
Thursday *n.* четвер chetver
thus *adv.* таким чином takym chynom
thwart *v.t.* перешкоджати pereshkodzhaty
tiara *n.* тіара tiara
tick *v.i.* цокати tsokaty
tick *n.* такт takt
ticket *n.* квиток kvytok
tickle *v.t.* лоскотати loskotaty
ticklish *a.* делікатне delikatne
tidal *a.* пов'язаний з приливом poviazanyi z prylyvom
tide *n.* хвиля khvylia
tidiness *n.* охайність okhainist
tidings *n. pl.* новини novyny
tidy *v.t.* приводити в порядок pryvodyty v poriadok

tidy *a.* охайний okhainyi
tie *v.t.* затягувати zatiahuvaty
tie *n* краватка kravatka
tier *n.* ярус yarus
tiger *n.* тигр tyhr
tight *a.* тугий tuhyi
tighten *v.t.* затягнути zatiahnuty
tigress *n.* тигриця tyhrytsia
tile *v.t.* крити кахлем kryty kakhlem
tile *n.* кахель kakhel
till *v.t.* орати oraty
till *n. conj.* поки poky
till *prep.* до do
tilt *v.i.* займатися хліборобством zaimatysia khliborobstvom
tilt *n.* опохиле положення opokhyle polozhennia
timber *n.* лісоматеріали lisomaterialy
time *v.t.* розрахувати за часом rozrakhuvaty za chasom
time *n.* час chas
timely *a.* доречно dorechno
timid *a.* полохливий polokhlyvyi
timidity *n.* боязкість boiazkist
timorous *a.* боязкий boiazkyi
tin *v.t.* покривати оловом pokryvaty olovom
tin *n.* олово olovo
tincture *v.t.* підфарбовувати pidfarbovuvaty
tincture *n.* настоянка nastoianka
tinge *v.t.* надавати відтінок nadavaty vidtinok
tinge *n.* відтінок vidtinok
tinker *n.* мідник midnyk
tinsel *n.* мішура mishura
tint *v.t.* відтіняти vidtiniaty
tint *n.* барва barva
tiny *a.* крихітний krykhitnyi
tip *n.* верхівка verkhivka
tip *v.t.* вивалювати vyvaliuvaty

tip *v.t.* давати на чай davaty na chai
tip *n.* підказка pidkazka
tip *v.t.* ходити навшпиньки khodyty navshpynky
tip *n.* наконечник nakonechnyk
tipsy *a.* підпилий pidpylyi
tirade *n.* тирада tyrada
tire *v.t.* надівати покришку nadivaty pokryshku
tiresome *a.* той, що втомлює toi, shcho vtomliuie
tissue *n.* тканина tkanyna
titanic *a.* титанічний tytanichnyi
tithe *n.* десятина desiatyna
title *n.* назва nazva
titular *a.* заголовний zaholovnyi
toad *n.* гадина hadyna
toast *v.t.* підрум'янювати pidrumianiuvaty
toast *n.* тост tost
tobacco *n.* тютюн tiutiun
today *n.* сьогордняшній день sohordniashnii den
today *adv.* сьогодні sohodni
toe *v.t.* торкатися носком torkatysia noskom
toe *n.* носок nosok
toffee *n.* іриска iryska
toga *n.* тога toha
together *adv.* разом razom
toil *v.i.* тягтися tiahtysia
toil *n.* важка праця vazhka pratsia
toilet *n.* туалет tualet
toils *n. pl.* тенета teneta
token *n.* прикмета prykmeta
tolerable *a.* терпимий terpymyi
tolerance *n.* терпимість terpymist
tolerant *a.* толерантний tolerantnyi
tolerate *v.t.* терпіти terpity
toleration *n.* терпимість terpymist

toll *v.t.* відбивати годинний vidbyvaty hodynnyi

toll *n* мито myto

toll *n.* дзвін dzvin

tomato *n.* помідор pomidor

tomb *n.* могила mohyla

tomboy *n.* шибеник shybenyk

tomcat *n.* кіт kit

tome *n.* том tom

tomorrow *adv.* завтра zavtra

tomorrow *n.* завтрашній день zavtrashnii den

ton *n.* світські люди svitski liudy

tone *v.t.* задавати тон zadavaty ton

tone *n.* тон ton

tongs *n. pl.* щипці shchyptsi

tongue *n.* язик yazyk

tonic *n.* основний тон osnovnyi ton

tonic *a.* тонізуючий tonizuiuchyi

tonight *adv.* сьогодні ввечері sohodni vvecheri

to-night *n.* сьогоднішній вечір sohodnishnii vechir

tonne *n.* тонна tonna

tonsil *n.* мигдалина myhdalyna

tonsure *n.* тонзура tonzura

too *adv.* занадто zanadto

tool *n.* верстат verstat

tooth *n.* зуб zub

toothache *n.* зубний біль zubnyi bil

toothsome *a.* смачний smachnyi

top *n.* верхній шар verkhnii shar

top *v.t.* перевищувати perevyshchuvaty

top *n.* верхня частина verkhnia chastyna

topaz *n.* топаз topaz

topic *n.* тема tema

topical *a.* актуальний aktualnyi

topographer *n.* топограф topohraf

topographical *a.* топографічний topohrafichnyi

topography *n.* топографія topohrafiia

topple *v.i.* повалити povalyty

topsy turvy *adv* вверх дном vverkh dnom

topsy turvy *a.* перевернутий perevernutyi

torch *n.* факел fakel

torment *n.* мука muka

torment *v.t.* заподіювати біль zapodiiuvaty bil

tornado *n.* торнадо tornado

torpedo *v.t.* торпедувати torpeduvaty

torpedo *n.* торпеда torpeda

torrent *n.* злива zlyva

torrential *a.* проливний prolyvnyi

torrid *a.* спекотний spekotnyi

tortoise *n.* черепаха cherepakha

tortuous *a.* ухильний ukhylnyi

torture *v.t.* катувати katuvaty

torture *n.* катування katuvannia

toss *n* метання metannia

toss *v.t.* метати metaty

total *v.t.* дорівнювати dorivniuvaty

total *n.* підсумок pidsumok

total *a.* тотальний totalnyi

totality *n.* сукупність sukupnist

touch *n* дотик dotyk

touch *v.t.* торкатися torkatysia

touchy *a.* образливий obrazlyvyi

tough *a.* щільний shchilnyi

toughen *v.t.* ставати міцним stavaty mitsnym

tour *v.i.* здійснювати поїздку zdiisniuvaty poizdku

tour *n.* тур tur

tourism *n.* туризм turyzm

tourist *n.* турист turyst

tournament *n.* турнір turnir
towards *prep.* до do
towel *v.t.* витирати рушником vytyraty rushnykom
towel *n.* рушник rushnyk
tower *v.i.* підноситися pidnosytysia
tower *n.* башта bashta
town *n.* містечко mistechko
township *a.* селище selyshche
toy *v.i.* крутити в руках krutyty v rukakh
toy *n.* іграшка ihrashka
trace *v.t.* слід slid
trace *n.* траєкторія traiektoriia
traceable *a.* якого можно відстежити yakoho mozhno vidstezhyty
track *v.t.* вистежувати vystezhuvaty
track *n.* слід slid
tract *n* тракт trakt
tract *n.* трактат traktat
traction *n.* тяга tiaha
tractor *n.* трактор traktor
trade *v.i* торгувати torhuvaty
trade *n.* торгівля torhivlia
trader *n.* торговець torhovets
tradesman *n.* крамар kramar
tradition *n.* традиція tradytsiia
traditional *a.* традиційний tradytsiinyi
traffic *v.i.* мати справу maty spravu
traffic *n.* транспорт transport
tragedian *n.* трагік trahik
tragedy *n.* трагедія trahediia
tragic *a.* трагічний trahichnyi
trail *v.t.* волочити volochyty
trail *n.* стежка stezhka
trailer *n.* трейлер treiler
train *v.t.* тренувати trenuvaty
train *n.* поїзд poizd

trainee *n.* стажист stazhyst
training *n.* навчання navchannia
trait *n.* особливість osoblyvist
traitor *n.* зрадник zradnyk
tram *n.* трамвай tramvai
trample *v.t.* топтати toptaty
trance *n.* транс trans
tranquil *a.* спокійний spokiinyi
tranquility *n.* спокій spokii
tranquillize *v.t.* заспокоюватися zaspokoiuvatysia
transact *v.t.* вести vesty
transaction *n.* угода uhoda
transcend *v.t.* долати dolaty
transcendent *a.* що перевершує shcho perevershuie
transcribe *v.t.* транскрибувати transkrybuvaty
transcription *n.* транскрипція transkryptsiia
transfer *v.t.* пересідати peresidaty
transfer *n.* перенесення perenesennia
transferable *a.* перекладний perekladnyi
transfiguration *n.* видозміна vydozmina
transfigure *v.t.* трансформувати transformuvaty
transform *v.t.* трансформувати transformuvaty
transformation *n.* трансформація transformatsiia
transgress *v.t.* переступати perestupaty
transgression *n.* провина provyna
transit *n.* транзит tranzyt
transition *n.* перехідний період perekhidnyi period
transitive *n.* перехідний perekhidnyi

transitory *a.* минущий mynushchyi

translate *v.t.* перекладати perevodyty

translation *n.* переклад pereklad

transmigration *n.* переселення pereselennia

transmission *n.* передача peredacha

transmit *v.t.* відправляти vidpravliaty

transmitter *n.* передавач peredavach

transparent *a.* прозорий prozoryi

transplant *v.t.* переселяти pereseliaty

transport *n.* транспорт transport

transport *v.t.* перевозити perevozyty

transportation *n.* транспортування transportuvannia

trap *v.t.* ставити капкани stavyty kapkany

trap *n.* капкан kapkan

trash *n.* сміття smittia

travel *n* подорож podorozh

travel *v.i.* мандрувати mandruvaty

traveller *n.* комівояжер komivoiazher

tray *n.* піднос pidnos

treacherous *a.* зрадницький zradnytskyi

treachery *n.* віроломство virolomstvo

tread *n* хода khoda

tread *v.t.* протоптувати protoptuvaty

treason *n.* зрадництво zradnytstvo

treasure *v.t.* високо цінувати vysoko tsinuvaty

treasure *n.* скарб skarb

treasurer *n.* скарбник skarbnyk

treasury *n.* казначейство kaznacheistvo

treat *n* пригощання pryhoshchannia

treat *v.t.* лікувати likuvaty

treatise *n.* трактат traktat

treatment *n.* поводження povodzhennia

treaty *n.* угода uhoda

tree *n.* дерево derevo

trek *n.* перехід perekhid

trek *v.i.* переселятися pereseliatysia

tremble *v.i.* тремтіти tremtity

tremendous *a.* гігантський hihantskyi

tremor *n.* тремтіння tremtinnia

trench *v.t.* скопувати skopuvaty

trench *n.* рів riv

trend *n.* тенденція tendentsiia

trespass *n.* посягання posiahannia

trespass *v.i.* провинитися provynytysia

trial *n.* судовий розгляд sudovyi rozhliad

triangle *n.* трикутник trykutnyk

triangular *a.* трикутний trykutnyi

tribal *a.* племінний pleminnyi

tribe *n.* плем'я plemia

tribulation *n.* нещастя neshchastia

tribunal *n.* трибунал trybunal

tributary *a.* другорядний druhoriadnyi

tributary *n.* приплив pryplyv

trick *v.t.* одурювати oduriuvaty

trick *n* трюк triuk

trickery *n.* хитрість khytrist

trickle *v.i.* сочитися sochytysia

trickster *n.* спритник sprytnyk

tricky *a.* хитрий khytryi

tricolour *n* триколор trykolor
tricolour *a.* триколірний trykolirnyi
tricycle *n.* триколісний велосипед trykolisnyi velosyped
trifle *v.i* ставитися несерйозно stavytysia neseriozno
trifle *n.* дрібниця dribnytsia
trigger *n.* детонатор detonator
trim *n* оздоблення ozdoblennia
trim *v.t.* привести в порядок pryvesty v poriadok
trim *a.* наведений у порядок navedenyi u poriadok
trinity *n.* трійця triitsia
trio *n.* тріо trio
trip *n.* мандрівка mandrivka
trip *v.t.* іти легко і швидко ity lehko i shvydko
tripartite *a.* тристоронній trystoronnii
triple *a.* протироєний protyroienyi
triple *v.t.,* потроювати potroiuvaty
triplicate *v.t.* виготовляти в трьох примірниках vyhotovliaty v trokh prymirnykakh
triplicate *n* тріплікат triplikat
triplicate *a.* потрійний potriinyi
triplication *n.* потроєння potroiennia
tripod *n.* штатив shtatyv
triumph *v.i.* тріумфувати triumfuvaty
triumph *n.* тріумф triumf
triumphal *a.* тріумфальний triumfalnyi
triumphant *a.* тріумфуючий triumfuiuchyi
trivial *a.* тривіальний tryvialnyi
troop *v.i* проходити строєм prokhodyty stroiem
troop *n.* зграя zhraia

trooper *n.* кавалерист kavaleryst
trophy *n.* трофей trofei
tropic *n.* тропік tropik
tropical *a.* тропічний tropichnyi
trot *n* рись rys
trot *v.i.* йти риссю yty ryssiu
trouble *v.t.* тривожитися tryvozhytysia
trouble *n.* проблема problema
troublesome *a.* клопіткий klopitkyi
troupe *n.* трупа trupa
trousers *n. pl* брюки briuky
trowel *n.* совок sovok
truce *n.* перемир'я peremyria
truck *n.* вантажний автомобіль vantazhnyi avtomobil
true *a.* істинний istynnyi
trump *v.t.* бити козирем byty kozyrem
trump *n.* козир kozyr
trumpet *v.i.* звіщати zvishchaty
trumpet *n.* труба truba
trunk *n.* стовбур stovbur
trust *v.t* вірити viryty
trust *n.* відповідальне положення vidpovidalne polozhennia
trustee *n.* опікун opikun
trustful *a.* довірливий dovirlyvyi
trustworthy *a.* той, що заслуговує довіри toi, shcho zasluhovuie doviry
trusty *n.* надійна людина nadiina liudyna
truth *n.* правда pravda
truthful *a.* правдивий pravdyvyi
try *n* спроба sproba
try *v.i.* спробувати sprobuvaty
trying *a.* втомливий vtomlyvyi
tryst *n.* побачення pobachennia
tub *n.* діжка dizhka
tube *n.* трубка trubka

tuberculosis *n.* туберкульоз tuberkuloz

tubular *a.* трубчастий trubchastyi

tug *v.t.* буксир buksyr

tuition *n.* тренування trenuvannia

tumble *n.* сум'яття sumiattia

tumble *v.i.* ворочатися vorochatysia

tumbler *n.* тумблер tumbler

tumour *n.* пухлина pukhlyna

tumult *n.* шум shum

tumultuous *a.* галасливий halaslyvyi

tune *v.t.* налаштовувати nalashtovuvaty

tune *n.* мотив motyv

tunnel *v.i.* прокладати тунель prokladaty tunel

tunnel *n.* тунель tunel

turban *n.* тюрбан tiurban

turbine *n.* турбіна turbina

turbulence *n.* турбулентність turbulentnist

turbulent *a.* турбулентний turbulentnyi

turf *n.* торф torf

turkey *n.* індичка indychka

turmeric *n.* куркума kurkuma

turmoil *n.* метушня metushnia

turn *n* черга cherha

turn *v.i.* спрямовувати spriamovuvaty

turner *n.* токар tokar

turnip *n.* ріпа ripa

turpentine *n.* скипидар skypydar

turtle *n.* черепаха cherepakha

tusk *n.* ікло iklo

tussle *v.i.* боротися borotysia

tussle *n.* боротьба borotba

tutor *n.* репетитор repetytor

tutorial *n.* навчальний navchalnyi

tutorial *a.* підручник pidruchnyk

twelfth *n.* дванадцята частина dvanadtsiata chastyna

twelfth *a.* дванадцятий dvanadtsiatyi

twelve *n* число дванадцять chyslo dvanadtsiat

twelve *n.* дванадцять dvanadtsiat

twentieth *n* двадцята частина dvadtsiata chastyna

twentieth *a.* двадцятий dvadtsiatyi

twenty *n* число двадцять chyslo dvadtsiat

twenty *a.* двадцятий dvadtsiatyi

twice *adv.* двічі dvichi

twig *n.* лоза loza

twilight *n* сутінки sutinky

twin *a* який є близнюком yakyi ye blyzniukom

twin *n.* близнюк blyzniuk

twinkle *n.* мигання myhannia

twinkle *v.i.* виблискувати vyblyskuvaty

twist *n.* закрутити zakrutyty

twist *v.t.* вигин vyhyn

twitter *v.i.* щебетати shchebetaty

twitter *n.* щебет shchebet

two *a.* двійка dviika

two *n.* два dva

twofold *a.* вдвічі vdvichi

type *v.t.* друкувати на машинці drukuvaty na mashyntsi

type *n.* тип typ

typhoid *n.* черевний тиф cherevnyi tyf

typhoon *n.* тайфун taifun

typhus *n.* висипний тиф vysypnyi tyf

typical *a.* типовий typovyi

typify *v.t.* уособлювати uosobliuvaty

typist *n.* друкарка drukarka

tyranny *n.* тиранія tyraniia

tyrant *n.* тиран tyran
tyre *n.* шина shyna

udder *n.* вим'я vymia
uglify *v.t.* спотворювати spotvoriuvaty
ugliness *n.* потворність potvornist
ugly *a.* потворний potvornyi
ulcer *n.* виразка vyrazka
ulcerous *a.* виразковий vyrazkovyi
ulterior *a.* наступний nastupnyi
ultimate *a.* кінцевий kintsevyi
ultimately *adv.* в кінцевому рахунку v kintsevomu rakhunku
ultimatum *n.* ультиматум ultymatum
umbrella *n.* парасолька parasolka
umpire *v.t.,* бути суддею buty suddeiu
umpire *n.* третейський суддя treteiskyi suddia
unable *a.* нездатний nezdatnyi
unanimity *n.* одностайність odnostainist
unanimous *a.* одностайний odnostainyi
unaware *a.* той, що не знає toi, shcho ne znaie
unawares *adv.* зненацька znenatska
unburden *v.t.* розвантажити rozvantazhyty
uncanny *a.* моторошний motoroshnyi
uncertain *a.* сумнівний sumnivnyi
uncle *n.* дядя diadia
uncouth *a.* необтесаний neobtesanyi
under *adv* внизу vnyzu

under *a* нижчий nyzhchyi
under *prep.* під pid
undercurrent *n.* підводна течія pidvodna techiia
underdog *n* невдаха nevdakha
undergo *v.t.* зазнавати zaznavaty
undergraduate *n.* студент student
underhand *a.* закулісний zakulisnyi
underline *v.t.* підкреслювати pidkresliuvaty
undermine *v.t.* підривати pidryvaty
underneath *adv.* знизу znyzu
underneath *prep.* під pid
understand *v.t.* знати znaty
undertake *v.t.* вживати vzhyvaty
undertone *n.* підтекст pidtekst
underwear *n.* натільна білизна natilna bilyzna
underworld *n.* підземний світ pidzemnyi svit
undo *v.t.* відмінити vidminyty
undue *a.* надмірний nadmirnyi
undulate *v.i.* рухатися хвилеподібно rukhatysia khvylepodibno
undulation *n.* хвилястість khvyliastist
unearth *v.t.* розкопувати rozkopuvaty
uneasy *a.* неспокійний nespokiinyi
unfair *a* упереджений uperedzhenyi
unfold *v.t.* розкриватися rozkryvatysia
unfortunate *a.* нещасний neshchasnyi
ungainly *a.* вайлуватий vailuvatyi
unhappy *a.* нещасливий neshchaslyvyi

unification *n.* об'єднання
obiednannia
union *n.* союз soiuz
unionist *n.* член профспілки
chlen profspilky
unique *a.* унікальний unikalnyi
unison *n.* унісон unison
unit *n.* одиниця odynytsia
unite *v.t.* об'єднувати obiednuvaty
unity *n.* єдність yednist
universal *a.* універсальний
universalnyi
universality *n.* універсальність
universalnist
universe *n.* всесвіт vsesvit
university *n.* університет
universytet
unjust *a.* необґрунтований
neobgruntovanyi
unless *conj.* якщо не yakshcho ne
unlike *prep* на відміну від na
vidminu vid
unlike *a* несхожий на neskhozhyi
na
unlikely *a.* неймовірний
neimovirnyi
unmanned *a.* безпілотний
bezpilotnyi
unmannerly *a* грубий hrubyi
unprincipled *a.* безпринципний
bezpryntsypnyi
unreliable *a.* ненадійний
nenadiinyi
unrest *n* заворушення
zavorushennia
unruly *a.* непокірний nepokirnyi
unsettle *v.t.* вибивати з колії
vybyvaty z kolii
unsheathe *v.t.* виймати з піхов
vyimaty z pikhov
until *prep.* до do
until *conj* до тих пір do tykh pir

untoward *a.* непокірний
nepokirnyi
unwell *a.* нездоровий nezdorovyi
unwittingly *adv.* мимоволі
mymovoli
up *prep.* до do
up *adv.* підвищується
pidvyshchuietsia
upbraid *v.t* докоряти dokoriaty
upheaval *n.* переворот perevorot
uphold *v.t* задовольняти
zadovolniaty
upkeep *n* утримання utrymannia
uplift *v.t.* піднімати pidnimaty
uplift *n* скид skyd
upon *prep* після pislia
upper *a.* верхній verkhnii
upright *a.* вертикально vertykalno
uprising *n.* повстання povstannia
uproar *n.* шум shum
uproarious *a.* бурхливий
burkhlyvyi
uproot *v.t.* виривати з коренем
vyryvaty z korenem
upset *v.t.* виводити з рівноваги
vyvodyty z rivnovahy
upshot *n.* розв'язка rozviazka
upstart *n.* вискочка vyskochka
up-to-date *a.* новітній novitnii
upward *adv.* наверх naverkh
upwards *adv.* вгору vhoru
urban *a.* міський miskyi
urbane *a.* люб'язний liubiaznyi
urbanity *n.* чемність chemnist
urchin *n.* вуличний хлопчик
vulychnyi khlopchyk
urge *v.t* примушувати
prymushuvaty
urge *n* спонукання sponukannia
urgency *n.* терміновість
terminovist
urgent *a.* терміновий terminovyi
urinal *n.* пісуар pisuar

urinary *a.* сечовий sechovyi
urinate *v.i.* мочитися mochytysia
urination *n.* сечовипускання sechovypuskannia
urine *n.* сеча secha
urn *n* урна urna
usage *n.* користування korystuvannia
use *n.* використання vykorystannia
use *v.t.* використовувати vykorystovuvaty
useful *a.* цінний tsinnyi
usher *v.t.* проводити provodyty
usher *n.* швейцар shveitsar
usual *a.* якій відповідає звичаю yakii vidpovidaie zvychaiu
usually *adv.* звичайно zvychaino
usurer *n.* лихвар lykhvar
usurp *v.t.* узурпувати uzurpuvaty
usurpation *n.* узурпація uzurpatsiia
usury *n.* лихварство lykhvarstvo
utensil *n.* начиння nachynnia
uterus *n.* матка matka
utilitarian *a.* утилітарний utylitarnyi
utility *n.* корисність korysnist
utilization *n.* утилізація utylizatsiia
utilize *v.t.* утилізувати utylizuvaty
utmost *n* все можливе vse mozhlyve
utmost *a.* найвіддаленіший naividdalenishyi
utopia *n .* утопія utopiia
utopian *a.* утопічний utopichnyi
utter *v.t.* виражати словами vyrazhaty slovamy
utter *a* повний povnyi
utterance *n.* висловлювання vyslovliuvannia
utterly *adv.* вкрай vkrai

V

vacancy *n.* вакансія vakansiia
vacant *a.* вакантний vakantnyi
vacate *v.t.* скасовувати skasovuvaty
vacation *n.* відпустка vidpustka
vaccinate *v.t.* вакцинувати vaktsynuvaty
vaccination *n.* вакцинація vaktsynatsiia
vaccinator *n.* провісник provisnyk
vaccine *n.* вакцина vaktsyna
vacillate *v.i.* хитатися khytatysia
vacuum *n.* вакуум vakuum
vagabond *a* бродячий brodiachyi
vagabond *n.* бродяга brodiaha
vagary *n.* примха prymkha
vagina *n.* піхва pikhva
vague *a.* розпливчастий rozplyvchastyi
vagueness *n.* невизначеність nevyznachenist
vain *a.* марний marnyi
vainglorious *a.* марнославний marnoslavnyi
vainglory *n.* хвастощі khvastoshchi
vainly *adv.* марно marno
vale *n.* юдоль yudol
valiant *a.* доблесний doblesnyi
valid *a.* дійсний diisnyi
validate *v.t.* перевіряти pereviriaty
validity *n.* дійсність diisnist
valley *n.* долина dolyna
valour *n.* доблесть doblest
valuable *a.* цінний tsinnyi
valuation *n.* валютування valiutuvannia
value *v.t.* цінувати tsinuvaty
value *n.* цінність tsinnist
valve *n.* клапан klapan

van *n.* фургон furhon
vanish *v.i.* зникати znykaty
vanity *n.* метушливість metushlyvist
vanquish *v.t.* перемагати peremahaty
vaporize *v.t.* випаровуватися vyparovuvatysia
vaporous *a.* пароподібний paropodibnyi
vapour *n.* туман tuman
variable *a.* змінюваний zminiuvanyi
variance *n.* дисперсія dyspersiia
variation *n.* коливання kolyvannia
varied *a.* змінний zminnyi
variety *n.* різноманітність riznomanitnist
various *a.* усілякий usiliakyi
varnish *v.t.* лакувати lakuvaty
varnish *n.* лак lak
vary *v.t.* змінюватися zminiuvatysia
vasectomy *n.* вазектомія vazektomiia
vaseline *n.* вазелін vazelin
vast *a.* численний chyslennyi
vault *v.i.* зводити склепіння zvodyty sklepinnia
vault *n.* льох lokh
vault *n.* сховище skhovyshche
vegetable *a.* овочевий ovochevyi
vegetable *n.* овоч ovoch
vegetarian *n.* вегетаріанець vehetarianets
vegetarian *a* вегетаріанський vehetarianskyi
vegetation *n.* рослинність roslynnist
vehemence *n.* гарячність hariachnist
vehement *a.* шалений shalenyi

vehicle *n.* засоб пересування zasob peresuvannia
vehicular *a.* автомобільний avtomobilnyi
veil *v.t.* приховувати prykhovuvaty
veil *n.* завіса zavisa
vein *n.* вена vena
velocity *n.* швидкість shvydkist
velvet *n.* оксамит oksamyt
velvety *a.* бархатистий barkhatystyi
venal *a.* продажний prodazhnyi
venality *n.* продажність prodazhnist
vendor *n.* роазнощик roaznoshchyk
venerable *a.* поважний povazhnyi
venerate *v.t.* шанувати shanuvaty
veneration *n.* шанування shanuvannia
vengeance *n.* помста pomsta
venial *a.* пробачний probachnyi
venom *n.* злоба zloba
venomous *a.* злісний zlisnyi
vent *n.* вентиляційний ventyliatsiinyi
ventilate *v.t.* вентилювати ventyliuvaty
ventilation *n.* вентиляція ventyliatsiia
ventilator *n.* вентилятор ventyliator
venture *v.t.* ризикнути ryzyknuty
venture *n.* підприємство pidpryiemstvo
venturesome *a.* азартний azartnyi
venturous *a.* безстрашний bezstrashnyi
venue *n.* місце зустрічі mistse zustrichi
veracity *n.* правдивість pravdyvist
veranda *n.* веранда veranda

verb *n.* дієслово diieslovo
verbal *a.* словесний slovesnyi
verbally *adv.* усно usno
verbatim *adv.* дослівно doslivno
verbatim *a.* дослівний doslivnyi
verbose *a.* багатослівний bahatoslivnyi
verbosity *n.* багатослівність bahatoslivnist
verdant *a.* нестиглий nestyhlyi
verdict *n.* вердикт verdykt
verge *n.* межа mezha
verification *n.* перевірка perevirka
verify *v.t.* перевірити pereviryty
verisimilitude *n.* правдоподібність pravdopodibnist
veritable *a.* справжній spravzhnii
vermillion *a.* яскраво-червоний yaskravo-chervonyi
vermillion *n.* яскраво-червоний колір yaskravo-chervonyi kolir
vernacular *a.* народний narodnyi
vernacular *n.* рідна мова ridna mova
vernal *a.* весняний vesnianyi
versatile *a.* різносторонній riznostoronnii
versatility *n.* гнучкість hnuchkist
verse *n.* віршований рядок virshovanyi riadok
versed *a.* досвічений dosvichenyi
versification *n.* віршування virshuvannia
versify *v.t.* складати вірши skladaty virshy
version *n.* версія versiia
versus *prep.* порівнюючи з porivniuiuchy z
vertical *a.* вертикальний vertykalnyi
verve *n.* сила syla

very *a.* справжній spravzhnii
vessel *n.* судно sudno
vest *v.t.* доручити doruchyty
vest *n.* жилетка zhyletka
vestige *n.* слід slid
vestment *n.* вбрання vbrannia
veteran *a.* заслужений zasluzhenyi
veteran *n.* ветеран veteran
veterinary *a.* ветеринарний veterynarnyi
veto *v.t.* накладати вето nakladaty veto
veto *n.* вето veto
vex *v.t.* докучати dokuchaty
vexation *n* досада dosada
via *prep.* через cherez
viable *a.* життєздатний zhyttiezdatnyi
vial *n.* флакон flakon
vibrate *v.i.* вібрувати vibruvaty
vibration *n.* вібрація vibratsiia
vicar *n.* вікарій vikarii
vicarious *a.* чужий chuzhyi
vice *n.* заступник zastupnyk
viceroy *n.* віце-король vitse-korol
vice-versa *adv.* навпаки navpaky
vicinity *n.* сусідство susidstvo
vicious *a.* порочний porochnyi
vicissitude *n.* мінливість minlyvist
victim *n.* жертва zhertva
victimize *v.t.* переслідувати peresliduvaty
victor *n.* переможець peremozhets
victorious *a.* переможний peremozhnyi
victory *n.* перемога peremoha
victuals *n.* провіант proviant
vie *v.i.* суперничати supernychaty
view *v.t.* оглянути ohlianuty
view *n.* краєвид kraievyd
vigil *n.* бдіння bdinnia

vigilance *n.* пильність pylnist
vigilant *a.* пильний pylnyi
vigorous *a.* сильний sylnyi
vile *a.* бридкий brydkyi
vilify *v.t.* поносити ponosyty
villa *n.* вілла villa
village *n.* село selo
villager *n.* сільський житель silskyi zhytel
villain *n.* пустун pustun
vindicate *v.t.* довести dovesty
vindication *n.* витребування vytrebuvannia
vine *n.* виноградна лоза vynohradna loza
vinegar *n.* оцет otset
vintage *n.* марочний marochnyi
violate *v.t.* паплюжити papliuzhyty
violation *n.* правопорушення pravoporushennia
violence *n.* насильство nasylstvo
violent *a.* насильницький nasylnytskyi
violet *n.* фіолетовий колір fioletovyi kolir
violin *n.* скрипка skrypka
violinist *n.* скрипаль skrypal
virgin *n* цілина tsilyna
virgin *n.* незаймана nezaimana
virginity *n.* незайманість nezaimanist
virile *a.* чоловічий cholovichyi
virility *n.* приналежність до чоловічої статі prynalezhnist do cholovichoi stati
virtual *a* віртуальний virtualnyi
virtue *n.* доброчесність dobrochesnist
virtuous *a.* доброчесний dobrochesnyi
virulence *n.* отруйність otruinist
virulent *a.* ворожий vorozhyi
virus *n.* вірус virus

visage *n.* вираз обличчя vyraz oblychchia
visibility *n.* видимість vydymist
visible *a.* зримий zrymyi
vision *n.* проникнення pronyknennia
visionary *n.* фантазер fantazer
visionary *a.* примарний prymarnyi
visit *n.* відвідування vidviduvannia
visit *v.t.* приходити в гості prykhodyty v hosti
visitor *n.* відвідувач vidviduvach
vista *n.* алея aleia
visual *a.* візуальний vizualnyi
visualize *v.t.* візуалізувати vizualizuvaty
vital *a.* життєво важливий zhyttievo vazhlyvyi
vitality *n.* життєвість zhyttievist
vitalize *v.t.* робити життєвим robyty zhyttievym
vitamin *n.* вітамін vitamin
vitiate *v.t.* псувати psuvaty
vivacious *a.* життєрадісний zhyttieradisnyi
vivacity *n.* жвавість zhvavist
viva-voce *a* усний usnyi
viva-voce *n* усний іспит usnyi ispyt
viva-voce *adv.* усно usno
vivid *a.* яскравий yaskravyi
vixen *n.* мегера mehera
vocabulary *n.* словник slovnyk
vocal *a.* вокальний vokalnyi
vocalist *n.* вокаліст vokalist
vocation *n.* професія profesiia
vogue *n.* популярність populiarnist
voice *v.t.* вимовляти vymovliaty
voice *n.* голос holos
void *v.t.* виділити vydilyty

void *n.* почуття спушеності pochuttia spushenosti

void *a.* недійсний nediisnyi

volcanic *a.* вулканічний vulkanichnyi

volcano *n.* вулкан vulkan

volition *n.* воля volia

volley *v.t* стріляти залпами striliaty zalpamy

volley *n.* залп zalp

volt *n.* вольт volt

voltage *n.* електрична напруга elektrychna napruha

volume *n.* об`єм ob`iem

voluminous *a.* об'ємистий obiemystyi

voluntarily *adv.* добровільно dobrovilno

voluntary *a.* добровільний dobrovilnyi

volunteer *v.t.* йти добровільно yty dobrovilno

volunteer *n.* волонтер volonter

voluptuary *n.* сластолюбець slastoliubets

voluptuous *a.* хтивий khtyvyi

vomit *n* блювота bliuvota

vomit *v.t.* нудити nudyty

voracious *a.* ненаситний nenasytnyi

votary *n.* чернець chernets

vote *v.i.* балотувати balotuvaty

vote *n.* балотування balotuvannia

voter *n.* учасник uchasnyk

vouch *v.i.* ручатися за ruchatysia za

voucher *n.* ваучер vaucher

vouchsafe *v.t.* удостоювати udostoiuvaty

vow *v.t.* давати обітницю davaty obitnytsiu

vow *n.* обітниця obitnytsia

vowel *n.* гласний hlasnyi

voyage *v.i.* робити подорож robyty podorozh

voyage *n.* політ polit

voyager *n.* мореплавець moreplavets

vulgar *a.* вульгарний vulharnyi

vulgarity *n.* вульгарність vulharnist

vulnerable *a.* уразливий urazlyvyi

vulture *n.* стерв'ятник sterviatnyk

waddle *v.i.* шкандибати shkandybaty

wade *v.i.* пробиратися probyratysia

waft *n* віяння viiannia

waft *v.t.* навіяти naviiaty

wag *n* жартівник zhartivnyk

wag *v.i.* махати makhaty

wage *n.* розплата rozplata

wage *v.t.* вести війну vesty viinu

wager *v.i.* укладати парі ukladaty pari

wager *n.* парі pari

wagon *n.* вагон vahon

wail *n* виття vyttia

wail *v.i.* волати volaty

wain *n.* віз viz

waist *n.* талія taliia

waistband *n.* пояс poias

waistcoat *n.* жилет zhylet

wait *n.* чекання chekannia

wait *v.i.* чекати chekaty

waiter *n.* офіціант ofitsiant

waitress *n.* офіціантка ofitsiantka

waive *v.t.* допускати відхилення dopuskaty vidkhylennia

wake *n* кільватер kilvater

wake *n* рубець rubets

wake *v.t.* пожвавити pozhvavyty

wakeful *a.* несплячий nespliachyi

walk *n* відстань vidstan
walk *v.i.* ходити khodyty
wall *v.t.* обносити стіною
obnosyty stinoiu
wall *n.* стіна stina
wallet *n.* гаманець hamanets
wallop *v.t.* побити pobyty
wallow *v.i.* валятися valiatysia
walnut *n.* волоський горіх
voloskyi horikh
walrus *n.* морж morzh
wan *a.* тьмяний tmianyi
wand *n.* паличка palychka
wander *v.i.* мандрувати
mandruvaty
wane *n* збиток zbytok
wane *v.i.* убувати ubuvaty
want *n* потреба potreba
want *v.t.* хотіти khotity
wanton *a.* безвідповідальний
bezvidpovidalnyi
war *v.i.* вести війну vesty viinu
war *n.* війна viina
warble *n* трель trel
warble *v.i.* заливатися zalyvatysia
warbler *n.* співочий птах
spivochyi ptakh
ward *v.t.* відвертати vidvertaty
ward *n.* підопічна особа
pidopichna osoba
warden *n.* доглядач dohliadach
warder *n.* тюремник tiuremnyk
wardrobe *n.* платтяна шафа
plattiana shafa
wardship *n.* піклування
pikluvannia
ware *n. pl.* вироби vyroby
warehouse *v.t* склад sklad
warfare *n.* військові дії viiskovi dii
warlike *a.* стосовний до війни
stosovnyi do viiny
warm *v.t.* гріти hrity
warm1 *a.* теплий teplyi

warmth *n.* тепло teplo
warn *v.t.* попереджати
poperedzhaty
warning *n.* застереження
zasterezhennia
warrant *v.t.* ручатися за
ruchatysia za
warrant *n.* ордер order
warrantee *n.* особа, якій дається
гарантія osoba, yakii daietsia
harantiia
warrantor *n.* особа, що дає
гарантію osoba, shcho daie
harantiiu
warranty *n.* гарантія harantiia
warren *n.* кролячий садок
kroliachyi sadok
warrior *n.* воїн voin
wart *n.* бородавка borodavka
wary *a.* насторожений
nastorozhenyi
wash *n* прання prannia
wash *v.t.* мити myty
washable *a.* що стирається
shcho styraietsia
washer *n.* мийник myinyk
wasp *n.* оса osa
waspish *a.* уїдливий uidlyvyi
wassail *n.* здравиця zdravytsia
wastage *n.* усушка usushka
waste *n.* відходи vidkhody
waste *v.t.* марнувати marnuvaty
waste *a.* стічний stichnyi
wasteful *a.* марнотратний
marnotratnyi
watch *n.* корабельний хронометр
korabelnyi khronometr
watch *v.t.* спостерігати
sposterihaty
watchful *a.* обережний
oberezhnyi
watchword *n.* пароль parol
water *v.t.* поїти poity

water *n.* вода voda
waterfall *n.* каскад kaskad
water-melon *n.* кавун kavun
waterproof *n* водонепроникна тканина vodonepronykna tkanyna
waterproof *v.t.* робити водонепроникним robyty vodonepronyknym
waterproof *a.* водонепроникний vodonepronyknyi
watertight *a.* непромокальний nepromokalnyi
watery *a.* водянистий vodianystyi
watt *n.* ват vat
wave *v.t.* завивати zavyvaty
wave *n.* хвиля khvylia
waver *v.i.* коливатися kolyvatysia
wax *v.t.* вощити voshchyty
wax *n.* віск visk
way *n.* шлях shliakh
wayfarer *n.* подорожній podorozhnii
waylay *v.t.* підстерігати pidsterihaty
wayward *a.* мінливий minlyvyi
weak *a.* слабкий slabkyi
weaken *v.t.* послаблювати poslabliuvaty
weakling *n.* слабка істота slabka istota
weakness *n.* слабкість slabkist
weal *n.* благо blaho
wealth *n.* добробут dobrobut
wealthy *a.* заможний zamozhnyi
wean *v.t.* відлучати vidluchaty
weapon *n.* знаряддя znariaddia
wear *v.t.* зносити znosyty
weary *a.* стомлений stomlenyi
weary *v.t.* стомлювати stomliuvaty
weary *v.i.* стомлюватися stomliuvatysia
weary *a.* втомлений vtomlenyi

weather *v.t.* вивітрювати vyvitriuvaty
weather *n* погода pohoda
weave *v.t.* ткати tkaty
weaver *n.* ткач tkach
web *n.* тасьма tasma
webby *a.* павутинний pavutynnyi
wed *v.t.* одружити odruzhyty
wedding *n.* одруження odruzhennia
wedge *v.t.* закріплювати клином zakripliuvaty klynom
wedge *n.* клин klyn
wedlock *n.* шлюб shliub
Wednesday *n.* середа sereda
weed *v.t.* полоти poloty
weed *n.* бур'ян burian
week *n.* тиждень tyzhden
weekly *adv.* раз на тиждень raz na tyzhden
weekly *adv.* щотижня shchotyzhnia
weekly *a.* тижневий tyzhnevyi
weep *v.i.* плакати plakaty
weevil *n.* довгоносик dovhonosyk
weigh *v.t.* важити vazhyty
weight *n.* вага vaha
weightage *n.* вагомість vahomist
weighty *a.* обтяжливий obtiazhlyvyi
weir *n.* водозлив vodozlyv
weird *a.* фантастичний fantastychnyi
welcome *v.t* привітно приймати pryvitno pryimaty
welcome *n* гостинність hostynnist
welcome *a.* довгоочікуваний dovhoochikuvanyi
weld *n* зварювання zvariuvannia
weld *v.t.* зварити zvaryty
welfare *n.* добробут dobrobut
well *adv.* добре dobre
well *n.* криниця krynytsia

well *v.i.* хлинути khlynuty
well *a.* хороший khoroshyi
wellington *n.* Веллінгтон Vellinhton
well-known *a.* відомий vidomyi
well-read *a.* начитаний nachytanyi
well-timed *a.* доречний dorechnyi
well-to-do *a.* забезпечений zabezpechenyi
welt *n.* бордюр bordiur
welter *n.* сумбур sumbur
wen *n.* жировик zhyrovyk
wench *n.* дівка divka
west *a.* західний zakhidnyi
west *adv.* на захід na zakhid
west *n.* вест vest
westerly *adv.* на захід na zakhid
westerly *a.* західний zakhidnyi
western *a.* вестовий vestovyi
wet *v.t.* промочити promochyty
wet *a.* мокрий mokryi
wetness *n.* вологість volohist
whack *v.t.* сильний удар sylnyi udar
whale *n.* кит kyt
wharfage *n.* портові митні збори portovi mytni zbory
what *interj.* що shcho
what *pron.* що за shcho za
what *a.* який yakyi
whatever *pron.* що б не shcho b ne
wheat *n.* пшениця pshenytsia
wheedle *v.t.* підлещуватися pidleshchuvatysia
wheel *v.t.* підкотити pidkotyty
wheel *a.* колесо koleso
whelm *v.t.* заливати zalyvaty
whelp *n.* цуценя tsutsenia
when *conj.* хоча khocha
when *adv.* коли koly
whence *adv.* звідки zvidky

whenever *adv. conj* коли б не koly b ne
where *conj.* де de
where *adv.* куди kudy
whereabout *adv.* місцезнаходження mistseznakhodzhennia
whereas *conj.* в той час як v toi chas yak
whereat *conj.* на що na shcho
wherein *adv.* в чому v chomu
whereupon *conj.* після чого pislia choho
wherever *adv.* де б не було de b ne bulo
whet *v.t.* точити tochyty
whether *conj.* чи chy
which *pron.* що shcho
which *a.* який yakyi
whichever *pron* який б не yakyi b ne
whiff *n.* подув poduv
while *conj.* поки poky
while *v.t.* проводити provodyty
while *n.* час chas
whim *n.* примха prymkha
whimper *v.i.* хникати khnykaty
whimsical *a.* химерний khymernyi
whine *n* пхикання pkhykannia
whine *v.i.* скиглити skyhlyty
whip *n.* батіг batih
whip *v.t.* січ sich
whipcord *n.* габардин habardyn
whir *n.* шум shum
whirl *n* вихор vykhor
whirl *v.i.* кружляти kruzhliaty
whirligig *n.* юла yula
whirlpool *n.* вир vyr
whirlwind *n.* смерч smerch
whisk *n* віник vinyk
whisk *v.t.* снувати snuvaty
whisker *n.* борода boroda

whisky *n.* віскі viski
whisper *n* шепіт shepit
whisper *v.t.* шепотіти shepotity
whistle *n* свисток svystok
whistle *v.i.* свистіти svystity
white *n* білизна bilyzna
white *a.* білий bilyi
whiten *v.t.* чистити до білого chystyty do biloho
whitewash *v.t.* білити bilyty
whitewash *n.* побілка pobilka
whither *adv.* для чого dlia choho
whitish *a.* білуватий biluvatyi
whittle *v.t.* стругати struhaty
whiz *v.i.* проноситися зі свистом pronosytysia zi svystom
who *pron.* хто khto
whoever *pron.* хто б не khto b ne
whole *n* ціле tsile
whole *a.* цілий tsilyi
whole-hearted *a.* щирий shchyryi
wholesale *a* оптовий optovyi
wholesale *adv.* оптом optom
wholesale *n.* оптова торгівля optova torhivlia
wholesaler *n.* оптовик optovyk
wholesome *a.* сприятливий spryiatlyvyi
wholly *adv.* повністю povnistiu
whom *pron.* кому komu
whore *n.* шльондра shlondra
whose *pron.* чий chyi
why *adv.* чому chomu
wick *n.* гніт hnit
wicked *a.* неприємний nepryiemnyi
wicker *n.* плетіння pletinnia
wicket *n.* хвіртка khvirtka
wide *adv.* широко shyroko
wide *a.* широкий shyrokyi
widen *v.t.* розширюватися rozshyriuvatysia

widespread *a.* дуже поширений duzhe poshyrenyi
widow *v.t.* знедолити znedolyty
widow *n.* вдова vdova
widower *n.* вдівець vdivets
width *n.* ширина shyryna
wield *v.t.* вміти поводитися vmity povodytysia
wife *n.* дружина druzhyna
wig *n.* перука peruka
wight *n.* особа osoba
wigwam *n.* вігвам vihvam
wild *a.* некультивований nekultyvovanyi
wilderness *n.* цілина tsilyna
wile *n.* хитрість khytrist
will *v.t.* веліти velity
will *n.* сила волі syla voli
willing *a.* схильний skhylnyi
willingness *n.* готовність hotovnist
willow *n.* верба verba
wily *a.* хитрий khytryi
wimble *n.* коловорот kolovorot
wimple *n.* бурав burav
win *n* виграш vyhrash
win *v.t.* виграти vyhraty
wince *v.i.* морщитися morshchytysia
winch *n.* лебідка lebidka
wind *v.t.* обмотати obmotaty
wind *v.t.* вертіти vertity
wind *n.* вітер viter
windbag *n.* пустодзвін pustodzvin
winder *n.* мотальна машина motalna mashyna
windlass *v.t.* брашпиль brashpyl
windmill *n.* вітряк vitriak
window *n.* вікно vikno
windy *a.* вітряний vitrianyi
wine *n.* вино vyno
wing *n.* крило krylo
wink *n* моргання morhannia

wink *v.i.* підморгувати
pidmorhuvaty
winner *n.* сторона, що виграла
storona, shcho vyhrala
winnow *v.t.* віяти viiaty
winsome *a.* чарівний charivnyi
winter *v.i* проводити зиму
provodyty zymu
winter *n.* зима zyma
wintry *a.* зимовий zymovyi
wipe *n.* глузування hluzuvannia
wipe *v.t.* витирати vytyraty
wire *v.t.* телеграфувати
telehrafuvaty
wire *n.* провід provid
wireless *n* радіоприймач
radiopryimach
wireless *a.* бездротовий
bezdrotovyi
wiring *n.* проводка provodka
wisdom *n.* мудрість mudrist
wisdom-tooth *n.* мудрості зуб
mudrosti zub
wise *a.* мудрий mudryi
wish *v.t.* хотіти khotity
wish *n.* бажання bazhannia
wishful *a.* жаданий zhadanyi
wisp *n.* пучок puchok
wistful *a.* що тужить shcho tuzhyt
wit *n.* дотепність dotepnist
witch *n.* відьма vidma
witchcraft *n.* чаклунство
chaklunstvo
witchery *n.* чаклунство
chaklunstvo
with *prep.* з z
withal *adv.* вдобавок vdobavok
withdraw *v.t.* знімати znimaty
withdrawal *n.* відведення
vidvedennia
withe *n.* вербовий прут verbovyi
prut
wither *v.i.* сохнути sokhnuty

withhold *v.t.* утримувати
utrymuvaty
within *adv.* в межах v mezhakh
within *adv.* всередені vseredeni
within *prep.* в v
without *adv.* без того, щоб bez
toho, shchob
without *n* простір за межами
чогось prostir za mezhamy
chohos
without *prep.* поза poza
withstand *v.t.* витримувати
vytrymuvaty
witless *a.* нерозумний
nerozumnyi
witness *v.i.* свідчити svidchyty
witness *n.* свідок svidok
witticism *n.* жарт zhart
witty *a.* дотепний dotepnyi
wizard *n.* чарівник charivnyk
wobble *v.i* хитатися khytatysia
woe *n.* скорбота skorbota
woebegone *a.* похмурий
pokhmuryi
woeful *n.* сумний sumnyi
wolf *n.* вовк vovk
woman *n.* жінка zhinka
womanhood *n.* жіночність
zhinochnist
womanise *v.t.* жити розпусно
zhyty rozpusno
womanish *n.* власний жінкам
vlasnyi zhinkam
womb *n.* чрево chrevo
wonder *v.i.* цікавитися
tsikavytysia
wonder *n* чудо chudo
wonderful *a.* дивний dyvnyi
wondrous *a.* чудовий chudovyi
wont *n* звичка zvychka
wont *a.* що має звичай shcho
maie zvychai

wonted *a.* звиклий до нових умов zvyklyi do novykh umov

woo *v.t.* доглядати dohliadaty

wood *n.* гай hai

wooden *a.* дерев'яний derevianyi

woodland *n.* лісиста місцевість lysysta mistsevist

woods *n.* ліси lisy

woof *n.* гавкання havkannia

wool *n.* вовна vovna

woollen *n* вовняна матерія vovniana materiia

woollen *a.* вовняний vovnianyi

word *v.t* висловлювати словами vyslovliuvaty slovamy

word *n.* слово slovo

wordy *a.* словесний slovesnyi

work *v.t.* прокладати шлях prokladaty shliakh

work *n.* робота robota

workable *a.* придатний для роботи prydatnyi dlia roboty

workaday *a.* буденний budennyi

worker *n.* робітник robitnyk

workman *n.* робочий robochyi

workmanship *n.* мистецтво mystetstvo

workshop *n.* майстерня maisternia

world *n.* світ svit

worldling *n.* людина, поглинена земними інтересами liudyna, pohlynena zemnymy interesamy

worldly *a.* суєтний suietnyi

worm *n.* черв'як cherviak

wormwood *n.* полин polyn

worn *a.* зношений znoshenyi

worry *v.i.* турбуватися turbuvatysia

worry *n.* мука muka

worsen *v.t.* погіршувати pohirshuvaty

worship *v.t.* поклонятися pokloniatysia

worship *n.* поклоніння pokloninnia

worshipper *n.* шанувальник shanuvalnyk

worst *n.* найгірше naihirshe

worst *a* найгірший naihirshyi

worst *v.t.* перемогти peremohty

worsted *n.* камвольний kamvolnyi

worth *a* вартий vartyi

worth *n.* що має цінність shcho maie tsinnist

worthless *a.* даремний daremnyi

worthy *a.* гідний hidnyi

would-be *a.* передбачуваний peredbachuvanyi

wound *v.t.* поранити poranyty

wound *n.* поранення poranennia

wrack *n.* повністю руйнувати povnistiu ruinuvaty

wraith *n.* мара mara

wrangle *n.* суперечка superechka

wrangle *v.i.* сперечатися sperechatysia

wrap *n* обгортка obhortka

wrap *v.t.* обернути obernuty

wrapper *n.* пакувальник pakuvalnyk

wrath *n.* лють liut

wreath *n.* вінок vinok

wreathe *v.t.* обвивати obvyvaty

wreck *v.t.* руйнувати ruinuvaty

wreck *n.* крах krakh

wreckage *n.* уламки ulamky

wrecker *n.* шкідник shkidnyk

wren *n.* кропив'яник kropvianyk

wrench *v.t.* вивихнути vyvykhnuty

wrench *n.* гайковий ключ haikovyi kliuch

wrest *v.t.* вирвати vyrvaty

wrestle *v.i.* вести наполегливу боротьбу vesty napolehlyvu borotbu

wrestler *n.* борець borets

wretch *n.* негідник nehidnyk

wretched *a.* кепський kepskyi

wrick *n* розтяг roztiah

wriggle *n* вигинання vyhynannia

wriggle *v.i.* просуватися вперед prosuvatysia vpered

wring *v.t* вичавлювати vychavliuvaty

wrinkle *v.t.* морщити morshchyty

wrinkle *n.* зморшка zmorshka

wrist *n.* зап'ясток zapiastok

writ *n.* судовий наказ sudovyi nakaz

write *v.t.* писати pysaty

writer *n.* письменник pysmennyk

writhe *v.i.* корчити korchyty

wrong *v.t.* бути несправедливим buty nespravedlyvym

wrong *adv.* неправильно nepravylno

wrong *a.* несправний nespravnyi

wrongful *a.* неправомірний nepravomirnyi

wry *a.* кривий kryvyi

xerox *v.t.* ксерокопіювати kserokopiiuvaty

xerox *n.* ксерокс kseroks

Xmas *n.* Різдво Rizdvo

x-ray *v.t.* просвічувати рентгенівськими променями prosvichuvaty renthenivskymy promeniamy

x-ray *n.* рентген renthen

x-ray *a.* рентгенівський renthenivskyi

xylophagous *a.* той, що живиться деревиною toi, shcho zhyvytsia derevynoiu

xylophilous *a.* зростаючий на деревині zrostaiuchyi na derevyni

xylophone *n.* ксилофон ksylofon

yacht *v.i* плавати на яхті plavaty na yakhti

yacht *n.* яхта yakhta

yak *n.* як yak

yap *n* пелька pelka

yap *v.i.* гавкати havkaty

yard *n.* подвір'я podviria

yarn *n.* пряжа priazha

yawn *n.* позіхання pozikhannia

yawn *v.i.* позіхати pozikhaty

year *n.* рік rik

yearly *a.* що триває рік shcho tryvaie rik

yearly *adv.* щорічно shchorichno

yearn *v.i.* тужити tuzhyty

yearning *n.* глибока туга hlyboka tuha

yeast *n.* дріжджі drizhdzhi

yell *v.i.* лементувати lementuvaty

yell *n* пронизливий крик pronyzlyvyi kryk

yellow *n* жовтизна zhovtyzna

yellow *a.* жовтий zhovtyi

yellow *v.t.* пожовтіти pozhovtity

yellowish *a.* жовтуватий zhovtuvatyi

Yen *n.* Ієна Iiena

yeoman *n.* йомен yomen

yes *adv.* так tak

yesterday *n.* вчора vchora

yesterday *adv.* учора uchora

yet *adv.* вже vzhe

yet *conj.* тільки tilky

yield *n* вихід vykhid
yield *v.t.* здати zdaty
yoke *v.t.* запрягти zapriahty
yoke *n.* ярмо yarmo
yolk *n.* жовток zhovtok
yonder *adv.* он там on tam
yonder *a.* он той on toi
young *n* молодь molod
young *a.* юний yunyi
youngster *n.* хлопчик khlopchyk
youth *n.* юнак yunak
youthful *a.* юний yunyi

Z

zany *a.* смішний smishnyi
zeal *n.* завзяття zavziattia
zealot *n.* фанатик fanatyk
zealous *a.* ревний revnyi
zebra *n.* зебра zebra
zenith *n.* зеніт zenit
zephyr *n.* зефір zefir
zero *n.* ніщо nishcho
zest *n.* родзинка rodzynka
zigzag *n.* зигзаг zyhzah
zigzag *a.* зигзагоподібний
zyhzahopodibnyi
zigzag *v.i.* робити зигзаги robyty
zyhzahy
zinc *n.* цинк tsynk
zip *v.t.* промайнути promainuty
zip *n.* свист кулі svyst kuli
zodiac *n* зодіак zodiak
zonal *a.* зональний zonalnyi
zone *n.* зона zona
zoo *n.* зоопарк zoopark
zoological *a.* зоологічний
zoolohichnyi
zoologist *n.* зоолог zooloh
zoology *n.* зоологія zoolohiia
zoom *n.* збільшення зображення
zbilshennia zobrazhennia

zoom *v.i.* рухатися з гудінням
rukhatysia z hudinniam

UKRAINIAN-ENGLISH

A

a same а саме *adv.* namely
a to а то *adv* else
abatstvo абатство *n.* abbey
abo ... abo або ... або *a.,* either
abo zh або ж *conj.* otherwise
abort аборт *n* abortion
aboryhennyi аборигенний *a*
  aboriginal
aboryheny аборигени *n. pl*
  aborigines
abreviatura абревіатура *n*
  abbreviation
abrykos абрикос *n.* apricot
absoliutno абсолютно *adv*
  absolutely
absoliutnyi абсолютний *a*
  absolute
abstrahuvaty абстрагувати *v.t*
  abstract
abstraktnyi абстрактний *a*
  abstract
abstraktsiia абстракція *n* abstract
abstses абсцес *n* abscess
absurdnyi абсурдний *a* absurd
absyda абсида *n.* conch
adamant адамант *n.* adamant
adaptatsiia адаптація *n.*
  adaptation
adaptuvatysia адаптуватися *v.t.*
  adapt
adekvatnist адекватність *n.*
  adequacy
adekvatnyi адекватний *a.*
  adequate
adiulter адюльтер *n.* adultery
administrator адміністратор *n.*
  administrator
administratyvnyi
  адміністративний *a.*
  administrative

admiral адмірал *n.* admiral
adresa адреса *n.* address
adresat адресат *n.* addressee
advokat адвокат *n* advocate
advokat naivyshchoho ranhu
  адвокат найвищого рангу *n.*
  barrister
advokatura адвокатура *n.*
  advocacy
aerodrom аеродром *n* aerodrome
aeronavtyka аеронавтика *n.pl.*
  aeronautics
aeroplan аероплан *n.* aeroplane
aeruvaty аерувати *v.t.* aerify
afektatsiia афектація *n*
  affectation
aforyzm афоризм *n* aphorism
agrus аґрус *n.* gooseberry
ahent агент *n* agent
ahent, shcho verbuie na
  vyiskovu sluzhbu obmanom
  агент, що вербує на військову
  службу обманом *n* crimp
ahentstvo агентство *n.* agency
ahitatsiia агітація *n* agitation
ahituvaty агітувати *v.t.* agitate
ahituvaty агітувати *v. t.* canvass
Ahni Агні *n* agnus
ahoniia агонія *n.* agony
ahorafobiia агорафобія *n.*
  agoraphobia
ahrarnyi аграрний *a.* agrarian
ahresiia агресія *n* aggression
ahresor агресор *n.* aggressor
ahresyvnyi агресивний *a.*
  aggressive
ahresyvnyi агресивний *a.*
  offensive
ahronom агроном *n.* agriculturist
ahronomiia агрономія *n.*
  agronomy
aisberh айсберг *n.* iceberg
akademiia академія *n* academy

akhromatychnyi ахроматичний *adj* achromatic

aklimatyzuvatysia акліматизуватися *v.t* acclimatise

akr акр *n.* acre

akrobat акробат *n.* acrobat

akt акт *n.* act

aktor актор *n.* actor

aktor-amator актор-аматор *adv* am

aktrysa актриса *n.* actress

aktsent акцент *n* accent

aktsentuvannia акцентування *n* emphasis

aktsentuvaty акцентувати *v. t* emphasize

aktsii акції *n.* stock

aktsiia акція *n* share

aktsyz акциз *n* excise

aktualnyi актуальний *a.* topical

aktyv актив *n.* asset

aktyvnyi активний *a.* active

aktyvuvaty активувати *v.t.* activate

akula акула *n.* shark

akumuliatsiia акумуляція *n* accumulation

akumuliuvaty акумулювати *v.t.* accumulate

akuratnyi акуратний *a.* neat

akusherka акушерка *n.* midwife

akustychnyi акустичний *a* acoustic

akustyka акустика *n.* acoustics

akvarium акваріум *n.* aquarium

akveduk акведук *n* aqueduct

Albion Альбіон *n* albion

albom альбом *n.* album

ale але *prep* but

ale але *conj.* but

alehoriia алегорія *n.* allegory

alehorychnyi алегоричний *a.* allegorical

alehorychnyi алегоричний *a.* allusive

aleia алея *n.* alley

aleia алея *n.* vista

alerhiia алергія *n.* allergy

alfa альфа *n* alpha

alfavit алфавіт *n.* alphabet

alfavitnyi алфавітний *a.* alphabetical

alhebra алгебра *n.* algebra

alians альянс *n.* alliance

alibi алібі *n.* alibi

alihator алігатор *n* alligator

alimenty аліменти *n.* alimony

aliteratsiia алітерація *n.* alliteration

aliteruvaty алітерувати *v.* alliterate

aliuminii алюміній *n.* aluminium

alkhimiia алхімія *n.* alchemy

alkohol алкоголь *n* alcohol

alkoholik алкоголік *n* drunkard

alkoholik алкоголік *n.* rummy

alkoholnyi napii алкогольний напій *n.* liquor

almanakh альманах *n.* almanac

alpinist альпініст *n* alpinist

alpinist альпініст *n.* mountaineer

alt альт *n* alto

altanka альтанка *n* belvedere

alternatyva альтернатива *n.* alternative

altymetr альтиметр *n* altimeter

amalhama амальгама *n* amalgam

amatorskyi аматорський *adj* amatory

amberit амберіт *n.* amberite

ambulatornyi khvoryi амбулаторний хворий *n.* outpatient

amelioratsiia амеліорація *n.*
amelioration
amenoreia аменорея *n*
amenorrhoea
amfiteatr амфітеатр *n*
amphitheatre
amin! амінь! *interj.* amen
amneziia амнезія *n* amnesia
amnistiia амністія *n.* amnesty
amoralnist аморальність *n.*
immorality
amoralnyi аморальний *a.* amoral
Amper Ампер *n* ampere
amplituda амплітуда *n.* span
amulet амулет *n.* amulet
anabaptyzm анабаптизм *n*
anabaptism
anafema анафема *n* ban
anakhronizm анахронізм *n*
anachronism
anaklaza анаклаза *n* anaclisis
analitychnyi аналітичний *a*
analytical
analityk аналітик *n* analyst
analiz аналіз *n.* analysis
analiz аналіз *n.* audit
analiz hry pislia yii zakinchennia
аналіз гри після її закінчення
n. post-mortem
analizuvaty аналізувати *v.t.*
analyse
analnyi анальний *adj.* anal
analohichnyi аналогічний *a.*
reciprocal
analohiia аналогія *n.* analogy
anamorfnyi анаморфний *adj*
anamorphous
ananas ананас *n.* pineapple
anarkhiia анархія *n* anarchy
anarkhist анархіст *n* anarchist
anarkhizm анархізм *n.* anarchism
anatomiia анатомія *n.* anatomy
androfah андрофаг *n.* androphagi

anekdot анекдот *n.* anecdote
aneksiia анексія *n* annexation
anemiia анемія *n* anaemia
anemometr анемометр *n*
anemometer
anestetyk анестетик *n.*
anaesthetic
anesteziia анестезія *n*
anaesthesia
anhina ангіна *n* angina
anhliiska mova англійська мова
n English
anis аніс *n* aniseed
anketa анкета *n.* questionnaire
annuitent аннуітент *n* annuitant
anomaliia аномалія *n* anomaly
anonimnist анонімність *n.*
anonymity
anonimnyi анонімний *a.*
anonymous
antahonist антагоніст *n.*
antagonist
antahonizm антагонізм *n*
antagonism
antarktychnyi антарктичний *a.*
antarctic
antatsydnyi антацидний *adj.*
antacid
antena антена *n.* aerial
antolohiia антологія *n.* anthology
antonim антонім *n.* antonym
antrakt антракт *n.* interlude
anty анти *pref.* anti
antydot антидот *n.* antidote
antyfon антифон *n.* antiphony
antykvar антиквар *n* antiquarian
antykvarnyi антикварний *a.*
antiquarian
antylopa антилопа *n.* antelope
antypatiia антипатія *n.* antipathy
antypatiia антипатія *n.*
repugnance
antypody антиподи *n.* antipodes

antyseptychnyi антисептичний
a. antiseptic
antyseptyk антисептик *n.*
antiseptic
antyteza антитеза *n.* antithesis
anuliuvannia анулювання *n.*
abolition
anuliuvannia анулювання *n.*
nullification
anuliuvannia анулювання *n.*
reversal
anuliuvaty анулювати *v. t.*
abrogate
anuliuvaty анулювати *v.t.* annul
aparat апарат *n.* apparatus
aparat dlia promyvannia vukha
апарат для промивання вуха
n. aurilave
apatiia апатія *n.* apathy
apatychnyi апатичний *a.* listless
apeliatsiia апеляція *v.t.* appeal
apelsyn апельсин *n.* orange
apendyks апендикс *n.* appendix
apendytsyt апендицит *n.*
appendicitis
aperytyv аперитив *n* appetizer
apetyt апетит *n.* appetite
aploduvaty аплодувати *v.t.*
applaud
apostol апостол *n.* apostle
apostol апостол *n* disciple
apostrof апостроф *n.* apostrophe
appeliant аппелянт *n.* appellant
apriornyi апріорний *a.*
antecedent
apteka аптека *n.* pharmacy
arbitr арбітр *n.* arbiter
areka арека *n* areca
arena арена *n.* lists
aresht арешт *n.* arrest
areshtant арештант *n* convict
arfa арфа *n.* harp

arhument аргумент *n.*
substantiation
arhumentatsiia zakhystu
аргументація захисту *n*
defence
arka арка *n.* arc
arkada аркада *n* arcade
arkhaichnyi архаїчний *a.* archaic
arkhanhel архангел *n* archangel
arkhiiepyskop архієпископ *n.*
archbishop
arkhitektor архітектор *n.* architect
arkhitektura архітектура *n.*
architecture
arkhivy архіви *n.pl.* archives
Arktyka Арктика *n* Arctic
armada армада *n.* armada
armatura арматура *n.* armature
armiia армія *n.* army
armuvannia армування *n.*
reinforcement
aromat аромат *n.* fragrance
aromatnyi ароматний *a.* fragrant
arrourut арроурут *n.* arrowroot
arsen арсен *n* arsenic
arsenal арсенал *n.* arsenal
artryt артрит *n* arthritis
artykuliuvaty артикулювати *a.*
articulate
artyleriia артилерія *n.* artillery
artyleriia артилерія *n.* ordnance
artyshok артишок *n.* artichoke
aryfmetyka арифметика *n.*
arithmetic
arystokrat аристократ *n.*
aristocrat
arystokratiia аристократія *n.*
aristocracy
asafetyda асафетида *n.*
asafoetida
asambleia асамблея *n.* assembly
asket аскет *n.* ascetic

asketychnyi аскетичний *a.*
ascetic
asortyment асортимент *n.* choice
asotsiatsiia асоціація *n.*
association
asotsiatyvnyi асоціативний *a.*
associate
asotsiiuvaty асоціювати *v.t.*
associate
aspekt аспект *n.* aspect
aspekt аспект *n* facet
asteryzm астеризм *n.* asterism
astma астма *n.* asthma
astroloh астролог *n.* astrologer
astrolohiia астрологія *n.*
astrology
astronavt астронавт *n.* astronaut
astronom астроном *n.*
astronomer
astronomiia астрономія *n.*
astronomy
asyhnuvannia асигнування *n.*
allocation
asyhnuvannia асигнування *n.*
appropriation
asystent асистент *n.* assistant
atakuvaty атакувати *v.t.* assault
atashe аташе *n.* attache
ateist атеїст *n* antitheist
ateizm атеїзм *n* atheism
atestat zrilosti атестат зрілості *n.*
matriculation
atestuvaty атестувати *v. t*
evaluate
atlas атлас *n.* atlas
atlet атлет *n.* athlete
atletychnyi атлетичний *a.* athletic
atletyka атлетика *n.* athletics
atmosfera атмосфера *n.*
atmosphere
atol атол *n.* atoll
atom атом *n.* atom
atomnyi атомний *a.* atomic

atrofovanyi атрофований *a.*
obsolete
audytor аудитор *n.* auditor
auktsionnyi zal аукціонний зал
n. mart
avanpost аванпост *n.* outpost
avans аванс *n.* advance
avantiura авантюра *n* adventure
avantiurnyi авантюрний *a.*
adventurous
avariia аварія *n* breakdown
aviatsiia авіація *n.* aviation
avtobiohrafiia автобіографія *n.*
autobiography
avtobus автобус *n* bus
avtohraf автограф *n.* autograph
avtomatychnyi автоматичний *a*
mechanic
avtomobil автомобіль *n.*
automobile
avtomobilist автомобіліст *n.*
motorist
avtomobilnyi автомобільний *a.*
vehicular
avtonomnyi автономний *a*
autonomous
avtor автор *n.* author
avtorytetnyi авторитетний *a.*
authoritative
azartna hra азартна гра *n* gamble
azartnyi азартний *a.* venturesome
azbest азбест *n.* asbestos
azot азот *n.* nitrogen

babuin бабуїн *n.* baboon
bachyty бачити *v. t* behold
badminton бадмінтон *n.*
badminton
badoryi бадьорий *a* awake
badoryi бадьорий *a.* sprightly
bahato багато *n.* lot

bahato багато *adv.* much
bahato khto багато хто *a.* many
bahatobozhzhia багатобожжя *n.* polytheism
bahatohrannyi багатогранний *a.* multifarious
bahatomovnyi багатомовний *a.* polyglot2
bahatonadiinyi багатонадійний *a.* likely
bahatonizhka багатоніжка *n.* millipede
bahatoobitsiaiuchyi багатообіцяючий *a.* promising
bahatorichna roslyna багаторічна рослина *n.* perennial
bahatoslivnist багатослівність *n.* verbosity
bahatoslivnyi багатослівний *a.* verbose
bahatostoronnii багатосторонній *a.* multilateral
bahatoznachnyi багатозначний *a.* meaningful
bahatoznachnyi багатозначний *a.* significant
bahatstvo багатство *n.* mammon
bahattia багаття *n* bonfire
bahatyi багатий *a.* opulent
bahatyi za narodzhenniam багатий за народженням *adj.* born rich
bahazh багаж *n.* luggage
bahnet багнет *n* bayonet
bahno багно *n.* slough
baiduzhist байдужість *n.* indifference
baiduzhyi байдужий *a.* immovable
baiduzhyi байдужий *a.* indifferent
baidykuvaty байдикувати *v.i.* dawdle

baika байка *n.* fable
bak бак *n* boiler
bakaliina lavka бакалійна лавка *n.* grocery
bakaliinyk бакалійник *n.* grocer
bakhroma бахрома *n.* fringe
baklazhan баклажан *n* brinjal
bakteriia бактерія *n.* bacteria
bakterytsyd бактерицид *n.* germicide
balada балада *n.* ballad
balakuchyi балакучий *a.* gassy
balans баланс *n.* balance
balansuvaty балансувати *v.t.* balance
balet балет *sn.* ballet
balkon балкон *n.* balcony
balotuvannia балотування *n.* vote
balotuvaty балотувати *v.i.* vote
baluvaty балувати *v. t* cocker
baluvaty балувати *v.t.* pamper
baluvaty балувати *v.t.* spoil
balzam бальзам *n.* balm
bambuk бамбук *n.* bamboo
bamper бампер *n.* bumper
banalnyi банальний *a.* banal
banan банан *n.* banana
banda банда *n.* gang
bandyt бандит *n.* dacoit
bandzho банджо *n.* banjo
banian баніан *n.* banyan
bank банк *n.* bank
banket банкет *n.* banquet
bankir банкір *n.* banker
bankrut банкрут *n.* bankrupt
bankrutstvo банкрутство *n.* insolvency
bant бант *n.* knot
baraban барабан *n* drum
barak барак *n.* barrack
baran баран *n.* ram
baranyna баранина *n.* mutton

bard бард *n.* bard
barier бар'єр *n.* barrier
barkhatystyi бархатистий *a.*
   velvety
barlih барліг *n.* lair
barometr барометр *n* barometer
barva барва *n.* tint
barvnyk барвник *n* dye
barvnyk барвник *n.* stain
barvystyi барвистий *a* flowery
barykada барикада *n.* barricade
barylo барило *n* cask
baryshnyk баришник *n.* coper
barzha баржа *n.* barge
bas бас *n.* bass
bashta башта *n.* tower
bastion бастіон *n* bulwark
batareia батарея *n* battery
batih батіг *n.* whip
batkivshchyna батьківщина *n.*
   habitat
batkivskyi батьківський *a.*
   parental
batkivstvo батьківство *n.*
   parentage
batko батько *n* father
batkovbyvstvo батьковбивство
   n. parricide
bavovna бавовна *n* clap
bavovna бавовна *n.* cotton
bavytysia бавитися *v.i.* play
bazhaiuchyi бажаючий *a*
   desirous
bazhannia бажання *n.* wish
bazhanyi бажаний *a* desirable
bazhaty бажати *v.t* desire
bazhaty shchastia бажати щастя
   v.t felicitate
bazika базіка *n.* jay
bazikaty базікати *v. t. & i* blab
bazioalveoliarnyi
   базіоальвеолярний *adv.* basial
bazovyi базовий *a.* base

bazylik базилік *n.* basil
bazys базис *n.* basis
bdinnia бдіння *n.* vigil
bdzhilnytstvo бджільництво *n.*
   apiculture
bdzhola бджола *n.* bee
bekannia бекання *n* bleat
bekaty бекати *v. i* bleat
belkotannia белькотання *n.*
   prattle
belkotaty белькотати *v.i.* prattle
benefitsii бенефіцій *n* benefice
benket бенкет *n* feast
benketnyi бенкетний *adj.*
   convivial
benketuvaty бенкетувати *v.t.*
   banquet
benzyn бензин *n.* petrol
bereh берег *n.* brink
bereh берег *n.* shore
berehty берегти *v.t.* preserve
berehtysia берегтися *v.i.* beware
bereza береза *n.* birch
berezen березень *n.* march
beriks берікс *n.* alphonsion
beshket бешкет *n* affray
beshketuvaty бешкетувати *v.t.*
   riot
besida бесіда *n.* chat1
besida бесіда *n* conversation
betel бетель *n* betel
beton бетон *n* concrete
betonnyi бетонний *a* concrete
bez без *prep.* less
bez hrosha без гроша *a.*
   penniless
bez toho, shchob без того, щоб
   adv. without
bezbozhnyk безбожник *n* atheist
bezchestia безчестя *n* dishonour
bezchestyty безчестити *v. t*
   dishonour

bezdiialnist бездіяльність *n.*
inaction
bezdiialnyi бездіяльний *a.*
inactive
bezdomna sobaka бездомна
собака *n* stray
bezdrotovyi бездротовий *a.*
wireless
bezhluzdist безглуздість *n*
absurdity
bezhluzdist безглуздість *n.*
stupidity
bezhluzdyi безглуздий *a.*
meaningless
bezhluzdyi безглуздий *a.*
senseless
bezholovyi безголовий *n.*
acephalus
bezkarnist безкарність *n.*
impunity
bezkarnyi безкарний *a.* scot-free
bezkoshtovnyi безкоштовний
adv. gratis
bezlad безлад *n* disorder
bezladdia безладдя *n.* mess
bezladdia безладдя *n.* muddle
bezladnyi безладний *a.* random
bezlich безліч *n.* multitude
bezlykist безликість *n.* anonymity
bezmezhnyi безмежний *a.* infinite
bezmezhnyi безмежний *a.*
limitless
bezmir безмір *n.* immensity
bezmirnyi безмірний *a.*
measureless
beznadiinyi безнадійний *a.*
hopeless
bezodnia безодня *n* abyss
bezodnia безодня *n.* profundity
bezosobovyi безособовий *a.*
impersonal
bezpechnist безпечність *n.*
security

bezpechnyi безпечний *a.* safe
bezpeka безпека *n.* safety
bezperechnyi безперечний *a.*
indisputable
bezperervnist безперервність *n*
continuity
bezperervnyi безперервний *adj.*
continual
bezperervnyi безперервний *a*
continuous
bezpidstavnyi безпідставний *a.*
baseless
bezpilotnyi безпілотний *a.*
unmanned
bezpomichnyi безпомічний *a.*
helpless
bezpomylkovyi безпомилковий
a. infallible
bezposerednii безпосередній *a*
direct
bezpryntsypnyi безпринципний
a. unprincipled
bezrezultatnyi безрезультатний
a. ineffective
bezrozsudnyi безрозсудний *a.*
reckless
bezshliubnist безшлюбність *n.*
celibacy
bezsmertia безсмертя *n.*
immortality
bezsmertnyi безсмертний *a.*
everlasting
bezsmertnyi безсмертний *a.*
immortal
bezsoromna diia безсоромна дія
n. indecency
bezsoromnyi безсоромний *a.*
lewd
bezsoromnyi безсоромний *a.*
shameless
bezstrashnyi безстрашний *a*
dauntless

bezstrashnyi безстрашний *a.* venturous

bezsumnivnyi fakt безсумнівний факт *n.* certainty

bezsyllia безсилля *n.* impotence

bezturbotnist безтурботність *n.* nonchalance

bezturbotnyi безтурботний *a.* gay

bezturbotnyi безтурботний *a.* serene

bezumets безумець *n.* lunatic

bezvidpovidalnyi безвідповідальний *a.* wanton

bezvykhidne polozhennia безвихідне положення *n.* stalemate

bezvykhidne stanovyshche безвихідне становище *n.* impasse

bezvynnyi безвинний *a.* innocent

bezzakonnyi беззаконний *a.* lawless

bezzhalisnyi безжалісний *a.* pitiless

bezzhurnyi безжурний *a.* cheerful

bi бі *pref* bi

bibliia біблія *n* bible

bibliohraf бібліограф *n* bibliographer

bibliohrafiia бібліографія *+n* bibliography

biblioteka бібліотека *n.* library

bibliotekar бібліотекар *n.* librarian

bida біда *n.* calamity

bidnist бідність *n.* necessity

bidnist бідність *n.* poverty

bidnyi бідний *a.* poor

bidolashnyi бідолашний *a.* miserable

bidon бідон *n.* can

bihaty бігати *v.i.* run

bihty бігти *v.i* flee

bihty makhovym krokom бігти маховим кроком *v.i.* stride

bihun бігун *n.* runner

bii бій *n* battle

biika бійка *n.* scuffle

biinytsia бійниця *n.* loop-hole

bil біль *n.* ache

bil u miazakh біль у м'язах *n.* myalgia

bilia біля *prep* by

bilia біля *adv* by

bilka білка *n.* squirrel

bilok білок *n.* protein

bilsh nizh dostatnii більш ніж достатній *a* abundant

bilshe більше *adv* more

bilshe toho більше того *adv.* moreover

bilshist більшість *n* most

biluvatyi білуватий *a.* whitish

bilyi білий *a.* white

bilyty білити *v.t.* whitewash

bilyty vapnom білити вапном *v.t* lime

bilyzna білизна *n* white

binokuliarnyi бінокулярний *n.* binocular

biohraf біограф *n* biographer

biohrafiia біографія *n* biography

bioloh біолог *n* biologist

biolohiia біологія *n* biology

bioskop біоскоп *n* bioscope

birzhovyi біржовий *a.* stock

birzhovyi broker біржовий брокер *n.* stag

bisyty бісити *v. t* enrage

bitseps біцепс *n* biceps

bity poperedu біти попереду *v.* precede

biudzhet бюджет *n* budget

biuleten бюлетень *n* ballot

biuro бюро *n.* bureau

biurokrat бюрократ *n* bureaucrat

biurokratiia бюрократія *n.* Bureacracy

bizhenets біженець *n.* refugee

biznes бізнес *n* business

biznesmen бізнесмен *n* businessman

bizon бізон *n* bison

blahannia благання *n* adjuration

blahannia благання *n* cry

blahannia благання *n.* oration

blahannia благання *n.* plea

blahaty благати *v.t.* adiure

blahaty благати *v. t.* beg

blaho благо *n.* weal

blahochestia благочестя *n.* piety

blahochestyvyi благочестивий *a.* pious

blahodatnyi благодатний *a.* grateful

blahodiiannia благодіяння *n.* benefaction

blahodiinist благодійність *n.* philanthropy

blahodiinyi благодійний *a.* charitable

blahohoviinyi благоговійний *a.* reverent

blahohovinnia благоговіння *n.* awe

blahoprystoinist благопристойність *n* decorum

blahorodnyi благородний *adj* alin

blahoslovennia благословення *n* benison

blahoslovliaty благословляти *v. t* bless

blahotvornyi благотворний *a* beneficial

blahovolinnia благовоління *n.* goodwill

blakytnyi блакитний *a* blue

blazen блазень *n* buffoon

blazen блазень *n* fool

blazenskyi kovpak блазенський ковпак *n* foolscap

blazhenstvo блаженство *n* bliss

blef блеф *n.* bluff

blefuvaty блефувати *v. t* bluff

blidnuty бліднути *v.i.* pale

blido-rozhevyi блідо-рожевий *a.* pinkish

blidyi блідий *a* pale

blindazh бліндаж *n* blindage

bliudo блюдо *n* dish

bliudtse блюдце *n.* saucer

bliuvota блювота *n* vomit

bliuznirskyi блюзнірський *a.* sacrilegious

blok блок *n* bloc

blokha блоха *n.* flea

blokuvannia блокування *v.t.* interlock

bloshytsia блошиця *n.* bug

bludyty блудити *v.i.* stray

blukaty блукати *v.i.* rove

blukaty bez mety блукати без мети *v.t.* ramble

blukaty navmannia блукати навмання *v.i.* meander

bluza блуза *n* blouse

blymaty блимати *v. t. & i* blink

blyshchaty блищати *v.i.* shine

blysk блиск *n* glitter

blyskotinnia блискотіння *n* flare

blyskucha mishura блискуча мішура *n.* glare

blyskuchyi блискучий *a* brilliant

blyskuchyi блискучий *a.* splendid

blyzhnii ближній *a.* near

blyzkist близькість *n.* proximity

blyzko близько *adv.* anigh

blyzniuk близнюк *n.* twin

boa боа *n.* necklet

bober бобер *n* beaver

bochka бочка *n.* bar

bochka бочка *n.* barrel

boh бог *n.* god
bohoslov богослов *n.* theologian
bohoslovia богослов'я *n* divinity
bohoslovia богослов'я *n.* theology
bohoslovskyi богословський *a.* theological
bohynia богиня *n.* goddess
boiahuz боягуз *n.* coward
boiahuzlyvyi боягузливий *a.* nerveless
boiahuztvo боягузтво *n.* cowardice
boiatysia боятися *v.t* dread
boiazkist боязкість *n.* timidity
boiazkyi боязкий *a.* timorous
boieprypasy боєприпаси *n.* ammunition
boiets боєць *n* militant
boikot бойкот *n* boycott
boikotuvaty бойкотувати *v. t.* boycott
boiovyi бойовий *a.* militant
boiovyi dukh бойовий дух *n.* morale
boiovyi poriadok бойовий порядок *n.* array
boks бокс *n* boxing
bolezaspokiilyvyi болезаспокійливий *a.* sedative
boliachka болячка *n* sore
boloto болото *n.* marsh
boloto болото *n.* swamp
bolotystyi болотистий *a.* marshy
bolvan болван *n.* loggerhead
bomba бомба *n* bomb
bombarduvalnyk бомбардувальник *n* bomber
bombarduvannia бомбардування *n* bombardment
bombarduvaty бомбардувати *v. t* bombard

bombyty бомбити *v. t* bomb
bordel бордель *n* brothel
bordiur бордюр *n.* welt
borets борець *n.* wrestler
borh борг *n* debt
borh борг *n.* score
borhovyi борговий *a.* obligatory
borhy борги *n.pl.* arrears
boroda борода *n* beard
boroda борода *n.* whisker
borodavka бородавка *n.* wart
boroshno борошно *n* flour
boroshnystyi борошнистий *a.* mealy
borotba боротьба *n* fight
borotba боротьба *n.* tussle
borotysia боротися *v. i.* battle
borotysia боротися *v. t.* combat
borotysia боротися *v.i.* tussle
borozna борозна *n.* furrow
borsuk борсук *n.* badger
borzhnyk боржник *n* debtor
borzhnyk za zastavnoiu боржник за заставною *n.* mortgagor
bos бос *n* boss
botanika ботаніка *n* botany
bovknuty бовкнути *v. t* blurt
bozhestvennist божественність *n.* godhead
bozhestvenyi божествений *a* divine
bozhestvo божество *n.* deity
bozhevillia божевілля *n.* frenzy
bozhevillia божевілля *n.* insanity
bozhevilnyi божевільний *a* crazy
bozhevilnyi божевільний *adj.* daft
brak брак *n.* paucity
brak брак *n.* scarcity
branets бранець *n.* captive
brashpyl брашпиль *v.t.* windlass
braslet браслет *n.* bangle
braslet браслет *n* bracelet
brat брат *n* brother

braterskyi братерський *a.* fraternal

bratovbyvstvo братовбивство *n.* fratricide

bratovbyvtsia братовбивця *n* cain

bratstvo братство *n* brotherhood

braty брати *v.t* take

braty na poruky брати на поруки *v. t.* bail

braty na sebe брати на себе *v.t.* incur

braty na vidhodivliu брати на відгодівлю *v.t.* agist

braty nazad брати назад *v.t.* resume

braty nazad брати назад *v.t.* revoke

braty pid sumniv брати під сумнів *v.t.* impeach

braty uchast брати участь *v.i.* partake

braty uchast u pikniku брати участь у пікніку *v.i.* picnic

braty uchast u skachkakh брати участь у скачках *v.i* race

braty v orendu брати в оренду *v.t.* rent

brekhaty брехати *v. t.* defame

brekhaty брехати *v.i* lie

brekhlyvyi брехливий *a.* mendacious

brekhnia брехня *n* lie

brekhun брехун *n.* liar

brendi бренді *n* brandy

briazkaltse брязкальце *n* rattle

briuky брюки *n. pl* trousers

brodiachyi бродячий *a* vagabond

brodiaha бродяга *n.* vagabond

brodinnia бродіння *n* fermentation

brodyty бродити *v.t* ferment

broker брокер *n* broker

brokkoli брокколі *n.* broccoli

bronia броня *n.* armour

bronza бронза *n. & adj* bronze

broshura брошура *n* brochure

broshura брошура *n* brochure

brova брова *n* brow

brud бруд *n* dirt

brudnyi брудний *a.* foul

brudnyty бруднити *v. t* blot

brudnytysia бруднитися *v.t.* soil

brukivka бруківка *n* causeway

brunka брунька *n* bud

brushchatka брущатка *n.* pitcher

brutalno povodytysia брутально поводитися *d* mistreat

brutalnyi брутальний *a* brutal

brutalnyi брутальний *a.* rude

brutto брутто *n.* gross

brydkyi бридкий *a.* horrible

brydkyi бридкий *a.* vile

brydzhi бриджі *n.* breeches

bryhada бригада *n.* brigade

bryhada бригада *n.* team

bryhadyr бригадир *n* brigadier

brytanskyi британський *adj* british

brytva бритва *n.* razor

bryz бриз *n* breeze

bryzhi брижі *n.* ripple

bryzkaty бризкати *v. t.* sprinkle

budennyi буденний *a.* workaday

bud-iakyi будь-який *adv.* either

bud-iakyi будь-який *a* every

budivelni lisy будівельні ліси *n.* scaffold

budivlia будівля *n* edifice

budivnytstvo будівництво *n* building

budka будка *n.* kennel

bud-khto будь-хто *n.* somebody

budova tila будова тіла *n* build

budova tila будова тіла *n.* habit

buduvaty будувати *v. t* build

budynochok будиночок *n.* lodge
budynok будинок *n.* home
budyty будити *v.t.* arouse
bufet буфет *n* cupboard
bufetna буфетна *n.* pantry
bufetnyk буфетник *n* drawer
bui буй *n* buoy
buinyi буйний *a.* rowdy
buinyi rist буйний ріст *n.* luxuriance
buivol буйвол *n.* buffalo
buivoliacha shkira буйволяча шкіра *n* buff
buk бук *n.* beech
buket букет *n* bouquet
buketyk kvitiv букетик квітів *n.* nosegay
bukhanets буханець *n.* loaf
bukhhalter бухгалтер *n* book-keeper
bukhhalterska sprava бухгалтерська справа *n.* accountancy
bukhta бухта *n* bay
buklet буклет *n* booklet
buksuvaty буксувати *v.i.* skid
buksyr буксир *v.t.* tug
bukvalnyi буквальний *a.* literal
buldoh бульдог *n* bulldog
bunhalo бунгало *n* bungalow
bunt бунт *n.* rebellion
bunt бунт *n.* riot
buntivnyk бунтівник *n.* rebel
buntuvaty бунтувати *v. i* mutiny
burav бурав *n.* wimple
burchannia бурчання *n* growl
burchaty бурчати *v.i.* growl
bure vuhillia буре вугілля *n.* lignite
buria буря *n.* tempest
buriak буряк *n* beet
burian бур'ян *n.* weed

burkhlyvo aploduvaty бурхливо аплодувати *v.t* acclaim
burkhlyvo vyrazhaty protest бурхливо виражати протест *v. i.* clamour
burkhlyvyi бурхливий *a.* tempestuous
burkhlyvyi бурхливий *a.* uproarious
burmotannia бурмотання *n.* murmur
burmotaty бурмотати *v.i.* gabble
burulka бурулька *n.* icicle
bushuvaty бушувати *v.i.* rage
busynka бусинка *n* bead
buterbrod бутерброд *n.* sandwich
buttia буття *n* being
buty бути *v.t.* be
buty бути *v.i* exist
buty hidnym бути гідним *v. t.* deserve
buty korysnym бути корисним *v.t.* avail
buty nerishuchym бути нерішучим *v.i.* shilly-shally
buty nespravedlyvym бути несправедливим *v.t.* wrong
buty poserednykom бути посередником *v.i.* mediate
buty skhozhym бути схожим *v.t.* resemble
buty suddeiu бути суддею *v.t.,* umpire
buty u velykii kilkosti бути у великій кількості *v.i.* abound
buty v konflikti бути в конфлікті *v. i* conflict
buty v zmozi бути в змозі *v.* can
buty zadovolenym бути задоволеним *v.t.* consent3
buvai бувай *interj.* bye-bye
buzok бузок *n.* lilac
bych бич *n.* scourge

bychuvaty бичувати *v.t.* scourge
byk бик *n* bull
byk бик *n.* ox
bynt бинт ~*n.* bandage
byntuvaty бинтувати *v.t* bandage
byttia биття *n.* throb
byty бити *v. t.* beat
byty kopytom бити копитом *n.* hoof
byty kozyrem бити козирем *v.t.* trump
byty lozynoiu бити лозиною *v.t.* switch
byty ostenem бити остенем *v.t.* spear
byty palytseiu бити палицею *v. i* bat
byty rukoiu бити рукою *v. t* cuff
byty strumenem бити струменем *v.i.* spout
byty strumynoiu бити струминою *v.i* flush
byty v baraban бити в барабан *v.i.* drum
bytysia битися *v.t* fight
bytysia битися *v.i.* pulse
bytysia битися *v.i.* scuffle
bytysia na dueli битися на дуелі *v. i* duel
byven бивень *n.* ivory

C

chaban чабан *n.* shepherd
chaharnyk чагарник *n.* shrub
chai чай *n* tea
chaika чайка *n* gull
chaika чайка *n.* gull
chainyk чайник *n.* kettle
chaklun чаклун *n.* sorcerer
chaklunka чаклунка *n.* hag
chaklunstvo чаклунство *n.* sorcery

chaklunstvo чаклунство *n.* witchcraft
chaklunstvo чаклунство *n.* witchery
chakluvaty чаклувати *v.t.* conjure
charivnist чарівність *n.* charm1
charivnist чарівність *n.* fascination
charivnist чарівність *n.* glamour
charivnyi чарівний *a.* winsome
charivnyk чарівник *n.* wizard
charuvaty чарувати *v. t* enchant
chary чари *n.* spell
chas час *n.* time
chas час *n.* while
chas do poludnia час до полудня *n* forenoon
chas liahaty spaty час лягати спати *n.* bed-time
chas vid chasu час від часу *adv.* occasionally
chasha чаша *n* bowl
chasha чаша *n* chaice
chashka чашка *n.* cup
chasnyk часник *n.* garlic
chasovyi часовий *n.* sentinel
chastka частка *n.* fraction
chastkovyi частковий *a.* partial
chasto часто *adv.* oft
chasto buvaty часто бувати *v.t.* haunt
chastota частота *n.* frequency
chastyi частий *a.* frequent
chastyna частина *n.* part
chastyna частина *n.* partition
chastyna частина *n* portion
chastyna частина *n.* residue
chastyna частина *n* stake
chavun чавун *n* cast-iron
chek чек *n.* cheque
chekannia чекання *n.* wait
chekaty чекати *v.t.* await
chekaty чекати *v. t* expect

chekaty чекати *v.i.* wait
chemnist чемність *n.* courtesy
chemnist чемність *n.* politeness
chemnist чемність *n.* urbanity
chemnyi чемний *a.* courteous
chempion чемпіон *n.* champion
chepliaty чепляти *v.i.* grapple
cherep череп *n.* skull
cherepakha черепаха *n.* tortoise
cherepakha черепаха *n.* turtle
chereshok черешок *n* stalk
cherevnyi черевний *a.* abdominal
cherevnyi tyf черевний тиф *n.* typhoid
cherevo черево *n* abdomen
cherez через *prep.* across
cherez через *prep.* along
cherez через *adv* over
cherez через *prep.* over
cherez через *prep.* through
cherez через *prep.* via
cherha черга *n.* queue
cherha черга *n* turn
cherhuvaty чергувати *v.t.* alternate
cherhuvatysia чергуватися *v.i.* rotate
chernets чернець *n.* monk
chernets чернець *n.* votary
chernetstvo чернецтво *n* monasticism
cherpaty черпати *v.t.* ladle
cherpaty lozhkoiu черпати ложкою *v.t.* spoon
cherstvist черствість *n.* obduracy
cherstvyi черствий *a.* callous
cherstvyi черствий *a.* stale
cherviak черв'як *n.* worm
chervone derevo червоне дерево *n.* mahogany
chervonity червоніти *v.i* blush
chervonity червоніти *v.t.* redden

chervonuvatyi червонуватий *a.* reddish
chervonyi червоний *a.* red
chervonyi kolir червоний колір *n.* red
chesnist чесність *n.* honesty
chesno чесно *adv.* fairly
chesnyi чесний *a.* honest
chest честь *n.* honour
chestoliubets честолюбець *n.* aspirant
chestoliubnyi честолюбний *a.* ambitious
chestoliubstvo честолюбство *n.* ambition
chetver четвер *n.* Thursday
chetvernyi четверний *a.* quadruple
chipkist чіпкість *n.* tenacity
chipkyi чіпкий *a.* tenacious
chipliannia чіпляння *n.* solicitation
chipliatysia чіплятися *v. t* cavil
chipliatysia чіплятися *v.t.* nag
chitkyi чіткий *a* distinct
chkhannia чхання *n* sneeze
chkhaty чхати *v.i.* sneeze
chlen член *n.* member
chlen profspilky член профспілки *n.* unionist
chlen tovarystva член товариства *n* co-partner
chlen zhuri член журі *n.* juror
chlenstvo членство *n.* membership
chmokane чмоканье *n* smack
chobit чобіт *n* boot
chokhol чохол *n.* sheet
cholo чоло *n.* front
cholovichyi чоловічий *a.* male
cholovichyi чоловічий *a.* manlike
cholovichyi чоловічий *a.* masculine

cholovichyi чоловічий *a.* virile
cholovik чоловік *n.* consort
cholovik чоловік *n* husband
cholovik чоловік *n* male
cholovik чоловік *n.* spouse
chomu чому *adv.* why
chorne derevo чорне дерево *n* ebony
chornobryvtsi чорнобривці *n.* marigold
chornorob чорнороб *n* coolie
chornorob чорнороб *n.* labourer
chornoshkiryi чорношкірий *n.* nigger
chornyi чорний *a* black
chornylo чорнило *n.* ink
chornysh чорниш *n.* slur
chornyty чорнити *v. t.* blacken
chortopolokh чортополох *n.* thistle
chotyrnadtsiat чотирнадцять *n.* fourteen
chotyry чотири *n.* four
chotyrykutnyi чотирикутний *a.* quadrangular
chotyrykutnyi чотирикутний *a.* quadrilateral
chotyrykutnyk чотирикутник *n.* quadrangle
chotyrynoha tvaryna чотиринога тварина *n.* quadruped
choven човен *n* boat
chovhannia човгання *n.* shuffle
chovhaty човгати *v.i.* shuffle
chovnyk човник *n.* shuttle
chrevo чрево *n.* womb
chub чуб *n* forelock
chudnyi чудний *a* rum
chudo чудо *n.* marvel
chudo чудо *n.* miracle
chudo чудо *n* wonder
chudotvornyi чудотворний *a.* miraculous

chudovyi чудовий *a.* remarkable
chudovyi чудовий *a.* wondrous
chudovysko чудовисько *n* beast
chuma чума *n.* plague
chutky чутки *n* bruit
chutlyvist чутливість *n.* sensibility
chutlyvyi чутливий *a.* sensitive
chutnyi чутний *a* audible
chuttia чуття *n.* antennae
chuttia чуття *v.t* nose
chuttievist чуттєвість *n.* sensuality
chuttievyi чуттєвий *a.* sensual
chuty чути *v.t.* hear
chuzhyi чужий *a.* vicarious
chvert чверть *n.* quarter
chy чи *conj.* whether
chyi чий *pron.* whose
chynovnyk чиновник *n* official
chynyty obstruktsiiu чинити обструкцію *v.t.* obstruct
chynyty opir чинити опір *v.t.* resist
chyselnyi чисельний *a.* numerical
chyselnyk чисельник *n.* numerator
chyslennishyi численніший *a.* more
chyslennyi численний *a.* numerous
chyslennyi численний *a.* vast
chyslo dvadtsiat число двадцять *n* twenty
chyslo dvanadtsiat число дванадцять *n* twelve
chyslo trydtsiat число тридцять *n.* thirty
chyslo trynadtsiat число тринадцять *n.* thirteen
chyslovyi числовий *a.* arithmetical
chystota чистота *n* clarity
chystota чистота *n* cleanliness

chystota чистота *n.* purity
chystyi чистий clean
chystyi чистий *a* clear
chystyi чистий *a* net
chystyi чистий *a* pure
chystyi чистий *a.* sheer
chystylnyk чистильник *n.* sweeper
chystylyshche чистилище *n.* purgatory
chystyty чистити *v. t* clean
chystyty чистити *v. t* cleanse
chystyty do biloho чистити до білого *v.t.* whiten
chystyty hubkoiu чистити губкою *v.t.* sponge
chystyty konia чистити коня *v.t* groom
chystyty shvabroiu чистити шваброю *v.t.* mop
chytach читач *n.* reader
chytaty читати *v.t.* read
chytaty lektsiiu читати лекцію *v* lecture

dacha дача *n* bower
dakh дах *n.* roof
daleka vidstan далека відстань *n* far
daleko далеко *adv.* far
dalekyi далекий *a* distant
dalekyi zviazok далекий зв'язок *n.* telecommunications
dali далі *adv.* onwards
dalnii дальній *a* far
dama дама *n.* dame
damba дамба *n* dam
dantyst дантист *n* dentist
dar дар *n.* donation
dar дар *n.* gift
daremnyi даремний *a.* worthless

daruvaty дарувати *v. t* bestow
daruvaty дарувати *v.t.* remember
data дата *n* date
datuvaty bilsh rannim chyslom датувати більш раннім числом *n* antedate
datuvaty piznishym chyslom датувати пізнішим числом *v.t.* post-date
daty liky дати ліки *v.t.* physic
daty poradu дати пораду *v. t.* counsel
daty prytulok дати притулок *v.t.* shelter
davaty давати *v.t.* afford
davaty давати *v.t.* impart
davaty khabar давати хабар *v. t.* bribe
davaty mozhlyvist давати можливість *v. t* enable
davaty na chai давати на чай *v.t.* tip
davaty obitnytsiu давати обітницю *v.t.* vow
davaty osichku давати осічку *v.i.* misfire
davaty osvitu давати освіту *v. t* educate
davaty perevahu давати перевагу *v.t.* advantage
davaty pokazannia давати показання *v.i.* testify
davaty pryvid давати привід *v.t* occasion
davaty sobi voliu давати собі волю *v.t.* indulge
davaty v borh давати в борг *v.t.* loan
davaty vidomosti давати відомості *v.t.* notify
davaty vidpochynok давати відпочинок *v.i.* repose

davaty vidsich давати відсіч *v.t.*
rebuff
davka давка *n.* jostle
davnii давній *a.* antique
dbailyvist дбайливість *n.*
solicitude
de де *conj.* where
de b ne bulo де б не було *adv.*
wherever
debatuvaty дебатувати *v. t.*
debate
debaty дебати *n.* debate
debet дебет *n* debit
debetuvaty дебетувати *v. t* debit
debosh дебош *n* debauch
defekt дефект *n* defect
defekt дефект *n.* shortcoming
defile дефіле *n.* defile
definitsiia дефініція *n* definition
defitsyt дефіцит *n* deficit
defitsytnyi дефіцитний *a.* scarce
defliatsiia дефляція *n.* deflation
dehraduvaty деградувати *v. t*
degrade
deist деїст *n.* deist
dekan декан *n.* dean
dekhto дехто *pron.* some
deklamatsiia декламація *n.*
recitation
deklamuvaty декламувати *v.t.*
recite
dekoratsii декорації *n.* scenery
dekoratsiia декорація *n*
decoration
dekoratyvnyi декоративний *a.*
ornamental
delehatsiia делегація *n*
delegation
delehuvaty делегувати *v. t*
delegate
delikatne делікатне *a.* ticklish
delta дельта *n* delta

demarkatsiia демаркація *n.*
demarcation
demokratiia демократія *n*
democracy
demokratychnyi демократичний
a democratic
demon демон *n.* demon
demonstratsiia демонстрація *n.*
demonstration
demonstruvaty демонструвати *v.*
t demonstrate
demonstruvaty smilyvist
демонструвати сміливість *v.t.*
stunt
demoralizuvaty деморалізувати
v. t. demoralize
den день *n* day
den vidpochynku день
відпочинку *n.* holiday
dendi денді *n* dandy
dennyi spektakl денний
спектакль *n.* matinee
depo депо *n* depot
deportuvaty депортувати *v.t.*
deport
depozyt депозит *n.* deposit
depresiia депресія *n* depression
deputat депутат *n* deputy
deputatsiia депутація *n*
deputation
deren дерен *n.* sod
derevianyi дерев'яний *a.* wooden
derevo дерево *n.* tree
dertysia дертися *v. i* clamber
derzhava держава *n.*
commonwealth
derzhavnyi diiach державний
діяч *n.* statesman
derzhavnyi strii державний стрій
n. regime
derzhavnyi ustrii державний
устрій *n.* polity
des десь *adv.* somewhere

des poruch десь поруч *adv.* hereabouts

desantnyi десантний *adj* amphibious

deshcho дещо *adv.* something

deshevshaty дешевшати *v. t.* cheapen

deshevyi дешевий *a* cheap

desiat десять *n.* ten

desiatkovyi десятковий *a* decimal

desiatylittia десятиліття *n.* decennary

desiatyna десятина *n.* tithe

desna десна *n.* gum

despot деспот *n* despot

detal деталь *n* detail

detali деталі *n.* belongings

detalizuvaty деталізувати *v. t* detail

detalno rozrobliaty детально розробляти *v. t* elaborate

detektyv детектив *a* detective

detektyvnyi детективний *n.* detective

detonator детонатор *n.* trigger

detsillion деціліон *n.* decillion

devianosto дев'яносто *n.* ninety

devianostyi дев'яностий *a.* ninetieth

deviat дев'ять *n.* nine

deviatnadtsiat дев'ятнадцять *n.* nineteen

deviatnadtsiatoho дев'ятнадцятого *a.* nineteenth

deviatsiia девіація *n* deviation

deviatyi дев'ятий *a.* ninth

deviz девіз *n.* motto

diadia дядя *n.* uncle

diafrahma діафрагма *n.* midriff

diahnostuvaty діагностувати *v. t* diagnose

diahnoz діагноз *n* diagnosis

dialekt діалект *n* dialect

dialoh діалог *n* dialogue

diamant діамант *n* diamond

diapazon діапазон *n.* range

diia vazhelia дія важеля *n.* leverage

diialnist діяльність *n.* activity

diialnyi діяльний *a.* live

diiaty діяти *v.i.* act

diiaty діяти *v.t.* operate

diiaty zanadto pospishno діяти занадто поспішно *v.t.* rush

diieslovo дієслово *n.* verb

diieta дієта *n* diet

diievist дієвість *n* efficacy

diievyi дієвий *a* forceful

diisnist дійсність *n.* validity

diisnyi дійсний *a.* valid

dilianka ділянка *n.* plot

dilianka zemli ділянка землі *n* dale

dilyty ділити *v.t.* portion

dilyty na sehmenty ділити на сегменти *v.t.* segment

dilyty navpil ділити навпіл *v. t* bisect

dilytysia ділитися *v.t.* share

dira діра *n* hole

diriavyty дірявити *v.t* hole

ditovbyvstvo дітовбивство *n.* infanticide

diuim дюйм *n.* inch

diuzhyna дюжина *n* dozen

diva діва *n.* maiden

divchyna дівчина *n.* girl

divchynka дівчинка *n.* lass

diviziia дівізія *n* division

divka дівка *n.* wench

divochyi дівочий *a.* girlish

dizhka діжка *n.* tub

diznannia дізнання *n* interrogative

diznavannia дізнавання *n.* recognition

diznavatysia дізнаватися *v.t.*
recognize
dlia для *prep* for
dlia choho для чого *adv.* whither
dlubatysia длубатися *v.t.* sap
dno дно *n* bottom
do до *prep* before
do до *prep.* pending
do до *prep.* till
do до *prep.* towards
do до *prep.* until
do до *prep.* up
do bereha до берега *adv.* ashore
do pobachennia до побачення
interj. good-bye
do rechi до речі *adv* appositely
do splaty до сплати *a.* payable
do tsykh pir до цих пір *adv.* still
do tykh pir до тих пір *conj* until
doba доба *n* epoch
dobir добір *n* adoption
dobirnyi добірний *a* select
doblesnyi доблесний *a.* valiant
doblest доблесть *n.* prowess
doblest доблесть *n.* valour
dobre добре *adv.* well
dobre znaiomyi добре знайомий
adj. conversant
dobrobut добробут *n.* wealth
dobrobut добробут *n.* welfare
dobrochesnist доброчесність *n.*
virtue
dobrochesnyi доброчесний *a.*
virtuous
dobrodiiannia добродіяння *n*
boon
dobrodushno zhartuvaty
добродушно жартувати *v.t.*
banter
dobroiakisnyi доброякісний *a.*
laudable
dobrosusidskyi добросусідський
a. neighbourly

dobrota доброта *n.* goodness
dobrovilno добровільно *adv.*
voluntarily
dobrovilnyi добровільний *a.*
voluntary
dobrozychlyvist
доброзичливість *n*
benevolence
dobrozychlyvo доброзичливо
adv. kindly
dobrozychlyvyi доброзичливий
adj. amicable
dobrozychlyvyi доброзичливий
a benevolent
dobryi добрий *a.* good
dobryvo добриво *n* fertilizer
dochirnia kompaniia дочірня
компанія *a.* subsidiary
dochka дочка *n* daughter
dodatkovi vybory додаткові
вибори *n* by-election
dodatkovo додатково *adv* extra
dodatkovyi додатковий *a.*
additional
dodatkovyi додатковий *a.* other
dodatkovyi podatok додатковий
податок *n.* surtax
dodatok додаток *n.* addition
dodatok додаток *n.* appendix
dodaty додати *v.t.* add
dodavaty додавати *v.t.* suffix
dohana догана *n.* rebuke
dohana догана *n.* reprimand
dohliad догляд *n.* care
dohliadach доглядач *n.* warden
dohliadaty доглядати *v.t.* woo
dohma догма *n* dogma
dohmatychnyi догматичний *a*
dogmatic
dohmatychnyi догматичний *a.*
oracular
dohot дьоготь *n.* tar
dohovir договір *n.* compact

doistorychnyi доісторичний *a.* prehistoric

doity доїти *v.t.* milk

dok док *n.* dock

dokaz доказ *n* evidence

dokaz доказ *n.* proof

dokhid дохід *n.* income

dokhody доходи *n.* revenue

dokir докір *n.* reproach

dokir докір *n.* reproof

dokladaty zusyllia докладати зусилля *v.i.* strive

dokladno докладно *adv.* minutely

dokoriaty докоряти *v.t.* reproach

dokoriaty докоряти *v.t* upbraid

dokory sovisti докори совісті *n.* remorse

doktor доктор *n.* medico

doktorska stupin докторська ступінь *n* doctorate

doktryna доктрина *n* doctrine

dokuchaty докучати *v.t.* vex

dokuchlyva liudyna докучлива людина *n* barnacles

dokument документ *n* document

dokument pro peredachu prava vlasnosti документ про передачу права власності *n* deed

dokument pro prava документ про права *n.* muniment

dolar долар *n* dollar

dolaty долати *v.t.* surmount

dolaty долати *v.t.* transcend

dolia доля *n* destiny

dolon долонь *n.* palm

dolyna долина *n.* valley

domahatysia домагатися *v.t.* attain

domahatysia uspikhu домагатися успіху *v.i.* succeed

domashnia ptytsia домашня птиця *n.* poultry

domashnia robota домашня робота *n* domestic

domashnia tvaryna домашня тварина *n.* pet

domashnii домашній *a* domestic

dominion домініон *n* dominion

dominuiuchyi домінуючий *a* dominant

dominuvaty домінувати *v. t* dominate

domovlenist домовленість *n.* covenant

donkikhotskyi донкіхотський *a.* quixotic

donor донор *n* donor

donos донос *n.* denunciation

donosyty доносити *v. t* denounce

donyzu донизу *adv* downward

doplata доплата *n.* surcharge

dopomahaty допомагати *v.t.* assist

dopomahaty допомагати *v.t.* help

dopomahaty допомагати *v.t.* support

dopomizhnyi допоміжний *a.* auxiliary

dopomizhnyi mekhanizm допоміжний механізм *n.* auxiliary

dopomizhnyi zasob допоміжний засоб *n.* supplement

dopomoha допомога *n* aid

dopomoha допомога *n.* succour

dopomohty допомогти *v.t* aid

dopovnennia доповнення *n.* adjunct

dopovnenyi доповнений *a* accomplished

dopovniuvaty доповнювати *v.t.* supplement

dopushchennia допущення *n.* admission

dopuskaty допускати *v.t.* admit

dopuskaty допускати *v.t.* own

dopuskaty vidkhylennia
допускати відхилення *v.t.*
waive

dopustymyi допустимий *a.*
admissible

dopytlyvyi допитливий *a.*
inquisitive

dopytuvaty допитувати *v.t.*
interrogate

dorechnist доречність *n.*
propriety

dorechno доречно *adj* apposite

dorechno доречно *a.* timely

dorechnyi доречний *a.*
appropriate

dorechnyi доречний *a.* pertinent

dorechnyi доречний *a.* well-timed

dorikaty дорікати *v.t.* rebuke

dorivniuvaty дорівнювати *v. t*
equal

dorivniuvaty дорівнювати *v.t.*
total

doroha дорога *n.* road

dorohotsinnyi дорогоцінний *a.*
precious

dorohotsinnyi kamin
дорогоцінний камінь *n.* jewel

dorohyi дорогий *a.* costly

dorosla liudyna доросла людина
n. adult

doroslyi дорослий *a* adult

doruchaty доручати *v. t.* commit

doruchaty доручати *v. t.* consign

doruchaty доручати *v. t* depute

doruchennia доручення *n.*
commission

doruchyty доручити *v.t.* vest

dosada досада *n.* annoyance

dosada досада *n* vexation

dosazhdaty досаждати *v.t.* annoy

doshch дощ *n* rain

doshchovyi дощовий *a.* moist

doshchovyi дощовий *a.* rainy

doshka дошка *n.* plank

doshliubnyi дошлюбний *adj.*
antenuptial

dosi досі *adv.* hitherto

dosiahaty досягати *v.t.* achieve

dosiahaty досягати *v.t.* obtain

dosiahaty naivyshchoi tochky
досягати найвищої точки *v.i.*
culminate

dosiahnennia досягнення *n.*
attainment

dosie досьє *n* file

doskonalyi досконалий *a.* perfect

doslidzhennia дослідження *n.*
examination

doslidzhuvaty досліджувати *v.t*
explore

doslivno дослівно *adv.* verbatim

doslivnyi дослівний *a.* verbatim

dostatnii достатній *a*
considerable

dostatnist достатність *n.*
sufficiency

dostatno достатньо *adv* enough

dostatok достаток *n.* affluence

dostatok достаток *n.* opulence

dostavka доставка *n* delivery

dostavliaty доставляти *v. t*
deliver

dostovirnyi достовірний *a.*
authentic

dostup доступ *n* access

dostup доступ *n.* admittance

dostupnyi доступний *a.*
obtainable

dosvichenyi досвічений *a*
conversant

dosvichenyi досвічений *a.*
versed

dosvid досвід *n* experience

dosvidchenyi povodyr
досвідчений поводир *n.* pilot

dosyt досить *adv.* enough
dosyt досить *adv.* pretty
dotep дотеп *n.* jest
dotepna vidpovid дотепна
   відповідь *n.* repartee
dotepnist дотепність *n.* wit
dotepnyi дотепний *a.* witty
dotrymannia дотримання *n.*
   adherence
dotrymannia дотримання *n.*
   observance
dotrymuvatysia дотримуватися
   v.i. adhere
dotsilnist доцільність *n*
   advisability
dotsilnist доцільність *n.* suitability
dotsilnyi доцільний *a.* advisable
dotychna дотична *n.* tangent
dotyk дотик *n* touch
dotykovyi дотиковий *a.* tactile
dovesty довести *v.t.* vindicate
dovesty do bidnosti довести до
   бідності *v.t.* impoverish
dovhastyi довгастий *a.* oblong
dovhastyi predmet довгастий
   предмет *n.* oblong
dovho довго *adv* long
dovhonosyk довгоносик *n.* weevil
dovhoochikuvanyi
   довгоочікуваний *a.* welcome
dovhota довгота *n.* longitude
dovhovichnist довговічність *n.*
   longevity
dovhovichnyi довговічний *a*
   durable
dovhozhytel довгожитель *n*
   centenarian
dovhyi довгий *a.* long
dovichnyi довічний *a.* lifelong
dovid довід *n.* argument
dovidatysia z dosvidu
   довідатися з досвіду *v. t.*
   experience

dovidka довідка *n.* reference
dovidnyk довідник *n* directory
dovidnyk turysta довідник
   туриста *n.* handbook
doviduvatysia довідуватися *v. t*
   consult
dovilnyi довільний *a.* arbitrary
dovira довіра *n* confidence
dovira довіра *n* faith
dovirena osoba довірена особа
   n confidant
dovirenist довіреність *n.* proxy
doviriaty довіряти *v. i* confide
dovirlyvist довірливість *adj.*
   credulity
dovirlyvyi довірливий *a.* trustful
dovodyty доводити *v.t.* prove
dovzhyna довжина *n.* length
doza доза *n* dose
doza likiv доза ліків *v. t* drench
dozrivaty дозрівати *v.i.* ripen
dozvil дозвіл *n.* assent
dozvil дозвіл *n.* leave
dozvil дозвіл *n.* permission
dozvillia дозвілля *n.* leisure
dozvolenyi дозволений *a.* legal
dozvolenyi дозволений *a.*
   permissible
dozvoliaty дозволяти *v.t.* allow
dozvoliaty дозволяти *v. i* consent
dozvoliaty demonstruvannia
   дозволяти демонстрування *v.t.*
   release
dozvolyty дозволити *v.t.* permit
drakhma драхма *n* dram
drakon дракон *n* dragon
drama драма *n* drama
dramaturh драматург *n* dramatist
dramatychnyi драматичний *a*
   dramatic
drapiruvalnyk драпірувальник *n*
   draper

drativlyvist дратівливість *n.* petulance

drativlyvyi дратівливий *a.* impatient

drativlyvyi дратівливий *a.* irritable

drativnyi дратівний *a.* irksome

dratuvaty дратувати *v.t.* incense

dratuvaty дратувати *v.t.* irritate

drazhe драже *n.* comfit

drazhnyty дражнити *v.t.* rag

drazhnyty дражнити *v.t.* taunt

drenazh дренаж *n* drainage

drenazhna truba дренажна труба *n.* culvert

drevnii древній *a.* immemorial

dribiazkovyi дріб'язковий *a.* minute

dribna chastka дрібна частка *n.* minim

dribnopomisne dvorianstvo дрібнопомісне дворянство *n.* gentry

dribnyi дрібний *a.* insignificant

dribnyi дрібний *a.* petty

dribnytsia дрібниця *n.* trifle

drimaty дрімати *v. i* doze

drimota дрімота *n.* doze

driuchok дрючок *n* cudgel

drizhdzhi дріжджі *n.* yeast

druhoriadnyi другорядний *a.* tributary

druhosortnyi другосортний *a.* middling

druhyi другий *a.* second

druk друк *n* print

drukarka друкарка *n.* typist

drukarska pomylka друкарська помилка *n.* misprint

drukuvaty друкувати *v.t.* print

drukuvaty na mashyntsi друкувати на машинці *v.t.* type

druzhni stosunky дружні стосунки *n.* amity

druzhyna дружина *n.* wife

druzi друзі *n.* kith

dub дуб *n.* oak

dublikat дублікат *n* duplicate

dubliuvaty дублювати *v. t* duplicate

dubylnyk дубильник *n.* tanner

dubyna дубина *n* bat

duel дуель *n* duel

duel дуель *n.* meeting

duha дуга *n* curve

dukh дух *n.* psyche

dukh дух *n.* spirit

dukhovenstvo духовенство *n* clergy

dukhovnist духовність *n.* spirituality

dukhovnyi духовний *a.* spiritual

dukhy духи *n.* perfume

dumaty думати *v.t.* think

dumka думка *n.* opinion

dupa дупа *n.* ass

duplo дупло *n.* cavern

duren дурень *n* blockhead

durist дурість *n* folly

durnuvatyi дурнуватий *a.* sheepish

durnyi дурний *a.* mindless

durnyi дурний *a* stupid

duryty дурити *v.t* gull

duryty дурити *v.t* hoax

dush душ *n.* shower

dusha душа *n.* soul

dushevnokhvoryi душевнохворий *a.* insane

dushyty душити *v.t.* stifle

dushyty душити *v.t* suffocate

dushytysia душитися *v. t.* choke

duty poryvamy дути поривами *v.t.* pull

duzhe дуже *adv.* highly

duzhe poshyrenyi дуже поширений *a.* widespread

duzhe smachnyi дуже смачний *a.* delicious

duzhe sylnyi дуже сильний *a.* herculean

duzhe tverda bryla дуже тверда брила *v. t* burk

duzhe zadovolenyi дуже задоволений *a.* overjoyed

dva два *n.* two

dva tyzhni два тижні *n.* fort-night

dvadtsiata chastyna двадцята частина *n* twentieth

dvadtsiatyi двадцятий *a.* twentieth

dvadtsiatyi двадцятий *a.* twenty

dvanadtsiat дванадцять *n.* twelve

dvanadtsiata chastyna дванадцята частина *n.* twelfth

dvanadtsiatyi дванадцятий *a.* twelfth

dveri двері *n* door

dvichi двічі *adv.* twice

dvichi na misiats двічі на місяць *adj.* bimonthly

dviika двійка *a.* two

dviikovyi двійковий *adj* binary

dviinyk двійник *n.* counterpart

dviinyk двійник *n* double

dvir двір *n.* courtyard

dvobukvenyi двобуквений *adj* biliteral

dvoiezhenstvo двоєженство *n* bigamy

dvoistyi двоїстий *a* dual

dvoiuridnyi brat двоюрідний брат *n.* cousin

dvokhosovyi двохосьовий *adj* biaxial

dvokhsotrichchia двохсотріччя *adj* bicentenary

dvokrapka двокрапка *n* colon

dvomovnyi двомовний *a* bilingual

dvonohe двоноге *n* biped

dvorianstvo дворянство *n.* nobility

dvorianyn дворянин *n.* nobleman

dvorichnyi дворічний *adj* biennial

dvostatevyi двостатевий *adj.* bisexual

dvoznachnist двозначність *n.* ambiguity

dvoznachnyi двозначний *a.* ambiguous

dvuuholnyi двуугольний *adj.* biangular

dvyhun двигун *n* engine

dydaktychnyi дидактичний *a* didactic

dyiakon диякон *n.* deacon

dyiavol диявол *n* devil

dykhannia дихання *n* breath

dykhaty дихати *v. i.* breathe

dykist дикість *n.* savagery

dyktator диктатор *n* dictator

dyktsiia дикція *n* diction

dyktuvannia диктування *n* dictation

dyktuvaty диктувати *v. t* dictate

dykun дикун *n* savage

dykyi дикий *a.* barbarous

dylema дилема *n* dilemma

dyler дилер *n* dealer

dym дим *n.* smoke

dymchastyi димчастий *a.* smoky

dymetr диметр *n* diameter

dymity диміти *v.i.* smoke

dynamichnyi динамічний *a* dynamic

dynamika динаміка *n.* dynamics

dynamit динаміт *n* dynamite

dynastiia династія *n* dynasty

dynia диня *n.* melon

dyplom диплом *n* diploma

dyplomat дипломат *n* diplomat

dyplomatiia дипломатія *n* diplomacy

dyplomatychnyi дипломатичний *a* diplomatic

dyrektor директор *n.* director

dyrektor директор *n.* principal

dysertatsiia дисертація *n.* thesis

dyshlo дишло *a.* neap

dysk диск *n.* disc

dyskryminatsiia дискримінація *n* discrimination

dyskryminuvaty дискримінувати *v. t.* discriminate

dyskvalifikatsiia дискваліфікація *n* disqualification

dyskvalifikuvaty дискваліфікувати *v. t.* disqualify

dyspanser диспансер *n* dispensary

dyspersiia дисперсія *n.* variance

dystsyplina дисципліна *n* discipline

dytia дитя *n.* kid

dytiacha koliaska дитяча коляска *n.* perambulator

dytiache lizhko дитяче ліжко *n.* cot

dytiachyi дитячий *a.* childish

dytiachyi budynok дитячий будинок *n.* orphanage

dytiachyi sad дитячий сад *n.* kindergarten ;

dytyna дитина *n.* baby

dytyncha дитинча *n* cub

dytynstvo дитинство *n.* childhood

dyvan диван *n.* couch

dyvanna podushka диванна подушка *n* cushion

dyvizion дивізіон *n* battalion

dyvnyi дивний *a.* queer

dyvnyi дивний *a.* strange

dyvnyi дивний *a.* wonderful

dyvoplit дивопліт *n.* hedge

dyvovyzhnyi дивовижний *a.* outlandish

dyvuvannia дивування *n.* amazement

dyvuvaty дивувати *v.t.* amaze

dyvuvatysia дивуватися *v.i.* astound

dyvuvatysia дивуватися *v.i* marvel

dyvyna дивина *n.* oddity

dyvytysia дивитися *v.t.* gaze

dyvytysia skosa дивитися скоса *v.i.* squint

dyvytysia vseredynu дивитися всередину *v.i.* introspect

dyvytysia zakokhanymy ochyma дивитися закоханими очима *v.t.* ogle

dyzenteriia дизентерія *n* dysentery

dzerkalo дзеркало *n* mirror

dzhem джем *n.* jam

dzhentlmen джентльмен *n.* gentleman

dzherelo джерело *n.* origin

dzherelo джерело *n.* source

dzherelo enerhii джерело енергії *n.* generator

dzherelo kharchuvannia джерело харчування *n* breast

dzhunhli джунглі *n.* jungle

dzhut джут *n.* jute

dzhynsova tkanyna джинсова тканина *n.* jean

dzob дзьоб *n* beak

dzvenity дзвеніти *v.i.* jingle

dzvin дзвін *n* bell

dzvin дзвін *n.* toll

dzvinkyi potsilunok дзвінкий поцілунок *n.* smack

dzvinok дзвінок *n.* call

dzvonyty дзвонити *v.t.* telephone

dzyzhchannia дзижчання *n.* buzz

dzyzhchaty дзижчати *v. i* buzz

efekt ефект *n* effect
efektyvnist ефективність *n* efficiency
efektyvnyi ефективний *a* effective
efektyvnyi ефективний *a* efficient
efir ефір *n* ether
ehoistychnyi егоїстичний *a.* selfish
ehoizm егоїзм *n* ego
ekipazh екіпаж *n.* crew
ekipiruvannia екіпірування *n.* kit
ekipiruvaty екіпірувати *v. t* equip
ekonomichnyi економічний *a* economic
ekonomiia економія *n* economy
ekonomika економіка *n.* economics
ekonomnyi економний *a.* thrifty
ekonomyty економити *v.t.* spare
ekran екран *n.* screen
ekskursiia екскурсія *n.* excursion
ekspansiia експансія *n.* expansion
ekspedytsiia експедиція *n* expedition
eksperiment експеримент *n* experiment
ekspert експерт *n* expert
ekspluatuvaty експлуатувати *v. t* exploit
eksponat експонат *n.* exhibit
ekstraordynarnyi екстраординарний *a.* extraordinary
ekstremalnyi екстремальний *a* extreme
ekstremist екстреміст *n* extremist
ekvator екватор *n* equator

ekvivalentnyi еквівалентний *a* equivalent
ekzamenator екзаменатор *n* examiner
ekzamenovanyi екзаменований *n* examinee
el ель *n* ale
elastychnyi еластичний *a* elastic
elehantnist елегантність *n* elegance
elehantnyi елегантний *adj* elegant
elehiia елегія *n* elegy
elektorat електорат *n* constituency
elektromotor електромотор *n.* motor
elektrychna napruha електрична напруга *n.* voltage
elektrychnyi електричний *a* electric
elektrychnyi strum електричний струм *n* current
elektryfikuvaty електрифікувати *v. t* electrify
elektryka електрика *n* electricity
element елемент *n* element
elementarnyi елементарний *a* elementary
elementarnyi елементарний *a.* simple
elf ельф *n* elf
emal емаль *n* enamel
emansypatsiia емансипація *n.* emancipation
emblema емблема *n* emblem
embrion ембріон *n* embryo
emotsiia емоція *n* emotion
emotsiinyi емоційний *a* emotional
enerhiia енергія *n.* energy
enerhiinyi енергійний *a* energetic
entomolohiia ентомологія *n.* entomology

entsyklopediia енциклопедія *n.*
encyclopaedia
entuziazm ентузіазм *n*
enthusiasm
epichna poema епічна поема *n*
epic
epidemiia епідемія *n* epidemic
epihrama епіграма *n* epigram
epilepsiia епілепсія *n* epilepsy
epiloh епілог *n* epilogue
epitafiia епітафія *n* epitaph
epizod епізод *n* episode
epokha епоха *n* era
erotychnyi еротичний *a* erotic
eroziia ерозія *n* erosion
ese есе *n.* essay
eseist есеїст *n* essayist
esentsiia есенція *n* essence
eskadron ескадрон *n.* squadron
eskiz ескіз *n.* sketch
estetychnyi естетичний *a.*
aesthetic
estetyka естетика *n.pl.* aesthetics
etap етап *n.* stage
etychnyi етичний *a* ethical
etyka етика *n.* ethics
etyket етикет *n* etiquette
etyketka етикетка *n.* tally
etymolohiia етимологія *n.*
etymology
evakuatsiia евакуація *n*
evacuation
evakuiuvaty евакуювати *v. t*
evacuate

F

fabryka фабрика *n* factory
faeton фаетон *n* chaise
fail файл *n* file
fakel факел *n.* torch
fakh фах *n* feat
faksymile факсиміле *n* facsimile

fakt факт *n* fact
faktor фактор *n* factor
faktychno фактично *adv.* actually
faktychnyi фактичний *a.* actual
fakultet факультет *n* faculty
falsyfikatsiia фальсифікація *n*
forgery
fanatychnyi фанатичний *a*
fanatic
fanatyk фанатик *n* bigot
fanatyk фанатик *n* fanatic
fanatyk фанатик *n.* zealot
fanatyzm фанатизм *n* bigotry
fantastychnyi фантастичний *a*
fantastic
fantastychnyi фантастичний *a.*
weird
fantazer фантазер *n.* visionary
fantaziinyi фантазійний *v.t* fancy
fantom фантом *n.* phantom
farba фарба *n.* paint
farbuvaty фарбувати *v. t* dye
farbuvaty фарбувати *v.t.* paint
farbuvaty za trafaretom
фарбувати за трафаретом *v.i.*
stencil
farfor фарфор *n.* china
farfor фарфор *n.* porcelain
farmatsevt фармацевт *n* druggist
fars фарс *n* farce
fartukh фартух *n.* apron
fasad фасад *n* facade
fatalnyi фатальний *a* fatal
fatum фатум *n* fate
fauna фауна *n* fauna
favoryt фаворит *n* favourite
favoryt фаворит *n.* minion
faza фаза *n.* phase
federalnyi федеральний *a*
federal
federatsiia федерація *n*
federation
feia фея *n* fairy

fenomenalnyi феноменальний *a.* phenomenal
feodalnyi феодальний *a* feudal
ferma ферма *n* farm
ferment фермент *n* ferment
fermer фермер *n* farmer
feston фестон *n* festoon
fial фіал *n.* phial
fiasko фіаско *n* fiasco
fihliar фігляр *n.* mummer
fihura фігура *n* figure
fihura фігура *n.* stature
fihuralnyi фігуральний *a* figurative
fiksuvaty фіксувати *v.t* fix
fiktsiia фікція *n* figment
fiktyvnyi фіктивний *a* sham
filantrop філантроп *n.* philanthropist
filantropichnyi філантропічний *a.* philanthropic
filiia філія *n* branch
filoloh філолог *n.* philologist
filolohichnyi філологічний *a.* philological
filolohiia філологія *n.* philology
filosof філософ *n.* philosopher
filosofiia філософія *n.* philosophy
filosofskyi філософський *a.* philosophical
filtr фільтр *n* filter
filtruvaty фільтрувати *v.t* filter
finansova sprava фінансова справа *n* finance
finansovyi фінансовий *a* financial
finansuvaty фінансувати *v.t* finance
finansyst фінансист *n* financier
fioletovyi фіолетовий *adj.* purple
fioletovyi kolir фіолетовий колір *n.* violet
firma фірма *n.* firm

fisharmoniia фісгармонія *n.* harmonium
fiskalnyi фіскальний *a* fiscal
fistula фістула *n* fistula
fizionomiia фізіономія *n.* physiognomy
fizychna vada фізична вада *n* handicap
fizychnyi фізичний *a.* physical
fizyk фізик *n.* physicist
fizyka фізика *n.* physics
flakon флакон *n.* vial
flanel фланель *n* flannel
fleita флейта *n* flute
fliaha фляга *n* flask
flihel флігель *n.* outhouse
flirt флірт *n* flirt
flirtuvaty фліртувати *v.i* flirt
fliuid флюїд *n* fluid
flora флора *n* flora
flot флот *n* fleet
foiie фойє *n.* lobby
fokalnyi фокальний *a* focal
fokus фокус *n* focus
fokusnyk фокусник *n.* juggler
fokusuvatysia фокусуватися *v.t* focus
folha фольга *v.t* foil
fon фон *n.* background
fond фонд *n.* fund
fonetychnyi фонетичний *a.* phonetic
fonetyka фонетика *n.* phonetics
fontan фонтан *n.* fountain
fora v tenisi фора в тенісі *n* bisque
forma форма *n* form
forma форма *n* mould
forma форма *n.* shape
formalnist формальність *n.* technicality
formalnyi формальний *a* formal
format формат *n* format

formula формула *n* formula
formuliuvaty формулювати *v.t* formulate
formuvannia формування *n* formation
formuvaty polk формувати полк *v.t.* regiment
fortetsia фортеця *n.* fortress
fortetsia фортеця *n.* stronghold
fosfat фосфат *n.* phosphate
fosfor фосфор *n.* phosphorus
foto фото *n* photo
fotohraf фотограф *n.* photographer
fotohrafichnyi фотографічний *a.* photographic
fotohrafiia фотографія *n* photograph
fotohrafuvannia фотографування *n.* photography
fotohrafuvaty фотографувати *v.t.* photograph
fotokadr фотокадр *n.* still
frahment фрагмент *n.* fragment
frakht фрахт *n.* freight
fraktsiia фракція *n* faction
fraktsiinyi фракційний *a* factious
frantsuzka mova французька мова *n* French
frantsuzkyi французький *a.* French
fraza фраза *n.* phrase
frazeolohiia фразеологія *n.* phraseology
freska фреска *n.* mural
frukt фрукт *n.* fruit
fruktovyi sad фруктовий сад *n.* orchard
fu фу *interj* fie
fufaika фуфайка *n.* jersey

fundamentalnyi фундаментальний *a.* fundamental
funktsiia функція *n.* function
funktsioner функціонер *n.* functionary
funktsionuvaty функціонувати *v.i* function
funt фунт *n.* pound
furazh фураж *n* fodder
furhon фургон *n.* van
futbolnyi miach футбольний м'яч *n* oval
fyrkaty фиркати *v.i.* snort

graty ґрати *n.* grate
gudzyk ґудзик *n* button

habardyn габардин *n.* whipcord
hachok гачок *n.* crotchet
hadaty гадати *v. t* conjecture
hadaty гадати *v.t.* presume
hadaty гадати *v.t.* repute
hadyna гадина *n.* toad
hai гай *n.* wood
haikovyi kliuch гайковий ключ *n.* wrench
hak гак *n.* hook
halaktyka галактика *n.* galaxy
halantnist галантність *n.* gallantry
halantnyi галантний *a.* gallant
halas галас *n* babel
halaslyvyi галасливий *a.* hilarious
halaslyvyi галасливий *a.* tumultuous
halereia галерея *n.* gallery
haliavyna галявина *n.* lawn
halka галька *n.* pebble
halmo гальмо *n* brake

halmuvaty гальмувати *v. t* brake
halon галон *n.* gallon
halop галоп *n.* gallop
halvanizuvaty гальванізувати *v.t.* galvanize
hamanets гаманець *n.* wallet
hanba ганьба *n* affront
hanba ганьба *n.* infamy
hanba ганьба *n.* odium
hanbyty ганьбити *v.* asperse
hanchirka ганчірка *n* duster
hanebnyi ганебний *a.* shameful
hanhster гангстер *n.* gangster
hanok ганок *n.* porch
harantiia гарантія *n.* warranty
harantiia vid zbytkiv гарантія від збитків *n.* indemnity
harantuvaty гарантувати *v. t* ensure
harazh гараж *n.* garage
harbuz гарбуз *n.* pumpkin
harchannia гарчання *n.* snarl
harchaty гарчати *v.i.* snarl
hariachkovyi oznob гарячковий озноб *n* ague
hariachnist гарячність *n.* vehemence
hariachyi гарячий *a* fervent
harmata гармата *n.* cannon
harmoniia гармонія *n.* harmony
harmoniinyi гармонійний *a.* harmonious
harnenkyi гарненький *a* pretty
harnyi гарний *a.* handsome
hartuvaty гартувати *v.t.* quench
has гас *n.* kerosene
haslo гасло *n.* slogan
hasyty гасити *v.t* extinguish
hatka гатка *n.* hurdle1
havan гавань *n.* harbour
havkannia гавкання *n.* woof
havkaty гавкати *v.i.* yap
haz газ *n.* gas

hazeta газета *n.* gazette
hazopodibnyi газоподібний *adj.* aeriform
hemoroi геморой *n.* piles
henerator генератор *n* dynamo
henii геній *n.* genius
heohraf географ *n.* geographer
heohrafichnyi географічний *a.* geographical
heohrafiia географія *n.* geography
heoloh геолог *n.* geologist
heolohichnyi геологічний *a.* geological
heolohiia геологія *n.* geology
heometriia геометрія *n.* geometry
heometrychnyi геометричний *a.* geometrical
hermetyzuvaty герметизувати *v.t.* pressurize
heroi герой *n.* hero
heroichnyi героїчний *a.* heroic
heroinia героїня *n.* heroine
heroizm героїзм *n.* heroism
hertsoh герцог *n* duke
herundii герундій *n.* gerund
het геть *adv.* away
hibon гібон *n.* gibbon
hibryd гібрид *n* hybrid
hibrydnyi гібридний *a.* hybrid
hidnist гідність *n* dignity
hidnyi гідний *a.* worthy
hidnyi pokhvaly гідний похвали *a.* praiseworthy
hihant гігант *n.* giant
hihantskyi гігантський *a.* gigantic
hihantskyi гігантський *a.* tremendous
hihiiena гігієна *n.* hygiene
hihiienichnyi гігієнічний *a.* hygienic
hiiena гієна *n.* hyaena, hyena
hildiia гільдія *n.* guild

hilka гілка *n* spray
hilochka гілочка *n.* sprig
himn гімн *n* anthem
himnast гімнаст *n.* gymnast
himnastychnyi гімнастичний *a.* gymnastic
himnastychnyi zal гімнастичний зал *n.* gymnasium
himnastyka гімнастика *n.* gymnastics
hiperbola гіпербола *n.* hyperbole
hipnotyzm гіпнотизм *n.* hypnotism
hipnotyzuvaty гіпнотизувати *v.t.* hypnotize
hipnotyzuvaty гіпнотизувати *v.t.* mesmerize
hipnoz гіпноз *n.* mesmerism
hipoteza гіпотеза *n.* hypothesis
hirchytsia гірчиця *n.* mustard
hirkota гіркота *n.* affliction
hirkyi гіркий *a* bitter
hirlianda гірлянда *n* anadem
hirska vershyna гірська вершина *n.* alp
hist гість *n.* guest
hitara гітара *n.* guitar
hladkyi гладкий *a.* sleek
hlasnist гласність *n.* publicity
hlasnyi гласний *n.* vowel
hlaukoma глаукома *n.* glaucoma
hlava глава *n.* chapter
hlazur глазур *n* glaze
hlechyk глечик *n.* jug
hliadach глядач *n.* on-looker
hliansuvatyi глянсуватий *a.* lustrous
hlianuty глянути *v.i* look
hlid глід *n.* hawthorn
hliser глісер *n.* glider
hlitseryn гліцерин *n.* glycerine
hliukoza глюкоза *n.* glucose
hlobalnyi глобальний *a.* global

hlobus глобус *n.* globe
hlosarii глосарій *n.* glossary
hlukhyi глухий *a* deaf
hlukhyi глухий *a.* hollow
hlukhyi stuk глухий стук *n.* thud
hlumytysia глумитися *v.i.* jeer
hlushnyk глушник *n.* silencer
hlushyty глушити *v.t.* muffle
hluzlyvo posmikhnutysia глузливо посміхнутися *v.i* sneer
hluzuvannia глузування *n.* wipe
hlyboka tuha глибока туга *n.* yearning
hlybokyi глибокий *a.* deep
hlybyna глибина *n* depth
hlyna глина *n* argil
hlynozem глинозем *n* clay
hnaty гнати *v. t* distil
hnii гній *n.* pus
hnit гніт *n.* wick
hnitiuchyi гнітючий *a.* oppressive
hnityty гнітити *v.t.* obsess
hnityty гнітити *v.t.* oppress
hniv гнів *n.* anger
hnivnyi гнівний *a.* irate
hnizdo гніздо *n.* nest
hnizdytysia гніздитися *v.t.* nest
hnobytel гнобитель *n.* oppressor
hnuchkist гнучкість *n.* versatility
hnuchkyi гнучкий *a* facile
hnuchkyi гнучкий *a* flexible
hnutysia гнутися *v. t* bow
hnyl гниль *n.* rot
hnyty гнити *v.i.* rot
hobelen гобелен *n.* tapestry
hoduvannia годування *n* feed
hoduvaty годувати *v.t* feed
hoduvaty hrudmy годувати грудьми *v.t.* suckle
hodyna година *n.* hour
hodynnyk годинник *n.* clock
hodytysia годитися *v.t* fit

hoidalky гойдалки *n* swing
hoidaty гойдати *v.i.* sway
hoidaty гойдати *v.t.* dandle
hoidatysia гойдатися *v. t* dangle
hoidatysia гойдатися *v.i.* oscillate
holf гольф *n.* golf
holinnia гоління *n* shave
holka голка *n.* needle
holod голод *n* dearth
holodna smert голодна смерть *n.* starvation
holodnyi голодний *a.* hungry
holodovka голодовка *n* famine
holoduvannia голодування *n* fast
holoduvaty голодувати *v.i* fast
holos голос *n.* voice
holosno hovoryty голосно говорити *v.i.* shout
holosuvannia голосування *n.* poll
holosuvaty голосувати *v.i.* ballot
holova голова *n.* head
holova komety голова комети *n.* coma
holoveshka головешка *n* brand
holovna pidtrymka головна підтримка *n.* mainstay
holovnyi головний *a.* basic
holovnyi головний *a.* cardinal
holovnyi головний *a.* chief
holovnyi bil головний біль *n.* headache
holovnym chynom головним чином *adv.* mainly
holovolomka головоломка *n.* puzzle
holovoriz головоріз *n.* thug
holovuiuchyi головуючий *n* chairman
holovuvaty головувати *v.i.* preside
holub голуб *n* dove
holub голуб *n.* pigeon
holubyty голубити *v.t* fondle

holyi голий *a.* bare
holyi голий *a.* nude
holytysia голитися *v.t.* shave
homeopat гомеопат *n.* homoeopath
homeopatiia гомеопатія *n.* homeopathy
homilka гомілка *n.* ankle
homin гомін *n* din
honchar гончар *n.* potter
honcharni vyroby гончарні вироби *n.* pottery
honh гонг *n.* gong
honky гонки *n.* race
honorar гонорар *n* fee
honytva гонитва *n.* pursuit
hora гора *n.* mount
horb горб *n.* hunch
horbok горбок *n.* hillock
hordist гордість *n.* pride
hordovytist гордовитість *n.* arrogance
hordovytyi гордовитий *a.* haughty
hordyi гордий *a.* proud
hore горе *n.* grief
horezvisnyi горезвісний *a.* notorious
horikh горіх *n* nut
hority горіти *v. t* burn
horiucha rechovyna горюча речовина *a.* inflammable
horiuvaty горювати *v.t.* grieve
horlianka горлянка *n.* gourd
horlo горло *n.* throat
horlovyi горловий *a.* guttural
horn горн *n.* furnace
horobets горобець *n.* sparrow
horokh горох *n.* pea
horoskop гороскоп *n.* nativity
horshchyk горщик *n.* pot
hortannyi гортанний *a.* throaty
horyla горила *n.* gorilla

horyshche горище *n.* loft
horystyi гористий *a.* mountainous
horyzont горизонт *n.* horizon
Hospoda Господа *n.* Messrs
hospodar господар *n.* host
hospodar господар *n.* proprietor
hostrokintsevyi гострокінцевий *a.* pungent
hostrota гострота *n.* keenness
hostryi гострий *adj* argute
hostryi bil гострий біль *n.* pang
hostynnist гостинність *n.* hospitality
hostynnist гостинність *n* welcome
hostynnyi гостинний *a.* hospitable
hotel готель *n.* hotel
hotivka готівка *n.* cash
hotovnist готовність *n.* willingness
hotovyi готовий *a.* ready
hotuvaty готувати *v. t* cook
hovirkyi говіркий *a.* talkative
hovoryty говорити *v.i.* talk
hovoryty natiakamy говорити натяками *v.t.* intimate
hovoryty zahadkamy говорити загадками *v.i.* riddle
hra гра *n.* game
hrabizh грабіж *n* plunder
hrabizhnyk грабіжник *n.* robber
hrabuvaty грабувати *v.t.* rob
hradatsiia градація *n.* gradation
hrafichnyi графічний *a.* graphic
hrafik графік *n.* chart
hrafik графік *n* diagram
hrafstvo графство *n.* shire
hrafynia графиня *n.* countess
hrak грак *n.* rook
hralna karta гральна карта *n.* card

hralna karta гральна карта *n.* play card
hralna kist гральна кість *n* die
hralni kosti гральні кості *n.* dice
hram грам *n.* gramme
hramatyka граматика *n.* grammar
hramatysty граматисти *n.* grammarian
hramofon грамофон *n.* gramophone
hramota грамота *n* charter
hramotnist грамотність *n.* literacy
hran грань *n* edge
hranata граната *n.* grenade
hrandioznyi грандіозний *a.* grand
hranychnyi граничний *a.* marginal
hranychnyi граничний *a* overall
hranytsia границя *n.* limit
hratsiia грація *n.* grace
hraty грати *v.i* game
hraty na fleiti грати на флейті *v.i* flute
hraty v azartni ihry грати в азартні ігри *v.i.* gamble
hraty v kosti грати в кості *v. i.* dice
hratysia гратися *v.i.* sport
hravets гравець *n.* gambler
hravets bytkoiu гравець биткою *n.* batsman
hraviruvaty гравірувати *v. t* engrave
hravitatsiia гравітація *n.* gravitation
hrebin гребінь *n* comb
hrebinets гребінець *n* crest
hreblia гребля *n.* barrage
hrebty гребти *v.t.* row
hrebty veslom гребти веслом *v.i.* paddle
hretska mova грецька мова *n.* Greek

hretskyi грецький *a* Greek
hriaz грязь *n.* mire
hriaznulia грязнуля *n.* slattern
hrikh гріх *n.* sin
hrilka грілка *n.* damsel
hrim грім *n.* thunder
hrish гріш *n.* mite
hrishnyi грішний *a.* sinful
hrishnyk грішник *n.* sinner
hrishyty грішити *v.i.* sin
hrity гріти *v.t.* warm
hrity na sontsi гріти на сонці *v.t.* sun
hritysia грітися *v.i.* bask
hriukaty грюкати *v.i.* rumble
hriznyi грізний *a* formidable
hrobnytsia гробниця *n* cist
hromada громада *n.* fraternity
hromadianstvo громадянство *n* citizenship
hromadianyn громадянин *n* citizen
hromadskist громадськість *n.* public
hromadskyi громадський *a.* public
hromizdkyi громіздкий *a* bulky
hromovyi громовий *a.* thunderous
hromyty громити *v.t.* smash
hroshi гроші *n.* money
hroshi гроші *n.* pelf
hroshovyi грошовий *a.* pecuniary
hroshovyi perekaz грошовий переказ *n.* remittance
hroshovyi podarunok грошовий подарунок *n.* gratuity
hrotesk гротеск *a.* grotesque
hroza гроза *n.* storm
hrozovyi грозовий *a.* stormy
hrubyi грубий *a* coarse
hrubyi грубий *a* unmannerly
hruden грудень *n* december

hrudka грудка *n.* clot
hrudna zaloza грудна залоза *n.* mamma
hrudnyi грудний *a.* mammary
hrudy груди *n* bosom
hrum грум *n.* groom
hrunt грунт *n.* soil
hruntovka грунтовка *n.* primer
hrupa група *n.* group
hrupa ministriv група міністрів *n.* cabinet
hrupa z desiaty група з десяти *n* decade
hrupuvaty групувати *v.t.* group
hrusha груша *n.* pear
hruzylo грузило *n.* lead
hryb гриб *n.* mushroom
hrybok грибок *n.* fungus
hrymasy гримаси *n* antic
hrymity гриміти *v.i.* thunder
hryp грип *n.* influenza
hryva грива *n.* mane
hryzha грижа *n.* hernia
hryzty гризти *v.t.* nibble
hryzun гризун *n.* rodent
huava гуава *n.* guava
huba губа *n.* lip
hubernator губернатор *n.* governor
hubka губка *n.* sponge
hubnyi губний *a.* labial
huchne vitannia гучне вітання *n* acclaim
huchni veseloshchi гучні веселощі *n.* hilarity
huchnyi гучний *a.* loud
hudinnia гудіння *n* hum
hudity гудіти *v. i* hum
huliaka гуляка *n.* reveller
hulianka гулянка *n.* jollity
huliannia гуляння *n.* revel
huma гума *n.* rubber

humanitarii гуманітарій *a* humanitarian
humanitarnyi гуманітарний *a* classical
humannyi гуманний *a.* humane
humor гумор *n.* humour
humoryst гуморист *n.* humorist
humorystychnyi гумористичний *a.* humorous
hurkit гуркіт *n.* rumble
hurkotity гуркотіти *v.i.* grumble
hurtka гуртка *n.* mug
hurtozhytok гуртожиток *n.* hostel
husak гусак *n.* goose
husenytsia гусениця *n* caterpillar
hushcha гуща *n* middle
hushchavyna гущавина *n.* thicket
husto густо *adv.* thick
hustonaselenyi густонаселений *a.* populous
hustyi густий *a* dense
huvernantka гувернантка *n.* governess
hvaltuvaty гвалтувати *v.t.* rape
hvozdyka гвоздика *n* clove
hvynt гвинт *n.* screw
hvyntivka гвинтівка *n* rifle
hykannia гикання *n.* hoot
hykavka гикавка *n.* hiccup
hynuty гинути *v.i.* perish
hyrlo shakhty гирло шахти *n.* outset

I

i і *conj.* and
i odyn i druhyi і один і другий *pron* both
i tak dali і так далі *a* etcetera
ideal ідеал *n* ideal
ideal ідеал *n.* nonpareil
idealist ідеаліст *n.* idealist

idealistychnyi ідеалістичний *a.* idealistic
idealizm ідеалізм *n.* idealism
idealizuvaty ідеалізувати *v.t.* idealize
idealnyi ідеальний *a.* ideal
ideia ідея *n.* idea
identychnist ідентичність *n.* identity
identychnyi ідентичний *a.* identical
identyfikatsiia ідентифікація *n.* indentification
identyfikuvaty ідентифікувати *v.t.* identify
idioma ідіома *n.* idiom
idioma ідіома *n.* locution
idiomatychnyi ідіоматичний *a.* idiomatic
idiot ідіот *n.* idiot
idiotskyi ідіотський *a.* idiotic
idiotyzm ідіотизм *n.* ideocy
idol ідол *n.* idol
idolopoklonnyk ідолопоклонник *n.* idolater
ihnoruvaty ігнорувати *v.t.* ignore
ihra sliv ігра слів *n.* quibble
ihrashka іграшка *n.* toy
iiena Ієна *n.* Yen
iierarkhiia ієрархія *n.* hierarchy
iklo ікло *n.* tusk
iliuminatsiia ілюмінація *n.* illumination
iliustratsiia ілюстрація *n.* illustration
iliustrovanyi ілюстрований *a.* pictorical
iliustruvaty ілюструвати *v.t.* illustrate
iliuziia ілюзія *n.* illusion
imbyr імбир *n.* ginger
imennyk іменник *n.* noun

imenuvaty іменувати *v.t.*
nominate
imenytyi іменитий *a* eminent
imia ім'я *n.* name
imitator імітатор *n* mimic
imituvaty імітувати *v.t* mimic
immihrant іммігрант *n.* immigrant
immihratsiia імміграція *n.*
immigration
immihruvaty іммігрувати *v.i.*
immigrate
imovirnyi імовірний *a.* possible
imperator імператор *n* emperor
imperatrytsia імператриця *n*
empress
imperializm імперіалізм *n.*
imperialism
imperiia імперія *n* empire
imperskyi імперський *a.* imperial
import імпорт *n.* import
importuvaty імпортувати *v.t.*
import
impozantnyi імпозантний *a.*
imposing
impuls імпульс *n.* impact
impulsyvnist імпульсивність *n.*
impetuosity
impulsyvnyi імпульсивний *a.*
impulsive
imunizuvaty імунізувати *v.t.*
immunize
imunnyi імунний *a.* immune
inakshe інакше *adv.* alias
inakshyi інакший *pron.* other
indiiskyi індійський *a.* Indian
indychka індичка *n.* turkey
indyho індиго *n.* indigo
indykator індикатор *n.* indicator
indyvidualizm індивідуалізм *n.*
individualism
indyvidualnist індивідуальність
n. individuality
inertnyi інертний *a.* inert

infantilnyi інфантільний *a.*
infantile
infektsiinyi інфекційний *a.*
infectious
informator інформатор *n.*
informer
informatsiia інформація *n.*
information
informatsiinyi інформаційний *a.*
informative
inhrediient інгредієнт *n.*
ingredient
initsial ініціал *n.* initial
initsiatyva ініціатива *n.* initiative
initsiatyvnist ініціативність *n*
enterprise
inkryminuvaty інкримінувати *v.t.*
incriminate
inodi іноді *adv.* sometimes
inozemets іноземець *n* foreigner
inozemna mova іноземна мова
n. lingo
inozemnyi іноземний *a* foreign
insektytsyd інсектицид *n.*
insecticide
inshyi інший *a* another
inshyi інший *a* else
inspektor інспектор *n.* inspector
inspektsiia інспекція *n.* inspection
inspektuvannia інспектування *n.*
survey
instantsiia інстанція *n.* instance
instinktyvnyi інстінктивний *a.*
intrinsic
instruktazh інструктаж *n.*
instruction
instruktor інструктор *n.* instructor
instrument інструмент *n.*
instrument
instrumentalist інструменталіст
n. instrumentalist

instrumentalnyi
інструментальний *a.*
instrumental
instsenuvaty інсценувати *v.t.*
stage
instynkt інстинкт *n.* instinct
instynktyvnyi інстинктивний *a.*
instinctive
instytut інститут *n.* institute
insynuatsiia інсинуація *n.*
insinuation
intelekt інтелект *n.* intellect
intelektualnyi інтелектуальний
a. inner
intelihent інтелігент *n.* intellectual
intelihentsiia інтелігенція *n.*
intelligentsia
intensyvnist інтенсивність *n.*
intensity
intensyvnyi інтенсивний *a.*
intensive
interes інтерес *n.* interest
interpretator інтерпретатор *n*
exponent
interval інтервал *n.* interim
interventsiia інтервенція *n.*
intervention
introspektsiia інтроспекція *n.*
introspection
intryha інтрига *n* intrigue
intryhuvaty інтригувати *v.t.*
intrigue
intsoliatsiia інтсоляція *n.*
installation
intsydent інцидент *n.* incident
intuitsiia інтуїція *n.* insight
intuitsiia інтуїція *n.* intuition
intuityvnyi інтуїтивний *a.* intuitive
intymnyi інтимний *a.* intimate
invalid інвалід *n* invalid
investuvaty інвестувати *v.t.*
invest

investytsii інвестиції *n.*
investment
inzhener інженер *n* engineer
inzhyr інжир *n* fig
irlandska mova ірландська мова
n. Irish
irlandskyi ірландський *a.* Irish
ironichnyi іронічний *a.* ironical
ironiia іронія *n.* irony
iryska ириска *n.* toffee
irzha іржа *n.* rust
irzhannia іржання *n.* neigh
irzhaty іржати *v.i.* neigh
irzhavity іржавіти *v.i* rust
irzhavyi іржавий *a.* rusty
iskra іскра *n.* spark
iskra іскра *n.* spark
iskrinnia іскріння *n.* sparkle
iskrytysia іскритися *v.i.* scintillate
iskrytysia іскритися *v.i.* spark
iskrytysia іскритися *v.i.* sparkle
isnuvannia існування *n* existence
isnuvannia існування *n.*
subsistence
isnuvaty існувати *v.i.* prevail
isnuvaty існувати *v.i.* subsist
ispanets іспанець *n.* Spaniard
ispanska mova іспанська мова
n. Spanish
ispanskyi іспанський *a.* Spanish
isteriia істерія *n.* hysteria
isterychnyi істеричний *a.*
hysterical
istoriia історія *n.* history
istoriia історія *n.* tale
istorychnyi історичний *a* . historic
istoryk історик *n.* historian
istotnyi істотний *a* essential
istynnyi істинний *a.* true
italiiska movu італійська мову *n.*
Italian
italiiska solomka італійська
соломка *n.* leghorn

italiiskyi італійський *a.* Italian
ity lehko i shvydko іти легко і
швидко *v.t.* trip
izhoi ізгой *n.* outlaw
izium ізюм *n.* raisin
izoliator ізолятор *n.* insulator
izoliatsiia ізоляція *n.* isolation
izoliatsiia ізоляція *n.* segregation
izoliuvaty ізолювати *v.t.* isolate
izoliuvaty ізолювати *a.* secluded
izoliuvatysia ізолюватися *v.t.*
segregate

kabala кабала *n* bondage
kaban кабан *n* boar
kabare кабаре *n.* cabaret
kabel кабель *n.* cable
kabinet кабінет *n.* closet
kabinet кабінет *n.* parlour
kachaty качати *v.t.* pitch
kachka качка *n* canard
kachka качка *n.* duck
kadmii кадмій *n* cadmium
kadylo кадило *n* censer
kadyty кадити *v. t* cense
kafe кафе *n.* cafe
kafedra кафедра *a.* pulpit
kafedralnyi sobor кафедральний
собор *n.* minster
kaiannyk каянник *a.* repentant
kaiattia каяття *n.* compunction
kaidany кайдани *n* bond
kaidany кайдани *n* fetter
kakhel кахель *n.* tile
kaktus кактус *n.* cactus
kal кал *n* dung
kalambur каламбур *n.* pun
kalamburyty каламбурити *v.i.*
pun
kalamutyty каламутити *v.t.*
puddle

kalendar календар *n.* calendar
kalibr калібр *n* bore
kalichyty калічити *v.t.* lame
kalihrafiia каліграфія *n*
calligraphy
kalii калій *n.* potassium
kalika каліка *n* cripple
kalitstvo каліцтво *n.* mutilation
kaliuzha калюжа *n.* puddle
kalkuliator калькулятор *n*
calculator
kaloriia калорія *n.* calorie
kaltsii кальцій *n* calcium
kamera камера *n.* camera
kamerher камергер *n*
chamberlain
kamfora камфора *n.* camphor
kamiana ukladka кам'яна
укладка *n.* masonry
kamianystyi кам'янистий *a.* stony
kamin камінь *n.* stone
kaminna doshka камінна дошка
n. mantel
kamlot камлот *n* camlet
kampaniia кампанія *n.* campaign
kamvolnyi камвольний *n.*
worsted
kanal канал *n.* canal
kanalizatsiia каналізація *n.*
sewerage
kanava канава *n* ditch
kanchuk канчук *n* lash
kandydat кандидат *n.* candidate
kanistra каністра *n.* canister
kanton кантон *n* canton
kantseliariia канцелярія *n*
chancery
kantseliarski tovary канцелярські товари *n.*
stationery
kantsler канцлер *n.* chancellor
kapannia капання *n* drip
kapaty капати *v. i* drip

kapeliukh капелюх *n.* hat
kapeliushnyk капелюшник *n.* milliner
kapitalist капіталіст *n.* capitalist
kapitalnyi remont капітальний ремонт *n.* overhaul
kapitan капітан *n.* captain
kapituliatsiia капітуляція *n* surrender
kapituliuvaty капітулювати *v. t* capitulate
kapiushon капюшон *n.* hood
kapkan капкан *n.* trap
kaplytsia каплиця *n.* chapel
kapot капот *n* bonnet
kapryz каприз *n.* caprice
kapsulnyi капсульний *adj* capsular
kapusta капуста *n.* cabbage
karakuli каракулі *n* scrawl
karalnyi каральний *a.* punitive
karat карат *n.* carat
karaty карати *v. t.* castigate
karaty карати *v.t.* punish
karaul караул *n.* sentry
karavan караван *n.* caravan
karbid карбід *n.* carbide
karbuvannia monety карбування монети *n* coinage
karbuvaty карбувати *v.t.* mint
kardamon кардамон *n.* cardamom
kardynal кардинал *n.* cardinal
karier кар'єр *n.* quarry
kariera кар'єра *n.* career
karioznyi каріозний *adj* carious
karkannia каркання *n.* caw
karkaty каркати *v. i.* caw
karliuchky карлючки *n.* scribble
karlyk карлик *n.* midget
karlykovyi карликовий *n.* pygmy
karnaval карнавал *n* carnival
karnyi карний *a.* penal

karta карта *n* map
karton картон *n.* cardboard
kartonka картонка *n* carton
kartoplia картопля *n.* potato
kartyna картина *n.* picture
karykatura карикатура *n.* caricature
kaseta касета *n.* cassette
kasha каша *n.* cereal
kashalot кашалот *n.* sperm
kashel кашель *n.* cough
kashliaty кашляти *v. i.* cough
kashne кашне *n.* muffler
kashtan каштан *n.* chestnut
kaskad каскад *n.* cataract
kaskad каскад *n.* waterfall
kasta каста *n* caste
kastorove maslo касторове масло *n.* castor oil
kasuvalnyi касувальний *a.* irritant
kasyr касир *n.* cashier
kat кат *n.* executioner
kataloh каталог *n.* catalogue
kataloh каталог *n.* schedule
katastrofa катастрофа *n* disaster
katastrofichnyi катастрофічний *a* disastrous
katatysia na chovni кататися на човні *v.i* boat
katatysia na kovzanakh кататися на ковзанах *v.t.* skate
katehorichnyi категорічний *a.* categorical
katehoriia категорія *n.* category
katok каток *v.i.* slide
katolitska zhinocha shkola католіцька жіноча школа *n* convent
katolytskyi католицький *a.* catholic
katuvannia катування *n.* torture
katuvaty катувати *v.t.* torture
kava кава *n* coffee

kavaler кавалер *n* chevalier
kavaler кавалер *n* gallant
kavaleriia кавалерія *n.* cavalry
kavaleryst кавалерист *n.* trooper
kavun кавун *n.* water-melon
kazhan кажан *n* bat
kaznacheistvo казначейство *n.* treasury
kedr кедр *n.* cedar
kelykh келих *n.* goblet
kepka кепка *n.* cap
kepkuvaty кепкувати *v.i.* jest
kepskyi кепський *a.* wretched
keramika кераміка *n* ceramics
kerivna posada керівна посада *n.* leadership
kerivnyk керівник *n.* leader
kerivnyk керівник *n.* superintendent
kerivnyk konferentsii керівник конференції *n* convener
kerivnytstvo керівництво *n.* governance
kerivnytstvo керівництво *n.* guidance
kermo кермо *n.* helm
kerovanyi керований *a.* manageable
keruvaty керувати *n* conduct
ketchup кетчуп *n.* ketchup
khabar хабар *n* bribe
khabarnyk хабарник *ns.* barrator
khalat халат *n.* robe
khalat халат *n.* smock
khalatnist халатність *n.* negligence
khalatnyi халатний *a.* negligent
khalupka халупка *n.* shanty
kham хам *n* cad
khandryty хандрити *v.i.* mope
khanzha ханжа *n* canter
khanzha ханжа *n.* noble
khanzha ханжа *n.* prude

khaos хаос *n.* chaos
khaotychnyi хаотичний *adv.* chaotic
khapaty хапати *v.t.* grab
kharakter характер *n.* character
kharakter характер *n.* kidney
kharakter характер *n.* mettle
kharakteryzuvaty характеризувати *v. t* define
kharchuvannia харчування *n.* nourishment
kharchuvannia харчування *n.* nutrition
khata хата *n* house
khatyna хатина *n.* cabin
khatyna хатина *n.* hut
khaziain хазяїн *n.* master
khid хід *n* stroke
khimichnyi хімічний *a.* chemical
khimichyty хімічити *v.i* fiddle
khimiia хімія *n.* chemistry
khimik хімік *n.* chemist
khimikat хімікат *n.* chemical
khinin хінін *n.* quinine
khiromant хіромант *n.* palmist
khiromantiia хіромантія *n.* palmistry
khirurh хірург *n.* surgeon
khirurhiia хірургія *n.* surgery
khlib хліб *n* bread
khliv хлів *n.* cote
khlopchyk хлопчик *n* boy
khlopchyk хлопчик *n.* youngster
khlopets хлопець *n* fellow
khlopets хлопець *n.* lad
khlor хлор *n* chlorine
khloroform хлороформ *n* chloroform
khlostaty хльостати *v.t.* lash
khlynuty хлинути *v.i.* surge
khlynuty хлинути *v.i.* well
khmara хмара *n.* cloud
khmarnist хмарність *a.* overcast

khmarnyi хмарний *a* cloudy
khmurytysia хмуритися *v.i* frown
khmurytysia хмуритися *v.i.* scowl
khnykaty хникати *v.i.* whimper
khobi хобі *n.* hobby
khocha хоча *conj.* albeit
khocha хоча *conj.* although
khocha хоча *adv* even
khocha хоча *conj.* nevertheless
khocha хоча *conj.* though
khocha хоча *conj.* when
khoda хода *n.* gait
khoda хода *n.* step
khoda хода *n* tread
khodovyi ходовий *a.* salable
khodyty ходити *v.i.* pace
khodyty ходити *v.i.* walk
khodyty navshpynky ходити навшпиньки *v.t.* tip
khokei хокей *n.* hockey
khol хол *n.* lounge
kholera холера *n.* cholera
kholod холод *n.* chill
kholod холод *n* cold
kholodnokrovnist холоднокровність *n.* composure
kholodnyi холодний *a* cold
kholodnyi холодний *a.* frigid
kholodylnyk холодильник *n* cooler
kholodylnyk холодильник *n.* fridge
kholodylnyk холодильник *n.* refrigerator
kholostiak холостяк *n.* bachelor
kholostiak холостяк *n.* single
khomut хомут *n* clamp
khor хор *n* choir
khor хор *n.* chorus
khoral хорал *n* chant
khorobrist хоробрість *n* bravery
khorobrist хоробрість *n.* courage

khorobryi хоробрий *a* brave
khorobryi хоробрий *a* daring
khoroshyi хороший *a.* well
khortytsia хортиця *n.* greyhound
khotity хотіти *v.t.* want
khotity хотіти *v.t.* wish
khotity pyty хотіти пити *v.i.* thirst
khovaty ховати *v. t.* bury
khovaty ховати *v. t.* conceal
khovaty ховати *v.t* hide
khovaty ховати *v.t.* secrete
khram храм *n.* temple
khrebet хребет *n.* backbone
khrebet хребет *n.* ridge
khrebet хребет *n.* spine
khreshchennia хрещення *n.* baptism
khrest хрест *n* cross
khrestyty хрестити +*v.t.* baptize
khronichnyi хронічний *a.* chronic
khronika хроніка *n.* chronicle
khronohraf хронограф *n* chronograph
khronolohiia хронологія *n.* chronology
khropinnia хропіння *n* snore
khropity хропіти *v.i.* snore
khrypkyi хрипкий *a.* hoarse
Khrystos Христос *n.* Christ
khrystyianskyi християнський *a.* Christian
khrystyianskyi svit християнський світ *n.* Christendom
khrystyianstvo християнство *n.* Christianity
khrystyianyn християнин *n* Christian
khto хто *pron.* who
khto b ne хто б не *pron.* whoever
khtos хтось *pron.* somebody
khtos хтось *pron.* someone
khtyvyi хтивий *a.* lascivious

khtyvyi хтивий *a.* lustful
khtyvyi хтивий *a.* voluptuous
khudnuty худнути *v.i.* slim
khudoba худоба *n.* cattle
khudozhnii художній *a.* artistic
khudozhnyk художник *n.* artist
khudozhnyk художник *n.* painter
khudyi худий *a.* lank
khudyi худий *n.* lean
khudyi худий *a.* scanty
khulihan хуліган *n* bully
khulihan хуліган *n.* hooligan
khulihan хуліган *n.* ruffian
khulihanskyi хуліганський *a.*
  obscene
khustka хустка *n.* kerchief
khutro хутро *n* bonten
khutro хутро *n.* fur
khvala хвала *n* laud
khvala хвала *n.* praise
khvalko хвалько *n* bouncer
khvalko хвалько *n* brag
khvalkuvatyi хвалькуватий *a.* tall
khvalyty хвалити *v. t* compliment
khvalyty хвалити *v.t.* praise
khvastaty хвастати *v.i* boast
khvastaty хвастати *v. i* brag
khvastaty хвастати *v.i.* swagger
khvastoshchi хвастощі *n* boast
khvastoshchi хвастощі *n.*
  vainglory
khvirtka хвіртка *n.* wicket
khvist хвіст *n.* stern
khvist хвіст *n.* tail
khvority хворіти *v.i.* ache
khvority хворіти *v.t.* pain
khvoroba хвороба *n.* ailment
khvoroba хвороба *n.* illness
khvoroba хвороба *n.* malady
khvoroba хвороба *n.* sickness
khvoroblyvyi хворобливий *a.*
  morbid

khvoroblyvyi хворобливий *a.*
  painful
khvoroblyvyi хворобливий *a.*
  sickly
khvoryi хворий *a.* ill
khvoryi хворий *a.* sick
khvyli хвилі *n.* surge
khvylia хвиля *n.* tide
khvylia хвиля *n.* wave
khvyliastist хвилястість *n.*
  undulation
khvyliuvannia хвилювання *n*
  commotion
khvyliuvannia хвилювання *n*
  disquiet
khvyliuvannia хвилювання *n.* fret
khvyliuvaty хвилювати *v. t* excite
khvyliuvaty хвилювати *v.t.*
  perturb
khvylyna хвилина *n.* minute
khyba хиба *n* fault
khykhykaty хихикати *v.i.* giggle
khylytysia хилитися *v.i.* slope
khymernyi химерний *adj* bizarre
khymernyi химерний *a.* quaint
khymernyi химерний *a.*
  whimsical
khytatysia хитатися *v.i.* stagger
khytatysia хитатися *v.i.* vacillate
khytatysia хитатися *v.i* wobble
khytkyi хиткий *a.* rickety
khytkyi хиткий *a.* shaky
khytrist хитрість *n* cunning
khytrist хитрість *n* deceit
khytrist хитрість *n.* ruse
khytrist хитрість *n.* stratagem
khytrist хитрість *n.* trickery
khytrist хитрість *n.* wile
khytryi хитрий *a* crafty
khytryi хитрий *a* cunning
khytryi хитрий *a.* sly
khytryi хитрий *a.* tricky
khytryi хитрий *a.* wily

khyzhyi хижий *adj* accipitral
khyzuvatysia хизуватися *v.t.* parade
kil кіл *n.* pale
kilka кілька *a* several
kilkisnyi кількісний *a.* quantitative
kilkist кількість *n.* quantity
kilochok кілочок *n.* peg
kiltse кільце *n.* ring
kiltsiuvaty кільцювати *v.t* girdle
kilvater кільватер *n* wake
kimnata кімната *n.* chamber
kin кінь *n.* steed
kinchatysia кінчатися *v. t* end
kinchatysia кінчатися *v.i.* expire
kinchyk pera кінчик пера *n.* nib
kinets кінець *n* last
kino кіно *n.* movies
kinoteatr кінотеатр *n.* cinema
kinovar кіновар *n* cinnabar
kintsevyi кінцевий *a.* ultimate
kintsivka кінцівка *n.* limb
kir кір *n* measles
kishka кішка *n.* cat
kistka кістка *n.* bone
kit кіт *n.* tomcat
kiuveta кювета *n.* cuvette
kivsh ківш *n.* ladle
kladovyshche кладовище *n.* churchyard
klapan клапан *n.* valve
klapot клапоть *n* patch
klapot клапоть *n.* rag
klaptyk клаптик *n.* scrap
klas клас *n* class
klasty класти *v.t.* lay
klasty krai класти край *v.t.* repress
klasty na polytsiu класти на полицю *v.t.* rack
klasty na stil класти на стіл *v.t.* table

klasty ne na mistse класти не на місце *v.t.* misplace
klasty u mishok класти у мішок *v. i.* bag
klasty v bank класти в банк *v. t* deposit
klasychnyi класичний *a* classic
klasyfikatsiia класифікація *n* classification
klasyfikuvaty класифікувати *v. t* classify
klasyk класик *n* classic
klatsannia клацання *n.* click
klatsaty клацати *v.t.* snap
klei клей *n.* adhesive
klei клей *n.* glue
kleikyi клейкий *a.* adhesive
kleity клеїти *v.t.* paste
klepaty клепати *v.t.* rivet
klerk клерк *n* clerk
klerykalnyi клерикальний *a* clerical
kliamka клямка *n.* latch
kliap кляп *n.* gag
kliient клієнт *n..* client
klimaks клімакс *n.* climax
klimat клімат *n.* climate
klinika клініка *n.* clinic
klishch кліщ *n* mite
klit кліть *n.* crate
klityna клітина *n.* cage
klitynnyi клітинний *adj* cellular
kliuch ключ *n* clue
kliuch ключ *n.* key
kliuvannia клювання *n* nibble
kliuvaty клювати *v.i.* peck
kliuvok клювок *n.* peck
klopitkyi клопіткий *a.* troublesome
klopotannia клопотання *n.* petition
klopotatysia клопотатися *v.t.* solicit

kloun клоун *n* clown
klub клуб *n* club
klubok клубок *n.* clew
klykaty кликати *v. t.* call
klyn клин *n.* wedge
kmitlyvist кмітливість *n.* acumen
kmitlyvyi кмітливий *a.* apprehensive
kmitlyvyi кмітливий *a.* intelligent
kniaziuvannia князювання *n* reign
kniazivskyi князівський *a.* princely
knyha книга *n* book
knyhoprodavets книгопродавець *n* book-seller
knyzhkovyi книжковий *n.* bookish
knyzhkovyi khrobak книжковий хробак *n* book-worm
koalitsiia коаліція *n* coalition
kobalt кобальт *n* cobalt
kobra кобра *n* cobra
kobyla кобила *n.* mare
kochehar кочегар *n.* stoker
kochivnyk кочівник *n.* nomad
kochovyi кочовий *a.* nomadic
kod код *n* code
kodlo кодло *n.* bantling
koefitsiient коефіцієнт *n.* coefficient
koika койка *n* berth
kokain кокаїн *n* cocaine
koketka кокетка *n.* minx
kokhanets коханець *n.* lover
kokhanka коханка *n.* paramour
kokhanyi коханий *n* beloved
kokos кокос *n* coconut
kokosovi volokna кокосові волокна *n* coir
kokpit кокпіт *n.* cock-pit
koks кокс *v. t* coke
kolechko колечко *n.* ringlet
koledzh коледж *n* college

koleha колега *n* colleague
kolektor колектор *a.* manifold
kolektsiia колекція *n* collection
kolektsionuvaty колекціонувати *v. t* collect
kolektyvnyi колективний *a* collective
koleso колесо *a.* wheel
koliaska коляска *n.* carriage
koliia колія *n.* rut
kolino коліно *n.* knee
kolir колір *n* colour
kolir oblychchia колір обличчя *n* complexion
koliuchist колючість *n* gibe
koliuchka колючка *n.* barb
koliuchyi колючий *a.* barbed
kolo коло *n.* circle
kolo коло *n.* circumference
koloda колода *n* block
koloda колода *n.* log
Kolon Колон *n* colon
kolona колона *n* column
kolonialnyi колоніальний *a* colonial
koloniia колонія *n* colony
kolonizatsiia колонізація *n.* settlement
kolonizuvaty колонізувати *v.t.* subjugate
kolorova kapusta кольорова капуста *n.* cauliflower
kolosalnyi колосальний *a.* stupendous
koloty колоти *n.* prick
kolovorot коловорот *n.* wimble
koly коли *conj.* now
koly коли *adv.* when
koly b ne коли б не *adv. conj* whenever
kolykhaty колихати *v.t.* lull
koly-nebud коли-небудь *adv* ever
kolys колись *adv.* sometime

kolyshnia vykhovanka колишня вихованка *n* alumna

kolyshnii колишній *a* former

kolyska колиска *n* cradle

kolyskova колискова *n.* lullaby

kolyvannia коливання *n.* hesitation

kolyvannia коливання *n.* variation

kolyvaty коливати *v.t.* rock

kolyvatysia коливатися *v.i.* hesitate

kolyvatysia коливатися *v.i.* waver

kolyvnyi коливний *a.* hesitant

kom ком *n.* clod

koma кома *n* comma

komakha комаха *n.* insect

komanda команда *n* command

komanduvaty командувати *v. t* command

komandyr командир *n* commander

komar комар *n.* mosquito

kombinatsiia комбінація *n* combination

kombinuvaty комбінувати *v. t* combine

komediant комедіант *n.* comedian

komediia комедія *n.* comedy

komendant комендант *n* commandant

komendantska hodyna комендантська година *n* curfew

komentar коментар *n* comment

komentar коментар *n* commentary

komentator коментатор *n* commentator

komentuvaty коментувати *v. i* comment

kometa комета *n* comet

komfort комфорт *n.* comfort1

komichnyi комічний *a* comic

komik комік *n* comic

komir комір *n* collar

komisioner комісіонер *n.* middleman

komitet комітет *n* committee

komiunike комюніке *n.* communiqué

komivoiazher комівояжер *n.* traveller

komora комора *n.* ambry

kompaniia компанія *n* bunch

kompaniia компанія *n.* company

kompas компас *n* compass

kompensatsiia компенсація *n* compensation

kompensuvaty компенсувати *v.t* compensate

kompetentnist компетентність *n* competence

kompetentnyi компетентний *a.* competent

kompetentsiia компетенція *n.* purview

kompiliuvaty компілювати *v. t* compile

kompleks комплекс *n* complex

kompleksnyi комплексний *a* complex

kompliment комплімент *n.* compliment

kompozytor композитор compositor

komprometuvaty компрометувати *v. t* compromise

kompromis компроміс *n* compromise

komu кому *pron.* whom

komunalnyi комунальний *a* communal

komunikatsiia комунікація *n.* communication

komunizm комунізм *n*
communism
konduktor кондуктор *n* conductor
kondyter кондитер *n* confectioner
kondyterski vyroby кондитерські
вироби *n* confectionery
konferentsiia конференція *n*
conference
konfidentsiinyi конфіденційний
a. confidential
konfiskatsiia конфіскація *n*
confiscation
konfiskuvaty конфіскувати *v. t*
confiscate
konflikt конфлікт *n.* conflict
konflikt конфлікт *n.* tangle
konfrontatsiia конфронтація *n.*
confrontation
konhres конгрес *n* congress
koniaka коняка *n.* horse
koniuktura кон'юктура *n.*
conjuncture
koniunktyva кон'юнктива *n.*
conjunctiva
konkretnyi конкретний *a.* specific
konkurentospromozhnyi
конкурентоспроможний *a*
competitive
konkursna propozytsiia
конкурсна пропозиція *n* bid
konkuruvaty конкурувати *v. i*
compete
konservant консервант *n.*
preservative
konservator консерватор *n*
conservative
konservator консерватор *n.*
square
konservatyvnyi консервативний
a conservative
konservuvaty консервувати *v. t*
conserve
konservy консерви *n.* preserve

konsolidatsiia консолідація *n*
consolidation
konsoliduvaty консолідувати *v. t.*
consolidate
konspekt конспект *n.* conspectus
konspekt конспект *n.* precis
konspekt конспект *n.* summary
konspekt конспект *n.* syllabus
konstatatsiia констатація *n.*
statement
konstebl констебль *n* constable
konstruiuvaty конструювати *v. t.*
construct
konstytutsiia конституція *n*
constitution
konsultatsiia консультація *n*
consultation
konsultuvaty консультувати *v.t.*
advise
kontakt контакт *n.* contact
kontaktuvaty контактувати *v. t*
contact
kontekst контекст *n* context
kontrabandyst контрабандист *n.*
smuggler
kontrakt контракт *n* contract
kontrast контраст *n* contrast
kontratseptsiia контрацепція *n.*
contraception
kontrol контроль *n* control
kontroler контролер *n.* controller
kontroler контролер *n.* supervisor
kontroliuvaty контролювати *v. t*
control
kontroliuvaty контролювати *v.t.*
supervise
kontsentratsiia концентрація *n.*
concentration
kontsentruvatysia
концентруватися *v. t*
concentrate
kontseptsiia концепція *n* concept
kontsert концерт *n.* concert

kontur контур *n* contour
kontuziia контузія *v.t.* contuse
kontynent континент *n* continent
kontynentalnyi континентальний *a* continental
kontynhent vybortsiv контингент виборців *n* electorate
konus конус *n* taper
konvert конверт *n* envelope
konvoi конвой *n* escort
konyk коник *n* fad
konyk коник *n.* hobby-horse
kooperatyvnyi кооперативний *a* co-operative
koordynatsiia координація *n* co-ordination
koordynovanyi координований *a* co-ordinate
koordynuvaty координувати *v.t* co-ordinate
kopaty копати *v.t.* dig
kopaty lopatoiu копати лопатою *v.t.* spade
kopiia копія *n* copy
kopiia копія *n.* repetition
kopiiuvaty копіювати *v. t* copy
kopiiuvaty копіювати *v.t.* imitate
koprolohiia копрологія *n.* coprology
kora кора *n.* bark
korabelnyi khronometr корабельний хронометр *n.* watch
koral корал *n* coral
korchyty корчити *v.i.* writhe
kordon кордон *n* border
korespondent кореспондент *n.* correspondent
korespondentsiia кореспонденція *n* mail
koriandr коріандр *n.* coriander
korin корінь *n.* root

korinnyi zub корінний зуб *n.* molar
korivnyk корівник *n* byre
kornet корнет *n.* cornet
korobka коробка *n* box
korol король *n.* king
koroleva королева *n.* queen
korolivskyi королівський *a.* regal
korolivstvo королівство *n.* kingdom
korolivstvo королівство *n.* realm
korona корона *n* crown
koronatsiia коронація *n* coronation
korosta короста *n.* scabies
korotenka pisenka коротенька пісенька *n* lay
korotko коротко *adv.* short
korotkochasnyi короткочасний *a.* momentary
korotkozorist короткозорість *n.* myopia
korotkozoryi короткозорий *a.* myopic
korotkyi короткий *a.* brief
korova корова *n.* cow
koroziinyi корозійний *adj.* corrosive
korporatsiia корпорація *n* corporation
korporatsiia корпорація *n.* incorporation
korporatyvnyi корпоративний *adj.* corporate
korpus корпус *n* corps
korsazh корсаж *n* bodice
korychnevyi коричневий *a* brown
korychnevyi kolir коричневий колір *n* brown
korydor коридор *n.* corridor
Korynf Коринф *n.* Corinth
koryslyvist користливість *n.* lucre

koryslyvyi користливий *a.* mercenary

korysnist користність *n.* utility

korysnyi корисний *a.* healthy

korysnyi корисний *a.* helpful

korysnyi корисний *a.* profitable

korystuvannia користування *n.* usage

korytsia кориця *n* cinnamon

korytysia коритися *v.t.* obey

kosa коса *n.* scythe

koshenia кошеня *n.* kitten

koshmar кошмар *n.* nightmare

koshtorys кошторис *n.* estimate

koshtovnist коштовність *n* gem

koshtovnosti коштовності *n.* jewellery

koshtuvaty коштувати *v.t.* cost

koshty кошти *n* means

koshyk кошик *n.* basket

kosmetychnyi косметичний *a.* cosmetic

kosmetyka косметика *n.* cosmetic

kosmichnyi космічний *adj.* cosmic

kosookist косоокість *n* squint

kostenity костеніти *v.t.* ossify

kostium костюм *n.* suit

kosulia косуля *n.* roe

kosyi косий *a.* oblique

kosyty косити *v.t.* scythe

kotedzh котедж *n* cottage

kotroho котрого *a.* implicit

kotushka котушка *n.* reel

kotyty котити *v.i.* roll

kovadlo ковадло *n.* anvil

koval коваль *n* blacksmith

koval коваль *n.* smith

kovbania ковбаня *n.* slough

kovdra ковдра *n* blanket

kovkyi ковкий *a.* malleable

kovtaty ковтати *v.t.* swallow

kovtok ковток *n.* gulp

kovtok ковток *n.* swallow

kovzannia ковзання *v.i.* slip

kovzaty ковзати *n* slide

koza коза *n.* goat

kozel vidpushchennia козел відпущення *n.* scapegoat

Kozerih Козеріг *n* Capricorn

kozhen кожен *a* each

kozhukh кожух *n.* casing

kozyr козир *n.* trump

krab краб *n* crab

kradena rich крадена річ *v.i.* steal

kradizhka крадіжка *n.* theft

kradizhka zi zlomom крадіжка зі зломом *n* burglary

kradkoma крадькома *adv.* stealthily

krai край *n* brim

kraievyd краєвид *n.* view

kraina країна *n.* country

krainii крайній *a.* last1

krainii крайній *a.* outside

krainist крайність *n* emergency

krainy Pivdnia країни Півдня *n.* south

krainy Zakhodu країни Заходу *n.* occident

krakh крах *n.* wreck

kramar крамар *n.* tradesman

kran кран *n.* tap

krapaty крапати *v. i* drop

kraplia крапля *n* drop

krasa краса *n* beauty

krashchaty кращати *v. t* brighten

krashchyi кращий *a* better

krasnomovnyi красномовний *a* eloquent

krasnomovstvo красномовство *n* eloquence

krasty красти *v.t.* pilfer

krastysia крастися *v.i.* sneak

krasunia красуня *n* belle

krasyvyi красивий *a* beautiful
kravatka краватка *n* tie
kravets кравець *n*. tailor
kredo кредо *n*. creed
kredyt кредит *n* credit
kredytor кредитор *n* creditor
kredytor po zastavnii кредитор
по заставній *n*. mortgagee
kreiser крейсер *n* cruiser
krematsiia кремація *n* cremation
kremuvaty кремувати *v. t*
cremate
kren крен *n*. lurch
krenytysia кренитися *v.i.* lurch
kreslennia креслення *n* draft
kreslennia креслення *n* drawing
Krez Крез *n*. croesus
kriakaty крякати *v.i.* quack
krim крім *prep* besides
krim toho крім того *adv* besides
kripak кріпак *n*. serf
kriposnyi riv кріпосний рів *n*.
moat
kripyty кріпити *v.t.* furl
kriz крізь *adv* around
krok крок *n*. pitch
krokhmal крохмаль *n*. starch
krokhmalyty крохмалити *v.t.*
starch
krokodyl крокодил *n* crocodile
krokuvaty крокувати *v.t.* advance
kroliachyi sadok кролячий садок
n. warren
krolyk кролик *n*. rabbit
kronshtein кронштейн *n*. corbel
kropitkyi кропіткий *a*. painstaking
kropyva кропива *n*. nettle
kropyvianyk кропив'яник *n*. wren
krov кров *n* blood
krovoprolyttia кровопролиття *n*
bloodshed
krovotochyty кровоточити *v. i*
bleed

kruhla duzhka кругла дужка *n*.
parenthesis
kruhliak кругляк *n*. rubble
kruhlyi круглий *a*. round
kruhom кругом *adv* about
kruhoobih кругообіг *n*. circuit
kruhovoi круговой *a* circular
kruhovorot круговорот *n*
circulation
kruiz круїз *v.i.* cruise
krupnyi крупний *a*. large
krupy крупи *n*. grain
krushyty крушити *v. t* distress
krutyi крутий *a*. steep
krutyty v rukakh крутити в руках
v.i. toy
kruzhliannia кружляння *n*. spin
kruzhliaty кружляти *v.i.* whirl
krychaty кричати *v. i* cry
kryk крик *n*. bawl
krykhitka крихітка *n* crumb
krykhitnyi крихітний *a*. tiny
krykhkyi крихкий *a*. frail
krykhkyi крихкий *a*. slight
krykhta крихта *n*. chit
krylatyi крилатий *adj*. aliferous
krylo крило *v.t.* annex
krylo крило *n*. wing
kryminalne peresliduvannia
кримінальне переслідування
n. prosecution
kryminalnyi кримінальний *a*
criminal
krynytsia криниця *n*. well
kryptohrafiia криптографія *n*.
cryptography
kryshka кришка *n*. lid
kryshtal кришталь *n* crystal
kryshyty кришити *v. t* chop
kryshyty кришити *v. t* crumble
kryterii критерій *n* canon
kryty крити *v.t.* roof

kryty kakhlem крити кахлем *v.t.* tile
kryty solomoiu крити соломою *v.t.* thatch
krytychnyi критичний *a* critical
krytyk критик *n* critic
krytyka критика *n* criticism
krytykuvaty критикувати *v. t* criticize
kryva крива *n.* graph
kryvava biinia кривава бійня *n* carnage
kryvavyi кривавий *a* bloody
kryvda кривда *n.* offence
kryvdnyk кривдник *n.* offender
kryvdyty кривдити *v.t.* aggrieve
kryvliaka кривляка *n.* monkey
kryvyi кривий *adj* anfractuous
kryvyi кривий *a.* wry
kryza криза *n* crisis
kryzhanyi крижаний *a.* icy
kserokopiiuvaty ксерокопіювати *v.t.* xerox
kseroks ксерокс *n.* xerox
ksylofon ксилофон *n.* xylophone
kub куб *n* cube
kubichnyi кубічний *a* cubical
kublo кубло *n* dive
kubok кубок *n* beaker
kubovydnyi кубовидний *adj.* cubiform
kucher кучер *n* coachman
kudkudakaty кудкудакати *v. i* cackle
kudy куди *adv.* where
kukhar кухар *n* cook
kukhnia кухня *n.* kitchen
kukhonna plyta кухонна плита *n* cooker
kukhovarstvo куховарство *n.* concoction
kukhovaryty куховарити *v. t* concoct

kukurikaty кукурікати *v. i* crow
kukurudza кукурудза *n.* maize
kulak кулак *n* fist
kulbaba кульбаба *n.* dandelion
kulhavyi кульгавий *a.* lame
kulia куля *n* bullet
kulinarne mystetstvo кулінарне мистецтво *n.* cuisine
kulminatsiia кульмінація *n.* superlative
kult культ *n* cult
kultura культура *n* culture
kulturnyi культурний *a* cultural
kumivstvo кумівство *n.* nepotism
kumkannia кумкання *n.* croak
kunytsia куниця *n.* marten
kupa купа *n.* heap
kupaty купати *v. t* bathe
kupe купе *n.* compartment
kupets купець *n.* merchant
Kupidon Купідон *n* Cupid
kupivlia купівля *v.t.* purchase
kuplet куплет *n.* couplet
kupol купол *n* dome
kupuvaty купувати *v. t* buy
kurcha курча *n.* chicken
kurhan курган *n.* mound
kurier кур'єр *n.* courier
kurierskyi кур'єрський *a* express
kurka курка *n.* hen
kurkuma куркума *n.* curcuma
kurkuma куркума *n.* turmeric
kurort курорт *n* resort
kurs курс *n.* course
kursant курсант *n.* cadet
kursyv курсив *n.* italics
kursyvnyi курсивний *a.* italic
kurtka куртка *n.* jacket
kurtyzanka куртизанка *n.* courtesan
kushak кушак *n.* girdle
kushch кущ *n* bush
kushtuvaty куштувати *v.t.* sip

kut кут *n.* angle
kutovyi кутовий *a.* angular
kuvalda кувалда *n.* maul
kuvaty кувати *v.t* forge
kuznia кузня *n* forge
kvadratnyi квадратний *a* square
kvalifikatsiia кваліфікація *n.*
  qualification
kvalifikuvaty кваліфікувати *v.i.*
  qualify
kvantovyi квантовий *n.* quantum
kvaplyvist квапливість *n* hurry
kvapyty квапити *v.t.* hurry
kvapyty квапити *v.i.* speed
kvartyra квартира *n.* apartment
kvasolia квасоля *n.* bean
kvintesentsiia квінтесенція *n.*
  quintessence
kvitka квітка *n* flower
kvitnykar квітникар *n* florist
kvituchyi квітучий *a.* prime
kvorum кворум *n.* quorum
kvota квота *n.* quota
kvytok квиток *n.* ticket
kydannia кидання *n* casting
kydaty кидати *v.t.* throw
kydaty zi stukom кидати зі
  стуком *v.t.* slam
kydok кидок *n.* bound
kyi кий *n.* staff
kylym килим *n.* carpet
kylymok килимок *n.* rug
kyndzhal кинджал *n.* baslard
kyndzhal кинджал *n.* dagger
kyparys кипарис *n* cypher
  cypress
kypinnia кипіння *n* boil
kypity кипіти *v.i.* boil
kypity na povilnomu vohni
  кипіти на повільному вогні *v.i.*
  simmer
kyrka кирка *n.* pick

kyrkomotyka киркомотика *n.*
  mattock
kysen кисень *n.* oxygen
kyshechnyk кишечник *n.* bowel
kyshenia кишеня *n.* pocket
kyshka кишка *n.* intestine
kyshkovyi кишковий *adj.* alvine
kyshkovyi кишковий *a.* intestinal
kyslota кислота *n* acid
kyslotnist кислотність *n.* acidity
kyslyi кислий *a* acid
kystovyi кистьовий *adj* carpal
kyt кит *n.* whale
kytovyi vus китовий вус *n.*
  baleen
kytytsia китиця *n* cluster
kyvaty holovoiu кивати головою
  v.i. nod
kyvok кивок *n.* beck

labirynt лабіринт *n.* labyrinth
laboratoriia лабораторія *n.*
  laboratory
ladan ладан *n.* incense
lahidnyi лагідний *a.* meek
lahodyty лагодити *v.t.* mend
lahuna лагуна *n.* lagoon
laiaty лаяти *v.t.* scold
laiatysia лаятися *v. t.* damn
laiatysia лаятися *v.t.* swear
laika лайка *n.* invective
laika лайка *n.* malediction
laika лайка *n.* obscenity
laim лайм *n.* lime
lak лак *n.* varnish
lakei лакей *n.* lackey
lakeiskyi лакейський *a.* menial
lakhmitnyk лахмітник *n.* tatter
lakonichnyi лаконічний *a.* laconic
laktometr лактометр *n.*
  lactometer

laktoza лактоза *n.* lactose
lakuvaty лакувати *v.t.* varnish
lama лама *n.* lama
lamaty ламати *v. t* break
lampa лампа *n.* bulb
lan лань *n* doe
lando ландо *n.* barouche
landshaft ландшафт *n.* landscape
lantset ланцет *a.* lancet
lantsiuh ланцюг *n* chain
lapa лапа *n.* paw
laska ласка *n.* endearment
lasoshchi ласощі *n.* dainty
lastivka ластівка *n.* swallow
lataty латати *v.t.* patch
latentnyi латентний *a.* latent
latun латунь *n.* brass
laureat лауреат *n* laureate
lava лава *n* bench
lava лава *n.* lava
lavanda лаванда *n.* lavender
lavr лавр *n.* laurel
lavyna лавина *n* billow
lebid лебідь *n.* swan
lebidka лебідка *n.* winch
led ледь *adv.* barely
ledachyi ледачий *a.* sluggish
ledar ледар *n.* loafer
ledar ледар *n.* sluggard
ledariuvaty ледарювати *v.i.* laze
ledariuvaty ледарювати *v.i.* loaf
ledarstvo ледарство *n.* idleness
ledi леді *n.* lady
ledve ne ледве не *adv.* nearly
lehalnist легальність *n.* legality
lehenda легенда *n.* legend
lehendarnyi легендарний *a.* legendary
lehion легіон *n.* legion
lehioner легіонер *n.* legionary
lehka koliaska легка коляска *n* chariot
lehke легке *n* lung
lehkist легкість *n* ease
lehkovazhnist легковажність *n* flippancy
lehkovazhnyi легковажний *a.* frivolous
lehkyi легкий *a* easy
lehkyi son легкий сон *n.* nap
lehkyi tuman легкий туман *n.* haze
lehshe легше *n.* lighter
leitenant лейтенант *n.* lieutenant
leksykohrafiia лексикографія *n.* lexicography
leksykon лексикон *n.* lexicon
lektor лектор *n.* lecturer
lektsiia лекція *n.* lecture
leleka лелека *n.* stork
lementuvaty лементувати *v.i.* yell
leopard леопард *n.* leopard
lepet лепет *n.* babble
lepetaty лепетати *v.i.* babble
lestoshchi лестощі *n* adulation
lestyty лестити *v.t* flatter
letalnyi летальний *a.* lethal
letarhichnyi летаргічний *a.* lethargic
letity летіти *v.i* fly
Lev Лев *n.* Leo
lev лев *n* lion
levynyi левиний *a* leonine
levytsia левиця *n.* lioness
lezhaty лежати *v.i.* lie
lezhyt hlyboko useredyni лежить глибоко усередині *a.* inmost
lezo лезо *n.* blade
liakaty лякати *v.t.* intimidate
lialka лялька *n* doll
lialka лялька *n.* puppet
liapas ляпас *n.* slap
liapaty ляпати *v. i.* clap
liapka ляпка *n.* blot

liaskannia ляскання *n.* pope
liberalizm лібералізм *n.* liberalism
liberalnyi ліберальний *a.* liberal
lichylnyi ochkiv лічильний очків
 n. scorer
lid лід *n.* ice
lift ліфт *n.* lift
liha ліга *n.* league
likar лікар *n* doctor
likarnia лікарня *n.* hospital
likarskyi лікарський *a.* medicinal
likarskyi retsept лікарський
 рецепт *n.* prescription
likhovisnyi ліховісний *a.* baleful
likhtar ліхтар *n.* lantern
likot лікоть *n* ancon
likuvalnyi лікувальний *a,*
 remedial
likuvannia лікування *n.* physic
likuvaty лікувати *v.t.* treat
likvidatsiia ліквідація *n.*
 liquidation
likviduvaty ліквідувати *v.t.*
 liquidate
liky ліки *n* cure
liky ліки *n.* medicament
liliia лілія *n.* lily
lin лінь *n.* laziness
linchuvaty лінчувати *v.t.* lynch
linhva franka лінгва франка *n.*
 lingua franca
linhvist лінгвіст *n.* linguist
linhvistychnyi лінгвістичний *a.*
 linguistic
liniia лінія *n.* line
liniiuvaty лініювати *v.t.* line
linoshchi лінощі *n.* sloth
linyvyi лінивий *n.* lazy
linza лінза *n.* lens
lipyty ліпити *v.t.* model
lira ліра *n.* lyre
lirychnyi ліричний *a.* lyric

lirychnyi virsh ліричний вірш *n.*
 lyric
liryk лірик *n.* lyricist
lis ліс *n* forest
lisnychyi лісничий *n.* ranger
lisnyk лісник *n* forester
lisnytstvo лісництво *n* forestry
lisomaterialy лісоматеріали *n.*
 timber
lisovyi лісовий *a.* sylvan
lisy ліси *n.* woods
lisysta mistsevist лісиста
 місцевість *n.* woodland
litak літак *n.* plane
litalnyi aparat літальний апарат
 n. aircraft
litaty літати *v.i.* navigate
literator літератор *n.* litterateur
literatura література *n.* literature
literaturnyi літературний *a.*
 literary
litnii літній *a.* aged
lito літо *n.* summer
litopysets літописець *n.* annalist
litopysi літописи *n.pl.* annals
litr літр *n.* litre
litsenziat ліцензіат *n.* licensee
litsenziia ліцензія *n.* licence
litsenzuvaty ліцензувати *v.t.*
 license
liturhiinyi літургійний *a.* liturgical
liubiaznist люб'язність *n.*
 amiability
liubiaznyi люб'язний *a.* amiable
liubiaznyi люб'язний *a.* urbane
liubliachyi люблячий *a.*
 affectionate
liubliachyi люблячий *a.* loving
liubov любов *n* love
liubovnyi zviazok любовний
 зв'язок *n* amour
liubytel любитель *n.* amateur
liubyty любити *v.t.* like

liubyty любити *v.t.* love
liudskyi людський *a.* human
liudskyi rid людський рід *n.* mankind
liudstvo людство *n.* humanity
liudy люди *n.* people
liudyna людина *n.* man
liudyna людина *n.* person
liudyna neznatnoho pokhodzhennia людина незнатного походження *n.* commoner
liudyna, pohlynena zemnymy interesamy людина, поглинена земними інтересами *n.* worldling
liudynopodibnyi людиноподібний *adj.* anthropoid
liuk люк *n.* manhole
liut лють *n.* fury
liut лють *n.* wrath
liutnia лютня *n.* lute
liutserna люцерна *n.* lucerne
liutyi лютий *n* February
liutyi лютий *a* ferocious
livak лівак *n* leftist
livo ліво *adv.* left
livreiaліврея *n.* livery
livyi лівий *a.* left
lizhko ліжко *n* bed
lliane nasinnia лляне насіння *n.* linseed
lob лоб *n* forehead
lodianyk na palychtsi льодяник на паличці *n.* lollipop
lodovyk льодовик *n.* glacier
loharyfm логарифм *n.* logarithim
lohichne poiasnennia логічне пояснення *n.* rationale
lohichnist логічність *n.* consistence,-cy
lohichnyi логічний *a* consequent

lohichnyi логічний *a.* logical
lohik логік *n.* logician
lohika логіка *n.* logic
loialnist лояльність *n* fidelity
loialnist лояльність *n.* loyalty
loialnyi лояльний *a.* loyal
lokalizuvaty локалізувати *v.t.* localize
lokh льох *n.* vault
lokomotyv локомотив *n.* locomotive
lokon локон *n.* curl
lopata лопата *n.* shovel
losion лосьйон *n.* lotion
loskotaty лоскотати *v.t.* tickle
lotereia лотерея *n.* lottery
lotos лотос *n.* lotus
lovyty ловити *v. t.* catch
lovyty na bleshniu ловити на блешню *v.i.* spin
lovyty sitkoiu ловити сіткою *v.t.* net
loza лоза *n.* rod
loza лоза *n.* twig
lozhka ложка *n.* spoon
luchka лучка *n.* meadow
luchnyk лучник *n* archer
luh луг *n* alkali
luh луг *n.* mead
luk dlia strilby лук для стрільби *n* bow
lukavist лукавість *n* duplicity
lukavyty лукавити *v. t* dodge
luna луна *n* echo
lunaty лунати *v. t* echo
lunatyk лунатик *n.* somnambulist
lupa лупа *n* dandruff
luptsiuvaty лупцювати *v. t* belabour
lushpaika лушпайка *n.* husk
lychyna личина *n.* guise
lykho лихо *n* evil
lykhodii лиходій *n* fiend

lykhomanka лихоманка *n* fever
lykhoslivia лихослів'я *n.* slander
lykhvar лихвар *n.* usurer
lykhvarstvo лихварство *n.* usury
lykhyi лихий *a* evil
lymon лимон *n.* lemon
lymonad лимонад *n.* lemonade
lymonnyi лимонний *adj.* citric
lynka линька *v.i.* moult
lypka hriaz липка грязь *n.* ooze
lypkyi липкий *n.* sticky
lyshe лише *conj.* only
lysk лиск *n.* gloss
lyskuchyi лискучий *a.* glossy
lyskuchyi лискучий *a.* shiny
lyst лист *n* letter
lyst лист *n.* message
lystia листя *n* foliage
lystochok листочок *n.* leaflet
lystok листок *n.* leaf
lystonosha листоноша *n.*
  postman
lystopad листопад *n.* november
lysukha лисуха *n.* coot
lysyi лисий *a.* bald
lysytsia лисиця *n.* fox
lytsar лицар *n.* knight
lytsarskyi лицарський *a.*
  chivalrous
lytsarstvo лицарство *n.* chivalry
lytse лице *n* face
lytsemir лицемір *n.* hypocrite
lytsemirnyi лицемірний *a.*
  hypocritical
lytsemirstvo лицемірство *n.*
  hypocrisy
lytsova storona лицьова
  сторона *n* outside
lytsovyi лицьовий *a* facial
lyty лити *v.i.* pour
lytysia литися *v.i.* rain
lytysia zlyvoiu литися зливою *v.t.*
  shower

lyzaty лизати *v.t.* lick
lzhesvidchennia лжесвідчення
  n. perjury
lzhesvidchyty лжесвідчити *v.i.*
  perjure

m'iakush м'якуш *n.* mush
mah маг *n.* magician
mahazyn магазин *n.* shop
mahichnyi магічний *a.* magical
mahistral магістраль *n.* artery
mahistratura магістратура *n.*
  magistracy
mahnat магнат *n.* magnate
mahnetyt магнетит *n.* loadstone
mahnetyzm магнетизм *n.*
  magnetism
mahnit магніт *n.* magnet
mahnitnyi магнітний *a.* magnetic
maiachyty маячити *v.i.* loom
maiak маяк *n* beacon
maiatnyk маятник *n.* pendulum
maibutnie майбутнє *n* future
maibutnii майбутній *a* after
maibutnii майбутній *a.* future
maidanchyk майданчик *n.*
  ground
maie pohanu reputatsiiu має
  погану репутацію *a.* infamous
maietok маєток *n.* manor
maino майно *n.* baggage
maino майно *n* estate
maino майно *n.* property
maior майор *n* major
maister майстер *n* foreman
maister vesluvannia майстер
  веслування *n.* oarsman
maisternia майстерня *n.*
  workshop
maisternist майстерність *n.*
  mastery

maisternyi майстерний *a.* skilful
maizhe майже *adv.* almost
maizhe майже *adv* much
maizhe майже *prep.* nigh
maket макет *n.* model
makh мах *n* bout
makhaty махати *v.i.* wag
makhaty krylamy махати
крилами *v.t* flutter
makler маклер *n.* jobber
maksymalnyi максимальний *a.*
maximum
maksymizuvaty максимізувати
v.t. maximize
maksymum максимум *n*
maximum
mala velychyna мала величина
n small
malenkyi маленький *a.* less
malenkyi kovtok маленький
ковток *n.* sip
malia маля *n.* babe
malia маля *n* child
maliariia малярія *n.* malaria
malist малість *n.* smallness
maliuvaty малювати *v.t* draw
maliuvaty малювати *v.t.* picture
maliuvaty olivtsem малювати
олівцем *v.t.* pencil
maliuvaty portret малювати
портрет *v.t.* portray
malo мало *adv.* little
malo ne мало не *prep.* near
malo toho мало того *adv.* nay
malovnychyi мальовничий *a.*
picturesque
malvaziia мальвазія *n.* malmsey
malyi малий *a.* least
malynovyi kolir малиновий колір
n crimson
mama мама *n* mum
mamasha мамаша *n* mummy
mamont мамонт *n.* mammoth

mandat мандат *n.* mandate
mandrivka мандрівка *n.* trip
mandrivnyk мандрівник *n.* rover
mandruvaty мандрувати *v.i.* stroll
mandruvaty мандрувати *v.i.*
travel
mandruvaty мандрувати *v.i.*
wander
mandry мандри *n* stroll
maneken манекен *n.* mannequin
manera манера *n.* manner
manera hovoryty манера
говорити *n.* parlance
manevr маневр *n.* manoeuvre
manevruvaty маневрувати *v.i.*
manoeuvre
manho манго *n* mango
manhusta мангуста *n.* mongoose
maniakalnyi syndrom
маніакальний синдром *n*
mania
manifest маніфест *n.* manifesto
maniia манія *n* craze
maniiak маніяк *n.* maniac
manikiur манікюр *n.* manicure
manipuliatsiia маніпуляція *n.*
manipulation
manipuliuvaty маніпулювати *v.t.*
manipulate
manirnist манірність *n.*
mannerism
manna манна *n.* manna
manorialnyi маноріальний *a.*
manorial
mantiia мантія *n* mantle
manzheta манжета *n* cuff
mara мара *n.* wraith
marafon марафон *n.* marathon
marhanets марганець *n.*
manganese
marharyn маргарин *n.* margarine
marharytka маргаритка *n* daisy

marionetka маріонетка *n.* marionette
marker маркер *n.* marker
marmelad мармелад *n.* marmalade
marmur мармур *n.* marble
marnist марність *n.* futility
marno марно *adv.* vainly
marnoslavnyi марнославний *a.* vainglorious
marnoslavstvo марнославство *n* conceit
marnotratnist марнотратність *n* extravagance
marnotratnyi марнотратний *a* extravagant
marnotratnyi марнотратний *a.* wasteful
marnovirstvo марновірство *n.* superstition
marnuvaty марнувати *v.t.* waste
marnyi марний *a* empty
marnyi марний *a* fond
marnyi марний *a.* futile
marnyi марний *a.* vain
marochnyi марочний *n.* vintage
maroder мародер *n.* marauder
maroderstvuvaty мародерствувати *v.i.* maraud
Mars Марс *n* Mars
marsh марш *n* march
marshal маршал *n* marshal
marshrut маршрут *n.* route
marshyruvaty марширувати *v.i* march
marynuvaty маринувати *v.t* pickle
maryty марити *v.i.* rave
marzha маржа *n.* margin
masa маса *n.* mass
masa маса *n.* mountain
masazh масаж *n.* massage
masazhuvaty масажувати *v.t.* massage

masazhyst масажист *n.* masseur
mashyna shvydkoi dopomohy машина швидкої допомоги *n.* ambulance
maska маска *n.* mask
maskarad маскарад *n.* masquerade
maskuvannia маскування *n* disguise
maskuvaty маскувати *v. t* disguise
maskuvaty маскувати *v.t.* mask
maslianystyi маслянистий *a.* oily
maslo масло *n* butter
maslorobnia маслоробня *n* dairy
masnyi масний *a* fat
masove vbyvstvo масове вбивство *n.* massacre
masove vynyshchennia масове винищення *n.* holocaust
masshtab масштаб *n.* scale
masturbuvaty мастурбувати *v.i.* masturbate
mastylo мастило *n* grease
mastyty мастити *v.t.* lubricate
masyvnyi масивний *a.* massive
mat мат *n* mate
matador матадор *n .* matador
match матч *n.* match
matematychnyi математичний *a.* mathematical
matematyk математик *n.* mathematician
matematyka математика *n* mathematics
materevbyvchyi матеревбивчий *a.* matricidal
materevbyvstvo матеревбивство *n.* matricide
material матеріал *n* material
materializm матеріалізм *n.* materialism

materializuvaty матеріалізувати
v.t. materialize
materiia матерія *n* fabric
materynskyi материнський *a.*
motherly
materynstvo материнство *n.*
maternity
materynstvo материнство *n.*
motherhood
matinka матінка *n* mother
matka матка *n.* uterus
matovyi матовий *a* dim
matrats матрац *n.* mattress
matrimonialnyi матрімоніальний
a. matrimonial
matros матрос *n.* sailor
matryarkh матриарх *n.* matriarch
matrytsia матриця *n* matrix
maty мати *v.t.* have
maty koryst мати користь *v. t.*
benefit
maty mozhlyvist мати
можливість *v* may
maty na uvazi мати на увазі *v.t*
mean
maty namir мати намір *v.t.* intend
maty nepravylne uiavlennia
мати неправильне уявлення
v.t. misconceive
maty pevni obov`iazky мати
певні обов`язки *v.t.* suppose
maty prysmak мати присмак *v.t.*
smack
maty skhylnist мати схильність
v.i. tend
maty spravu мати справу *v.i.*
traffic
mavpa мавпа *n* ape
mavpiachyi мавпячий *a.* apish
mavpuvaty мавпувати *v.t.* ape
mavzolei мавзолей *n.* mausoleum
maz мазь *n.* ointment
mazaty мазати *v.t.* anoint

mazaty мазати *v. t* butter
mazaty dohtem мазати дьогтем
v.t. tar
mazok мазок *n.* daub
mech меч *n.* sword
mechet мечеть *n.* mosque
med мед *n.* honey
medal медаль *n.* medal
medalion медальйон *n.* locket
medalist медаліст *n.* medallist
mediana медіана *a.* median
medovi soty медові соти *n.*
honeycomb
medovyi misiats медовий місяць
n. honeymoon
medsestra медсестра *n.* nurse
medychnyi медичний *a.* medical
medykament медикамент *n* drug
medytatyvnyi медитативний *a.*
meditative
medytsyna медицина *n.* medicine
mehafon мегафон *n.* megaphone
mehalit мегаліт *n.* megalith
mehalitychnyi мегалітичний *a.*
megalithic
mehera мегера *n.* vixen
mekhanichnyi механічний *a.*
mechanical
mekhanik механік *n.* mechanic
mekhanika механіка *n.*
mechanics
mekhanizm механізм *n.*
mechanism
melankholiia меланхолія *n.*
melancholia
melankholiinyi меланхолійний *a.*
melancholic
melioruvaly меліорували *v.t.*
meliorate
melnyk мельник *n.* miller
melodiia мелодія *n.* melody
melodiinyi мелодійний *a.*
melodious

melodrama мелодрама *n.*
melodrama
melodramatychnyi
мелодраматичний *a.*
melodramatic
membrana мембрана *n.*
membrane
memorandum меморандум *n*
memorandum
memorial меморіал *n.* memorial
memorialnyi меморіальний *a*
memorial
memuary мемуари *n.* memoir
menedzher менеджер *n.*
manager
meni мені *pron.* me
meninhit менінгіт *n.* meningitis
meniu меню *n.* menu
menopauza менопауза *n.*
menopause
mensh za vse менш за все *adv.*
least
menshe менше *adv.* less
menshist меншість *n.* minority
menshyi менший *a.* lesser
menstrualnyi менструальний *a.*
menstrual
menstruatsii менструації *n.*
menses
menstruatsiia менструація *n.*
menstruation
mentalitet менталітет *n.* mentality
mer мер *n.* mayor
merekhtinnia мерехтіння *n* flicker
merekhtity мерехтіти *v.t* flicker
merezha мережа *n.* network
merezhyvnyi мереживний *a.* lacy
merezhyvo мереживо *n.* lace
merhel мергель *n.* marl
merkantylnyi меркантильний *a.*
mercantile
mersyryzuvaty мерсиризувати
v.t. mercerise

mertvo-blidyi мертво-блідий *a.*
ghastly
mertvyi мертвий *a* dead
merydian меридіан *a.* meridian
merzennyi мерзенний *a*
despicable
merzliakuvatyi мерзлякуватий *a*
chilly
merzota мерзота *n* filth
merzotnyi мерзотний *a* filthy
meshkanets мешканець *n.*
inmate
meshkaty мешкати *v. i* dwell
mesiia месія *n.* messiah
meta мета *n.* aim
metafizychnyi метафізичний *a.*
metaphysical
metafizyka метафізика *n.*
metaphysics
metafora метафора *n.* metaphor
metal метал *n.* metal
metalevyi металевий *a.* metallic
metalnyi метальний *a* projectile
metalnyi spys метальний спис *n.*
javelin
metalurhiia металургія *n.*
metallurgy
metamorfoza метаморфоза *n.*
metamorphosis
metannia метання *n* toss
metaty метати *v. t.* cast
metaty метати *v.t.* toss
metaty ikru метати ікру *v.i.* spawn
metelyk метелик *n* butterfly
metempsykhoz метемпсихоз *n.*
rebirth
meteor метеор *n.* meteor
meteornyi метеорний *a.* meteoric
meteoroloh метеоролог *n.*
meteorologist
meteorolohiia метеорологія *n.*
meteorology
metod метод *n* device

metod метод *n.* method
metodychnyi методичний *a.*
    methodical
metr метр *n.* meter
metr метр *n.* metre
metropoliia метрополія *n.*
    metropolis
metrychnyi метричний *a.* metric
metushlyvist метушливість *n.*
    vanity
metushnia метушня *n.* fuss
metushnia метушня *n.* turmoil
metushytysia метушитися *v.i*
    fuss
mezalians мезальянс *n.*
    misalliance
mezha межа *n* boundary
mezha межа *n.* verge
mezhuvaty межувати *v.t* border
mezonin мезонін *n.* mezzanine
miach м'яч *n.* ball
miakist м'якість *n.* lenience,
    leniency
miakot plodu м'якоть плоду *n.*
    pulp
miakyi м'який *a.* gentle
miasnyk м'ясник *n* butcher
miaso м'ясо *n.* meat
miasystyi м'ясистий *a.* pulpy
miata м'ята *n.* mint
miatnyi м'ятний *n* mint
miaz м'яз *n.* muscle
miazystyi м'язистий *a.* muscular
mid мідь *n* copper
midnyk мідник *n.* tinker
mif міф *n.* myth
mifichnyi міфічний *a.* mythical
mifolohichnyi міфологічний *a.*
    mythological
mifolohiia міфологія *n.* mythology
mihrant мігрант *n.* migrant
mihratsiia міграція *n.* migration
mihren мігрень *n.* migraine

mihruvaty мігрувати *v.i.* migrate
mii мій *pron.* mine
mii мій *a.* my
mikhur міхур *n* bubble
mikhy міхи *n.* bellows
mikrob мікроб *n.* germ
mikrofilm мікрофільм *n.* microfilm
mikrofon мікрофон *n.*
    microphone
mikrokhvylova pich
    мікрохвильова піч *n.*
    microwave
mikrometr мікрометр *n.*
    micrometer
mikroskop мікроскоп *n.*
    microscope
mikroskopichnyi мікроскопічний
    a. microscopic
mikroskopiia мікроскопія *n.*
    micrology
miliard мільярд *n* billion
milion мільйон *n.* million
milioner мільйонер *n.* millionaire
militsiia міліція *n.* militia
mility міліти *v.t.* shoal
milkyi мілкий *a.* shallow
mim мім *n.* mime
mimichnyi мімічний *a.* mimic
mimika міміка *n* mimicry
mimikriia мімікрія *n.* mimesis
minaret мінарет *n.* minaret
mineral мінерал *n.* mineral
mineralnyi мінеральний *a*
    mineral
mineraloh мінералог *n.*
    mineralogist
mineralohiia мінералогія *n.*
    mineralogy
miniatiura мініатюра *n.* miniature
miniatiurnyi мініатюрний *a.*
    miniature
miniaty міняти *v.t.* barter1
miniaty міняти *v.t.* supersede

minimalnyi мінімальний *a.*
minimal
minimalnyi мінімальний *a*
minimum
minimizuvaty мінімізувати *v.t.*
minimize
minimum мінімум *n.* minimum
ministerstvo міністерство *n.*
ministry
ministr міністр *n.* minister
minlyvist мінливість *n.* vicissitude
minlyvyi мінливий *a* fickle
minlyvyi мінливий *a.* wayward
minus мінус *n* minus
miozis міозіс *n.* myosis
mira міра *n.* measure
mirazh міраж *n.* mirage
miriady міріади *n.* myriad
mirkuvannia міркування *n.*
speculation
mirkuvaty міркувати *v.t.* meditate
mirylo мірило *n* criterion
mishanyna мішанина *n.*
miscellany
mishok мішок *n.* sack
mishura мішура *n.* tinsel
misiachnyi місячний *a.* lunar
misiats місяць *n.* month
misiats місяць *n.* moon
misiia місія *n.* mission
misioner місіонер *n.* missionary
misis місіс *n..* missis, missus
miska mytnytsia міська митниця
n. octroi
miskyi міський *a.* urban
mist міст *n* bridge
mistechko містечко *n.* town
mister містер *n.* mister
mistkist місткість *n.* capacity
mistkyi місткий *a.* ample
mistkyi місткий *a.* roomy
misto місто *n* city
mistse місце *n.* lieu

mistse місце *n.* place
mistse dii місце дії *n.* locale
mistse podii місце подій *n* arena
mistse prozhyvannia місце
проживання *n.* residence
mistse roztashuvannia місце
розташування *n.* location
mistse zustrichi місце зустрічі *n.*
venue
mistsepolozhennia
місцеположення *n.* locus
mistsevist місцевість *n.* locality
mistsevyi місцевий *a.* indigenous
mistsevyi місцевий *a.* local
mistsevyi zhytel місцевий
житель *n* native
mistseznakhodzhennia
місцезнаходження *adv.*
whereabout
mistychnyi містичний *a.* mystic
mistyfikatsiia містифікація *n.*
hoax
mistyfikuvaty містифікувати *v.t.*
mystify
mistyk містик *n* mystic
mistyt містить *a.* inclusive
mistytsyzm містицизм *n.*
mysticism
mistyty містити *v.t.* contain
mistyty v sobi містити в собі *v.t.*
imply
mistyty v sobi містити в собі *v.t.*
presuppose
mitla мітла *n* broom
mits міць *n.* power
mitsnist міцність *n.* strength
mitsnyi міцний *a* firm
mitsnyi міцний *a.* sound
mizantrop мізантроп *n.*
misanthrope
mizernyi мізерний *a.* minuscule
mizh між *prep.* amongst
mizh між *prep* between

mizhnarodnyi міжнародний *a.* international

mliavist млявість *n.* lethargy

mliavyi млявий *a* flat

mlyn млин *n.* mill

mnozhene множене *n.* multiplicand

mnozhennia множення *n.* multiplication

mnozhynnist множинність *n.* multiplicity

mnozhynnyi множинний *a.* multiple

mnozhyty na chotyry множити на чотири *v.t.* quadruple

mobilizuvaty мобілізувати *v.t.* mobilize

mobilnist мобільність *n.* mobility

mobilnyi мобільний *a.* mobile

mochka vukha мочка вуха *n.* lobe

mochytysia мочитися *v.i.* urinate

moda мода *n* fashion

modalnist модальність *n.* modality

model модель *n* make

modernizuvaty модернізувати *v.t.* modernize

modni tovary модні товари *n.* millinery

modnyi модний *a* fashionable

moduliuvaty модулювати *v.t.* modulate

modyfikatsiia модифікація *n.* modification

modystka модистка *n.* milliner

mohty могти *v. t.* can

mohutnii могутній *adj.* mighty

mohutnist могутність *n.* might

mohyla могила *n.* grave

mohyla могила *n.* tomb

mohylnyk могильник *n.* mortuary

mokh мох *n.* moss

mokhove boloto мохове болото *n.* moor

mokrota мокрота *n.* sputum

mokryi мокрий *a.* wet

mol моль *n.* mole

molekula молекула *n.* molecule

molekuliarnyi молекулярний *a.* molecular

moliarnyi молярний *a* molar

molochnyi молочний *a.* milch

molochnyi молочний *a.* milky

molod молодь *n* young

molodist молодість *n.* adolescence

molodshyi za zvanniam молодший за званням *n.* junior

molodyi молодий *a.* junior

moloko молоко *n.* milk

molotarka молотарка *n.* thresher

molotok молоток *n.* hammer

moloty молоти *v.t.* mill

molotyty молотити *v.t.* thrash

molytva молитва *n.* prayer

molyty молити *v. t.* entreat

molytysia молитися *v.i.* pray

moment момент *n.* moment

monakhynia монахиня *n.* nun

monarkh монарх *n.* monarch

monarkhiia монархія *n.* monarchy

monastyr монастир *n.* cloister

monastyr монастир *n.* monastery

moneta монета *n* coin

monetnyi монетний *a.* monetary

monohamiia моногамія *n.* monogamy

monohinnyi моногінний *a.* monogynous

monohrafiia монографія *n.* monograph

monohrama монограма *n.* monogram

monokhromatychnyi
монохроматичний *a.*
monochromatic
monokl монокль *n.* monocle
monokuliar монокуляр *a.*
monocular
monolit моноліт *n.* monolith
monoloh монолог *n.* monologue
monopoliia монополія *n.*
monopoly
monopolist монополіст *n.*
monopolist
monopolizuvaty монополізувати
v.t. monopolize
monoteist монотеїст *n.*
monotheist
monoteizm монотеїзм *n.*
monotheism
monotonnist монотонність *n*
monotony
monstr монстр *n.* monster
monumentalnyi монументальний
a. monumental
moral мораль *n.* moral
moralist мораліст *n.* moralist
moralizuvaty моралізувати *v.t.*
moralize
moralnist моральність *n.* morality
moralnyi моральний *a.* moral
morda морда *n.* muzzle
more море *a.* profound
more море *n.* sea
morekhidnyi морехідний *a.*
nautic(al)
moreplavets мореплавець *n.*
voyager
morfii морфій *n.* morphia
morh морг *n.* morgue
morhanatychnyi морганатичний
a. morganatic
morhannia моргання *n* wink
moriak моряк *n.* mariner
morkva морква *n.* carrot

moroz мороз *n.* frost
morshchyty морщити *v.t.* wrinkle
morshchytysia морщитися *v. i*
cockle
morshchytysia морщитися *v.i.*
wince
morska sazhen морська сажень
n fathom
morskyi морський *a.* marine
morzh морж *n.* walrus
moskvych москвич *n.* muscovite
mostyty мостити *v.t.* pave
mostyty kamenem мостити
каменем *v.t.* stone
mot мот *n.* spendthrift
motalna mashyna мотальна
машина *n.* winder
motaty мотати *v.i.* reel
motel мотель *n.* motel
motok priazhi моток пряжі *n.*
skein
motornyi моторний *adj.* deft
motoroshnyi моторошний *a.*
uncanny
motuzka мотузка *n.* rope
motuzka мотузка *v.t.* string
motyka мотика *v.t.* hack
motyv мотив *n.* motif
motyv мотив *n.* motive
motyv мотив *n.* tune
motyvatsiia мотивація *n.*
motivation
motyvuvaty мотивувати *v*
motivate
mova мова *n* discourse
movchannia мовчання *n.* quiet
movchaznyi мовчазний *a.* mum
movchaznyi мовчазний *a.* mute
movnyi мовний *a.* lingual
movoznavstvo мовознавство *n.*
linguistics
mozaika мозаїка *n.* mosaic

mozhlyvist можливість *n.*
occasion
mozhlyvist можливість *n.*
probability
mozhlyvo можливо *adv.* perhaps
mozhlyvyi можливий *a.*
hypothetical
mozok мозок *n* brain
mriachyty мрячити *v. i* drizzle
mriiaty мріяти *v. i.* dream
mriilyvist мрійливість *n.* reverie
msprytnyi мспритний *a* slick
mstyty мстити *v.t.* avenge
mstyvyi мстивий *a.* revengeful
muchenyk мученик *n.* martyr
muchenytstvo мучеництво *n.*
martyrdom
muchyty мучити *v. t* bedevil
muchytysia мучитися *v.t.* agonize
mudrets мудрець *n.* sage
mudrist мудрість *n.* wisdom
mudrosti zub мудрості зуб *n.*
wisdom-tooth
mudryi мудрий *a.* sage
mudryi мудрий *a.* wise
muka мука *n.* torment
muka мука *n.* worry
mukannia мукання *n.* low
mukaty мукати *v.i* moo
mukha муха *n* fly
mul мул *n.* mule
mulat мулат *n.* mulatto
muliar муляр *n.* mason
muliar муляр *n.* paddy
mulla мулла *n.* mullah
multfilm мультфільм *n.* cartoon
mumiia мумія *n.* mummy
munitsypalitet муніципалітет *n.*
municipality
munitsypalnyi муніципальний *a.*
municipal
murakha мураха *n* ant
murkotannia муркотання *n.* purr

murkotity муркотіти *v.i.* purr
mushka мушка *n* foresight
mushket мушкет *n.* musket
mushketer мушкетер *n.*
musketeer
mushtabel муштабель *n.*
maulstick
muskus мускус *n.* musk
muslin муслін *n.* muslin
muson мусон *n.* monsoon
mustanh мустанг *n.* mustang
mutatsiia мутація *n.* mutation
mutatsiinyi мутаційний *a.*
mutative
muza муза *n* muse
muzei музей *n.* museum
muzhnii мужній *a.* manly
muzhnist мужність *n* manliness
muzhyk мужик *n* boor
muzychnyi музичний *a.* musical
muzyka музика *n.* music
muzykant музикант *n.* musician
myhannia мигання *n.* twinkle
myhdal мигдаль *n.* almond
myhdalyna мигдалина *n.* tonsil
myinyk мийник *n.* washer
mylia миля *n.* mile
mylna pina мильна піна *n.* lather
mylnyi мильний *a.* soapy
mylo мило *n.* soap
myloserdia милосердя *n.* charity
myloserdia милосердя *n.* mercy
myloserdnyi милосердний *a.*
merciful
mylostynia милостиня *n.* alms
mylostyvo милостиво *adv*
benignly
mylostyvyi милостивий *adj*
benign
mylostyvyi милостивий *a.*
gracious
mylovydnist миловидність *n.*
prettiness

mylyi милий *a* dear
mymovoli мимоволі *adv.* unwittingly
mymryty мимрити *v.i.* mutter
mynule минуле *n.* antecedent
mynulyi минулий *a.* past
mynushchyi минущий *a.* transitory
mynuty минути *n* escape
myr мир *n.* peace
myrianyn мирянин *n.* layman
myrnyi мирний *a.* peaceful
myroliubnyi миролюбний *a.* pacific
myrovyi poserednyk мировий посередник *n.* compounder
myrra мирра *n.* myrrh
myrskyi мирський *a.* mundane
myrt мирт *n.* myrtle
mysha миша *n.* mouse
myslennia мислення *n* thought
myslytel мислитель *n.* thinker
myslyty мислити *v.i.* reason
myslyvets мисливець *n.* hunter
myslyvskyi sobaka мисливський собака *n.* hound
mystetstvo мистецтво *n.* art
mystetstvo мистецтво *n.* workmanship
myt мить *n.* instant
myto мито *n* toll
mytra митра *n.* mitre
mytropolyt митрополит *n.* metropolitan
myttievyi миттєвий *a.* instant
myty мити *v.t.* wash
myty shampunem мити шампунем *v.t.* shampoo
mzhychka мжичка *n* drizzle

N

na на *adv.* on
na на *prep.* on
na bortu на борту *adv* aboard
na hirshe на гірше *adv.* backward
na pershyi pohliad на перший погляд *adv.* prima facie
na pivnich на північ *adv.* north
na pivnich на північ *adv.* northerly
na shchastia на щастя *adv.* luckily
na shcho на що *conj.* whereat
na skhid на схід *adv* east
na sotniu на сотню *adv.* per cent
na viddali на віддалі *adv.* apart
na vidminu vid на відміну від *prep* unlike
na vodi на воді *adv.* afloat
na zakhid на захід *adv.* west
na zakhid на захід *adv.* westerly
na zakinchennia на закінчення *adv.* lastly
na zhal на жаль *interj.* alas
na zvoroti на звороті *adv.* overleaf
nabahato набагато *adv.* better
nabih набіг *n.* irruption
nabir набір *n* set
nablyzhatysia наближатися *v.i.* near
nabob набоб *n.* nabob
nabrydaty набридати *v. t* bore
nabrydaty набридати *v. t* bother
nabukhaty набухати *v.i.* swell
nabuttia набуття *n* commencement
nabuttia chynnosti набуття чинності *n* acquest
nabuvaty набувати *v.t.* acquire
nabyvaty набивати *v.t.* pad
nabyvka набивка *n.* gasket

nachalnyk начальник *n.* senior

nachebto начебто *adv.* like

nachis начіс *n* nap

nachynnia начиння *n.* utensil

nachytanyi начитаний *a.* well-read

nad над *prep.* above

nadannia надання *n.* provision

nadaty formu надати форму *v.t* shape

nadavaty надавати *v.t.* grant

nadavaty надавати *v. t* entrust

nadavaty dvorianskyi tytul надавати дворянський титул *v. t.* ennoble

nadavaty kvadratnu formu надавати квадратну форму *v.t.* square

nadavaty pravo надавати право *v. t.* entitle

nadavaty vidtinok надавати відтінок *v.t.* tinge

nadavaty zhorstkosti надавати жорсткості *v.t.* stiffen

nadavaty zhytlo надавати житло *v.t* house

nadhrobna plyta надгробна плита *n.* ledger

nadiahaty namordnyk надягати намордник *v.t* muzzle

nadiia надія *n* hope

nadiia надія *n.* reliance

nadiina liudyna надійна людина *n.* trusty

nadiinyi надійний *a.* reliable

nadiinyi надійний *a.* sterling

nadil наділ *n.* allotment

nadiliaty наділяти *v.t.* allot

nadity naruchnyky надіти наручники *v.t* handcuff

nadivaty pokryshku надівати покришку *v.t.* tire

nadkhodyty надходити *v. i.* behave

nadkhodyty надходити *v.t.* reach

nadliudskyi надлюдський *a.* superhuman

nadlyshkovyi надлишковий *a.* redundant

nadlyshok надлишок *n* abundance

nadlyshok надлишок *n* excess

nadmir надмір *n.* plenty

nadmirna kilkist надмірна кількість *n.* superabundance

nadmirnist надмірність *n* extreme

nadmirnist надмірність *n.* redundance

nadmirno napruzhuvaty надмірно напружувати *v.t.* tax

nadmirno optymistychnyi надмірно оптимістичний *a.* roseate

nadmirnyi надмірний *a.* prodigal

nadmirnyi надмірний *a.* undue

nadpryrodnyi надприродний *a.* supernatural

nadpysuvaty надписувати *v. t.* endorse

naduty надути *v.i.* blow

naduvannia надування *n.* inflation

nadzvukovyi надзвуковий *a.* supersonic

nadzvychaino shchedryi надзвичайно щедрий *a.* munificent

nafarshyruvaty нафарширувати 2 *v.t.* stuff

nafta нафта *n.* petroleum

nahaduiuchyi нагадуючий *a.* reminiscent

nahaduvannia нагадування *n.* reminder

nahaduvaty нагадувати *v.t.*
remind
nahar na svichtsi нагар на свічці
n. snuff
nahliad нагляд *n.* oversight
nahliadach наглядач *n.* overseer
nahliadaty наглядати *v.t.*
invigilate
nahori нагорі *adv* above
nahoroda нагорода *n.* award
nahorodyty ordenom нагородити
орденом *v.t.* star
nahorodzhuvaty нагороджувати
v.t. award
nahorodzhuvaty ordenamy
нагороджувати орденами *v. t*
decorate
nahota нагота *n.* nudity
nahrabovane награбоване *n.*
prey
nahromadzhuvaty
нагромаджувати *v.t* heap
naiavnist наявність *n.* presence
naiavnyi наявний *a* available
naibilsh найбільш *adv.* most
naiblyzhchyi найближчий *a.*
proximate
naichastishe найчастіше *adv.*
often
naihirshe найгірше *n.* worst
naihirshyi найгірший *a* worst
naihlybshyi найглибший *a.*
innermost
naimach наймач *n.* lessee
naimanets найманець *n.* hireling
naimannia наймання *n.* hire
naimaty наймати *v. t* employ
nainyzhchyi riven найнижчий
рівень *n.* nadir
naitonshyi найтонший *a.*
superfine
naivazhlyvishyi найважливіший
a. momentous

naividdalenishyi
найвіддаленіший *a.* utmost
naivnist наївність *n.* naivete
naivnyi наївний *a.* naive
naivyshcha tochka найвища
точка *n* sublime
naivyshchyi найвищий *a.*
superlative
nakaz наказ *n.* conge
nakazovyi наказовий *a.*
imperative
nakazuvaty наказувати *v.t* order
nakazuvaty наказувати *v.t.*
prescribe
nakazuvaty наказувати *v.t.*
require
nakhaba нахаба *n.* swine
nakhabnyi нахабний *a.*
impertinent
nakhabstvo нахабство *n.*
insolence
nakhlibnyk нахлібник *n*
dependant
nakhyl нахил *n* bias
nakhylennia нахилення *n.*
inclination
nakhyliaty нахиляти *v.t.* slant
nakladaty aresht накладати
арешт *v.t.* sequester
nakladaty veto накладати вето
v.t. veto
nakladennia накладення *n.*
imposition
naklasty накласти *v.t.* impose
nakleika наклейка *n.* sticker
nakleity наклеїти *v.t.* stick
nakleiuvaty наклеювати *v.t.* affix
naklep наклеп *n* defamation
naklepnytskyi наклепницький *a.*
slanderous
nakoloty наколоти *v.t.* prick
nakonechnyk наконечник *n.* tip
nakydaty накидати *v.t.* sketch

nakydatysia накидатися *v.i.*
pounce
nakydka накидка *n.* cape
nakyp накип *n.* ream
nalashtovuvaty налаштовувати
v.t. tune
nalezhaty належати *v. i* belong
nalezhne належне *n* due
nalezhnyi належний *adv* due
nalezhnyi належний *a* due
nalezhnyi належний *a.* proper
nalezhnyi належний *a.* requisite
nalezhnyi належний *a.* sufficient
nalezhnym chynom належним
чином *adv* duly
nalezhnym chynom належним
чином *adv* right
naliakaty налякати *v.t.* frighten
naliakaty налякати *v.t.* scare
naliakaty налякати *v.t.* startle
namahatysia намагатися *v.t.*
attempt
namatsuvaty намацувати *v.t.*
grope
namet намет *n.* tent
namichatysia намічатися *v.i.*
teethe
namir намір *n* animus
namir намір *n.* design
namir намір *n.* purpose
namir намір *n.* scope
namylyty намилити *v.t.* soap
namysto намисто *n.* necklace
nanosnyi наносний *a.* superficial
nanosyty наносити *v.t.* inflict
nanosyty na kartu наносити на
карту *v.t.* map
nanosyty smuhy наносити смуги
v.t. stripe
nanyzuvaty нанизувати *v.t* thread
napad напад *n.* assault
napadaty нападати *v.t.* attack

napakhuvaty parfumamy
напахувати парфумами *v.t.*
perfume
naparnyk напарник *n.* mate
napererik наперерік *prep.* athwart
naperstok наперсток *n.* thimble
napii напій *n* beverage
napolehlyvist наполегливість *n.*
perseverance
napolehlyvyi наполегливий *a.*
insistent
napoliahaty наполягати *v.t.* insist
napoval наповал *adv.* outright
napravliaty направляти *v. t* direct
napravliaty na mistse roboty
направляти на місце роботи
v.t. station
napriam напрям *n* direction
napruha напруга *n* strain
napruzhenist напруженість *n.*
tension
napruzhenyi напружений *a.*
strenuous
napruzhuvaty напружувати *v. t*
bend
napys напис *n.* inscription
narada нарада *n* deliberation
narazhaty na nebezpeku
наражати на небезпеку *v.t.*
imperil
narechena наречена *n* bride
nariad наряд *n.* attire
nariadnist нарядність *n.* gaiety
nariadzhaty наряджати *v.t.* attire
narikannia нарікання *n.*
lamentation
narikaty нарікати *v.t.* murmur
narizaty skybkamy нарізати
скибками *v.t.* slice
narizaty u dovzhynu нарізати у
довжину *v.t.* slit
narizno нарізно *adv.* asunder
narkoman наркоман *n.* addict

narkotychnyi наркотичний *n.*
narcotic
narkoz наркоз *n.* narcosis
narochnyi нарочний *n* express
narodnyi народний *a.* vernacular
narodzhennia народження *n*
bearing
narodzhennia народження *n.*
inception
narodzhenyi pislia smerti batka
народжений після смерті
батька *a.* posthumous
narodzhuvaty народжувати *v. t*
beget
naroshchuvaty koru нарощувати
кору *v.t.* bark
nartsys нарцис *n* narcissus
nartsys zhovtyi нарцис жовтий
n. daffodil
naruchnyk наручник *n.* handcuff
naruha наруга *n.* outrage
narukavnyk нарукавник *a* armlet
naryv нарив *n* blain
naselennia населення *n.*
population
naseliaty населяти *v.t.* inhabit
naseliaty населяти *v.t.* populate
nash наш *pron.* our
nashchadky нащадки *n.* posterity
nashchadok нащадок *n*
descendant
nasinnia насіння *n.* seed
nasinnievyi насіннєвий *a.*
seminal
naskochyty наскочити *v.t.*
surprise
naskok наскок *n* pounce
naslidky наслідки *n.* repercussion
naslidok наслідок *n* consequence
naslidok наслідок *n.* outcome
naslidok наслідок *n.* progeny
naslidok наслідок *n.* sequel

nasliduvach наслідувач *n.*
imitator
nasliduvannia наслідування *n.*
imitation
nasliduvanyi наслідуваний *a.*
heritable
nasliduvaty наслідувати *v.i* mime
nasmikhatysia насміхатися *v.i.*
gibe
nasmishka насмішка *n.* ridicule
nasmishnyk насмішник *n.* joker
nasoloda насолода *n.* luxury
nasoloda насолода *n* relish
nasolodzhuvatysia
насолоджуватися *v.t.* relish
nasos насос *n.* pump
naspravdi насправді *adv.* really
nastavnyk наставник *n.* mentor
nastii настій *n* extract
nastoianka настоянка *n.* tincture
nastoiatel настоятель *n* prior
nastoiatelka настоятелька *n.*
prioress
nastorozhenist настороженість
n. alertness
nastorozhenyi насторожений *a.*
alert
nastorozhenyi насторожений *a.*
wary
nastrii настрій *n.* mood
nastrii настрій *n.* sentiment
nastroiuvaty настроювати *v. t*
bias
nastup наступ *n.* attack
nastup наступ *n* offensive
nastupnist наступність *n.*
succession
nastupnyi наступний *a.*
forthcoming
nastupnyi наступний *a.* next
nastupnyi наступний *a.*
successive
nastupnyi наступний *a.* ulterior

nastupnyi den наступний день *n.*
morrow
nastupnyk наступник *n.*
successor
nastylaty doshky настилати
дошки *v.t.* plank
nastylaty palubu настилати
палубу *v. t* deck
nastylaty pidlohu настилати
підлогу *v.t* floor
nastyrlyvist настирливість *n.*
molestation
nasuvaietsia насувається *a.*
imminent
nasychennia насичення *n.*
saturation
nasychuvaty насичувати *v.t.*
satiate
nasylaty neshchastia насилати
нещастя *v.t.* plague
nasylnytskyi насильницький *a*
forcible
nasylnytskyi насильницький *a.*
violent
nasylstvo насильство *n.* violence
nasylu насилу *adv.* hardly
nasyp насип *n* embankment
natalnyi натальний *a.* natal
natiahuvaty натягувати *v.t.* strain
natiak натяк *n* allusion
natiak натяк *n.* hint
natiakaty натякати *v.i* hint
natilna bilyzna натільна білизна
n. underwear
natkhnennia натхнення *n.*
inspiration
natkhnennyi натхненний *a.*
animate
natovp натовп *n* crowd
natrapyty натрапити *v.t.* jostle
natsiia нація *n.* nation
natsionalistychnyi
націоналістичний *n.* nationalist

natsionalizatsiia націоналізація
n. nationalization
natsionalizm націоналізм *n.*
nationalism
natsionalizuvaty націоналізувати
v.t. nationalize
natsionalnist національність *n.*
nationality
natsionalnyi національний *a.*
internal
natsionalnyi національний *a.*
national
naturalist натураліст *n.* naturalist
naturalizuvaty натуралізувати
v.t. naturalize
natyraty натирати *v.t.* smear
natysk натиск *n.* onrush
natysk натиск *n.* onset
natyskaty pedal натискати
педаль *v.t.* pedal
nauka наука *n.* science
naukovets науковець *n.* scientist
naukovyi науковий *a* academic
navala навала *n.* invasion
navaliuvaty навалювати *v.t.* pile
navantazhennia навантаження
n. load
navantazhuvaty навантажувати
v.t. load
navazhuvatysia наважуватися
v.t. risk
navchalnyi навчальний *n.* tutorial
navchalnyi plan навчальний
план *n* curriculum
navchalnyi sudovyi protses
навчальний судовий процес
n. moot
navchannia навчання *n.* learning
navchannia навчання *n.* training
navchaty навчати *v.t.* teach
navedennia наведення *n* offer
navedenyi u poriadok наведений
у порядок *a.* trim

naverkh наверх *adv.* upward
naviazlyva ideia нав'язлива ідея
n. obsession
naviazuvaty нав'язувати *v. t.*
enforce
navidnyi навідний *a.* suggestive
navihator навігатор *n.* navigator
navihatsiia навігація *n.* navigation
naviiaty навіяти *v.t.* waft
naviiuvaty навіювати *v.t.* inspire
navis навіс *n* shed
navkolo навколо *adj.* ambient
navkolo навколо *adv.* round
navkolyshnie seredovyshche
навколишнє середовище *n.*
environment
navmysne vbyvstvo навмисне
вбивство *n.* murder
navmysnist навмисність *n.*
premeditation
navmysno навмисно *adv.*
purposely
navmysno vvodyty v omanu
навмисно вводити в оману *v. t*
deceive
navmysnyi навмисний *a.*
intentional
navodyty dokazy наводити
докази *v.t.* adduce
navpaky навпаки *adv.* vice-versa
navriad chy навряд чи *adv.* ill
navriad chy навряд чи *adv.*
scarcely
navyk навик *n.* skill
nazad назад *adv.* back
nazavzhdy назавжди *adv* forever
nazdohnaty наздогнати *v.t.*
overtake
nazhyty нажити *v.t.* profit
nazhyvka наживка *n* bait
nazovni назовні *prep* outside
nazovni назовні *adv* outward
nazva назва *n.* title

nazvanyi batko названий батько
n. parent
nazvaty назвати *v.t.* name
ne не *conj* nor
ne не *adv.* not
ne buty не бути *v.t* absent
ne diiaty не діяти *v.i.* slumber
ne doviriaty не довіряти *v.t.*
mistrust
ne dozvoliaty не дозволяти *v. t.*
debar
ne dozvoliaty не дозволяти *v.t*
forbid
ne liubyty не любити *v. t* dislike
ne pidkoriatysia не підкорятися
v. t disobey
ne podobatysia не подобатися *v.*
t displease
ne potrapyty не потрапити *v.t.*
miss
ne skhodytysia v pohliadakh
не сходитися в поглядах *v. i*
disagree
ne skhvaliuvaty не схвалювати
v. t disapprove
ne vidpovidaty не відповідати
v.t. mismatch
neabyiakyi неабиякий *a.* hefty
neaktyvnyi неактивний *a.* silent
neakuratno pysaty неакуратно
писати *v.t.* scribble
nebahatoslivnyi небагатослівний
a. terse
nebazhannia небажання *n.*
reluctance
nebesa небеса *n.* heaven
nebesnyi небесний *adj* celestial
nebezpechnist небезпечність *n.*
insecurity
nebezpechnyi небезпечний *a*
dangerous
nebezpechnyi небезпечний *a.*
insecure

nebezpeka небезпека *n.* danger
nebezpeka небезпека *n.* jeopardy
nebezpeka небезпека *n* menace
nebo небо *n.* sky
nechemnist нечемність *n.* indiscretion
nechesno нечесно *adv* malafide
nechesnyi нечесний *a* dirty
nechesnyi нечесний *a* dishonest
nechistokrovnyi нечістокровний *a* mongrel
nechutlyvist нечутливість *n.* insensibility
nechutlyvyi нечутливий *a.* insensible
nechutnyi нечутний *a.* inaudible
nechuvanyi нечуваний *a* fabulous
nechyslennyi нечисленний *a* few
nechystota нечистота *n.* impurity
nechystyi нечистий *a.* impure
nedarma недарма *adv.* justly
nedavnii недавній *a.* latter
nedavnii недавній *a.* new
nedavno недавно *adv.* recently
nedbailyvyi недбайливий *n.* slothful
nedbalyi недбалий *a.* careless
nedbalyi недбалий *a.* nonchalant
nedbalyi недбалий *a.* slipshod
nediisnyi недійсний *a.* invalid
nediisnyi недійсний *a.* void
nediiuchyi недіючий *a.* inoperative
nedilia неділя *n.* Sunday
nedohliad недогляд *n.* omission
nedoidannia недоїдання *n.* malnutrition
nedolik недолік *n* blemish
nedootsiniuvaty недооцінювати *v.t.* misjudge
nedopalok недопалок *n.* stub
nedorechna veselist недоречна веселість *n.* levity

nedorechnist недоречність *n.* impropriety
nedorechnyi недоречний *a.* inopportune
nedorechnyi недоречний *a.* irrelevant
nedorohyi недорогий *a.* inexpensive
nedoskonalist недосконалість *n.* imperfection
nedoskonalyi недосконалий *a* faulty
nedostacha недостача *n.* shortage
nedostatnii недостатній *adj.* deficient
nedostupnyi недоступний *a.* impenetrable
nedosvidchenist недосвідченість *n.* inexperience
nedotorkannyi недоторканний *a.* sacrosanct
nedoumkuvatyi недоумкуватий *a.* silly
nedovira недовіра *n.* mistrust
nedozvolenyi недозволений *a.* illicit
nedruh недруг *n* foe
nedystsyplinovanist недисциплінованість *n.* indiscipline
nef неф *n.* nave
nehaino негайно *adv.* straightway
nehainyi негайний *a.* instantaneous
neharazdy негаразди *n.* adversity
nehatyv негатив *n.* negative
nehatyvnyi негативний *a* minus
nehidnyk негідник *n.* wretch
nehnuchkyi негнучкий *a.* inflexible
nehnuchkyi негнучкий *n.* stiff

nehostynnyi негостинний *a.*
inhospitable
nehovirkyi неговіркий *a.* taciturn
nehr негр *n.* negro
nehramotnist неграмотність *n.*
illiteracy
nehrytianka негритянка *n.*
negress
neiaskravyi неяскравий *a.* sullen
neiasnyi неясний *a* equivocal
neiasnyi неясний *a.* indescribable
neiasnyi неясний *a.* indistinct
neilon нейлон *n.* nylon
neimovirnyi неймовірний *a.*
incredible
neimovirnyi неймовірний *a.*
unlikely
neitralizm нейтралізм *n.* non-
alignment
neitralizuvaty нейтралізувати *v.t.*
neutralize
neitralnyi нейтральний *a.* neutral
neitron нейтрон *n.* neutron
nekhtuvaty нехтувати *v. t.* disdain
nekhtuvaty нехтувати *v.t.* slight
nekompetentnyi некомпетентний
a. incompetent
nekonkuruiuchyi неконкуруючий
a complementary
nekroloh некролог *a.* obituary
nekromant некромант *n.*
necromancer
nekropol некрополь *n.* necropolis
nektar нектар *n.* nectar
nekultyvovanyi некультивований
a. wild
nekvaplyvo неквапливо *adv.*
leisurely
nekvaplyvyi неквапливий *a.*
leisurely
neliudianist нелюдяність *n*
barbarity

neliudskyi нелюдський *a.*
inhuman
nelohichnyi нелогічний *a.* illogical
neloialnyi нелояльний *a* disloyal
nematerialnyi нематеріальний *a.*
immaterial
nemich неміч *n.* infirmity
nemichnyi немічний *a.* infirm
nemitsnyi неміцний *a* flimsy
nemovlia немовля *n.* infant
nemozhlyvist неможливість *n.*
impossibility
nemozhlyvist prochytaty
неможливість прочитати *n.*
illegibility
nemozhlyvyi неможливий *a.*
impossible
nemyloserdnyi немилосердний
adj. merciless
nemynuchyi неминучий *a.*
inevitable
nenadiinyi ненадійний *a.*
unreliable
nenadovho ненадовго *adv.*
awhile
nenalezhna povedinka
неналежна поведінка *n.*
misbehaviour
nenasytno ненаситно *a.*
insatiable
nenasytnyi ненаситний *a.*
voracious
nenavydity ненавидіти *v.t.* abhor
nenavydity ненавидіти *v.t.* hate
nenavydity ненавидіти *v.t.* loathe
nenavyst ненависть *n.* hate
nenazhera ненажера *n.*
cormorant
nenormalnyi ненормальний *a*
abnormal
neobachnyi необачний *a.* rash
neobdumanyi необдуманий *a.*
haphazard

neobdumanyi необдуманий *a.*
inconsiderate
neoberezhnyi необережний *a.*
imprudent
neobgruntovanyi
необґрунтований *a.* unjust
neobhruntovanyi
необгрунтований *a.* invalid
neobkhidna umova необхідна
умова *n.* requirement
neobkhidne необхідне *a.* needful
neobkhidnist необхідність *n.*
must
neobkhidnist необхідність *n.*
need
neobkhidno необхідно *n.*
necessary
neobkhidnyi необхідний *a.*
indispensable
neoboviazkovyi необов'язковий
a. optional
neobroblenyi необроблений *a*
crude
neobroblenyi необроблений *a.*
rough
neobtesanyi необтесаний *a.*
uncouth
neodnakovyi неоднаковий *a.*
matchless
neofitsiinyi неофіційний *a.*
informal
neokhainyi неохайний *a.*
slatternly
neokhainyi неохайний *a.* slovenly
neokhoche zhodzhuvatysia
неохоче згоджуватися *v.i.*
acquiesce
neokhochyi неохочий *a.* loath
neolitychnyi неолітичний *a.*
neolithic
neonovyi неоновий *n.* neon
neosiazhnyi неосяжний *a.*
immense

neosvichenyi неосвічений *a.*
ignorant
neotsinennyi неоціненний *a.*
invaluable
neparnyi непарний *a.* odd
neperebornyi непереборний *a.*
insurmountable
neperekhidnyi неперехідний *a.*
(verb) intransitive
neperekhidnyi неперехідний *a.*
neuter
neperemozhnyi непереможний
a. invincible
neperenosnyi непереносний *a.*
intolerable
neperevershuvanyi
неперевершуваний *a.* peerless
neplatospromozhnyi
неплатоспроможний *a.*
insolvent
nepodalik неподалік *adv.*
thereabouts
nepodilnyi неподільний *a.*
indivisible
nepokhytnyi непохитний *a.*
adamant
nepokhytnyi непохитний *a.*
resolute
nepokirlyvyi непокірливий *a.*
insubordinate
nepokirnyi непокірний *a.* unruly
nepokirnyi непокірний *a.*
untoward
nepokora непокора *n.*
insubordination
nepomirnist непомірність *n.*
surfeit
nepomitno vseliaty непомітно
вселяти *v.t.* insinuate
nepomitnyi непомітний *a.*
obscure
nepopravnyi непоправний *a.*
irrecoverable

neporiadnyi непорядний *a.* indecent

neporivniannyi непорівнянний *a.* incomparable

neporozuminnia непорозуміння *n* misapprehension

neporozuminnia непорозуміння *n.* mistake

neporozuminnia непорозуміння *n.* misunderstanding

neporushnyi непорушний *a.* still

neposhtyvyi непоштивий *a* discourteous

nepotribnyi непотрібний *a.* needless

nepovaha неповага *n* disrespect

nepovnolitnii неповнолітній *a.* minor

nepovnolitnii pidlitok неповнолітній підліток *n* minor

nepovnotsinnist неповноцінність *n.* inferiority

nepovnyi неповний *a* . incomplete

nepovtornyi неповторний *a.* inimitable

nepratsezdatnyi непрацездатний *a* disabled

nepravomirnyi неправомірний *a.* wrongful

nepravosuddia неправосуддя *n.* injustice

nepravylna nazva неправильна назва *n.* misnomer

nepravylne неправильне *n.* misdirection

nepravylne kerivnytstvo неправильне керівництво *n.* mismanagement

nepravylne uiavlennia неправильне уявлення *n.* misconception

nepravylni administratyvni dii неправильні адміністративні дії *n.* maladministration

nepravylnist неправильність *n.* irregularity

nepravylno неправильно *adv.* wrong

nepravylno adresuvaty неправильно адресувати *v.t.* misdirect

nepravylno tlumachyty неправильно тлумачити *v.t.* misconstrue

nepravylno zrozumity неправильно зрозуміти *v.t.* misunderstand

nepravylnyi неправильний *a* anomalous

nepravylnyi неправильний *a* erroneous

nepravylnyi неправильний *a.* illegitimate

nepriamyi непрямий *a.* indirect

neprofesiinyi непрофесійний *a.* lay

neprokhidnist непрохідність *n.* obstruction

neprokhidnyi непрохідний *a.* impassable

nepromokalnyi непромокальний *a.* watertight

nepronyknyi непроникний *a* proof

neprozorist непрозорість *n.* opacity

neprozoryi непрозорий *a.* opaque

nepryborkanyi неприборканий *a.* indomitable

neprydatnyi непридатний *a.* inapplicable

nepryiazn неприязнь *n* dislike

nepryiaznyi неприязний *a.*
inimical
nepryiemnist неприємність *n.*
nuisance
nepryiemno volohyi неприємно
вологий *adj.* dank
nepryiemnyi неприємний *a.*
disagreeable
nepryiemnyi неприємний *a.*
obnoxious
nepryiemnyi неприємний *a.*
wicked
nepryiemnyi zvuk неприємний
звук *n.* jar
nepryiniattia неприйняття *n.*
rejection
neprykhovanyi неприхований *a.*
obvious
neprykhylnist неприхильність *a.*
indisposed
neprykhylnyi неприхильний *a.*
averse
neprykhylnyi неприхильний *a.*
reluctant
neprymyrennyi непримиренний
a. irreconcilable
neprypustymyi неприпустимий
a. inadmissible
neprytomnist непритомність *n.*
swoon
neprytomnity непритомніти *v.i*
swoon
Neptun Нептун *n.* Neptune
nepysmennyi неписьменний *a.*
illiterate
nepytushcha liudyna непитуща
людина *n.* teetotaller
nepytushchyi непитущий *a.*
teetotal
neratsionalnyi нераціональний
a. irrational
nerazni obrysy неразні обриси
n blur

nerehuliarnyi нерегулярний *a.*
irregular
nerehuliarnyi нерегулярний *a.*
occasional
nerishuchist нерішучість *n.*
indecision
nerishuchyi нерішучий *n.* shilly-
shally
nerivnist нерівність *n* disparity
neroba нероба *n.* idler
nerozbirlyvo pysaty
нерозбірливо писати *v.t.* scrawl
nerozbirlyvyi нерозбірливий *a.*
indiscriminate
nerozchynnyi нерозчинний *n.*
insoluble
nerozdilnyi нероздільний *a.*
inseparable
nerozsudlyvist нерозсудливість
n. imprudence
nerozsudlyvyi нерозсудливий *a*
foolish
nerozumnyi нерозумний *a.*
witless
nerukhomist нерухомість *n.*
stillness
nerukhomyi нерухомий *a.*
motionless
nerushymyi нерушимий *a.*
imperishable
Nerv Нерв *n.* Nerve
nervovyi нервовий *a.* nervous
nerzhaviiuchyi нержавіючий *a.*
stainless
neshchadnyi нещадний *a.*
ruthless
neshchaslyvyi нещасливий *a.*
unhappy
neshchasnyi нещасний *a* forlorn
neshchasnyi нещасний *a.*
unfortunate
neshchasnyi vypadok нещасний
випадок *n.* misadventure

neshchasnyi vypadok нещасний випадок *n.* mishap

neshchastia нещастя *n.* tribulation

neshchyrist нещирість *n.* insincerity

neshchyryi нещирий *a.* insincere

neskhozhyi несхожий *a* dissimilar

neskhozhyi na несхожий на *a* unlike

neskhvalennia несхвалення *n* disapproval

neskhvalennia несхвалення *n.* objection

neskinchennist нескінченність *n.* infinity

neskinchennyi нескінченний *a.* interminable

neskinchennyi нескінченний *a.* perpetual

neskladnist нескладність *n* facility

neskorochenyi нескорочений *a.* full

neskromne нескромне *a.* immodest

neskromnist нескромність *n.* immodesty

neskromnyi нескромний *a.* indiscreet

neslukhnianyi неслухняний *a.* naughty

nesmachnyi несмачний *a.* insipid

nespliachyi несплячий *a.* wakeful

nespodivanka несподіванка *n.* sudden

nespokii неспокій *n* botheration

nespokiinyi неспокійний *a.* uneasy

nespravedlyvyi несправедливий *a* crook

nespravnyi несправний *a.* wrong

nespromozhnist неспроможність *n.* bankruptcy

nespryiatlyvyi несприятливий *a* adverse

nespryiniatlyvist несприйнятливість *n.* immunity

nestabilnyi нестабільний *adj.* astatic

nestacha нестача *n.* lack

nestalist несталість *n.* instability

nestandartnyi нестандартний *a.* outsize

nestatky нестатки *n.* hardship

nesterpnyi нестерпний *a.* insupportable

nesterpnyi нестерпний *a.* repugnant

nesterpnyi bil нестерпний біль *n.* throe

nestiamnyi нестямний *a.* rampant

nestiikist нестійкість *n.* insistence

nestravnyi нестравний *a.* indigestible

nesty нести *v. t* bring

nestyhlyi нестиглий *a.* immature

nestyhlyi нестиглий *a.* verdant

nesumlinnist несумлінність *n.* dishonesty

nesumlinnyi несумлінний *a.* malafide

nesuvoryi несуворий *a.* mild

nesvidomyi несвідомий *a.* automatic

nesvoiechasnyi несвоєчасний *a.* injudicious

netaktovnyi нетактовний *a* clumsy

neterpymist нетерпимість *n.* impatience

neterpymyi нетерпимий *a.* intolerant

netochnyi неточний *a.* inexact

netolerantnist нетолерантність *n.* intolerance

netri нетрі *n.* slum

neuperedzhenist неупередженість *n.* impartiality

neuperedzhenyi неупереджений *a.* impartial

neuspikh неуспіх *n* failure

neutstvo неуцтво *n.* ignorance

neuvazhnyi неуважний *a.* inattentive

nevarenyi неварений *a.* raw

nevblahannyi невблаганний *a.* inexorable

nevdacha невдача *n.* mischance

nevdacha невдача *n.* misfortune

nevdachlyvyi невдачливий *a.* luckless

nevdakha невдаха *n* underdog

nevdalyi невдалий *a.* maladroit

nevdiachnist невдячність *n.* ingratitude

nevdiachnyi невдячний *a.* thankless

nevdovolenist невдоволеність *n* displeasure

nevdovolennia невдоволення *n* dissatisfaction

nevelyka kilkist невелика кількість *n.* little

nevelykyi невеликий *a.* small

nevhaslyi невгаслий *a.* living

nevianuchyi нев'янучий *a.* perennial

nevidchutnyi невідчутний *a.* intangible

nevidomist невідомість *n.* obscurity

nevidpovidalnyi невідповідальний *a.* irresponsible

nevidpovidnist невідповідність *n.* maladjustment

nevidpovidnyi невідповідний *a.* improper

nevidstupnyi невідступний *a.* relentless

nevirno невірно *adv.* amiss

nevirno nazyvaty невірно називати *v.t.* miscall

nevirnyi невірний *a.* incorrect

nevlovymyi невловимий *a* elusive

nevmilo pratsiuvaty невміло працювати *v. t* bungle

nevmilyi невмілий *a.* incapable

nevpynnyi невпинний ~*a.* ceaseless

nevroloh невролог *n.* neurologist

nevrolohiia неврологія *n.* neurology

nevroz невроз *n.* neurosis

nevtrymnyi невтримний *adv.* headlong

nevvichlyvyi неввічливий *a.* impolite

nevybahlyvyi невибагливий *a.* lowly

nevydymyi невидимий *a.* invisible

nevyhadlyvyi невигадливий *a.* plain

nevyhnutyi невигнутий *a.* straight

nevylikovnyi невиліковний *a.* incurable

nevymovnyi невимовний *a.* nefandous

nevynnist невинність *n.* innocence

nevypravnyi невиправний *a.* incorrigible

nevyznachenist невизначеність *n.* vagueness

nevyznachenyi невизначений *a.* indefinite

nevyznachenyi artykl
невизначений артикль *art* an
nevzhe невже *adv.* indeed
nezabarom незабаром *adv.*
shortly
nezadovilnyi незадовільний *a.*
insufficient
nezadovolenist незадоволеність
n discontent
nezadovolenyi незадоволений *a.*
malcontent
nezaimana незаймана *n.* virgin
nezaimanist незайманість *n.*
virginity
nezaimanyi незайманий *a.* intact
nezainiatyi незайнятий *a.* idle
nezakhyshchenyi незахищений
a. indefensible
nezakonne pryvlasnennia
незаконне привласнення *n.*
misappropriation
nezakonnyi незаконний *a.* illegal
nezalezhnist незалежність *n.*
independence
nezalezhno незалежно *adv.* solo
nezalezhnyi незалежний *a.*
irrespective
nezamizhnia незаміжня *a* maiden
nezaperechnyi незаперечний *a.*
irrefutable
nezapliamovanyi
незаплямований *a.* spotless
nezavershenyi незавершений *a.*
imperfect
nezbahnenyi незбагнений *a.*
marvellous
nezchyslennyi незчисленний *a.*
countless
nezdatnist нездатність *n* disability
nezdatnist нездатність *n.*
incapacity
nezdatnyi нездатний *a.* unable
nezdibnist нездібність *n.* inability

nezdiisnennist нездійсненність
n. impracticability
nezdiisnennyi нездійсненний *a.*
impracticable
nezdorovyi нездоровий *a.* unwell
nezduzhannia нездужання *n.*
malaise
nezhrabnyi незграбний *a.*
awkward
nezhyvyi неживий *a.* inanimate
nezlichenni незліченні *a.*
incalculable
nezlichennyi незліченний *a*
myriad
nezlichnyi незлічний *a.*
innumerable
nezmirnyi незмірний *a.*
immeasurable
neznachnist незначність *n.*
insignificance
neznachnyi незначний *a.* puny
neznaiomets незнайомець *n.*
stranger
neznannia незнання *n.* nescience
nezrilist незрілість *n.* immaturity
nezrilyi незрілий *adj* callow
nezrilyi незрілий *a.* puerile
nezrivniannyi незрівнянний *a.*
nonpareil
nezrozumilyi незрозумілий *a.*
inexplicable
nezruchnist незручність *n*
discomfort
nezruchnyi незручний *a.*
inconvenient
nezvazhaiuchy na незважаючи
на *conj.* notwithstanding
nezviazno hovoryty незв'язно
говорити *v.t.* maunder
nezviaznykh незв'язних *a.*
incoherent
nezvychainist незвичайність *n.*
singularity

nezzakonno pryvlasniuvaty
незаконно привласнювати *v.t.*
misappropriate
ni ні *a.* no
ni odyn ні один *adv.* none
niavkannia нявкання *n.* mew
niavkaty нявкати *v.i.* mew
nich ніч *n.* night
nichnyi нічний *a.* nocturnal
nichnyi metelyk нічний метелик
n. moth
nichoho нічого *adv.* nothing
nide ніде *adv.* nowhere
nihilizm нігілізм *n.* nihilism
nihot ніготь *n.* nail
niiakyi ніякий *adv.* no
nikchema нікчема *n.* nonentity
nikchema нікчема *n.* nought
nikel нікель *n.* nickel
nikhto ніхто *pron.* nobody
nikoly ніколи *adv.* never
nikotyn нікотин *n.* nicotine
nimb німб *n.* nimbus
nimfa німфа *n.* nymph
nimyi німий *a* dumb
nis ніс *n.* nose
nisenitnyi нісенітний *a.*
nonsensical
nisenitnyi нісенітний *a.*
quarrelsome
nisenitnytsia нісенітниця *n.*
nonsense
nisha ніша *n.* niche
nishcho ніщо *n.* zero
niuans нюанс *n.* nuance
niukh нюх *n.* smell
niukhaty нюхати *v.t.* smell
nivechyty нівечити *v.t.* mutilate
nizdria ніздря *n.* nostril
nizh ніж *n.* knife
nizhno vorkuvaty ніжно
воркувати *v. i* coo
nizhnyi ніжний *n.* soft

nizhnyi ніжний *a* tender
nizhytysia ніжитися *v.i.* loll
nochnushka ночнушка *n.* nightie
noha нога *n* foot
noha нога *n.* leg
nomenklatura номенклатура *n.*
nomenclature
nomer номер *n.* number
nominal номінал *n.* par
nominalnyi номінальний *a.*
nominal
nora нора *n* burrow
norka норка *n.* mink
norma норма *n.* norm
norma норма *n.* regulation
normalizuvaty нормалізувати *v.t.*
normalize
normalnist нормальність *n.*
normalcy
normalnyi нормальний *a.* normal
normalnyi нормальний *a.* sane
normuvannia нормування *n.*
measurement
norovlyvyi норовливий *a.* restive
nosha ноша *n* burden
noshi ноші *n.* litter
nosok носок *n.* toe
nosorih носоріг *n.* rhinoceros
nosova kistka носова кістка *n*
nasal
nosovychok носовичок *n.*
handkerchief
nosovyi носовий *a.* nasal
nostalhiia ностальгія *n.* nostalgia
nosyk носик *n.* spout
nosylky носилки *n.* sedan
nosylky носилки *n.* stretcher
nosylnyk носильник *n.* carrier
nosytysia носитися *v.i* scamper
notarius нотаріус *n.* notary
novator новатор *n.* innovator
novitnii новітній *a.* up-to-date

novonavernenyi новонавернений *n* convert
novovvedennia нововведення *n.* innovation
novyi новий *a.* novel
novyi protektor новий протектор *n.* retread
novynka новинка *n.* novelty
novyny новини *n.* news
novyny новини *n. pl.* tidings
nozhnyi braslet ножний браслет *n* anklet
nozhytsi ножиці *n.* scissors
nozhytsi ножиці *n. pl.* shears
nudha нудьга *n.* tedium
nudnyi нудний *a.* lifeless
nudota нудота *n.* nausea
nudotnyi нудотний *a.* mawkish
nudyty нудити *v.t.* vomit
nudytysia нудитися *v.i.* pine
nul нуль *n.* nil
nulovyi нульовий *a.* null
numeruvaty storinky нумерувати сторінки *v.t.* page
nutroshchi нутрощі *n.* entrails
nuzhda нужда *n* distress
nyshchivnyi udar нищівний удар *n* smash
nyshporyty нишпорити *v.i.* fumble
nytka нитка *n.* thread
nytsyi ниций *a.* low
nyzhche нижче *adv* below
nyzhche нижче *prep* below
nyzhche нижче *v.t.* lower
nyzhchyi нижчий *a* under
nyzhnia spidnytsia нижня спідниця *n.* petticoat
nyzhnii нижній *a.* nether
nyzkopoklonstvo низькопоклонство *n.* sycophancy
nyzkyi низький *a.* ignoble

nyzkyi низький *a.* short
nyzyna низина *n.* low

O

oazys оазис *n.* oasis
**ob`iekt** об`єкт *n.* object
**ob`iekt zazdroshchiv** об`єкт заздрощів *n* envy
**ob`iekt znevahy** об`єкт зневаги *n.* scorn
**ob`iem** об`єм *n.* volume
obbyty оббити *v.t.* stud
obbyvka оббивка *n.* padding
obchyslennia обчислення *n.* calculation
obchysliuvaty обчислювати *v.t.* rate
obdarovanyi обдарований *a.* gifted
obdumanyi обдуманий *a* deliberate
obdyraty обдирати *v.t.* peel
obdyraty обдирати *v.t.* rook
obdyvliatysia обдивлятися *v.t.* survey
oberezhnist обережність *n.* safeguard
oberezhnyi обережний *adj.* circumspect
oberezhnyi обережний *a.* watchful
oberihaty оберігати *v.t.* reserve
oberihaty оберігати *v.t.* retain
obernuty обернути *v.t.* wrap
obertalnyi обертальний *a.* rotary
obertannia обертання *n.* rotation
obertaty обертати *v.t.* reverse
obertatysia обертатися *v.i.* revolve
obez- обез- *pref.* be
obezholovyty обезголовити *v. t.* behead

obezzbroiuvaty обеззброювати *v. t* disarm

obgruntovanyi обґрунтований *a.* reasonable

obgruntovuvaty обґрунтовувати *v.t.* substantiate

obhorodzhuvaty tynom обгороджувати тином *v.t* hurdle2

obhortka обгортка *n* wrap

obhovorennia обговорення *n.* counsel

obhovoriuvaty обговорювати *v. i* deliberate

obhovoriuvaty обговорювати *v. t.* discuss

obid обід *n.* lunch

obid обід *n.* rim

obidaty обідати *v.i.* lunch

obiednannia об'єднання *n.* unification

obiednanyi об'єднаний *a.* incorporate

obiednuvaty об'єднувати *v.t.* unite

obiekt об'єкт *n.* target

obiektyvnyi об'єктивний *a.* objective

obiemystyi об'ємистий *a.* voluminous

obiiednannia обйєднання *n* rally

obiimatysia обійматися *v.t.* pet

obiimy обійми *n* embrace

obiiniaty обійняти *v. t.* embrace

obitnytsia обітниця *n.* vow

obitsianka обіцянка *n* promise

obitsiaty обіцяти *v.t* promise

obiznanyi обізнаний *a.* adept

obiznanyi обізнаний *a.* proficient

obkhid обхід *n* bypass

obkhodyty обходити *v.t.* skirt

obkladannia обкладання *n.* assessment

obkladaty обкладати *v.t.* levy

obkladaty podatkom обкладати податком *v.t.* geld

obkraiaty обкраяти *v.t.* lop

oblachaty облачати *v.t.* robe

obladnannia обладнання *n* equipment

oblahorodzhuvaty облагороджувати *v.t* dignify

oblast область *n* domain

obliahaty облягати *v. t* besiege

obliamovuvaty облямовувати *v.t* fringe

oblihatsiia облігація *n.* obligation

obliteratsiia облітерація *n.* obliteration

obloha облога *n.* siege

obluda облуда *n* deception

oblychchia обличчя *n.* countenance

oblyzuvannia облизування *n* lick

obman обман *n.* imposture

obmaniuvaty обманювати *v.t.* juggle

obmanshchyk обманщик *n.* impostor

obmazuvaty обмазувати *v. t.* daub

obmezhennia обмеження *n.* infringement

obmezhennia обмеження *n.* restriction

obmezhenyi обмежений *adj.* borne

obmezhuvalnyi обмежувальний *a.* restrictive

obmezhuvaty обмежувати *v. t* confine

obmezhuvaty обмежувати *v.t.* straiten

obmin обмін *n* exchange

obmin rechovyn обмін речовин *n.* metabolism

obminiuvaty обмінювати *v. t* exchange

obminiuvatysia обмінюватися *v.* interchange

obmirkovuvaty обмірковувати *v. t* consider

obmirkovuvaty обмірковувати *v.t.* premeditate

obmotaty обмотати *v.t.* wind

obmovliaty обмовляти *v.t.* backbite

obmundyruvannia обмундирування *n* clothing

obmundyruvannia обмундирування *n.* outfit

obmundyruvaty обмундирувати *v.t* outfit

obmyvannia обмивання *n* ablution

obnosyty rovom обносити ровом *v.t.* moat

obnosyty stinoiu обносити стіною *v.t.* wall

obolonka оболонка *n.* shell

oborka оборка *n.* frill

oborona оборона *adv.* defensive

oboroniaty обороняти *v. t* defend

oboronozdatnyi обороноздатний *a.* tenable

oborotna storona оборотна сторона *n* reverse

oborotnyi оборотний *a.* negotiable

oboviazkovyi обов'язковий *a* compulsory

obozhniuvannia обожнювання *n.* adoration

obozhniuvanyi обожнюваний *a.* adorable

obozhniuvaty обожнювати *v.t.* adore

obpaliuvaty опалювати *v.t.* singe

obramovuvaty обрамовувати *v.t.* frame

obraty обрати *v. t* elect

obraz образ *n.* image

obraza образа *n* hurt

obraza образа *n.* snub

obrazhaty ображати *v.t.* abuse

obrazhaty ображати *v.t.* offend

obrazlyve hluzuvannia образливе глузування *n* taunt

obrazlyvyi образливий *a.* touchy

obrazyty образити *v.t.* affront

obriad обряд *n.* rite

obrobka обробка *n* manufacture

obrobliaty обробляти *v. t* cultivate

obrubok обрубок *n.* stump

obrubuvaty обрубувати *v.t* stump

obruchyty обручити *v. t* betroth

obrys обрис *n.* outline

observatoriia обсерваторія *n.* observatory

obshyvaty paneliamy обшивати панелями *v.t.* panel

obsiah обсяг *n* bulk

obsluhovuvannia обслуговування *n.* service

obsluhovuvaty обслуговувати *v.t* service

obstanovka обстановка *n.* furniture

obstavliaty обставляти *v.t.* furnish

obstavyna обставина *n* circumstance

obstavyny, shcho vypravdovuiut обставини, що виправдовують *n.* justification

obstriliuvaty artyleriiskym vohnem обстрілювати артилерійським вогнем *v. t.* cannonade

obstupaty обступати *v.t.* surround

obtiazhenyi обтяжений *a.* fraught

obtiazhlyvyi обтяжливий *a*
burdensome
obtiazhlyvyi обтяжливий *a.*
weighty
obtiazhuvaty обтяжувати *v. t*
burden
obtikannia обтікання *n.*
circumfluence
obtsukrovuvaty обцукровувати
v.t. sugar
obumovlenyi обумовлений *a*
conditional
obumovliuvaty обумовлювати *v.*
t. calumniate
oburennia обурення *n.*
indignation
oburenyi обурений *a.* indignant
oburiuvatysia обурюватися *v.t.*
resent
obval обвал *v. i* collapse
obvodyty обводити *v. t.* encircle
obvynuvach обвинувач *n.*
prosecutor
obvynuvachenyi обвинувачений
n. accused
obvynuvachyty обвинувачити
v.t. accuse
obvynuvalnyi akt обвинувальний
акт *n.* indictment
obvyvaty обвивати *v.t.* wreathe
obydva обидва *adj.* both
obzherlyvist обжерливість *n.*
gluttony
ocheret очерет *n.* rush
ochevydets очевидець *n.*
spectator
ochevydnyi очевидний *a.* evident
ochikuvannia очікування *n.*
expectation
ochikuvaty очікувати *v.i* abide
ochne yabluko очне яблуко *n*
eyeball
ochnyi очний *a.* ocular

ocholiuvaty очолювати *v.t.*
spearhead
ochyshchaty очищати *v. t* clear
ochyshchaty vid shkarlupy
очищати від шкарлупи *v.t.* shell
ochyshchatysia очищатися *v.t.*
purify
ochyshchennia очищення *n*
clearance
ochyshchennia kyshechnyka
очищення кишечника *n.*
purgation
ochysnyi очисний *a* purgative
ochysnyi zavod очисний завод
n. refinery
oda ода *n.* ode
oderzhuvach одержувач *n.*
receiver
oderzhuvach platezhu
одержувач платежу *n.* payee
oderzhuvaty одержувати *v.t.*
score
odiah одяг *n.* costume
odiahaty одягати *v.t.* bedight
odiahatysia одягатися *v.t* garb
odiiannia одіяння *n.* garb
odioznyi одіозний *a.* odious
odkrovennia одкровення *n.*
revelation
odnak однак *adv.* notwithstanding
odnakovyi однаковий *a* equal
odnakovyi однаковий *a.* same
odnochasnyi одночасний *a.*
simultaneous
odnomanitnyi одноманітний *a.*
monotonous
odnoridnyi однорідний *a.*
homogeneous
odnoskladove slovo
односкладове слово *n.*
monosyllable
odnoskladovyi односкладовий
a. monosyllabic

odnostainist одностайність *n.* unanimity

odnostainyi одностайний *a.* unanimous

odnostoronnii односторонній *a* ex-parte

odr одр *n* bier

odruzhennia одруження *n.* wedding

odruzhuvatysia одружуватися *v.t.* marry

odruzhyty одружити *v.t.* wed

oduriuvaty одурювати *v.t.* trick

odurmaniuvaty одурманювати *v.t.* intoxicate

odyn один *pron.* one

odyn odnoho один одного *pron.* each

odynadtsiat одинадцять *n* eleven

odynychnyi одиничний *a.* singular

odynytsia одиниця *n.* unit

ofis офіс *n.* office

ofitser офіцер *n.* officer

ofitsiant офіціант *n.* waiter

ofitsiantka офіціантка *n.* waitress

ofitsiine rozporiadzhennia офіційне розпорядження *n.* requisition

ofitsiino офіційно *adv.* officially

ofitsiino praznachuvaty na posadu офіційно празначувати на посаду *v.t.* install

ofitsiino vvodyty na posadu офіційно вводити на посаду *n.* induction

ofitsiinyi офіційний *a.* official

ofitsioznyi офіціозний *a.* officious

ohirok огірок *n* cucumber

ohliad огляд *n* browse

ohliadaty оглядати *v.t.* review

ohlianuty оглянути *v.t.* view

ohlushaty оглушати *v.t.* stun

oholene tilo оголене тіло *n* nude

oholenyi оголений *a.* naked

oholiuvaty оголювати *v.t.* bare

oholoshennia оголошення *n.* announcement

oholoshuvaty оголошувати *v.t.* announce

oholoshuvaty оголошувати *v.t.* publicize

oholoshuvaty poza zakonom оголошувати поза законом *v.t.* attaint

oholoshuvaty poza zakonom оголошувати поза законом *v.t* outlaw

ohornuty огорнути *v.t* mantle

ohorodzhuvaty огороджувати *v.t* fence

ohorozha огорожа *n.* enclosure

ohortaty огортати *v. t* envelop

ohriadnyi огрядний *a* gross

ohuzok огузок *n.* rear

ohyda огида *n.* horror

ohydnyi огидний *a.* heinous

ohynaty огинати *v.t.* round

okean океан *n.* ocean

okeanichnyi океанічний *a.* oceanic

okhainist охайність *n.* tidiness

okhainyi охайний *a.* tidy

okholodyty охолодити *v.t.* refrigerate

okholodzhennia охолодження *n.* refrigeration

okholodzhuvaty охолоджувати *v. i.* cool

okhorona охорона *n.* guard

okhoronets охоронець *n.* bodyguard

okhoroniaty охороняти *v.i.* guard

oklad оклад *n.* salary

oko око *n* ogle

oko око *n* eye
okolytsi околиці *n.* surroundings
okolytsia околиця *n.* outskirts
okozamyliuvannia
окозамилювання *n* eyewash
okremo окремо *adv.* aside
okremyi окремий *a.* separate
okreslyty окреслити *v.t.* outline
okruh округ *n* district
oksamyt оксамит *n.* velvet
oktava октава *n.* octave
okulist окуліст *n.* oculist
okultnyi окультний *a.* occult
okun окунь *n.* perch
okupant окупант *n.* occupier
okynuty pohliadom окинути
поглядом *v.i.* glance
olen олень *n* deer
oleniachyi rih оленячий ріг *n.*
antler
oliharkhiia олігархія *n.* oligarchy
oliia олія *n.* oil
oliinytsia олійниця *n.* churn
olimpiada олімпіада *n.* olympiad
oliudniuvaty олюднювати *v.t.*
humanize
olivets олівець *n.* pencil
olovo олово *n.* tin
olyvkovyi оливковий *n.* olive
omana омана *n* fallacy
omanlyvyi оманливий *adj*
bimenasl
omar омар *n.* lobster
omeha омега *n.* omega
omela омела *n.* mistletoe
omlet омлет *n.* omelette
omolodzhennia омолодження *n.*
rejuvenation
omolodzhuvatysia
омолоджуватися *v.t.* rejuvenate
on tam он там *adv.* yonder
on toi он той *a.* yonder
onimilyi онімілий *a.* numb

onovlennia оновлення *n.* renewal
onovyty оновити *v.t.* refresh
opadaty опадати *v. t* diminish
opal опал *n.* opal
opera опера *n.* opera
operator оператор *n.* operator
operatsii операції *n.* interchange
operatsiia операція *n.* operation
operatyvnyi оперативний *a.*
operative
operizuvaty оперізувати *v.t.*
begird
opik опік *n* burn
opik опік *n* singe
opika опіка *v* custody
opikun опікун *n.* trustee
opir опір *n.* resistance
opir опір *n.* revolt
opium опіум *n.* opium
oplachuvaty оплачувати *v.t.*
remunerate
oplakuvaty оплакувати *v. t* bewail
oplata оплата *n* pay
oplata pratsi оплата праці *n.*
remuneration
oplesky оплески *n.* applause
oplot оплот *n.* support
opodatkovuvanyi
оподатковуваний *a.* taxable
opodatkuvannia оподаткування
n. taxation
opokhyle polozhennia опохиле
положення *n.* tilt
oponent опонент *n.* opponent
opora опора *n* crutch
oportunizm опортунізм *n.*
opportunism
opovidach оповідач *n.* teller
opovidannia оповідання *n.*
narrative
opovidannia оповідання *n.* story
opovidaty оповідати *v.t.* narrate
opozytsiia опозиція *n.* opposition

opozytsioner опозиціонер *n* malcontent

oprominiuvaty опромінювати *v.t.* illuminate

oprotestuvannia опротестування *n.* protestation

opryliudnyty оприлюднити *v. t* divulge

optom оптом *adv.* wholesale

optova torhivlia оптова торгівля *n.* wholesale

optovyi оптовий *a* wholesale

optovyk оптовик *n.* wholesaler

optsiia опція *n.* option

optsion опціон *n.* refusal

optychnyi оптичний *a.* optic

optyk оптик *n.* optician

optymalnyi оптимальний *a* optimum

optymist оптиміст *n.* optimist

optymistychnyi оптимістичний *a.* optimistic

optymizm оптимізм *n.* optimism

optymum оптимум *n.* optimum

opublikuvannia опублікування *n.* publication

opuklist опуклість *n.* prominence

opuklyi опуклий *a* arch

opuskaty опускати *v.t.* avale

opustyty опустити *v.t.* omit

opys опис *n* description

opys опис *n.* portrait

opysovyi описовий *a* descriptive

opysuvaty описувати *v. t* describe

opysuvaty описувати *v.t.* report

orach орач *n.* ploughman

orakul оракул *n.* oracle

oranzhereia оранжерея *n.* greenery

orator оратор *n.* orator

oratorske mystetstvo ораторське мистецтво *n.* oratory

oratorskyi ораторський *a.* oratorical

oraty орати *v.t.* plough

oraty орати *v.t.* till

orbita орбіта *n.* orbit

orda орда *n.* horde

order ордер *n.* warrant

orel орел *n* eagle

orenda оренда *n.* lease

orendar орендар *n.* tenant

orhan орган *n.* organ

orhanichne dobryvo органічне добриво *n.* manure

orhanichnyi органічний *a.* organic

orhanizatsiia організація *n.* organization

orhanizm організм *n.* organism

orhanizuvaty організувати *v.t.* organize

orhiia оргія *n* debauchery

oriientovnyi орієнтовний *a.* tentative

oriientuvaty орієнтувати *v.t.* orient

oriientuvatysia орієнтуватися *v.t.* orientate

orkestr оркестр *n.* orchestra

orkestrovyi оркестровий *a.* orchestral

ornament орнамент *n.* ornament

ornyi орний *adj* arable

ortodoksalnist ортодоксальність *n.* orthodoxy

ortodoksalnyi ортодоксальний *a.* orthodox

oryhinal оригінал *n* original

oryhinalnist оригінальність *n.* originality

osa оса *n.* wasp

osel осел *n* donkey
oseledets оселедець *n.* herring
oselennia v seli оселення в селі *n.* rustication
oselia оселя *n* dwelling
oseredok осередок *n.* cell
oshchadlyvist ощадливість *n.* thrift
oshchadlyvyi ощадливий *a* economical
oshchadlyvyi ощадливий *a.* prudent
oshukanets ошуканець *n.* swindler
oshukuvannia ошукування *n.* swindle
oshukuvaty ошукувати *v.t.* swindle
osiazhnyi осяжний *a.* tangible
osichka осічка *n.* miss
osin осінь *n.* autumn
oskarzhuvaty оскаржувати *v. t* contest
oskolok осколок *n.* splinter
oskverniaty осквернятu *v.t.* profane
oslabliaty ослабляти *v.t.* abate
oslabliaty opir protyvnyka ослабляти опір противника *v.t.* soften
osliachyi ослячий *adj.* asinine
osnova основа *n.* base
osnovnyi основний *a* main
osnovnyi основний *a* staple
osnovnyi ton основний тон *n.* tonic
osnovy hromadianskosti основи громадянськості *n* civics
osoba особа *n.* wight
osoba, shcho daie harantiiu особа, що дає гарантію *n.* warrantor

osoba, shcho zaimaie posadu особа, що займає посаду *n.* incumbent
osoba, yaka zazhyla durnoi slavy особа, яка зажила дурної слави *n.* notoriety
osoba, yakii daietsia harantiia особа, якій дається гарантія *n.* warrantee
osoblyvist особливість *n.* peculiarity
osoblyvist особливість *n.* trait
osoblyvo особливо *adv.* singularly
osoblyvyi особливий *a* especial
osobniak особняк *n.* mansion
osobovyi особовий *a* finite
osobystist особистість *n.* personality
osobysto особисто *adv.* bodily
osobystyi особистий *a.* individual
ostannii останній *a.* recent
ostannim chasom останнім часом *adv.* lately
ostatochnyi остаточний *a* final
ostoron осторонь *adv.* aloof
ostriv острів *n.* island
ostrivets острівець *n.* isle
ostrivnyi острівний *a.* insular
osud осуд *n* blame
osudnist осудність *n.* sanity
osudzhuvaty осуджувати *v. t.* censure
osushennia осушення *n* arefaction
osushuvaty осушувати *v. t* drain
osviachennia освячення *n.* sanctification
osviachuvaty освячувати *v.t.* sanctify
osvichenist освіченість *n.* accomplishment
osvichenyi освічений *a.* literate

osvidchennia освідчення *n.*
proposal
osvita освіта *n* education
osvitlennia освітлення *n.*
lightening
otochennia оточення *n.* milieu
otochuvaty оточувати *v. t* enclose
otochyty kiltsem оточити
кільцем *v.t.* ring
otrotstvo отроцтво *n* boyhood
otruinist отруйність *n.* virulence
otruinyi отруйний *a.* poisonous
otruity отруїти *v.t.* poison
otruta отрута *n.* poison
otrymannia отримання *n.* receipt
otrymuvaty отримувати *v.t.*
receive
otrymuvaty zadovolennia
отримувати задоволення *v. t*
enjoy
otset оцет *n.* vinegar
otsiniuvaty оцінювати *v.t.* price
otsinka оцінка *n.* appreciation
otvir отвір *n.* aperture
ovalnyi овальний *a.* oval
ovatsiia овація *n.* ovation
Oven Овен *n* aries
overdraft овердрафт *n.* overdraft
oves овес *n.* oat
ovoch овоч *n.* vegetable
ovochevyi овочевий *a.* vegetable
ovolodity soboiu оволодіти
собою *v.t.* rally
ovolodivaty оволодівати *v.t.*
possess
ozbroiennia озброєння *n.*
armament
ozbroiuvaty озброювати *v.t.* arm
ozdoblennia оздоблення *n.*
ornamentation
ozdoblennia оздоблення *n* trim
ozdobliuvaty оздоблювати *v.t.*
ornament

ozero озеро *n.* lake
ozhyrinnia ожиріння *n.* obesity
ozhyvliaty оживляти *v. t.* enliven
ozhyvyty оживити *v.t.* animate
ozlobliaty озлобляти *v. t* embitter
oznachaty означати *v.i.* matter
oznaiomyty ознайомити *v.t.*
initiate
oznaka ознака *n* feature
oznaka ознака *n.* omen

P

pachka пачка *n* batch
padaty падати *v.i.* fall
padaty nyts падати ниць *v.t.*
prostrate
padinnia падіння *n* fall
padliuka падлюка *n.* scoundrel
pafos пафос *n.* pathos
pahin пагін *n* sprout
pahoda пагода *n.* pagoda
pahorb пагорб *n.* hill
pai пай *n.* share
paket пакет *n.* packet
pakhnuty пахнути *v.i.* smack
pakhta пахта *n* buttermilk
pakt пакт *n.* pact
pakuvalnyk пакувальник *n.*
wrapper
palaiuchyi палаючий *adv.* ablaze
palaiuchyi палаючий *adv.* aglow
palankin паланкін *n.* palanquin
palatka палатка *n* booth
palats палац *n.* palace
palatsovyi палацовий *a.* palatial
palaty палати *v.i* blaze
palets палець *n* finger
palia паля *n.* pile
palia паля *n.* stilt
palitra палітра *n.* palette
palkist палкість *n* fervour

palko bazhaty палко бажати *v.t.*
crave
palkyi палкий *a.* ardent
palma пальма *n.* palm
palomnyk паломник *n.* pilgrim
palomnytstvo паломництво *n.*
pilgrimage
palto пальто *n* coat
paluba палуба *n* deck
palychka паличка *n.* wand
palytsia палиця *n.* stick
palyty палити *v.t.* scorch
palyvo паливо *n.* fuel
pamflet памфлет *n.* pamphlet
pamfletyst памфлетист *n.*
pamphleteer
pamiat пам'ять *n.* memory
pamiataty пам'ятати *v.t.* mind
pamiatnyi пам'ятний *a.*
memorable
pamiatnyk пам'ятник *n.*
monument
pan пан *n.* lord
panatseia панацея *n.* panacea
panchishni vyroby панчішні
вироби *n.* hosiery
panehiryk панегірик *n.* panegyric
panel панель *n.* panel
pani пані *n.* mistress
panichna vtecha панічна втеча
n. stampede
panichno tikaty панічно тікати *v.i*
stampede
panika паніка *n.* panic
paniruvaty панірувати *v. t. & i*
breaden
panorama панорама *n.* panorama
panorama панорама *n.* prospect
panskyi панський *a.* lordly
panteist пантеїст *n.* pantheist
panteizm пантеїзм *n.* pantheism
pantera пантера *n.* panther

pantomima пантоміма *n.*
pantomime
panuvannia панування *n*
domination
panuvannia панування *n.*
prevalence
panuvaty панувати *v.t.* rule
paperovyi zmii паперовий змій
n. kite
papir папір *n.* paper
papliuzhyty паплюжити *v.t.*
slander
papliuzhyty паплюжити *v.t.*
violate
papskyi папський *a.* papal
papstvo папство *n.* papacy
papuha папуга *n.* parrot
par пар *n* steam
para пара *n* couple
para пара *n.* pair
parad парад *n.* parade
paradoks парадокс *n.* paradox
paradoksalnyi парадоксальний
a. paradoxical
parafin парафін *n.* paraffin
parafraz парафраз *n.* paraphrase
parahon парагон *n.* paragon
parahraf параграф *n.* item
paralelizm паралелізм *n.*
parallelism
paralelnyi паралельний *a.*
parallel
paralelohram паралелограм *n.*
parallelogram
paralich параліч *n.* paralysis
paralitychnyi паралітичний *a.*
paralytic
paralizuvaty паралізувати *v.t.*
paralyse
parashut парашут *n.* parachute
parashutyst парашутист *n.*
parachutist

parasolka парасолька *n.*
umbrella
parazyt паразит *n.* parasite
parazytnyi паразитний *a.*
spurious
parcha парча *n* brocade
pari парі *n.* wager
pariia парія *n.* leper
park парк *n.* park
parkan паркан *n* fence
parkuvaty паркувати *v.t.* park
parlament парламент *n.*
parliament
parlamentarii парламентарій *n.*
parliamentarian
parlamentskyi парламентський
a. parliamentary
parodiia пародія *n.* parody
parodiia пародія *n.* skit
parodiiuvaty пародіювати *v.t.*
parody
parol пароль *n.* watchword
paroplav пароплав *n.* steamer
paropodibnyi пароподібний *a.*
vaporous
parostok паросток *n.* sapling
parta парта *n* desk
partiia партія *n.* consignment
partner партнер *n.* partner
partnerstvo партнерство *n.*
partnership
partyzan партизан *n.* guerilla
partyzaniv партизанів *a.* partisan
partyzanskyi партизанський *n.*
partisan
parusyna парусина *n.* canvas
paryruvannia парирування *n.*
parry
paryruvaty парирувати *v.t.* parry
parytet паритет *n.* parity
paryty парити *v.i.* soar
pasazhyr пасажир *n.* passenger
pasha паша *v.t.* pasture

pasika пасіка *n.* apiary
paskvil пасквіль *n.* libel
pasmo пасмо *n* strand
pasovyshchi пасовищі *n.* lea
pasovyshchi пасовищі *n.* pasture
pasport паспорт *n.* passport
pasta паста *n.* paste
pastelnyi пастельний *n.* pastel
pastka пастка *n.* snare
pastoralnyi пасторальний *a.*
pastoral
pastukh пастух *n.* herdsman
pastva паства *n.* sheep
pasty пасти *v.i.* graze
pasyvnyi пасивний *a.* passive
patent патент *n* patent
patentovanyi патентований *a.*
patent
patentovanyi zasob
патентований засоб *n.* nostrum
patentuvaty патентувати *v.t.*
patent
patetychnyi патетичний *a.*
pathetic
patly патли *n.* manes
patoka патока *n* molasses
patriot патріот *n.* patriot
patriotychnyi патріотичний *a.*
patriotic
patriotyzm патріотизм *n.*
patriotism
patron патрон *n.* cartridge
patronazh патронаж *n.* patronage
patrul патруль *n* patrol
patruliuvaty патрулювати *v.i.*
patrol
patsiient пацієнт *n* patient
pauza пауза *n.* pause
pava пава *n.* peahen
pavilion павільйон *n.* pavilion
pavuk павук *n.* spider
pavutyna павутина *n* cobweb
pavutynnyi павутинний *a.* webby

pavych павич *n.* peacock
paz паз *n.* notch
pazur пазур *n* claw
pechal печаль *n.* sorrow
pechatka печатка *n.* seal
pechenia печеня *n* roast
pechera печера *n.* cave
pechinka печінка *n.* liver
pechyvo печиво *n* biscuit
pedahoh педагог *n.* pedagogue
pedahohika педагогіка *n.*
　pedagogy
pedal педаль *n.* pedal
pedant педант *n.* pedant
pedantychnist педантичність *n.*
　pedantry
pedantychnyi педантичний *n.*
　pedantic
pederast педераст *n.* sodomite
pekar пекар *n.* baker
pekarnia пекарня *n* bakery
pekelnyi пекельний *a.* infernal
peklo пекло *a.* hell
pekty пекти *v.t.* bake
pekuchyi пекучий *a.* hot
pekuchyi bil пекучий біль *n*
　smart
peliustka пелюстка *n.* petal
pelka пелька *n* yap
penka пенька *n.* hemp
penni пенні *n.* penny
pensiia пенсія *n.* pension
pensioner пенсіонер *n.* pensioner
penzlyk пензлик *n* brush
perchyty перчити *v.t.* pepper
perebilshennia перебільшення
　n. exaggeration
perebilshuvaty перебільшувати
　v.t. amplify
perebilshuvaty перебільшувати
　v. t. exaggerate
perebuvannia перебування *n*
　stay

perebyty tsinu перебити ціну *v.t.*
　outbid
peredacha передача *n.*
　transmission
peredaty передати *v.t* hand
peredavach передавач *n.*
　transmitter
peredavaty передавати *v.t*
　forward
peredavaty po radio передавати
　по радіо *v.t.* radio
peredavaty po telebachenniu
　передавати по телебаченню
　v.t. telecast
peredavaty v suborendu
　передавати в суборенду *v.t.*
　sublet
peredbachaty передбачати *v.t*
　forestall
peredbachennia передбачення
　n. foreknowledge
peredbachennia передбачення
　n. prescience
peredbachlyvist
　передбачливість *n* forethought
peredbachlyvyi передбачливий
　a. cautious
peredbachuvanyi
　передбачуваний *a.* would-be
peredbachyty передбачити *v.t.*
　anticipate
peredbachyty передбачити *v.t*
　foresee
peredchasnyi передчасний *a.*
　premature
peredchasnyi передчасний *a.*
　previous
peredchuttia передчуття *n.*
　premonition
peredchuvaty передчувати *v.t.*
　apprehend
peredmistia передмістя *n.*
　suburb

peredmova передмова *n*
foreword
perednia lapa передня лапа *n*
foreleg
perednii передній *a* front
peredovyi передовий *a* foremost
peredovyi передовий *a.* forward
peredovytsia передовиця *n*
editorial
peredozuvannia передозування
n. overdose
peredplichchia передпліччя *n*
forearm
peredrukovuvaty
передруковувати *v.t.* reprint
peredshliubnyi передшлюбний
a. premarital
peredumova передумова *n.*
presupposition
pereduvaty передувати *v.t.*
antecede
peredvishchaty передвіщати *v.t.*
portend
peredzvin передзвін *n.* jingle
perehaniaty переганяти *v.t.* still
perehaniaty litaky переганяти
літаки *v.t* ferry
perehliad перегляд *n.* revision
perehliadaty переглядати *v.t.*
revise
perehlianuty переглянути *v.t.*
peruse
perehovory переговори *n.*
negotiation
perehovory переговори *n.* parley
perehravaty перегравати *v.t.*
overact
pereimaty переймати *v.t.* adopt
perekazuvaty переказувати *v.t.*
paraphrase
perekhid перехід *n.* trek
perekhidnyi перехідний *n.*
transitive

perekhidnyi period перехідний
період *n.* transition
perekhopliuvannia
перехоплювання *n.*
interception
perekhopyty перехопити *v.t.*
intercept
perekhrestia перехрестя *n.*
intersection
perekhytryty перехитрити *v.t.*
outwit
pereklad переклад *n.* translation
perekladach перекладач *n.*
interpreter
perekladnyi перекладний *a.*
transferable
perekladyna перекладина *n.*
girder
perekladyny перекладини *n.*
rung
pereklychka перекличка *n.* roll-
call
pereklyk переклик *n* muster
perekonanist переконаність *n*
conviction
perekonannia переконання *n.*
persuasion
perekonanyi переконаний *a*
earnest
perekonanyi kholostiak
переконаний холостяк *n*
agamist
perekonaty переконати *v. t*
convince
perekonlyvyi переконливий *adj.*
cogent
perekonuvaty переконувати *v.i.*
dehort
perekonuvaty переконувати *v.t.*
reassure
perekruchuvaty перекручувати
v.t. sophisticate
perekryttia перекриття *n* overlap

perekryvaty перекривати *v.t.*
overlap

perekydannia перекидання *n.*
somersault

perekydaty перекидати *v.t.*
overthrow

perekydatysia перекидатися *v. i.*
capsize

pereliakanyi переляканий *a.*
afraid

perelit переліт *n* flight

pereliub перелюб *n.* adulteration

pereliubstvuvaty
перелюбствувати *v.t.*
adulterate

perelyvannia переливання *n.*
supervision

perelyvatysia cherez krai
переливатися через край *v.t*
overrun

peremahaty перемагати *v.t.*
vanquish

peremezhovuvaty
перемежовувати *v.t.* punctuate

peremishchaty переміщати *v.t.*
shift

peremishchennia переміщення
n. permutation

peremizhnyi переміжний *a.*
alternate

peremoha перемога *n.* victory

peremohty перемогти *v. t.* defeat

peremohty перемогти *v.t.* worst

peremozhets переможець *n.*
victor

peremozhnyi переможний *a.*
victorious

peremychky перемички *n.* lintel

peremykach перемикач *n.* switch

peremykaty перемикати *v. t*
commute

peremyria перемир'я *n.* truce

perenesennia перенесення *n.*
transfer

perenesty перенести *v.* born

perenosnyi переносний *a.*
portable

perenosyty переносити *v.t* bear

pereobtiazhuvaty
переобтяжувати *v.t.*
overburden

pereotsiniuvaty переоцінювати
v.t. overrate

perepel перепел *n.* quail

pereplutaty переплутати *v.t.* mull

perepochynok перепочинок *v.t.*
bait

perepolokh переполох *v.i.* stir

perepona перепона *n.* obstacle

perepovnenyi переповнений *a.*
replete

pereprava переправа *n* ferry

perepravliaty переправляти *v. t.*
convey

perepustka перепустка *n.* permit

perepys перепис *n.* census

perepysuvaty переписувати *v. t.*
enumerate

pererobliaty переробляти *v.t.*
alter

pererobliaty переробляти *v. t.*
change

pererva перерва *n.* interruption

perervaty перервати *v.i* abort

pereryvaty переривати *v.t.*
interrupt

pereryvchastyi переривчастий
a fitful

peresadzhuvaty пересаджувати
v.t graft

pereselennia переселення *n.*
transmigration

pereseliaty переселяти *v.t.*
transplant

pereseliatysia переселятися *v.i.*
trek

pereshkoda перешкода *n*
drawback

pereshkodzhaiuchyi
перешкоджаючий *a.*
obstructive

pereshkodzhaty перешкоджати
v.i. interfere

pereshkodzhaty перешкоджати
v.t. thwart

peresidaty пересідати *v.t.*
transfer

peresliduvannia переслідування
n. pursuance

peresliduvaty переслідувати *v.t.*
victimize

**peresliduvaty v sudovomu
poriadku** переслідувати
в судовому порядку *v.t.*
prosecute

perestaratysia перестаратися *v.t.*
overdo

perestavaty переставати *v. i.*
cease

perestrilka перестрілка *n.*
skirmish

perestromliuvaty
перестромлювати *v.t.* spike

perestupaty переступати *v.t.*
transgress

peresuvannia пересування *n.*
movement

peresuvaty пересувати *v.t.* shunt

peresuvatysia пересуватися *v.t*
ambulate

peresuvatysia kolonoiu
пересуватися колоною *v.i.* file

peresyliuvaty пересилювати *v.t.*
overpower

peresyliuvaty пересилювати *v.t.*
overrule

perets перець *n.* pepper

perets chervonyi перець
червоний *n* capsicum

perets hostryi перець гострий *n.*
chilli

peretvorennia перетворення *n.*
reduction

peretvoriuvaty перетворювати *v.
t* convert

peretvoriuvaty na ridynu
перетворювати на рідину *v.t.*
liquefy

peretvoriuvaty v hotivku
перетворювати в готівку *v. t.*
cash

peretvoriuvatysia
перетворюватися *v.t.* pivot

peretvoriuvatysia na otset
перетворюватися на оцет *v.*
acetify

peretvoryty na miaku masu
перетворити на м'яку масу *v.t.*
pulp

peretyn перетин *n.* crossing

peretynaty перетинати *v. t* cross

peretynatysia перетинатися *v.t.*
intersect

perevaha перевага *n.* advantage

perevaha перевага *n* start

perevaliuvannia перевалювання
n. preponderance

perevaliuvaty перевалювати *v.i.*
preponderate

perevantazhennia
перевантаження *n* overload

perevantazhuvaty
перевантажувати *v.t.* overload

perevariuvaty переварювати *v.
t.* digest

perevazhannia переважання *n.*
predominance

perevazhaty переважати *v.i.*
predominate

perevazhuvaty переважувати *v.t.*
outweigh
perevernutyi перевернутий *a.*
topsy turvy
perevershuvaty перевершувати
v.t. out-balance
perevershuvaty chyselno
перевершувати чисельно *v.t.*
outnumber
perevershyty перевершити *v.t.*
outdo
perevertaty перевертати *v.t.*
invert
perevertaty перевертати *v.t.*
subvert
perevezennia перевезення *n.*
cartage
pereviriaty перевіряти *v.t.*
validate
pereviriaty zvitnist перевіряти
звітність *v.t.* audit
perevirka перевірка *n.* verification
pereviryty перевірити *v.t.* verify
perevizny zasoby перевізни
засоби *n* conveyance
perevodyty переводити *v.t.*
translate
perevorot переворот *n.* upheaval
perevozyty перевозити *v.t.*
transport
perevtoma перевтома *n.*
overwork
perevtomliuvatysia
перевтомлюватися *v.i.*
overwork
perevydannia перевидання *n.*
reprint
perevyshchennia перевищення
n. surplus
perevyshchuvaty перевищувати
v.t exceed
perevyshchuvaty перевищувати
v.i excel

perevyshchuvaty перевищувати
v.t. top
perevytrachaty перевитрачати
v.t. overdraw
perezariad перезаряд *n*
overcharge
perezariadzhaty перезаряджати
v.t. overcharge
perezhovuvaty пережовувати *v.t.*
masticate
perezhyty пережити *v.t.* outlive
perforuvaty перфорувати *v.t.*
perforate
period період *n.* period
periodychne vydannia
періодичне видання *n.*
periodical
periodychnyi періодичний *a.*
periodical
perlyna перлина *n.* pearl
pero перо *n* feather
perpendykuliar перпендикуляр
n. perpendicular
perpendykuliarnyi
перпендикулярний *a.*
perpendicular
persh перш *adv.* before
pershoriadnyi першорядний *n.*
paramount
pershyi перший *a* first
pershyi перший *a.* premier
pershyi prymirnyk перший
примірник *n* first
personal персонал *n.* personnel
personalnyi персональний *a.*
personal
personazh персонаж *n.*
personage
personifikatsiia персоніфікація
n. personification
perspektyva перспектива *n.*
opportunity

perspektyvnyi перспективний *a.* prospective

perspektyvy перспективи *n.* possibility

persyk персик *n.* peach

peruka перука *n.* wig

perukar перукар *n.* barber

pervisnyi первісний *a.* primeval

pervynnyi первинний *a.* primary

peryferiia периферія *n.* periphery

peryla перила *n.* rail

pestytsyd пестицид *n.* pesticide

pestyty пестити *v. t.* caress

pestytysia пеститися *v.t* endear

pesymist песиміст *n.* pessimist

pesymistychnyi песимістичний *a.* pessimistic

pesymizm песимізм *n.* pessimism

petelka петелька *n* eyelet

petlia петля *n.* loop

pevna kilkist певна кількість *n.* aliquot

pevnyi певний *a* decisive

pevnyi певний *a* definite

pianino піаніно *n.* piano

pianist піаніст *n.* pianist

pianytsia п'яниця *n* bibber

piat п'ять *n* five

piata п'ята *n.* heel

piatdesiat п'ятьдесят *n.* fifty

piatnadtsiat п'ятнадцять *n* fifteen

piatnytsia п'ятниця *n.* Friday

piatykutnyk п'ятикутник *n.* pentagon

piavka п'явка *n.* leech

pich піч *n.* oven

pich піч *n.* stove

pid під *prep* beneath

pid під *prep.* under

pid під *prep.* underneath

pid chas під час *prep* during

pid uklon під уклон *adv* downwards

pidbadoriuvaty підбадьорювати *v. t* encourage

pidbir підбір *n* match

pidboriddia підборіддя *n.* chin

pidburiuvalnyi підбурювальний *a.* seditious

pidburiuvannia підбурювання *n.* instigation

pidburiuvannia do zakolotu підбурювання до заколоту *n.* sedition

pidburiuvaty підбурювати *v.t.* abet

pidburiuvaty підбурювати *v.t* foment

piddatlyvist піддатливість *v.t.* give

piddatlyvyi піддатливий *a.* supple

piddavaty піддавати *v.t.* subject

piddavaty nebezpetsi піддавати небезпеці *v. t.* endanger

piddavaty nebezpetsi піддавати небезпеці *v.t.* peril

piddavaty ostrakizmu піддавати остракізму *v.t.* ostracize

piddavaty sumnivu піддавати сумніву *v.t* query

piddavatysia піддаватися *v.i.* succumb

pidfarbovuvaty підфарбовувати *v.t.* tincture

pidhaniaty підганяти *v. t* bustle

pidhliadaty підглядати *v.i.* peep

pidhonka підгонка *n* fit

pidhotovchyi підготовчий *a.* preparatory

pidhotovchyi zakhid підготовчий захід *n* preliminary

pidhotovka підготовка *n.* preparation

pidhotovliaty підготовляти *v.t.* prepare

pidiom підйом *n.* climb1
pidiom підйом *n.* rise
pidiomnyi kran підйомний кран
n crane
pidkabluchnyk підкаблучник *n.*
henpecked
pidkazka підказка *n.* tip
pidkazuvaty підказувати *v.t.*
suggest
pidkhid підхід *n.* approach
pidkhodyty підходити *v.t.*
approach
pidkhozhyi підхожий *a* eligible
pidkladaty podushku підкладати
подушку *v. t* cushion
pidkladka підкладка *n* lining
pidkladka підкладка *n* pillow
pidkorennia підкорення *n.*
subjugation
pidkoriatysia підкорятися *v. i*
comply
pidkotyty підкотити *v.t.* wheel
pidkresliuvaty підкреслювати *v.t.*
underline
pidkydaty підкидати *v.t.* palm
pidlabuznyk підлабузник *n.*
sycophant
pidlehlyi підлеглий *a.* inferior
pidlehlyi підлеглий *n* subordinate
pidleshchuvatysia
підлещуватися *v.t.* wheedle
pidlisok підлісок *n.* coppice
pidlist підлість *n.* meanness
pidlitkovyi vik підлітковий вік *n.*
teens
pidlitok підліток *n.* teenager
pidloha підлога *n* floor
pidlokitnyk підлокітник *n* elbow
pidlyi підлий *a.* abject
pidlyi підлий *a.* nefarious
pidmaister підмайстер *n.*
apprentice
pidmitannia підмітання *n.* sweep

pidmitaty підмітати *v.i.* sweep
pidmorhuvaty підморгувати *v.i.*
wink
pidnebinnia піднебіння *n.* palate
pidnebinnyi піднебінний *a.*
palatal
pidnesenist піднесеність *n.* fort
pidnesenist піднесеність *n.*
sublimity
pidnesennia піднесення *n*
elevation
pidnesenyi піднесений *a.* sublime
pidneslyvist піднесливість *n.*
servility
pidniaty підняти *v.t.* hoist
pidniatyi піднятий *a* erect
pidnimaty піднімати *v.i.* heave
pidnimaty піднімати *v.t.* uplift
pidnimaty na smikh піднімати на
сміх *v.t.* ridicule
pidnimaty za dopomohoiu
vazhilia піднімати за
допомогою важіля *v.t.* lever
pidnimaty zakolot піднімати
заколот *v.i.* rebel
pidnimatysia підніматися *v.i.*
scramble
pidnos піднос *n.* tray
pidnoshennia підношення *n.*
offering
pidnosyty підносити *v.t.* present
pidnosytysia підноситися *v.i.*
tower
pidopichna osoba підопічна
особа *n.* ward
pidopichnyi підопічний *n.*
responsibility
pidoshva підошва *n.* sole
pidozra підозра *n.* surmise
pidozra підозра *n.* suspicion
pidozrilyi підозрілий *a.* suspect
pidozriuvanyi підозрюваний *n*
suspect

pidozriuvaty підозрювати *v.t.*
suspect
pidpal підпал *n* arson
pidperizuvaty підперізувати *v.t.*
gird
pidpirka підпірка *n.* prop
pidporiadkovanist
підпорядкованість *n*
dependence
pidporiadkovuvaty
підпорядковувати *v.t.*
subordinate
pidporiadkuvannia
підпорядкування *n.* conformity
pidpryiemstvo підприємство *n.*
venture
pidpylyi підпилий *a.* tipsy
pidpyraty підпирати *v.t.* prop
pidpys підпис *n.* signature
pidpysaty підписати *v.t.* sign
pidpyska підписка *n.* subscription
pidpysuvatysia підписуватися
v.t. subscribe
pidrakhovuvaty підраховувати *v.*
t. count
pidrakhovuvaty підраховувати
v.t. reckon
pidrakhovuvaty holosy
підраховувати голоси *v.t.* poll
pidrakhuvaty підрахувати *v.t.*
tally
pidriadnyi підрядний *a.*
subordinate
pidriadnyk підрядник *n* contractor
pidrizaty підрізати *v.t.* prune
pidroblenyi підроблений *a* bogus
pidrobliaty підробляти *a.*
counterfeit
pidrobliuvach підроблювач *n.*
counterfeiter
pidruchnyk підручник *a.* tutorial
pidrumianiuvaty підрум'янювати
v.t. toast

pidryvaty підривати *v.t.*
undermine
pidryvna diialnist підривна
діяльність *n.* subversion
pidryvnyi підривний *a.*
subversive
pidshtovkhnuty підштовхнути
v.t. nudge
pidshyty підшити *v.t* file
pidslipuvatyi підсліпуватий *n.*
purblind
pidslukhovuvaty підслуховувати
v.t. overhear
pidsolodzhuvaty підсолоджувати
v.t. sweeten
pidstava підстава *n.* basement
pidstava підстава *n.* cause
pidsterihaty підстерігати *v.t.*
waylay
pidstupnist підступність *n.* guile
pidsudnyi підсудний *n* defendant
pidsumok підсумок *n.* total
pidsumovuvaty підсумовувати
v.t. summarize
pidsushuvaty підсушувати *v.t.*
parch
pidsyliuvach підсилювач *n*
amplifier
pidtekst підтекст *n.* undertone
pidtochuvaty підточувати *v.t.* fret
pidtrymka підтримка *n* behalf
pidtrymuvaty підтримувати *v.t.*
maintain
pidtrymuvaty підтримувати *v.t.*
second
pidtrymuvaty vohon
підтримувати вогонь *v.t.* stoke
pidtverdzhennia підтвердження
n confirmation
pidtverdzhuvaty підтверджувати
v.t. corroborate
pidviazka підв'язка *n.* garter

pidvodna techiia підводна течія *n.* undercurrent
pidvodnyi підводний *a* submarine
pidvodnyi choven підводний човен *n.* submarine
pidvyshchennia підвищення *v.t.* raise
pidvyshchuietsia підвищується *adv.* up
pidvyshchuvaty підвищувати *v.t.* heighten
pidvyshchuvaty po sluzhbi підвищувати по службі *v. t* elevate
pidzemnyi підземний *a.* subterranean
pidzemnyi svit підземний світ *n.* underworld
pidzhaty піджати *v.t.* purse
piedestal п'єдестал *n.* pedestal
pihmei пігмей *n.* pigmy
piimannia піймання *n.* catch
piimaty v pastku піймати в пастку *v.t.* snare
piimaty v siti піймати в сіті *v.t* mesh
pik пік *n.* peak
pikantnist пікантність *n.* poignancy
pikantnyi пікантний *a.* piquant
pikantnyi пікантний *a.* poignant
piket пікет *n.* picket
piketuvaty пікетувати *v.t.* picket
pikhota піхота *n.* infantry
pikhotynets піхотинець *n.* peon
pikhva піхва *n.* vagina
pikhvy піхви *n.* scabbard
pikiruvannia пікірування *n* swoop
pikluvannia піклування *n.* wardship
pikluvatysia піклуватися *v. i.* care
piknik пікнік *n.* picnic
pilhovyi пільговий *a.* preferential

piliulia пілюля *n.* pill
pilot пілот *n.* aviator
pilotuvaty пілотувати *v.t.* pilot
pina піна *n* foam
pioner піонер *n.* pioneer
pioreia піорея *n.* pyorrhoea
piramida піраміда *n.* pyramid
pirat пірат *n.* pirate
piratstvo піратство *n.* piracy
pirnannia пірнання *n* plunge
pirnaty пірнати *v. i* dive
pishchanyi піщаний *a.* sandy
pishokhid пішохід *n.* pedestrian
pislia після *prep.* since
pislia після *prep* upon
pislia choho після чого *conj.* whereupon
pislia vsikh після всіх *adv.* last
pisnia пісня *n.* song
pisnyi пісний *a* fast
pisok пісок *n.* sand
pistolet пістолет *n.* pistol
pisuar пісуар *n.* urinal
pit піт *n.* perspiration
pit піт *n.* sweat
piton пітон *n.* python
piure пюре *n.* mash
pivden південь *n.* south
pivdennyi південний *a.* south
piven півень *n* cock
pivkulia півкуля *n.* hemisphere
pivnich північ *n.* north
pivnichnyi північний *a.* northerly
pivnoch північ *n.* midnight
piznannia пізнання *n.* knowledge
piznii пізній *a.* late
pizno пізно *adv.* late
pkhaty пхати *v.t.* jab
pkhykannia пхикання *n* whine
plachushchyi плачущий *a.* tearful
plakalnyky плакальники *n.* mourner
plakat плакат *n.* poster

plakaty плакати *v.i.* weep

plaksyvyi плаксивий *a.* lachrymose

plan план *n.* plan

planeruvaty планерувати *v.t.* plane

planeta планета *n.* planet

planetarnyi планетарний *a.* planetary

plantatsiia плантація *n.* plantation

planuvaty планувати *v.t.* plan

plany na maibutnie плани на майбутнє *n.* outlook

plashch плащ *n.* cloak

plata плата *n.* premium

plata za prostii плата за простій *n.* demurrage

platan платан *n.* sycamore

platforma платформа *n.* platform

plato плато *n.* plateau

platonichnyi платонічний *a.* platonic

platospromozhnist платоспроможність *n.* solvency

plattia плаття *n* dress

plattia плаття *n.* frock

plattiana shafa платтяна шафа *n.* wardrobe

platyty платити *v.t.* pay

platyty vdruhe платити вдруге *v.t.* repay

plavaty плавати *v.i* float

plavaty na yakhti плавати на яхті *v.i* yacht

plavaty v chomus плавати в чомусь *v.i.* swim

plavets плавець *n.* swimmer

plavka плавка *n* fuse

plavlennia плавлення *n.* fusion

plavno rukhatysia плавно рухатися *v.t.* glide

plavnyi плавний *a.* smooth

plavnyk плавник *n* fin

plavuchist плавучість *n* buoyancy

plavuchyi плавучий *a.* natant

plavylna chasha плавильна чаша *n.* crevet

plavylnia плавильня *n.* foundry

plavyty плавити *v.t.* fuse

plazuvaty плазувати *v. i* creep

plebistsyt плебісцит *n.* plebiscite

pleche плече *n.* shoulder

plekaty плекати *v. t.* cherish

plekaty плекати *v.t.* mother

plemia плем'я *n.* tribe

pleminnyi племінний *a.* tribal

pleminnyk племінник *n.* nephew

pleminnytsia племінниця *n.* niece

plentatysia плентатися *v. t* crawl

pleskaty плескати *v.i.* pop

pleskaty yazykom плескати язиком *v.t.* jabber

pleskatysia плескатися *v.i.* splash

plesty intryhy плести інтриги *v.t.* plot

plesty z ocheretu плести з очерету *v. t.* cane

pletinnia плетіння *n.* wicker

pliama пляма *n.* smear

pliamkaty плямкати *v.t.* munch

pliamochka плямочка *n.* speck

pliamuvaty плямувати *v.t.* spot

pliashka пляшка *n* bottle

pliazh пляж *n* beach

plidnyi плідний *a.* fruitful

plidnyi плідний *a.* prolific

plitka плітка *n.* gossip

pliumazh плюмаж *n* aigrette

plius плюс *n* plus

pliushch плющ *n* ivy

pliuvalnytsia плювальниця *n.* spittoon

pliuvaty плювати *v.i.* spit

pliuvok плювок *n* spittle
plivka плівка *n* film
plodyty плодити *v.t.* propagate
ploshcha площа *n* area
ploshcha zemli v akrakh площа
землі в акрах *n.* acreage
ploshchyna площина *n* flat
ploskyi плоский *a* level
ploskyi плоский *a.* plane
plot плоть *n* flesh
plotskyi плотський *a.* sensuous
pluh плуг *n.* plough
plutanyna плутанина *n.* maze
plutaty плутати *v.t.* muddle
plyn плин *n* lapse
plyta плита *n.* plate
plyvun пливун *n.* quicksand
pnevmoniia пневмонія *n.*
pneumonia
po по *prep.* around
po по *prep* down
po batkovi по батькові *a.* paternal
po vsomu по всьому *adv.*
throughout
pobachennia побачення *n.*
appointment
pobachennia побачення *n.* tryst
pobachyty побачити *v.t.* sight
pobichnyi побічний *a.* incidental
pobilka побілка *n.* whitewash
pobizhnyi побіжний *a.* fugitive
poblazhlyvist поблажливість *n.*
indulgence
poblazhlyvyi поблажливий *a.*
indulgent
poblyzu поблизу *adv.* near
poboiuvannia побоювання *n.*
anticipation
poboiuvannia побоювання *n.*
misgiving
poboiuvatysia побоюватися *v.i*
fear
pobornyk поборник *n.* protagonist

pobyty побити *v.t.* wallop
pochatkivets початківець *n.*
novice
pochatkovyi початковий *a.* initial
pochatkovyi початковий *a.*
original
pochatok початок *n.* beginning
pochatok початок *n.* prime
pochesnyi почесний *a.* honorary
pochet почет *n.* suite
pochuttia почуття *n* feeling
pochuttia obrazy почуття образи
n. resentment
pochuttia spushenosti почуття
спушеності *n.* void
pochynaty починати *v.t.*
auspicate
pochynatysia починатися *v. t*
commence
pochytaty почитати *v.t.* revere
podacha подача *n.* innings
podacha m`iacha подача м'яча
n. serve
podahra подагра *n.* gout
podali подалі *adv.* further
podalshyi подальший *a* further
podarunok подарунок *n.* present
podarunok na pamiat подарунок
на пам'ять *n.* keepsake
podatok податок *n* duty
podatok na nadprybutok
податок на надприбуток *n.*
supertax
podavaty подавати *v.i.* provide
podavaty miach подавати м'яч
v.i bowl
podavaty prokhannia подавати
прохання *v.t.* petition
podiaka подяка *n.* gratitude
podiaka подяка *n.* thanks
podiakuvaty подякувати *v.t.*
thank
podibnist подібність *n.* likeness

podibno подібно *adv* alike
podibnyi подібний *a.* analogous
podibnyi do zhinky подібний до
    жінки *a* effeminate
podiia подія *n.* happening
podil поділ *n.* separation
podilyty navpil поділити навпіл
    v.t. halve
podobatysia подобатися *v.i.*
    please
podolaty подолати *v.t.* overcome
podorozh подорож *n* travel
podorozhnii подорожній *n.*
    wayfarer
podorozhnyk подорожник *n.*
    plantain
podorozhuvaty подорожувати
    v.i. journey
podovzhuvaty подовжувати *v.t.*
    lengthen
podraznyk подразник *n.* irritant
podriapaty подряпати *v.t.* scratch
podriapyna подряпина *n.* scratch
podribniuvaty подрібнювати *v.t.*
    pound
podrimaty подрімати *v.i.* nap
podrizaty zhyvoplit подрізати
    живопліт *v.t* hedge
podruzhnii подружній *n.* spousal
podruzhzhia подружжя *n.*
    matrimony
podushka подушка *n.* pad
poduv подув *n.* whiff
podviinyi подвійний *a* double
podviria подвір'я *n.* yard
podvoity подвоїти *v.t.* redouble
podvyh подвиг *n.* coup
podvyh подвиг *n* exploit
podyv подив *n* daze
poet поет *n.* poet
poetesa поетеса *n.* poetess
poetychnist поетичність *n.* poetry
poetychnyi поетичний *a.* poetic

poetyka поетика *n.* poetics
poeziia поезія *n.* poesy
pohan погань *n.* muck
pohana robota погана робота *n*
    bungle
pohana slava погана слава *n*
    disrepute
pohane stavlennia погане
    ставлення *n.* misuse
pohane upravlinnia погане
    управління *n.* misrule
pohano погано *adv.* badly
pohano povodytysia погано
    поводитися *v.i.* misbehave
pohanyi поганий *a.* sinister
pohanyty поганити *v.t.* pollute
pohashaty погашати *v.t.* satisfy
pohashennia погашення *n.*
    redemption
pohirshuvaty погіршувати *v.t.*
    worsen
pohladzhuvaty погладжувати *v.t.*
    stroke
pohliad погляд *n* gaze
pohliad nazad погляд назад *n.*
    retrospect
pohlynaty поглинати *v.t* absorb
pohlynennia поглинення *n.*
    merger
pohoda погода *n* weather
pohodzhenist погодженість *n.*
    conformity
pohodzhuvatysia погоджуватися
    v.i. agree
pohodzhuvatysia погоджуватися
    v.t. concede
pohonia погоня *v. t.* chase1
pohonych sloniv погонич слонів
    n. mahout
pohrabuvannia пограбування *n.*
    robbery
pohrabuvaty пограбувати *v.t.*
    plunder

pohrib погріб *n* cellar
pohrozhuvaty погрожувати *v.t.* threaten
poias пояс *n.* waistband
poiasnennia пояснення *n* explanation
poiasniuvaty пояснювати *v. t.* explain
poiasok kolony поясок колони *n* annulet
poiava поява *n* appearance
poiednuvaty поєднувати *v.t.* mate
poity поїти *v.t.* water
poizd поїзд *n.* train
poizdka поїздка *n.* journey
poizdka поїздка *n* ride
pokaiannia покаяння *n.* repentance
pokarannia покарання *n.* punishment
pokaz показ *n.* signification
pokazannia показання *n.* testimony
pokazhchyk покажчик *n.* index
pokaznyi показний *a.* conspicuous
pokaznyk показник *n.* quotient
pokazuvaty показувати *v.t.* show
pokazuvaty zhestom показувати жестом *v.i.* motion
pokazuvatysia показуватися *v.i.* appear
pokhid похід *n* crusade
pokhmuryi похмурий *a.* moody
pokhmuryi похмурий *a.* woebegone
pokhmuryi pohliad похмурий погляд *n.* frown
pokhmuryi vyhliad похмурий вигляд *n.* scowl
pokhodzhennia походження *n.* ancestry

pokhoron похорон *n.* funeral
pokhoronna pisnia похоронна пісня *n.* monody
pokhoronne bahattia похоронне багаття *n.* pyre
pokhovannia поховання *n.* sepulture
pokhvala похвала *n* commendation
pokhvalnyi похвальний *a.* commendable
pokhvalnyi похвальний *a* creditable
pokhyloho viku похилого віку *a* elderly
pokhylyi похилий *adj.* declivous
pokhytuvannia похитування *n.* stagger
pokirnist покірність *n.* acquiescence
pokirnist покірність *n.* humility
pokirnyi покірний *a* dutiful
pokirnyi покірний *a.* submissive
pokladatysia покладатися *v.i.* rely
pokladenyi покладений *a* incumbent
poklasty покласти *v.t.* put
poklasty kinets покласти кінець *v.t* abolish
pokloniatysia поклонятися *v.t.* worship
pokloninnia поклоніння *n.* worship
pokloninnia odnomu Bohu поклоніння одному Богу *n.* monolatry
poklykannia покликання *n.* calling
poklykaty покликати *v.t.* summon
pokoivka покоївка *n.* maid
pokolinnia покоління *n.* generation

pokora покора *n.* submission
pokrovytel покровитель *n.* patron
pokryshka покришка *n.* cover
pokryty покрити *v.t.* sheet
pokryty sazheiu покрити сажею *v.t.* soot
pokrytyi lystiam покритий листям *a.* leafy
pokrytyi shvamy покритий швами *a.* seamy
pokryvalo покривало *n.* coverlet
pokryvaty bryzhamy покривати брижами *v.t.* ripple
pokryvaty merezheiu покривати мережею *v.t.* net
pokryvaty metalom покривати металом *v.t.* plate
pokryvaty olovom покривати оловом *v.t.* tin
pokryvaty shkiroiu покривати шкірою *v.t* skin
pokryvaty tonkoiu plivkoiu покривати тонкою плівкою *v.t* film
pokupets покупець *n.* buyer
pokupka покупка *n.* purchase
poky поки *n. conj.* till
poky поки *conj.* while
pokydaty покидати *v.t.* abandon
pokydky покидьки *n.* refuse
pola пола *n.* lap
pole поле *n* field
polehshennia полегшення *n.* alleviation
polehshennia полегшення *n.* relief
polehshuvaty полегшувати *v.t.* appease
polehshuvaty полегшувати *v. t* ease
polehshuvaty полегшувати *v.t* facilitate

polehshuvaty полегшувати *v.i.* lighten
poliahaty полягати *v. i* consist
Poliarna zirka Полярна зірка *n.* loadstar
poliarnyi полярний *n.* polar
polihamiia полігамія *n.* polygamy
polihamnyi полігамний *a.* polygamous
polihlot поліглот *n.* polyglot1
polipshennia поліпшення *n.* improvement
polipshuvaty поліпшувати *v. t* better
polipshuvatysia поліпшуватися *v.t.* ameliorate
polirovka поліровка *n* polish
poliruvaty полірувати *v.t.* polish
polit політ *n.* voyage
politeist політеїст *n.* polytheist
politeistychnyi політеїстичний *a.* polytheistic
politekhnichnyi політехнічний *a.* polytechnic
politekhnikum політехнікум *n.* polytechnic
politseiskyi поліцейський *n.* policeman
politsiia поліція *n.* police
politychnyi політичний *a.* politic
polityk політик *n.* politician
polityka політика *n.* policy
polityka політика *n.* politics
polius полюс *n.* pole
poliuvannia полювання *n.* chase2
poliuvannia полювання *n* hunt
poliuvaty полювати *v.t.* hunt
polk полк *n.* regiment
polkovnyk полковник *n.* colonel
polo поло *n.* polo
poloh полог *n.* canopy
polokhatysia полохатися *v.i.* shy

polokhlyvyi полохливий *a.* timid
polomka поломка *n* breakage
polonennia полонення *n.* captivity
polonenyi полонений *a.* captive
polonyty полонити *v. t.* captivate
polosa полоса *n.* strip
poloskaty полоскати *v.i.* gargle
polotno полотно *n.* linen
poloty полоти *v.t.* weed
polovyi hravets na livii storoni vid boulera v kryketi польовий гравець на лівій стороні від боулера в крикеті *n.* mid-off
polovyi hravets na pravii storoni vid boulera v kryketi польовий гравець на правій стороні від боулера в крикеті *n.* mid-on
polovyna половина *n.* half
polovynnyi половинний *a* half
polozhennia положення *n.* case
poluden полудень *n.* midday
poluden полудень *n.* noon
polumia полум'я *n* blaze
polumia полум'я *n* flame
polumianity полум'яніти *v.i* flame
polunytsia полуниця *n.* strawberry
polyn полин *n.* wormwood
pomaranchevyi помаранчевий *a* orange
pomerty померти *v. i* decease
pomerty померти *v. i* die
pomiakshennia пом'якшення *n.* mitigation
pomiakshuvaty пом'якшувати *v.t.* alleviate
pomiakshuvatysia пом'якшуватися *v.i.* relent
pomichaty помічати *v.t.* remark
pomichnyk помічник *n* help
pomidor помідор *n.* tomato

pomirnist помірність *n.* temperance
pomirnyi помірний *a* medium
pomirnyi помірний *a.* moderate
pomishchaty поміщати *v.t.* place
pomishchaty poseredyni поміщати посередині *v.t.* sandwich
pomist поміст *n.* dais
pomitno помітно *adj* perceptible
pomitnyi помітний *a.* appreciable
pomnozhyty помножити *v.t.* multiply
pompeznist помпезність *n.* pomposity
pompeznyi помпезний *a.* pompous
pomsta помста *n.* revenge
pomsta помста *n.* vengeance
pomstytysia помститися *v.i.* retaliate
pomyliatysia помилятися *v. i* err
pomyliatysia помилятися *v.t.* mistake
pomylka помилка *n* error
pomylka помилка *n.* miscarriage
pomylkova dumka помилкова думка *n.* misbelief
pomylkovyi помилковий *a.* inaccurate
pomyluvannia помилування *n.* pardon
pomyluvaty помилувати *v.t.* pardon
ponad понад *adv.* beyond
ponadnormovyi понаднормовий *adv.* overtime
ponadnormovyi chas понаднормовий час *n* overtime
ponedilok понеділок *n.* Monday
ponevoliuvaty поневолювати *v.t.* enslave
poni поні *n.* pony

poniattia поняття *n.* notion
ponosyty поносити *v.t.* vilify
po-novomu по-новому *adv.* anew
ponuryi понурий *a.* morose
ponyzhuvaty понижувати *v.t.* abase
poperechnyi поперечний *a* cross
poperechyna поперечина *n.* spoke
poperednii попередній *a.* preliminary
poperednyk попередник *n* forerunner
poperednyk попередник *n.* predecessor
poperedu попереду *adv.* ahead
poperedzhaty попереджати *v.t.* warn
poperedzhaty zazdalehid попереджати заздалегідь *v.t* forewarn
poperedzhennia попередження *n.* notification
poperedzhuvalnyi попереджувальний *a.* precautionary
poperek поперек *n.* loin
po-pershe по-перше *adv* first
popil попіл *n.* ash
popleskuvannia поплескування *n* pat
poplin поплін *n.* poplin
popovniuvaty поповнювати *v.t.* replenish
popravky поправки *n.pl.* amends
poprosyty попросити *v.t.* request
populiarnist популярність *n.* popularity
populiarnist популярність *n.* vogue
populiarnyi популярний *n* pop
populiarnyi популярний *a.* popular

populiaryzuvaty популяризувати *v.t.* popularize
popusk попуск *n.* connivance
popyt попит *n* request
porada порада *n* advice
poranennia поранення *n.* wound
poranyty поранити *v.t.* wound
poratysia поратися *v.t* handle
porazka поразка *n.* affection
poriadok порядок *n.* order
poriatunok порятунок *n* rescue
poriatunok порятунок *n.* salvation
porih поріг *n.* threshold
porivnialnyi порівняльний *a* comparative
porivniannia порівняння *n* comparison
porivniannia порівняння *n.* simile
porivniuiuchy z порівнюючи з *prep.* versus
porivniuvaty порівнювати *v. t* compare
porivniuvaty порівнювати *v.t.* parallel
poriz поріз *n* cut
porochnyi порочний *a.* vicious
poroda порода *n* breed
porodzhuvaty породжувати *v.t.* generate
poroshok порошок *n.* powder
poroshyty порошити *v.t.* dust
porozhnia poroda порожня порода *n* spoil
porozhnie mistse порожнє місце *n.* nothing
porozhnii порожній *a* blank
porozhnyna порожнина *n.* cavity
porshen поршень *n.* piston
port порт *n.* port
portal портал *n.* portal
portatyvnyi портативний *a.* handy
portfel портфель *n.* portfolio

portovi mytni zbory портові митні збори *n.* wharfage
portret портрет *n* portrayal
portretnyi zhyvopys портретний живопис *n.* portraiture
portsiia порція *n.* allowance
portyk портик *n.* portico
poruch поруч *adv.* nigh
poruch z поруч з *prep.* beside
poruchchia поруччя *n.* railing
poruchytel поручитель *n.* guarantee
poruchytelstvo поручительство *n.* surety
porushennia порушення *n* breach
porushennia travlennia порушення травлення *n.* indigestion
porushuvaty порушувати *v.t.* incite
porushuvaty spravu порушувати справу *v.t.* sue
porushuvaty zakon порушувати закон *v.t.* outrage
pory пори *n.* pore
porynaty поринати *v.t.* plunge
poselenets поселенець *n.* settler
poserednii посередній *a.* ordinary
poserednist посередність *n.* mediocrity
poserednyk посередник *n.* intermediary
poserednyk посередник *n.* mediator
poserednytstvo посередництво *n.* mediation
poserednytstvo посередництво *n.* mediation
posharpanyi пошарпаний *a.* threadbare
poshest пошесть *n.* pestilence

poshkodzhennia пошкодження *n.* damage
poshkodzhuvaty пошкоджувати *v. t.* damage
poshta пошта *n.* mail
poshtmeister поштмейстер *n.* postmaster
poshtove viddilennia поштове відділення *n.* post-office
poshtovi vytraty поштові витрати *n.* postage
poshtovkh поштовх *n.* push
poshtovyi поштовий *a.* postal
poshuk пошук *n.* quest
poshuky пошуки *n* rummage
poshyrennia поширення *n.* spread
poshyrenyi поширений *a.* prevalent
poshyriuvaty поширювати *v.t.* shed
poshyriuvaty chutky поширювати чутки *v.t.* rumour
poshyriuvatysia поширюватися *v.i.* spread
posiahannia посягання *n.* trespass
posiahaty посягати *v.t.* infringe
posibnyk посібник *n* manual
poslablennia послаблення *n.* abatement
poslabliaty послабляти *v.t.* mitigate
poslabliuvaty послаблювати *v. t.* enfeeble
poslabliuvaty послаблювати *v.t.* weaken
poslannia послання *n.* missive
poslaty послати *v.t.* send
poslatysia послатися *v.t.* refer
poslidovnist послідовність *n.* sequence

poslidovno послідовно *adv*
consecutively
poslidovnyi послідовний *adj.*
consecutive
poslidovnyk послідовник *n*
follower
posliduvaty послідувати *v.t* follow
posluzhlyvyi послужливий *adj.*
complacent
posluzhlyvyi послужливий *adj.*
complaisant
posmertnyi посмертний *a.* post-mortem
posmiiuvatysia посміюватися *v. i* chuckle
posmikhatysia посміхатися *v.i.* smile
posmikhovysko посміховисько *n.* scoff
posol посол *n.* ambassador
posolstvo посольство *n* embassy
pospikh поспіх *n.* haste
pospishaty поспішати *v.i.* hasten
pospishnyi поспішний *a* snap
post пост *n.* post
postachalnyk постачальник *n.* supplier
postachannia постачання *n.* procurement
postachaty постачати *v.t.* supply
postanova постанова *n* bylaw, bye-law
postava постава *n.* posture
postavliaty proviziiu поставляти провізію *v. i* cater
postiine mistse prozhyvannia постійне місце проживання *n* domicile
postiinyi постійний *a* abiding
postilni prynalezhnosti постільні приналежності *n.* bedding
postril постріл *n.* shot

postskryptum постскриптум *n.* postscript
postupalnyi поступальний *a.* onward
postupatysia поступатися *v.t.* surrender
postupka поступка *n* concession
postupovyi поступовий *a.* gradual
posud посуд *n.* crockery
posukha посуха *n* dry
posviachuvaty v lytsari посвячувати в лицарі *v.t.* knight
posylannia посилання *n.* link
posylaty povidomlennia посилати повідомлення *v.t.* notice
posylatysia посилатися *v.t* link
posylatysia na посилатися на *v.t.* allege
posyliuvaty посилювати *v.t.* reinforce
posyliuvatysia посилюватися *v.t.* intensify
posylka посилка *n.* parcel
posylnyi посильний *n.* messenger
posypaty посипати *v.t.* strew
potai prosuvatysia потай просуватися *v.i.* stalk
potainyi потайний *a.* secretive
potash поташ *n.* potash
potentsial потенціал *n.* potential
potentsiia потенція *n.* potency
potentsiinist потенційність *n.* potentiality
potentsiinyi потенційний *a.* potential
potertyi потертий *a.* shabby
potiah потяг *n.* appetence
potik потік *n* flow
potim потім *adv.* next

potity потіти *v.i.* perspire
potity потіти *v.i.* sweat
potmianity потьмяніти *v. t* dim
potochnyi поточний *a* current
potochnyi поточний *a* routine
potomstvo потомство *n.* offspring
potreba потреба *n* want
potrebuvaty потребувати *v.t.*
  need
potreby потреби *adv.* needs
po-tretie по-третє *adv.* thirdly
potribne потрібне *n* requisite
potribnyi потрібний *a* necessary
potriinyi потрійний *a.* triplicate
potriskuvaty потріскувати *v.t.*
  crackle
potroiennia потроєння *n.*
  triplication
potroiuvaty потроювати *v.t.*, triple
potsilunok поцілунок *n.* kiss
poturannia потурання *n.*
  condonation
potuzhnyi потужний *a.* potent
potuzhnyi потужний *a.* powerful
potvornist потворність *n.*
  ugliness
potvornyi потворний *a.* hideous
potvornyi потворний *a.* ugly
potylytsia потилиця *n.* nape
povaha повага *n* deference
povaha повага *n.* respect
povalennia повалення *n*
  overthrow
povalyty повалити *v.i.* topple
povazhaty поважати *v. t* esteem
povazhaty поважати *v. t* honour
povazhnyi поважний *a.* venerable
povchalna baza повчальна база
  n apologue
povchaty повчати *v.i.* sermonize
povedinka поведінка *n* behaviour
poverennnia повереннния *n.*
  resumption

poverkh поверх *n.* storey
poverkhnevyi поверхневий *a.*
  outward
poverkhnia поверхня *n.* surface
poverkhovist поверховість *n.*
  superficiality
poverkhovyi поверховий *a*
  cursory
povernennia повернення *n.*
  return
povernennia do zhyttia
  повернення до життя *n.* revival
povernuty повернути *v.i.* return
povertaty повертати *v.t.* restore
povertaty hroshi повертати
  гроші *n.* refund
povertatysia повертатися *v.i.*
  revert
poviazanyi z ictoriieiu
  пов'язаний з історією *a.*
  historical
poviazanyi z polizzkoiu
  пов'язаний з політикою *a.*
  political
poviazanyi z prylyvom
  пов'язаний з приливом *a.* tidal
poviazka пов'язка *n* deligate1
poviazuvaty пов'язувати *v.t* bind
povidomlennia повідомлення *n.*
  intimation
povidomliaty повідомляти *v.t.*
  inform
povidomliaty po telebachenniu
  повідомляти по телебаченню
  v.t. televise
poviia повія *n.* strumpet
povilnist повільність *n.* slowness
povilno повільно *adv.* slowly
povilnyi повільний *a* slow
povin повінь *n* flood
povirenyi повірений *n.* solicitor
povist повість *n.* novelette
povistka повістка *n.* agenda

povitria повітря *n* air
povitriana kulia повітряна куля *n.* balloon
povitrianyi повітряний *a.* aerial
povitrianyi повітряний *a.* airy
povna lozhka повна ложка *n.* spoonful
povnistiu повністю *adv* entirely
povnistiu повністю *adv.* wholly
povnistiu ruinuvaty повністю руйнувати *n.* wrack
povnolitnii повнолітній *a.* major
povnolittia повноліття *n.* majority
povnota повнота *n.* fullness
povnyi повний *a* complete
povnyi повний *adj.* crass
povnyi повний *a* downright
povnyi повний *a* utter
povnyi bazhannia повний бажання *a.* solicitous
povnyi komplekt повний комплект *n* complement
povody поводи *n.* rein
povodzhennia поводження *n.* treatment
povstalyi повсталий *a.* insurgent
povstanets повстанець *n.* insurgent
povstannia повстання *n.* uprising
povstavaty повставати *v.i.* revolt
povtorennia повторення *n.* reiteration
povtorennia повторення *n.* relapse
povtoriuvanyi повторюваний *a.* recurrent
povtoriuvaty повторювати *v.t.* repeat
povtoryty повторити *v.t.* reiterate
povynen повинен *v.* must
povz повз *prep.* past
povzannia повзання *n* crawl
povzty повзти *v.i.* snake

povzucha roslyna повзуча рослина *n* creeper
poza поза *n.* pose
poza поза *prep.* without
poza mezhamy поза межами *a.* outdoor
pozadu позаду *adv* after
pozadu позаду *prep* behind
pozashliubne spivzhyttia позашлюбне співжиття *n.* concubinage
pozashliubnyi позашлюбний *a* bastard
pozbavlennia позбавлення *n* forfeiture
pozbavlennia voli позбавлення волі *n.* confinement
pozbavlennia zhyttia позбавлення життя *n.* homicide
pozbavlenyi позбавлений *a* devoid
pozbavlenyi holovy позбавлений голови *adj.* acephalous
pozbavlenyi prostoty позбавлений простоти *a.* sophisticated
pozbavliaty позбавляти *v.t.* denude
pozbavliaty позбавляти *v.t.* relieve
pozbavliaty zakonnoi syly позбавляти законної сили *v.t.* invalidate
pozbavyty позбавити *v. t* deprive
pozbavyty vlady позбавити влади *v. t* depose
pozbutysia позбутися *v.t* forfeit
pozdorovlennia поздоровлення *n* congratulation
pozdorovliaty поздоровляти *v. t* congratulate
pozdorovliaty поздоровляти *v.t* hail

pozhadlyvist пожадливість *n.*
avidity
pozhadlyvyi пожадливий *a.*
greedy
pozhertvuvannia пожертвування
n. sacrifice
pozhovtity пожовтіти *v.t.* yellow
pozhvavlennia пожвавлення *n*
animation
pozhvavyty пожвавити *v.t.* wake
pozhylets пожилець *n.* occupant
pozhynaty пожинати *v.t.* reap
pozhyvnist поживність *n.*
richness
pozhyvnyi поживний *a.* nutritive
pozikhannia позіхання *n.* yawn
pozikhaty позіхати *v.i.* gape
pozikhaty позіхати *v.i.* yawn
poznachaty позначати *v. i* denote
poznachaty позначати *v.t.* label
poznachaty позначати *v.t* mark
poznachennia позначення *n.*
notation
poznachka позначка *n.* mark
poznaiomyty познайомити *v.t.*
acquaint
pozolota позолота *a.* gilt
pozov позов *n* claim
pozovna позовна *n.* count
pozuvaty позувати *v.i.* pose
pozychaty позичати *v.t.* lend
pozyka позика *n.* loan
pozytsiia позиція *n.* position
pozytyvnyi позитивний *a.* plus
pozytyvnyi позитивний *a.*
positive
pozyvach позивач *n* claimant
pozyvach позивач *n.* plaintiff
ppohane povodzhennia ппогане
поводження *n.* mal-treatment
prabatko прабатько *n* forefather
prachka прачка *n.* laundress

prahmatychnyi прагматичний *a.*
pragmatic
prahmatyzm прагматизм *n.*
pragmatism
prahnennia прагнення *n.*
aspiration
prahnennia прагнення *n.*
intention
prahnuchyi прагнучий *adj.* athirst
prahnuty прагнути *v.t.* aspire
prahnuty прагнути *v.i.* hanker
praktychni znannia практичні
знання *n.* lore
praktychnyi практичний *a.*
practical
praktyka практика *n.* practice
praktykuiuchyi likar
практикуючий лікар *n.*
practitioner
pralnia пральня *n.* laundry
prannia прання *n* wash
prapor прапор *n.* banner
praska праска *n.* iron
pratsia праця *n.* labour
pratsiuvaty працювати *v.i.* labour
pratsiuvaty nasosom працювати
насосом *v.t.* pump
pratsiuvaty stameskoiu
працювати стамескою *v. t.*
chisel
pratsiuvaty, yak rab працювати,
як раб *v.i.* slave
pratsivnyk працівник *n* employee
pratsovytyi працьовитий *a.*
industrious
praty прати *v. t* erase
praty i prasuvaty прати і
прасувати *v.t.* launder
pravda правда *n.* truth
pravdopodibnist
правдоподібність *n.*
verisimilitude

pravdopodibnyi правдоподібний *a.* probable

pravdyvist правдивість *n.* veracity

pravdyvyi правдивий *a.* truthful

pravednyi праведний *a.* godly

pravliachyi правлячий *n.* ruling

pravo право *n* right

pravoporushennia правопорушення *n.* violation

pravyi правий *a.* right

pravylno правильно *adv* aright

pravylnyi правильний *a* correct

pravylo правило *n.* rule

pravytel правитель *n.* ruler

pravyty правити *v.t.* rein

preambula преамбула *n.* preamble

predmet предмет *n.* matter

predmet bazhannia предмет бажання *n* desire

predmet odiahu предмет одягу *n.* garment

predmet zakhoplennia предмет захоплення *n.* admiration

predmety odiahu предмети одягу *n.* apparel

predok предок *n.* ancestor

predstavliaty представляти *v.t.* submit

predstavnyk представник *n.* representative

predstavnytskyi представницький *a.* representative

predykat предикат *n.* predicate

prefekt префект *n.* prefect

preferentsiia преференція *n.* preference

prefiks префікс *a.* particle

prefiks префікс *n.* prefix

prekrasnyi прекрасний *a.* admirable

prekrasnyi прекрасний *a.* lovely

prelat прелат *n.* prelate

preliudiia прелюдія *n.* prelude

premiera прем'єра *n.* premiere

premier-ministr прем'єр-міністр *n* premier

premiia премія *n* bonus

prepodobnyi преподобний *a.* reverend

prerohatyva прерогатива *n.* prerogative

presa преса *n* press

prestyzh престиж *n.* prestige

prestyzhnyi престижний *a.* prestigious

pretendent претендент *n* nominee

pretenziinist претензійність *n.* pretension

pretenziinyi претензійний *a.* pretentious

pretsedent прецедент *n.* precedent

preventyvnyi превентивний *a.* preventive

prezentatsiia презентація *n.* presentation

prezumptsiia презумпція *n.* presumption

prezydent президент *n.* president

prezydentskyi президентський *a.* presidential

prezyrlyva usmishka презирлива усмішка *n* sneer

prezyrlyvyi презирливий *a* contemptuous

prezyrstvo презирство *n* contempt

priakha пряха *n.* spinner

priama kyshka пряма кишка *n.* rectum

priamo прямо *adv.* straight

priamokutnyi прямокутний *a.*
rectangular
priamokutnyk прямокутник *n.*
rectangle
priamota прямота *n.* integrity
priamyi прямий *a* through
prianyi пряний *a.* spicy
priazha пряжа *n.* yarn
priazhka пряжка *n* buckle
priorytet пріоритет *n.* precedence
prizvyshche прізвище *n.*
surname
prizvysko прізвисько *n.* alias
pro про *prep* about
proba проба *n.* hallmark
probachnyi пробачний *a.* venial
probachyty пробачити *v.t.* remit
probih пробіг *n.* mileage
probii пробій *n.* rupture
probil пробіл *n* blank
probizhka пробіжка *n* scamper
problema проблема *n.* trouble
problematychnyi
проблематичний *a.* problematic
problysk проблиск *n.* ray
probudzhuvatysia
пробуджуватися *v.t.* awake
probyratysia пробиратися *v.i.*
wade
probyty пробити *v.t.* punch
probyvaty otvir пробивати отвір
v.t. puncture
prochyshchaty прочищати *v.t.*
purge
prochytannia прочитання *n.*
perusal
prodavaty продавати *v.t.* sell
prodavaty v rozdrib продавати в
роздріб *v.t.* retail
prodavaty z auktsionu
продавати з аукціону *v.t.*
auction

prodavets продавець *n.*
salesman
prodazh продаж *n.* sale
prodazhnist продажність *n.*
venality
prodazhnyi продажний *a.* venal
prodovzhennia продовження *n.*
continuation
prodovzhuvaty продовжувати *v.*
i. continue
prodovzhuvatysia
продовжуватися *v.i.* last
prodovzhyty продовжити *v.i.*
proceed
prodovzhyty продовжити *v.t.*
prolong
produkt продукт *n.* product
produktsiia продукція *n.* produce
produktsiia продукція *n.*
production
produktyvnist продуктивність *n.*
performance
produktyvnist продуктивність *n.*
productivity
produktyvnyi продуктивний *a.*
productive
proekt проект *n.* project
proektor проектор *n.* projector
proektsiia проекція *n* plane
proektsiia проекція *n.* projection
proektuvaty проектувати *v. t.*
design
profanuvaty профанувати *v.t.*
profile
profesiia професія *n.* profession
profesiia професія *n.* vocation
profesiinyi професійний *a.*
professional
profesor професор *n.* professor
profil профіль *n.* profile
prohalyna прогалина *n.* lacuna
prohnoz прогноз *n* forecast
prohnoz прогноз *n.* prediction

prohnozuvaty прогнозувати *v.t.*
predict
proholoshennia проголошення
n. proclamation
proholoshuvaty проголошувати
v.t. proclaim
prohrama програма *n.*
programme
prohrama програма *v.t.* project
prohres прогрес *n.* advancement
prohres прогрес *n.* progress
prohresuvaty прогресувати *v.i.*
progress
prohresyvnyi прогресивний *a.*
progressive
prohulianka прогулянка *n* ramble
prohulianka za muzhi mista
прогулянка за мужі міста *n.*
outing
prohulnyk прогульник *n.* shirker
proiasnennia прояснення *n*
clarification
proiasnyty прояснити *v. t* clarify
proiav прояв *n* display
proiavliaty проявляти *v. t* display
proizd проїзд *n.* thoroughfare
prokaza проказа *n.* lark
prokaza проказа *n.* leprosy
prokazhenyi прокажений *a.*
leprous
prokhach прохач *n.* petitioner
prokhannia прохання *n.* entreaty
prokhidnyi прохідний *a.*
practicable
prokhodyty проходити *v. t* elapse
prokhodyty проходити *v.i.* pass
prokhodyty stroiem проходити
строєм *v.i* troop
prokhodzhennia проходження *n.*
passage
prokhodzhuvatysia
проходжуватися *v.t.* saunter

prokholodnyi прохолодний *a*
cool
prokladaty shliakh прокладати
шлях *v.t.* pioneer
prokladaty shliakh прокладати
шлях *v.t.* work
prokladaty tunel прокладати
тунель *v.i.* tunnel
prokliattia прокляття *n* curse
prokliatyi проклятий *a.* accursed
proklin проклін *n.* damnation
proklynaty проклинати *v. t* curse
prokol прокол *n.* puncture
prokoliuvaty проколювати *v.t.*
pierce
proktor проктор *n.* proctor
prokuror прокурор *n.* attorney
prokysaty прокисати *v.t.* sour
prokyslyi прокислий *a.* sour
proloh пролог *n.* preface
proloh пролог *n.* prologue
prolom пролом *n.* fracture
prolom пролом *n* gap
prolyvaty проливати *v.i.* spill
prolyvnyi проливний *a.* torrential
promainuty промайнути *v.t.* zip
promakh промах *n* blunder
promakhuvatysia промахуватися
v.i blunder
promenystyi променистий *a.*
radiant
promin промінь *n* beam
promizhnyi проміжний *adj.*
annectant
promizhnyi проміжний *a.*
intermediate
promizhok проміжок *n.* interval
promochyty промочити *v.t.* wet
promova промова *n.* speech
promovets промовець *n.*
spokesman

promyslova pich dlia sushinnia промислова піч для сушіння *n.* kiln

pronos пронос *n* diarrhoea

pronosne проносне *n.* purgative

pronosnyi проносний *a* laxative

pronosnyi zasib проносний засіб *n.* laxative

pronosytysia zi svystom проноситися зі свистом *v.i.* whiz

pronykaiuchyi проникаючий *a.* ingrained

pronykaty проникати *v.t.* penetrate

pronyklyvist проникливість *n.* sagacity

pronyklyvyi проникливий *a.* shrewd

pronyknennia проникнення *n.* vision

pronyrlyvyi пронирливий *a.* nosy

pronyzlyvo krychaty пронизливо кричати *v. i* bray

pronyzlyvyi пронизливий *a.* shrill

pronyzlyvyi kryk пронизливий крик *n* yell

pronyzuvaty пронизувати *v.t.* saturate

pronyzuvaty spysom пронизувати списом *v.t.* lance

propahanda пропаганда *n.* propaganda

propahandyst пропагандист *n.* propagandist

propoloskaty прополоскати *v.t.* rinse

proponuvaty пропонувати *v. t* enact

proponuvaty tsinu пропонувати ціну *v.t* bid

proponuvaty vykonannia uhody пропонувати виконання угоди *v.t.* tender

proportsiia пропорція *n.* proportion

proportsiinyi пропорційний *a.* proportional

propovid проповідь *n.* gospel

propovidnyk проповідник *n.* preacher

propoviduvaty проповідувати *v.i.* preach

propozytsiia пропозиція *n* tender

propusk пропуск *n* pass

propuskaty пропускати *v.i.* skip

propyshchaty пропищати *v. i* cheep

prorakhunok прорахунок *n.* miscalculation

prorakhuvatysia прорахуватися *v.t.* miscalculate

prorochyi пророчий *a.* prophetic

prorok пророк *n.* prophet

prorokuvaty пророкувати *v.t.* prophesy

proroshchuvannia пророщування *n.* germination

prorostaty проростати *v.i.* sprout

prorosty прорости *v.i.* germinate

prorotstvo пророцтво *n.* prophecy

prorubuvaty прорубувати *v.t.* hew

proryv прорив *n* break

proryv прорив *n.* penetration

proryvaty проривати *v.t.* rupture

proshchalnyi pryiom hostei прощальний прийом гостей *n* farewell

proshchannia прощання *n.* adieu

proshchaty прощати *v.t* excuse

proshchavai! прощавай! *interj.* farewell

proshchavai(te)! прощавай(те)! *interj.* adieu

proshchupuvaty прощупувати *v.t.* probe

proshtovkhuvatysia проштовхуватися *v.t.* shoulder

prosivaty просівати *v.t.* sift

proslavliannia прославляння *n.* apotheosis

proslavliaty прославляти *v.t.* laud

proso просо *n.* millet

prosochuvannia просочування *n.* leakage

prosochuvaty просочувати *v.t.* pervade

prosochuvatysia просочуватися *v.i.* seep

prosodiia просодія *n.* prosody

prospekt проспект *n.* avenue

prostak простак *n.* simpleton

prostatstvo простацтво *n.* naivety

prostiahatysia простягатися *v.t.* span

prostir простір *n.* space

prostir za mezhamy chohos простір за межами чогось *n* without

prostodushnist простодушність *n.* simplicity

prostoliudyn простолюдин *n.* jack

prostorovyi просторовий *a.* spatial

prostoryi просторий *a.* spacious

prostota простота *n.* rusticity

prostratsiia прострація *n.* prostration

prostrochenyi прострочений *a.* overdue

prostrochuvaty прострочувати *v.i.* procrastinate

prostupok проступок *n.* misconduct

prostyi простий *a.* artless

prostyi простий *a.* straightforward

prostyi narod простий народ *n.* populace

prostymyi простимий *a.* pardonable

prostytutka проститутка *n.* prostitute

prostytutsiia проституція *n.* prostitution

prosuvannia просування *n.* promotion

prosuvatysia vpered просуватися вперед *v.i.* wriggle

prosvichuvaty renthenivskymy promeniamy просвічувати рентгенівськими променями *v.t.* x-ray

prosvishchaty просвіщати *v. t.* enlighten

prosvit просвіт *n.* glimpse

prosvit просвіт *n.* rent

prosyty просити *v.t.* ask

prosyty просити *v.t.* implore

prote проте *adv.* nonetheless

protehuvannia протегування *n.* protection

protehuvaty протегувати *v.t.* patronize

protest протест *n.* protest

protestuvaty протестувати *v.i.* protest

protiahom протягом *conj.* for

protoka протока *n.* strait

protoptuvaty протоптувати *v.t.* tread

prototyp прототип *n.* prototype

protsedura процедура *n.* procedure

protses процес *n.* process

protsesiia процесія *n.* procession

protsvitaiuchyi процвітаючий *a.* prosperous

protsvitannia процвітання *n.* prosperity

protsvitaty процвітати *v.i.* prosper

proty проти *prep.* against

proty- проти- *pref.* contra

protydiiaty протидіяти *v.t.* counteract

protylezhnyi протилежний *a.* opposite

protyotruta протиотрута *n.* mithridate

protyrichchia протиріччя *n* contradiction

protyrichchia v zakoni протиріччя в законі *n.* antinomy

protyroienyi протироєний *a.* triple

protystavliaty протиставляти *v.t.* contrapose

protystoiaty протистояти *v. t* counter

protyvnyi противний *a.* nasty

protyvnyk противник *n.* adversary

proverbialnyi провербіальний *a.* proverbial

provesty провести *v.t.* guide

provesty opytuvannia провести опитування *v.t.* quiz

provesty rozvidku провести розвідку *v.i* scout

provezennia провезення *n.* portage

proviant провіант *n.* victuals

provid провід *n.* wire

providentsialne провіденціальне *a.* providential

providna pozytsiia провідна позиція *n.* lead

providnyi провідний *a* principal

providnyk провідник *n.* porter

provintsializm провінціалізм *n.* provincialism

provintsiia провінція *n.* province

provintsiinyi провінційний *a.* provincial

provisnyk провісник *n.* vaccinator

provodka проводка *n.* wiring

provodyty проводити *v.t.* pursue

provodyty проводити *v.t.* usher

provodyty проводити *v.t.* while

provodyty liniiu проводити лінію *v.t.* line

provodyty spivbesidu проводити співбесіду *v.t.* interview

provodyty vidbir проводити відбір *v.t.* select

provodyty zymu проводити зиму *v.i* winter

provokatsiia провокація *n.* provocation

provokatsiinyi провокаційний *a.* provocative

provokuvaty провокувати *v.t.* provoke

provozyty kontrabandoiu провозити контрабандою *v.t.* smuggle

provulok провулок *n.* row

provydets провидець *n.* seer

provydinnia провидіння *n.* providence

provyna провина *n.* guilt

provyna провина *n.* transgression

provynytysia провинитися *v.i.* trespass

proza проза *n.* prose

prozaichnyi прозаїчний *a.* prosaic

prozhyvannia проживання *n.* habitation

prozhyvaty проживати *v. t* bide

prozhyvaty проживати *v.i.* reside

prozorlyvyi прозорливий *a.*
sagacious
prozoryi прозорий *a.* transparent
prozvaty прозвати *v.t.* nickname
pry при *prep.* at
pry smerti при смерті *adj.* alamort
pry tsomu при цьому *conj*
however
pryberezhnyi прибережний *a.*
littoral
prybii прибій *n.* surf
pryblyzno приблизно *a.*
approximate
pryborkaty приборкати *v. t* daunt
pryborkuvaty приборкувати *v. t*
curb
prybulets прибулець *a.* alien
prybutkovyi прибутковий *a.*
lucrative
prybuttia прибуття *n.* arrival
prybuty прибути *v.i.* arrive
prybyralnyk vulyts
прибиральник вулиць *n.*
orderly
prybyraty прибирати *v.t.* remove
prybyvaty прибивати *v.t* hammer
prychal причал *n.* moorings
prychastia причастя *n.* supper
prychisuvaty причісувати *v. t*
dress
prychyna причина *n.* reason
prychynnist причинність *n*
causality
prychynnyi причинний *adj.*
causal
prydane придане *n* dowry
prydatnist придатність *n.*
aptitude
prydatnyi придатний *a*
convenient
prydatnyi придатний *n* fitter
prydatnyi придатний *a.* suitable

prydatnyi dlia roboty придатний
для роботи *a.* workable
prydatnyi dlia yizhy придатний
для їжи *a* edible
prydatnyi dlia zhytla придатний
для житла *a.* habitable
prydatok придаток *n.* appendage
prydbannia придбання *n.*
acquirement
prydushennia придушення *n.*
suppression
prydushuvaty придушувати *v.t.*
nail
prydvornyi придворний *n.*
courtier
pryhaduvannia пригадування *n*
anamnesis
pryhaniaty приганяти *v.i* surface
pryhladzhuvaty пригладжувати
v.t. smooth
pryhnichennia пригнічення *n.*
oppression
pryhnichuvaty пригнічувати *v. t*
deject
pryhnobliuvaty пригноблювати
v. t depress
pryhoda пригода *n.* occurrence
pryholomshlyvyi
приголомшливий *a.* terrific
pryholomshuvaty
приголомшувати *v.t.* stupefy
pryholomshyty приголомшити *v.
t* bemuse
pryholosnyi приголосний *n.*
consonant
pryhoshchannia пригощання *n*
treat
pryhvynchuvaty пригвинчувати
v.t. screw
pryiatel приятель *n* chum
pryiatel приятель *n.* friend
pryiatel приятель *n.* pal

pryiednannia приєднання *n.*
affiliation
pryiednatysia приєднатися *v.t.*
rejoin
pryiednuvaty приєднувати *v.t.*
append
pryiednuvatysia приєднуватися
v.t. accede
pryiednuvatysia приєднуватися
v.t. join
pryiemne provedennia chasu
приємне проведення часу *n.*
pastime
pryiemnyi приємний *a.* cosy
pryiemnyi приємний *a.* glad
pryiemnyi приємний *a.* pleasant
pryimaty приймати & accept
pryiniatnyi прийнятний *a*
acceptable
pryiniattia прийняття *n*
acceptance
pryiniattia yizhy прийняття їжи
n. meal
pryiniaty duzhe velyku dozu
прийняти дуже велику дозу *v.t.*
overdose
pryiom прийом *n.* reception
pryiom hostei прийом гостей *n.*
party
prykazka приказка *n* byword
prykhid прихід *n.* advent
prykhid прихід *n.* parish
prykhodyty приходити *v. i.* come
prykhodyty na dopomohu
приходити на допомогу *v.t.*
succour
prykhodyty v hosti приходити в
гості *v.t.* visit
prykhovanyi прихований *a* inside
prykhovuvaty приховувати *v.t.*
veil
prykhylnist прихильність *n*
favour1

prykhylnyk прихильник *n*
devotee
prykhylnyk прихильник *n.* stickler
prykhylnyk suvoroi dystsypliny
прихильник суворої
дисципліни *n.* martinet
pryklad приклад *n* example
prykladaty прикладати *v.t.* adhibit
prykmeta прикмета *n.* token
prykmetnyk прикметник *n.*
adjective
prykoliuvaty приколювати *v.t.* pin
prykrasa прикраса *n* dressing
prykrashaty прикрашати *v.t.*
adorn
prykrashaty прикрашати *v. t*
beautify
prykrashaty прикрашати *v.t.* gild
prykrashaty hirliandoiu
прикрашати гірляндою *v.t.*
garland
prykripliuvaty kilochkom
прикріплювати кілочком *v.t.*
peg
prykryi прикрий *a* deplorable
prykryty прикрити *v.t.* screen
prykydatysia прикидатися *v.t*
feign
prylad прилад *n.* appliance
prylavok прилавок *n.* counter
prylehlyi прилеглий *a.* adjacent
pryliahaty прилягати *v* abutted
prylypannia прилипання *n.*
adhesion
prylypaty прилипати *v. i.* cling
prymaniuvaty приманювати *v.t.*
lure
prymanka приманка *n.* lure
prymara примара *n.* spectre
prymarnyi примарний *a.*
visionary
prymishchennia приміщення *n.*
accommodation

prymishchennia приміщення *n.* room

prymitka примітка *n.* note

prymitnyi примітний *a.* notable

prymityvnyi примітивний *a.* primitive

prymkha примха *n.* vagary

prymkha примха *n.* whim

prymorskyi приморський *a.* maritime

prymus примус *n* compulsion

prymushuvaty примушувати *v.t* force

prymushuvaty примушувати *v.t* urge

prymusovyi примусовий *a.* mandatory

prymusyty примусити *v.t* block

prymykaty примикати *v.t.* adjoin

prymyrennia примирення *n.* reconciliation

prymyriaty примиряти *v.t.* conciliate

prymyriaty примиряти *v.t.* reconcile

prymyrytel примиритель *n.* lubricant

prynada принада *n.* attraction

prynalezhnist приналежність *n* appurtenance

prynalezhnist do cholovichoi stati приналежність до чоловічої статі *n.* virility

prynesty принести *v.t* fetch

prynosyty приносити *v.t.* get

prynosyty v zhertvu приносити в жертву *v.t.* sacrifice

prynter принтер *n.* printer

prynts принц *n.* prince

pryntsesa принцеса *n.* princess

pryntsyp принцип *n.* principle

pryntsyp принцип *n.* tenet

prynyzhenist приниженість *n.* humiliation

prynyzhennia приниження *n* abasement

prynyzhuvaty принижувати *v.t.* humiliate

prynyzyty принизити *v.t.* snub

prypadok припадок *n* fit

prypii припій *n.* solder

pryplyv приплив *n.* influx

pryplyv приплив *n.* tributary

prypravliaty приправляти *v.t.* spice

prypushchennia припущення *n.* supposition

prypuskaty припускати *v.t.* surmise

prypynennia припинення *n* defeat

prypynennia припинення *n.* termination

prypynennia viiskovykh dii припинення військових дій *n.* armistice

prypyniaty припиняти *v. t* discontinue

prypyniaty припиняти *v.t.* leave

prypyniaty припиняти *v.t.* terminate

prypys припис *n.* injunction

prypysanyi приписаний *adj.* adscript

prypysuvaty приписувати *v.t.* ascribe

prypysuvaty приписувати *v.t.* attribute

pryrechennia приречення *n.* predestination

pryrikaty прирікати *v. t.* doom

pryrist приріст *n.* increment

pryroda природа *n.* nature

pryrodno природно *adv.* naturally

pryrodnyi природний *a.* natural

pryruchaty приручати *v.t.* tame
pryshch прищ *n* acne
pryshchyk прищик *n.* spot
pryshporyty пришпорити *v.t.* spur
prysiaha присяга *n.* oath
prysiazhnyi присяжний *n.* juryman
prysidaty присідати *v.i.* duck
pryskiplyvyi прискіпливий *adj* censorious
pryskorennia прискорення *n* acceleration
pryskoriuvaty прискорювати *v.t* accelerate
pryskoriuvaty прискорювати *v. t* boost
pryslivia прислів'я *n.* adage
pryslivia прислів'я *n.* proverb
pryslivnyk прислівник *n.* adverb
pryslivnykovyi прислівниковий *a.* adverbial
prysmak присмак *n.* smack
pryspiv приспів *n* refrain
prystavaty приставати *v.t.* molest
prystavliaty speredu приставляти спереду *v.t.* prefix
prystoinist пристойність *n* decency
prystoinyi пристойний *a.* seemly
prystosovuvaty пристосовувати *v.t* accommodate
prystrasnyi пристрасний *a.* passionate
prystrast пристрасть *n.* appetite
prystrii пристрій *n* establishment
prystup приступ *n* flush
prysviachuvaty присвячувати *v.t.* consecrate
prysypliaty присипляти *v.t.* sedate
prytcha притча *n.* parable
prytiahaty do sudu притягати до суду *v.* arraign

pryton притон *n* den
prytuliaty притуляти *v.i.* lean
prytulok притулок *n.* haven
prytupliatysia притуплятися *v. t.* dull
prytysnutysia притиснутися *v.i.* nestle
prytysnutysia притиснутися *v.* nuzzle
pryvablyvyi привабливий *a.* attractive
pryvablyvyi привабливий *a.* lovable
pryval привал *n* halt
pryvatnist приватність *n.* particular
pryvatnyi приватний *a.* private
pryvchaty привчати *v.t.* accustom
pryvchaty привчати *v. t.* habituate
pryvertaty привертати *v. t* engage
pryvertaty uvahu привертати увагу *v.t.* preoccupy
pryvesty v poriadok привести в порядок *v.t.* trim
pryviaz прив'язь *n.* tether
pryviazaty прив'язати *v.t.* tether
pryvid привід *n.* preposition
pryvilei привілей *n* benefit
pryvilei привілей *n.* franchise
pryvilei привілей *n.* privilege
pryvitannia привітання *n.* salutation
pryvitaty привітати *v.t.* salute
pryvitno pryimaty привітно приймати *v.t* welcome
pryvitnyi привітний *a.* affable
pryvlasnennia привласнення *n.* acquisition
pryvlasniuvaty привласнювати *v.t.* appropriate
pryvlasnyty привласнити *v.t.* pocket

pryvnesenyi привнесений *adj* adscititious

pryvodyty u vidchai приводити у відчай *v. t* dishearten

pryvodyty v liut приводити в лють *v.t.* infuriate

pryvodyty v poriadok приводити в порядок *v.t.* tidy

pryvodyty v skladne stanovyshche приводити в складне становище *v.t.* puzzle

pryvodyty v zamishannia приводити в замішання *v.t.* nonplus

pryz приз *n.* prize

pryznachaty призначати *v.t.* allocate

pryznachaty pensiiu призначати пенсію *v.t.* pension

pryznachatysia призначатися *v.t.* mean

pryznachennia призначення *n* destination

pryznachennia призначення *n.* intent

pryzovnyi призовний *a.* military

pryzovnyk призовник *n.* recruit

pryzupynennia призупинення *n.* suspension

pryzupyniaty призупиняти *v.t.* suspend

psalom псалом *n.* psalm

psevdonim псевдонім *n.* pseudonym

pshenytsia пшениця *n.* wheat

psuietsia псується *a.* incorruptible

psuvannia псування *n.* corruption

psuvaty псувати *v.t.* vitiate

psykhiatr психіатр *n.* psychiatrist

psykhiatriia психіатрія *n.* psychiatry

psykhiatrychna likarnia психіатрична лікарня *n* asylum

psykhichnyi психічний *a.* psychic

psykholoh психолог *n.* psychologist

psykholohichnyi психологічний *a.* psychological

psykholohiia психологія *n.* psychology

psykhopat психопат *n.* psychopath

psykhoterapiia психотерапія *n.* psychotherapy

psykhoz психоз *n.* psychosis

ptakh птах *n* bird

ptakholov птахолов *n.* fowler

ptashenia пташеня *n.* nestling

ptashnyk пташник *n.* aviary

ptashynyi klei пташиний клей *n* birdlime

ptytsia птиця *n.* fowl

publika публіка *n.* audience

publikatsiia публікація *n.* prospectus

publikuvaty публікувати *v.t.* publish

puchok пучок *n.* wisp

pudryty пудрити *v.t.* powder

pudynh пудинг *n.* pudding

pukh пух *n* over

pukhkyi пухкий *adv.* full

pukhlyna пухлина *n.* tumour

pukhyr пухир *n* bleb

pulover пуловер *n.* pullover

puls пульс *n.* pulse

pulsatsiia пульсація *n.* pulsation

pulsuvaty пульсувати *v.i.* pulsate

punkt пункт *n.* paragraph

punktualnist пунктуальність *n.* nicety

punktualnyi пунктуальний *a.* punctual

punktuatsiia пунктуація *n.* punctuation

punsh пунш *n.* punch

purkhannia пурхання *n* flutter
puryst пурист *n.* purist
purytanskyi пуританський *a.* puritanical
purytanyn пуританин *n.* puritan
pushynka пушинка *n* flock
puskaty korinnia пускати коріння *v.i.* root
puskaty pid ukis пускати під укіс *v. t.* derail
pustelia пустеля *n* desert
pustodzvin пустодзвін *n.* windbag
pustoporozhnie пустопорожнє *a.* indolent
pustoshchi пустощі *n.* frolic
pustota пустота *n.* hollow
pustotlyvyi пустотливий *a.* mischievous
pustun пустун *n.* villain
pustuvaty пустувати *v.i.* frolic
pustyn пустинь *n.* hermitage
pustyr пустир *n* barren
puta пута *n.* shackle
puzyr пузир *n* blister
pyiachyty пиячити *v.i.* revel
pyiatyka пиятика *n.* revelry
pykhatyi пихатий *a.* insolent
pykhtinnia пихтіння *n.* pant
pyl пил *n* dust
pyliaty пиляти *v.t* file
pyliaty пиляти *v.t.* saw
pylnist пильність *n.* vigilance
pylno dyvytysia пильно дивитися *v.i* glare
pylnyi пильний *a.* vigilant
pylnyi pohliad пильний погляд *n.* stare
pylok пилок *n.* pollen
pyrih пиріг *n.* cake
pyrkhannia пирхання *n.* snort
pysaty писати *v.t.* write

pysaty pamflety писати памфлети *v.t.* lampoon
pysaty paskvili писати пасквілі *v.t.* libel
pyshatysia пишатися *v.t.* pride
pyshchaty пищати *v.i* pipe
pyshnist пишність *n.* pageantry
pyshnota пишнота *n.* pomp
pyshnyi пишний *a.* luxuriant
pyshnyi пишний *a.* magnificent
pysmennyk письменник *n.* writer
pysmove svidchennia письмове свідчення *n* affidavit
pytalnyi питальний *a.* interrogative
pytannia питання *n.* interrogation
pytannia питання *n.* question
pytaty питати *v.t.* question
pytvo питво *n* drink
pyvo пиво *n* beer
pyvovarnia пивоварня *n* brewery

rab раб *n.* slave
rab chohos раб чогось *n.* thrall
rabolipnyi раболіпний *a.* subservient
rabolipstvo раболіпство *n.* subservience
rabolipstvuvaty раболіпствувати *v. i.* cringe
rabolipstvuvaty раболіпствувати *v. i.* crouch
rabovlasnytstvo рабовласництво *n.* slavery
rabskyi рабський *a.* servile
rabskyi рабський *a.* slavish
rabstvo рабство *n.* thralldom
rada рада *n.* council
radiatsiia радіація *n.* radiation
radii радій *n.* radium
radio радіо *n.* radio

radioperedacha радіопередача *n* broadcast

radiopryimach радіоприймач *n* wireless

radisnyi радісний *a*. mirthful

radist радість *n*. glee

radity радіти *v.i.* rejoice

radius радіус *n*. radius

radnyk радник *n*. councillor

radnyk радник *n*. counsellor

raduvaty радувати *v.t.* gladden

radykalnyi радикальний *a*. radical

radyty радити *v.t.* recommend

radytysia радитися *v. i* confer

rahu z miasa z ovochamy рагу з м'яса з овочами *n*. hotchpotch

rai рай *n*. paradise

raion район *n* corner

rak рак *n*. cancer

raketa ракета *n*. missile

rakhit рахіт *n*. rickets

rakhunok рахунок *n*. account

rakhunok-faktura рахунок-фактура *n*. invoice

rakhuvaty рахувати *v.t.* compute

rakovyna раковина *n* sink

rama рама *n* frame

rana рана *n*. injury

randevu рандеву *n*. rendezvous

ranets ранець *n*. satchel

ranh ранг *n*. rank

ranishe раніше *adv* formerly

rankova zoria ранкова зоря *n* aurora

rannie dytynstvo раннє дитинство *n*. infancy

rannii ранній *a* early

rano рано *adv* early

ranok ранок *n*. morning

rapira рапіра *n*. rapier

raptova zlyva раптова злива *n*. spate

raptovo раптово *adv.* suddenly

raptovyi раптовий *a* abrupt

rasovyi расовий *a*. racial

rasyzm расизм *n*. racialism

ratsion раціон *n*. ration

ratsionalizuvaty раціоналізувати *v.t.* rationalize

ratsionalnist раціональність *n*. rationality

ratsionalnyi раціональний *a* expedient

ratyfikuvaty ратифікувати *v.t.* ratify

ratyshche ратище *n*. shaft

ravlyk равлик *n*. snail

raz раз *adv*. once

raz na dva tyzhni раз на два тижні *adj* bi-weekly

raz na tyzhden раз на тиждень *adv*. weekly

razmeliuvaty размелювати *v.i.* grind

razom разом *adv*. together

reabilitatsiia реабілітація *n*. rehabilitation

reabilituvaty реабілітувати *v.t.* rehabilitate

reahuvannia реагування *n*. response

reahuvaty реагувати *v.i.* react

reaktsiia реакція *n*. reaction

reaktsiinyi реакційний *a*. reactionary

reaktyvnyi dvyhun реактивний двигун *n*. jet

reaktyvnyi snariad реактивний снаряд *n*. rocket

realist реаліст *n*. realist

realistychnyi реалістичний *a*. realistic

realizatsiia реалізація *n*. realization

realizm реалізм *n*. realism

realnist реальність *n.* reality
realnyi реальний *a.* real
rebernyi реберний *adj.* costal
rebro ребро *n.* rib
rechovyi речовий *a.* material
rechovyna речовина *n.* stuff
redahuvaty редагувати *v. t* edit
redaktorckii редакторскій *a.*
  editorial
redys редис *n.* radish
referendum референдум *n.*
  referendum
refleks рефлекс *n.* reflex
reflektornyi рефлекторний *a.*
  reflex
reflektyvnyi рефлективний *a.*
  reflective
reforma реформа *n.* reform
reformator реформатор *n.*
  reformer
reformuvannia реформування *n.*
  reformation
reformuvaty реформувати *v.t.*
  reform
reheneratsiia регенерація *n.*
  regeneration
reheneruvaty регенерувати *v.t.*
  regenerate
rehion регіон *n.* region
rehionalnyi регіональний *a.*
  regional
rehit регіт *n.* laughter
rehuliarnist регулярність *n.*
  regularity
rehuliarnyi регулярний *a.* regular
rehuliator регулятор *n.* regulator
rehuliuvannia регулювання *n.*
  alignment
rehuliuvaty регулювати *v.t.*
  temper
reid рейд *n.* raid
reiestr реєстр *n.* register

reiestrator реєстратор *n.*
  recorder
reiestratsiia реєстрація *n.*
  registration
reiestratura реєстратура *n.*
  registry
reiestruvaty реєструвати *v.t.*
  incorporate
reiestruvaty реєструвати *v.t.*
  register
reika рейка *n.* lath
reituzy рейтузи *n.* pantaloon
reket рекет *n.* racket
reklama реклама *n* advertisement
reklamnyi lystok рекламний
  листок *n.* handbill
reklamuvannia рекламування *n*
  boost
reklamuvaty рекламувати *v.t.*
  advertise
rekomendatsiia рекомендація *n.*
  recommendation
rekomenduvaty рекомендувати
  v. t commend
rektifikuvaty ректіфікувати *v.i.*
  rectify
rektyfikatsiia ректифікація *n.*
  purification
rekviiem реквієм *n.* requiem
rekvizuvaty реквізувати *v.t.*
  requisition
relaksatsiia релаксація *n.*
  relaxation
rele реле *n.* relay
relevantnist релевантність *n.*
  relevance
relevantnyi релевантний *a.*
  relevant
relihiia релігія *n.* religion
relihiinyi релігійний *a.* religious
relikviia реліквія *n.* relic
remeslo ремесло *n* craft
remin ремінь *n* belt

reminets ремінець *n.* strap
remisiia ремісія *n.* remission
remisnyk ремісник *n.* artisan
remont ремонт *n.* renovation
remontuvaty ремонтувати *v.t.*
overhaul
renesans ренесанс *n.*
renaissance
renthen рентген *n.* x-ray
renthenivskyi рентгенівський *a.*
x-ray
repatriant репатріант *n* repatriate
repatriatsiia репатріація *n.*
repatriation
repatriiuvaty репатріювати *v.t.*
repatriate
repelent репелент *n* repellent
repetyruvaty репетирувати *v.t.*
rehearse
repetytor репетитор *n.* tutor
repetytsiia репетиція *n.* rehearsal
replika репліка *n* cue
reporter репортер *n.* reporter
represiia репресія *n.* repression
reproduktsiia репродукція *n.*
replica
reptyliia рептилія *n.* reptile
reputatsiia репутація *n.*
reputation
resheto решето *n.* riddle
reshitka решітка *n.* lattice
respublika республіка *n.* republic
respublikanets республіканець *n*
republican
respublikanskyi
республіканський *a.* republican
restavruvaty реставрувати *v.t.*
renovate
restoran ресторан *n.* restaurant
restoratsiia ресторація *n.*
restoration
resurs ресурс *n.* resource

retelni poshuky ретельні пошуки
n research
retelnyi ретельний *a* careful
retelnyi ретельний *a* thorough
retrospektsiia ретроспекція *n.*
retrospection
retrospektyvnyi
ретроспективний *a.*
retrospective
retsept рецепт *n.* recipe
retsesiia рецесія *n.* recession
retsydyv рецидив *n.* recurrence
retsydyvuvaty рецидивувати *v.i.*
recur
retsypiient реципієнт *n.* recipient
retushuvaty ретушувати *v.t.*
retouch
rev рев *n.* roar
reverans реверанс *n.* obeisance
reversyvnyi реверсивний *a.*
reversible
revinnia ревіння *n* bray
revity ревіти *v. i* bellow
revmatychnyi ревматичний *a.*
rheumatic
revmatyzm ревматизм *n.*
rheumatism
revnoshchi ревнощі *n.* jealousy
revnyi ревний *a.* zealous
revnyvyi ревнивий *a.* jealous
revokatsiia революція *n.*
revocation
revoliutsiia революція *n.*
revolution
revoliutsiinyi революційний *a.*
revolutionary
revoliutsioner революціонер *n*
revolutionary
revolver револьвер *n.* revolver
rezerv резерв *n.* store
rezervuar резервуар *n.* basin
rezervuvannia резервування *n.*
reservation

rezhym режим *n.* mode
reziume резюме *n.* resume
rezonans резонанс *n.* resonance
rezonansnyi резонансний *a.* resonant
rezultat результат *n.* result
rezydent резидент *n* resident
riabyty рябити *v.t.* ruffle
riad ряд *n.* row
riasnity рясніти *v.i.* teem
riasnyi рясний *a* fertile
riasnyi рясний *a.* profuse
riativnyk рятівник *n.* saviour
riatuvaty рятувати *v.t.* rid
riatuvaty sudno рятувати судно *v.t.* salvage
rich річ *n.* thing
richechka річечка *n.* rivulet
richka річка *n.* river
richnyi річний *adj* aestival
richnytsia річниця *n.* anniversary
richyshche річище *n* channel
rid рід *n.* gender
ridka yizha рідка їжа *n* liquid
ridkisnyi рідкісний *a.* rare
ridkisnyi рідкісний *a.* sparse
ridko рідко *adv.* seldom
ridkyi рідкий *a.* liquid
ridna mova рідна мова *n.* vernacular
ridnia рідня *n.* kin
ridnyi рідний *a.* native
rifmopletstvo ріфмоплетство *n.* crambo
rih ріг *n.* horn
rik рік *n.* year
rikoshetuvaty рікошетувати *v.i.* rebound
ripa ріпа *n.* turnip
rishaty рішати *v.t.* resolve
rishennia рішення *n* decision
rishennia рішення *n* decree

rishuche bratysia рішуче братися *v.t* fling
rishuchist рішучість *n* dash
rishuchist рішучість *n.* resolution
rishuchyi рішучий *a.* manful
rishymist рішимість *n.* determination
riv рів *n.* trench
riven рівень *n.* level
riven zapasiv рівень запасів *n.* stocking
rivnia рівня *n* equal
rivniannia рівняння *n* equation
rivnist рівність *n* equality
rivnomirnyi рівномірний *a* even
rivnostoronnii рівносторонній *a* equilateral
rivnosylnyi рівносильний *a.* tantamount
rivnyi рівний *n.* peer
rivnyna рівнина *n.* plain
rizak різак *n* colter
rizanyna різанина *n.* slaughter
rizaty різати *v. t* cut
rizba різьба *n.* imagery
Rizdvo Різдво *n* Christmas
Rizdvo Різдво *n.* Xmas
rizhok ріжок *n* bugle
rizko padaty різко падати *v.i.* slump
rizko zaperechuvaty різко заперечувати *v.t.* retort
rizkyi різкий *adj* absonant
rizkyi різкий *a.* acute
rizkyi різкий *a.* smart
rizkyi rukh різкий рух *n.* jerk
rizkyi vypad різкий випад *n.* shy
riznomanitnist різноманітність *n.* variety
riznomanitnyi різноманітний *a* diverse
riznomanitnyi різноманітний *a.* miscellaneous

riznomanitnyi різноманітний *a.* multiform

riznostoronnii різносторонній *a.* versatile

riznovyd різновид *n.* kind

riznyi різний *a.* sundry

riznytsia різниця *n* difference

roaznoshchyk роазнощик *n.* vendor

robitnyk робітник *n.* worker

robochyi робочий *n.* workman

robot робот *n.* robot

robota робота *n.* job

robota робота *n.* work

robotodavets роботодавець *n* employer

robyty робити *v. t* do

robyty робити *v.t.* make

robyty dohanu робити догану *v.t.* reprimand

robyty eskiz робити ескіз *v. t* draft

robyty hnuchkym робити гнучким *v.t.* limber

robyty karnym робити карним *v.t.* penalize

robyty krashchym робити кращим *v.t.* reclaim

robyty nedbalo робити недбало *v. t* botch

robyty neobkhidnym робити необхідним *v.t.* necessitate

robyty neprydatnym робити непридатним *v. t* disable

robyty ochevydnym робити очевидним *v.t.* manifest

robyty pauzu робити паузу *v.i.* pause

robyty pereklyk робити переклик *v.t.* muster

robyty pobytym робити побитим *v.t.* stereotype

robyty podorozh робити подорож *v.i.* voyage

robyty pokupky робити покупки *v.i.* shop

robyty poperedzhennia робити попередження *v. t.* caution

robyty rivnym робити рівним *v.t.* level

robyty shcheplennia робити щеплення *v.t.* inoculate

robyty shcho-nebud u vidpovid робити що-небудь у відповідь *v.i.* respond

robyty skladky робити складки *v.t.* crimple

robyty syrotoiu робити сиротою *v.t* orphan

robyty tonkym робити тонким *v.t.* thin

robyty tverdym робити твердим *v.t.* harden

robyty vodonepronyknym робити водонепроникним *v.t.* waterproof

robyty vstup робити вступ *v.t.* preface

robyty vybir робити вибір *v.i.* opt

robyty vylazku робити вилазку *v.i.* sally

robyty vypad робити випад *v.i* lunge

robyty zhyttievym робити життєвим *v.t.* vitalize

robyty zyhzahy робити зигзаги *v.i.* zigzag

robytysia робитися *v.t.* grow

rodiuchist родючість *n* fertility

rodiuchyi родючий *a* rank

rodiuchyi родючий *a.* rich

rodovid родовід *n.* lineage

rodovid родовід *n.* pedigree

rodych родич *n.* relative

rodychka родичка *n.* relation

rodzynka родзинка *n.* zest
rohivka рогівка *n* cornea
rohonosets рогоносець *n.* cuckold
roialist рояліст *n.* royalist
roialti роялті *n.* royalty
roitysia роїтися *v.i.* swarm
rokhkannia рохкання *n.* grunt
rokhkaty рохкати *v.i.* grunt
rol роль *n.* role
rom ром *n.* rum
roman роман *n* novel
romanist романіст *n.* novelist
romantychnyi романтичний *a.* romantic
romantyka романтика *n.* romance
ropa ропа *v.t.* leach
rosa роса *n.* dew
roslyi рослий *a.* stalwart
roslyna рослина *n.* plant
roslynnist рослинність *n.* vegetation
roslynnyi slyz рослинний слиз *n.* mucilage
rosomakha росомаха *n.* glutton
rot рот *n.* mouth
rovisnyk ровісник *n.* precursor
rozarii розарій *n.* rosary
rozbavlenyi розбавлений *a* dilute
rozbavliaty розбавляти *v. t* dilute
rozbazariuvaty розбазарювати *v.t.* squander
rozbihatysia розбігатися *v. t* disperse
rozbii розбій *n.* dacoity
rozbiinychaty розбійничати *v.t* pirate
rozbiinyk розбійник *n.* bandit
rozbirlyvo розбірливо *adv.* legibly
rozbirlyvyi розбірливий *a.* legible
rozbizhnist розбіжність *n.* disagreement

rozbrat розбрат *n.* strife
rozbyty vshchent розбити вщент *v.t.* rout
rozbyty z hriukotom розбити з грюкотом *v. i* crash
rozbyvaty tabir розбивати табір *v. i.* camp
rozcharovuvaty розчаровувати *v. t.* disappoint
rozchyn розчин *n.* solution
rozchyniaty розчиняти *v.t* dissolve
rozchynnist розчинність *n.* solubility
rozchynnyi розчинний *a.* soluble
rozchynnyk розчинник *n* solvent
rozdacha роздача *n.* dealing
rozdaty роздати *v. i* deal
rozdavaty роздавати *v. t* distribute
rozdavliuvaty роздавлювати *v.t* mash
rozdavliuvaty роздавлювати *v.t.* squash
rozdavyty роздавити *v. t* crush
rozdil розділ *n.* section
rozdiliaty розділяти *v. t* divide
rozdiliaty розділяти *v.t.* partition
rozdilyty na chotyry розділити на чотири *v.t.* quarter
rozdobuty роздобути *v.t.* procure
rozdratuvannia роздратування *n.* ire
rozdratuvannia роздратування *n.* irritation
rozdribna torhivlia роздрібна торгівля *n.* retail
rozdribnyi роздрібний *a* retail
rozdribnyi torhovets роздрібний торговець *n.* retailer
rozdum роздум *n.* rumination
rozdvoiuvatysia роздвоюватися *v. t.* double

rozdyraty роздирати *v.t.* tear
rozetka розетка *n.* socket
rozfarbovuvaty розфарбовувати *v. t* colour
rozhevyi рожевий *a* pink
rozhevyi рожевий *n.* pink
rozhliad розгляд *n.* approval
rozhliad розгляд *n* consideration
rozhliad розгляд *n* review
rozhliad розгляд *n.* scrutiny
rozhliadaty розглядати *v. t* examine
rozhortaty розгортати *v.t.* deploy
rozhrabuvaty розграбувати *v.t.* ransack
rozhrom розгром *n* rout
roziasnyty роз'яснити *v.i.* irradiate
rozibratysia розібратися *v.t.* grasp
roziednaty роз'єднати *v.t.* insulate
roziednuvaty роз'єднувати *v. t* disconnect
rozihrash розіграш *n.* bam
rozihrash розіграш *n* draw
rozivdka розівдка *n* exploration
rozkaiuvatysia розкаюватися *v.i.* repent
rozkazaty розказати *v.t.* tell
rozkhvaliuvaty розхвалювати *v. t.* extol
rozkish розкіш *n.* superfluity
rozkishnyi розкішний *a.* sumptuous
rozkladannia розкладання *n.* decomposition
rozkladaty розкладати *v. t.* decompose
rozkleiuvaty розклеювати *v.t.* post
rozkol розкол *n.* secession
rozkoliuvaty розколювати *v.i.* split

rozkoliuvaty розколювати *v.t.* sunder
rozkoliuvatysia розколюватися *v.t* fracture
rozkopka розкопка *n.* excavation
rozkopuvaty розкопувати *v.t.* unearth
rozkryty розкрити *v. t* disclose
rozkrytyi розкритий *a.* open
rozkryvatysia розкриватися *v.t.* unfold
rozkvartyruvannia розквартирування *n.* cantonment
rozkvit розквіт *n* bloom
rozkvit розквіт *n.* heyday
rozkvitaty розквітати *v.i.* bloom
rozkydaty розкидати *v.t.* scatter
rozlad розлад *n* discord
rozlad розлад *n.* frustration
rozladnuvaty розладнувати *v.t.* frustrate
rozluchaty розлучати *v. t* divorce
rozluchennia розлучення *n* divorce
rozlyvochna mashyna розливочна машина *n* bottler
rozmir розмір *n.* gauge
rozmir розмір *n.* size
rozmiriaty розміряти *v.t.* proportion
rozmistyty розмістити *v.t.* locate
rozmnozhuvalnyi aparat розмножувальний апарат *n* cyclostyle
rozmnozhuvaty розмножувати *v. t* cyclostyle
rozmova розмова *n* talk
rozmovliaty розмовляти *v. i.* chat2
rozorennia розорення *n.* ruin
rozpad розпад *n* decay
rozpiattia розп'яття *n.* rood

rozplata розплата *n.* wage
rozplavlenyi розплавлений *a.*
molten
rozplidnyk розплідник *n.* nursery
rozplyvchastyi розпливчастий *a.*
vague
rozpochynaty розпочинати *v.t.*
begin
rozpodil розподіл *n* distribution
rozpodiliaty розподіляти *v.t.*
apportion
rozpodiliaty розподіляти *v.i.*
participate
rozporiadzhennia
розпорядження *n* disposal
rozporoshuvaty розпорошувати
v.t. spray
rozpovid розповідь *n.* narration
rozpovidach розповідач *n.*
narrator
rozpovidaty розповідати *v.t.*
recount
rozpovidnyi розповідний *a.*
narrative
rozprostertyi розпростертий *a.*
prostrate
rozpushchenyi розпущений *a.*
licentious
rozpusnyi розпусний *a.* profligate
rozpusnyk розпусник *n*
debauchee
rozpusta розпуста *n.* profligacy
rozputnyi розпутний *a.* immoral
rozpytuvaty розпитувати *v.t.*
inquire
rozrada розрада *n.* balsam
rozrakhovuvaty розраховувати *v.*
t. calculate
rozrakhunok розрахунок *n.*
computation
rozrakhunok розрахунок *n*
estimation

rozrakhuvaty za chasom
розрахувати за часом *v.t.* time
rozriadzhaty розряджати *v. t*
discharge
rozrizaty розрізати *v.t.* rip
rozrizniaty розрізняти *v. i*
distinguish
rozrobliaty karier розробляти
кар'єр *v.i.* quarry
rozrostannia tkanyny
розростання тканини *n*
accrementition
rozrostatysia розростатися *v.i*
flourish
rozryv розрив *n* abruption
rozryvaty розривати *v.t.* sever
rozshchepliuvannia
розщеплювання *n* split
rozshchepliuvaty розщеплювати
v.t. splinter
rozshchepliuvaty na tonki shary
розщеплювати на тонкі шари
v.t. laminate
rozshuk розшук *n.* search
rozshyriuvaty розширювати *v. t*
enlarge
rozshyriuvatysia розширюватися
v.t. widen
rozsichennia розсічення *n*
dissection
rozsikaty розсікати *v. t* dissect
rozsil розсіл *n* brine
rozsistysia розсістися *v.i.* lounge
rozslabliatysia розслаблятися
v.t. relax
rozsliduvannia розслідування *n.*
investigation
rozsliduvaty розслідувати *v.t.*
investigate
rozstavliaty za velychynoiu
розставляти за величиною *v.t.*
size

rozstavyty z promizhkamy
розставити з проміжками *v.t.*
space
rozstroiuvatysia розстроюватися
v.t. shatter
rozsud розсуд *n* discretion
rozsudlyvist розсудливість *n.*
prudence
rozsudlyvyi розсудливий *a.*
judicious
rozsudlyvyi розсудливий *a.*
rational
rozsypchastyi розсипчастий *a*
crisp
roztashovanyi useredeni krainy
розташований усередені
країни *a.* inland
roztashovuvaty розташовувати
v. t dispose
roztashovuvatysia
розташовуватися *v.t.* pair
roztiah розтяг *n* wrick
roztiahnennia suhloba
розтягнення суглоба *n.* sprain
roztiahnuty zviazky розтягнути
зв'язки *v.t.* sprain
roztiahuvannia розтягування *n*
stretch
roztiahuvaty розтягувати *v.t.*
stretch
roztrachuvaty розтрачувати *v.t.*
spend
roztriskuvannia розтріскування
v. i crack
roztsiniuvaty розцінювати *v.t.*
appraise
roztsiniuvaty розцінювати *v.t.*
regard
roztyrannia розтирання *n* rub
rozum розум *n.* judgement
rozum розум *n.* mind
rozuminnia розуміння *n.*
apprehension

rozuminnia розуміння *n*
comprehension
rozumnyi розумний *a.* clever
rozumovyi розумовий *a.*
intellectual
rozumovyi розумовий *a.* mental
**rozv`iazuvaty** розв`язувати *v.t.*
loosen
rozvaha розвага *n.* fun
rozval розвал *n* downfall
rozvantazhuvannia
розвантажування *n.* discharge
rozvantazhyty розвантажити *v.t.*
unburden
rozvazhaty розважати *v. t*
entertain
rozvazhlyvyi розважливий *a.*
prudential
rozvedennia розведення *n.*
propagation
rozviazka розв'язка *n.* upshot
rozviaznist розв'язність *n*
swagger
rozviazuvaty розв'язувати *v.t.*
loose
rozvidka розвідка *n.* intelligence
rozvidnyk розвідник *n.* guide
rozvidnyk розвідник *n* scout
rozvodyty розводити *v.t* breed
rozvytok розвиток *n.*
development
rozvytok розвиток *n* evolution
rozvyvaty розвивати *v. t.* develop
rozvyvaty розвивати *v.t.* expand
rozzbroiennia роззброєння *n.*
disarmament
rozzhariuvatysia розжарюватися
v.i. glow
rozziavyvshy rot роззявивши рот
adv., agape
rtut ртуть *n.* mercury
rtut ртуть *n.* quicksilver
rtutnyi ртутний *a.* mercurial

rubaty рубати *v.t.* slash

rubaty miaso рубати м'ясо *v.t.* mince

rubaty shableiu рубати шаблею *v.t.* sabre

rubets рубець *n* wake

rubin рубін *n.* ruby

rubizh рубіж *n.* frontier

rubl рубль *n.* rouble

ruchatysia ручатися *v.t* guarantee

ruchatysia za ручатися за *v.i.* vouch

ruchatysia za ручатися за *v.t.* warrant

ruchka ручка *n.* pen

ruchna robota ручна робота *n.* handicraft

ruchna robota ручна робота *n.* handiwork

ruchnyi ручний *a.* manual

ruchnyi ручний *a.* tame

ruda руда *n.* ore

rudyment рудимент *n.* rudiment

rudymentarnyi рудиментарний *a.* rudimentary

ruinuvannia руйнування *n* destruction

ruinuvaty руйнувати *v.t.* wreck

ruinuvatysia руйнуватися *v. i* decay

ruka рука *n.* arm

ruka рука *n* hand

rukav рукав *n* sleeve

rukavychka рукавичка *n.* glove

rukavytsia рукавиця *n.* gauntlet

rukavytsia рукавиця *n.* mitten

rukh рух *n.* motion

rukhatysia рухатися *v.t.* move

rukhatysia khvylepodibno рухатися хвилеподібно *v.i.* undulate

rukhatysia nazad i vpered рухатися назад і вперед *v.t.* shuttle

rukhatysia z hudinniam рухатися з гудінням *v.i.* zoom

rukhlyvyi рухливий *a.* agile

rukhome maino рухоме майно *n.* movables

rukhomyi рухомий *a.* movable

rukoiatka рукоятка *n.* handle

rukopashna рукопашна *n.* melee

rukopys рукопис *n.* manuscript

rulka рулька *n.* shin

rulon рулон *n.* roll

rumianets рум'янець *n* blush

rumianyi рум'яний *a.* rosy

runo руно *n* fleece

rupiia рупія *n.* rupee

rusalka русалка *n.* mermaid

rushiina syla рушійна сила *n.* momentum

rushiina syla рушійна сила *n.* mover

rushnyk рушник *n.* towel

ruta рута *v.t.* rue

rutyna рутина *n.* routine

rvaty рвати *v.t.* gather

rvaty рвати *v.t.* lacerate

rvaty na shmatky рвати на шматки *v.t* tatter

ryba риба *n* fish

rybalka рибалка *n* fisherman

rychaty ричати *v.i.* roar

rydannia ридання *n* sob

rydaty ридати *v.i.* sob

rydykiul ридикюль *n.* purse

ryksha рикша *n.* rickshaw

rylo рило *n.* snout

ryma рима *n.* rhyme

rymuvaty римувати *v.i.* rhyme

rynok ринок *n* market

rynok ринок *v.t* market

rys рис *n.* rice

rys рись *n* trot
rytm ритм *b.* rhythm
rytmichnyi ритмічний *a.* rhythmic
rytorychnyi риторичний *a.* rhetorical
rytoryka риторика *n.* rhetoric
rytual ритуал *n.* ritual
rytualnyi ритуальний *a.* ritual
ryty рити *v. t.* excavate
rytysia ритися *v.i.* rummage
ryvok ривок *n.* hitch
ryvok ривок *n* spurt
ryzyk ризик *n.* peril
ryzyk ризик *n.* risk
ryzyknuty ризикнути *v.t.* venture
ryzykovanyi ризикований *a.* risky
ryzykuvaty ризикувати *v.t.* jeopardize

sabotazh саботаж *n.* sabotage
sabotuvaty саботувати *v.t.* sabotage
sad сад *n.* garden
sadivnyk садівник *n.* gardener
sadivnyk садівник *n.* grower
sadivnytstvo садівництво *n.* horticulture
sadno садно *n* graze
sadyba садиба *n.* barton
sadyst садист *n.* sadist
sadyzm садизм *n.* sadism
sadzhaty саджати *v.t.* plant
sadzhaty u vulyk саджати у вулик *n.* hive
sait сайт *n.* site
sake саке *n.* sake
sakharinovyi сахаріновий *a.* saccharine
sakharyn сахарин *n.* saccharin
salat салат *n.* salad
saliut салют *n* salute

salo сало *n.* bacon
salo сало *n.* tallow
sam сам *pron.* myself
samist самість *n.* self
samit саміт *n.* summit
samitnyk самітник *n.* hermit
samitnyk самітник *n.* recluse
samka самка *n* bitch
samoderzhavnyi самодержавний *a* autocratic
samoderzhavstvo самодержавство *n* autocracy
samoderzhets самодержець *n* autocrat
samohubnyi самогубний *a.* suicidal
samohubstvo самогубство *n.* suicide
samoobman самообман *n* flattery
samorodok самородок *n.* nugget
samostiinyi самостійний *a.* independent
samota самота *n.* solitude
samotnii самотній *a.* alone
samotnii самотній *a.* single
samotnist самотність *n.* loneliness
samovdovolenyi самовдоволений *a.* smug
samoviddanyi самовідданий *a.* selfless
samovpevnenist самовпевненість *n.* assumption
samozakokhanist самозакоханість *n.* narcissism
samozrechennia самозречення *n.* renunciation
samyi самий *a.* most
samytsia самиця *n* female
sanatorii санаторій *n.* sanatorium
sanchata санчата *n.* skate
sandal сандал *n.* sandal

sandalove derevo сандалове дерево *n.* sandalwood
sanhvinichnyi сангвінічний *a.* sanguine
sanitarnyi санітарний *a.* sanitary
sanktsiia санкція *n.* sanction
sanktsionuvaty санкціонувати *v.t* approbate
sanktsionuvaty санкціонувати *v. t* confirm
sanktsionuvaty санкціонувати *v.t.* sanction
sapfir сапфір *n.* sapphire
sarai сарай *n.* barn
sarana сарана *n.* locust
sardonichnyi сардонічний *a.* sardonic
sarkastychnyi саркастичний *a.* sarcastic
sarkazm сарказм *n.* sarcasm
sarzha саржа *n.* serge
satana сатана *n.* satan
satyra сатира *n.* satire
satyrychnyi сатиричний *a.* satirical
satyryk сатирик *n.* satirist
savan саван *n.* shroud
sazha сажа *n.* soot
secha сеча *n.* urine
sechovyi сечовий *a.* urinary
sechovyi mikhur сечовий міхур *n* bladder
sechovypuskannia сечовипускання *n.* urination
sehment сегмент *n.* segment
seif сейф *n.* safe
seismichnyi сейсмічний *a.* seismic
sekret секрет *n.* secret
sekretar секретар *n.* secretary
sekretariat секретаріат *n.* secretariat (e)
sekretnist секретність *n.* secrecy

sekretnyi секретний *a.* secret
sekretsiia секреція *n.* secretion
seksapilnyi сексапільний *a.* sexy
seksualnist сексуальність *n.* sexuality
seksualnyi сексуальний *a.* sexual
sekta секта *n.* schism
sekta секта *n.* sect
sektantskyi сектантський *a.* sectarian
sektor сектор *n.* sector
sekunda секунда *n* second
selektyvnyi селективний *a.* selective
selezinka селезінка *n.* spleen
selianstvo селянство *n.* peasantry
selianyn селянин *n.* peasant
selianyn селянин *n* rustic
seliuk селюк *n* carl
seliuk селюк *n* churl
selo село *n.* village
selyshche селище *n.* hamlet
selyshche селище *a.* township
semestr семестр *n.* semester
semestrovyi семестровий *a.* terminal
seminar семінар *n.* seminar
semyrichnyi семирічний *a* seven
senat сенат *n.* senate
senator сенатор *n.* senator
senatorskyi сенаторський *a.* senatorial
sens сенс *n.* meaning
sens сенс *n.* purport
sens сенс *n.* sense
sensatsiinyi сенсаційний *a.* sensational
sententsiia сентенція *n.* maxim
sentymentalni сентиментальнй *a* maudlin

sentymentalnyi
сентиментальний *a.*
sentimental
separatyst сепаратист *n.*
secessionist
sepsys сепсис *n.* sepsis
septychnyi септичний *a.* septic
ser сер *n.* sir
serdyty сердити *v.i.* rouse
sered серед *prep.* among
sered серед midst
sereda середа *n.* Wednesday
serednia velychyna середня
величина *n.* average
serednii середній *a.* mediocre
serednii середній *a.* mid
serednii середній *a.* middle
serednii rid середній рід *n* neuter
serednovichnyi середньовічний
a. medieval
serednovichnyi середньовічний
a. medieval
serednyk середник *n.* mullion
seredyna lita середина літа *n.*
midsummer
serial серіал *n.* serial
seriia серія *n.* series
seriinyi серійний *a.* serial
serioznist серйозність *n.* gravity
serioznyi серйозний *a* serious
serp серп *n.* sickle
serpen серпень *n.* August
sertse серце *n.* heart
sertsebyttia серцебиття *n.*
palpitation
sertsepodibnyi серцеподібний
adj. cordate
sertsevo серцево *adv.* heartily
sertsevyi серцевий *adjs* cardiacal
sertsevyi серцевий *a* cordial
sertyfikat сертифікат *n.* certificate
servetka серветка *n.* napkin
serzhant сержант *n.* sergeant

sesiia сесія *n.* session
sestra сестра *n.* sister
sestrynskyi сестринський *a.*
sisterly
sestrynstvo сестринство *n.*
sisterhood
sezon сезон *n.* season
sezonnyi сезонний *a.* seasonal
sfera сфера *n.* sphere
sferychnyi сферичний *a.*
spherical
shabash шабаш *n.* sabbath
shablia шабля *n.* sabre
shablon шаблон *n.* pattern
shafa шафа *n.* locker
shafran шафран *n.* saffron
shafrannyi шафранний *a* saffron
shakal шакал *n.* jackal
shakh i mat шах і мат *n*
checkmate
shakhrai шахрай *n.* knave
shakhrai шахрай *n.* rascal
shakhrai шахрай *n.* sharper
shakhraiskyi шахрайський *a.*
fraudulent
shakhraiskyi шахрайський *a.*
roguish
shakhraistvo шахрайство *n.*
cheat
shakhraistvo шахрайство *n.*
fraud
shakhraistvo шахрайство *n.*
knavery
shakhraistvo шахрайство *n.*
roguery
shakhraiuvaty шахраювати *v. t.*
cheat
shakhta шахта *n* mine
shakhtar шахтар *n.* miner
shal шаль *n.* shawl
shalenity шаленіти *v.i.* rampage
shalenstvo шаленство *n.*
rampage

shalenyi шалений *adv.* amuck
shalenyi шалений *a* fierce
shalenyi шалений *a.* frantic
shalenyi шалений *a.* vehement
shamkaty шамкати *v.i.* mumble
shampun шампунь *n.* shampoo
shana шана *n* esteem
shanoblyvyi шанобливий *a.* respectful
shanoblyvyi шанобливий *a.* reverential
shanovnyi шановний *a.* honourable
shans шанс *n.* chance
shansy шанси *n.* odds
shantazh шантаж *n* blackmail
shantazhuvaty шантажувати *v.t* blackmail
shanuvalnyk шанувальник *n.* suitor
shanuvalnyk шанувальник *n.* worshipper
shanuvannia шанування *n.* homage
shanuvannia шанування *n.* reverence
shanuvannia шанування *n.* veneration
shanuvaty шанувати *v.t.* hallow
shanuvaty шанувати *v.t.* respect
shanuvaty шанувати *v.t.* venerate
shar шар *n* coating
shar шар *n.* layer
shar шар *n.* orb
shar шар *n* ply
shar шар *n.* stratum
sharf шарф *n.* scarf
sharf шарф *n.* throw
sharlatan шарлатан *n* quack
sharlatanstvo шарлатанство *n.* quackery
sharm шарм *n* spell
shatun шатун *n.* pitman

shchabel щабель *n.* round
shchaslyvyi щасливий *a.* fortunate
shchaslyvyi щасливий *a.* happy
shchaslyvyi щасливий *a.* joyful, joyous
shchaslyvyi щасливий *a.* lucky
shchastia щастя *n.* happiness
shchebet щебет *n.* twitter
shchebetaty щебетати *v.i.* twitter
shchedrist щедрість *n* bounty
shchedrist щедрість *n.* generosity
shchedrist щедрість *n.* liberality
shchedro razdavaty щедро раздавати *v.t.* lavish
shchedryi щедрий *a* bountiful
shchedryi щедрий *a.* generous
shchedryi щедрий *a.* lavish
shchedryi dar щедрий дар *n.* largesse
shchelepa щелепа *n.* jaw
shcheplennia щеплення *n.* graft
shcheplennia щеплення *n.* inoculation
shchetyna щетина *n* bristle
shchilnist щільність *n* density
shchilnyi щільний *a.* compact
shchilnyi щільний *a* consistent
shchilnyi щільний *a.* tough
shchilyna щілина *n.* opening
shchilyna щілина *n.* slit
shchipka щіпка *n.* pinch
shcho що *conj.* that
shcho що *interj.* what
shcho що *pron.* which
shcho b ne що б не *pron.* whatever
shcho lezhyt v osnovi що лежить в основі *adj.* basal
shcho maie formu vukha що має форму вуха *adj.* auriform
shcho maie tsinnist що має цінність *n.* worth

shcho maie zvychai що має
звичай *a.* wont

shcho ne maie nomera що не
має номера *a.* numberless

shcho ne maie plodiv що не має
плодів *adj.* acarpous

shcho perebuvaie v rusi що
перебуває в русі *adv.* astir

shcho perekhodyt z odnoho
mistsia na inshe що
переходить з одного місця на
інше *adj* ambulant

shcho perevazhaie що
переважає *a.* predominant

shcho perevershuie що
перевершує *a.* transcendent

shcho rozchyniaie що розчиняє
a. solvent

shcho styraietsia що стирається
a. washable

shcho tryvaie rik що триває рік
a. yearly

shcho tryvaie vsiu nich що
триває всю ніч *a* overnight

shcho tuzhyt що тужить *a.* wistful

shcho vyklykaie strakh що
викликає страх *a.* awful

shcho vyklykaie vidrazu що
викликає відразу *a.* loathsome

shcho za що за *pron.* what

shchob щоб *adv.* that

shchob... ne щоб... не *conj.* lest

shchodenna hazeta щоденна
газета *n.* daily

shchodenno щоденно *adv* adays

shchodenno щоденно *adv.* daily

shchodennyi щоденний *a* daily

shchodennyk щоденник *n* diary

shchohla щогла *n.* mast

shchoka щока *n* cheek

shchokvartalnyi щоквартальний
a. quarterly

shchomisiachno щомісячно *adv*
monthly

shchomisiachnyi щомісячний *a.*
monthly

shchomisiachnyk щомісячник *n*
monthly

shchorichna renta щорічна
рента *n.* annuity

shchorichno щорічно *adv.* yearly

shchorichnyi щорічний *a.* annual

shchos щось *n.* aught

shchos щось *pron.* something

shchos podibne щось подібне
n. like

shchotyzhnia щотижня *adv.*
weekly

shchur щур *n.* rat

shchypaty щипати *v.t* nip

shchypaty щипати *v.t.* pinch

shchyptsi щипці *n. pl.* tongs

shchyrist щирість *n.* sincerity

shchyroserdnyi щиросердний *a.*
sincere

shchyryi щирий *a.* candid

shchyryi щирий *a.* frank

shchyryi щирий *a.* whole-hearted

shchyt щит *n.* shield

shchzabezpechuvaty
instrumentamy
щзабезпечувати
інструментами *v.t.* implement

shchzhoda щзгода *n.* compliance

shedevr шедевр *n.* masterpiece

shelf шельф *n.* shelf

shelma шельма *n.* rogue

shepeliavist шепелявість *n* lisp

shepeliavyty шепелявити *v.t.* lisp

shepit шепіт *n* whisper

shepotity шепотіти *v.t.* whisper

shershen шершень *n.* hornet

shevron шеврон *n.* stripe

shist шість *n., a* six

shistdesiat шістьдесят *n., a.* sixty

shistdesiatyi шістдесятий *a.* sixtieth

shistnadtsiat шістнадцять *n., a.* sixteen

shistnadtsiatyi шістнадцятий *a.* sixteenth

shkandybaty шкандибати *v.i.* waddle

shkapa шкапа *n.* jade

shkapa шкапа *n.* nag

shkarpetka шкарпетка *n.* sock

shkatulka шкатулка *n* casket

shkidlyvyi шкідливий *a.* injurious

shkidlyvyi шкідливий *a.* noxious

shkidlyvyi шкідливий *a.* pernicious

shkidnyk шкідник *n.* pest

shkidnyk шкідник *n.* wrecker

shkiper шкіпер *n.* skipper

shkira шкіра *n.* cutis

shkira шкіра *n.* leather

shkira шкіра *n.* skin

shkirianyi zavod шкіряний завод *n.* tannery

shkirka шкірка *n.* peel

shkiv шків *n.* pulley

shkoda шкода *n.* harm

shkoda шкода *n* ill

shkoduvaty шкодувати *v.t.* grudge

shkodyty шкодити *v.i* blast

shkodyty шкодити *v.t* harm

shkola школа *n.* school

shkval шквал *n.* gust

shlam шлам *n.* silt

shlanh шланг *n.* hose

shliakh шлях *n* medium

shliakh шлях *n.* path

shliakh шлях *n.* way

shliakhetnist шляхетність *n.* splendour

shliakhetnyi шляхетний *a.* noble

shlifuvalnyk шліфувальник *n.* grinder

shliub шлюб *n.* marriage

shliub шлюб *n.* wedlock

shliubnyi шлюбний *a* conjugal

shliubnyi шлюбний *a.* marriageable

shliubnyi шлюбний *a.* nubile

shliubnyi шлюбний *a.* nuptial

shliuz шлюз *n.* sluice

shlondra шльондра *n.* slut

shlondra шльондра *n.* whore

shlopaty шльопати *v.t.* pat

shlopaty шльопати *v.t.* slap

shlunkovyi шлунковий *a.* gastric

shlunok шлунок *n.* stomach

shmahaty шмагати *v.t.* lambaste

shmatochok шматочок *n.* morsel

shmatok шматок *n* bit

shmatok шматок *n.* lump

shmatok шматок *n.* mouthful

shmatok шматок *n.* piece

shmatok шматок *n.* slab

shmatuvaty шматувати *v.t.* mangle

shnek шнек *n.* auger

shnur шнур *n* cord

shnuruvaty шнурувати *v.t.* lace

shofer шофер *n.* chauffeur

shok шок *n.* shock

shokolad шоколад *n* chocolate

shokuvaty шокувати *v.t.* horrify

shokuvaty шокувати *v.t.* scandalize

shokuvaty шокувати *v.t.* shock

sholom шолом *n.* helmet

shorstkuvatyi шорсткуватий *a.* rugged

shorty шорти *n. pl.* shorts

shose шосе *n.* highway

shostyi шостий *a.* sixth

shotlandets шотландець *n.* Scot

shotlandskyi шотландський *a.* scotch

shou шоу *n.* show

shov шов *n.* joint

shov шов *n.* seam

shovk шовк *n.* silk

shovkovyi шовковий *a.* silken

shovkovystyi шовковистий *a.* silky

shovkovytsia шовковиця *n.* mulberry

shpora шпора *n.* spur

shpryts шприц *n.* syringe

shpurliaty шпурляти *v.t.* shove

shpyhun шпигун *n* emissary

shpyhun шпигун *n.* spy

shpyhuvaty шпигувати *v.i.* spy

shpyl шпиль *n.* steeple

shpylka шпилька *n.* pin

shpylka шпилька *n.* spike

shpylka шпилька *n.* stud

shpynat шпинат *n.* spinach

shpyndel шпиндель *n.* spindle

shram шрам *n* scar

shryft Brailia шрифт Брайля *n* braille

shtamp штамп *n.* imprint

shtamp штамп *n.* stamp

shtampuvaty штампувати *v.t.* manufacture

shtatyv штатив *n.* tripod

shtofkhaty штофхати *v.t.* spurn

shtorm шторм *n.* gale

shtovkhannia штовхання *n.* shove

shtovkhaty штовхати *v.t.* jog

shtovkhaty штовхати *v.t.* poke

shtovkhaty штовхати *v.t.* push

shtraf штраф *n* fine

shtraf штраф *n* forfeit

shtraf штраф *n.* penalty

shtrafuvaty штрафувати *v.t* fine

shtrafuvaty штрафувати *v.t.* surcharge

shtrykhuvaty штрихувати *v.t.* shade

shtuchnyi штучний *a.* artificial

shtuchnyi штучний *a* false

shtukaturka штукатурка *n.* plaster

shtukaturyty штукатурити *v.t.* plaster

shturmuvaty штурмувати *v.* assail

shturmuvaty штурмувати *v.i.* storm

shukaty шукати *v.t.* search

shukaty шукати *v.t.* seek

shum шум *n.* ado

shum шум *n* clamour

shum шум *n.* hubbub

shum шум *n.* noise

shum шум *n.* tumult

shum шум *n.* uproar

shum шум *n.* whir

shumno svarytysia шумно сваритися *v. t* brangle

shumnyi шумний *a.* noisy

shuntuvalnyi шунтувальний *a.* shut

shvabra швабра *n.* mop

shvartuvatysia швартуватися *v.t* moor

shveitsar швейцар *n.* usher

shveitsarets швейцарець *n.* swiss

shveitsarskyi швейцарський *a* swiss

shvets швець *n* cobbler

shvets швець *n* sewer

shvydke zbilshennia швидке збільшення *n.* proliferation

shvydkist швидкість *n.* gear

shvydkist швидкість *n.* rapidity

shvydkist швидкість *n.* speed

shvydkist швидкість *n.* velocity
shvydko швидко *adv.* apace
shvydko швидко *adv.* speedily
shvydko poshyriuvatysia швидко поширюватися *v.i.* proliferate
shvydko vykonuvaty швидко виконувати *v. t.* expedite
shvydkoplynnyi швидкоплинний *a.* temporal
shvydkopsuvnyi швидкопсувний *a.* perishable
shvydkyi швидкий *a* fast
shvydkyi швидкий *a.* lively
shvydkyi швидкий *a.* prompt
shvydkyi швидкий *a.* quick
shvydkyi швидкий *a.* rapid
shvydkyi швидкий *a.* speedy
shvydkyi швидкий *a.* swift
shvydkyi pohliad швидкий погляд *n.* glance
shvydkyi pohliad швидкий погляд *n* peep
shvydshe швидше *adv.* rather
shvydshe, nizh швидше, ніж *conj* before
shybenyk шибеник *n.* romp
shybenyk шибеник *n.* tomboy
shybenytsia шибениця *n. .* gallows
shyfer шифер *n.* slate
shyfr шифр *n.* cipher, cipher
shyia шия *n.* neck
shykuvaty v sherenhu шикувати в шеренгу *v.t.* rank
shylinh шилінг *n.* shilling
shympanze шимпанзе *n.* chimpanzee
shyna шина *n.* tyre
shynel шинель *n.* overcoat
shynok шинок *n.* saloon
shyp шип *n.* thorn
shypinnia шипіння *n* hiss
shypinnia шипіння *n.* sizzle
shypity шипіти *v.i* hiss
shypity шипіти *v.i.* sizzle
shyroko широко *adv.* wide
shyrokyi широкий *a* broad
shyrokyi широкий *a.* general
shyrokyi широкий *a.* wide
shyrota широта *n.* latitude
shyryna ширина *n* breadth
shyryna ширина *n.* width
shyshka шишка *n.* cone
shyty шити *v.t.* sew
shyty шити *v.t.* tailor
siaiania сяяня *n* shine
siaiaty сяяти *v. i* beam
siaiuchyi сяючий *a.* refulgent
siaiuchyi сяючий *a.* resplendent
siaivo сяйво *n.* radiance
siaivo сяйво *n.* refulgence
sich січ *v.t.* whip
sidalo сідало *n.* roost
sidlaty сідлати *v.t.* saddle
sidlo сідло *n.* saddle
siiaty сіяти *v.t.* seed
siiaty сіяти *v.t.* sow
siiesta сієста *n.* siesta
sik сік *n* juice
sil сіль *n.* salt
silske hospodarstvo сільське господарство *n* agriculture
silskohospodarskyi сільськогосподарський *a* agricultural
silskyi сільський *a.* rural
silskyi сільський *a.* rustic
silskyi zhytel сільський житель *n.* villager
sim сім *n.* seven
simdesiat сімдесят *n., a* seventy
simdesiatyi сімдесятий *a.* seventieth
simeinyi сімейний *a.* marital
simia сім'я *n* family

simnadtsiat сімнадцять *n.* seventeen
simnadtsiatyi сімнадцятий *a.* seventeenth
sino сіно *n.* hay
sirchanyi сірчаний *a.* sulphuric
sirka сірка *n.* sulphur
siryi сірий *a.* grey
sisty na korabel сісти на корабель *v. t.* board
sisty na milynu сісти на мілину *v.i.* strand
sit сіть *n.* net
siti сіті *n.* mesh
sitkivka сітківка *n.* retina
siudy сюди *adv.* hither
siurpryz сюрприз *n.* surprise
skakaty скакати *v.t.* gallop
skakaty скакати *v.i.* spring
skalp скальп *n* scalp
skamianilist скам'янілість *n.* fossil
skandal скандал *n* scandal
skanuvaty сканувати *v.t.* scan
skarb скарб *n.* treasure
skarbnyk скарбник *n.* treasurer
skarby скарби *n.* riches
skarha скарга *n* complaint
skarha скарга *n.* grievance
skarhy скарги *n* lament
skarzhytysia скаржитися *v. i* complain
skasovuvaty скасовувати *v.t.* lift
skasovuvaty скасовувати *v.t.* repeal
skasovuvaty скасовувати *v.t.* vacate
skasuvannia скасування *n* cancellation
skasuvannia скасування *n* repeal
skasuvaty скасувати *v.t.* nullify
skaz сказ *n.* rabies
skazaty сказати *v.t.* say

skazhenist скаженість *n.* rage
skazhenyi скажений *a.* furious
skelet скелет *n.* skeleton
skelia скеля *n.* rock
skeptychnyi скептичний *a.* sceptical
skeptyk скептик *n.* sceptic
skeptytsyzm скептицизм *n.* scepticism
skhema схема *n.* scheme
skhid схід *n* east
skhid схід *n.* orient
skhidnyi східний *a* east
skhidnyi східний *a* eastern
skhidnyi східний *a.* oriental
skhody сходи *n.* ladder
skhodynka сходинка *n.* stair
skhodyty сходити *v.t.* ascend
skhodzhennia сходження *n.* ascent
skholastychnyi схоластичний *a.* scholastic
skhopliuvaty схоплювати *v.t.* grip
skhovyshche сховище *n.* refuge
skhovyshche сховище *n.* repository
skhovyshche сховище *n.* vault
skhozhist схожість *n.* resemblance
skhozhist схожість *n.* similitude
skhozhyi схожий *a.* alike
skhozhyi схожий *a.* like
skhozhyi схожий *a.* similar
skhozhyi na mamonta схожий на мамонта *a* mammoth
skhreshchuvaty схрещувати *v.t* fold
skhvalennia схвалення *n.* approbation
skhvalennia схвалення *n* rush
skhvalnyi vyhuk схвальний вигук *n.* cheer
skhyblenyi схиблений *a.* lunatic

skhyl схил *n* slant
skhyl схил *n.* slope
skhyliaty схиляти *v.i.* incline
skhylnist схильність *n* bent
skhylnist схильність *n.* proclivity
skhylnyi схильний *a.* intent
skhylnyi схильний *a.* prone
skhylnyi схильний *a.* willing
skipetr скіпетр *n.* sceptre
sklad склад *n.* storage
sklad склад *n.* syllable
sklad склад *v.t* warehouse
sklad tovariv склад товарів *n.* godown
sklad zbroi склад зброї *n.* armoury
skladalnyk складальник *n* collector
skladannia складання *n* composition
skladannia tablyts складання таблиць *n.* tabulation
skladaty складати *v. t* compose
skladaty складати *v. t* constitute
skladaty складати *v.t.* sum
skladaty koshtorys складати кошторис *v. t* estimate
skladaty v yamu складати в яму *v.t.* pit
skladaty virshy складати вірши *v.t.* versify
skladaty zakonoproekt складати законопроект *n* draught
skladenyi складений *a* compound
skladka складка *n* crease
skladka складка *n* fold
skladnist складність *n.* complication
skladnyi складний *a* difficult
skladnyi складний *a.* multiplex
skladovyi складовий *adj.* component
skladovyi складовий *a.* syllabic

sklasty rozklad скласти розклад *v.t.* schedule
skleiuvaty склеювати *v.t.* conglutinat
sklep склеп *n.* sepulchre
skliar скляр *n.* glazier
sklo скло *n.* glass
sklobii склобій *n.* cullet
sklykannia скликання *n.* convocation
sklykaty скликати *v. t* convene
sklykaty скликати *v.t.* convoke
sklyty склити *v.t.* glaze
sknara скнара *n.* miser
sknara скнара *n.* niggard
sknarist скнарість *n* cupidity
skoba скоба *n* brace
skoba скоба *n.* staple
skopuvaty скопувати *v.t.* trench
skorbota скорбота *n.* woe
skorbotnyi скорботний *n.* mournful
skoriaty скоряти *v.t.* subdue
skoro скоро *adv.* anon
skoro скоро *adv.* soon
skorochennia скорочення *n* abridgement
skorochennia скорочення *n.* breviary
skorochennia скорочення *n.* retrenchment
skorochuvaty скорочувати *v.t* abridge
skorochuvaty скорочувати *v.t.* abbreviate
skorochuvaty скорочувати *v. t* contract
skorochuvaty скорочувати *v. t* curtail
skorochuvaty скорочувати *v.t.* shorten
skorochuvatysia скорочуватися *v. t* dwindle

skorochuvatysia скорочуватися *v.i* shrink

skorpion скорпіон *n.* scorpion

skorynka скоринка *n.* crust

skotch скотч *n.* scotch

skotokrad скотокрад *n* abactor

skotokradstvo скотокрадство *n* abaction

skovuvaty сковувати *v.t* fetter

skovznuty сковзнути *n.* slip

skripliuvaty pidpysom скріплювати підписом *v. t.* countersign

skripyty скріпити *v.t.* tag

skromnist скромність *n* modesty

skromnyi скромний *a.* frugal

skromnyi скромний *a.* humble

skromnyi скромний *a.* modest

skronia скроня *n* temple

skrutne stanovyshche скрутне становище *n.* predicament

skrutne stanovyshche скрутне становище *n.* quandary

skrutnyi скрутний *a.* needy

skrutnyi скрутний *a.* onerous

skryp скрип *n* creak

skryp скрип *n* squeak

skrypal скрипаль *n.* violinist

skrypity скрипіти *v. i* creak

skrypity скрипіти *v.i.* squeak

skrypka скрипка *n* fiddle

skrypka скрипка *n.* violin

skrypuchyi скрипучий *a.* strident

skrytnist скритність *n.* reticence

skubty скубти *v.t.* pluck

skulptor скульптор *n.* sculptor

skulptura скульптура *n.* sculpture

skulpturnyi скульптурний *a.* sculptural

skupchennia narodu скупчення народу *n* confluence

skupchuvaty скупчувати *v.t.* amass

skupchuvatysia скупчуватися *v.i* flock

skupist скупість *n.* avarice

skupyi скупий *a.* mean

skupyi скупий *a.* miserly

skupyi скупий *a.* niggardly

skupyi скупий *a.* stingy

skupyty скупити *v.t* engross

skuter скутер *n.* scooter

skuvaty скувати *v.t.* shackle

skybochka скибочка *n.* slice

skyd скид *n* uplift

skydaty скидати *v.t.* oust

skydaty z tronu скидати з трону *v. t* dethrone

skyhlyty скиглити *v.i.* whine

skynuty shkiru скинути шкіру *v.t.* slough

skypydar скипидар *n.* turpentine

skyrtuvaty скиртувати *v.t.* mow

slabka istota слабка істота *n.* weakling

slabka pidozra слабка підозра *n.* inkling

slabkist слабкість *n* debility

slabkist слабкість *n.* laxity

slabkist слабкість *n.* weakness

slabkyi слабкий *a* delicate

slabkyi слабкий *a* faint

slabkyi слабкий *a* feeble

slabkyi слабкий *a.* impotent

slabkyi слабкий *a.* lax

slabkyi слабкий *a.* little

slabkyi слабкий *a.* slack

slabkyi слабкий *a.* weak

slabnuty слабнути *v.i* faint

slaboumnyi слабоумний *n.* moron

slabshaty слабшати *v.i.* languish

slabshaty слабшати *v.t.* slacken

slabyna слабина *n.* slacks

slastoliubets сластолюбець *n.* sensualist

slastoliubets сластолюбець *n.* voluptuary

slava слава *n* fame

slava слава *n.* glory

slava слава *n.* hail

slava слава *n.* lustre

slava слава *n.* renown

slavetna liudyna славетна людина *n* celebrity

slavetnyi славетний *a* famous

slavnyi славний *a* decent

slavnyi славний *a.* glorious

slavyty славити *v.t.* glorify

slenh сленг *n.* slang

slid слід *v.t.* trace

slid слід *n.* track

slid слід *n.* vestige

slidstvo слідство *n.* inquest

sliduvaty слідувати *v.i* ensue

slipe zakhoplennia сліпе захоплення *n.* infatuation

slipen сліпень *n.* gadfly

slipota сліпота *n* ablepsy

slipota сліпота *n* amauriosis

slipota сліпота *n* blindness

slipuchyi blysk сліпучий блиск *n* dazzle

slipyi сліпий *a* blind

sliuda слюда *n.* mica

sloika слойка *n.* puff

slon слон *n* elephant

slota сльота *n.* slush

slotavyi сльотавий *a.* slushy

slovesnyi словесний *a.* verbal

slovesnyi словесний *a.* wordy

slovnyk словник *n* dictionary

slovnyk словник *n.* vocabulary

slovo слово *n.* say

slovo слово *n.* word

slovo chesti слово честі *n.* parole

sloza сльоза *n.* tear

sloza сльоза *n.* tear

sluha слуга *n* menial

sluha слуга *n.* servant

slukh слух *n.* hearsay

slukh слух *n.* rumour

slukhach слухач *n.* listener

slukhaty слухати *v.i.* listen

slukhnianist слухняність *n.* obedience

slukhnianyi слухняний *a.* obedient

slukhovyi слуховий *adj.* auditive

sluzhyty служити *v.t.* serve

sluzhyty podushkoiu служити подушкою *v.t.* pillow

sluzhyty vstupom служити вступом *v.t.* prelude

slyna слина *n.* saliva

slyna слина *n* spit

slynyty слинити *v. t* beslaver

slyva слива *n.* plum

slyz слиз *n.* mucus

slyz слиз *n.* slime

slyzkyi слизький *a.* slippery

slyzovyi слизовий *a.* mucous

slyzovyi слизовий *a.* slimy

smachnyi смачний *a.* palatable

smachnyi смачний *a.* tasty

smachnyi смачний *a.* toothsome

smahliavyi смаглявий *a.* swarthy

smak смак *n* flavour

smak смак *n.* liking

smak смак *n.* savour

smak смак *n.* taste

smakuvaty смакувати *v.t.* savour

smarahd смарагд *n* emerald

smazhene смажене *n* fry

smazhenyi смажений *a* roast

smazhyty смажити *v.t.* fry

smazhyty смажити *v.t.* roast

smerch смерч *n.* whirlwind

smerdity смердіти *v.i.* stink

smert смерть *n* death

smert смерть *n* decease

smert смерть *n.* end

smert смерть *n.* exit
smertelnyi смертельний *a* deadly
smertnist смертність *n.* mortality
smertnyi смертний *n* mortal
smertnyi смертний *a.* mortal
smiiatysia сміятися *v.i* laugh
smikh сміх *n.* laugh
smilyvist сміливість *n* boldness
smilyvist сміливість *n.* daring
smilyvist сміливість *n.* intrepidity
smilyvyi сміливий *a.* courageous
smilyvyi сміливий *a.* spirited
smishnyi смішний *a* comical
smishnyi смішний *a.* laughable
smishnyi смішний *a.* ridiculous
smishnyi смішний *a.* zany
smittia сміття *n.* garbage
smittia сміття *n.* rubbish
smittia сміття *n.* trash
smittiar сміттяр *n.* scavenger
smity сміти *v. i.* dare
smoh смог *n.* smog
smoktaty смоктати *v.t.* suck
smorid сморід *n.* stench
smorid сморід *n* stink
smorodyna смородина *n.* currant
smykannia смикання *n* pluck
smykannia смикання *n.* pull
smyrennist смиренність *n.* lowliness
smyslovyi смисловий *a.* notional
snariad снаряд *n.* projectile
snasti снасті *n.* tackle
snidanok сніданок *n* breakfast
snih сніг *n.* snow
snip сніп *n.* sheaf
snizhnyi сніжний *a.* snowy
snob сноб *n.* snob
snobistskyi снобістський *v* snobbish
snobizm снобізм *n.* snobbery
snuvaty снувати *v.t.* whisk
sobaka собака *n* dog

sobor собор *n.* cathedral
sochevytsia сочевиця *n.* lentil
sochytysia сочитися *v.i.* trickle
sodomiia содомія *n.* sodomy
sofa софа *n.* sofa
sofist софіст *n.* sophist
sofizm софізм *n.* sophism
sohodni сьогодні *adv.* today
sohodni vvecheri сьогодні ввечері *adv.* tonight
sohodnishnii vechir сьогоднішній вечір *n.* to-night
sohordniashnii den сьогордняшній день *n.* today
soiuz союз *n.* union
soiuznyk союзник *n.* ally
sokhnuty сохнути *v. i.* dry
sokhnuty сохнути *v.i.* wither
sokil сокіл *n* falcon
sokilnyk сокільник *n* hawker
sokovytyi соковитий *a.* juicy
sokovytyi соковитий *a.* lush
sokyra сокира *n.* axe
sokyrka сокирка *n.* hatchet
soldat солдат *v.i.* soldier
solidnyi солідний *a.* massy
solinnia соління *n.* pickle
solist соліст *n.* soloist
solnyi сольний *a.* solo
solnyi kontsert сольний концерт *n.* recital
solo соло *n* solo
solod солод *n.* malt
solodkist солодкість *n.* sweetness
solodkyi солодкий *a.* luscious
solodkyi солодкий *a.* sweet
solodovyi otset солодовий оцет *n* alegar
soloma солома *n.* straw
soloma солома *n.* thatch
solonist солоність *n.* salinity
solonyi солоний *a.* salty

solovei соловей *n.* nightingale
solovyi сольовий *a.* saline
solyty солити *v.t.* condite
solyty солити *v.t* salt
somnabulizm сомнабулізм *n.* lunacy
somnambulizm сомнамбулізм *n.* somnambulism
somyi сьомий *a.* seventh
son сон *n* dream
son сон *n* rest
son сон *n.* sleep
son сон *n.* slumber
sonet сонет *n.* sonnet
sonia соня *n.* sleeper
soniachnyi сонячний *a.* solar
soniachnyi сонячний *a.* sunny
sonlyvist сонливість *n.* somnolence
sonlyvyi сонливий *a.* somnolent
sonnyi сонний *a.* sleepy
sontse сонце *n.* sun
sopinnia сопіння *n* sniff
sopity сопіти *v.i.* sniff
soplo сопло *n.* nozzle
sorochka сорочка *n.* shirt
sorochyty сорочити *v. t* beguile
sorok сорок *n.* forty
soroka сорока *n.* magpie
sorokonizhka сороконіжка *n.* centipede
sorom сором *n.* shame
soromiazlyvyi сором'язливий *a.* bashful
soromyty соромити *v.t.* abash
soromyty соромити *v.t.* shame
sort сорт *a* kind
sort сорт *n.* sort
sortuvaty сортувати *v.t.* assort
sortuvaty сортувати *v.t* grade
sortuvaty сортувати *v.t* sort
sosna сосна *n.* pine
sosok сосок *n.* nipple

sosok сосок *n.* teat
sotnia сотня *n.* hundred
sotsialist, sotsialistychnyi соціаліст, соціалістичний *n,a* socialist
sotsializm соціалізм *n* socialism
sotsialnyi соціальний *n.* social
sotsiolohiia соціологія *n.* sociology
sous соус *n.* sauce
sova сова *n.* owl
sovisno совісно *a.* ashamed
sovist совість *n* conscience
sovok совок *n.* trowel
spad спад *n.* slump
spadaty спадати *v.i.* subside
spadkoiemets спадкоємець *n.* heir
spadkoiemne maino спадкоємне майно *n.* patrimony
spadkovist спадковість *n.* heredity
spadkovyi спадковий *a.* ancestral
spadkovyi спадковий *a.* hereditary
spadshchyna спадщина *n.* heritage
spadshchyna спадщина *n.* legacy
spaika спайка *n.* commissure
spalakh спалах *n* burst
spalakh спалах *n* flash
spalakh спалах *n.* outbreak
spalakh спалах *n.* outburst
spalne mistse спальне місце *n* bunk
spaniiel спанієль *n.* spaniel
spantelychuvaty спантеличувати *v. t.* baffle
spantelychuvaty спантеличувати *v.t.* perplex
spariuvatysia спарюватися *v. t* couple

sparovuvatysia спаровуватися
v.i. copulate
spaty спати *v.i.* sleep
spazm спазм *n.* spasm
spazmatychnyi спазматичний *a.*
spasmodic
speka спека *n* glow
speka спека *n.* heat
spekotnyi спекотний *a.* sultry
spekotnyi спекотний *a.* torrid
spektakl спектакль *n.* play
spekuliant спекулянт *n.* profiteer
spekuliatsiia спекуляція *n.*
jobbery
spekuliuvaty спекулювати *v.i.*
profiteer
spekuliuvaty спекулювати *v.i.*
speculate
sperechannia сперечання *n.*
altercation
sperechatysia сперечатися *v.t.*
argue
sperechatysia сперечатися *v.i*
bet
sperechatysia сперечатися *v. t*
bicker
sperechatysia сперечатися *v. i*
dispute
sperechatysia сперечатися *v.i.*
wrangle
sperma сперма *n.* semen
spetsialist спеціаліст *n.* specialist
spetsializatsiia спеціалізація *n.*
specialization
spetsializuvatysia
спеціалізуватися *v.i.* specialize
spetsialnist спеціальність *n.*
speciality
spetsialnyi спеціальний *a* extra
spetsialnyi спеціальний *a.*
special
spetsii спеції *n.* spice
spetsodiah спецодяг *n.* overall

spetsyfikatsiia специфікація *n.*
specification
spianinnia сп'яніння *n.*
intoxication
spidnytsia спідниця *n.* skirt
spiker спікер *n.* speaker
spilkuvannia спілкування *n.*
intercourse
spilkuvatysia спілкуватися *v. t*
commune
spilkuvatysia спілкуватися *v. t*
communicate
spilkuvatysia спілкуватися *v.t.*
converse
spilkuvatysia спілкуватися *v.t.*
intermingle
spilne navchannia спільне
навчання *n.* co-education
spilno спільно *adv.* jointly
spilnyk спільник *n* accomplice
spilnyk спільник *n.* associate
spilyi спілий *a.* mellow
spir спір *n* controversy
spir спір *n* dispute
spiral спіраль *n.* spiral
spiralnyi спіральний *a.* spiral
spirnyi спірний *a.* objectionable
spirytualist спіритуаліст *n.*
spiritualist
spirytyzm спіритизм *n.*
spiritualism
spishno спішно *adj.* post
spishnyi спішний *a* immediate
spivak співак *n.* singer
spivak співак *n.* songster
spivaty співати *v.i.* sing
spivbesida співбесіда *n.*
interview
spivchuttia співчуття *n*
compassion
spivchuttia співчуття *n*
condolence
spivchuttia співчуття *n.* sympathy

spivchuvaty співчувати *v. t*
commiserate

spivchuvaty співчувати *v. i.*
condole

spivchuvaty співчувати *v.i.*
sympathize

spivisnuvannia співіснування *n*
co-existence

spivisnuvaty співіснувати *v. i*
co-exist

spivmeshanka співмешанка *n*
concubine

spivmeshkaty співмешкати *v. t*
cohabit

spivochyi ptakh співочий птах *n.*
warbler

spivpadaty співпадати *v.i.* match

spivpratsiuvaty співпрацювати *v.*
i collaborate

spivpratsiuvaty співпрацювати *v.*
i co-operate

spivrobitnytstvo співробітництво
n collaboration

spivrobitnytstvo співробітництво
n co-operation

spivrozmirnyi співрозмірний *a.*
proportionate

spivuchasnyk співучасник *n*
accessory

spivvidnoshennia
співвідношення *n.* ratio

spivzvuchchia співзвуччя *n.*
consonance

splachuvaty сплачувати *v.t.*
reimburse

splata сплата *n.* payment

splata сплата *n.* repayment

splata borhu сплата боргу *n.*
satisfaction

splavliaty сплавляти *n.* alloy

splesk сплеск *n* splash

spliachyi сплячий *adv.* asleep

spodivatysia сподіватися *v.t.*
hope

spohad спогад *n.* recollection

spohad спогад *n.* reminiscence

spohliadannia споглядання *n*
contemplation

spohliadaty споглядати *v. t*
contemplate

spohliadaty споглядати *v.i.* muse

spoiuvaty споювати *n.* soldier

spokii спокій *n.* calm

spokii спокій *n.* repose

spokii спокій *n.* tranquility

spokii спокій *n.* serenity

spokiinyi спокійний *a.* peaceable

spokiinyi спокійний *a.* placid

spokiinyi спокійний *a.* secure

spokiinyi спокійний *a.* tranquil

spokusa спокуса *n* allurement

spokusa спокуса *n.* temptation

spokushaty спокушати *v. t.* court

spokushaty спокушати *v. t.*
debauch

spokushaty спокушати *v. t.* entice

spokushaty спокушати *n.* seduce

spokushaty спокушати *v.t.* tempt

spokuslyvyi спокусливий *a*
seductive

spokusnyk спокусник *n.* tempter

spokuta спокута *n.* atonement

spokutuvaty спокутувати *v.i.*
atone

spoluchennia сполучення *n*
compound

spoluchnyi сполучний *a* binding

spoluka сполука *n* compound

sponsor спонсор *n.* sponsor

sponsoruvaty спонсорувати *v.t.*
sponsor

spontannist спонтанність *n.*
spontaneity

spontannyi спонтанний *a.*
spontaneous

sponukannia спонукання *n.*
incentive
sponukannia спонукання *n.*
inducement
sponukannia спонукання *n* urge
sponukaty спонукати *v.t* goad
sponukaty спонукати *v.t.* induce
sponukaty спонукати *v.t.* instigate
sponukaty спонукати *v.t.* prompt
sporadychnyi спорадичний *a.*
sporadic
sporiadzhaty споряджати *v.t.*
apparel
sporiadzhennia спорядження *n.*
munitions
sporidnenist спорідненість *n*
affinity
sporidnenist спорідненість *n.*
kinship
sporidnenyi споріднений *a.* akin
sporidnenyi споріднений *adj*
cognate
sporozhnyty спорожнити *v* empty
sport спорт *n.* sport
sportsmen спортсмен *n.*
sportsman
sportyvnyi спортивний *a.*
sportive
sporudyty спорудити *v. t* erect
sporudzhennia спорудження *n*
construction
sporudzhennia спорудження *n*
erection
sporudzhuvaty споруджувати *v.t.*
rear
sposib zhyttia спосіб життя *n*
living
sposterezhennia спостереження
n. observation
sposterezhennia спостереження
n. surveillance

sposterezhennia za tymy,
khto prokhodyt ispyt
спостереження за тими, хто
проходить іспит *n.* invigilation
sposterezhlyvyi спостережливий
a. observant
sposterihaty спостерігати *v.t.*
observe
sposterihaty спостерігати *v.t*
shadow
sposterihaty спостерігати *v.t.*
watch
spotvoriuvaty спотворювати *v. t.*
corrupt
spotvoriuvaty спотворювати *v. t*
distort
spotvoriuvaty спотворювати *v.t.*
mar
spotvoriuvaty спотворювати *v.t.*
misrepresent
spotvoriuvaty спотворювати *v.t.*
uglify
spotykatysia спотикатися *v.i.*
stumble
spovid сповідь *n* confession
spoviduvaty сповідувати *v. t.*
confess
spoviduvaty сповідувати *v.t.*
profess
spovilnennia сповільнення *n.*
moderation
spovilniuvaty сповільнювати *v.t.*
retard
spovishchaty сповіщати *v.t.*
apprise
spovishchaty сповіщати *v.t*
herald
spovnenyi hidnosti сповнений
гідності *a.* stately
spovniuvaty сповнювати *v.t.*
overwhelm
spozhyvannia споживання *n*
consumption

spozhyvannia споживання *n* expenditure
spozhyvaty споживати *v. t* consume
spraha спрага *n.* thirst
sprahlyi спраглий *adj.* appetent
sprahlyi спраглий *a.* thirsty
sprava справа *n.* affair
sprava справа *n* concern
sprava справа *n* deal
sprava справа *n* file
sprava справа *n.* proposition
spravedlyvist справедливість *n.* justice
spravedlyvyi справедливий *a* equitable
spravedlyvyi справедливий *a* fair
spravedlyvyi справедливий *a.* just
spravedlyvyi справедливий *a.* righteous
spravnyi справний *a.* serviceable
spravytysia справитися *v. i* cope
spravzhnii справжній *a.* genuine
spravzhnii справжній *a.* present
spravzhnii справжній *a.* veritable
spravzhnii справжній *a.* very
spriamovuvaty спрямовувати *v.i.* turn
spriamuvatysia vnyz спрямуватися вниз *v.i.* swoop
sprintovat спрінтовать *v.i.* sprint
sproba спроба *n.* attempt
sproba спроба *n* effort
sproba спроба *v.i* endeavour
sproba спроба *n* try
sprobuvaty спробувати *v.i.* try
spromozhnii спроможній *a* able
sproshchennia спрощення *n.* simplification
sprostiahaty спростягати *v. t* extend

sprostovuvaty спростовувати *v.t.* confute
sprostovuvaty спростовувати *v. t* disprove
sprostovuvaty спростовувати *v.t.* stale
sprostuvannia спростування *n.* refutation
sprostuvaty спростувати *v.t.* refute
sprostyty спростити *v.t.* simplify
sprychyniaty bezlad спричиняти безлад *v. t* clutter
spryiannia сприяння *n.* abetment
spryiannia сприяння *n.* assistance
spryiatlyvyi сприятливий *a.* auspicious
spryiatlyvyi сприятливий *a* congenial
spryiatlyvyi сприятливий *a* favourable
spryiatlyvyi сприятливий *a.* opportune
spryiatlyvyi сприятливий *a.* wholesome
spryiaty сприяти *v. t* contribute
spryiaty сприяти *v.t* favour
spryiaty сприяти *v.t* further
spryiaty сприяти *v.i.* minister
spryiaty сприяти *v.t.* promote
spryiaty zaienniu сприяти заєнню *v.i.* heal
spryimaty сприймати *v.t.* perceive
spryiniatlyvyi сприйнятливий *a.* perceptive
spryiniatlyvyi сприйнятливий *a.* receptive
spryiniattia сприйняття *n.* perception
sprynt спринт *n* sprint

spryntsiuvaty спринцювати *v.t.* syringe
sprytnist спритність *n.* agility
sprytnist спритність *n.* readiness
sprytnist спритність *n.* sleight
sprytnyi спритний *a.* nimble
sprytnyi спритний *a.* resourceful
sprytnyk спритник *n.* trickster
spusk спуск *n.* descent
spusk спуск *n.* launch
spuskaty спускати *v.t.* launch
spustoshennia спустошення *n.* havoc
spustoshennia спустошення *n.* ravage
spustoshuvaty спустошувати *v.t.* depredate
spustoshuvaty спустошувати *v.t.* ravage
spyna спина *n.* back
spynnyi спинний *a.* spinal
spyrtohorilchanyi zavod спиртогорілчаний завод *n* distillery
spys спис *n.* lance
spys спис *n.* spear
spysok список *n* bill
spysok список *n.* list
sriblo срібло *n.* silver
sriblyty сріблити *v.t.* silver
sribnyi срібний *a* silver
ssavets ссавець *n.* mammal
stabilizatsiia стабілізація *n.* stabilization
stabilizuvatysia стабілізуватися *v.t.* stabilize
stabilnist стабільність *n.* stability
stabilnyi стабільний *a.* stable
stadion стадіон *n.* stadium
stado стадо *n.* herd
stainia стайня *n* stable
stal сталь *n.* steel
stalist сталість *n.* permanence

stalyi сталий *a* constant
stameska стамеска *n* chisel
stan стан *n.* fortune
stan стан *n.* state
stan nepevnosti стан непевності *n.* abeyance
stan povnoi bezporadnosti стан повної безпорадності *n.* palsy
stan sprav стан справ *n.* juncture
stan viiny стан війни *n* belligerency
standart стандарт *n.* norm
standart стандарт *n.* standard
standartnyi стандартний *a* standard
standartyzatsiia стандартизація *n.* standardization
standartyzuvaty стандартизувати *v.t.* standardize
stanovyty становити *v.i* amount
stantsiia станція *n.* station
stara diva стара діва *n.* spinster
starannia старання *n* endeavour
starannist старанність *n* diligence
starannyi старанний *a* diligent
starannyi старанний *a* eager
starannyi старанний *a.* studious
starechyi старечий *a.* senile
stareznyi старезний *a.* antiquated
starist старість *n.* senility
starodavnii стародавній *a.* ancient
staromodnyi старомодний *a.* outmoded
starosta староста *n* elder
starosta староста *n.* monitor
starovyna старовина *n.* antiquity
starshyi старший *a* elder
starshyi старший *a.* senior
starshynstvo старшинство *n.* priority

starshynstvo старшинство *n.* superiority

staryi старий *a.* old

stat стать *n.* sex

statechnyi статечний *a.* sedate

statechnyi статечний *a.* staid

stateva zrilist статева зрілість *n.* puberty

statevyi chlen статевий член *n.* penis

statsionarnyi стаціонарний *a.* stationary

stattia стаття *n* article

stattia стаття *n* clause

statuia статуя *n.* statue

statura статура *n.* physique

status статус *n.* status

statut статут *n.* statute

staty na yakir стати на якір *v.t* harbour

statychnyi статичний *n.* static

statyka статика *n.* statics

statysia статися *v.t.* happen

statyst статист *n.* mute

statystychnyi статистичний *a.* statistical

statystyk статистик *n.* statistician

statystyka статистика *n.* statistics

stavaty ставати *v. i* become

stavaty mitsnym ставати міцним *v.t.* toughen

stavka ставка *n* bet

stavka ставка *n.* rate

stavlennia ставлення *n.* attitude

stavnyi ставний *a.* lofty

stavok ставок *n.* pond

stavyty ставити *v.t.* impute

stavyty ставити *v.t* set

stavyty ставити *v.t.* stake

stavyty chyslo ставити число *v. t* date

stavyty initsialy ставити ініціали *v.t* initial

stavyty kapkany ставити капкани *v.t.* trap

stavyty kran ставити кран *v.t.* tap

stavyty krapky nad ставити крапки над *v. t* dot

stavyty liudei (do harmaty) ставити людей (до гармати) *v.t.* man

stavyty na kartu ставити на карту *v.t* hazard

stavyty naholos ставити наголос *v.t* stress

stavyty pechatku ставити печатку *v.t.* seal

stavyty pechatku ставити печатку *v.i.* stamp

stavyty pidmetku ставити підметку *v.t* sole

stavyty po poriadku ставити по порядку *v.t.* range

stavyty umovoiu ставити умовою *v.t.* stipulate

stavyty v stainiu ставити в стайню *v.t.* stable

stavytysia ставитися *v.i.* pertain

stavytysia ставитися *v.t.* relate

stavytysia druzhno ставитися дружньо *v. t.* befriend

stavytysia neseriozno ставитися несерйозно *v.i* trifle

stazhyst стажист *v.t.* intern

stazhyst стажист *n.* probationer

stazhyst стажист *n.* trainee

steblo стебло *n.* stalk

steblo стебло *n.* stem

stehno стегно *n* hip

stehno стегно *n.* thigh

stelazh стелаж *n.* rack

stelia стеля *n.* ceiling

stenohrafiia стенографія *n.* stenography

stenohrafistka стенографістка *n.* stenographer

step степ *n.* steppe
stereotyp стереотип *n.* stereotype
stereotypnyi стереотипний *a.* stereotyped
sterlinh стерлінг *n.* sterling
sternia стерня *n.* stubble
sterpity стерпіти *v.t.* stomach
sterpnyi стерпний *a* endurable
sterty стерти *v. t* efface
sterviatnyk стерв'ятник *n.* vulture
sterylizatsiia стерилізація *n.* sterilization
sterylizuvaty стерилізувати *v.t.* sterilize
sterylnist стерильність *n.* sterility
sterylnyi стерильний *a.* sterile
stetoskop стетоскоп *n.* stethoscope
stezhka стежка *n.* lane
stezhka стежка *n.* trail
stiah стяг *n* flag
stiahnuty remenem стягнути ременем *v.t.* strap
stibaty стібати *v.t.* thresh
stibok стібок *n.* stitch
stichni vody стічні води *n.* sewage
stichnyi стічний *a.* waste
stih стіг *n.* rick
stiikist стійкість *n.* steadiness
stiikyi стійкий *a.* persistent
stiikyi стійкий *a.* resistant
stiikyi стійкий *a.* staunch
stiikyi стійкий *a.* steadfast
stiikyi стійкий *a.* steady
stiikyi стійкий *a.* sturdy
stiikyi prykhylnyk стійкий прихильник *n* stalwart
stiilo стійло *n.* stall
stil стіл *n.* table
stilets стілець *n.* chair
stilets стілець *n.* stool

stina стіна *n.* wall
stinnyi стінний *a.* mural
stiuard стюард *n.* steward
sto tysiach сто тисяч *n* lac, lakh
stobana kovdra стьобана ковдра *n.* quilt
stobaty стьобати *v.t* flog
stobaty стьобати *v.t.* stitch
stohin стогін *n* groan
stohin стогін *n.* moan
stohnaty стогнати *v.i.* groan
stohnaty стогнати *v.i.* lament
stohnaty стогнати *v.i.* moan
stohradusnyi стоградусний *a.* centigrade
stoiachyi стоячий *n.* standing
stoiak стояк *n.* stand
stoiak стояк *n* strut
stoiaty стояти *v.i.* stand
stoiaty na kolinakh стояти на колінах *v.i.* kneel
stoiaty oblychchiam do стояти обличчям до *v.t* face
stoichnyi стоїчний *n.* stoic
stokratnyi стократний *n. & adj* centuple
stoliar столяр *n.* joiner
stolitnii столітній *adj.* centennial
stolittia століття *n.* century
stolychnyi столичний *a.* capital
stolychnyi столичний *a.* metropolitan
stolytsia столиця *n.* capital
stomlenyi стомлений *a.* weary
stomliuiuchyi стомлюючий *a.* laborious
stomliuvaty стомлювати *v.t* fatigue
stomliuvaty стомлювати *v.t.* weary
stomliuvatysia стомлюватися *v.i.* weary
stop стоп *n* stop

stopor стопор *n.* throttle
storichchia сторіччя *n.* centenary
storinka сторінка *n.* page
storona сторона *n.* side
storona u spravi сторона у справі *n.* litigant
storona, shcho vyhrala сторона, що виграла *n.* winner
storona, yaka pidpysalasia сторона, яка підписалася *n.* signatory
storonnia liudyna стороння людина *n.* outsider
storozh сторож *n.* keeper
stos стос *n.* pack
stosovnyi do viiny стосовний до війни *a.* warlike
stosuvatysia стосуватися *v. t* concern
stosuvatysia стосуватися *v. t* encompass
stovbur стовбур *n.* trunk
stovp стовп *n.* pillar
stovp стовп *n* post
stovpotvorinnia стовпотворіння *n.* pandemonium
straik страйк *n* strike
straikari страйкарі *n.* striker
straikuvaty страйкувати *v.t.* strike
strakh страх *n* fear
strakh страх *n.* scare
strakhatysia страхатися *a* dread
strakhovka страховка *n.* insurance
strakhovyshche страховище *n* bogle
strakhuvannia страхування *n.* assurance
strakhuvaty страхувати *v.t.* insure
strashennyi страшенний *a.* terrible
strashnyi страшний *a.* fearful

strata страта *n* execution
strateh стратег *n.* strategist
stratehichnyi стратегічний *a.* strategic
stratehiia стратегія *n.* strategy
stratyty стратити *v.t.* decimate
stratyty стратити *v. t* execute
straus страус *n.* ostrich
strazh страж *n.* guardian
strazhdannia страждання *n.* anguish
strazhdannia страждання *n.* pain
strazhdaty страждати *v.t.* suffer
stremeno стремено *n.* stirrup
stres стрес *n.* stress
strichka стрічка *n.* band
strichka стрічка *n.* ribbon
strichka стрічка *n.* tape
strila стріла *n* arrow
strila стріла *n.* dart
strilianyna стрілянина *n* shoot
striliaty стріляти *v.t.* shoot
striliaty z hvyntivky стріляти з гвинтівки *v.t.* rifle
striliaty zalpamy стріляти залпами *v.t* volley
strimchak стрімчак *n.* cliff
strimka ataka стрімка атака *n.* onslaught
strimkyi стрімкий *a.* impetuous
strofa строфа *n.* stanza
strohist строгість *n.* rigour
strohist строгість *n.* severity
strohist строгість *n.* stringency
stroiovyi стройовий *a.* combatant
strok davnosti строк давності *n.* limitation
strokatyi строкатий *a.* motley
strokatyi строкатий *a.* plural
strokovyi строковий *a.* terminable
strop строп *n.* sling
struchok стручок *n.* pod

struhachka стругачка *n.* sharpener
struhaty стругати *v.t.* whittle
struktura структура *n.* structure
strukturnyi структурний *a.* structural
strumin струмінь *n.* spray
strumochok струмочок *n.* streamlet
strumok струмок *n.* brook
strumok струмок *n.* creek
struna струна *n.* chord
strunkyi стрункий *a.* shapely
strunkyi стрункий *n.* slender
strybaty стрибати *v. i* hop
strybaty стрибати *v.i* jump
strybaty стрибати *v.i.* leap
strybaty perevertom стрибати перевертом *v.i.* somersault
strybok стрибок *n* hop
strybok стрибок *n.* jump
strybok стрибок *n* leap
strybok стрибок *n* skip
stryhty ovets стригти овець *v.t* fleece
stryhuchyi lyshai стригучий лишай *n.* ringworm
stryktura стриктура *n.* stricture
strymanyi стриманий *a.* reticent
strymanyi стриманий *a.* temperate
strymuvannia стримування *n.* inhibition
strymuvaty стримувати *v.t.* moderate
strymuvaty стримувати *v.t.* restrain
strymuvaty стримувати *v.i.* stay
stryzhen стрижень *n.* pivot
stryzhka стрижка *n* coif
stsena сцена *n.* scene
stsena сцена *n.* spectacle
stsenarii сценарій *n.* script

stsenichnyi сценічний *a.* scenic
stsyntylliatsyia сцинтилляция *n.* scintillation
student студент *n.* student
student студент *n.* undergraduate
studiia студія *n.* studio
stukaty стукати *v.t.* knock
stukaty стукати *v.t.* thump
stuknuty стукнути *v.t.* bang
stupin ступінь *n* degree
stupin ступінь *n.* extent
stupin ступінь *n.* grade
stupnuty ступнути *v.i.* step
stverdnyi ствердний *a* affirmative
stverdzhuvaty стверджувати *v.t.* affirm
stverdzhuvaty стверджувати *v.t* state
stvorennia створення *n* creation
stvorennia створення *n.* invention
stvorinnia створіння *n* creature
stvoriuvaty створювати *v. t* create
styhlyi стиглий *a* ripe
styhmat стигмат *n.* stigma
stykhnuty стихнути *v.t.* quiet
styl стиль *n.* language
styl стиль *n.* style
stymul стимул *n.* goad
stymul стимул *n.* stimulus
stymuliator стимулятор *n.* stimulant
stymuliuvaty стимулювати *v.t.* propel
stymuliuvaty стимулювати *v.t.* stimulate
stypendiia стипендія *n.* stipend
styskannia стискання *n* grasp
styskaty стискати *v. t.* compress
styskaty стискати *v.t.* constrict
styskaty стискати *v.t.* throttle
stysle chyslo стисле число *n* multiple

styslist стислість *n* brevity

styslo zapysaty стисло записати *v.t.* jot

styslyi стислий *a* concise

stysnuty стиснути *v.t.* squeeze

**sub`iekt** суб`єкт *n* entity

subiektyvnyi суб'єктивний *a.* subjective

sublimuvaty сублімувати *v.t.* sublimate

subordynatsiia субординація *n.* subordination

subota субота *n.* Saturday

subprodukty субпродукти *n* by-product

substantsiia субстанція *n.* substance

subsydiia субсидія *n.* subsidy

subsydiiuvaty субсидіювати *v.t.* subsidize

suchasnist сучасність *n.* modernity

suchasnyi сучасний *a* contemporary

suchasnyi сучасний *a.* modern

suchkorub сучкоруб *n* limber

sud суд *n.* court

suddia суддя *n.* judge

suddia суддя *n.* magistrate

suddivskyi суддівський *a.* magisterial

sudno судно *n.* ship

sudno судно *n.* vessel

sudnoplavnyi судноплавний *a.* navigable

sudochynstvo судочинство *n.* judicature

sudoustrii судоустрій *n.* judiciary

sudova povistka судова повістка *n.* summons

sudovchynstvo судовчинство *n.* proceeding

sudovo karanyi prostupok судово караний проступок *n.* misdemeanour

sudovyi судовий *a.* judicial

sudovyi nakaz судовий наказ *n.* writ

sudovyi nakaz pro peredachu areshtovanoho do sudu dlia nalezhnoho sudovoho rozhliadu судовий наказ про передачу арештованого до суду для належного судового розгляду *n.* habeas corpus

sudovyi protses судовий процес *n.* litigation

sudovyi prystav судовий пристав *n.* bailiff

sudovyi rozhliad судовий розгляд *n.* trial

sudovyi rozporiadnyk судовий розпорядник *n.* referee

sudynna obolonka судинна оболонка *n* choroid

sudyty судити *v.i.* judge

sudytysia судитися *v.t.* litigate

sufiks суфікс *n.* suffix

sufler суфлер *n.* prompter

suietnyi суєтний *a.* worldly

suk сук *n* bough

sukhar сухар *n* cracker

sukhyi сухий *adj.* arid

sukhyi сухий *a* dry

sukhyi сухий *a.* husky

suknia сукня *n.* gown

sukupnist сукупність *n.* constellation

sukupnist сукупність *n.* totality

suky суки *n.* lop

suma сума *n* amount

suma сума *n.* sum

sumarno сумарно *adv.* summarily

sumarnyi сумарний *a* summary

sumbur сумбур *n.* welter

sumchastyi сумчастий *n.* marsupial

sumiattia сум'яття *n.* tumble

sumish суміш *n* blend

sumish суміш *n.* mixture

sumisnyi сумісний *adj.* compliant

sumisnytstvo сумісництво *n.* plurality

sumka сумка *n.* bag

sumka сумка *n.* pouch

sumlinno сумлінно *adv* bonafide

sumlinnyi сумлінний *a* bonafide

sumniv сумнів *n* distrust

sumniv сумнів *n* doubt

sumniv сумнів *n.* query

sumnivatysia сумніватися *v. t.* distrust

sumnivatysia сумніватися *v. i* doubt

sumnivnyi сумнівний *a.* questionable

sumnivnyi сумнівний *a.* uncertain

sumnyi сумний *a.* grievous

sumnyi сумний *a.* lamentable

sumnyi сумний *a.* pitiful

sumnyi сумний *a.* rueful

sumnyi сумний *a.* sad

sumnyi сумний *n.* woeful

sumovaty сумовати *v.t.* sadden

sumovytyi сумовитий *a* cheerless

sumuvaty сумувати *v.i* long

sumuvaty сумувати *v.i.* mourn

sup суп *n.* soup

superechka суперечка *n.* contest

superechka суперечка *n.* wrangle

superechyty суперечити *v. t* contradict

superechyty суперечити *v. t* contrast

superechyty суперечити *v.t.* gainsay

supermen супермен *n.* superman

supernychaty суперничати *v.t.* rival

supernychaty суперничати *v.i.* vie

supernyk суперник *n* agonist

supernyk суперник *n.* rival

supernytstvo суперництво *n.* rivalry

suprotyvnyi супротивний *a* contrary

suprovid супровід *n* accompaniment

suprovidne maino супровідне майно *n.* paraphernalia

suprovodzhuvaty супроводжувати *v.t.* accompany

suprovodzhuvaty супроводжувати *v. t* escort

suputnyk супутник *n.* companion

suputnyk супутник *n.* satellite

suputnyk супутник *n.* sputnik

surmyty сурмити *v. t* blare

susha суша *n.* land

susid сусід *n.* neighbour

susidstvo сусідство *n.* neighbourhood

susidstvo сусідство *n.* vicinity

suspilstvo суспільство *n.* community

suspilstvo суспільство *n.* society

sut суть *n* content

sut суть *n.* gist

sutinkovyi сутінковий *n* dusk

sutinky сутінки *n* twilight

sutulist сутулість *n* stoop

sutulytysia сутулитися *v.i.* stoop

sutychka сутичка *n* collision

sutychka сутичка *n* combat1

sutychka сутичка *n.* encounter

sutychka сутичка *n.* grapple

suvenir сувенір *n.* memento

suvenir сувенір *n.* remembrance

suvenir сувенір *n.* souvenir
suveren суверен *n.* sovereign
suverenitet суверенітет *n.*
  sovereignty
suverennyi суверенний *a.*
  sovereign
suvii сувій *n.* scroll
suvoryi суворий *a.* austere
suvoryi суворий *a.* rigorous
suvoryi суворий *a.* stern
suvoryi суворий *a.* strict
suvoryi суворий *a.* stringent
svarka сварка *n* fray
svarka сварка *n.* quarrel
svaryty сварити *v. t.* chide
svarytysia сваритися *v. i. & n*
  brawl
svarytysia сваритися *v.i.* quarrel
svavilnyi свавільний *a.*
  headstrong
sverbity свербіти *v.i.* itch
sverbizh свербіж *n.* itch
sverdlo свердло *n* drill
sverdlyty свердлити *v. t.* drill
svetr светр *n.* sweater
Sviashchenne pysannia
  Священне писання *n.* scripture
sviashchennyi священний *a.*
  heavenly
sviashchennyi священний *a.*
  sacred
sviashchenstvo священство *n.*
  priesthood
sviashchenyk священик *a.*
  ministrant
sviashchenyk священик *n.*
  parson
sviashchenyk священик *n.* priest
sviatist святість *n.* sanctity
sviatkovyi святковий *a* festive
sviatkuvannia святкування *n.*
  celebration

sviatkuvannia святкування *n.*
  commemoration
sviatkuvaty святкувати *v. t. & i.*
  celebrate
sviatkuvaty святкувати *v.t.*
  solemnize
sviato свято *n* festival
sviato свято *n.* jubilee
sviatotatstvo святотатство *n.*
  sacrilege
sviatyi святий *a.* holy
sviatyi святий *n.* saint
sviatyi святий *a.* saintly
sviatylyshche святилище *n.*
  sanctuary
svichka свічка *n.* candle
svidchyty свідчити *v.i.* witness
svidchyty proty свідчити проти
  v.i. militate
svidok свідок *n.* witness
svidok, yakyi daie pokazannia
  pid prysiahoiu свідок, який
  дає показання під присягою *n.*
  deponent
svidomyi свідомий *a.* aware
svidotstvo свідоцтво *n.*
  testimonial
svit світ *n.* world
svitanok світанок *n* dawn
svitaty світати *v. i.* dawn
svitlist світлість *n.* lordship
svitlo світло *n.* light
svitlyi світлий *a* light
svitski liudy світські люди *n.* ton
svitskyi світський *a.* profane
svitylo світило *n.* lamp
svitytsia світиться *a.* luminous
svizhyi свіжий *a.* fresh
svoboda свобода *n.* freedom
svoboda свобода *n.* liberty
svoiaky свояки *n.* in-laws
svoiechasno своєчасно *adv* pat

svoiechasnyi своєчасний *a.* seasonable

svoieridnyi своєрідний *a.* peculiar

svynarnyk свинарник *n.* sty

svynia свиня *n.* pig

svynia свиня *n.* sow

svyniache salo свиняче сало *n.* lard

svynka свинка *n.* mumps

svyntsevyi свинцевий *a.* leaden

svynyna свинина *n.* pork

svyst kuli свист кулі *n.* zip

svystity свистіти *v.i.* whistle

svystok свисток *n* whistle

svyta свита *n.* retinue

svydchyty свідчити *v.t.* attest

sydiachyi сидячий *a.* sedentary

sydinnia сидіння *n.* seat

sydity сидіти *v.t.* seat

sydity сидіти *v.i.* sit

sydity navpochipkakh сидіти навпочіпках *v.i.* squat

syhara сигара *n* cheroot

syhara сигара *n.* cigar

syhareta сигарета *n.* cigarette

syhnal сигнал *n.* signal

syhnalizuvaty сигналізувати *v.t.* signal

syhnalnyi сигнальний *v.t* alarm

syhnalnyi сигнальний *a.* signal

syla сила *n* force

syla сила *n.* verve

syla dukhu сила духу *n.* fortitude

syla inertsii сила інерції *n.* inertia

syla voli сила волі *n.* will

sylf сильф *n.* sylph

sylna storona сильна сторона *n.* forte

sylne bazhannia сильне бажання *n.* longing

sylno сильно *adv.* sharp

sylnodiinyi сильнодійний *a.* drastic

sylnyi сильний *a.* strong

sylnyi сильний *a.* vigorous

sylnyi udar сильний удар *v.t.* whack

syluet силует *n.* silhouette

symetriia симетрія *n.* symmetry

symetrychnyi симетричний *a.* symmetrical

symfoniia симфонія *n.* symphony

sympatychnyi симпатичний *a.* sympathetic

sympozium симпозіум *n.* symposium

symptom симптом *n.* symptom

symptomatychnyi симптоматичний *a.* symptomatic

symuliuvaty симулювати *v.i.* sham

symvol символ *n.* symbol

symvolichnyi символічний *a.* symbolic

symvolizm символізм *n.* symbolism

symvolizuvaty символізувати *v.t.* symbolize

syn син *n.* son

syniak синяк *n* bruise

synii kolir синій колір *n* blue

synonim синонім *n.* synonym

synonimichnyi синонімічний *a.* synonymous

synopsys синопсис *n.* synopsis

syntaksys синтаксис *n.* syntax

syntetychnyi синтетичний *a.* synthetic

syntetychnyi produkt синтетичний продукт *n* synthetic

syntez синтез *n.* synthesis

sypatysia сипатися *v.i* hail

syr сир *n.* cheese
syr сир *n* curd
syrena сирена *n.* siren
syrity сиріти *v. t.* damp
syrop сироп *n.* syrup
syrota сирота *n.* orphan
syryi сирий *a.* humid
systema система *n.* system
systematychnyi систематичний *a.* systematic
systematyzuvaty систематизувати *v.t.* systematize
sytist ситість *n.* satiety
syto сито *n.* sieve
sytuatsiia ситуація *n.* situation

T

ta, shcho narodzhuvala та, що народжувала *a.* multiparous
tabir табір *n.* camp
tabirnyi табірний *adj* castral
tabletka таблетка *n.* tablet
tablychnyi табличний *a.* tabular
tabu табу *n.* taboo
tabuliator табулятор *n.* tabulator
taiemna uhoda таємна угода *n* collusion
taiemnychyi таємничий *a.* mysterious
taiemnyi таємний *adj.* clandestine
taiemnytsia таємниця *n* dark
taiemnytsia таємниця *n* enigma
taiemnytsia таємниця *n.* mystery
taifun тайфун *n.* typhoon
tainstvo таїнство *n.* sacrament
tainyk тайник *n* cache
taitysia таїтися *v.i.* lurk
tak так *adv.* so
tak так *adv.* yes
tak chy inakshe так чи інакше *adv.* anyhow

tak samo, yak так само, як *conj* both
tak yak так як *conj.* as
takhta тахта *n.* ottoman
takozh також *adv.* also
takozh також *adv.* likewise
taksi таксі *n.* cab
taksi таксі *n.* taxi
takt такт *n.* tick
taktovnist тактовність *n.* tact
taktovnyi тактовний *a.* tactful
taktyk тактик *n.* tactician
taktyka тактика *n.* tactics
takyi такий *a.* such
takym chynom таким чином *conj.* so
takym chynom таким чином *adv.* thus
talant талант *n.* talent
taliia талія *n.* waist
talisman талісман *n.* mascot
talisman талісман *n.* talisman
tam там *adv.* there
tamarynd тамаринд *n.* tamarind
tanets танець *n* dance
tanker танкер *n.* tanker
tantsiuvaty танцювати *v. t.* dance
tanuty танути *v.i.* melt
tanuty танути *v.i* thaw
tapochky тапочки *n. pl* slipper
taranyty таранити *v.t.* ram
tarhan тарган *n* cockroach
taryf тариф *n.* tariff
tasma тасьма *n.* string
tasma тасьма *n.* web
tato, tatus тато, татусь *n* dad, daddy
tatuiuvannia татуювання *n.* tattoo
tatuiuvaty татуювати *v.i.* tattoo
taverna таверна *n.* tavern
teatr театр *n.* theatre
teatralnyi театральний *a.* theatrical

teist теїст *n.* theist
teizm теїзм *n.* theism
tekhnichne obsluhovuvannia технічне обслуговування *n.* maintenance
tekhnichnyi технічний *a.* scientific
tekhnichnyi технічний *n.* technical
tekhnik технік *n.* technician
tekhnika техніка *n.* technique
tekhnoloh технолог *n.* technologist
tekhnolohichnyi технологічний *a.* technological
tekhnolohiia технологія *n.* technology
tekst текст *n.* text
tekstovyi текстовий *n.* textual
tekstura текстура *n.* texture
tekstylnyi текстильний *a.* textile
tekty текти *v.i* flow
tekty текти *v.i.* leak
tekty текти *v.i.* stream
tekuchyi текучий *a* fluid
telebachennia телебачення *n.* television
telefon телефон *n.* phone
telefon телефон *n.* telephone
telehrafiia телеграфія *n.* telegraphy
telehrafist телеграфіст *n.* telegraphist
telehrafnyi телеграфний *n.* telegraph
telehrafnyi телеграфний *a.* telegraphic
telehrafuvaty телеграфувати *v.t.* telegraph
telehrafuvaty телеграфувати *v.t.* wire
telehrama телеграма *n.* telegram
telepat телепат *n.* telepathist
telepatiia телепатія *n.* telepathy

telepatychnyi телепатичний *a.* telepathic
telepen телепень *n.* laggard
teleperedacha телепередача *n.* telecast
teleskop телескоп *n.* telescope
teleskopichnyi телескопічний *a.* telescopic
telia теля *n.* calf
tema тема *n.* subject
tema тема *n.* theme
tema тема *n.* topic
tematychnyi тематичний *a.* thematic
temnity темніти *v.i.* darkle
temno-bordovyi темно-бордовий *a* maroon
temno-bordovyi kolir темно-бордовий колір *n.* maroon
temnyi темний *a.* backward
temnyi темний *a* dark
temnyi темний *a.* gloomy
temnyi темний *a.* shadowy
temnyi темний *a.* sombre
temp темп *n* pace
temperament темперамент *n.* temperament
temperamentnyi темпераментний *a.* temperamental
temperatura температура *n.* temperature
tendentsiia тенденція *n.* tendency
tendentsiia тенденція *n.* trend
tender тендер *n* tender
tenditnyi тендітний *a.* brittle
tenditnyi тендітний *a.* fragile
tenditnyi тендітний *a.* slight
teneta тенета *n. pl.* toils
tenis теніс *n.* tennis
teokratiia теократія *n.* theocracy
teorema теорема *n.* theorem

teoretychnyi теоретичний *a.* theoretical

teoretyk теоретик *n.* theorist

teoretyzuvaty теоретизувати *v.i.* theorize

teoriia теорія *n.* theory

teplo тепло *n.* warmth

teplovyi тепловий *a.* thermal

teplyi теплий *a.* lukewarm

teplyi теплий *a.* warm1

terapevt терапевт *n.* physician

terapiia терапія *n.* therapy

terasa тераса *n.* terrace

terier тер'єр *n.* terrier

termin термін *n.* term

termin orendy термін оренди *n.* tenancy

terminal термінал *n* terminal

terminolohichnyi термінологічний *a.* terminological

terminolohiia термінологія *n.* terminology

terminovist терміновість *n.* urgency

terminovyi терміновий *a.* urgent

termometr термометр *n.* thermometer

termos (kolba) термос (колба) *n.* thermos (flask)

ternystyi тернистий *a.* thorny

teror терор *n.* terror

teroryst терорист *n.* terrorist

teroryzm тероризм *n.* terrorism

teroryzuvaty тероризувати *v.t.* terrorize

terpinnia терпіння *n.* patience

terpity терпіти *v.t.* tolerate

terpliachist терплячість *n.* endurance

terpliachyi терплячий *a.* patient

terpymist терпимість *n.* tolerance

terpymist терпимість *n.* toleration

terpymyi терпимий *a.* lenient

terpymyi терпимий *a.* tolerable

tertia тертя *n.* friction

terty терти *v.t* grate

terty терти *v.t.* rub

terytorialnyi територіальний *a.* territorial

terytoriia територія *n.* territory

terzaty терзати *v.t* maul

terzaty терзати *v.i.* prey

tesliar тесляр *n.* carpenter

tesliarski roboty теслярські роботи *n.* carpentry

test тест *n* test

testuvaty тестувати *v.t.* test

tezka тезка *n.* namesake

ti, khto ті, хто *dem. pron.* that

tiaha тяга *n.* traction

tiahar тягар *n.* onus

tiahar тягар *n.* tax

tiahty тягти *v. t* drag

tiahty тягти *v.t.* manhandle

tiahtysia тягтися *v.i.* plod

tiahtysia тягтися *v.i.* toil

tiamushchyi тямущий *a* docile

tiara тіара *n.* tiara

tiazhity тяжіти *v.i.* gravitate

tikaty тікати *v. i* decamp

tikaty тікати *v.i* escape

tilesnyi тілесний *a* corporal

tilky тільки *adv.* just

tilky тільки *adv.* only

tilky тільки *conj.* yet

tilo тіло *n* body

tilo тіло *n.* solidarity

tin тінь *n.* ghost

tin тінь *n.* shade

tin тінь *n.* shadow

tipatysia тіпатися *v.i.* pant

tisnyi zviazok тісний зв'язок *n.* intimacy

tisto тісто *n* dough

titka тітка *n.* aunt

tiulen тюлень *n.* seal
tiurban тюрбан *n.* turban
tiuremnyk тюремник *n.* jailer
tiuremnyk тюремник *n.* warder
tiurma тюрма *n.* prison
tiutiun тютюн *n.* tobacco
tkach ткач *n.* weaver
tkanyna тканина *n* cloth
tkanyna тканина *n* textile
tkanyna тканина *n.* tissue
tkatskyi verstat ткацький
  верстат *n* loom
tkaty ткати *v.t.* weave
tlity тліти *v.i.* smoulder
tlumachyty тлумачити *v.t.*
  interpret
tmianist тьмяність *v.t.* tarnish
tmianyi тьмяний *a.* lacklustre
tmianyi тьмяний *a.* wan
tochka точка *n* dot
tochka точка *n.* point
tochka zoru точка зору *n* angle
tochka zoru точка зору *n.*
  standpoint
tochna kopiia точна копія *n.* ditto
tochnist точність *n.* accuracy
tochnist точність *n.* precision
tochnist точність *n.* punctuality
tochnyi точний *a.* accurate
tochnyi точний *a* exact
tochnyi точний *a.* precise
tochnyi postril точний постріл *n*
  bull's eye
tochyty точити *v.t.* sharpen
tochyty точити *v.t.* whet
todi тоді *adv.* then
todishnii тодішній *a* then
toha тога *n.* toga
toi той *pron.* such
toi той *rel. pron.* that
toi, khto boretsia той, хто
  бореться *n* combatant1

toi, khto ne pidkhodyt той, хто
  не підходить *n.* misfit
**toi, khto pidtrymuie
  kandydaturu** той, хто
  підтримує кандидатуру *n.*
  seconder
**toi, kto slidkuie za tym, shchob
  studenty ne spysuvaly pid
  chas ispytiv** той, кто слідкує
  за тим, щоб студенти не
  списували під час іспитів *n.*
  invigilator
toi, shcho ne maie tsentru той,
  що не має центру *adj* acentric
toi, shcho ne znaie той, що не
  знає *a.* unaware
**toi, shcho vidnosytsia
  do Arystofana** той, що
  відноситься до Аристофана
  adj aristophanic
toi, shcho vtomliuie той, що
  втомлює *a.* tiresome
toi, shcho vysoko lytaie той, що
  високо літає *adj* altivalent
toi, shcho zablukav той, що
  заблукав *adv.,* astray
toi, shcho zasluhovuie doviry
  той, що заслуговує довіри *a.*
  trustworthy
toi, shcho zhyvytsia derevynoiu
  той, що живиться дерев иною
  a. xylophagous
**toi, shcho znakhodytsia v stani
  viiny** той, що знаходиться в
  стані війни *a* belligerent
toi, shcho zrostaie той, що
  зростає *adj.* adnascent
tokar токар *n.* turner
tokarnyi verstat токарний
  верстат *n.* lathe
toksychna rechovyna токсична
  речовина *n.* intoxicant

tolerantnyi толерантний *a.* tolerant
tom том *n.* tome
tomu тому *adv.* ago
tomu тому *adv.* since
tomu тому *adv.* therefore
tomu shcho тому що *conj.* because
ton тон *n.* tone
tonizuiuchyi тонізуючий *a.* tonic
tonkist тонкість *n.* subtlety
tonko spryimaiuchyi тонко сприймаючий *a.* keen
tonkyi тонкий *a* fine
tonkyi тонкий *a.* slim
tonkyi тонкий *a.* subtle
tonkyi тонкий *a.* thin
tonkyi muslin тонкий муслін *n.* mull
tonna тонна *n.* tonne
tonuty тонути *v.i* drown
tonzura тонзура *n.* tonsure
topaty топати *v.t.* conculcate
topaz топаз *n.* topaz
topohraf топограф *n.* topographer
topohrafichnyi топографічний *a.* topographical
topohrafiia топографія *n.* topography
topolia тополя *n.* poplar
toptaty топтати *v.t.* trample
topyty топити *v.i.* sink
torf торф *n.* turf
torh торг *n* auction
torhivlia торгівля *n* commerce
torhivlia торгівля *n.* trade
torhovets торговець *n.* monger
torhovets торговець *n.* seller
torhovets торговець *n.* trader
torhovets kantseliarskym pryladdiam торговець канцелярським приладдям *n.* stationer

torhovyi торговий *a* commercial
torhuvaty торгувати *v.i* trade
torhuvatysia торгуватися *v.i.* haggle
torkaty lapoiu торкати лапою *v.t.* paw
torkatysia торкатися *v.t.* touch
torkatysia noskom торкатися носком *v.t.* toe
tornado торнадо *n.* tornado
torpeda торпеда *n.* torpedo
torpeduvaty торпедувати *v.t.* torpedo
torzhestvo торжество *n.* jubilation
tost тост *n.* pledge
tost тост *n.* toast
totalnyi тотальний *a.* total
totozhnist тотожність *n.* oneness
totozhnist тотожність *n.* similarity
tovar товар *n.* commodity
tovar товар *n* good
tovar товар *n.* merchandise
tovarnyi товарний *a.* marketable
tovaroobmin товарообмін *n.* barter2
tovarysh товариш *n.* comrade
tovarysh товариш *n.* helpmate
tovaryskist товариськість *n.* joviality
tovaryskist товариськість *n.* sociability
tovaryskyi товариський *a.* jovial
tovaryskyi товариський *a.* sociable
tovarystvo товариство *n.* confraternity
tovkotnecha товкотнеча *n.* throng
tovkty v stupi товкти в ступі *v.t.* mortar
tovpytysia товпитися *v.t.* mob
tovpytysia товпитися *v.t.* throng
tovstyi товстий *a.* stout

tovstyi товстий *a.* thick
tradytsiia традиція *n.* tradition
tradytsiinyi традиційний *a.* traditional
trafaret трафарет *n.* stencil
trahediia трагедія *n.* tragedy
trahichnyi трагічний *a.* tragic
trahik трагік *n.* tragedian
traiektoriia траєкторія *n.* trace
trakt тракт *n* tract
traktat трактат *n.* tract
traktat трактат *n.* treatise
traktor трактор *n.* tractor
traktyr трактир *n.* inn
tramvai трамвай *n.* tram
trans транс *n.* trance
transformatsiia трансформація *n.* transformation
transformuvaty трансформувати *v.t.* transfigure
transformuvaty трансформувати *v.t.* transform
transkrybuvaty транскрибувати *v.t.* transcribe
transkryptsiia транскрипція *n.* transcription
transliuvaty транслювати *v. t* broadcast
transport транспорт *n.* traffic
transport транспорт *n.* transport
transportuvannia транспортування *n.* transportation
tranzyt транзит *n.* transit
trapliatysia траплятися *v. t* befall
trapliatysia траплятися *v.t.* offer
traur траур *n.* mourning
trava трава *n* grass
trava трава *n.* herb
traven травень *n.* May
travlennia травлення *n* digestion
treiler трейлер *n.* trailer
trel трель *n* warble

tremtinnia тремтіння *n* quake
tremtinnia тремтіння *n* shake
tremtinnia тремтіння *n* shudder
tremtinnia тремтіння *n.* tremor
tremtity тремтіти *v.i.* quake
tremtity тремтіти *v.i.* shiver
tremtity тремтіти *v.i.* tremble
trener тренер *n* coach
trenuvannia тренування *n.* tuition
trenuvaty тренувати *v.t.* train
trepet трепет *n.* quiver
trepet трепет *n.* thrill
treteiskyi sud третейський суд *n.* arbitration
treteiskyi suddia третейський суддя *n.* arbitrator
treteiskyi suddia третейський суддя *n.* umpire
tretii третій *a.* third
tretii третій *a* three
tretyna третина *n.* third
triasinnia трясіння *n.* jolt
triaska тряска *n.* jumble
triasovyna трясовина *n* bog
triasty трясти *v.t.* jolt
triasty трясти *v.i.* shake
triastysia трястися *v.t.* jumble
triitsia трійця *n.* trinity
trio тріо *n.* trio
triplikat тріплікат *n* triplicate
tripotity тріпотіти *v.i.* palpitate
tripotity тріпотіти *v.i.* quiver
tripotity тріпотіти *v.t.* thrill
tripotity тріпотіти *v.i.* throb
trishchaty тріщати *v. i* blether
trishchaty тріщати *v. i* brustle
trishchaty тріщати *n. & v. i* clack
trishchaty тріщати *v.i.* rattle
trishchyna тріщина *n* cleft
trishchyna тріщина *n* fissure
trishchyna тріщина *n* flaw
trishchyna тріщина *n.* rift
trishky трішки *n.* modicum

trisk тріск *n* crack
triuk трюк *n* trick
triumf тріумф *n.* triumph
triumfalnyi тріумфальний *a.* triumphal
triumfuiuchyi тріумфуючий *a.* triumphant
triumfuvaty тріумфувати *v. i* exult
triumfuvaty тріумфувати *v.i.* triumph
trofei трофей *n.* loot
trofei трофей *n.* trophy
troianda троянда *n.* rose
trokhy трохи *adv.* somewhat
tron трон *n.* throne
tropichna lykhomanka тропічна лихоманка *n.* dengue
tropichnyi тропічний *a.* tropical
tropik тропік *n.* tropic
trotuar тротуар *n.* pavement
truba труба *n.* chimney
truba труба *n.* pipe
truba труба *n.* trumpet
trubchastyi трубчастий *a.* tubular
trubka трубка *n.* tube
trudnoshchi труднощі *n* difficulty
trudovyi stazh трудовий стаж *n.* seniority
truna труна *n* coffin
trup труп *n* corpse
trupa трупа *n.* troupe
truskyi труський *a.* jerky
try три *n.* three
trybuna трибуна *n.* rostrum
trybunal трибунал *n.* tribunal
trychi тричі *adv.* thrice
trydtsiat тридцять *n.* thirty
trydtsiatyi тридцятий *a.* thirtieth
trykolirnyi триколірний *a.* tricolour
trykolisnyi velosyped триколісний велосипед *n.* tricycle
trykolor триколор *n* tricolour
trykutnyi трикутний *a.* triangular
trykutnyk трикутник *n.* triangle
trymaty тримати *v.t* hold
trymaty тримати *v.t.* keep
trymaty pid vartoiu тримати під вартою *v. t* detain
trymaty v pevnykh mezhakh тримати в певних межах *v.t.* restrict
trymatysia триматися *v. t.* carry
trynadtsiat тринадцять *n.* thirteen
trynadtsiata chastyna тринадцята частина *n* thirtieth
trynadtsiatyi тринадцятий *a.* thirteenth
trystoronnii тристоронній *a.* tripartite
tryvala vorozhnecha тривала ворожнеча *n.* feud
tryvale nedoidannia тривале недоїдання *n* hunger
tryvalist тривалість *n* duration
tryvalist тривалість *a.* lasting
tryvalyi тривалий *a.* lengthy
tryvialnyi тривіальний *a.* trivial
tryvkyi тривкий *a.* substantial
tryvoha тривога *n* alarm
tryvoha тривога *n* anxiety
tryvozhytysia тривожитися *v.t.* trouble
trysk тріск *n* crash
tsarevbyvstvo царевбивство *n.* regicide
tsariuvaty царювати *v.i.* reign
tsarskyi царський *a.* royal
tseberka цеберка *n.* pail
tsehla цегла *n* brick
tsehla povitrianoho sushinnia цегла повітряного сушіння *n.* adobe
tselibat целібат *n.* celibacy
tsement цемент *n.* cement

tsementuvaty цементувати *v. t.* cement

tsent цент *n* cent

tsentr центр *n* center

tsentr центр *n* centre

tsentr центр *n.* thick

tsentr uvahy центр уваги *n.* limelight

tsentralnyi центральний *a.* central

tsentralnyi центральний *n.* midland

tsenzor цензор *n.* censor

tsenzura цензура *n.* censorship

tsenzura цензура *n.* censure

tsenzuruvaty цензурувати *v. t.* censor

tserebralnyi церебральний *adj* cerebral

tseremonialnyi церемоніальний *a.* ceremonial

tseremoniia церемонія *n.* ceremony

tseremonnyi церемонний *a.* ceremonious

tserkovnyi himn церковний гімн *n.* hymn

tserkovnyi storozh церковний сторож *n.* beadle

tserkva церква *n.* church

tsiatka цятка *n.* mottle

tsiatochka цяточка *n.* mote

tsikavist цікавість *n* curiosity

tsikavyi цікавий *a* curious

tsikavyi цікавий *a.* interesting

tsikavyi цікавий *a.* nosey

tsikavytysia цікавитися *v.i.* wonder

tsil ціль *n.* objective

tsile ціле *n* whole

tsilespriamovanyi цілеспрямований *a* outright

tsiliushchyi цілющий *a* curative

tsiliushchyi цілющий *a.* salutary

tsilkom цілком *adv* all

tsilkom цілком *a* bodily

tsilkom цілком *adv.* fully

tsilkom цілком *adv.* quite

tsilkom цілком *adv.* stark

tsilkovytyi цілковитий *a.* mere

tsiluvaty цілувати *v.t.* kiss

tsilyi цілий *a* entire

tsilyi цілий *a.* whole

tsilyna цілина *n* virgin

tsilyna цілина *n.* wilderness

tsilyty цілити *v.i.* aim

tsina ціна *n.* expense

tsina ціна *n.* price

tsinnist цінність *n.* value

tsinnyi цінний *a.* useful

tsinnyi цінний *a.* valuable

tsinuvaty цінувати *v.t.* value

tsipok ціпок *n.* cane

tskuvannia цькування *n.* persecution

tskuvaty sobakamy цькувати собаками *v. t* dog

tsnotlyvist цнотливість *n.* chastity

tsnotlyvyi цнотливий *a.* chaste

tsokaty цокати *v.i.* tick

tsokotity цокотіти *v. t.* chatter

tsukaty цукати *n.* sweetmeat

tsukerka цукерка *n.* candy

tsukerka цукерка *n* sweet

tsukor цукор *n.* sugar

tsukrovyi diabet цукровий діабет *n* diabetes

tsutsenia цуценя *n.* puppy

tsutsenia цуценя *n.* whelp

tsvil цвіль *n.* mildew

tsvirinkannia цвірінькання *n* chirp

tsvirinkaty цвірінькати *v.i.* chirp

tsvirkun цвіркун *n* cricket

tsvisty цвісти *v.i* blossom

tsvisty цвісти *v.i.* thrive
tsvitinnia цвітіння *n* blossom
tsvyntar цвинтар *n.* cemetery
tsybulia цибуля *n.* onion
tsybulia-porei цибуля-порей *n.*
  leek
tsyferblat циферблат *n.* dial
tsyfra цифра *n* digit
tsyfra цифра *a.* numeral
tsykl цикл *n* cycle
tsyklichnyi циклічний *a* cyclic
tsyklon циклон *n.* cyclone
tsylindr циліндр *n* cylinder
tsynik цинік *n* cynic
tsynk цинк *n.* zinc
tsynovka циновка *n.* mat
tsyrk цирк *n.* circus
tsyrkuliar циркуляр *n.* circular
tsyrkuliuvaty циркулювати *v. i.*
  circulate
tsysterna цистерна *n.* tank
tsytadel цитадель *n.* citadel
tsytata цитата *n.* quotation
tsytuvaty цитувати *v.t.* quote
tsyvilizatsiia цивілізація *n.*
  civilization
tsyvilizuvaty цивілізувати *v. t*
  civilize
tsyvilna osoba цивільна особа *n*
  civilian
tsyvilnyi цивільний *a* civic
tsyvilnyi цивільний *a* civil
tualet туалет *n.* lavatory
tualet туалет *n.* toilet
tuberkuloz туберкульоз *n.*
  tuberculosis
tudy туди *adv.* thither
tuflia туфля *n.* shoe
tuhyi тугий *a.* tight
tuman туман *n* fog
tuman туман *n.* mist
tuman туман *n.* vapour
tumannist туманність *n.* nebula

tumannyi туманний *a.* hazy
tumannyi туманний *a.* misty
tumbler тумблер *n.* tumbler
tunel тунель *n.* tunnel
tupyi тупий *a* blunt
tupyi тупий *a* dull
tupyi тупий *a.* obtuse
tupyk тупик *n* deadlock
tur тур *n.* tour
turbina турбіна *n.* turbine
turbotlyvyi турботливий *a.*
  respective
turbulentnist турбулентність *n.*
  turbulence
turbulentnyi турбулентний *a.*
  turbulent
turbuvaty турбувати *v.t.* ail
turbuvaty турбувати *v. t*
  commove
turbuvaty турбувати *v. t* disturb
turbuvaty турбувати *v.t.* harass
turbuvatysia турбуватися *v.i.*
  worry
turnir турнір *n.* tournament
turyst турист *n.* tourist
turyzm туризм *n.* tourism
tushkovane miaso тушковане
  м'ясо *n.* stew
tushkuvaty тушкувати *v.t.* stew
tut тут *adv.* here
tut i dali тут і далі *adv.* hereafter
tuz туз *n* ace
tuzhlyvyi тужливий *adj*
  melancholy
tuzhyty тужити *v.i.* yearn
tvan твань *n.* mud
tvaryna тварина *n.* animal
tvaryna тварина *n* brute
tvaryna, shcho maie bahato nih
  тварина, що має багато ніг *n.*
  multiped
tvarynnyi тваринний *a* beastly
tverdity твердіти *v. t* concrete

tverdo твердо *adv.* surely
tverdyi твердий *a.* harsh
tverdyi твердий *a.* severe
tverdyi твердий *n* solid
tverdyty твердити *v. i* contend
tverdzhennia твердження *n.* allegation
tverdzhennia твердження *n* contention
tverezist тверезість *n.* sobriety
tverezyi тверезий *a.* sober
tvorchyi творчий *adj.* creative
tvorchyi творчий *a.* imaginative
tvorets творець *n* creator
tvorets творець *n.* originator
tvoryty творити *v.t.* pen
tychok тичок *n* dig
tychok тичок *n.* poke
tyhr тигр *n.* tiger
tyhrytsia тигриця *n.* tigress
tyk тик *n.* teak
tykaty тикати *v.t.* thrust
tykhyi тихий *a.* quiet
tylna storona ruky тильна сторона руки *n.* backhand
tym chasom тим часом *adv.* meanwhile
tym ne mensh тим не менш *adv.* however
tym samym тим самим *adv.* thereby
tymchasove perebuvannia тимчасове перебування *n* sojourn
tymchasove zhytlo тимчасове житло *n.* lodging
tymchasovo prozhyvaty тимчасово проживати *v.i.* sojourn
tymchasovo zhyty тимчасово жити *v.t.* lodge
tymchasovyi тимчасовий *a.* casual

tymchasovyi тимчасовий *a.* provisional
tymchasovyi тимчасовий *a.* temporary
tyniatysia тинятися *v.i.* roam
tyniatysia bez dila тинятися без діла *v.i.* loiter
typ тип *n.* cast
typ тип *n.* type
typovyi типовий *a.* typical
tyrada тирада *n.* tirade
tyran тиран *n.* tyrant
tyraniia тиранія *n.* tyranny
tysha тиша *n* hush
tysha тиша *n.* silence
tysiacha тисяча *n.* chiliad
tysiacha тисяча *n.* thousand
tysiachnyi тисячний *a* thousand
tysiacholittia тисячоліття *n.* millennium
tysk тиск *n.* pressure
tysniava тиснява *n* squash
tytanichnyi титанічний *a.* titanic
tytr титр *n.* caption
tyzhden тиждень *n.* week
tyzhnevyi тижневий *a.* weekly

u у *prep.* in
u у *prep.* into
u lizhku у ліжку *adv.* abed
u podyvi у подиві *adv* agaze
u poli у полі *adv.* afield
u seredyni у середині *adv.* inside
u vohni у вогні *adv.* aflame
uberihaty уберігати *v.t.* save
ubliudok ублюдок *n.* bastard
ubohyi убогий *a.* meagre
ubohyi убогий *a.* scant
ubohyi убогий *a* spare
ubohyi убогий *a.* squalid
uboztvo убозтво *n.* misery

uboztvo убозтво *n.* squalor
ubrannia убрання *n.* clothes
ubuvaty убувати *v.i.* wane
ubyty убити *v.t.* slay
ubyvtsia убивця *n.* murderer
uchasnyk учасник *n.* participant
uchasnyk учасник *n.* voter
uchasnyk biiky учасник бійки *n* belligerent
uchasnyk hry учасник гри *n.* player
uchasnyk perehovoriv учасник переговорів *n.* negotiator
uchasnyk torhiv учасник торгів *n* bidder
uchast участь *n.* participation
uchen учень *n.* learner
uchora учора *adv.* yesterday
uchuvaty учувати *v.t.* scent
uchytel учитель *n.* preceptor
udacha удача *n.* godsend
udacha удача *n.* luck
udalyni удалині *adv.* afar
udar удар *n.* bang
udar удар *n* beat
udar удар *n* blow
udar удар *n* hit
udar удар *n* slam
udar удар *n.* stab
udar удар *n* thrust
udar nohoiu удар ногою *n.* kick
udariaty ударяти *v.t.* hit
udariaty pro zemliu ударяти про землю *v.i.* dap
udariatysia iz hlukhym stukom ударятися із глухим стуком *v.i.* thud
udavannia удавання *n.* pretence
udavannia удавання *n* sham
udavanyi удаваний *adj* mock
udavaty удавати *v.t.* assume
udobriuvaty удобрювати *v.t* fertilize

udobriuvaty удобрювати *v.t.* manure
udobriuvaty kompostom удобрювати компостом *n* compost
udoskonalennia удосконалення *n.* perfection
udoskonaliuvaty удосконалювати *v.t.* perfect
udoskonaliuvaty удосконалювати *v.t.* refine
udostal удосталь *adv.* galore
udostoiuvaty удостоювати *v.t.* grace
udostoiuvaty удостоювати *v.t.* vouchsafe
udrukovane удруковане *v.t.* imprint
udushennia удушення *n.* strangulation
udushennia удушення *n.* suffocation
uhlyb krainy углиб країни *adv.* inland
uhoda угода *n.* agreement
uhoda угода *n.* bargain
uhoda угода *n.* consent
uhoda угода *n.* convention
uhoda угода *n* fix
uhoda угода *n.* transaction
uhoda угода *n.* treaty
uiava уява *n* fancy
uiava уява *n.* imagination
uiavliaty уявляти *v.t.* imagine
uiavnyi уявний *a.* imaginary
uidlyvyi уїдливий *a.* caustic
uidlyvyi уїдливий *a.* waspish
ukaz указ *n.* ordinance
ukazuvaty указувати *v.t.* point
ukhyliannia ухиляння *n* evasion
ukhyliatysia ухилятися *v.t.* shirk
ukhylnyi ухильний *a.* tortuous
ukladach укладач *n* draftsman

ukladach укладач *n.* former
ukladaty укладати *v. t* conclude
ukladaty укладати *v. t* encase
ukladaty укладати *v.t.* infer
ukladaty укладати *v.t.* stow
ukladaty pari укладати парі *v.i.* wager
ukladaty uhodu укладати угоду *v.t.* bargain
uklin уклін *n* bow
ukomplektuvaty shtat укомплектувати штат *v.t.* staff
ukripliuvaty укріплювати *v.t.* steady
ukryttia укриття *n.* hide
ukryttia укриття *n.* lee
ukryttia укриття *n.* shelter
ukus укус *n* bite
ukus укус *n.* sting
ulamky уламки *n* debris
ulamky уламки *n.* wreckage
ulamok zuba уламок зуба *n.* snag
ulan улан *n.* lancer
uliublene mistse улюблене місце *n* haunt
uliublenets улюбленець *n* darling
uliublenyi улюблений *a* beloved
uliublenyi улюблений *a* darling
uliublenyi улюблений *a* favourite
uliuliukaty улюлюкати *v.i* hoot
ultymatum ультиматум *n.* ultimatum
uminnia уміння *n.* proficiency
umova умова *n* condition
umova умова *n* prerequisite
umova умова *n.* proviso
umova умова *n.* stipulation
umovliaty умовляти *v. t* coax
umovne zvilnennia uviaznenoho z viaznytsi умовне звільнення ув'язненого з в'язниці *v.t.* parole

umyrotvoriaty умиротворяти *v.t.* pacify
unikalnyi унікальний *a.* unique
unison унісон *n.* unison
universalnist універсальність *n.* universality
universalnyi універсальний *a.* universal
universytet університет *n.* university
untsiia унція *n.* ounce
unykaty уникати *v.i* abscond
unykaty уникати *v.t.* avoid
unykaty уникати *v. t* elude
unykaty уникати *v. t* evade
unykaty уникати *v.t.* shun
unyknuty уникнути *n.* avoidance
uosoblennia уособлення *n.* impersonation
uosoblennia уособлення *n.* incarnation
uosobliuvaty уособлювати *v.t.* impersonate
uosobliuvaty уособлювати *v.t.* personify
uosobliuvaty уособлювати *v.t.* typify
upakovka упаковка *n.* packing
upakovuvaty упаковувати *v.t.* pack
upakuvannia упакування *n.* package
upered уперед *adv* forward
uperedzhenist упередженість *n.* partiality
uperedzhennia упередження *n.* prejudice
uperedzhenyi упереджений *a.* interested
uperedzhenyi упереджений *a* unfair
uperemish упереміш *adv.* pell-mell

upertist упертість *n.* obstinacy
upertyi упертий *a.* stubborn
upodibniuvaty уподібнювати *v.t.* liken
uporiadkovanyi упорядкований *a.* orderly
uporiadkovuvaty упорядковувати *v.t.* adjust
uporskuvannia упорскування *n.* injection
upovilnennia уповільнення *n.* retardation
upovnovazhenyi уповноважений *n.* assignee
upovnovazhenyi уповноважений *n.* commissioner
upovnovazhuvaty уповноважувати *v.t.* accredit
upovnovazhuvaty уповноважувати *v.t.* assign
upovnovazhuvaty уповноважувати *v.t.* authorize
upovnovazhyty уповноважити *v.t* empower
upravliaty управляти *v.t.* administer
upravliaty управляти *v.t.* govern
upravliaty управляти *v.t.* lead
upravliaty управляти *v.t.* manage
upravliaty управляти *v.t.* steer
upravliaty управляти *v.t.* superintend
upravlinnia управління *n.* administration
upravlinnia управління *n* board
upravlinnia управління *n.* government
upravlinnia управління *n.* management
upravlinskyi управлінський *a.* managerial
upriazh упряж *n.* harness

upuskaty z uvahy упускати з уваги *v.t.* overlook
upyratysia упиратися *v.i.* persevere
ura ура *interj.* hurrah
urahan ураган *n.* hurricane
urazlyvyi уразливий *a.* vulnerable
urehulovuvaty урегульовувати *v.t.* regulate
urizuvaty урізувати *v.t.* retrench
urna урна *n* urn
urochysta promova урочиста промова *a.* inaugural
urochyste vidkryttia урочисте відкриття *n.* inauguration
urochystist урочистість *n.* solemnity
urochystyi урочистий *a.* solemn
urodzhenyi уроджений *a.* inborn
urok урок *n.* lesson
urozhai урожай *n* crop
urozhai урожай *n.* harvest
urvaty урвати *v.t.* snatch
uryvchastyi уривчастий *a* curt
uryvchastyi уривчастий *a.* sketchy
usadka усадка *n.* shrinkage
usamitnennia усамітнення *n.* privacy
usamitnennia усамітнення *n.* seclusion
usamitniuvatysia усамітнюватися *v.t.* seclude
useredniuvaty усереднювати *v.t.* average
useredyni усередині *prep.* inside
useredynu усередину *adv.* inwards
ushchelyna ущелина *n.* ravine
usiliakyi усілякий *a.* various
usiudy усюди *prep.* throughout
uskladnennia ускладнення *n.* impediment

uskladnennia ускладнення *n.* perplexity

uskladniuvaty ускладнювати *v.t.* aggravate

uskladniuvaty ускладнювати *v. t* complicate

uskladniuvaty ускладнювати *v. t* embarrass

uskladniuvaty ускладнювати *v.t.* handicap

uskladniuvaty ускладнювати *v.t.* involve

usmishka усмішка *n.* smile

usno усно *adv.* orally

usno усно *adv.* verbally

usno усно *adv.* viva-voce

usnyi усний *a.* oral

usnyi усний *a* viva-voce

usnyi ispyt усний іспит *n* viva-voce

uspadkovuvaty успадковувати *v.t.* inherit

uspadkuvannia успадкування *n.* inheritance

uspikh успіх *n.* joy

uspikh успіх *n.* success

uspishnyi успішний *a* successful

ustanova установа *n.* foundation

ustanova установа *n.* institution

ustanovka установка *n* mount

ustrytsia устриця *n.* oyster

usunennia усунення *n* elimination

usushka усушка *n.* wastage

usuvaty усувати *v. t* eliminate

usuvaty усувати *v.t* remedy

usvidomliuvaty усвідомлювати *v.* acknowledge

usvidomliuvaty усвідомлювати *v.t.* appreciate

usvidomliuvaty усвідомлювати *v.t.* sense

usypalnytsia усипальниця *n.* shrine

utikach утікач *n.* fugitive

utikha утіха *n* consolation

utishaty утішати *v.t.* solace

utopichnyi утопічний *a.* utopian

utopiia утопія *n .* utopia

utrudnene dykhannia утруднене дихання *n.* gasp

utrymannia утримання *n.* retention

utrymannia утримання *n* upkeep

utrymuvach reiestru утримувач реєстру *n.* registrar

utrymuvaty утримувати *v.t.* deduct

utrymuvaty утримувати *v.t.* withhold

utrymuvatysia утримуватися *v.i.* abstain

utrymuvatysia утримуватися *v.i.* refrain

utrymuvatysia vid утримуватися від *v.t* forgo

utvoriuvaty утворювати *v.t.* form

utyl утиль *n.* junk

utylitarnyi утилітарний *a.* utilitarian

utylizatsiia утилізація *n.* utilization

utylizuvaty утилізувати *v.t.* utilize

uvaha увага *n.* attention

uvaha увага *n* heed

uvaha увага *n.* regard

uvazhno ohliadaty уважно оглядати *v.t.* inspect

uvazhnyi уважний *a.* attentive

uvazhnyi уважний *a.* considerate

uvazhnyi уважний *a.* mindful

uvertiura увертюра *n.* overture

uviaznenyi ув'язнений *n.* prisoner

uviazniuvaty ув'язнювати *v.t.* imprison

uvichniuvaty увічнювати *v.t.* perpetuate

uvichnyty увічнити *v.t.* immortalize

uvihnutyi увігнутий *adj.* concave

uzahalnennia узагальнення *n.* abstraction

uzakonyty узаконити *v.t.* legalize

uzberezhzhia узбережжя *n* coast

uzbichchia узбіччя *n* curb

uzda узда *n* bridle

uzdovzh уздовж *adv.* along

uzhalyty kropyvoiu ужалити кропивою *v.t.* nett¹e

uzhodzhennia узгодження *n.* concord

uzhodzhuvaty узгоджувати *v.t.* accord

uzmoria узмор'я *n.* offing

uzurpatsiia узурпація *n.* usurpation

uzurpuvaty узурпувати *v.t.* usurp

V

v в *prep.* within

v chomu в чому *adv.* wherein

v hori в горі *adv.* aloft

v inshomu vypadku в іншому випадку *adv.* otherwise

v kintsevomu rakhunku в кінцевому рахунку *adv.* ultimately

v kupi в купі *adv* aheap

v mezhakh в межах *adv.* within

v pershu cherhu в першу чергу *adv.* primarily

v riad в ряд *adv* abreast

v rozdrib в роздріб *adv.* retail

v rusi в русі *adv.* afoot

v seredeni в середені *prep.* amid

v toi chas yak в той час як *conj.* whereas

v znachnii miri в значній мірі *adv.* substantially

vabyty вабити *v.t.* beckon

vada вада *n* demerit

vaha вага *n.* weight

vahannia вагання *n* demur

vahatysia вагатися *v. t* demur

vahitna вагітна *a.* pregnant

vahitnist вагітність *n.* pregnancy

vahomishyi вагоміший *a.* prior

vahomist вагомість *n.* weightage

vahomyi вагомий *a.* grave

vahon вагон *n.* wagon

vahon tramvaia вагон трамвая *n.* car

vailuvatyi вайлуватий *a.* ungainly

vakansiia вакансія *n.* vacancy

vakantnyi вакантний *a.* vacant

vaktsyna вакцина *n.* vaccine

vaktsynatsiia вакцинація *n.* vaccination

vaktsynuvaty вакцинувати *v.t.* vaccinate

vakuum вакуум *n.* vacuum

val вал *n.* rampart

valiatysia валятися *v.i.* wallow

valiuta валюта *n* currency

valiutuvannia валютування *n.* valuation

valka валка *n.* stream

valun валун *n* boulder

valyk валик *n.* roller

valyty валити *v.t* fell

vanna ванна *n* bath

vantazh вантаж *n.* cargo

vantazhivka вантажівка *n.* lorry

vantazhnyi avtomobil вантажний автомобіль *n.* truck

vantazhyty вантажити *v.t.* lade

vantazhyty na korabel вантажити на корабель *v. t* embark

vapno вапно *n.* lime

vartist вартість *n.* cost

vartist proizdu вартість проїзду *n* fare

vartyi вартий *a* worth

varvar варвар *n.* barbarian

varvarskyi варварський *a.* barbarian

varvarskyi варварський *a.* savage

varvarstvo варварство *n.* barbarism

varyty pyvo варити пиво *v. t.* brew

vat ват *n.* watt

vaucher ваучер *n.* voucher

vazektomiia вазектомія *n.* vasectomy

vazelin вазелін *n.* vaseline

vazhil важіль *n.* lever

vazhka pratsia важка праця *n.* toil

vazhka robota важка робота *v.i.* moil

vazhko dykhaty важко дихати *v.i* gasp

vazhko stupaty важко ступати *v.t.* lump

vazhkyi важкий *a.* arduous

vazhkyi важкий *a.* muggy

vazhkyi udar важкий удар *n.* thump

vazhlyvist важливість *n.* importance

vazhlyvyi важливий *a.* important

vazhlyvyi важливий *a.* responsible

vazhyty важити *v.t.* weigh

vbrannia вбрання *n.* vestment

vbyraty вбирати *v.t.* soak

vbyty вбити *v.t.* assassinate

vbyvaty вбивати *v.t.* kill

vbyvaty вбивати *v.t.* murder

vbyvchyi вбивчий *a.* murderous

vbyvstvo вбивство *n* assassination

vbyvstvo batka вбивство батька *n.* patricide

vbyvtsia вбивця *n.* assassin

vchenist вченість *n.* scholarship

vchenyi вчений *a.* learned

vchenyi вчений *n.* scholar

vchora вчора *n.* yesterday

vchyniaty zmovu вчиняти змову *v. i.* conspire

vchynok вчинок *n.* action

vchytel вчитель *n.* teacher

vchyty вчити *v.t.* instruct

vchytysia вчитися *v.i.* learn

vdacha вдача *n.* temper

vdalist вдалість *n* felicity

vdaryty nohoiu вдарити ногою *v.t.* kick

vdavaty вдавати *v.t.* pretend

vdavatysia вдаватися *v.i.* resort

vdiachnyi вдячний *a.* thankful

vdivets вдівець *n.* widower

vdobavok вдобавок *adv.* withal

vdoskonalenyi вдосконалений *a* elaborate

vdoskonaliuvaty вдосконалювати *v.t.* improve

vdova вдова *n.* widow

vdumlyvyi вдумливий *a.* thoughtful

vduvaty вдувати *v.i.* puff

vdvichi вдвічі *a.* twofold

vdykh вдих *n.* respiration

vdykhaty вдихати *v.i.* inhale

vdykhaty вдихати *v.i.* respire

vecheria вечеря *n* dinner

vecheriaty вечеряти *v. t.* dine

vechir вечір *n* evening

vedmid ведмідь *n* bear

vehetarianets вегетаріанець *n.* vegetarian

vehetarianskyi вегетаріанський *a*
vegetarian
velity веліти *v.t.* will
Vellinhton Веллінгтон *n.*
wellington
velosyped велосипед *n.* bicycle
velosypedyst велосипедист *n*
cyclist
velych велич *n.* grandeur
velychavist величавість *n.*
stateliness
velycheznyi величезний *a*
enormous
velycheznyi величезний *a.* huge
velycheznyi величезний *a.*
monstrous
velychnist величність *n.* majesty
velychnyi величний *a.* august
velychnyi величний *a.* majestic
velychyna величина *n.*
magnitude
velyka kilkist велика кількість *n.*
prodigality
velyka kilkist велика кількість *n.*
profusion
velykden великдень *n* easter
velykodushnist великодушність
n. magnanimity
velykodushnyi великодушний *a.*
magnanimous
velykyi великий *a* big
velykyi krok великий крок *n*
stride
velykyi palets великий палець *n.*
thumb
velykyi vidkladnyi komir великий
відкладний комір *n.* rabato
vena вена *n.* vein
ventyliator вентилятор *n.*
ventilator
ventyliatsiia вентиляція *n.*
ventilation

ventyliatsiinyi вентиляційний *n.*
vent
ventyliuvaty вентилювати *v.t.*
ventilate
veranda веранда *n.* veranda
verba верба *n.* willow
verbliud верблюд *n.* camel
verbovyi prut вербовий прут *n.*
withe
verbuvaty вербувати *v.t.* recruit
verdykt вердикт *n.* verdict
veredlyvyi вередливий *a.*
capricious
veresen вересень *n.* September
vereshchaty верещати *v.i.* shriek
veresk вереск *n.* shriek
verkhivka верхівка *n.* apex
verkhivka верхівка *n.* tip
verkhnia chastyna верхня
частина *n.* top
verkhnia shchelepa верхня
щелепа *n.* maxilla
verkhnii верхній *a.* upper
verkhnii shar верхній шар *n.* top
verkhovenstvo верховенство *n.*
supremacy
verkhovnyi верховний *a.*
supreme
vershky вершки *n* cream
vershnyk вершник *n.* rider
vershyna вершина *n.* pinnacle
versiia версія *n.* version
verstat верстат *n.* lathe
verstat верстат *n.* tool
vertity вертіти *v.t.* wind
vertykalno вертикально *a.*
upright
vertykalnyi вертикальний *a.*
vertical
ves весь *a.* all
vesela pisnia весела пісня *n*
carol
veselist веселість *n* festivity

veselist веселість *n.* mirth
veseloshchi веселощі *n.* merriment
veselyi веселий *a* merry
vesillia весілля *n.* nuptials
vesliar весляр *n.* oar
veslo весло *n* paddle
vesluvannia веслування *n* row
vesna весна *n* spring
vesnianyi весняний *a.* vernal
vest вест *n.* west
vestovyi вестовий *a.* western
vesty вести *v. t* conduct
vesty вести *v.t* head
vesty вести *v.t.* transact
vesty napolehlyvu borotbu вести наполегливу боротьбу *v.i.* wrestle
vesty perehovory вести переговори *v.t.* negotiate
vesty perehovory вести переговори *v.i* parley
vesty viinu вести війну *v.t.* wage
vesty viinu вести війну *v.i.* war
veteran ветеран *n.* veteran
veterynarnyi ветеринарний *a.* veterinary
veto вето *n.* veto
vezty na avtomobili везти на автомобілі *v.i.* motor
vhamovuvaty вгамовувати *v.t.* allay
vhamovuvaty вгамовувати *v.t.* mortify
vholos вголос *adv.* aloud
vhoru вгору *adv.* upwards
vianuty в'янути *v.i* fade
viazanka в'язанка *n* faggot
viazaty в'язати *v.t.* knit
viazaty u vuzly в'язати у вузли *v.t.* bale
viaznytsia в'язниця *n.* jail
vibratsiia вібрація *n.* oscillation

vibratsiia вібрація *n.* vibration
vibruvaty вібрувати *v.i.* vibrate
vich-na-vich віч-на-віч *n.* tete-a-tete
vichnist вічність *n* eternity
vichnozelena roslyna вічнозелена рослина *n* evergreen
vichnozelenyi вічнозелений *a* evergreen
vichnyi вічний *a* eternal
vid від *prep.* from
vidbiliuvaty відбілювати *v. t. & i* blanch
vidbiliuvaty відбілювати *v. t* bleach
vidbutysia відбутися *v.i.* stem
vidbuvaty відбувати *v. i.* depart
vidbuvatysia відбуватися *v.i.* occur
vidbyraty відбирати *v.t.* pick
vidbyraty probu відбирати пробу *v.t.* sample
vidbytok відбиток *n* cachet
vidbyvach відбивач *n.* reflector
vidbyvaty відбивати *v.t.* repulse
vidbyvaty hodynnyi відбивати годинний *v.t.* toll
vidbyvatysia відбиватися *v.i.* struggle
vidchai відчай *n* despair
vidchaidushna holova відчайдушна голова *n.* bayard
vidchaidushnyi відчайдушний *a* desperate
vidchutnyi відчутний *a.* palpable
vidchutnyi відчутний *a.* sensible
vidchuttia відчуття *n.* sensation
vidchuvaty відчувати *v.t* feel
vidchuvaty brak відчувати брак *v.t.* lack
vidchuvaty hostryi bil відчувати гострий біль *v.t.* sting

vidchuvaty sylnyi bil відчувати сильний біль *v.i* smart
vidchuzhuvaty відчужувати *v.t.* alienate
viddacha віддача *n.* recoil
viddalenyi віддалений *a.* remote
viddalenyi vid moria віддалений від моря *a.* interior
viddanist відданість *n* dedication
viddanist відданість *n* devotion
viddannia віддання *n.* subjection
viddaty віддати *v.t.* render
viddavaty na muky віддавати на муки *v.t.* tantalize
viddavaty perevahu віддавати перевагу *v.t.* prefer
viddavatysia віддаватися *v. t* devote
viddilennia відділення *n* department
viddilennia відділення *n.* severance
viddilnyi віддільний *a.* separable
viddrukovuvaty віддруковувати *v.t.* impress
vidhaluzhennia відгалуження *n.* offshoot
vidibrannia dytyny vid hrudei відібрання дитини від грудей *n* ablactation
vidibraty відібрати *v.t.* single
vidiity відійти *v.i.* retreat
vidkhody відходи *n.* waste
vidkhozhe mistse відхоже місце *n.* latrine
vidkhylennia відхилення *n.* aberrance
vidkhyliaty відхиляти *v. t.* decline
vidkhyliatysia відхилятися *v. i* deviate
vidkladaty відкладати *v.t.* adjourn
vidkladennia відкладення *n.* adjournment

vidklasty відкласти *v.t.* shelve
vidklykannia відкликання *n.* recall
vidklykaty відкликати *v.t.* countermand
vidklykaty відкликати *v.t.* recall
vidkryte more відкрите море *n* main
vidkryto відкрито *adv.* openly
vidkryttia відкриття *n.* discovery
vidkryty відкрити *v.t.* open
vidkrytyi відкритий *adv.* ajar
vidkrytyi відкритий *a.* free
vidkryvaty відкривати *v. t.* dedicate
vidkydaty відкидати *v.t.* negative
vidkydaty відкидати *v.t.* reject
vidluchaty відлучати *v.t.* wean
vidluchyty vid tserkvy відлучити від церкви *v. t.* excommunicate
vidlyha відлига *n* thaw
vidlyty відлити *v. i* ebb
vidlyv відлив *n* ebb
vidlyvaty u formu відливати у форму *v.t.* mould
vidma відьма *n.* witch
vidminiuvatysia відмінюватися *v.t. & i.* conjugate
vidminnist відмінність *n* distinction
vidminnyi відмінний *a* different
vidminnyi відмінний *a.* excellent
vidminyty відмінити *v.t.* undo
vidmiriaty відміряти *v.t* mete
vidmitka відмітка *n* check
vidmova відмова *n* abnegation
vidmova відмова *n.* repulse
vidmova відмова *n* no
vidmovka відмовка *n* pretext
vidmovliaty відмовляти *v. t* dissuade
vidmovliaty відмовляти *v.t.* refuse

vidmovliaty sobi v chomu-nebud відмовляти собі в чому-небудь *v. t* abnegate

vidmovliatysia відмовлятися *v.t.* forsake

vidmovliatysia відмовлятися *v.t.* relinquish

vidmovliatysia vid perekonan відмовлятися від переконань *v.i.* backslide

vidmovyty відмовити *v.t.* persuade

vidniaty відняти *v.t.* subtract

vidnimannia віднімання *n.* subtraction

vidnimaty віднімати *v. t.* bereave

vidnimaty vid hrudei віднімати від грудей *v. t* ablactate

vidnosnyi відносний *a.* relative

vidnovlennia відновлення *n.* reinstatement

vidnovliuvaty відновлювати *v.t.* redress

vidnovliuvaty відновлювати *v.t.* reinstate

**vidnovliuvaty u pam`iati** відновлювати у пам`яті *v.t.* retrace

vidnovyty відновити *v.t.* renew

vidnovyty protektor відновити протектор *v.t.* retread

vidobrazhaty відображати *v.t* fend

vidobrazhaty відображати *v.t.* mirror

vidobrazhaty відображати *v.t.* reflect

vidobrazhennia відображення *n.* reflection

vidokremlene mistse відокремлене місце *n.* recess

vidokremlennia відокремлення *n.* insulation

vidokremlenyi відокремлений *a.* lone

vidokremliuvaty відокремлювати *v.t.* part

vidokremliuvaty відокремлювати *v.t.* separate

vidokremliuvatysia відокремлюватися *v.i.* secede

vidoma liudyna відома людина *n.* notability

vidomyi відомий *a.* well-known

vidosoblenist відособленість *n.* insularity

vidplachuvaty відплачувати *v.t.* requite

vidplata відплата *n.* nemesis

vidplata відплата *n.* retaliation

vidpochynok відпочинок *n.* recreation

vidpochyvaty відпочивати *v.i.* rest

vidpovid відповідь *n.* rejoinder

vidpovidach відповідач *n.* accountant

vidpovidach відповідач *n.* respondent

vidpovidalne polozhennia відповідальне положення *n.* trust

vidpovidalnist відповідальність *n.* liability

vidpovidalnyi відповідальний *a* accountable

vidpovidaty відповідати *v. i* correspond

vidpovidaty vzaiemnistiu відповідати взаємністю *v.t.* reciprocate

vidpovidnist відповідність *n.* correspondence

vidpovidno відповідно *adv.* accordingly

vidpovidnyi відповідний *a.* apposite

vidpovisty відповісти *v.t* answer

vidpravliaty відправляти *v.t.* post

vidpravliaty відправляти *v.t.* transmit

vidpravliaty poshtoiu відправляти поштою *v.t.* mail

vidpravliatysia відправлятися *v.t.* repair

vidpuskaty відпускати *v. t.* dismiss

vidpuskaty na voliu відпускати на волю *v.t.* enfranchise

vidpuskna hramota відпускна грамота *n.* manumission

vidpustka відпустка *n.* vacation

vidradzhuvaty відраджувати *v. t.* discourage

vidrakhuvannia відрахування *n* remand

vidrakhuvaty відрахувати *v.t.* remand

vidraza відраза *n.* abhorrence

vidraza відраза *n.* aversion

vidrazlyvyi відразливий *a.* repulsive

vidrazu відразу *adv.* instantly

vidriadzhannia відряджання *n* detachment

vidriadzhaty відряджати *v. t* detach

vidrikatysia відрікатися *v.t,* abdicate

vidrizniatysia відрізнятися *v. i* differ

vidro відро *n* bucket

vidrodzhennia відродження *n.* resurgence

vidrodzhuvaty відроджувати *v.i.* revive

vidryv відрив *n.* avulsion

vidryvnyi talon відривний талон *n.* coupon

vidryzhka відрижка *n* belch

vidshkodovuvaty відшкодовувати *v.t.* refund

vidshkoduvannia відшкодування *n.* recompense

vidshkoduvannia відшкодування *n.* recovery

vidshkoduvannia відшкодування *n* redress

vidshkoduvannia відшкодування *n.* remedy

vidshkoduvaty відшкодувати *v.t.* recoup

vidshtovkhuvannia відштовхування *n.* repulsion

vidshtovkhuvaty відштовхувати *v.t.* repel

vidsich відсіч *n.* rebuff

vidsivaty відсівати *v.t.* sieve

vidskochyty відскочити *v.i.* recoil

vidskok відскок *n.* rebound

vidsorbuvaty відсьорбувати *v.i.* sup

vidsotok відсоток *n.* percentage

vidstalyi відсталий *n.* straggler

vidstan відстань *n* distance

vidstan відстань *n* walk

vidstavaty відставати *v.i.* straggle

vidstavka відставка *n.* resignation

vidstii відстій *n.* sediment

vidstoiuvaty відстоювати *v.t.* assert

vidstrochka відстрочка *n.* postponement

vidstrochka відстрочка *n.* prolongation

vidstrochuvaty відстрочувати *v.t.* prorogue

vidstupaty відступати *v.i.* recede

vidsutnii відсутній *a* absent

vidsutnist відсутність *n* absence

vidsutnist відсутність *n.* privation
vidsutnist smaku відсутність смаку *n.* insipidity
vidteper відтепер *adv.* henceforward
vidterminovuvaty відтерміновувати *v.t.* postpone
vidtik відтік *n* drain
vidtiniaty відтіняти *v.t.* tint
vidtinok відтінок *n.* tinge
vidtodi відтоді *adv.* thereafter
vidtsentrovyi відцентровий *adj.* centrifugal
vidtvorennia відтворення *n* reproduction
vidtvoriuvalnyi відтворювальний *a.* reproductive
vidtvoriuvaty відтворювати *v.t.* reproduce
vidvantazhennia відвантаження *n.* shipment
vidvazhnyi відважний *adj.* hardy
vidvazhnyi відважний *a.* intrepid
vidvedennia відведення *n.* withdrawal
vidvernennia відвернення *n.* prevention
vidvertaty відвертати *v.t.* ward
vidvertist відвертість *n.* candour
vidvertyi відвертий *a.* outspoken
vidvesty відвести *v.t.* avert
vidviduvach відвідувач *n.* attendant
vidviduvach відвідувач *n.* visitor
vidviduvanist відвідуваність *n.* attendance
vidviduvannia відвідування *n.* visit
vidviduvaty відвідувати *v.t.* attend
vidvolikaty відволікати *v. t* divert
vidvyslyi відвислий *a* flabby

vidznachaty відзначати *v. t.* commemorate
vidzyv відзив *n* reply
vihvam вігвам *n.* wigwam
viia вія *n* eyelash
viialo віяло *n* fan
viiannia віяння *n* waft
viiaty віяти *v.t.* winnow
viina війна *n.* war
viiska війська *n* military
viiskovi dii військові дії *n.* warfare
viiskovo-morskyi військово-морський *a.* naval
viiskovo-morskyi flot військово-морський флот *n.* navy
viiskovyi військовий *a.* martial
vik вік *n.* age
vikarii вікарій *n.* vicar
vikha віха *n.* milestone
vikno вікно *n.* window
vikonna rama віконна рама *n.* chess
vikonne sklo віконне скло *n.* pane
viktoryna вікторина *n.* quiz
vil віл *n* bullock
villa вілла *n.* villa
vilnodumets вільнодумець *n.* libertine
vilnyi вільний *a* fluent
vilnyi вільний *a.* loose
vilnyi chas вільний час *n.* leisure
vin він *pron.* he
vinchaty вінчати *v. t* crown
vinochok віночок *n.* coronet
vinok вінок *n.* garland
vinok вінок *n.* wreath
vinyk віник *n* whisk
vira віра *n* belief
virnist вірність *n.* allegiance
virno вірно *adv.* aright

virnopiddanyi вірнопідданий *n.* loyalist

virnyi вірний *a* faithful

virolomstvo віроломство *n.* perfidy

virolomstvo віроломство *n.* treachery

virospovidannia віросповідання *n* creed

virsh вірш *n.* poem

virshomaz віршомаз *n.* poetaster

virshomaz віршомаз *n.* rhymester

virshovanyi riadok віршований рядок *n.* verse

virshuvannia віршування *n.* versification

virshyk віршик *n.* clink

virtualnyi віртуальний *a* virtual

virtuoznyi віртуозний *a.* masterly

virus вірус *n.* virus

viryty вірити *v. t* believe

viryty вірити *v.t* trust

vis вісь *n.* axis

vis вісь *n.* axle

vishaty вішати *v.t.* hang

vishaty вішати *v.i.* swing

vishaty pid steliu вішати під стелю *v.t.* sky

visim вісім *n* eight

visimdesiat вісімдесят *n* eighty

visimdesiatyrichnyi вісімдесятирічний *a.* octogenarian

visimdesiatyrichnyi staryi вісімдесятирічний старий *n.* octogenarian

visimnadtsiat вісімнадцять *n* eighteen

visk віск *n.* wax

viski віскі *n.* whisky

visnyk вісник *n.* herald

vispa віспа *n.* smallpox

vistria вістря *n.* spearhead

vitalni vyhuky вітальні вигуки *n* acclamation

vitalnia вітальня *n* drawing-room

vitamin вітамін *n.* vitamin

vitaty вітати *v. t.* cheer

vitatysia вітатися *v.t.* greet

viter вітер *n.* wind

vitriak вітряк *n.* windmill

vitrianyi вітряний *a.* windy

vitrylo вітрило *n.* sail

vitse-korol віце-король *n.* viceroy

vivsianka вівсянка *n.* porridge

vivtar вівтар *n.* altar

vivtsia вівця *n* ewe

viyzvoliaty визволяти *v.t.* liberate

viz віз *n.* wain

vizok візок *n.* cart

vizualizuvaty візуалізувати *v.t.* visualize

vizualnyi візуальний *a.* visual

vizyter візитер *n* caller

vkazivka вказівка *n.* indication

vkazivka вказівка *n.* suggestion

vkazivnyi palets вказівний палець *n* forefinger

vkazuvaty вказувати *v.t.* indicate

vkhid вхід *n* entrance

vkhodyty входити *v. t* enter

vkladannia вкладання *n.* insertion

vkladaty вкладати *v.t.* attach

vkladennia вкладення *n.* attachment

vkliuchaty включати *v. t* comprehend

vkliuchaty включати *v.t.* include

vkliuchennia включення *n.* inclusion

vkrai вкрай *adv.* utterly

vkryvaty вкривати *v. t* clothe

vlada влада *n.* authority

vlada влада *n* sway

vlashtovuvaty влаштовувати *v.t.* arrange

vlashtuvaty rizanynu
влаштувати різанину *v.t.*
massacre
vlashtuvatysia влаштуватися *v.i.*
perch
vlasnist власність *n.* ownership
vlasnyi власний *a.* own
vlasnyi zhinkam власний жінкам
n. womanish
vlasnyk власник *n.* owner
vlasnytskyi власницький *a.*
proprietary
vlastyvyi властивий *a.* inherent
vlastyvyi materi властивий
матері *a.* maternal
vlastyvyi vchenym властивий
вченим *a.* scholarly
vlastyvyi zhinkam властивий
жінкам *a* feminine
vliublyvyi влюбливий *a.* amorous
vlyvannia вливання *n.* infusion
vlyvaty вливати *v.t.* infuse
vlyvaty po kraplyni вливати по
краплині *v.t.* instil
vmishchuvaty вміщувати *v.t.*
store
vmity povodytysia вміти
поводитися *v.t.* wield
vmyraiuchyi вмираючий *a.*
moribund
vnesok внесок *n* contribution
vnochi вночі *adv.* nightly
vnosyty do spysku вносити до
списку *v. t* enrol
vnosyty do spysku вносити до
списку *v.t.* list
vnutrishnia storona внутрішня
сторона *n.* inside
vnutrishnii внутрішній *a.* indoor
vnutrishnii внутрішній *a.* inward
vnutrishnii monoloh внутрішній
монолог *n.* soliloquy

vnutrishnist внутрішність *n.*
interior
vnyz вниз *adv* down
vnyzu внизу *adv* beneath
vnyzu внизу *adv* under
voda вода *n.* water
voden водень *n.* hydrogen
vodianyi водяний *n.* merman
vodianystyi водянистий *a.* watery
vodii водій *n* driver
vodoima водойма *n.* reservoir
Vodolii Водолій *n.* aquarius
vodonepronykna tkanyna
водонепроникна тканина *n*
waterproof
vodonepronyknyi
водонепроникний *a.* waterproof
vodoprovidnyk водопровідник *n.*
plumber
vodospad водоспад *n.* cascade
vodozlyv водозлив *n.* weir
vodyty avtomobil водити
автомобіль *v. t* drive
vohkist вогкість *n* damp
vohnennyi вогненний *a* fiery
vohnyshche вогнище *n.* hearth
vohon вогонь *n* fire
voin воїн *n.* warrior
voiovnychyi войовничий *a*
bellicose
vokalist вокаліст *n.* vocalist
vokalnyi вокальний *a.* vocal
vokzal вокзал *n.* terminus
volan волан *n.* shuttlecock
volaty волати *v.i.* low
volaty волати *v.i.* scream
volaty волати *v.i.* wail
voleiu-nevoleiu волею-неволею
adv. perforce
volia воля *n.* volition
volochinnia волочіння *n* drag
volochyty волочити *v.t.* trail
volodinnia володіння *n.* hold

volodinnia володіння *n.* tenure
volodity володіти *v.t.* master
voloha волога *n.* moisture
volohist вологість *n.* humidity
volohist вологість *n.* wetness
volohyi вологий *a* damp
volokno волокно *n* fibre
volonter волонтер *n.* volunteer
voloskyi horikh волоський горіх *n.* walnut
volossia волосся *n* hair
volt вольт *n.* volt
volynka волинка *n.* bagpipe
vona вона *pron.* she
vono воно *pron.* it
vorkuvannia воркування *n* coo
vorochatysia ворочатися *v.i.* tumble
voroh ворог *n* enemy
vorohuvaty ворогувати *v.t.* antagonize
voron ворон *n.* raven
vorona ворона *n* crow
vorota ворота *n.* gate
vorozhe stavlennia вороже ставлення *n.* hostility
vorozhist ворожість *n* animosity
vorozhnecha ворожнеча *n* enmity
vorozhyi ворожий *a.* hostile
vorozhyi ворожий *a.* virulent
vorsuvaty ворсувати *v.t.* tease
vorushytysia ворушитися *v. i. & n* budge
vosha воша *n.* louse
voshchyty вощити *v.t.* wax
voskovanyi воскований *adj.* cerated
vosma chastyna myli восьма частина милі *n.* furlong
vosmykutnyi восьмикутний *a.* octangular
vosmykutnyk восьмикутник *n.* octagon

vostanskyi востанський *a.* rebellious
vovk вовк *n.* wolf
vovna вовна *n.* wool
vovniana materiia вовняна матерія *n* woollen
vovnianyi вовняний *a.* woollen
vozhd вождь *n.* chieftain
vozytysia возитися *v.i.* romp
vpadaty впадати *v.i.* lapse
vpered вперед *adv.* forth
vpertyi впертий *a.* mulish
vpertyi впертий *a.* obstinate
vpevnenyi впевнений *a.* confident
vpevnenyi впевнений *a.* sure
vpiddavaty honinniam впіддавати гонінням *v.t.* persecute
vplutuvaty вплутувати *v.t.* implicate
vplyv вплив *n.* influence
vplyvaty впливати *v.t.* affect
vplyvaty впливати *v. t* effect
vplyvova osoba впливова особа *v.t.* influence
vplyvovyi впливовий *a.* influential
vpoperek впоперек *adv.* across
vporiadkuvannia впорядкування *n.* arrangement
vprava вправа *n.* exercise
vpravliatysia вправлятися *v.t.* practise
vpravnyi вправний *a.* artful
vpravnyi maister вправний майстер *n* craftsman
vpravnyi strilets вправний стрілець *n.* marksman
vprovadzhuvaty впроваджувати *v.t.* inculcate
vpysuvaty вписувати *v.t.* inscribe
vrakhovuiuchy враховуючи *prep.* considering

vrazhaiuchyi вражаючий *a.* impressive

vrazhaty вражати *v.t.* astonish

vrazhaty вражати *v.t.* invade

vrazhennia враження *n.* impression

vrazhenyi zhakhom вражений жахом *a.* aghast

vrazlyvyi вразливий *a.* intense

vrehuliuvannia врегулювання *n.* adjustment

vrehuliuvaty врегулювати *v.i.* settle

vreshti-resht врешті-решт *adv.* eventually

vrivnovazhenist врівноваженість *n* poise

vrivnovazhuvaty врівноважувати *v.t.* poise

vrodzhenyi вроджений *a.* innate

vse все *pron* all

vse mozhlyve все можливе *n* utmost

vsebichnyi всебічний *a* comprehensive

vseliaty poboiuvannia вселяти побоювання *v.t.* misgive

vseliaty shanoblyvyi strakh вселяти шанобливий страх *v.t.* overawe

vsemohutnii всемогутній *a.* almighty

vsemohutnist всемогутність *n.* omnipotence

vseosiazhnyi всеосяжний *a.* integral

vseredeni всередені *adv.* within

vseredyni всередині *adv.* indoors

vsesvit всесвіт *n.* universe

vsesylnyi всесильний *a.* omnipotent

vsevidannia всевідання *n.* omniscience

vseznaiuchyi всезнаючий *a.* omniscient

vshanovuvaty вшановувати *v.i* feast

vsi всі *n* all

vsi razom всі разом *adv.* altogether

vsistysia na sidalo всістися на сідало *v.i.* roost

vsiu nich всю ніч *adv.* overnight

vsiudysushchist всюдисущість *n.* omnipresence

vsiudysushchyi всюдисущий *a.* omnipresent

vsmoktuvannia всмоктування *n.* suck

vspiniuvaty вспінювати *v.t* foam

vstanovlenyi встановлений *a* set

vstanovliuvaty встановлювати *v.t.* mount

vstanovliuvaty встановлювати *v.t.* specify

vstanovliuvaty mezhi встановлювати межі *v.t.* limit

vstanovyty встановити *v.t* finger

vstavaty вставати *v.* rise

vstavaty na chyius storonu вставати на чиюсь сторону *v.i.* side

vstavliaty вставляти *v.t.* insert

vstavliaty kameni вставляти камені *v.t.* jewel

vstup вступ *n* accession

vstup вступ *n* entry

vstupaty u soiuz вступати у союз *v.t.* ally

vstupaty v taiemni vidnosyny вступати в таємні відносини *v.i.* tamper

vstupnyi вступний *a.* introductory

vsuperech всупереч *prep.* notwithstanding

vsypaty всипати *v. t* bestrew

vtamuvaty втамувати *v.t.* slake
vtecha втеча *n.* run
vtekty втекти *v. i* elope
vtilennia втілення *n* embodiment
vtilenyi втілений *a.* incarnate
vtiliuvaty втілювати *v. t.* embody
vtiliuvaty втілювати *v.t.* incarnate
vtim втім *adv.* though
vtishaty втішати *v. t* comfort
vtishaty втішати *v.t.* soothe
vtoma втома *n* fatigue
vtomlenyi втомлений *a.* weary
vtomlyvyi втомливий *a.* trying
vtorhatysia вторгатися *v.t.* intrude
vtorhnennia вторгнення *n.* intrusion
vtorynna syrovyna вторинна сировина *n.* salvage
vtorynnyi вторинний *a.* secondary
vtrachaty втрачати *v.t.* lose
vtrata втрата *n* bereavement
vtrata втрата *n.* loss
vtraty втрати *n.* casualty
vtruchannia втручання *n.* interference
vtruchannia втручання *n.* interjection
vtruchatysia втручатися *v.i.* intervene
vtulka втулка *n.* hub
vtykaty втикати *v.t.* stab
vtyskuvaty втискувати *v. t* cram
vudyty вудити *v.i* fish
vuhillia вугілля *n* coal
vuhlets вуглець *n.* carbon
vuhor вугор *n.* pimple
vukho вухо *n* ear
vulharnist вульгарність *n.* vulgarity
vulharnyi вульгарний *a.* vulgar
vulkan вулкан *n.* volcano

vulkanichnyi вулканічний *a.* volcanic
vulychnyi khlopchyk вуличний хлопчик *n.* urchin
vulyk вулик *n.* beehive
vulytsia вулиця *n.* street
vus вус *n.* moustache
vusa вуса *n.* mustache
vushna sirka вушна сірка *n* cerumen
vusyk вусик *n.* cornicle
vuzkyi вузький *a.* narrow
vuzlovyi punkt вузловий пункт *n.* node
vuzol вузол *n* bundle
vvazhaty вважати *v.i.* deem
vvazhaty vynnym вважати винним *v. t* blame
vvazhaty za вважати за *v.t.* account
vvedennia введення *n.* input
vverhaty u morok ввергати у морок *v. t* benight
vverkh dnom вверх дном *adv* topsy turvy
vvesty v omanu ввести в оману *v.t.* hoodwink
vvichlyvist ввічливість *n.* complaisance
vvichlyvyi ввічливий *adj.* bland
vviriaty ввіряти *v.t.* consign
vvodyty вводити *v.t.* inject
vvodyty v omanu вводити в оману *v.t.* misguide
vvodyty v posadu вводити в посаду *v.t.* induct
vvodytysia вводитися *v.i* mix
vybachaty вибачати *v.t* forgive
vybachatysia вибачатися *v.i.* apologize
vybachennia вибачення *n.* apology
vybir вибір *n.* selection

vyblyskuvaty виблискувати *v.t* flash

vyblyskuvaty виблискувати *v.i.* glitter

vyblyskuvaty виблискувати *v.i.* twinkle

vyboina вибоїна *n.* groove

vyboina вибоїна *n.* pitfall

vyboistyi вибоїстий *adj* bumpy

vyborche pravo виборче право *n.* suffrage

vyborets виборець *n.* constituent

vybory вибори *n* election

vybudovuvaty вибудовувати *v.t* marshal

vybudovuvaty v liniiu вибудовувати в лінію *v.t.* align

vybukh вибух *n* blast

vybukh вибух *n.* explosion

vybukh pochuttiv вибух почуттів *n.* passion

vybukhnuty вибухнути *v. t.* explode

vybukhova rechovyna вибухова речовина *n.* explosive

vybukhovyi вибуховий *a* explosive

vybyraty вибирати *v. t.* choose

vybyvaty z kolii вибивати з колії *v.t.* unsettle

vychavliuvaty вичавлювати *v.t* wring

vycherpuvaty вичерпувати *v. t.* exhaust

vyd вид *n.* perspective

vyd вид *n.* species

vyd dyialnosti вид дияльності *n.* occupation

vydacha видача *n* grant

vydalennia видалення *n.* removal

vydalyty видалити *v. t* delete

vydannia видання *n* edition

vydatky na zbilshennia vartosti vlasnosti видатки на збільшення вартості власності *n* betterment

vydatnyi видатний *a.* laureate

vydatnyi видатний *a.* pre-eminent

vydavaty видавати *v. t* emit

vydavaty dekret видавати декрет *v. i* decree

vydavaty zakony видавати закони *v.i.* legislate

vydavets видавець *n* editor

vydavets видавець *n.* publisher

vydiliaty виділяти *v.t* accent

vydiliaty виділяти *v.t* evolve

vydiliaty moloko виділяти молоко *v.i.* lactate

vydiliatysia виділятися *v.i.* ooze

vydilyty виділити *v.t.* void

vydnyi видний *a.* prominent

vydnyi видний *a.* sightly

vydobutok видобуток *n* booty

vydovbuvaty видовбувати *v.t* hollow

vydovyshche видовище *n.* entertainment

vydovyshche видовище *n.* pageant

vydozmina видозміна *n.* transfiguration

vydra видра *n.* otter

vyduzhuvaty видужувати *v.t.* recover

vydymist видимість *n.* visibility

vydymyi видимий *a.* apparent

vydyrannia видирання *n* scramble

vydyratysia видиратися *v.i* climb

vyhadanyi вигаданий *a* fictitious

vyhadaty вигадати *v. t* devise

vyhadka вигадка *n* fiction

vyhaduvaty вигадувати *v.t* fabricate

vyhaniaty виганяти *v.t.* banish
vyhidnyi вигідний *a.* remunerative
vyhnanets вигнанець *n.* outcast
vyhnannia вигнання *n.* expulsion
vyhnaty вигнати *v. t.* eject
vyhoda вигода *n.* profit
vyhodovuvaty dytynu
вигодовувати дитину *v.t* nurse
vyhotovlennia виготовлення *n*
fabrication
vyhotovliaty v trokh
prymirnykakh виготовляти в
трьох примірниках *v.t.* triplicate
vyhrash виграш *n* gain
vyhrash виграш *n* win
vyhrashnyi виграшний *a.*
advantageous
vyhrashnyi виграшний *a.*
meritorious
vyhraty виграти *v.t.* win
vyhribaty вигрібати *v.t.* shovel
vyhribna yama вигрібна яма *n.*
cesspool
vyhuk вигук *n* exclamation
vyhuk вигук *n.* outcry
vyhuk вигук *n.* shout
vyhukuvaty вигукувати *v.i*
exclaim
vyhyn вигин *v.t.* twist
vyhynannia вигинання *n* wriggle
vyhynaty вигинати *v. t* curve
vyhynaty spynu вигинати спину
v.i bog
vyiav sumnivu вияв сумніву *n.*
impeachment
vyiav zakhoplennia вияв
захоплення *n.* rapture
vyiavlennia виявлення *n.*
manifestation
vyiavliaty виявляти *v. t* detect
vyiavliaty виявляти *v. t* exhibit
vyiavliaty виявляти *v.t.* signify

vyimaty z pikhov виймати з
піхов *v.t.* unsheathe
vyizd виїзд *n* drive
vykhid вихід *n* yield
vykhid na pensiiu вихід на
пенсію *n.* retirement
vykhodyty виходити *n.* issue
vykhodyty na виходити на *v.t*
front
vykhor вихор *n* whirl
vykhovannia виховання *n.*
nurture
vykhovuvaty виховувати *v.t.*
foster
vykhvaliannia вихваляння *n.*
glorification
vykladaty викладати *v. t* expose
vykliuchaty виключати *v. t* except
vykliuchaty, ne rakhuiuchy
виключати, не рахуючи *v.t* bar
vyklyk виклик *n.* challenge
vyklykaty викликати *v. t.*
challenge
vyklykaty nevdovolennia
викликати невдоволення *v. t.*
dissatisfy
vyklykaty revnoshchi викликати
ревнощі *v.t.* jaundice
vyklykaty zakhoplennia
викликати захоплення *v. t*
enrapture
vykonannia виконання *n.*
achievement
vykonannia виконання *n.* acting
vykonavets виконавець *n.*
performer
vykonuvaty виконувати *v.t.* fulfill
vykonuvaty виконувати *v.t.*
perform
vykonuvaty oboviazky
виконувати обов'язки *v.i.*
officiate

vykoriniuvaty викорінювати *v. t* eradicate

vykorystannia використання *n.* use

vykorystovuvaty використовувати *v.t.* use

vykradaty викрадати *v.t.* abduct

vykradennia викрадення *n* abduction

vykrasty викрасти *v.t.* kidnap

vykresliuvaty викреслювати *v.t.* obliterate

vykrut викрут *n* elusion

vykrutas викрутас *v.i.* quibble

vykup викуп *n.* ransom

vykupovuvaty викуповувати *v.t.* ransom

vykydaty викидати *v.t.* spurt

vykyden викидень *adv* abortive

vykynuty викинути *v.i.* miscarry

vylazka вилазка *n.* sally

vylikovnyi виліковний *a* curable

vylikovuvaty виліковувати *v. t.* cure

vylit виліт *n* departure

vylochnyi kliuch вилочний ключ *n.* spanner

vyluchaty вилучати *v. t.* exempt

vyluchaty z obihu вилучати з обігу *v.t.* demonetize

vylyvok виливок *n* mould

vymahaty вимагати *v. t* claim

vymia вим'я *n.* udder

vymir вимір *n* dimension

vymiriuvalnyi вимірювальний *a.* metrical

vymiriuvaty вимірювати *v. t* determine

vymiriuvaty вимірювати *v.t* measure

vymiriuvaty hlybynu вимірювати глибину *v.t* fathom

vymiriuvaty hlybynu вимірювати глибину *v.i.* sound

vymirnyi вимірний *a.* measurable

vymochuvaty вимочувати *v.t.* steep

vymoha вимога *n* demand

vymova вимова *n.* pronunciation

vymovliaty вимовляти *v.t.* pronounce

vymovliaty вимовляти *v.t.* voice

vymovliaty z shypinniam вимовляти з шипінням *v.* assibilate

vympel вимпел *n.* streamer

vymuchenyi вимучений *a.* laboured

vymykaty вимикати *v. t* exclude

vynahoroda винагорода *n.* gratification

vynahoroda винагорода *n.* honorarium

vynahoroda винагорода *n.* reward

vynahorodzhuvaty винагороджувати *v.t.* recompense

vynahorodzhuvaty винагороджувати *v.t.* reward

vynakhid винахід *n.* artifice

vynakhidlyvyi винахідливий *a.* inventive

vynakhidnyk винахідник *n.* inventor

vynakhodyty винаходити *v.t.* invent

vyniatkovyi винятковий *a* exclusive

vyniatkovyi винятковий *a.* particular

vyniatkovyi винятковий *a* sole

vyniatok виняток *n* exception

vynnyi винний *a* culpable

vyno вино *n.* wine

vynohrad виноград *n.* grape

vynohradna loza виноградна лоза *n.* vine

vynosyty na noshakh виносити на ношах *v.t.* litter

vynosyty treteiske rishennia виносити третейське рішення *v.t.* arbitrate

vynosyty vypravdalnyi vyrok виносити виправдальний вирок *v.t.* acquit

vynosyty vyrok виносити вирок *v.t.* adjudge

vynuvatets винуватець *n* culprit

vynuvatyi винуватий *a.* guilty

vynykaty виникати *v.i.* arise

vypad випад *n.* lunge

vypadkovist випадковість *n.* contingency

vypadkovyi випадковий *a* accidental

vypadok випадок *n* accident

vypadok випадок *n* event

vyparovuvaty випаровувати *v. i* evaporate

vyparovuvatysia випаровуватися *v.t.* vaporize

vyperedzhaty випереджати *v.t.* outrun

vyperedzhaty випереджати *v.t.* surpass

vyplachuvaty виплачувати *v.t.* redeem

vyplavliaty виплавляти *v.t.* smelt

vyplodok виплодок *n.* spawn

vypravdannia виправдання *n.* acquittal

vypravdovuvaty виправдовувати *v.t.* justify

vypravdovuvaty po sudu виправдовувати по суду *v.t.* assoil

vypravlennia виправлення *n* correction

vypravlennia виправлення *n* reclamation

vypravliaty виправляти *v. t* correct

vypravliaty виправляти *v. t* exercise

vypravnyi виправний *a* reformatory

vypravnyi zaklad виправний заклад *n.* reformatory

vypravyty виправити *a.* reparable

vypriamlennia випрямлення *n.* rectification

vypriamliaty випрямляти *v.t.* straighten

vypriamytysia випрямитися *v.t.* right

vyprobnyi termin випробний термін *n.* probation

vyprobovuvaty випробовувати *v. t.* essay

vyprobuvannia випробування *n.* ordeal

vyprobuvaty випробувати *v.t.* taste

vyprominiuvaty випромінювати *v.t.* radiate

vypuklyi випуклий *a.* salient

vypusk випуск *n.* instalment

vypusk випуск *v.t.* number

vypuskaty випускати *v.i.* graduate

vypuskaty par випускати пар *v.i.* steam

vypusknyi випускний *n* graduate

vypyvaty випивати *v. t* drink

vypyvka випивка *v. i* booze

vypzvoliaty випзволяти *v.t* free

vyr вир *n.* whirlpool

vyraz вираз *n.* expression

vyraz oblychchia вираз обличчя *n.* visage

vyrazhaty виражати *v.t.* term
vyrazhaty slovamy виражати
словами *v.t.* utter
vyrazka виразка *n.* ulcer
vyrazkovyi виразковий *a.*
ulcerous
vyraznyi виразний *a* emphatic
vyraznyi виразний *a.* sharp
vyrikaty вирікати *v.t.* mouth
vyrishalnyi вирішальний *adj.*
crucial
vyrishennia вирішення *n* answer
vyrishuvaty вирішувати *v. t*
decide
vyrishyty вирішити *v.t.* solve
vyrivniuvaty вирівнювати *v. t*
even
vyrizaty вирізати *v. t.* carve
vyrobliaty виробляти *v.t.* produce
vyrobnychyi виробничий *a.*
industrial
vyrobnyk виробник *n.* maker
vyrobnyk виробник *n*
manufacturer
vyrobnytstvo виробництво *n.*
industry
vyroby вироби *n. pl.* ware
vyrok вирок *n* condemnation
vyrok вирок *n.* sentence
vyroshchuvaty вирощувати *v.t.*
nurture
vyrostaty z виростати з *v.t.*
outgrow
vyrubka вирубка *n* slash
vyruchka виручка *n.* proceeds
vyrushaty v dorohu вирушати в
дорогу *v.t.* start
vyruvaty вирувати *v.i.* seethe
vyrvaty вирвати *v.t.* wrest
vyryvaty z korenem виривати з
коренем *v.t.* uproot
vysadka висадка *n.* landing

vysadzhuvaty висаджувати *v.i.*
land
vyselennia виселення *n* eviction
vyseliaty виселяти *v. t* evict
vyshche вище *prep.* afore
vyshchist вищість *n.* pre-
eminence
vyshchoi yakosti вищої якості *a.*
superb
vyshchyi вищий *a.* superior
vyshtovkhuvaty виштовхувати *v.
t.* expel
vyshukanist вишуканість *n.*
refinement
**vyshykovuvaty v boiovyi
poriadok** вишиковувати в
бойовий порядок *v.t.* array
vyshyvannia вишивання *n*
embroidery
vyskochka вискочка *n.* upstart
vysliv вислів *n* dictum
vysliv вислів *n.* saw
vyslovliuvannia висловлювання
n. utterance
vyslovliuvaty висловлювати *v. t.*
express
vyslovliuvaty dumku
висловлювати думку *v.t.* opine
vyslovliuvaty slovamy
висловлювати словами *v.t*
word
vyslovliuvatysia
висловлюватися *v.i.* speak
vyslovyty висловити *v.t.* phrase
vyslyzaty вислизати *v. t.* bilk
vysmiiuvaty висміювати *v.t.*
satirize
vysnazhenyi виснажений *a.*
haggard
vysnazhlyvyi виснажливий *a.*
tedious
vysnazhuvaty виснажувати *v.t.*
depauperate

vysnovok висновок *n.* conclusion
vysoka yakist висока якість *n.* excellence
vysoke polozhennia високе положення *n* eminence
vysokist високість *n.* Highness
vysoko tsinuvaty високо цінувати *v.t.* prize
vysoko tsinuvaty високо цінувати *v.t.* treasure
vysokyi високий *a.* high
vysota висота *n.* altitude
vystachyty вистачити *v.i.* suffice
vystavka виставка *n.* exhibition
vystezhuvaty вистежувати *v.t.* track
vystupaty proty виступати проти *v.t.* oppose
vystupaty v sudi виступати в суді *v.i.* plead
vysuvannia висування *n.* nomination
vysuvaty висувати *v.t.* propose
vysuvaty висувати *v.t.* propound
vysuvaty obvynuvachennia висувати обвинувачення *v.t.* indict
vysuvaty vymohu висувати вимогу *v. t* demand
vysvitliuvaty висвітлювати *v.t.* alluminate
vysydzhuvaty висиджувати *v.i.* incubate
vysylka висилка *n.* banishment
vysypnyi tyf висипний тиф *n.* typhus
vyterpity витерпіти *v.t.* endure
vytiahaty витягати *v. t* extract
vytiahuvaty витягувати *v.t.* retrieve
vytik витік *n.* leak
vytikannia витікання *n* expiry
vytikaty витікати *v.i.* result

vytisniaty витісняти *v. t* displace
vytivka витівка *n* mischief
vytonchenist витонченість *n.* sophistication
vytonchenyi витончений *a.* dainty
vytonchenyi витончений *a.* nice
vytonchenyi витончений *a.* polite
vytrachaty витрачати *v. t* expend
vytrata витрата *n* consumption
vytrebuvannia витребування *n.* vindication
vytrebuvaty spravu z nyzhchoho sudu do vyshchoho витребувати справу з нижчого суду до вищого *v. t* evoke
vytrishchatysia витріщатися *v.i.* stare
vytrymuvaty витримувати *v.t.* withstand
vytryvalist витривалість *n.* stamina
vyttia виття *n* wail
vyty вити *v.t.* howl
vytyraty витирати *v.t.* wipe
vytyraty rushnykom витирати рушником *v.t.* towel
vyvaliuvaty вивалювати *v.t.* tip
vyvchaty вивчати *v.t.* scrutinize
vyvchaty вивчати *v.i.* study
vyvchennia вивчення *n.* inquisition
vyvchennia вивчення *n.* study
vyvedennia виведення *n.* inference
vyverhaty вивергати *v. t* belch
vyverhatysia вивергатися *v. i* erupt
vyvershennia вивершення *n.* completion
vyvert виверт *n* dodge
vyvertkyi вивертий *a.* shifty

vyverzhennia виверження *n*
eruption
vyvezennia вивезення *n* export
vyvitriuvaty вивітрювати *v.t.*
weather
vyvodok виводок *n* brood
vyvodyty виводити *v. t.* derive
vyvodyty z rivnovahy виводити з
рівноваги *v.t.* upset
vyvozyty вивозити *v. t.* export
vyvykhnuty вивихнути *v.t.*
wrench
vyzhyvannia виживання *n.*
survival
vyzhyvaty виживати *v.i.* survive
vyznachaty визначати *v.t.* assess
**vyznachaty
mistseznakhodzhennia**
визначати місцезнаходження
v.t. position
vyznachennia визначення *n.*
attribute
vyznachnyi визначний *a.*
noteworthy
vyznannia визнання *n.*
acknowledgement
vyznanty vynnym визнанти
винним *v. t.* convict
vyznavaty визнавати *v.t.* avow
vyznavaty визнавати *v. t.* declare
vyzvolennia визволення *n.*
liberation
vyzvolytel визволитель *n.*
liberator
vzahali взагалі *adv.* any
vzaiemnyi взаємний *a.* mutual
vzaiemodiia взаємодія *n.*
interplay
vzaiemodiia взаємодія *n.* liaison
vzaiemorozuminnia
взаєморозуміння *n.* rapport

vzaiemozalezhnist
взаємозалежність *n.*
interdependence
vzaiemozalezhnyi
взаємозалежний *a.*
interdependent
vzaiemozviazok взаємозв'язок *n.*
correlation
vzhe вже *adv.* already
vzhe вже *adv.* yet
vzhyvaty вживати *v.t.* undertake
vzhyvaty vidpovidnykh zakhodiv
вживати відповідних заходів
v.i. reply
vzirets взірець *n.* sample
vzuvaty взувати *v.t.* shoe
vzvod взвод *n.* platoon

ya я *pron.* I
yabluko яблуко *n.* apple
yachmin ячмінь *n.* barley
yachmin na otsi ячмінь на оці *n.*
stye
yadernyi ядерний *a.* nuclear
yadro ядро *n.* core
yadro ядро *n.* nucleus
yahnia ягня *n.* lamb
yahniatko ягнятко *n.* lambkin
yaiechko яєчко *n.* testicle
yaiechnyi bilok яєчний білок *n*
albumen
yaiechnyk яєчник *n.* ovary
yaitse яйце *n* egg
yak як *adv.* as
yak як *adv.* how
yak як *n.* yak
yak maty як мати *adj.* motherlike
yak pravylo як правило *adv.*
generally
yakhta яхта *n.* yacht

yakii vidpovidaie zvychaiu якій
відповідає звичаю *a*. usual
yakir якір *n*. anchor
yakirna stoianka якірна стоянка
n anchorage
yakisnyi якісний *a*. qualitative
yakist якість *n*. quality
yakoho mozhno vidstezhyty
якого можно відстежити *a*.
traceable
yakos якось *adv*. somehow
yakshcho якщо *conj*. if
yakshcho ne якщо не *conj*.
unless
yakyi який *pron*. as
yakyi який *a*. that
yakyi який *a*. what
yakyi який *a* which
yakyi b ne який б не *pron*
whichever
yakyi dme z pivnochi який дме з
півночі *a*. northern
yakyi dopovniuie який доповнює
a. supplementary
yakyi doroho koshtuie який
дорого коштує *a* expensive
yakyi holosuie «za» який
голосує «за» *a*. content
**yakyi korystuietsia
nedotornkanistiu** який
користується недоторканістю
a. inviolable
yakyi liubyt rozkish який любит
розкіш *a*. luxurious
yakyi maie pidozru який має
підозру *a*. suspicious
**yakyi maie pravo na zvilnennia
z uviaznennia pid zastavu**
який має право на звільнення
з ув'язнення під заставу *a*.
bailable
yakyi maietsia na uvazi який
мається на увазі *a*. tacit

yakyi mistyt zoboviazannia
який містить зобов'язання *a*.
promissory
yakyi narodzhuietsia який
народжується *a*. nascent
yakyi navivaie tuhu який навіває
тугу *a*. lonely
yakyi ne beretsia do uvahy
який не береться до уваги *a*.
negligible
yakyi ne pamiataie який не
пам'ятає *a*. oblivious
yakyi nese vidpovidalnist який
несе відповідальність *a*.
answerable
yakyi obyraie який обирає *adj*.
constituent
yakyi pasuie який пасує *a*
becoming
yakyi perebuvaie na rozhliadi
який перебуває на розгляді *a*.
subjudice
yakyi pidliahaie skasuvanniu
який підлягає скасуванню *a*.
revocable
yakyi postiino meshkaie який
постійно мешкає *a*. resident
yakyi rozhliadaietsia який
розглядається *a* pending
yakyi sluzhyt do vyrazhennia
який служить до вираження *a*.
expressive
yakyi spodivaietsia який
сподівається *a*. hopeful
yakyi spuskaietsia який
спускається *a* downward
**yakyi stosuietsia vyboriv u
senat** який стосується виборів
у сенат *a* senatorial
yakyi usvidomliuie який
усвідомлює *a* conscious
yakyi vazhko chytaietsia який
важко читається *a*. illegible

yakyi vidbuvsia do narodzhennia який відбувся до народження *adj.* antenatal

yakyi vidchuvaie який відчуває *a.* sentient

yakyi vidrodzhuietsia який відроджується *a.* resurgent

yakyi vidshtovkhuie який відштовхує *a.* repellent

yakyi vilno teche який вільно тече *a.* affluent

yakyi vkazuie який вказує *a.* indicative

yakyi vykhodyt na pivnich який виходить на північ *a* north

yakyi vymahaietsia zazdalehid який вимагається заздалегідь *a.* prerequisite

yakyi vyplyvaie який випливає *a.* subsequent

yakyi yde lyshe vid odniiei storony який йде лише від однієї сторони *a* ex-parte

yakyi ye blyzniukom який є близнюком *a* twin

yakyi zadovolniaietsia який задовольняється *a.* satiable

yakyi zberihaie який зберігає *a.* retentive

yakyi zlyvaietsia який зливається *adj.* confluent

yakyi-nebud який-небудь *a.* any

yakyis якийсь *a* certain

yakyis якийсь *a.* some

yalovychyna яловичина *n* beef

yalyna ялина *n* fir

yama яма *n.* pit

yamka ямка *n* bunker

yamka pid hrudmy ямка під грудьми *n* anticardium

yanhol янгол *n* angel

yarlyk ярлик *n.* label

yarlyk ярлик *n.* tag

yarmarok ярмарок *n.* fair

yarmo ярмо *n.* yoke

yarus ярус *n.* tier

yashchirka ящірка *n.* lizard

yashchyk ящик *n* ark

yashchyk ящик *n* chest

yaskravist яскравість *n* brilliance

yaskravo spalakhnuty яскраво спалахнути *v.i* flare

yaskravo-chervonyi яскраво-червоний *a.* vermillion

yaskravo-chervonyi kolir яскраво-червоний колір *n.* vermillion

yaskravyi яскравий *a* bright

yaskravyi яскравий *a.* gaudy

yaskravyi яскравий *a.* gorgeous

yaskravyi яскравий *a.* lucent

yaskravyi яскравий *a.* vivid

yasla ясла *n.* crib

yasla ясла *n.* manger

yasnist ясність *n.* lucidity

yasno ясно *adv* clearly

yasnovelmozhnist ясновельможність *n* excellency

yasnyi ясний *a.* lucid

yastrub яструб *n* hawk

yavno явно *adv* downright

yavnyi явний *a.* explicit

yavnyi явний *a.* manifest

yavnyi явний *a.* overt

yavyshche явище *n.* phenomenon

yazyk язик *n.* tongue

ye є *v. t* eat

yednist єдність *n.* unity

yedynyi єдиний *a.* one

yedynyi єдиний *a.* only

yeher єгер *n.* huntsman

yemnyi ємний *a.* capacious

yepyskop єпископ *n* bishop

yeretyk єретик *n.* miscreant

Yevanheliie Євангеліє *n.* gospel

yevnukh євнух *n* eunuch
yevrei єврей *n.* Jew
yidalnia їдальня *n.* canteen
yidkist їдкість *n.* pungency
yii їй *pron.* her
yii її *a* her
yikh їх *a.* their
yikhaty zaliznytseiu їхати залізницею *v.t.* rail
yikhnii їхній *pron.* theirs
yim їм *pron.* them
yistivne їстівне *n.* eatable
yistivnyi їстівний *a* eatable
yizdyty їздити *v.t.* ride
yizdyty na taksi їздити на таксі *v.i.* taxi
yizha їжа *n* food
ymovirnist ймовірність *n.* likelihood
ymovirno ймовірно *adv.* probably
ymovirnyi ймовірний *a* credible
yoho його *pron.* his
yolop йолоп *n* dunce
yolop йолоп *n.* gander
yomen йомен *n.* yeoman
yomu йому *pron.* him
yota йота *n.* jot
yty йти *v.i.* go
yty dobrovilno йти добровільно *v.t.* volunteer
yty na pensiiu йти на пенсію *v.i.* retire
yty pid vitrylamy йти під вітрилами *v.i.* sail
yty ryssiu йти риссю *v.i.* trot
yty u vidstavku йти у відставку *v.t.* resign
yudol юдоль *n.* vale
yula юла *n.* whirligig
yunak юнак *n.* youth
yunatskyi юнацький *a.* juvenile
yunyi юний *a.* adolescent
yunyi юний *a.* young

yunyi юний *a.* youthful
Yupiter Юпітер *n.* jupiter
yurba юрба *n.* mob
yurysdyktsiia юрисдикція *n.* jurisdiction
yurysprudentsiia юриспруденція *n.* jurisprudence
yuryst юрист *n.* jurist
yuryst юрист *n.* lawyer
yushka юшка *n* broth
yuvelir ювелір *n.* goldsmith
yuvelir ювелір *n.* jeweller
yzobar изобар *n.* isobar

z з *prep.* with
z druhoho boku з другого боку *adv.* again
z harnymy maneramy з гарними манерами *a.* mannerly
z hotovnistiu з готовністю *adv.* readily
z obmezhenoiu vidpovidalnistiu з обмеженою відповідальністю *a.* limited
z pivdnia з півдня *a.* southerly
z tsoho chasu з цього часу *adv.* henceforth
z tykh pir з тих пір *conj.* since
za за *prep.* after
za за *prep.* beyond
za bort за борт *adv.* overboard
za khvylynu за хвилину *adv.* presently
za kordonom за кордоном *adv* abroad
za mezhamy за межами *adv* outside
za mezhi за межі *adv* outwards
za minusom за мінусом *prep.* minus

za vyniatkom за винятком *prep* except

za vyniatkom за винятком *prep* save

za vyrakhuvanniam за вирахуванням *adv.* less

zaareshtovuvaty заарештовувати *v.t.* arrest

zaareshtuvaty заарештувати *v.t.* nab

zaarkanyty заарканити *v.t.* noose

zabalzamuvaty забальзамувати *v. t* embalm

zabavliaty забавляти *v.t.* amuse

zabavnyi забавний *n.* funny

zabezpechenyi забезпечений *a.* well-to-do

zabezpechuvaty postiinym dokhodom забезпечувати постійним доходом *v. t* endow

zabiiaka-korotun забіяка-коротун *n.* bantam

zabludlyi заблудлий *a* stray

zabobonnyi забобонний *a.* superstitious

zaborhuvaty заборгувати *v.t* owe

zaborona заборона *n.* ban

zaborona заборона *n.* prohibition

zaboronenyi заборонений *a* taboo

zaboroniaiuchyi забороняючий *a.* prohibitory

zaboroniaty забороняти *v.t.* inhibit

zaboroniaty забороняти *v.t.* suppress

zaboroniaty забороняти *v.t.* taboo

zaboronnyi заборонний *a.* prohibitive

zabrudnennia забруднення *n.* pollution

zabrudniuvaty забруднювати *v.t.* contaminate

zabrudnyty забруднити *v.t.* stain

zabryzkuvaty brudom забризкувати брудом *v. t* bemire

zabudkuvatyi забудькуватий *a* forgetful

zabudovuvaty забудовувати *v. t.* encumber

zabuttia забуття *n.* oblivion

zabuvaty забувати *v.t* forget

zabyraty nahrabovane dobro забирати награбоване добро *v.i.* loot

zabyty забити *v.t.* injure

zabyvaty забивати *v. t* butcher

zacharovuvaty зачаровувати *v.t.* spell

zacharovuvaty pohliadom зачаровувати поглядом *v.t* fascinate

zacharuvaty зачарувати *v.t* bewitch

zad зад *n* buttock

zadacha задача *n.* problem

zadaty robotu задати роботу *v.t.* task

zadavaty ton задавати тон *v.t.* tone

zadnii prokhid задній прохід *n.* anus

zadovilnyi задовільний *a.* satisfactory

zadovolenist задоволеність *n* contentment

zadovolennia задоволення *n.* content

zadovolennia задоволення *n* enjoyment

zadovolennia задоволення *n.* pleasure

zadovolenyi задоволений *a.* jubilant

zadovolniaty задовольняти *v. t* content

zadovolniaty задовольняти *v.t* uphold

zadovolniaty vymoham задовольняти вимогам *v.t.* suit

zadubilyi задубілий *n.* stark

zadukha задуха *n* apnoea

zadum задум *n* conception

zadumuvaty задумувати *v. t* conceive

zadushlyvyi задушливий *a.* stuffy

zadushyty задушити *v.t.* strangle

zadykhnutysia задихнутися *v.t.* smother

zadyraty задирати *v. t.* bully

zahadka загадка *n.* conundrum

zahalna dumka загальна думка *n.* repute

zahalne mistse загальне місце *a.* commonplace

zahalne mistse загальне місце *a.* humdrum

zahalnyi загальний *a.* common

zahar загар *n., a.* tan

zahartovuvaty загартовувати *v.t.* season

zahin загін *n.* squad

zahin dlia khudoby загін для худоби *n.* bawn

zahlushka заглушка *n.* plug

zahlushyty заглушити *v.t.* silence

zahoiennia загоєння *n.* repair

zaholovnyi заголовний *a.* titular

zaholovok заголовок *n.* heading

zahoriaty загоряти *v.i.* tan

zahoritysia загорітися *v.t.* kindle

zahornuty v savan загорнути в саван *v.t.* shroud

zahortaty v paket загортати в пакет *v.t.* parcel

zahostrennia загострення *n.* aggravation

zahostrenyi загострений *adj.* cultrate

zahotovliuvaty pro zapas заготовлювати про запас *v.t.* pot

zahroza загроза *n.* hazard

zahroza загроза *n.* threat

zahrozhuvaty загрожувати *v.t* menace

zahrozlyvyi загрозливий *a.* ominous

zahybel загибель *n* doom

zahybel загибель *v.t.* ruin

zaiava заява *n* declaration

zaiavnyk заявник *n.* applicant

zaiets заєць *n.* hare

zaikannia заїкання *n* stammer

zaikatysia заїкатися *v.i.* stammer

zaimannia займання *n.* inflammation

zaimaty stiilo займати стійло *v.t.* stall

zaimaty vysoke stanovyshche займати високе становище *v.t.* throne

zaimatysia chyms poverkhovo займатися чимсь поверхово *v. i.* dabble

zaimatysia khliborobstvom займатися хліборобством *v.i.* tilt

zaimatysia prostytutsiieiu займатися проституцією *v.t.* prostitute

zaimennyk займенник *n.* pronoun

zainiatist зайнятість *n* employment

zainiatyi зайнятий *a* busy

zaivyi зайвий *a* excess

zaivyi зайвий *a.* superabundant

zaivyi зайвий *a.* superfluous

zakhid захід *n* decline
zakhidnyi західний *a.* occidental
zakhidnyi західний *a.* west
zakhidnyi західний *a.* westerly
zakhody bezpeky заходи
безпеки *n.* precaution
zakhoplennia захоплення *n.*
seizure
zakhoplenyi захоплений *a*
enthusiastic
zakhoplenyi захоплений *a.* lyrical
zakhopliuiuchyi захоплюючий *a.*
spectacular
zakhopliuvaty захоплювати *v. t.*
delight
zakhopliuvaty захоплювати *v.t.*
occupy
zakhopliuvaty syloiu
захоплювати силою *v. t.*
capture
zakhopliuvatysia захоплюватися
v.t. admire
zakhoronennia захоронення *n*
burial
zakhvat захват *n* delight
zakhvataty захватати *v.t.* thumb
zakhvoriuvanist захворюваність
n morbidity
zakhvoriuvannia захворювання
n disease
zakhyshchaty захищати *v.t.*
advocate
zakhyshchaty захищати *v. t.*
champion
zakhyshchaty захищати *v.t.*
protect
zakhysnyi захисний *a.* protective
zakhysnyk захисник *n.* pleader
zakhysnyk захисник *n.* protector
zakinchennia закінчення *n* finish
zakinchuvaty закінчувати *v.t*
finish

zakinchuvatysia закінчуватися
v.i. issue
zakladaty закладати *v. t.*
establish
zakladka закладка *n.* book-mark
zaklepka заклепка *n.* rivet
zakliuchnyi заключний *a*
conclusive
zaklopotanist заклопотаність *n.*
preoccupation
zaklopotanyi заклопотаний *a.*
anxious
zaklyk заклик *n.* appeal
zaklykaty закликати *v.t.* invoke
zaklynannia заклинання *n.*
invocation
zaklynaty заклинати *v. t.* charm2
zaklynaty заклинати *v.i.* conjure
zakokhuvaty закохувати *v. t*
enamour
zakolot заколот *n.* insurrection
zakolot заколот *n.* mutiny
zakolotnyi заколотний *a.*
mutinous
zakon закон *n.* law
zakonnist законність *n.*
legitimacy
zakonnyi законний *a.* justifiable
zakonnyi законний *a.* lawful
zakonnyi законний *a.* statutory
zakonodavcha vlada
законодавча влада *n.*
legislature
zakonodavchyi законодавчий *a.*
legislative
zakonodavets законодавець *n.*
legislator
zakonodavstvo законодавство *n.*
legislation
zakononarodzhenyi
закононароджений *a.*
legitimate
zakrep закреп *n.* constipation

zakresliuvannia закреслювання
v. t. cancel
zakripliuvaty закріплювати *v.i.*
strut
zakripliuvaty kanatom
закріплювати канатом *v. t.*
cable
zakripliuvaty klynom
закріплювати клином *v.t.*
wedge
zakripyty snastiamy закріпити
снастями *v.t.* tackle
zakrut закрут *n* bight
zakrutyty закрутити *n.* twist
zakrutyty holovu закрутити
голову *v.t.* infatuate
zakryttia закриття *n.* closure
zakryty закрити *v. t* close
zakrytyi закритий *a.* close
zakryvaty закривати *v. t.* cover
zakryvaty kryshkoiu закривати
кришкою *v. t.* cap
zakulisnyi закулісний *a.*
underhand
zakuska закуска *n.* snack
zakusky ta napoi закуски та
напої *n.* refreshment
zal зал *n.* hall
zal dlia hliadachiv зал для
глядачів *n.* auditorium
zalezhaty залежати *v.t.* addict
zalezhaty залежати *v. i.* depend
zalezhna teritoriia залежна
теріторія *n.* possession
zalezhnist залежність *n.* addiction
zalezhnyi залежний *a* dependent
zalezhnyi залежний *a* subject
zaliakuvannia залякування *n.*
harassment
zaliakuvannia залякування *n.*
intimidation
zaliakuvaty залякувати *v. t.* cow
zaliznyi залізний *v.t.* iron

zaliznytsia залізниця *n.* railway
zalomliuvaty заломлювати *v.t. &*
i. deflect
zaloza залоза *n.* gland
zalp залп *n.* volley
zaluchaty залучати *v.t.* attract
zaluchennia залучення *n.*
implication
zalyshaty залишати *v. t.* desert
zalyshaty shram залишати шрам
v.t. scar
zalyshatysia залишатися *v.i.*
remain
zalyshatysia v bezvykhidnomu
stanovyshchi залишатися в
безвихідному становищі *v.t*
maroon
zalyshkovyi залишковий *a.*
permanent
zalyshkovyi залишковий *a.*
residual
zalyshky залишки *n.* remains
zalyshok залишок *n.* remainder
zalyshyty залишити *v.t.* jack
zalytsiannia залицяння *n.*
courtship
zalyvaty заливати *v.t.* whelm
zalyvatysia заливатися *v.i.*
warble
zamakh замах *n.* stroke
zamaniuvaty заманювати *v.t.*
allure
zamanyty заманити *v. t.* entrap
zametil заметіль *n* blizzard
zamiaty зам'яти *v.i* falter
zamina заміна *n.* change
zamina заміна *n.* substitution
zaminiuvaty замінювати *v.t.*
replace
zaminnyk замінник *n.* substitute
zaminyty замінити *v.t.* substitute
zamishchennia заміщення *n.*
replacement

zamishuvannia замішування *n* confusion

zamishuvaty замішувати *v. t* entangle

zamiskyi заміський *a.* suburban

zamizhnia zhinka заміжня жінка *n.* matron

zamochuvannia замочування *n.* soak

zamok замок *n.* castle

zamok замок *n.* lock

zamorozhuvaty заморожувати *v.i.* freeze

zamovchuvannia замовчування *n.* default

zamovchuvaty замовчувати *v. t* bemask

zamovnyk замовник *n* customer

zamozhnyi заможний *a.* wealthy

zamuliuvatysia замулюватися *v.t.* silt

zamykaty замикати *v.t* key

zamykaty na zamok замикати на замок *v.t* lock

zamykaty na zasuv замикати на засув *v. t* bolt

zamyshliaty замишляти *v.t.* purpose

zamyslenyi замислений *a.* pensive

zamyslyty замислити *v.i.* scheme

zanadto занадто *adv.* too

zanedbanyi занедбаний *a.* lonesome

zanedbanyi занедбаний *a.* solitary

zanepad занепад *n* blight

zanepad занепад *n* decline

zanepadnytskyi занепадницький *a* decadent

zanepokoiennia занепокоєння *n.* suspense

zaniattia заняття *n.* occupancy

zanos занос *n* skid

zanosyty snihom заносити снігом *v.i.* snow

zanurennia занурення *n.* dip

zanurennia занурення *n.* immersion

zanuriuvaty занурювати *v.t.* immerse

zanuriuvatysia занурюватися *v. t* dip

zanuryty занурити *v.t.* ship

zaokhochuvaty заохочувати *v. t.* embolden

zapakh запах *n.* odour

zapakh запах *n.* scent

zapal запал *n.* ardour

zapalenyi запалений *a.* sore

zapaliuvaty запалювати *v.t* fire

zapaliuvatysia запалюватися *v.i.* inflame

zapalnyi запальний *a.* hasty

zapamorochennia запаморочення *n* swim

zapamorochlyva shvydkist запаморочлива швидкість *n* breakneck

zapamorochlyvyi запаморочливий *a.* giddy

zapas запас *n* supply

zapashnyi запашний *a.* odorous

zapasni chastyny запасні частини *n.* spare

zapasnyi запасний *a* duplicate

zapeklyi запеклий *n.* arrant

zaperechennia заперечення *n* denial

zaperechennia заперечення *n.* negation

zaperechennia заперечення *n.* retort

zaperechnyi заперечний *a.* negative

zaperechuvaty заперечувати *v.*
t. deny
zaperechuvaty заперечувати *v.t.*
object
zapevniaty запевняти *v.t.* pledge
zapiastok зап'ясток *n.* wrist
zapii запій *n.* spree
zapikatysia запікатися *v. t* clot
zapiznilyi запізнілий *adj.* belated
zapizniuvatysia запізнюватися
v.i. lag
zaplisnilyi запліснілий *a.* mouldy
zaplutanyi заплутаний *a.* intricate
zaplutuvaty заплутувати *v. t*
bewilder
zaplutuvaty заплутувати *v.t.*
tangle
zapobihaty запобігати *v.t.* prevent
zapobizhnyi запобіжний *a.*
preservative
zapochatkovuvaty
започатковувати *v.t.* originate
zapodiiuvaty заподіювати *v.t*
cause
zapodiiuvaty bil заподіювати
біль *v.t.* hurt
zapodiiuvaty bil заподіювати
біль *v.t.* torment
zapopadlyvyi запопадливий *adj*
alacrious
zapovid заповідь *n.* precept
zapovidaty заповідати *v. t.*
bequeath
zapovit заповіт *n.* testament
zapovniuvaty заповнювати *v.t* fill
zapozychuvaty запозичувати *v.*
t borrow
zapriahaty запрягати *v.t* harness
zapriahty запрягти *v.t.* yoke
zaprohramuvaty запрограмувати
v.t. programme
zaproshennia запрошення *n.*
invitation

zaproshuvaty запрошувати *v.t.*
invite
zaprovadzhuvaty
novovvedennia
запроваджувати
нововведення *v.t.* innovate
zapynky запинки *n.* stumble
zapys запис *n.* record
zapysuvaty записувати *v.t.* record
zapysuvatysia записуватися *v.*
t. book
zapyt запит *n.* inquiry
zarakhuvaty do vyshchoho
navchalnoho zakladu
зарахувати до вищого
навчального закладу *v.t.*
matriculate
zaraz зараз *adv.* forthwith
zaraz зараз *adv.* now
zaraza зараза *n.* taint
zarazhaty заражати *v.t.* infect
zarazhennia зараження *n.*
infection
zarazlyvyi заразливий *a*
contagious
zarazyty заразити *v.t.* taint
zariad заряд *n.* charge
zariadzhaty заряджати *v. t.*
charge
zarikatysia зарікатися *v.t.*
forswear
zarizaty зарізати *v.t.* slaughter
zarobliaty заробляти *v. t* earn
zarobotok заработок *n*
emolument
zarodzhennia зародження *n.*
birth
zarozumilist зарозумілість *n*
egotism
zarozumilyi зарозумілий *a.*
arrogant
zarplatnia зарплатня *n.* livelihood
zarubka зарубка *n.* nick

zaruchnyk заручник *n.* hostage
zaruchyny заручини *n.* betrothal
zaruchyny заручини *n.* plight
zasadyty lisom засадити лісом *v.t.* afforest
zaseliaty заселяти *v.t.* people
zashmorh зашморг *n.* noose
zasib засіб *n.* mean
zasidka засідка *n.* ambush
zasknilyi заскнілий *a.* obdurate
zaslanets засланець *n.* exile
zaslaty заслати *v. t* exile
zaslipliuvaty blyskom засліплювати блиском *v. t.* dazzle
zaslona заслона *n* curtain
zasluha заслуга *n.* merit
zasluhovuvaty заслуговувати *v.t* merit
zasluzhenyi заслужений *a.* veteran
zasmoktuvaty засмоктувати *v.t* engulf
zasmuchenyi засмучений *a.* sorry
zasmuchuvaty засмучувати *v.t.* afflict
zasmuchuvatysia засмучуватися *v.i.* sorrow
zasnovnyk засновник *n.* founder
zasnovuvaty засновувати *v.t.* found
zasnuvaty заснувати *v.t.* base
zasob peresuvannia засіб пересування *n.* vehicle
zasoby do isnuvannia засоби до існування *n.* sustenance
zaspokiilyve заспокійливе *n* sedative
zaspokiilyvyi заспокійливий *adj* calmative
zaspokoiennia заспокоєння *n.* calm

zaspokoiennia заспокоєння *n.* solace
zaspokoity заспокоїти *v.t.* assuage
zaspokoiuvaty заспокоювати *v. t.* calm
zaspokoiuvaty заспокоювати *v. t* console
zaspokoiuvaty заспокоювати *v.t.* quell
zaspokoiuvatysia заспокоюватися *v.t.* tranquillize
zastarilyi застарілий *a.* outdated
zastava застава *n.* bail
zastavliaty заставляти *v.t.* mortgage
zastavna заставна *n.* mortgage
zastavne pravo заставне право *n.* lien
zasterezhennia застереження *n.* admonition
zasterezhennia застереження *n.* caution
zasterezhennia застереження *n.* warning
zasterezhlyvyi застережливий *a.* monitory
zasterihaty застерігати *v.t.* admonish
zastibaty застібати *v. t.* button
zastibka застібка *n* clasp
zastii застій *n.* stagnation
zastiinyi застійний *a.* stagnant
zastoiuvatysia застоюватися *v.i.* stagnate
zastosovnist застосовність *n.* application
zastosovnyi застосовний *a.* applicable
zastosovuvaty застосовувати *v.t.* apply
zastrakhuvaty застрахувати *v.t.* secure

zastup заступ *n.* spade
zastupnyk заступник *n.* vice
zastupnytstvo заступництво *n.* auspice
zasudyty засудити *v. t.* condemn
zasudzhuvaty засуджувати *v.t.* sentence
zasuv засув *n* bolt
zasuv засув *n* lock
zasuvka засувка *n* snap
zasvichuvaty засвічувати *v.t.* light
zasvidchuvaty засвідчувати *v. t.* certify
zasvoiennia засвоєння *n* assimilation
zasvoiuvaty засвоювати *v.* assimilate
zasypaty засипати *v.t.* ply
zatemnennia затемнення *n* eclipse
zatemniuvaty затемнювати *v.t.* obscure
zatiahnuty затягнути *v.t.* tighten
zatiahuvaty затягувати *v.t.* tie
zatiniuvaty затінювати *v.t.* overshadow
zatkhlyi затхлий *a.* musty
zatmariuvaty затьмарювати *v.t.* outshine
zatoka затока *n.* gulf
zatopliaty затопляти *v.t* flood
zatopliuvaty затоплювати *v.t.* swamp
zatopliuvatysia затоплюватися *v.i.* submerge
zator затор *n* blockade
zatovarennia затоварення *n* glut
zatrymka затримка *n* stoppage
zatrymuvaty затримувати *v.t. & i.* delay
zatrymuvaty затримувати *v.t.* impede

zatrymuvatysia затримуватися *v.i.* linger
zatsukrovuvaty зацукровувати *v. t.* candy
zatuliaty затуляти *v.t.* shield
zatumaniuvaty затуманювати *v. t* blear
zatverdzhennia затвердження *n* affirmation
zatverdzhuvaty затверджувати *v.t.* appoint
zatverdzhuvaty затверджувати *v.t.* approve
zatvor затвор *n.* shutter
zatychka затичка *n* spill
zatykaty затикати *n.* cork
zatykaty затикати *v.t.* plug
zatykaty rot затикати рот *v.t.* gag
zatyshne mistechko затишне містечко *n.* snug
zatyshne mistse затишне місце *n.* cosier
zatyshnyi затишний *adj.* cozy
zatyshnyi kutochok затишний куточок *n.* nook
zatyshshia затишшя *n.* lull
zatyskaty затискати *v.t.* jam
zatysnennia затиснення *n* grip
zaukhvalyi заухвалий *a.* petulant
zauvazhennia зауваження *n.* remark
zauvazhennia, zroblene «pro sebe» зауваження, зроблене «про себе» *n.* aside
zauvazhyty зауважити *v.t.* note
zavada завада *n.* hindrance
zavaliuvaty tovaramy завалювати товарами *v.t.* glut
zavarnyi krem заварний крем *n* custard
zavazhaty заважати *v.t.* hinder
zavazhaty заважати *v.t.* prohibit
zavbachaty завбачати *v.t* foretell

zavbachennia завбачення *v.t* forecast

zavbachlyvyi завбачливий *a.* provident

zavchasno завчасно *adv.* beforehand

zavdannia завдання *n* errand

zavdannia завдання *n.* goal

zavdannia завдання *n.* task

zavdavaty obrazy завдавати образи *v.t.* insult

zaverbuvatysia завербуватися *v. t* enlist

zavershennia завершення *n.* close

zavershuvaty завершувати *v. t* complete

zaviazaty perestrilku зав'язати перестрілку *v.t.* skirmish

zaviazaty vuzlom зав'язати вузлом *v.t.* knot

zaviaznuty v bahniutsi зав'язнути в багнюці *v.t.* mire

zaviazuvaty зав'язувати *v.t* fasten

zaviazuvaty ochi зав'язувати очі *v. t* blindfold

zaviduvannia завідування *n.* superintendence

zaviriaty завіряти *v.t.* assure

zavisa завіса *n.* veil

zavoiovuvaty завойовувати *v. t* conquer

zavoiuvannia завоювання *n* conquest

zavolikatysia заволікатися *n.* gloom

zavolodity заволодіти *v.t.* seize

zavorushennia заворушення *n* unrest

zavtra завтра *adv.* tomorrow

zavtrashnii den завтрашній день *n.* tomorrow

zavydnyi завидний *a* enviable

zavyvannia завивання *n* howl

zavyvaty завивати *v.t.* wave

zavzhdy завжди *adv* always

zavziatist завзятість *n.* persistence

zavziattia завзяття *n.* zeal

zavziatyi завзятий *a.* mettlesome

zazdalehid ozbroiuvatysia заздалегідь озброюватися *v.t* forearm

zazdrisnyi заздрісний *a* envious

zazdrist заздрість *n* grudge

zazdryty заздрити *v. t* envy

zazikhaty зазіхати *v. i* encroach

zaznachyty зазначити *v. t.* check

zaznavaty зазнавати *v.t.* undergo

zaznavaty nevdachi зазнавати невдачі *v.i* fail

zazvychai зазвичай *adv.* ordinarily

zbahachuvaty збагачувати *v. t* enrich

zbentezhenyi збентежений *adv* ablush

zberezhennia збереження *n.* preservation

zberihach зберігач *n* custodian

zberihaty зберігати *v. t* enshrine

zberihaty na skladi зберігати на складі *v.t.* stock

zberihatysia зберігатися *v.i.* persist

zbihatysia збігатися *v. i* coincide

zbilshennia збільшення *n.* augmentation

zbilshennia zobrazhennia збільшення зображення *n.* zoom

zbilshuvaty збільшувати *v.t.* augment

zbilshuvaty збільшувати *v.t.* magnify

zbilshuvatysia збільшуватися *v.i.* accrue

zbilshuvatysia збільшуватися *n* increase

zbir збір *n.* meet

zbirnyk збірник *n.* digest

zbochenets збоченець *v.t.* pervert

zbochenist збоченість *n.* perversity

zbochennia збочення *n.* perversion

zbochenyi збочений *a.* perverse

zbory збори *n.* forum

zbroia зброя *n.* gun

zbroienosets зброєносець *n.* henchman

zbroienosets зброєносець *n.* squire

zbudlyvyi збудливий *a.* inflammatory

zbudzhennia збудження *n.* impulse

zbudzhennia збудження *n.* tense

zbudzhenyi збуджений *adj.* agog

zbudzhenyi збуджений *a.* tense

zbyrach starovynnykh rechei збирач старовинних речей *n.* antiquary

zbyrach vrozhaiu збирач врожаю *n.* harverster

zbyrannia збирання *n.* levy

zbyraty збирати *v.t.* aggregate

zbyraty material збирати матеріал *v.i.* research

zbyratysia збиратися *v.t.* assemble

zbyratysia natovpom збиратися натовпом *v.i* mass

zbytok збиток *n* disadvantage

zbytok збиток *n* wane

zbyty збити *v. t* down

zbyvaty збивати *v. t. & i.* churn

zbyvaty z shliakhu збивати з шляху *v.t.* mislead

zcheplennia зчеплення *n* clutch

zcheplenyi зчеплений *a* coherent

zdatnist здатність *n* ability

zdatnist do volovoho rukhu здатність до вольового руху *n.* conation

zdatnist vidchuvaty здатність відчувати *n.* sentience

zdatnyi здатний *a.* capable

zdatnyi do zcheplennia здатний до зчеплення *adj* cohesive

zdaty здати *v.t.* yield

zdavaty v orendu здавати в оренду *v.t.* lease

zdavaty vnaim здавати внайм *v.t.* let

zdavatysia здаватися *v.i.* seem

zdavyty здавити *v.t.* press

zdibnist здібність *n.* capability

zdibnyi здібний *a.* apt

zdiimatysia здійматися *v.i* billow

zdiisnennia здійснення *n.* fulfilment

zdiisnennist здійсненність *n.* practicability

zdiisnennyi здійсненний *a* feasible

zdiisniavaty nahliad здійснявати нагляд *v.t.* oversee

zdiisniuvaty здійснювати *v.t.* accomplish

zdiisniuvaty nabih здійснювати набіг *v.t.* raid

zdiisniuvaty poizdku здійснювати поїздку *v.i.* tour

zdiisniuvaty poshuk здійснювати пошук *v.t* quest

zdiisnyty здійснити *v.t.* realize

zdobuvaty здобувати *v.t.* gain

zdobych здобич *n.* capture

zdobych здобич *n.* kill

zdohad здогад *n* conjecture
zdohadka здогадка *n.* guess
zdohaduvatysia здогадуватися *v.i* guess
zdorovia здоров'я *n.* health
zdorovyi здоровий *a.* hale
zdorovyi здоровий *a.* lusty
zdorovyi здоровий *a.* robust
zdravytsia здравиця *n.* wassail
zdryhatysia здригатися *v.i.* shudder
zduttia здуття *n* swell
zdyraty здирати *v.t.* strip
zdyvovanyi pohliad здивований погляд *n.* goggles
zdyvuvannia здивування *n.* astonishment
zdyvuvaty здивувати *v. t* daze
zebra зебра *n.* zebra
zefir зефір *n.* zephyr
zelenyi зелений *a.* green
zelenyi kolir зелений колір *n* green
zemlerobstvo землеробство *n.* husbandry
zemleryika землерийка *n.* shrew
zemletrus землетрус *n* earthquake
zemlia земля *n* earth
zemlia pid parom земля під паром *n* fallow
zemlianyi земляний *a* earthly
zemnyi земний *a* earthen
zenit зеніт *n.* zenith
zenitnyi зенітний *a.* anti-aircraft
zerniatko зернятко *n.* kernel
zerno зерно *n* corn
zhaba жаба *n.* frog
zhadanyi жаданий *a.* wishful
zhadaty жадати *v.t.* covet
zhadibnist жадібність *n.* greed
zhadibno жадібно *adv* avidly
zhadibnyi жадібний *adj.* avid

zhadka згадка *n.* mention
zhadoba pomsty жадоба помсти *v.t.* revenge
zhaduvaty згадувати *v. t* cite
zhaduvaty згадувати *v.t.* mention
zhaha жага *n.* lust
zhaket жакет *n.* jerkin
zhakh жах *n.* fright
zhakhaty жахати *v.t.* terrify
zhakhlyvo monotonnyi жахливо монотонний *a.* monostrous
zhakhlyvyi жахливий *a* abominable
zhakhlyvyi жахливий *a* dire
zhakhlyvyi жахливий *a* flagrant
zhal жаль *n* regret
zhalibnyi жалібний *a.* piteous
zhalist жалість *n.* pity
zhality жаліти *v.t.* pity
zhaliuhidni hroshi жалюгідні гроші *n.* pittance
zhaliuhidnyi жалюгідний *a.* paltry
zhaliuhidnyi жалюгідний *a.* pitiable
zhalkuvaty жалкувати *v.i.* regret
zhaloby жалоби *v.t* groove
zhalyty жалити *v. t.* bite
zharhon жаргон *n.* jargon
zhart жарт *n.* joke
zhart жарт *n.* prank
zhart жарт *n.* witticism
zhartivlyva besida жартівлива бесіда *n.* banter
zhartivlyvist жартівливість *n.* pleasantry
zhartivlyvyi жартівливий *a.* jocular
zhartivnyk жартівник *n* wag
zhartuvaty жартувати *v.i.* joke
zharty жарти *n.* raillery
zhaslyi згаслий *a* extinct
zhasmyn жасмин *n.* jasmine, jessamine

zhburliaty жбурляти *v.t.* hurl
zhburnuty жбурнути *v. i.* dash
zhebrak жебрак *n* beggar
zhebrakuvaty жебракувати *v. i* cadge
zhele желе *n.* jelly
zhenykh жених *n.* bridegroom
zhereb жереб *n.* lot
zherebets жеребець *n.* stallion
zhertovnyi жертовний *a.* sacrificial
zhertva жертва *n.* victim
zhertvoprynesennia жертвопринесення *n.* oblation
zhertvuvaty жертвувати *v. t* donate
zherty жерти *n.* gobble
zhest жест *n.* gesture
zhezl жезл *n* baton
zhidno згідно *prep.* per
zhidno z згідно з *conj.* after
zhinka жінка *n.* woman
zhinocha sorochka жіноча сорочка *n* chemise
zhinochnist жіночність *n.* womanhood
zhinochyi жіночий *a* female
zhinochyi monastyr жіночий монастир *n.* nunnery
zhmenia жменя *n.* handful
zhnets жнець *n.* reaper
zhoda згода *n.* accord
zhoda згода *n.* consensus
zhoden жоден *a.* neither
zhoden жоден *pron.* none
zhodnyi згодний *a.* agreeable
zhodom згодом *adv.* afterwards
zhodzhuvatysia згоджуватися *v.i.* assent
zholob жолоб *n.* gutter
zholodnity зголодніти *v.i.* starve
zholud жолудь *n.* acorn
zhorstkyi жорсткий *a.* hard

zhorstkyi жорсткий *a.* rigid
zhorstokist жорстокість *n* cruelty
zhorstokyi жорстокий *a* abusive
zhorstokyi жорстокий *a* cruel
zhortaty згортати *v.t.* convolve
zhovch жовч *n* bile
zhovchnist жовчність *n* acrimony
zhovirlyvyi зговірливий *a* amenable
zhovta farba жовта фарба *n* chrome
zhovten жовтень *n.* October
zhovtianytsia жовтяниця *n.* jaundice
zhovtok жовток *n.* yolk
zhovtuvatyi жовтуватий *a.* yellowish
zhovtyi жовтий *a.* yellow
zhovtyzna жовтизна *n* yellow
zhraia зграя *n.* shoal
zhraia зграя *n.* swarm
zhraia зграя *n.* troop
zhribaty v kupu згрібати в купу *v.t.* bank
zhrytsia жриця *n.* priestess
zhubnyi згубний *a.* maleficent
zhubnyi згубний *a.* perilous
zhuinu tvaryna жуйну тварина *n.* ruminant
zhuinyi жуйний *a.* ruminant
zhuk жук *n* beetle
zhuri журі *n.* jury
zhurnal журнал *n.* journal
zhurnalist журналіст *n.* journalist
zhurnalistyka журналістика *n.* journalism
zhurtovanyi згуртований *a.* solid
zhushchuvaty згущувати *v. t* condense
zhustyty згустити *v.i.* thicken
zhut жуть *n* dread
zhuvaty жувати *v. t* chew

zhuvaty zhuiku жувати жуйку *v.i.* ruminate
zhvaltuvannia згвалтування *n.* rape
zhvavist жвавість *n.* alacrity
zhvavist жвавість *n.* vivacity
zhvavyi жвавий *adj* brisk
zhvavyi жвавий *a.* jolly
zhylet жилет *n.* waistcoat
zhyletka жилетка *n.* vest
zhylyi жилий *a.* inhabitable
zhyn згин *n* bend
zhynaty згинати *v.t.* arch
zhyr жир *n* fat
zhyraf жираф *n.* giraffe
zhyrnyi жирний *a.* greasy
zhyrovyk жировик *n.* wen
zhytel житель *n.* inhabitant
zhytel Skhodu житель Сходу *n* oriental
zhyteli hrafstva жителі графства *n.* county
zhytlo житло *n* abode
zhytnytsia житниця *n.* granary
zhyto жито *n.* rye
zhyttia життя *n* life
zhyttia liudyny життя людини *n.* past
zhyttieradisnyi життєрадісний *a.* vivacious
zhyttievist життєвість *n.* vitality
zhyttievo vazhlyvyi життєво важливий *a.* vital
zhyttiezdatnyi життєздатний *a.* viable
zhyty жити *v.i.* live
zhyty rozpusno жити розпусно *v.t.* womanise
zhyty v seli жити в селі *v.t.* rusticate
zhyva ohorozha жива огорожа *n* quick
zhyvit живіт *n* belly

zhyvopys живопис *n.* painting
zhyvyi живий *a* alive
zhyvylnyi живильний *a.* nutritious
zhyvytsia живиця *n.* sap
zhyvyty живити *v.t.* nourish
zhyvyty syly живити сили *v.t.* sustain
zi smakom зі смаком *a.* tasteful
ziasovuvaty з'ясовувати *v.t.* ascertain
ziasuvaty з'ясувати *v. t* elucidate
ziavytysia з'явитися *v. i* emerge
ziednanyi з'єднаний *adj.* conjunct
ziednaty shvamy з'єднати швами *v.t.* seam
ziednuvaty з'єднувати *v. i* compound
ziednuvaty з'єднувати *v.t.* piece
ziednuvatysia з'єднуватися *v. t.* connect
zihrivaty зігрівати *v.t* heat
ziity зійти *v. i.* descend
zinytsia зіниця *n.* pupil
zipsovanyi зіпсований *adj* addle
zipsovanyi зіпсований *a.* bad
zipsovanyi зіпсований *a.* corrupt
zir зір *n.* sight
zirka зірка *n.* star
zirkopodibnyi зіркоподібний *adj.* asteroid
zirochka зірочка *n.* asterisk
zishchuliuvatysia зіщулюватися *v.i.* cower
zishtovkhuvaty зіштовхувати *v. i.* collide
zishtovkhuvatysia зіштовхуватися *v. t.* clash
zistavliaty зіставляти *v.t.* correlate
zitkhannia зітхання *n.* sigh
zitkhaty зітхати *v.i.* sigh
zitknennia зіткнення *n.* clash
ziuidovyi зюйдовий *a.* southern

zkhrustkyi зхрусткий *adj.* crump
zla satyra зла сатира *n.* lampoon
zlakovyi злаковий *a* cereal
zlamuvaty зламувати *v. i.* burst
zlamuvaty зламувати *v.i.* pry
zlehka злегка *adv.* lightly
zlipok зліпок *n.* mould
zlisnyi злісний *a.* malignant
zlisnyi злісний *a.* venomous
zlist злість *n.* spite
zlizty злізти *v.i.* alight
zloba злоба *n.* venom
zlochyn злочин *n* crime
zlochyn злочин *n.* misdeed
zlochynets злочинець *n* criminal
zlodii злодій *n.* thief
zlodiistvo злодійство *n.* snatch
zlodiuzhka злодюжка *n* sneak
zloiakisnist злоякісність *n.*
  malignancy
zloiakisnyi злоякісний *a* malign
zlomshchyk зломщик *n* burglar
zlopamiatnist злопам'ятність *n.*
  rancour
zloslovyty злословити *v.t.* malign
zlovisnyi зловісний *a.*
  inauspicious
zlovmysnyi зловмисний *a.*
  malicious
zlovmysnyk зловмисник *n.*
  malefactor
zlovzhyvannia зловживання *n*
  abuse
zlovzhyvannia зловживання *n.*
  misapplication
zlovzhyvannia doviroiu
  зловживання довірою *n.*
  malpractice
zlovzhyvaty зловживати *v.t.*
  misuse
zlydar злидар *n.* pauper
zlydennyi злиденний *a.* sordid
zlyi злий *a.* angry

zlyi umysel злий умисел *n.*
  malice
zlyttia злиття *n* amalgamation
zlyttia злиття *n.* junction
zlyva злива *n* downpour
zlyva злива *n.* torrent
zlyvatysia зливатися *v.t.*
  amalgamate
zlyvatysia зливатися *v.t.* merge
zmahannia змагання *n.*
  competition
zmahatysia змагатися *v. t*
  emulate
zmashchuvannia змащування *n.*
  lubrication
zmashchuvaty змащувати *v.t* oil
zmastyty змастити *v.t* grease
**zmenshene im`ia** зменшене ім`я
  n. nickname
zmenshennia зменшення *n.*
  decrement
zmenshuvaty зменшувати *v.t.*
  delibate
zmenshuvatysia зменшуватися
  v.t lessen
zmenshyty зменшити *v.t.* reduce
zmiia змія *n.* serpent
zmiiovyk змійовик *n.* serpentine
zmina зміна *n* alteration
zmina зміна *n.* amendment
zmina зміна *n* conversion
zmina зміна *n* shift
zmina polozhennia зміна
  положення *n.* move
zminiaty зміняти *v.t.* relay
zminiuvanyi змінюваний *a.*
  variable
zminiuvaty змінювати *v.t.* modify
zminiuvatysia змінюватися *v.t.*
  vary
zminnyi змінний *a.* alternative
zminnyi змінний *a.* removable
zminnyi змінний *a.* varied

zminyty змінити *v.t.* amend
zmishchennia зміщення *n* offset
zmishuvaty змішувати *v. t* blend
zmishuvaty змішувати *v. t* confuse
zmishuvatysia змішуватися *v.t.* mingle
zmist зміст *n.* aliment
zmitsniuvaty зміцнювати *v.t.* strengthen
zmorshka зморшка *n.* wrinkle
zmova змова *n.* conspiracy
zmovliatysia змовлятися *v. t* concert2
zmovnyk змовник *n.* conspirator
zmushuvaty змушувати *v. t* compel
zmushuvaty zamovchaty змушувати замовчати *v.i* hush
zmuzhnilist змужніліість *n.* manhood
znachennia значення *n.* significance
znachnyi значний *a* great
znachnyi значний *a.* sizable
znachok значок *n.* badge
znaiomstvo знайомство *n.* acquaintance
znaiomstvo знайомство *n.* introduction
znaiomyi знайомий *a* familiar
znaiomyty знайомити *v.t.* introduce
znaiuchyi знаючий *a* expert
znak знак *n.* sign
znakhodytsia v borhu знаходиться в боргу *a.* indebted
znakhodyty знаходити *v. t* discover
znakhodyty знаходити *v.t* find
znakhodyty знаходити *v.t.* see

znamenytist знаменитість *n.* luminary
znamenytyi знаменитий *a.* outstanding
znamenytyi знаменитий *a.* renowned
znannia знання *n* cognizance
znariaddia знаряддя *n.* implement
znariaddia знаряддя *n.* weapon
znaty знати *v.t.* know
znaty знати *v.t.* understand
znavets знавець *n.* adept
znedolenyi знедолений *a* outcast
znedolyty знедолити *v.t.* widow
znekhtuvaty знехтувати *v. t* disregard
znenatska зненацька *adv.* unawares
znetsiniuvaty знецінювати *v.t.i.* depreciate
znetsiniuvatysia знецінюватися *v. t* erode
znevaha зневага *n* disregard
znevaha зневага *n* neglect
znevazhannia зневажання *n* disdain
znevazhaty зневажати *v. t* despise
znevazhaty зневажати *v.t.* neglect
znevazhaty зневажати *v.t.* scorn
znevira зневіра *n* dejection
znevira зневіра *n.* melancholy
zneviriatysia зневірятися *v. i* despair
zniattia зняття *n* dismissal
zniaty kontrol зняти контроль *v.t.* decontrol
znimaty знімати *v.t* hire
znimaty знімати *v.t.* withdraw
znimaty z posady знімати з посади *v.t.* sack
znoshenyi зношений *a.* worn

znosyty зносити *v. t.* demolish
znosyty зносити *v.t.* wear
znovu знову *adv.* afresh
znovu robyty знову робити *v.i.* relapse
znovu zibraty знову зібрати *v.t.* recollect
znushchannia знущання *n.* insult
znushchannia знущання *n.* mockery
znushchatysia знущатися *v.i.* mock
znushchatysia знущатися *v.i.* scoff
znykaty зникати *v.i.* vanish
znyknennia зникнення *n* disappearance
znyknennia зникнення *n.* output
znyknuty зникнути *v. i* disappear
znyshchennia знищення *n* annihilation
znyshchuvaty знищувати *v.t.* annihilate
znyshchuvaty знищувати *v. t* devour
znyshchyty знищити *v. t* destroy
znyzhennia зниження *n* decrease
znyzhka знижка *n* discount
znyzhuvaty знижувати *v. t* decrease
znyzhuvaty yakist знижувати якість *v. t.* debase
znyzu знизу *adv.* underneath
znyzuvannia знизування *n* shrug
znyzuvaty plechyma знизувати плечима *v.t.* shrug
zob зоб *n.* craw
zoboviazannia зобов'язання *n.* engagement
zoboviazanyi зобов'язаний *a.* liable
zoboviazuvaty зобов'язувати *v.t.* oblige

zobovzannia зобов'зання *n* must
zobrazhaty зображати *v. t.* depict
zobrazhaty зображати *v.t.* represent
zobrazhennia зображення *n* effigy
zobrazhennia зображення *n.* representation
zobrazyty зобразити *v.t* figure
zodiak зодіак *n* zodiac
zoik зойк *n* scream
zoloto золото *n.* gold
zolotyi золотий *a.* golden
zona зона *n.* zone
zonalnyi зональний *a.* zonal
zond зонд *n* probe
zooloh зоолог *n.* zoologist
zoolohichnyi зоологічний *a.* zoological
zoolohiia зоологія *n.* zoology
zoopark зоопарк *n.* zoo
zorianyi зоряний *a.* starry
zorianyi зоряний *a.* stellar
zoseredzhenyi зосереджений *a.* rapt
zovni зовні *adv.* out
zovni зовні *adv.* outwardly
zovnishnii зовнішній *a* external
zovnishnii зовнішній *a.* outer
zovnishnii slukhovyi prokhid зовнішній слуховий прохід *n* alveary
zovnishnist зовнішність *n.* look
zovnishnist зовнішність *n.* semblance
zovsim зовсім *adv.* through
zozulia зозуля *n* cuckoo
zposylatysia зposilатися *v.i.* allude
zrada зрада *n* betrayal
zradnyk зрадник *n.* snake
zradnyk зрадник *n.* traitor

zradnytskyi зрадницький *a.*
treacherous
zradnytstvo зрадництво *n.*
treason
zradzhuvaty зраджувати *v.t.*
betray
zrazok зразок *n.* specimen
zrechennia зречення *n* abdication
zrechennia зречення *n.*
repudiation
zrikatysia зрікатися *v.t.* renounce
zrikatysia зрікатися *v.t.* repudiate
zrilist зрілість *n.* maturity
zrilyi зрілий *a.* mature
zrist зріст *n.* height
zrity зріти *v.i* mature
zrivniaty iz zemleiu зрівняти із
землею *v.t.* raze
zrivniuvaty зрівнювати *v. t.*
equalize
zrivniuvaty зрівнювати *v. t* equate
zrobyty bezlad зробити безлад
v.i mess
zrobyty mat зробити мат *v.t.*
mate
zrobyty pomylku зробити
помилку *v.t.* misprint
zrobyty pryval зробити привал
v. t. halt
zrobyty znak зробити знак *v. t*
beckon
zroshchennia зрощення *n.*
concrescence
zroshennia зрошення *n.* irrigation
zroshuvaty зрошувати *v.t.* irrigate
zrostaiuchyi na derevyni
зростаючий на деревині *a.*
xylophilous
zrostannia зростання *n.* growth
zrostaty зростати *v.t.* increase
zrostaty hronamy зростати
гронами *v. i.* cluster

zrostatysia зростатися *v.t.*
accrete
zrozumilyi зрозумілий *a.*
intelligible
zrozumity nepravylno зрозуміти
неправильно *v.t.* misapprehend
zruchnist зручність *n.*
convenience
zruchnyi зручний *a* comfortable
zrushennia зрушення *v.t.* shear
zrymyi зримий *a.* visible
zryvaty зривати *v. t* disrupt
zub зуб *n.* tooth
zubets зубець *n* cog
zubnyi bil зубний біль *n.*
toothache
zubrinnia зубріння *n.* rote
zukhvala povedinka зухвала
поведінка *n* defiance
zukhvalist зухвалість *n.*
impertinence
zukhvalstvo зухвальство *n.*
hardihood
zukhvalyi зухвалий *a.* bold
zumovliuvaty зумовлювати *v.t.*
predetermine
zupyniaty rozvytok зупиняти
розвиток *n* dwarf
zupynka зупинка *n.* standstill
zupynka zrostannia зупинка
зростання *n* stunt
zupynyty зупинити *v.t.* stop
zustrichatysia зустрічатися *v.t.*
meet
zustrichne zvynuvachennia
зустрічне звинувачення *n.*
countercharge
zustrity зустріти *v. t* encounter
zusyllia зусилля *n* amplification
zusyllia зусилля *n* struggle
**zv`iazok** зв`язок *n* connection
zvaba зваба *n.* delusion
zvaba зваба *n.* seduction

zvabliuvaty зваблювати *n.t.* delude

zvannia kapitana звання капітана *n.* captaincy

zvariuvannia зварювання *v.t.* solder

zvariuvannia зварювання *n* weld

zvaryty зварити *v.t.* weld

zvazhuvaty зважувати *v.t.* ponder

zvazhuvaty зважувати *v.t.* scale

zvedennia зведення *n* bulletin

zvelychuvaty звеличувати *v. t* exalt

zvernennia звернення *n.* recourse

zvernuty uvahu звернути увагу *v.t.* heed

zvernutysia звернутися *v.t.* address

zvertaty uvahu звертати увагу *v.t.* notice

zvertatysia звертатися *v.* advert

zveseliannia звеселяння *n* amusement

zviazaty motuzkoiu зв'язати мотузкою *v.t.* rope

zviazaty shnurom зв'язати шнуром *v.t* tape

zviazka зв'язка *n.* bale

zvid звід *n.* arch

zvidky звідки *adv.* whence

zvidnyk звідник *n.* bawd

zvidsy звідси *adv.* hence

zvidty звідти *adv.* thence

zvilnennia звільнення *n* release

zvilnennia vid oboviazku звільнення від обов'язку *n* excuse

zvilnenyi vid звільнений від *a* exempt

zvilniaty звільняти *v.t* absolve

zvilniaty звільняти *v. t* discard

zvilniaty звільняти *v.t.* manumit

zvilniaty звільняти *v.t.* quit

zvilniaty звільняти *v.t.* rescue

zviriachyi звірячий *a.* atrocious

zvirstvo звірство *n* atrocity

zvishchaty звіщати *v.i.* trumpet

zvit звіт *n.* report

zvodyty balans зводити баланс *v.t.* offset

zvodyty na prestol зводити на престол *v. t* enthrone

zvodyty sklepinnia зводити склепіння *v.i.* vault

zvodyty ukriplennia зводити укріплення *v.t.* fortify

zvodyty v tablytsiu зводити в таблицю *v.t.* tabulate

zvodyty z rozumu зводити з розуму *v.t* dement

zvodytysia зводитися *v.* amount

zvolikannia зволікання *n.* procrastination

zvolikaty зволікати *v.i.* slow

zvolozhuvaty зволожувати *v.t.* moisten

zvorotnyi зворотний *a* reflexive

zvorotnyi зворотний *a.* reverse

zvuchaty звучати *v.i.* resound

zvuchnist звучність *n.* sonority

zvuk звук *n* sound

zvuk rizhka звук ріжка *n.* clarion

zvukonasliduvannia звуконаслідування *n.* onomatopoeia

zvukovyi звуковий *a.* sonic

zvuzhuvaty звужувати *v.t.* narrow

zvuzhuvatysia do kintsia звужуватися до кінця *v.i.* taper

zvychai звичай *n.* custom

zvychaino звичайно *adv.* certainly

zvychaino звичайно *adv.* usually

zvychainyi звичайний *a.* average

zvychainyi звичайний *a* customary

zvychka звичка *n* wont

zvykhnutysia звихнутися *v.i.*
    maddle

zvyklyi звиклий *a.* accustomed

zvyklyi do novykh umov звиклий
    до нових умов *a.* wonted

zvynuvachennia звинувачення *n*
    accusation

zvyvatysia звиватися *v.t.* crankle

zvyvystyi звивистий *a.* sinuous

zyhzah зигзаг *n.* zigzag

zyhzahopodibnyi
    зигзагоподібний *a.* zigzag

zyma зима *n.* winter

zymivlia зимівля *n.* hibernation

zymovyi зимовий *a.* wintry

zzadu ззаду *adv* behind